Contemporary Social Issues in East Asian Societies:

Examining the Spectrum of Public and Private Spheres

Mika Markus Merviö
Kibi International University, Japan

A volume in the Advances in Religious and Cultural Studies (ARCS) Book Series

Information Science REFERENCE
An Imprint of IGI Global

Managing Director: Lindsay Johnston
Production Manager: Jennifer Yoder
Development Editor: Austin DeMarco
Acquisitions Editor: Kayla Wolfe
Typesetter: Mike Brehm
Cover Design: Jason Mull

Published in the United States of America by
Information Science Reference (an imprint of IGI Global)
701 E. Chocolate Avenue
Hershey PA 17033
Tel: 717-533-8845
Fax: 717-533-8661
E-mail: cust@igi-global.com
Web site: http://www.igi-global.com

Library of Congress Cataloging-in-Publication Data

Contemporary social issues in East Asian societies : examining the spectrum of public and private spheres / Mika Markus Mervio, editor.
pages cm
Includes bibliographical references and index. ISBN 978-1-4666-5031-2 (hardcover) -- ISBN 978-1-4666-5032-9 (ebook) -- ISBN 978-1-4666-5033-6 (print & perpetual access) 1. East Asia--Social conditions. I. Mervio, Mika Markus, 1961-
HN720.5.A8C665 2014 306.095--dc23
2013037502

This book is published in the IGI Global book series Advances in Religious and Cultural Studies (ARCS) (ISSN: Pending; eISSN: Pending)

British Cataloguing in Publication Data
A Cataloguing in Publication record for this book is available from the British Library.

All work contributed to this book is new, previously-unpublished material. The views expressed in this book are those of the authors, but not necessarily of the publisher.

For electronic access to this publication, please contact: eresources@igi-global.com.

Advances in Religious and Cultural Studies (ARCS) Book Series

ISSN: Pending
EISSN: Pending

Mission

In the era of globalization, the diversity of the world and various cultures becomes apparent as cross-cultural interactions turn into a daily occurrence for individuals in all professions. Understanding these differences is necessary in order to promote effective partnerships and interactions between those from different religious and cultural backgrounds.

The **Advances in Religious and Cultural Studies (ARCS)** book series brings together a collection of scholarly publications on topics pertaining to religious beliefs, culture, population studies, and sociology. Books published within this series are ideal for professionals, theorists, researchers, and students seeking the latest research on collective human behavior in terms of religion, social structure, and cultural identity and practice.

Coverage

- Cross-Cultural Interaction
- Cults and Religious Movements
- Cultural Identity
- Gender
- Globalization and Culture
- Group Behavior
- Human Rights and Ethics
- Impact of Religion on Society
- Politics and Religion
- Social Stratification and Classes
- Sociology
- Stereotypes and Racism

IGI Global is currently accepting manuscripts for publication within this series. To submit a proposal for a volume in this series, please contact our Acquisition Editors at Acquisitions@igi-global.com or visit: http://www.igi-global.com/publish/.

The Advances in Religious and Cultural Studies (ARCS) Book Series (ISSN Pending) is published by IGI Global, 701 E. Chocolate Avenue, Hershey, PA 17033-1240, USA, www.igi-global.com. This series is composed of titles available for purchase individually; each title is edited to be contextually exclusive from any other title within the series. For pricing and ordering information please visit http://www.igi-global.com/book-series/advances-religious-cultural-studies/84269. Postmaster: Send all address changes to above address.

Titles in this Series

For a list of additional titles in this series, please visit: www.igi-global.com

Contemporary Social Issues in East Asian Societies Examining the Spectrum of Public and Private Spheres
Mika Markus Merviö (Kibi International University, Japan)
Information Science Reference • copyright 2014 • 327pp • H/C (ISBN: 9781466650312) • US $175.00 (our price)

New Media and Communication Across Religions and Cultures
Isaac Nahon-Serfaty (University of Ottawa, Canada) and Rukhsana Ahmed (University of Ottawa, Canada)
Information Science Reference • copyright 2014 • 335pp • H/C (ISBN: 9781466650350) • US $175.00 (our price)

Editorial Advisory Board

Table of Contents

Detailed Table of Contents

Namely, public authority is quite often measured by only analyzing how citizens obey the norms and rules of the society. However, these analyses are not very plausible, because the definition of privacy can manifest itself in the claim of individuals, groups, or institutions to determine for themselves when, how, and to what extent information about them is communicated to others. The authors call for more diversity and different viewpoints in public-private research to get beyond the simple dichotomy of approaches focusing on state and market as opposing ends.

Section 2
Family Institution and the Spectrum of Public and Private Spheres

This section focuses on the family institution in the East Asian context and proceeds to analyze family-related policies and social issues in different societies in the region. Family is the basic institution of any society, but in the East Asian context, it has played and continues to play a particularly important role in social development, often adopting roles that elsewhere belong to other social actors and institutions. Furthermore, in reference to public and private spheres, the family institution in the East Asian context provides a good chance to test how these spheres interact and how East Asian models are evolving.

Family plays an unusually important role in Taiwanese society, and this chapter analyzes the consequences of global financial crises on the family in Taiwan. With its export-oriented economy, Taiwan is vulnerable to global vacillations. In the periods from 1997 to 2004 and from 2008 to the 2009, Taiwan experienced mass unemployment and family suffering. This chapter deals with the effects of the economic recession on family finances and family attitudes involved. The study shows how the anxiety affected the willingness of people to have children and/or support their parents. Furthermore, the victims of financial crises had a greater awareness of the necessity of providing intergenerational support, but they also wanted to have fewer children. The data clearly presents that economic hardship changes the traditional generational contract as well.

This chapter analyzes the importance of protective factors in family relationships. In Confucian societies, where services for older people may be limited, intergenerational family relationships are crucial in providing care for the elderly. Confucian societies are better at recognizing the protective influence of the family, but scholars from these areas suggest that the culture may be changing. As the "One child" norm extends (not only in China) across many Asian societies, the challenges for young people in supporting their parents and grandparents may become overwhelming. This chapter suggests that at every stage of the life cycle, some families will need state support in order to carry out their protective role in mitigating the risks experienced by both the young and the old. A state/family partnership approach is likely to be more acceptable, more effective, and more economic than state care alone.

This chapter deals with the situation of family and care work in Japan, and, in particular, the Conjunction between Family, Care Work, and Immigration in Japan. The chapter is aimed to elucidate the complex interplay between family and care work from both paid and unpaid work. Furthermore, Japan currently does not have an immigration policy that would include social integration policies. Since the care needs cannot be met solely by the families or the domestic labor market, globalization of care will become a salient trend for a foreseeable future. Moreover, the chapter proceeds to analyze the globalization thesis within the Japanese context. According to the author, one should be able to see the convergence of welfare states in many countries, but as in the case of Japan, the process of globalization is not linear but contingent. Instead, what one has seen is a dialectical process of how the domestic factors are differently shaping the well-being of the people within their own institutional histories and strategies.

This chapter examines how the foreign aid policy should and should have supported families facing risks by using the case study of Myanmar. The chapter starts by addressing the issue of poverty, which continues to be the gravest risk in the developing countries, and how family could be the cause of poverty as well as the solution of poverty in foreign aid policy discussion. The situation of poverty and migration as a risk management tool are then examined in the second section of the chapter. Interviews with migrant workers in Thailand and Japan were conducted. Finally, there is a discussion about the developments of Myanmar and how the foreign aid and international community has inadequately responded to the democratization of Myanmar and to the needs of its people.

Many Japanese researchers have suggested that both Japanese and Western societies are experiencing individualization of the family; whether or not this is the case in Japanese rural farming villages remains unclear. The purpose of this chapter is to investigate this question using a case study. The research involves interviews of families living in rural areas within the Shimane Prefecture, each engaged in agriculture, forestry, and/or fishery. The emerging picture is that it is increasingly difficult to find traditional Ie in rural farming villages today. For the rural farming family, individual freedom is important. However, respecting individuals seems to occur for the purposes of maintaining unity of the family as a group rather than for the purpose of individual self-realization. Therefore, emphasizing individual freedom does not mean conflict among family members (i.e., enforcement of competition with other family members or compromises by them).

While family structure continues to diversify in Korean society, society's rejection of unmarried mothers continues to be a strong obstacle. However, Korean teenage mothers increasingly are deciding to raise their own children and live their daily lives in communities that hold biases and express rejection towards them. At present, the Single-Parent Family Support Act is central to the development of support policies for unmarried mothers, but as pointed out in this study, it is important to implement detailed, individualized, comprehensive, and continual assistance, not limited to those who opt for childrearing but also towards all unmarried mothers who opt for adoption. While raising one's own child, it is important to provide long-term and continual support and support that helps the recipient foresee how she can step her way up to independence, rather than short-term and sporadic handouts.

In order to extend the understandings of work-family reconciliation patterns and following problems in Taiwan, this chapter reviews the development of employment and childcare trends in Taiwan to show how these changing phenomena affect Taiwanese families and contribute to families' difficulties in work-family reconciliation. This chapter includes three main sections. The first section demonstrates the changes of household structure and employment in Taiwan. The second section focuses on childcare arrangements to demonstrate Taiwanese families' decisions between work and childcare. Finally, there is a concluding section to sum up the implications of these phenomena.

This chapter examines the low fertility phenomenon in Taiwan and argues that the low fertility problem can be identified as a type of new social risk. Existing studies on new social risks tend to focus on the social risks that have negative influences on individuals but ignore those that have more negative influences on the whole society, such as the low fertility problem. This chapter illustrates how the Taiwanese government recognizes low fertility as a social risk and how such recognition facilitated the recent development of policies that support families and children.

Section 3
Health and Care Sector and the Spectrum of Public and Private Spheres

In this section, the book tackles the health and care-related issues and policies. In fact, health and care-related issues often inhibit the grey area between the private and public spheres. Furthermore, families are still very much involved in these issues, as the East Asian examples clearly demonstrate.

This chapter analyzes the issue of primary health care utilization in Hong Kong and introduces the case of Hong Kong where a special division between public and private sectors has developed in the field of primary health services. The chapter argues that in the foreseeable future, it is likely that the division of health care between the public and private sector will be maintained. In recent years, more and more individuals and families have purchased private health insurance so as to gain more options. The idea of universal health insurance was rejected by the public in recent consultations; the current alternative is government-regulated private insurance. Although private primary health services will continue as usual in the near future, public primary health services should be maintained or even expanded. Given the costliness of private services (especially specialist services), it is recommended that more resources should be invested in corresponding public health services.

Since the late 1950s, Hong Kong's public health services have increased. They are mainly funded by taxes, supplemented by minimal user fees. In the late 1980s, the government recognized the limitations of this financing model and has subsequently proposed alternative methods of funding. Their proposals have been rejected by various stakeholders, who represent different, and even conflicting, values and interests. This chapter describes the development of health services and the debates that have surrounded health financing since the late 1980s. It shows that the health finance debate in Hong Kong is not a simple issue that can be tackled by rational planning; instead, it is a complex consequence of welfare politics in an increasingly mobilized society.

To address the risks to families of the availability of care for their older family members, this chapter explores the impact of different care systems on the way that relevant care actors contribute to the long-term care of older people. It focuses on how front-line professionals and formal/informal carers meet the needs of older people who are frail and disabled, since caring for older people has become one of the potential family risks in East Asia and many industrial countries in the West for a number of reasons. On the one hand, the rise in life expectancy and multiple disabilities means the number of older people requiring long-term care has increased. On the other hand, the decreased younger population with increased female employment calls into question the continued availability of family carers and requires support from public and formal carers to help them to care for their older family members for as long as possible.

Section 4
Risk Society and the Spectrum of Public and Private Spheres

This section deals with modern societies dealing with contemporary social issues and social risks. While societies have modernized and people have become aware of the risks and global connectedness of the modern global society, the particular modes of "risk societies" are rather varied, reflecting various cultural and social traditions.

This research applies social quality framework to analyze the current social development of Taiwan by utilizing the governmental database as a secondary dataset and using meta-analysis as a further check in data collection. This study found that the social development of current Taiwanese society keeps progressing along with requirements and indicators of social quality. Among them, Taiwan's performance of social development within the dimension of social economic security attains the best results. Furthermore, in the fields of social inclusion and social empowerment dimensions, the indicators show much progress. However, the biggest room for further improvement and development clearly is in social cohesion.

Fiji is a very interesting case for studying the bridges between private and public spheres and social and cultural background. Despite its idyllic setting and concentration of resources, Fiji has one of the highest rates of violence against women, outside of conflict zones, in the world. The state, legal system, and society have simply failed to protect the women against different forms of violence and discrimination. The lack of parliamentary democratic process certainly has contributed to the deplorable situation. After analyzing the roots of the problem, the authors introduce comprehensive policy recommendations to help rectify the situation. The problems in Fiji are rather extreme, and there is a lot to learn for everyone about the weakness of state and institutions to perform some of their most fundamental functions.

Japan, two years after the triple catastrophe of earthquake, tsunami, and Fukushima nuclear plant crisis, is only slowly wakening to the new reality of a new kind of reflexive relationship with nuclear power and, more generally, the use of modern technology and the social risks linked with modern life. In Japan, the idea that Japan's very own catastrophe is, instead, a global catastrophe has not really sunk in. Coping with the disasters may be the most urgent and visible task of the government, but the Japanese society can hardly wait to find solutions to many long-term policy choices. This chapter analyzes the Japanese model of risk society, the risk society discourse in Japan, and the challenges of risk society to Japanese public policy.

Preface

This book focuses on modern, highly developed East Asian societies and their social issues, particularly ones that are related to family and health. The examples are from Japan, South Korea, Taiwan, Myanmar, Singapore, and the Pacific Islands, while references are made to contrasting examples in other Asian societies, especially China, because of its regional and global importance as well as its cultural importance in the region. Since discourses on the delicate balance between private and public sectors are very much global and based primarily on the experiences of the affluent societies in Western Europe and North America, we have also taken a look at parallels with relevant counterparts elsewhere. In short, the East Asian discourses and developments have been deeply influenced by developments elsewhere while East Asian societies are bound to influence other societies, due to the global reach of East Asian economies and the increased political weight of East Asian societies. This book shows that the East Asian discourses have raised new concerns, and quite often the distinctive features are connected with local social and cultural traditions. However, the traditions are constantly being reinterpreted and surely there is nowhere any simple and coherent East Asian model that would be based on shared cultural traditions. Instead, tradition itself is a highly contested terrain, and the demarcation between private and public spheres in East Asia needs to take into account the changing meanings attached to all relevant institutions.

HISTORY AND CONCEPTUAL RICHNESS OF "PUBLIC" AND "PRIVATE": FROM EUROPE TO EAST ASIA

The concepts of public and private themselves are very much Western in origin and are closely associated with particular historical developments in Europe. The fragmented and culturally diverse Greek ancient system of governance produced much of the foundation of Western philosophy and political science, from *politeia* (organized politics within *poleis*) and *dêmokratia* (democracy) to *koinônia politikê* (community politics, the ancestor of civil society) and *koinôn* (commonwealth or rapidly changing political league among poleis). It is the Greek world that left the heritage of critical thinking about the best possible solution to the practical issues of governance. The model also tied together the idea of manliness *(adreia)* and politics. It was the free men who took care of managing the public sphere and responding to all challenges in a rational manner after frank discussions. Aristotle also makes the observation that the hoplite warfare made it possible for many men to achieve military virtue while it was far more difficult to achieve the whole range of human virtues. There have always been limits on political participation, but some of the Greek *poleis* went the extra mile to encourage participation, Athens being the most important *polis* to do so. The consequences have been important for the European thinking on political participation and also on thinking about politics/society and gender roles. However, it was Aristotle who discussed in an honest manner the importance of maintaining the rule of law (*nomos*) while warning about the practical difficulties of choosing the wisest action or *praxis* (practice) in a specific context. The laws (*nomoi*), after all, are universal and as such (too) abstract. The sphere of politics for Aristotle is one of the prime examples of (many) paradoxes of human life: the actual politics involves an endless succession of compromises that will never do much justice to real philosophy and the beauty of laws, on which the whole activity is built (for more, see, Salkever, 2009, pp. 232-241).

While the thinking of Aristotle gives a good idea about the flexibility of the ancient Greeks to respond to changing social and political situations, the ancient Greeks also had more than their fair share of conservatism when it came to political ideas and attitudes. The concept of revolution was often expressed by *"neôtera pragmata"* (*too* new affairs) and the opposite of "new," and potentially threatening ideas was seen to be *ta patria*, the ways of the ancestors. The real Greek patriotism meant more or less the same as keeping to the tradition (Cartledge, 2009, p. 87). The different Greek *poleis* were not mentally prepared to modify their *ta patria,* which was one of the main reasons why the poleis could never truly unify and ultimately protect their way of life against the other civilizations.

Much of the vocabulary and cultural package has been passed to the English language from Latin, and in the process, it was shaped by the experiences of the Roman Empire. The Roman Empire presented a model of a ruthless centralized authority that was capable of ruling huge areas with diverse cultures and traditions. The Roman thinking was very much based on earlier Greek ideas, but the Romans created a long-lived empire that developed further (or simplified) the ideas and made them a permanent fixture of the European scene. In terms of public/private distinction, it was the Roman Empire that established a well-functioning and unambiguous legal system that clearly defined the public and private spheres and what kind of legal principles applied to both of them. The idea of autonomous legal systems for different spheres was later only strengthened in Europe by the important role that the church carved for itself as an independent actor. However, the Roman Empire also kept alive some ideals of its Republican origins.

Res publica and *societas civilis* both are associated with the serious ideals of the Roman republic: the Roman civil duties and rights were a basis that made Rome a superpower and distinguished it from its neighbors. Even in eroded forms, they continued to inspire people for centuries, and, for instance, the French revolution in politics and art found great inspiration from the Roman republic. Of course, Imperial Rome with its excesses and military repression (or glory) has also inspired many subsequent European political systems. The modern state with its emphasis on effective administration, rule of law, and homogeneity in terms of culture owes much to the example of the Roman Empire.

In the field of the private sphere, the key concepts owe much to an understanding shaped by the Greek *oikos* (home, house), which still serves even in English as the root of such terms as economy and ecology. *Oikos* stood in clear contrast to public sphere and the specific ideas about political participation that were discussed above. Furthermore, *oikos* established a clear differentiation of gender roles within the unit. Meanwhile, *domus* is the Latin for house or home and normally refers to a range of houses from a palace to city houses that the wealthy and middle classes owned. The masses, the vast majority of people, in Rome lived in *insulae*, incredibly cramped apartment blocks, while many wealthy people lived in countryside *villas*. The Roman *domus* was interestingly multifunctional, as there was no clear distinction between rooms meant solely for private use. Public rooms and front rooms were sometimes even rented out to merchants if the house was next to a busy street. As the slaves took care of most household tasks (and slept outside), the original, quite elitist *domus* is a strange root for modern understanding of "domestic" as a unit that isolates the "family" from the rest of the society. What we can learn from the Roman *domus* is that people of different classes and gender did have a remarkable variety of life styles and that the Romans had little reason for making a strong separation between their domestic and (other) social life. However, it was the state, through legislation and strict enforcement of that legislation, which clearly distinguished the public and private spheres.

The elitist interpretation of the family unit in the sense of *domus*/domestic is by no means restricted to only English and other European languages, which operate with the words related to the Latin original. Japanese counterparts *ie* and *kateinai* use, in a very similar manner, a concept of house/household that is associated with a quite restricted concept of suitable "house" as a unit for social life. Originally, the Chinese *kanji* for house stood for an affluent house that could keep a pig/swine under its roof. By definition *ie* (house) in Japan came to signify a kind of model family, which was relatively well off and in good esteem. The Confucian thinking in its great variety in Japan, Korea, and China has always added a lot of weight to the continuation of the family unit, although in these societies and during the centuries, the unit itself has been interpreted very differently. It should also be noted that with modernization the *ie* system (*ie seido*) was elevated by legislative means into a state policy in Japan. Furthermore, the uniform paternalistic family register system with the "heads of family" (usually men) with their official duties was a key component of the Meiji *ie* system, and it has survived all the democratization and other changes in Japanese politics and society until these days (cf. Merviö, 2008). This book has many articles (section 2) dealing with the issue of family institution in East Asia and the easiest way to introduce the variety of experiences is to state that family continues to serve as the basic unit of society and culture in East Asia. However, this does not mean that families would be immune to social transformations and policy changes. Furthermore, Yoshimi Kataoka's chapter provides a very insightful discussion about the specific pressures that the *ie* institution is facing in Japan.

When we move to the East Asian scene, it becomes evident that societies have developed in different ways in different cultural, political, social, and economic contexts. In addition, academic disciplines are developed differently, and both the key concepts and fields of study are often understood differently. This book demonstrates how public policies in East Asian societies tend to reflect both the cultural traditions and dynamic changes in society and economic conditions. Having discussed above the origins of public sphere in Europe, there is a clear contrast in East Asia in terms of traditional ideas about social participation and activism, and about the social rules that grew up in Europe to support that kind of behavior. Among these are equality (among peers), openness, tolerance, and all the small niceties of civilised behavior on which civil society is built. It would be an enormous mistake to dismiss East Asian democratization as a doomed cultural implant, which has no chance of success. It would also be dishonest to use a reconstructed tradition of a mixed bag of Western ideals and use it as a proof that the Western societies have made these ideals part of their social DNA and cannot go wrong with these issues.

For instance, Japan has, due to its history of modernization, a political tradition of central state dominating social development. Civil society remains weak in the Western sense of the word, and, for instance, Japanese politics leaves little room for NGOs in anything resembling "high politics," and the expectation is that this realm belongs to the government. In addition, the business sector and media are all too happy to seek close cooperation with the government rather than defend their autonomy. On the other hand, the family institution continues to play an important role in Japan, as well as in all East Asian societies. In fact, the states prefer to leave many policy areas for the families to take care of. However, there are limits to how much the family institution can be stretched to respond to new and all needs alike.

SCOPE OF THE BOOK

This book includes discussions of many different related topics, all adding to understanding the delicate interplay between the public and private spheres in East Asia. In section 1, the authors analyze the mechanisms and reality of public and private spheres, with a special reference to East Asia. This section analyses the theoretical ramifications of distinguishing the public and private spheres in the context of East Asia and its cultural and social traditions. This book helps to transcend all kind of boundaries, including the national boundaries and boundaries of academic disciplines to search explanations to developments in East Asia. East Asia-specific discussions, of course, are linked to developments elsewhere, but there is also a need to analyze the impact of local traditions without becoming blind to changes in these traditions.

In section 2, the book takes the issue of family institution in the East Asian context and proceeds to analyse family-related policies and social issues in different societies in the region. Of course, family is the key institution of any society, but in the East Asian context, it has played and continues to play a particularly important role in social development, often adopting roles that elsewhere belong to other social actors and institutions. Furthermore, in reference to public and private spheres, the family institution in the East Asian context provides a good chance to test how these spheres interact and how East Asian models are evolving.

In section 3, the book moves to health and care-related issues and policies. These issues often inhabit the grey area between the private and public spheres. Furthermore, families are still very much involved in these issues, as the East Asian examples clearly demonstrate, and in many ways, this section builds on the discussion in the preceding chapter while the issue of health finance tends to place these discussions more to the realm of public policy.

Section 4 deals with the modern societies facing social problems and social risks. While societies have modernized and people have become aware of the risks and global connectedness of the modern global society, the particular modes of "risk societies" are rather varied, reflecting various cultural and social traditions. The chapters in the preceding sections already discussed at length the particular problems and social risks that accompany social development in different Asian countries, especially the fields of family, health, and care. In this section, the book continues to areas where social development has been going astray for reasons that may have something to do with domestic developments, but also with dramatic developments and occurrences of risks that have posed challenges to the usual methods of social development, such as the parliamentary democratic process. For instance, the chapter by Lih-Rong Lillian Wang, Yun-Tung Wang, and Peishan Yung introduces the idea of using social quality as a framework for analyzing social development in Taiwan. Of course, the approaches focusing on social quality provide very different perspective than ones that emphasize primarily economic and political development. Once again, this study shows the importance of the family institution in the Taiwanese context. Furthermore, it shows that Taiwanese social development and social quality itself has taken its own path that is quite different from the European one (which gave rise to the use of social quality as a concept and indicator within the context of the European Union).

However, among the societies covered in this book, Japan is different from all societies in the region and elsewhere, while it shares so many social problems—and risks—with the rest of the world. In many ways, Japan, with its experiences and problems, is paving the way for a very different kind of modernity and relationship with risk – and the limitations of public policy. Japan was unfortunate to encounter the impact of highly improbable catastrophe, or more precisely, a triple catastrophe, in 2013. Furthermore, Japan stands alone in its corner of the world, politically more isolated from its neighbors than any other highly developed affluent society. In times of sudden crisis, it is easy to see how societies cope very differently in their response and how the rest of the world perceives and reacts to the same event. After the crisis, Japanese politics have rapidly turned to more nationalistic in their orientation and distanced themselves from the traditions that gave birth to and nurtured democracy, civil society, and direct social participation. After gaining political support largely to its economic initiatives and strong posture against Chinese aggression, the Abe cabinet decided to spend its political capital to push through a vaguely phrased secrecy legislation, which surely highlights how different Japan is from its last remaining allies. While the baffling legislation was pushed through the Diet the number two LDP leader, Secretary-General Shigeru Ishiba, likened peaceful public protests against the new secrecy bill being introduced by his government to "acts of terrorism." The message was clear: politics belongs to politicians while transparency and too many questions or making noise are not part of the genuine Japanese political tradition. While the government may not want to immediately use the law to silence the media and make everything secret in the legislation, there are too many similarities with the pre-war Japanese laws and politics that did not end well. Surveys have indicated that the majority of Japanese people did not see much need for such a legislation but few worried about civil liberties either. The cabinet was right in calculating that most people do not like noisy demonstrators or media anymore than whistleblowers shaking the social order. The Japanese policy choices and strong continued support for the Abe administration so soon after the triple catastrophe surely look unusual. Nuclear power enjoys government support while the situation in Fukushima is far from being under control. Meanwhile, the government appears to equate basic civil liberties and freedoms as subversive activities. Of course, these opinions would find much support in neighboring countries like China, North Korea, and Russia.

Nassim Nicholas Taleb (2010) uses the term "black swan" to discuss such events in social development and (human) history. The real insight of Taleb's book is that a naïve projection of the future from the past is often pointless and misleading. Taleb's example of the turkey's feeling of safety based on consistently good experiences of human race (until the big surprise; Taleb, 2010, pp. 40-41) has a lot in common with the complacency and security that people in Japan have felt as long as it seemed that modern orderly society and a well-functioning public sector can prepare for anything. Japanese society has gone through such catastrophes of epic proportion as the Hiroshima/Nagasaki bombings and the triple shock of 2011, which help to teach the lesson that there is no such thing as perpetual social progress and infallible leadership. Human life is fragile, and unexpected dangerous things happen all the time. Human societies often deal with the very basic issues of organizing themselves. Politics rarely are successful in meeting the changing needs of people or even guiding societies to their chosen policy goals, but for the first time in history, there is emerging some kind of understanding that people of the world share a common planet and increasingly similar social problems. Cooperation and learning would always beat other more "traditional" policy choices, no matter which level of policy choices we focus on.

Mika Markus Merviö
Kibi International University, Japan

REFERENCES

Cartledge, P. (2009). *Ancient Greek political thought in practice*. Cambridge, UK: Cambridge University Press. doi:10.1017/CBO9780511801747

Merviö, M. (2008). *Domestic violence: Political and ethical analysis of power relationships.* Paper presented at the East Asia Social Policy 5th International Conference. Taipei, Taiwan. Retrieved from http://www.welfareasia.org/5thconference/papers/Mervio%20M_domestic%20violence%20and%20power%20relationships.pdf

Taleb, N. N. (2010). *The black swan: The impact of the highly improbable* (Rev. Ed.). London: Penguin Books. doi:10.2139/ssrn.1669317

Section 1

Spectrum of Public and Private Spheres in East Asia

This section analyzes the theoretical ramifications of distinguishing the public and private spheres in the context of East Asia and its cultural and social traditions.

Chapter 1
Spectrum of Public and Private Spheres in East Asia:
Theoretical Inspirations from Past and Present

Mika Markus Merviö
Kibi International University, Japan

ABSTRACT

This chapter discusses the significance of cultural traditions for social development in East Asian societies, in particular Japan and Korea. The chapter treats culture and society in a broad sense in order to find out what makes the East Asian case specific. Moreover, the chapter provides a reinterpretation of Japanese social realities and social models in 2013 when Japanese politics and society are going through the transformation known as Abenomics.

1. REFLECTIONS OF JAPANESE AND KOREAN MODERNITY AND TRADITIONS

This book helps to transcend all kind of boundaries, including the national boundaries and boundaries of academic disciplines to search explanations to developments in East Asia. East Asia- specific discussions, of course, are linked to developments elsewhere, but there is also a need to analyse the impact of local traditions without becoming blind to changes in these traditions. In this chapter there is discussion about the significance of cultural traditions for social developments in East Asian societies, in particular, Japan and Korea. Social development and policies are made by people within the possibilities created by existing social and cultural realities. As this chapter will show,

DOI: 10.4018/978-1-4666-5031-2.ch001

there is always room for real ingenuity in seeking new directions for societies or their culture. In the end of the chapter I also draw together ideas about Japanese social model and how it is faring in 2013.

To make sense of the specific model of Korean social development, Korean authors often make references to the use of Confucian traditions to strengthen and legitimise state-led authoritarian development (see e.g. Han 1998, p. 5-27). Of course, Confucianism is the most natural starting point for any policy analysis that takes place in Korea or China. However, this should always be done with caution and by bearing in mind that Confucianism itself is a very diverse and rich intellectual tradition spanning a very long time. Furthermore, in contemporary context it is always mixed with a constantly transforming social theory and social reality. For instance, Korean social analysis may be built on the foundations of Confucianism, but it also needs to explain how Korea functions in the context of contemporary global community as a full and very important member and how Korean society deals with many of the same challenges that other societies are facing. On the basis of Korean social development, Kim Dae Hwan creates a most original analytical tool of dual-risk approach to explain how both the insufficiency of modernisation and modernisation in their peculiar mix have created risks and dangers for Koreans. Another name for this Korean model of modernisation would be "rush-to" growth or limping modernisation (Kim Dae Hwan 1998, p. 28-45). For me it appears that the dual-risk approach would also fit particularly well for Japan. In his comment on Kim's article Beck argues that the concept of "dual-risk society" enriches the analysis of Western societies, too, because what is a dominant aspect in the Korean context might be an additive aspect in many parts of the West as well (Beck 1998, p. 201). This is a very important point. For me a better term would be "multiple-risk societies", because in all societies there are multiple risk narratives and the whole idea of rigid classifications between traditional (pre-modern), modern and post-modern fit badly with most societies. It is even more so with dualistic classification of reflexivity either being there or being absent. In some other disciplines (than some branches of sociology) there has been far more sensitivity to traces of Eurocentrism, colonialism, racism, sexism and other forms of imposing one's own values on other cultures without finding out about all the multiple ways of constructing the world. For me Korea is a perfect example of a multiple risk society and Kim Dae Hwan's analysis merits compliments for raising the issue of the need to modify Beck's idea of singular-risk approach and uniform reflexivity with something else that would make more sense in the Korean case. Beck seems to miss the point if he thinks that there is only a difference of "dominant" and "additive" elements. Instead, there is a whole range of alternatives and mixes, which would make far more sense in a context of multiple risk society.

For me the most problematic part in Beck's comment is the use of such terms as "the West", which goes directly against Beck's own claim that risk society is already borderless, although Beck himself in other part of his essay includes the dichotomy between Western and non-Western on the list of boundaries that have collapsed. Beck uses reflexive modernisation in measuring whether risk society has arrived, but actual measuring of reflexivity or lack of it in modernisation is most difficult to accomplish. In its narrowest sense, reflexivity is used to measure who has understood the theories of Beck and others and only a slightly more open-minded interpretation would be juxtapose the enlightened intelligentsia of the world to the ignorant masses. This, of course, it not Beck's main point, but a lack of cultural sensitivity is a major problem in applying the contemporary European social risk discourse globally. This is unfortunately true although for Beck reflexive modernity means going beyond most post-modern theories and not being bothered by boundaries in time and space. Beck's concept of reflexive modernity in its mockery of boundaries has very appealing qualities but the reader often is returned to the boring and narrow-minded realities of academic discourses when different societies are treated with different criteria and such labels as "the West" are used to differentiate when Beck does not want to make claims about the degree of reflexivity found in different societies. When Beck says that risk society analysis in Korean cases has crossed cultural boundaries he at the same claims that the cultural boundary in the Korean case is highly significant. When he contrasts Korea with the West he also claims that Korea is not like the West without telling where his West is. We can only speculate what Beck would think about the cultural boundaries, reflexivity or Westerness of such societies as Japan, China, Finland, Russia, Croatia, Lithuania or Hungary. The classical modernisation of Japanese society took place very much at the same time as that of Prussia and Germany and with carefully chosen indicators it would be easy to argue that Japan in many ways beats many Western European countries in reflexivity and in many of the traditional criteria of being regarded as part of the West, such as GDP per capita, level of science and technology or support for the U.S. military (compare with Beck's surprisingly strong criticism of European pacifism). Moreover, if the first thing that catches Beck's eye in the Korean case is the height of the cultural boundary, the same apparently should apply not only to Japan and China but also to many of the current Member States of the European Union.

Furthermore, the concept of modernity has been contested in Korean studies as providing justification first for Japanese rule and then for other forms of imperialism. Many Korean scholars have noted with satisfaction that the modernisation theory has become increasingly discredited in past decades and that when the concept of modernity is used it is most often relativised. In short, the assumed unity of the diverse phenomena subsumed under the title of "modernity" is dubious. There is no single modernity package containing the right mix of democracy, rule of law, liberal legality, bureaucracy, science, rationalisation in thought, etc. The Korean nationalist scholars (there are many) have a tendency to dismiss many important changes taking place during the colonial rule as being results of the premodern character of Japanese rule. In short, these Korean scholars have a rather fixed idea what real modernity is and the abuses and crimes of Japanese rule, which certainly blocked democratisation in Korea, make the whole colonial period appear to be premodern. The legal-administrative changes and the intensification of control imposed to subjugate the Koreans were also something that covered areas of life left relatively untouched by the traditional Korean state. After the colonial period there was no going back to the old political and administrative practices, nor was any gratitude to the Japanese for having invaded Korea and disrupted its social and political development (Cf. Lee 1999, p. 21-23). Lee continues with an analysis of Japanese colonial practices, such as strict enforcement of sanitation standards and monopolies, and even tried to resume and enforce some of the policies of the Chôson reform Cabinet (1895) such as short hair for males and wearing coloured clothes instead of traditional white dress. The Japanese rationale in trying to revolutionalize Korean fashion was that in their eyes topknots and white dresses were unhygienic and impeded hard work. Ibid, p. 39-42).

Of course, any policy of forcing or encouraging or banning people to have topknots or wearing clothes of some particular colour or style limits in a very direct way the freedom of people to express their individuality. Whether the stated reason to require a particular type of conformity in terms of fashion is related to tradition or any rational modern explanation, such as hygiene or need to wear a uniform to distinguish the members of the group from other groups, continuation of rather inflexible dress codes in both Korea and Japan tells much about the Confucian or feudal traditions of these societies. Meanwhile, both Japan and South Korea are also societies where people are very conscious about fashion and about the possibilities of fashion statements. However, social pressures and dress codes often leave little room for people to express their personality through fashion, but whatever room there exists, it is often used effectively. Furthermore, people who are free from occupational pressures often have a very creative approach to fashion and both Japan and Korea are among the fashion centres of the world.

It is quite telling that in Japan there are government policies about enforcing particular type of little bit less formal dress code for civil servants during hot and humid summers in order to conserve energy and set the air conditioning to 28 Celsius. The original so called Cool Biz dress code was introduced during the term of Prime Minister Koizumi and it included such features as starched collars and short-sleeved shirts. The idea was that the private sector would emulate the behaviour of the bureaucrats and there would be significant energy savings. The issue was not that people would be free to choose lighter dress code during summer months if they wished so. After the energy shortages caused by the Fukushima crisis even more stringent rules for the use of air conditioning and dress codes were enforced both in public and private sectors in Japan. This time the Ministry of Environment started a Super Cool Biz campaign that included the wear of colourful Okinawan *kariyushi* shirts. The Okinawan shirts remained an exotic photo opportunity item but there was a renewed social pressure to put up with working in 28 Celsius. The actual clothing styles did not change dramatically since the formal wear strongly associated with social status and employment status. In the hot and humid weather of the East Asian summers maintaining the formal European dress code is clearly a very irrational and uncomfortable thing to do. While Europe and the United States with their much milder climate have gone through drastic changes in dress code in working life, Japan and Korea have made a rather premodern Western tradition a part of their modern tradition, also combining aspects of their political and social traditions in the lack of flexibility and use of common sense.

While modernisation *(kindaika)* in Japan refers to the period when Japan left behind the premodern era of Edo period and became a modern society, not many Japanese scholars are ready to dismiss the quality of modernisation or modernity simply on the basis of absence of democracy and civil liberties in Japan. If it is argued that Japan essentially modernised only after 1945 the argument comes close to the interpretation of Japanese and German history repeatedly put forward by George W. Bush, claiming that there is an analogy between the occupation of Iraq and the democratisation of Japan and Germany. For instance, in his nationally broadcast speech on September 7, 2003 President Bush claimed that "America has done this kind of work before. Following World War II, we lifted up the defeated nations of Japan and Germany, and stood with them as they built representative governments. We committed years and resources to this cause. And that effort has been repaid many times over in three generations of friendship and peace. America today accepts the challenge of helping Iraq in the same spirit -- for their sake, and our own." (The White House, http://www.whitehouse.gov/news/releases/2003/09/20030907-1.html).

This kind of argument basically claims that prewar Japan and Germany had similarities with contemporary Iraq in terms of foundations for democracy, modernity and affluence, and in Japan the greatest insult of all is to give the whole credit of contemporary Japanese democracy to the U.S. military occupation (while the U.S. military itself as a racially segregated occupation force in the 1940s and 1950s was not the ideal model for all the years to come). For many Japanese historians the ability to build up and run a colonial empire itself was a sign of modernity rather than absence of it. What appears to so many Koreans as a premodern monster bullying its neighbours and its own citizens with arbitrary and harsh policies is seen by most Japanese as the modern Japanese state gradually establishing foundations for post-war modernity and post-modernity – and prosperity in East Asia. In short, the modernity concepts in Korea and Japan have very different meanings and for any researcher touching these issues, especially in a comparative analysis, it means entering a political minefield. Interestingly, also Western researchers such as Beck in his analysis also jumps over the sensitive years of Japanese colonialism and contrasts the contemporary South Korea with Confucian Korea. In Japan, it would be almost impossible to forget or leap over the years 1905-1945 in any serious analysis of modernisation/modernity.

However, in the Korean case there are also policies and social practices that can easily be extended to pre-colonial Korea. For instance, Kim Jung Wk argues that the Korean environmental policy and thinking are firmly based on old Korean traditions, and many of these traditions actually predating Confucianism. According to Kim, Korean people, being pantheists, used to revere nature and have very strict environmental ethics. They did not regard nature as a resource for human exploitation but regarded human beings as parts of nature, and sought a life in harmony with it. They regarded such acts as destroying or polluting nature or the wasteful use of resources as crimes, which would incur divine wrath (Kim Jung Wk 1998, p. 220).

Kim cites examples of the severe punishments that were reserved for people who, for instance, wasted useful fertiliser resources or were caught at illegal logging. There were also strict rules for building towns and houses so as to minimise damage to the environment. The Korean *ondol* heating system serves (still used in many variations both in contemporary South and North Korea) as a specific example of thrifty use of energy when the cooking fireplace exhaust-gases were used to warm all rooms through channels built under the floor. This heating method alone was able to save a lot of firewood. Furthermore, forests were also protected through banning all logging in designated areas of "Forbidden Mountains". The methods of nightsoil collection and food waste recycling closely resemble practices found in Japan. However, the tone in Kim's research is that the policy priority of government in Korea for centuries was management of mountains and water and that this policy was carried out so effectively that people thought that even pouring hot water on soil was sinful because it would kill the soil (Ibid, p. 220-221). In other words, traditional Korea can provide material for constructing a rather extreme example of how clearly pre-modern society designed and implemented an environmental policy that was effective in protecting nature and natural resources while allowing people to benefit from relatively flourishing nature. Some aspects of that policy go to such extremes that with good reason it can be claimed that the policy became embedded in ritual and that its cosmological and ontological foundations helped to raise environmental risk control to the position of a civil religion (in the absence of a better term to describe the spiritual content of these practices).

According to Kim all this was reversed when Japan occupied Korea. The deforestation activities were at the heart of the conflict between Russia and Japan and it is no wonder that Japanese colonialists did not waste time in exploiting the Korean natural resources. As a result forests were cut down without mercy and for instance the Korean tiger soon became extinct.

Korean tigers were not the only animals to become extinct during those years, but in Korean culture tigers and magpies *(Pica pica)* are the animals with the greatest symbolic role. The demise of the tigers is something that is still deeply felt by contemporary Koreans, while magpies are luckily still found everywhere. The true mystery bird of Korean tradition and birdwatching is the Korean Crested Shelduck *(wonangsachon, Tadorna cristata)*. The species is known to science from a few individuals in what is nowadays South Korea and Primorye, Russia. Of the three known specimens, two are in Japan at the Yamashina Institute and one in Copenhagen. However, there are Japanese records indicating that these birds were still regularly hunted by the Japanese in Korea as late as in the 1920s. The bird had been known for years in Japan as the *chôsenoshi* ("Korean Mandarin Duck", whereas the modern Japanese name is *kanmuritsukushigamo*) and is depicted and described in many Japanese documents in the 18th, 19th and 20th centuries. There is also a certain wild record from Hokkaidô in 1822 (Brazil 1991, p. 76 and Fuller 2000, p. 96-97). There have been unconfirmed reports and rumours of sightings in North Korea, the Russian Far East and Northern China during the past decades. BirdLife International is still optimistic that a small population may actually survive somewhere (BirdLife 2000, p. 94). In fact, the Korean crested shelduck would be a perfect symbol for the destruction of Korean environment and for the lack of interest in the rest of the world for Korea and its nature.

Other consequences included serious problems with flood control and drought. There has also been heavy soil erosion. This is directly connected with flood control and riparian habitat destruction since eroded soil accumulates in rivers and river banks need to be built high simply to control flood risk. The erosion has also made even many major rivers including Han'gang largely unsuitable for navigation making it necessary to develop railway and highway transportation. Erosion and an enormous amount of eroded soil deposits are also connected with large-scale reclamation projects in the West Coast area, which have destroyed some of the most unique natural treasures of Korea. The environmental destruction started with the Japanese colonialism, but the end of it did not bring back the lost paradise. The Korean war and rapid industrialisation without much concern for the environment simply continued the process of environmental degradation. Such Japanese policies as the forced monoculture of rice (instead of the former practices based on mixed-culture and crop rotation) also irrevocably changed Korean agriculture and the rice monoculture in turn led to heavy dependence on chemical fertilisers and pesticides (Kim Jung Wk 1998, p. 221-227). The history of Korean environmental degradation has clear parallels with the developments in Japan, but the distinguishing factor is that the Japanese colonial administrators had little concern for the Korean people and for Korean nature and that they were in a position during the colonial rule (1905-1945) to totally exterminate traditional environmental policy. The Korean people can blame the Japanese for these sins but after the end of colonialism there has been little sign of efforts to revive the foundations of traditional environmental policy.

Kim Jung Wk's concise description of traditional Korean environmental practices summarises well ideas that have been presented in more detailed and more conservatively focused research. One of the best available sources is Totman 2004, which presents a picture of pre-modern agricultural regimes in Korea and Japan. Totman discusses in detail the different phases in the development of agricultural orders. The overall picture is that pre-modern farming and forestry practices were remarkably rationally planned and implemented in both countries. For instance, in both countries there is a wealth of essays and farm manuals that discuss farming problems and describe remedies. These writings are often based on direct observation and in their method often comes very close to modern natural sciences. In some points Totman is less convinced than Kim on the ecological sustainability of pre-modern Korean practices. For instance, Totman notes that large cities consumed so much wood (for fuel and timber) that by the eighteenth century little valuable timber seems to have survived on accessible sites across peninsular Korea (Totman 2004, p. 147).

The other side of the Korean social system was that the rigidity of the class society (with large numbers of slaves) and strict social control meant that everything took place top-down in society, where the authority of the ruling *yangban* class was not questioned. The social and environmental stability was accompanied even with demographic stability: the population of Korea fluctuated within the 10-14 million range during the 170 years to 1870 and only after that started to increase rapidly (having clear parallels with Japan). For the environment stability meant that especially vast areas of mountainous high country continued to flourish as wild realms, sustaining indigenous flora and fauna. However, Totman also cites Western visitors from the 1890s and around 1900, who observed large deforested areas and signs of serious erosion and, for instance, talked about the brown, bare hills of Pusan (Ibid, p. 149-160). All in all, the evidence points to less dramatic transition between the pre-modern and modern, or traditional Korean environmental regime and the Japanese occupation mindlessly destroying a sustainable and stable system. The hierarchical traditions in Korea have made it difficult then and now to create environmental regimes that enjoy the free support of the people. In the end the *yangban* served Korean nature much better than either the Japanese colonialists or modern Korean political leaders, and in some aspects, one could think that the *yangban* actually were not so bad in terms of reflexivity, but it surely was a pre-modern rather than a post-modern variant. In terms of legitimacy, of course, the rule of *yangban* beats hands down the Japanese occupation, but the lack of democracy and tight control of people with particularly strong dose of patriarchy are parts of Korean tradition, that have created particularly severe obstacles for modern Korean society.

Furthermore, it may be misleading to treat pantheism and Confucianism as inseparable parts of Korean tradition. When pantheism is usually discussed in the Korean context the first thing to come up is shamanism. However, most contemporary Koreans talk about shamanism by using such modern terms as superstition *(mishin)* and the whole issue is subject to prejudices and stigma. Shamanism is often equated with irrationality and therefore scientists and administrators especially want to have nothing to do with it. Similarly, the *yangban* legitimised their rule with far more rational Confucianism. Nowadays the scorn of shamanism is particularly strong in the medical field, where the healing powers of shamans are not much appreciated, although many ordinary people also seek additional treatment from shamans. Kim Chongho argues that it is precisely the irrationality of shamanism which appeals to many Koreans and gives the tradition its value and healing power. Kim points out that the experience of misfortune does not really make sense to the sufferer in rational terms. Furthermore, the dominant culture, which for a very long time has looked down on shamanism, is often itself identified as one of the main sources of misfortunes. As Kim elegantly puts it, shamans are experts in dealing with cultural nonsense – the cultural problems which cannot be solved within the framework of Korean public culture. Kim goes as far to juxtapose shamanism to all other ideologies and religions in Korea, which all are less subject to prejudice and less frequently seen as superstition (Kim 2003).

By analysing Korean traditions somewhat more closely it is easy to see much cultural heterogeneity and co-existence of seemingly incompatible elements. Kim's main point is that shamanism has been able to survive throughout Korean history just because it has maintained its relevance to people on the margins of society. By offering glimpses of a worldview which is at odds with the modern rational worldview shamanism offers an escape from contemporary Korean society. This may not be very different from Marx's understanding of religion as opium for the people to be able to carry on with their miserable lives. However, Kim in his original analysis of Korean shamanism also shows how shamanism has had a deep impact on Korean Buddhist and Christian sects, many of which have rituals with a close resemblance to shamanic rituals. Some churches even have developed their own techniques of ecstasy and exorcism rites. Kim also makes the point that people make a difference between the religions traditions and, for instance, the Christians explain their rites by their own theological dogmas (Ibid, p. 36-37).

Taking this argument slightly further one could also see that much of the ritualistic behaviour or leadership behaviour so typical to both Korean states and so many social organisations has a lot in common with the irrational and marginalised, but, yet so appealing shamanistic tradition intermingled with the narrative of Korean history – even if not all the rituals involve mastering spirits or talking with them. Unfortunately, shamanism has the greatest use for contemporary people as a type of cultural paradox providing alternative views on modernity and rationality. This means that while many Koreans continue to practice shamanism in some form they also fail to seriously study the cosmology and views of nature, which after all, are central to the original Eurasian shamanist tradition.

2. AN INTERPRETATION OF JAPANESE VISUAL TRADITIONS IN THEIR SOCIAL AND CULTURAL CONTEXT

The tradition of Japanese visual arts has developed in close interaction with Asian and Western arts. However, Japanese visual arts have created a new tradition of re-presentation of reality that represents and reflects the changes in society and by doing so has served as an agent of change itself. However, even the use of basic terminology of visual arts in Japanese reveals that there are different ideas about how "Japanese" different traditions of artistic expression are. The terms of *yôga* (literally Western painting, oil painting) and *kaiga* (picture, painting and increasingly, movies and animations) both refer primarily to art that is seen to fall under the category of Western art, while Asian art forms *(tôyôbijutsu,* primarily Chinese, Korean, "Silkroad" and Indian art traditions) and Japanese art forms are normally addressed by more specific names such as *emakimono* (picture scroll), *nihonga* (Japanese painting) or *ukiyoe* (woodblock prints of the floating world). Many Japanese art forms have been labelled outside Japan as crafts or are not understood as arts that would easily fit the hierarchy of artistic expression, that had been developed primarily on the basis of European tradition.

Ernest Fenollosa, the first foreigner that seriously tried to understand the whole variety of Japanese art forms, already complained about the tendency to analyze and classify Japanese art by the technique or material rather than power of the imagination (Fenellosa 1912/2007, p. xxxii-xxxiii). By focusing on that power of imagination and creativity Fenellosa was far more successful than most of his contemporaries, either Western or Japanese, to see how Japanese art clearly differed from Chinese art and who were the most interesting representatives of Japanese tradition, although also Fenellosa quite often also explicitly compared to the European tradition and with his deep knowledge of European arts was, indeed, able to detect faraway influences and parallels. Although Fenellosa complained about the other scholars' insensitive framework of analysis, he did not really try to cover the whole field of Japanese artistic expression, regardless of the technique or material. In fact, that task has not been completed by anyone and the lack of trying means that we do not have a good theoretical foundation that would easily accomodate Japanese artistic tradition and serve as a basis of further discussion.

One might easily assume that things have changed totally with modern art and a more liberal attitude towards a great diversity of techniques and ideas about art. However, when it comes to basic writing on Japanese art history both in Japan and elsewhere the concerns that Fenellosa raised are still very much with us. Among the many Japanese attempts to cover the long narrative of Japanese visual arts is a book by Tsuji Nobuo, the director of Miho Museum, *'Nihon bijutsu no rekishi. Jômon kara manga-anime made'* [The history of Japanese Arts. From Jômon period to Manga and Anime]. However, the short theoretical parts of the books simply discuss the awkwardness of translating *bijutsu* into "fine arts" and pointing out to Fenellosa's ideas. The book follows very much the traditional descriptive mode and gets to *manga* & *anime* and the really contemporary art (that is promised in the subtitle) only on page 428. The remaining 12 pages of the book fails to tell much how the contemporary Japanese art connects with all the preceding Japanese art. This kind of treatment of contemporary art is very common in art history everywhere: it is difficult to sum up the latest developments in art and say something meaningful about the contemporary art against the long tradition of arts. Tsuji's conclusion concludes with idea taken from Langdon Warner's The Enduring Art of Japan (1952) that Japanese art keeps on enduring and continuing its history while going through changes (Tsuji 2005, p. 440, Warner 1952). The book serves well its role of following the narrative of "fine arts" in Japan from Jômon Period to present, but it does not analyze the special character of Japanese arts, nor the selection of art pieces in the book or analyze how the art reflects all the changes in society since the Jômon Period. Of course, it is better not to dishonestly claim that there is an unbroken tradition of distinctly Japanese art starting from the Haniwa clay figures and continuing to the most original contemporary Japanese art, unless someone wants to write a history of Japanese art that selects only works that are unmistakably different from any other traditions. Therefore, the Japanese art history, as it is usually understood in Japan and elsewhere, is very much part of the global history of art and global cultural traditions, and making sense out of it requires that both the global and Japanese cultural context is taken into account. Easy to say but this is not the easiest task to accomplish as it requires both a good knowledge of the both and an open mind.

There is also another way to analyse the past and present of Japanese art. In *Furu/ima. Kurabete wakaru nippon bijutsu nyûmon* (Wada ed. 2010) such very basic ideas as composition, space, allusion, diorama, animism, jest and nothingness in Japanese visual arts are illustrated by showing one selected comtemporary piece of art next to one old piece of art. In some cases it is obvious that the artist has been using a classic work as a source of inspiration or copied some part of it whereas in some cases the parallels are more general but work well enough to serve the purpose of the book to illustrate how much contemporary Japanese art owes to past Japanese art. In her introductory chapter Wada Kyôko argues that the distinguishing character of the Japanese art is that the tradition and present, foreign and domestic influences are all combined and adjusted to the natural features *(fûdo)* of Japan. Wada herself describes her method as seeking analogies *(anarojî)* between past and present works and art and then using them to illustrate some of the most basic conceptual ideas of Japanese art, such as the *wabisabi* and simplicity (Wada 2010, p. 18-19).

The book makes good reading, the selections are thought evoking and provide interesting comparisons. Of course, the idea of analogy (Greek *analogia)* is something that the classical philosophers already discussed at length. Analogies as shared abstractions are closely related to metaphors, allegories and other kinds of comparisons. In short, analogies make thinking and understanding of abstractions easier. Although Wada does not go any deeper to analyse her use of a term that is very much part of classical art theory, it is worth noticing that her approach is very close to the idea of classical art education in Europe where artists were closely studying past art and getting fluent using visual clues and references in interesting ways to enrich the meaning of their work and show their knowledge. Furthermore, such vocabulary as allegories, metaphors and analogies are something that any classical European painter would have felt very familiar with. Of course, the idea of analogy can be used analogically with *mimêsis* to point out that both comparison and representation include both aspects of finding similarities and contrasting or new features. The danger of this approach is that the same method could easily be used to demonstrate that the Japanese artists often base their work on past foreign works of art.

The Japanese language still distinquishes the art forms largely on the basis of technique and material, and shows great concern to "foreign" origins of techniques – after about 150 years of very mixed traditions. Furthermore, both Western and Japanese art communities still find it problematic to locate, for instance, such important parts of Japanese artistic tradition as garden design or tea ceremony within the tradition of Japanese arts. Nowadays it is quite difficult to decide what should be included within the Western art tradition as the borders of expression are all the time deliberately crossed. The often quite rigid categorization used in Japanese language, art education and museums looks rather unusual from a European perspective. Furthermore, it is commonplace in Japan to find generalizations about rational world view being the basis of Western arts in a direct contrast to the less dogmatic and less naturalistic world view that defines the Japanese traditions of art, especially *nihonga*. Sometimes the Japanese art philosophy is extended to cover also the Chinese and Indian traditions (see e.g. Hatanaka 1986, p. 176-177).

Of course, the reality is far more complex and interesting. Both Western and Japanese (or Asian) art traditions are impossible to capture by neat definitions as the whole idea of modern and contemporary art rests on the strive to seek new ways to create art and constant reinterpretation of all traditions, often in interesting cross-fertilized mixes. Anyway, Japanese tradition of art also has strong roots in realism. Curator Sherman E. Lee wrote many books and curated several splendid exhibitions focusing on realism in Japanese art. His point was that in Japanese art there is a strong tradition of boldness and pragmatic and frank realism. Someone reading only Lee's books would certainly reach the conclusion that Japanese tradition of visual art is particularly realist in its orientation and that artists focused primarily on depicting the human foibles and personalities with candor (Lee 1983).

The labels and names have not stopped the Japanese artists from adopting influences from everywhere and from mixing techniques. With art it is not only important what is being created but it also matters how works of art are received. Japan has developed its own way of appreciating art and artists and this relationship is constantly changing. It is a serious problem if the tastes and lifestyles of people do not have room for art in their lives, as art often makes people to think and feel more deeply about everything: life, society, environment, politics, people themselves and the meaning of everything. Culture tells much about the nation and its people. In political science culture is increasingly seen in the context of soft power, which is based on the attractiveness and admiration of the values on which the culture rests (Nye 2004). However, the idea of "getting others to want the outcomes you want" (Ibid, p. 5) is a bit naive in the complicated modern societies, when most people and nations are at loss to think what they really want. Culture may be the ultimate tool of influence, but it can not be easily used in a manipulated way, although Joseph Nye and Prime Minister Abe seem to think so. Instead, in culture there is always present an element of honesty and widely shared values and views. What is exactly that the Japanese state wants to show to the rest of the world by promoting the export of *manga* and *anime* and the idea that Japan is cool?

The Abe administration presented its new Cool Japan agenda in May 2013. *Manga* and *anime* are still there but the new addition was the Japanese food culture and the idea that Japan will send its cultural missionaries to convert the rest of the world. One new aspect is that the government will support the Japanese creators to contribute internationally. The overall purpose seems to tell to the Japanese public that the Trans Pacific Partnership treaty would also create new opportunities to Japanese agriculture and that Japanese culture can be exploited as a cash cow with little investment. The way the agenda was presented to the public made the whole idea appear as a business and marketing event rather than a serious attempt to change Japanese image and do something to facilitate that change. The whole campaign seems to be at least as much aimed to the domestic audience than to the world. The latest version includes such bizarre elements as sending Japanese food missionaries to teach the virtues of tea ceremony and Japanese sake to the rest of the world. Someone must have seen a great untapped global market for *macha* that would solve all the problems caused by the liberalization of farm trade (Mainichi Shimbun 2013b).

Most likely the result is just fine as the impact of this kind of "policy change" will be limited, but there is no telling what will be the actual reception and whether it is anywhere near what the policy-makers wanted. Japanese politicians introduced the whole idea of Cool Japan after Japan started to cut its ODA and seemed to abandon many of the goals of its foreign policy of the 1990s. Japan will not be admitted to the UN Security Council as long as it depends on China and Russia and the UN diplomacy has little to offer to help with the acute problems of Japanese international relations. Heng Yee-Kuan has compared the soft power competition between Japan and China and puts forward the argument that Japanese popular cultural efforts are 'decentered' and often present the non-dogmatic and non-nationalist side of Japan. Hello Kitty, for instance, is surnamed White, her parents are called George and Mary and they live in London (Heng 2010, p. 275-304). The decentered Japanese cultural products surely find a market and positive reception abroad. However, Hello Kitty apparently was not in the mind of Joseph Nye when he thought about using culture to influence others. The Cool Japan policy is presented primarily as a sales pitch to the Japanese audience and one should not think that Japanese diplomacy will be outsourced to Hello Kitty and Totoro anytime soon as a shrewd effort to win the hearts and minds of everyone.

My point is that cultural values should be shared by a large segment of the society to become socially relevant and to really matter. Style in art can cover both individual style and the styles of groups of artists, schools of art or national or international style. As art becomes labelled and placed into these boxes, it also becomes evaluated by different specialist communities and by the larger society, whose tastes are often guided from above, but not nearly always. In fact, the Japanese art provides ample evidence of the constant interplay between the high art and popular art, and the popular art is often winning.

The Japanese modern lifestyles leave little room for traditional visual arts in the narrow sense of tradition. The number of households that have space to exhibit properly traditional Japanese art, especially *kakejiku* scrolls and *nihonga* are increasingly rare. Small sized Western paintings would be easier to hang on the walls of modern Japanese houses, but unlike with proper bourgeois households in Europe there are not so many ordinary people who have oil paintings covering all the walls. The European bureaucrat who used the expression *'cage à lapin'* (rabbit hutch) to describe Japanese modern houses and invited the anger of the Japanese side and created an immortal description of the reality of modern Japanese living simply compared the life style of his own social class to that of the wealthy Japanese in Japanese urban centres. Even the most luxurious and spacious rabbit hutches are not ideal for art collecting, but are real homes with their own aesthetic standards. The Japanese art market is much more dependent on museums and corporate customers, but these customers tend to have somewhat narrow interests.

From a broader persective, the Japanese tradition of visual arts is doing just fine: Japanese artists use every available opportunity to make use of the new wealthy consumer society and its rapidly shifting tastes. After all, there are not anymore enough wealthy connoisseurs of art available for the artists and, instead, there is a new much bigger target audience. The potential visual arts audience is everyone with their varying possessions of wealth and, at least, some knowledge of Japanese artistic traditions, sometimes simply as a result of school education, but even more from the exposure to popular culture. Graphic art is everywhere in Japan and the upper end of graphic art is just very good by any comparison, with an eye to detail, clarity and beauty. Some of the best known and commercially most successful Japanese painters have blended their art and careers with commercial graphic design, such as Yokoo Tadanori, Tanaami Kei'ichi, Ôtake Shinrô and Hibino Katsuhiko. The contemporary art after them owes much to the success of these artists in the 1970s and the 1980s. The internationally recognized artists, Murakami, Nara and Aida have went further with the elements of graphic design and commentary of contemporary society, as well as branding and marketing their own art.

The visual environment of modern Japan is different from the Western traditions largely because of commercial aesthetics, which range from subdued and sensitive colours and forms derived from old traditions to the most blatant disrespect to harmony and good manners, which is the essence of visual culture using simple messages or images of sex and violence simply to make people stop and take notice. The presence of *kanji* characters, of course, brings a special visual effect everywhere. Some Westerns observers seem to be confused with the *kanji* and what they tell about Japanese society. One prominent example is Roland Barthes who interpreted the whole Japanese culture as an extraordinary case of an empire of signs (Barthes 1982) (without much of focus or clear significance if we believe Barthes, who attempted to understand Japanese culture without any knowledge of Japanese culture and only marginally more knowledge about its art traditions).

The other end of Japanese popular culture and its visual aesthetics, the one of unmistakably and often decidedly bad taste, is the one that has not been frequently analyzed. Much of *manga* falls into this category. During the Edo Period many artists started to produce so called toba-e comical and satirizing coloured prints produced by woodblocks the same way as *ukiyoe*. The common people kept buying these cheap and funny works and many more ambitious *ukiyoe* artists produced also these works as a sidejob. In other words, the artists often had an open mind about producing very different kind of art to different audiences. *Manga* was used sometimes in the meaning of a sketch, but Imaizumi Ippyô used it in the Newspaper Jiji Shinpô in 1890 to translate Italian *caricatura* with the result that *toba-e* gradually was renamed to *manga* (Shimizu 2013, p. 9-10).

During the 20th century the manga artists were quick to adopt ideas from Europe, such as Art Deco. A significant new development was a creation of mass market of childrens' *manga*. Meanwhile, many older art forms were in decline and manga artists were mostly professionals, who now could make their living with manga. Nowadays Japan has too many *mangaka* (*manga* artists), who struggle to get their work published and to survive in a market where the rules are made by the publishers. The result is that it does not pay to produce quality and to survive one needs to produce vast amounts of substandard work. Many artists also also know very well the dark attics of their audience and society and by their art create a "more balanced" picture of the Japanese traditions and culture. The Japanese artists who show the ugly condition of modern society with the occasional beauty in ugliness are often using the medium of commercial art, *anime* or *manga*. Also the big names of Japanese contemporary art sometimes have no worries to mix their art with images that would be branded as glorifying pedophilia, violence, racism or religious/ cultural insensitivity outside Japan. The rest of the world simply often has different set of rules concerning hypocrisy than Japan and some Japanese art may end up being a bit too much for art lovers elsewhere, while in

Japan it is just interpreted against the reality of the other end of popular culture.

The art of Aida Makoto is a good example of a contemporary artist who touches every aspect of Japanese cultural tradition and by doing so demonstrates his originality and ability to renew himself. His art also is far more social in its character as it is not made to fall into some easily definable, sellable or exportable brand. When Mori Art Museum curator Kataoka Mami introduced Aida's exhibition in 2012 she characterised Aida as an artist of chaos and disorder and confinued to argue that Western rational worldview refutes ambiquity and paradox whereas Japanese society is based on contradiction and incomprehensibility (Kataoka 2012, p. 33-46).

Kataoka certainly has a point about Aida's ability to show how in Japan art, politics, economy and society are interwoven in a complex way. However, the Western art can hardly be claimed to be dominated by the Western rational worldview only and the power of artistic expression everywhere and at most times has been associated very closely with the ability of art to express ideas in ways that are different from other modes of expression. Furthermore, paradoxes (word derives from Greek *paradoxos*, "contrary to expectations/ opinions") have a long history as a source of art and philosophy in Europe. The Japanese version of the text uses terms *mujun* and *aimaisa*. *Mujun* (contradiction/paradox) is derived from Chinese philosophy and is based on Han Feizi's (3rd century B.C.) story about a merchant's self-contradictory claim that he had an invincible spear and shield for sale. However, the point of Han Feizi was to show how the logical approach works while paradoxes were often used by the Greek philosophers as a stylistic and artistic tool to make their story more interesting and to illustrate the weaknesses of too simple thinking/ expectations.

Contemporary Japanese society has a wealth of examples of both rather rigid categorization of cultural tradition and very open and playful approach to high and low culture and everything between them. The best way to define popular culture is to note that it is popular and that alone is no reason to suspect low standards. Japan does have a mass market for popular culture and many artists want to navigate the both worlds. Such issues as former stereotypes, either Japanese or foreign, or narrow ideas about culture based on social class, gender or social convention can also seen as an opportunity to make art or make fun. Historically many genres of Japanese culture have travelled from rather humble origins to the top category and general respect, such as the journey of Kabuki from Edo period bourgeois pastime to an icon of Japanese traditional culture. Some of the most famous Kabuki stars have occasionally wanted to bring more dynamism and new tricks to keep the interest of the audience (for a discussion on the special characteristics of Japanese popular culture, Treat 1996).

3. JAPANESE HISTORY AS A TREASURE CHEST OF POLICY STUDIES

As I have discussed above, the world is full of ingenious, often indigenous, solutions to organize living in modern societies. I have also shown that some kind of multiple risk framework would serve better to put modern reflexivity in a more fitting cultural and historical context. What ever we think about the degree of reflexivity among Japanese people (of various personalities and social/ educational backgrounds) in different phases and periods of Japanese history it becomes clear that Japanese history provides (just like the previous examples from Korea) a particularly interesting treasure chest from which both the contemporary Japanese people and the rest of the world can learn a lot. In the following I present a variety of cases to demonstrate the types of opportunities that Japanese history provides for researchers interested in policy studies. My intention is not to chronicle Japanese history of policies, although there clearly would be a demand for such books. Instead, I provide a variety of narratives, which together open windows on Japanese history and can serve as an alternative introduction to modern Japanese history.

3.1. Alternative Japanese Narratives of Health Policy: The Case of Hygiene and Sanitation in the Edo Period in Japan

Nowadays Japan is known as a model of longevity and relatively healthy life-styles. The premodern Japanese household in most cases was relatively poor, but in terms of hygiene and sanitation Japan was well ahead of all the European countries in the 19th century, after industrialisation had already had abundant time to change such societies as Britain. To start from water, the population density of Japan reached high levels relatively early, and people had to pay attention to hygiene in a country where climatic conditions could easily pollute the water. One practical way to ensure the safety of drinking water has been, and continues to be, drinking water in the form of tea. Water has also contributed to public health in Japan by being used for bathing. In addition, the bodily wastes of people and animals had been taken into good use for centuries as fertiliser and therefore they did not contaminate water resources. The water distribution and sanitation systems of such major Japanese cities as Edo and Kyôto during the Edo period had no parallel in the rest of the world. When the city of Edo (later, Tôkyô) was selected as the capital Shôgun Tokugawa Ieyasu realised that major works were needed to secure an adequate water supply. He ordered Ôkubo Tôgorô Tadayuki to build a system, which has then served the city for centuries and has for its part made it possible that Tôkyô is today the largest city on earth (Merviö 2001, p. 2-3 and Steele 2000, p. 39-50). The old Edo system was so effective that when it was modernised at the end of the 19th century the only major work was in replacing the wooden pipes with metal ones (Hanley 1997, p. 107-109. For the history of the Tama River and Tôkyô water system, see Steele 2000, p. 39-50). In addition to a rapidly increasing number of private family bathing facilities, the city of Edo had some 600 public baths in operation at the beginning of the 19th century and most people seem to have had good access to them, while, for instance, most contemporary European city populations had very poor bathing facilities (Cf. Hanley 1997, p. 97-101).

The examples from the Edo period in Japan illustrate how a country that by definition was supposed to be premodern and due to its security concerns even limited foreign contacts to a minimum, was still able to design effective large-scale systems that that effectively minimised health risks, contributed to public health and avoided wasting and polluting environment and scarce natural resources. The key policy element was an optimal use of water and other natural resources in the long run rather than maximum use in the short run. Without the early successes of these policies Japanese society would not have been able to increase its population so rapidly or maintain such large and dynamic urban concentrations as it did. Modern Japan for a long time turned its back on its premodern roots and the wisdom of many earlier achievements did get lost in many cases. However, designing sustainable life-styles and "managing the risks" of our times may in Japan produce solutions that, for instance, in the optimal use of water resources come remarkably close to some of the premodern practices.

One of the most important lesson from Edo history is that social infrastructure can serve people well and minimise a whole range of risks. However, neglect in investment in the social infrastructure has resulted in imbalances, distortions and anomalies. Public monies are wasted without regret and public outcry on purposes that in many cases are best described as being absurd while there are no funds available for removing the most appalling and visible defects of the cityscape. While many modern Japanese cities and houses have no effective municipal sewage systems (and are far behind both the premodern Japanese models and modern European cities) Japan has all too many bridges and roads that lead nowhere and other public projects whose official purposes and financial calculations are less logical than most fairy tales (Cf. Hanley 1997, p. 176-198).

3.2. Alternative Japanese Narratives of History: The Case of Umesao Tadao and His Ecological View of History

Umesao Tadao is one of the best-known and most influential Japanese anthropologists. He has had very diverse interests, but already relatively early in his career, in the 1950s, he developed his distinctive theories on Japanese history narratives being linked with ecological views. His ideas and writings ranging from the 1950s to 2002, all related to an ecological view of history, were meticulously edited by Befu in an English language volume in 2003. The book contains as its core the Japanese classic *Bunmei no seitaishikan* in its 1967 version but also includes a number of articles that help to put the work in a context of rapidly developing academic discourses. The main original points of Umesao's work were such as: Japan's civilisation is structurally the same as that of Western Europe and is radically different from China. Umesao paints a picture where such people as the Chinese, Russians, Huns, Mongols, Tungus or Ottomans, all of relatively arid regions, had to always remain on guard against outside violence, especially against nomadic people. By solving the challenges of cultivation and irrigation people were able to build great civilisations. These cultures were characterised by a never-ending cycle of construction and destruction. By contrast, Japan and Western Europe appeared to Umesao almost as a greenhouse with perfect conditions for agriculture and with a certain level of technological development people could easily live well with the temperate forests, which were easier to control than tropical rainforests. For Umesao the ecological basis had already helped to form a modern citizenry when Western technology was introduced to Japan and as Japan modernised, it was not aiming at modernisation then or even today and instead always had its own agenda. Umesao uses the term hybrid culture (borrowed from Katô Shûichi) to describe modern Japanese culture not as a product of grafting Western imports onto Japanese roots but to describe how an entirely new hybrid plant has been crossbred. Umesao ends up dismissing both the concept of modernisation and the dichotomy of East/West as being unsuitable to describe Japanese culture (Umesao 2003, p. 38-61).

Umesao's theories are most interesting as they provide a contrast to all the theories treating Japan as an Eastern civilisation and having many links with Chinese culture. Furthermore, the critique related to modernisation as a uniform process has many implications, even to such discourses as risk society, with its focus on reflexivity and stages of modernity. Umesao's use of ecology (or *seitai*, including the diverse associations with life, ecology and biology) as the key concept of his theory was rather unusual for a Japanese scholar in the 1950s, and it is no wonder that even today he is regarded as one of the most original living scientists. Unfortunately, Umesao never developed further his ideas related to ecology in the sense of modern environmental studies or environmental ethics. Instead, he clarified his ideas and provided further arguments consolidating his theory that Japanese culture was very different from its neighbours. In his writing in 2000 he strongly defends the view that Japanese people have not originated from elsewhere but were in the archipelago from the very beginning. While admitting that Africa is the most likely birthplace of humans, Umesao sees a strong continuity from the Jômon culture to contemporary Japanese culture and goes to great lengths to show that, for instance, the nomadic horseback-riders never played a significant role in Japanese culture. Umesao argues that the lack of a tradition in milking and neutering proves that the nomads never invaded Japan or established the Japanese state (Ibid, p. 164-183). On the other hand, the Korean historians tend to present the "Horseriders" as people of Eastern Puyo, who first moved out of Manchuria, then established the kingdom of Koguryo and while moving out their horses southward on boats and invaded Japan in 369 A.D., bringing to Japan their practices of Shamanism and Shaman-kings, and giving rise to Shintô (See e.g. Covel 1988, p. 144-145 and for an analysis of Korean cultural influences/ exports and early Japanese culture, especially Shintô, Kimu 2001).

The way that Umesao's argument reads today makes him appear to many as a researcher who collaborated in crafting theories that fit well with the political needs of the time and, in particular, legitimised Japanese nationalism and the views of Japanese uniqueness. Yes, there is that aspect making it clear that Umesao is not a great friend of Chinese or Korean culture and has not been very perceptive in keeping up with the cultural, social and political developments in China and Korea.

To understand Umesao's intellectual development one clue is provided by the fact that his mentor and predecessor at the Kyôto University was Imanishi Kinji, one of the best known figures of Japanese biology and philosophy of science. While Umesao's career has been far more international and focused on culture than that of Imanishi, both shared a fondness for explaining society and culture by ecology in broad terms and seeing both people and nature as parts of the same web of life. Of the two, Imanishi firmly fixed his focus on nature and shows a clear respect for nature in all his writing. Imanishi is still greatly respected as a scientist, whose research on the social behaviour of Japanese monkeys, even showing some characteristics commonly shared by Japanese people, once made him a household name in Japan and is still one of the best known Japanese biologists outside Japan. Some of Imanishi's social theories also appear somewhat heterodox. In particular, Imanishi opposed Darwinism and in his later career even used as strong expressions as 'anti-science' to describe his opposition to such ideas that organisms had to compete with each other for survival. Many of Imanishi's books in the 1970s and early 1980s specifically focused on criticising Darwinism and Darwin's concepts of evolution and survival. Instead, Imanishi saw in nature more proof of co-operation and everything living as part of a harmonised whole (for Imanishi's views of nature, see Imanishi 2002. The English translation of this 1941 classic also includes a superb Introduction by Pamela J. Asquith, where she introduces Imanishi's work and puts even his somewhat more unusual ideas in a context, Asquith 2002, p. xxix-xliii).

Just as some of Umesao's views were convenient for Japanese nationalists, Imanishi is another of those famous Japanese scholars who at times have become used as evidence of a unique Japanese approach in science or as justifying some claims of popular Japaneseness discourse *(nihonjinron)* (Cf. Asquith: xxi). The picture of all living things living as part of a harmonised whole comes so close to the ideals of harmony *(wa)* and the ideals of Japanese society in the long harmony narrative that it is no wonder that many people in Japan and elsewhere immediately make the connection that when Imanishi is talking about harmony in the world he is somehow projecting the ideas of Japanese harmony to the word of natural science (for the harmony tradition in Japan, see e.g. Merviö 1988 and 1991). From the point of risk society the discourses of Umesao and Imanishi both provide a wealth of alternatives to test the ideas of reflexivity and modernity and how the Japanese (and other) views of nature have emerged. To clarify, for me the theories of neither Umesao or Imanishi represent particularly well the Japanese views of nature, but the very popularity of their views tells a lot about a need to find alternatives to standard theories, such as those relating to modernisation or Darwinism (although Imanishi's work can hardly be recommended as the best introduction to Darwinism).

The issue of nature concepts and their relation to modernisation has been a subject of several serious studies, the best one being Julia Adeney Thomas's book *Reconfiguring Modernity. Concepts of Nature in Japanese Political Ideology* (Thomas 2001). Thomas, first of all, makes the point that nature in Japanese intellectual history is not necessarily in any way related to environmental concerns. The concept *'shizen'* (usually translated as 'nature') was established in the 1890's replacing such terms as *'tenri', 'tenzen', 'tempu', 'tenchi', 'ûchû'* and *'banbutsu'*. '*Shizen*, and its alternative pronunciation, *'jinen'* suggested idleness and purposelessness in addition to spontaneity. This process of constructing the original meaning of the concept itself is quite different from 'nature', which has its etymological roots going back to the Latin root of *nasci* (to be born), sharing them with such words as the 'nation'. In Japan, *'shizen'* has been closely associated with the idea/myth of love of nature being a permanent Japanese national characteristic. The proof for this love is usually found in such fields of culture as poetry, arts and architecture, which undoubtedly symbolise all that is best in Japanese society. The problem of this myth is that it simply ignores all the proof of Japanese people and society being insensitive to nature and involved in its destruction (Ibid, p. 2-15).

As for modernisation and modernity, Thomas notes that she first thought that naturalised politics always had to mean the antithesis of modernity. However, she discovered that in the Japanese case the concepts related to modernisation and modernity were often used in the most confusing ways. The Japanese story or narrative of nature and modernity in intellectual history that emerged to her involved different historical phases when nature was interpreted very differently. In the Edo period, it was widely assumed that the static, hierarchical pattern of the physical cosmos promised universal social harmony if social forms accorded with the model provided by the external world. By the 1870's, nature everywhere was in flux, driving toward the progressive future of social Darwinism with the natural hierarchy produced by fierce competition. Finally, by the 1930's there was a changeover to a nationalised nature, no longer progressive or even universal (Ibid, p. 29-31). What is striking in this modern nature discourse is how removed the nature concepts were from environmentalist concerns and how much even in the Edo period nature concepts there was an emphasis that nature was part of human society. In Japan, modernity never left nature behind because nature was all along understood in ways making it easy to reconfigure both nature and modernity so as to fit in with the needs to interpret the changing Japanese society. Thomas's analysis provides a good basis to understand the kind of idea that scholars such as Umesao and Imanishi have held on nature and why they keep coming back to such issues as social harmony.

4. SECURITY ILLUSION: THE CASE OF JAPAN

Security perceptions in Japan are to a large extent built and reinforced by media and, for instance, the perceptions and fears of crime do not reflect the actual levels of criminality in society. I next move to analyse security from the assumption that insecurity has become a major political tool to sell public policies and political agendas that utilise vaguely defined concepts of security, often described by using nationalist rhetoric. In the political agendas of Japan such issues as national security in the sense of specific issues as the threat of China or North Korea or the war against terror are linked with broader social issues of public security and safety, which are much closer to the lives of most people.

4.1. Changing Traditional Security Environment

The Japanese constitution forbids the use of the military in international relations and the very existence and role of the Self-Defense Forces *(jieitai)* was for a long time a very sensitive issue. The official Japanese policy is that the SDF is exclusively defence-oriented *(senshû bôei)* and that to guarantee this there are constitution based limitations and prohibitions on Japan's use of military power. What follows is that Japan should limit its military capacity to the minimum necessary for the purposes of self-defence. This phase also opens the window of opportunity to make actual changes to the military capacity since the government has for decades argued that the minimum limit depends on the prevailing international situation and on existing military technology – and that it is the Japanese government, which can at its discretion identify needs to make changes to SDF capability. In short, it has never been very clear what kind of weapons *per se* would be unconstitutional, although in the past such rather scholastic discussions have characterised Japanese defence discourses. While most Japanese people take this kind pedantry at its face value they would not be happy to see their neighbours practising similar equivocating. Basically the line of North Korean leaders is that nuclear weapons constitute the bare minimum that North Korea needs for self-defence (and that they have got ever more powerful weapons if anyone is still not convinced) (for the legal and other norms relating to the Self-Defense Forces, see Katzenstein 1996, p. 99-130 and Hughes 2004, p. 136-137).

With all the political and legal constraints surrounding defence issues in Japan most Japanese politicians have been cautious about increasing the role of the Self-Defense Forces. The categorical constitutional ban on collective security *(shûdan-teki jieiken)* is even more difficult to explain in a way to leave any meaningful role for the SDF in the real world, where Japan happens to be allied with the United States. For instance, the process to gradually open United Nations peace-keeping to the Self-Defense Forces was a difficult one and Japanese peace-keepers certainly have more limitations than any other forces in their use of force. The excuse that was used that time made the distinction that the SDF can constitutionally support the military forces of other countries if the actions do not involve military combat (Cf. Hughes 2004, p. 137). However, the dispatch of Japanese troops to Iraq by the Koizumi Cabinet without more opposition was a clear sign that the Japanese government and many Japanese people are ready to accept a far more traditional role for their fighting forces and are ready for deaths in combat, if that is the price that they have to pay for the new government policies and for a new type of credibility in foreign policy.

Against the background of constitutional pacifism and the bitter lessons of past wars it is easy to understand that Japanese people, including politicians, have generally been glad to welcome challenges to 'traditional' security approaches. The Japanese foreign policy liturgy has already for years been using "human security" to characterise its policy approach. In reality Japan has been far less assertive in its diplomacy than its main partner especially, the United States, and therefore there is no abrupt change if Japan adopts "soft" security approaches when it has already had "soft" policies and political liturgy for a half a century (for more on the issues of "human security" and "ecological security" in Japan, see Merviö 2002). What is new for Japan is that, after almost 60 years, it is once again sending soldiers overseas with a clear understanding of the risks involved. In other words, from a Japanese perspective traditional security can be interpreted to mean the Japanese tradition of constitutional pacifism focusing on welfare, democracy and human rights while the military security approach is most closely identified with sending the troops to Iraq and challenging the rationale of sticking to the 9th article when China and North Korea have adopted a far more hostile defense policy.

For most of the post-war era most Japanese have believed that Japan can best avoid conflicts by maintaining close relations with its key allies and keeping a low profile, especially in security policies. With the globalisation of the world economy and the growing global presence of Japanese economic interests it became clear from the 1970s and 1980s that Japan needed more active foreign policies. The United States, Japan's security partner, had been steadily asking Japan ever since the 1950s to adopt a more assertive defence policy, but Japan had felt that the minimum level acceptable for the US and the security treaty obligations would serve Japanese interests much better and would contribute more to the security and welfare of people by maximising their economic wealth. The Soviet threat during the Cold War was a rather abstract risk for most Japanese. The main theatre of Cold War was in Europe and stronger military capabilities in Japan did not seem to do much to deter the Soviet Union. The security treaty with the US made any Soviet attack seem unrealistic and for much of the time the only scenario of military attack to Japan was based on the assumption that the Soviet Union would attack US forces and military installations in Japan in the event of full-blown nuclear war. On the other hand, the Soviets did not seem to appreciate Japanese pacifism, either, and the deadlock over the Northern Territories partly explains why the relations between Japan and the Soviet Union remained so bad for so long. This territorial dispute, and more recently, rising Russian nationalism, has also spoiled much of the potential for a new start in Russo-Japanese relations, as well. Moreover, in the end, Russia and the Soviet Union have been difficult neighbours for Japan, but most of the time there has been little reason to worry about a military attack after the United States stopped advancing Soviet troops in 1945 before they could reach Hokkaidô. With the new Russia with far weaker military power and with less assertive foreign policies there is naturally less reason (so far) to worry about Russian intentions.

In the 1990s the situation changed rapidly with the emergence of North Korea as a country posing a direct military threat to Japan with its nuclear and missile programmes and its hostility to the Japanese government and even Japanese people due to bitter experiences of Japanese colonialism. For the Japanese public the abductions of Japanese citizens by North Korean spies and the public outrage that has followed after the North Korean government partly admitted its role in the abductions have convinced many Japanese people that the North Korean government cannot be trusted. At the same time the quality of media coverage of North Korea has not been high: the smallest details of the private lives of former abductees have been followed with avid interest while serious discussion on North Korean social, political and humanitarian issues has been relatively rare. In this kind of atmosphere it has been easy for Japanese politicians to seek political support by simply appearing to be tough towards North Korea. The result is that North Korean behaviour has greatly added to Japanese determination to strengthen her military capabilities and reliance on military power as a means to respond to perceived threats from North Korea (see Hughes 2004, p. 87-91).

In addition, China's gradual emergence as a regional and global superpower in all fields, including economy and military, has been perceived as a potential long-term risk, especially, because 1) Taiwan is so close to Japan, and because 2) China's political modernisation and democratisation has not proceeded with the same speed as other parts of China's modernisation process. The sporadic outbreaks of Chinese nationalism and anti-Japanese feelings serve as a reminder that Japan is not viewed as a friend and ally in China. Modern Chinese nationalism and notions of Chinese identity themselves are often rooted in narratives about past humiliations (Cf. Gries 2004).

On the other hand, Sino-Japanese relations are also characterised by an increasing interdependence in economic relations and significant co-operation in many fields. After all, Japanese technology, investments and foreign aid have played an important role in the Chinese modernisation process. Furthermore, in such fields as environmental aid Japan has done more than any other country to change Chinese environmental behaviour, although the magnitude of environmental problems is so large in China that Japanese environmental aid may look quite modest. In short, Sino-Japanese relations are characterised by both rivalry and co-operation and behind all the official friendly talk there are serious reservations about the real motives of the counterpart. The worst fears on both sides certainly include scenarios of greater militarisation of the counterpart and the possibility that an unexpected turn in (North) Korea, Taiwan or elsewhere will create a situation where Chinese and Japanese military forces find themselves on opposing sides (Cf. Green 2003, p. 77-109). Against this growing sense of interdependence the Chinese aggressive behaviour in the Senkaku Islands dispute became as a surprise to most people in Japan and there are very few people who see any justification in the Chinese increasingly vocal position that essentially is disputing the legitimacy of the international treaties concluded during the colonial era when China was weak. From the Japanese point of view Chinese policy has drastically changed when Chinese government has started to claim a superpower position and has started to seek confrontation in East Asia instead of trying to deepen regional and global cooperation that in the first place helped to raise China into a global economic power.

The rise of old type of military threats together with the erosion of Cold War camps has made some Japanese turn to old solutions of national security, which would include an independent strong military. The Koizumi Cabinet already wanted to step up Japanese defence capabilities and actual battle readiness. However, this activity was carefully done within the context of the U.S.-Japan Security Treaty and the Bush administration certainly greatly valued Japanese new defence contributions, which demonstrated that the Japanese have finally started to accept the view that Japanese and global security need strong military defences, and that Japan is doing its part in the global fight against terror and those governments that the U.S. claims to be behind terror or have anything to do with the "axis of evil". North Korean hostility to Japan gave new life and meaning to the old U.S.-Japan Security Treaty, but the Senkaku Island dispute with China raises the stakes enormously and has became a serious issue also for the Sino-US relations. The years of DPJ administrations in Japan saw a lower profile in defense issues and in US-Japan relations. However, the new Chinese threat was a major force helping Abe administration to power and Abe used the opportunity without hesitation to show his determination to respond to the Chinese threat in a way that the Chinese would understand: the use of nationalist language and the strengthening Japanese defense capabilities. The next step will be to get rid of the 9th article and deepen political, economic and defense cooperation with the United States. All this represents a major change in Japanese politics and will be accompanied by major policy changes in such fields as economy, foreign policy, education, environment and defence. The more assertive and nationalist Japanese foreign policy most likely will only worsen relations with China – and also with South Korea, which should be an ally, if seen through the alliance mechanics.

The new Chinese nationalistic and aggressive policies certainly remind Japanese of the fundamental differences between Japan and China and it is easy for the Abe administration to push forward with its own foreign and defense policies that quite ironically have some similarities with the Chinese policies and style. The big difference is that Abe administration has overwhelming popular support that has been measured in free elections. However, if Abe administration is succesfull in revising the Constitution and in changing the status of defense forces, Japan will surely be a different country for its neighbours to deal with in the future. From the point of view of the Abe administration the other immediate burning concern is to find a more sustainable solution to trade relations. The quickest, most rational and most realistic choice was the Trans Pacific Partnership and closer trade relations also with the EU countries and emerging economies everywhere. After all, Japan has already wasted a lot of time and fallen behind countries like South Korea in fixing its trade policies. Something like nuclear-free Japan would not qualify as a policy goal for the LDP under these circumstances. For the common people the LDP policy choices appear primarily as rational ones that may be chosen by the LDP but apparently also enjoy the support of the Japanese specialists and bureaucrats, as well.

4.2. Safety as a Psychological State of Mind

The modern welfare systems and advances of modern medicine have considerably lengthened the life span of people, Japan being the ultimate example. Meanwhile, Japanese society is also a prime example of societies where technocratic decision-making and futuristic dreams have few serious political critics. In Japan technology has played its role well in supporting the business and political establishments. The final test of the value of technological innovations has been whether they will sell on domestic and on international markets, rather than usefulness for people in Japan or elsewhere. In Japan, the current distribution of labour within the world economic system and the Japanese economy with close participation of the engineering sector and technological innovations have obviously worked well to produce unforeseen material benefits for the people. In the minds of people also the successes of welfare systems and medical advances are also closely associated with "modern science", to a degree little short of elevating the technology and (natural) sciences to the status of religion (in the sense of determining the meaning and future of life as we know it). Another aspect of this phenomenon is that organised religion does not do too well in Japan (nor in many other modern societies). However, in the end people continue to be mortal and highly vulnerable to diseases and endless miseries of life. It may be that modern science can identify ways for people to reduce everyday risks and health risks, but in the end the lives of people are not and will never be safe (Cf. Wahlstedt 2004, p. 50-51, reviewing the thought of philosopher Torsti Lehtinen).

In Japan, the triple crisis of 2011 (tsunami, earthquake and Fukushima) with its death toll and reminder of fragility of life for a short moment stopped many people to reflect about the vulnerability of Japanese society and every single individual. However, the teaching seems to have lost quickly and the policy makers rather skillfully hijacked the crisis to bolster their old preferred agendas. The policies of both DPJ and LDP administrations after 2011 show little attempt of trying to learn from the mistakes. Instead the politicians were quick to use to their benefit the talk of social solidarity and social bonds that understandably had become widespread (Cf. Samuels 2013).

It is interesting how quickly the criticism against Japanese nuclear policy vanished or became marginalized after Fukushima when the political mainstream was just ignoring those concerns and was presenting other themes as the real solution to burning social and economic problems. The success of Abenomics (with the support rate of Abe administration rapidly climbing to above 70% and staying there) tells how Abe as a skilful politician could come up with an assortment of policies that appeared to provide a more credible promise of hope than anything that Japanese people have seen for a long time. However, Prime Minister Abe has remained committed to his own ideas and principles and quite bravely he has pushing a pro-nuclear agenda in a country that not even put behind itself the Fukushima crisis and very complex contamination issue. Prime Minister Abe surely knows his people better than any surveys: while post-Fukushima surveys indicate that the majority of Japanese people has become very suspicious of nuclear energy, Abe has with no serious opposition made revitalization of nuclear energy sector a key part of his policy agenda and has even aggressively supported the export of Japanese nuclear technology abroad, especially in the Middle East and Southeast Asia.

After the Hubris and Nemesis reminding of the Japanese people of their short-sightedness they are already back to life as usual – back to modernity and rationality providing an illusion of safety and hope of a better future. Even people who have doubts about some particular aspects of Japanese modern project have very little to present as an alternative. Japanese politics, especially, is void of real alternatives. The real strength of LDP lies in its track record of having nurtured a bureaucratic system that is reasonably efficient and capable of working together with the Japanese style of economic system. It may be too much to say that the politicians should be entitled to take credit for the successes of Japanese economy, but the erratic behaviour of the DPJ administrations during their stay in power clearly sent a powerful message to the Japanese public that the best hope that they have for future is to trust the LDP, especially if it works in cooperation with the bureaucracy and business sector. While the LDP is more or less promising the return to past safety and feeling of normalcy, that also means that LDP will not introduce drastic changes unless the external environment clearly requires them and those policy changes also happen to be ideologically acceptable.

Being left at the mercy of "modernity" without values, both modern science and most religious systems reduce nature and reality to something that can be defined and explained from chosen principles or dogmas. Natural sciences and religion both use knowledge and conceptual thinking to bring nature/ reality under control and for most people the feeling of being in control is the next thing to security or feelings of safety and familiarity. The feeling of familiarity kills all spontaneity and diminishes the ability to respect the uniqueness of life in all its details. Most of good poetry and art has for centuries derived its vitality from the untamed conflicts and chaos of life, far from trying to sanitise and make it all too familiar.

Philosophers like Heidegger and Nishida have written at length about the richness and variety of being. For Heidegger 'Being' remained beyond analytical thinking and one of his most useful concepts to deal with reality was *Gelassenheit.* Nishida opted for such mysterious concepts as *'junsui keiken'* (pure experience) (which he loosely attributed to the Rinzai Zen Schools) to explain how reality can be met in its original undistorted state. Japanese society, of course, has had and continues to have individuals who practice *Gelassenheit* effectively in their private lives and the sensitivity of many Japanese artists and artisans serves as a constant reminder of this. The similarities between Heidegger's thought and the various schools of Eastern thought, in particular Japanese Zen traditions, has frequently been pointed out (see e.g. Hempel 1987). However, turning one's back on society does not necessarily signify opening up to the 'Being' as it is.

The phenomena of *'otaku'* and *'furîtâ'* in Japan tell about young people who do not want to meet the contemporary Japanese social expectations to compete for education, career and social success and, instead, either spend their lives at home (*'otaku'*) or take up short-term low-pay employment without (or with) worrying much about the future. *Otaku* means literally a home, but in Japanese discourses it also has the meaning of young people who stay at home and in most extreme cases spend years inside in their own rooms, possibly communicating with the outside world with a computer. Meanwhile, the term of *furîtâ* is a mix between *arubaito* (derived from German 'Arbeit', work, meaning in Japanese part-time non-regular work) and things associated with 'free'.

For me the *'otaku'* and *'furîtâ'*both serve as critics of modern Japanese society and its social values. However, both *'otaku'* and *'furîtâ'* know well what they reject in Japanese society but as far as I can see both these forms of social escapism are likely to lead to a rather dull existence and in the worst cases filling minds with the instant satisfaction of 'entertainment'. Furthermore, the inflexibility of Japanese social institutions almost guarantees that the drop-outs never get a second chance. In this respect there is a notable difference between Japan and, for instance, Hong Kong, where people can far more easily return to school and where it is in the nature of things that people as a matter of personal risk management create alternative strategies for survival, and, for instance, regard juggling with two jobs as a good strategy just in case they lose one of them.

For instance, life-long learning is nowhere to be seen in Japan and a total rejection of the salaryman *(sararîman)* ideal is likely to lead to problems of establishing alternative lifestyles that still could include some degree of stability and, for instance, family life. The other part of missing safety nets is that most people have some sense of solidarity and are not ready to use every available opportunity to ostracise others. For instance, in schools this can sometimes lead to absurd situations, where students graduate from schools even if they have not even shown up at school for extended periods of time, but the teachers are kind enough not to be the ones who officially 'destroy' the future of young people.

While a common criticism in Japan of younger generations is that they have received everything too easily and it is the relative safety, welfare and affluence that has made some spoiled kids think that they have no need to think about tomorrow. This criticism fails to grasp why there are so many young people who, against all the social pressure, do not want to do as their elders did and as most of their peers still do. Social alienation in Japan nowadays tends to be turned inside and there is remarkably little of anything like social radicalism among young people in Japan. Playing computer games at home is neither a form of social radicalism nor a sign of feeling safe or happy. I would rather be afraid that the contemporary forms of social escapism are prone to nurture a state of mind characterised by a lack of strong feelings or opinions and that the end result in many cases will be resignation and depression rather than a desire to do something to improve the personal or wider social situation.

The safety illusion of modern people may manifestate itself in an attempt to deliberately alienate oneself from the unwanted facts of life. The medical profession in Japan is a keen accomplice in making people believe that everything human is done to control their lives. The most innocent part is when people start taking medicine to fight any new symptom without giving much thought whether the medicine is really needed. A huge portion of medicines consumed in modern societies is done in order to treat colds and flues that normally do not require extensive treatment. The Japanese peculiarity is that medical doctors normally do not properly explain in a professional manner their diagnosis and treatment to the patients and only in the recent years have the pharmacies started to list the names and chemical components of prescribed medicines. However, it is still commonplace in Japan to go to the doctor and receive a bunch of blue and red pills with only instructions of how many are taken in a day before having to visit the doctor again. The lack of transparency in the medical profession has made it easy for the whole profession in Japan to sell unneeded or even harmful medicines.

Hospitalisations are used more frequently in Japan than in most other similar affluent industrialised countries and the average length of hospitalisation in Japan is often many times longer than that in other countries. There are many reasons for this state of affairs, but it is certainly not within the best interest of either the patients or hospitals. Japanese hospitals and clinics also make use of the most modern technology in the world and once the expensive gadgets are procured they must also be used. For instance, Japanese clinics and hospitals have nowadays about half of the CAT scans in the world and have few inhibitions about using them. However, the use of CAT scans entails excessive amounts of radiation and when used without restraints there is a real danger of causing cancer (as shown especially in British studies). The motive of the hospitals, medical doctors and pharmacies, of course, all too often is to keep people in the dark about (some of) the medical details and maximise their economic gain, while people have little choice when they shop for good care, especially if they need acute care or if they know from experience that all the clinics and hospitals in the city are just as bad. Yet, most people in Japan do not read foreign medical journals or pay too much attention to the scandal weeklies and instead trust their doctors and hospitals with the result that there is a widespread belief that the Japanese medical sector has greatly contributed to making Japan the safest country in the world (and the best measurement in the end is always the longest average life span, which, however, does not exclusively measure the quality of medical care or quality of life).

Safety is not only measured by medical or other measurable standards, but is more often a psychological state of mind. Medicines, drugs or alcohol are used deliberately to make all the anxiety and *Angst* of life disappear. Furthermore, whole lifestyles can be created for the same purpose. Television, videos, DVDs and the virtual reality of Internet all fill the emptiness of life without much effort being asked. Much of the modern "entertainment" simply helps people fill their time without making them think, and especially think about the unpleasant facts of life. Having painted a somewhat depressing picture of the use of modern technology to find the lowest common denominator of consumers (Japanese TV getting quite close to that goal) I still believe that information societies can be developed so that technological innovation strengthens the social participation and transparency of society, and in the end contributes to the welfare of the people. One attempt to set up a real world model of how information society and welfare society can be combined is Castells and Himanen 2003. The Japanese example of information society, anyway, is rather depressing: the "information" that people actually are interested in is all too often not fit to be called information and there is good reason to take a critical look at the "improvements" that the technology and modernity have delivered to people in recent years.

5. JAPAN AND THE JAPANESE SOCIAL MODEL: A REINTERPRETATION OF THE SITUATION IN 2013

The global political and economic influence of East Asia has increased especially because of the economic performance of the East Asian societies and the steadily increased co-dependency between East Asian and other developed economies. The new economic status has increased interest on East Asia elsewhere, but it is difficult to provide easy answers about societies that are, first of all, very different from each other when it comes to social systems and even political systems. The first wave of serious Western interest on modern Asian societies and their social models and policies was probably Japan in the 1970s when it's economy for the first time was perceived to pose a serious challenge to American and European political and economic systems. At that time such Japanese social innovations or characteristics as the life-long employment, loyalty to the elderly, employers and authorities, the high savings rate of Japanese households or the close cooperation between the Japanese politicians, bureaucrats and businesses created an image of a society that has re-invented the wheel and had become unbeatable in economic terms.

However, Japanese society soon lost its momentum and in the beginning of the 1990s the Japanese economic bubble burst with the result that much of the interest in Japanese model and in Japanese social and economic policies vanished rapidly. The Japanese model, after all, was not nearly as unique and successful as it had appeared during its emergence as a rival to other established systems and models. In Japan, many corporations soon started to question the cornerstones of the Japanese model such as the company-as-a-family and life-long employment and turned to similar kind of cost-cutting and productivity increase measures that had previously seen as the proof of the shortsightedness of other models. Once the post-bubble problems in Japan proved to be more or less permanent in their nature also politicians increasingly started to voice opinions that legitimized the harsh measures of corporate sector and asked for serious cost-cutting within the public sector to bring the budget deficit within a more sustainable terrain. However, for the opposition politicians it is easy to tell that the foundations of the economy and nation's future are built on sand. It is quite a different story for a government filled with quarreling politicians who share little in terms political ideology and can under no circumstances alienate their own support organization and all the many people who helped them to their position. Furthermore, the new governments in Japan have usually been facing a life-expectancy of a few months and a need to do something just to survive to the next week and month rather than have the luxury to think about the future of nation and civilization.

The weak governments in Japan have proved unable to balance the national and local budgets as they are afraid of antagonizing the voters with increased taxation or significant cuts to public services. During the prolonged recession populist politicians in Japan have tried to find unpopular symbols and waste and have made them the cornerstone of their policy. In reality changes both in spending and savings have been insignificant. Meanwhile, the Japanese society has developed the most extreme case of ageing society, a mix of longevity, low birth rates and low levels of immigration. The longevity of the Japanese people is based both on policy successes, such as relatively well-functioning medical sector, and also on cultural issues such as sense of moderation in terms of culinary habits. Also the tendency to keep working as long as possible seems to keep at least some Japanese away from less healthy activities. The low birth rates are a result of policies that are hostile to child rearing: inflexibility of working life to permit parents to take care of their children and keep working, and lack of public childcare and support for raising children, including economic support for education.

Finally, Japanese society has proved to be unprepared to accept significant numbers of immigrants and make best use of ones that have managed to settle this far. Most foreigners in Japan are from China and Korea and political problems between these societies have made the Japanese people very worried about increased immigration. If anything, the atmosphere has turned even more hostile to foreigners with the Senkaku Islands and Takeshima Island controversies and there is a small but vocal Japanese minority that has turned against the Chinese and Koreans and goes to their neighborhoods with loudspeakers asking to "kill all the cockroaches, Koreans and Chinese" – while the police has reacted only in cases of fistfights, Japan having no specific or effective legislation against either hate speech or racial discrimination. Furthermore, Japan lacks any serious policies on multiculturalism. On the other hand, most Japanese people have at least some interest in the rest of the world and world cultures and have never had personal problems with foreigners. However, the Japanese media does make its best to report the crimes of foreigners, such as the rather rare cases of Chinese snakehead triad activities (often in cooperation with Japanese organized Yakuza crime). While the foreigners in Japan as a whole are even more law obedient than the rest of the population, the image and media coverage matters and most Japanese seem to believe that larger presence of foreigners would automatically involve an increase in crime and social problems, while there is very little discussion about potential benefits of immigration, in a country that has a declining and rapidly ageing population. However, the Japanese society has very strict rules on acceptable behavior and it is clear that most foreigners could never fulfill all the expectations as these norms have proved to be increasingly difficult to met even by native Japanese people, especially the younger ones who do not necessarily share the social norms and ideologies or older generations.

The prolonged recession has created a situation where most people seem to see no need for increased immigration. Instead, with recession the Japanese authorities were quick to invent policies with cash incentives to send back home so called *Nikkeijin* (people with Japanese ancestry from Latin America) who had once been given preferential treatment to come to Japan to work. The idea was that people who ideally had Japanese names, looks and cultural habits would more easily settle down and cause no trouble with their neighbors. The reality was that the *Nikkeijin* who largely lived in their own communities had particularly difficult time to assimilate and after this kind of setbacks and failed policies the Japanese authorities are even more reluctant to design policies to accept larger numbers of immigrants.

Against the background of a long succession of short-lived LDP and DPJ governments it is understandable that many Japanese people were tempted to believe that things could drastically improve if there was a government with a broad enough political mandate to present a comprehensive political agenda that would address a multitude of policy issues from foreign policy to trade policies and social policy. Abe Shinzô may appear as an unlike Messiah with already one recently failed administration that is best remembered because of his health problems and his hawkish views on defense and foreign policies. However, Abe apparently has learnt from his and other people's past failures and has energetically initiated and pushed through policies. His Abenomics is based very much on the idea that even people who are opposed to many of his ideas are happy to see that there is overall support rate exceeding 70 percent for Abe administration and that at least some of the policies appear to be working. Abe started with bold monetary policy and fiscal spending which immediately weakened Japanese yen by about 20 percent against other major currencies. Rather unorthodox method for a country that imports more than exports. Timely fiscal spending, of course, is exactly the same wasteful spending that other Japanese administrations have done for decades.

However, the weakening yen was promoted in Japanese media as a method to kickstart Japanese export industries. It did produce something like a boom in stock market as some people actually believed that Abenomics would actually bring a sustained economic revival. Meanwhile others noticed that the new conditions would certainly help some companies and will immediately change their profit outlook. Moreover, weaker yen, at least, meant that most companies appeared more valuable when evaluated in their yen value. After the first major stock market corrections Abe started to talk about the "third arrow" of his policies, the structural challenges of overcoming deflation, improving labor productivity and maintaining fiscal discipline. Of course, these policies will take far longer to implement and, may actually be contradictory to his initial policies. The Abenomics package apparently has not been put together to impress economists. More specifically, the idea of deliberately weakening own currency or printing more money is something that goes against everything that was the foundation of EU monetary policy. That is, the policy that failed when the majority of European countries demonstrated that they never seriously considered following the same fiscal discipline than Germany. By succeeding Abe would surely secure his place in the Pantheon of economic theory and would invite others to try similar tricks elsewhere. The main difference is that Abe does not need to ask a permission from anyone to weaken yen while the Greek, Italian or Spanish states had never got into their current mess without the help of the more disciplined and wealthy Euro peers who will in the end also spread the pain of failed economic policies.

Anyway, Abe has already been successful in winning the support of most Japanese voters and in addition to reorganising the foreign relations of Japan and introducing his most controversial economic policies he has put forward a wide range of initiatives that address many burning social issues and somehow seem to relate to his other policies. Abe has suggested that he will raise the consumption tax to 8 percent from current 5 percent as soon as April 2014 if the political and economic situation allows it. The increase is justified primarily on the grounds of ballooning social security costs. However, at the same time Abe government has also tried to present especially the increased need for nursing care services for elderly people and medical businesses as an opportunity rather than an unavoidable necessity. Government funding for both sectors is likely to increase rapidly.

As for convincing the rest of the world that Japan will turn its budget balance to a surplus, the new target is year 2020, close enough to appear as a serious target and far enough for a Japanese politician to be able to do very little about it. It remains to be seen whether Abe is also able to convince foreign investors and politicians. The initial reaction abroad has been surprisingly positive, the only major criticism has been voiced by Chancellor Merkel, who has warned about credit-easing policies and tampering with exchange rates. Of course, Japan is also showing a very bad example to economically undisciplined European countries and the last thing that Merkel wants is that there is a global contagion of Abenomics. Meanwhile, the foreign investment to Japan has been quite undeveloped area during the time when foreign investors were often happy to leave Japan and seek new opportunities elsewhere in Asia, but the situation may change if Japan will move ahead with Trans pacific Partnership and a FTA with European Union, and if Japanese government under Abe is able to improve the domestic economy and woo investors with tax breaks and other measures that promote investments – and keep up the perception that Abenomics might work. The support to Abenomics will be tested quite soon when the impact of more expensive imports and higher inflation will start to show in economy. The initial reaction of Japanese consumers to perceived improvement in economy was to increase consumption and there are also some signs of increased investments, but if the actual purchasing power will drop, there will be no sustained economic boom and Abenomics will be discredited sooner or later. However, for the Abe administration it is important to translate high support rates to election victories that will secure a freedom for LDP to put their ideas to test, as next lower and upper house elections need to be held only in 2016. This is most unusual in Japan where there have been 15 prime ministers in last 20 years.

Soon after becoming Prime Minister Abe antagonized China and South Korea with statements concerning history and territorial issues and instead of trying to repair the damage he continued moving closer to the United States economically and politically and pushed Japan to build closer economic ties with other Asian countries. For the years to come Japan will not be pursuing anything resembling Asian regionalism or integration. During the DPJ administrations some short-lived Prime Ministers such as Hatoyama talked kindly about closer relations with Asian neighbors, but nothing substantial was done or proposed by any government to take the relationships to another level. In the light of present problems Japan is experiencing with both China and Korea it seems that there are few people in East Asia who believe in constructive political, economic and social cooperation between Japan, Korea and China.

Japan has chosen the path of relying even more heavily on the United States politically and economically and the United States also is moving during Obama administration to have more comprehensive trade policies with its allies under forthcoming Trans Pacific and Trans Atlantic Partnership agreements. However, TPP, a trade agreement, is not a good substitute to close neighborly relations for Japan. In particular, Japan is missing many opportunities when it fails to develop closer relations with Korea and China, the only countries with a substantial number of nationals living in Japan and a potential for major movement of people across borders.

In addition too high profile economic and foreign policy initiatives, Abe has also come up with other domestic policy initiatives. Among his major initiatives are the ones to reform educational policies and to address the shortage of kindergarten places. In educational field his administration has voiced the need to drastically reform the English language education that has failed to make Japanese people able to use English. The new focus is on business English and practical English and the idea is to make Japanese people able to discuss and express themselves in English. Of course, this initiative in closely linked to Abe administration's trade policies and to renewed sense of alliance and a special relationship with the United States. To accomplish the new goals it is proposed that English teaching should start from the third grade and that English should be treated as a regular subject. Moreover, English teachers should themselves have demonstrated their fluency and studied the language abroad. Nowadays the English teaching starts usually in the Junior High School and the actual abilities of English teachers leave lot of room for improvement, while the classes are conducted mostly in Japanese. One major change will be replacing the Japanese English testing schemes with the American TOEFL test and the idea is to make the TOEFL testing an integral part of university level English education, as well.

Meanwhile, the Abe administration has also shown its interest in doing something to alleviate the chronic shortage of childcare and kindergarten places. The issue is directly related to female participation in work life as well as to the low birth rate. It is interesting that in the Japanese discourses it is the conservative politicians who have started to talk in earnest about the need to improve women's participation in work life and to have more children. The reason to their concern has more to do with the worries that economy and pension systems will collapse if there are no workers. If the conservatives have to choose between accepting larger immigration and tapping the female labor reserve, which would require reassessment of family policies, they will surely choose the latter one. The issues of gender equality or children's rights are not the first things in the minds of these politicians, but they may end up doing much more than all the weak and softer hearted DPJ administrations ever accomplished. The city of Yokohama is famous in Japan as having able to fix the childcare situation with a coordinated approach involving both public and private sectors and increased municipal funding. The result is that among the major cities Yokohama has turned from one of the worst cases into one where it is easiest to find professional childcare – and a model city for the Abe administration. This far Abe administration has primarily tried to convince the corporations of the need to show understanding and flexibility to the needs of working mothers (and working fathers). It is too early to tell whether this administration will be serious in drafting a national policy that would drastically alter the situation and ultimately help to support Japanese to have more children and also tap the last remaining labor reserve, females with higher education, who have been forced to quit their jobs due to lack of flexibility and availability with child care arrangements, as well as nursing arrangements for the elderly. In short, Japan in the beginning of the Abe administration is a showcase how different public and private policies are interdependent and fall or stand together.

6. JAPANESE MEDIA STRUGGLING TO FIND ITS VOICE AND ROLE IN THE PUBLIC SPHERE

Finally, there is the issue of media shaping the minds and hearts of people and whether it serves its role of informing the public and keeping public watch over politicians' behavior. In Japan, the mass media has traditionally worked together with the government and the political elite and, therefore, limited open discussion rather than promoted it. Japan simply has a very different tradition concerning civil society and and social discourses than, for instance, different European societies have developed. Without publicity and transparency public sphere is severy incapacitated. The Internet has potential to change that situation, but when one takes a look at web discussions in Japanese about politics those all too often confirm the worst fears as the loss of "civility" and public virtue seems to be a permanent feature. Unfortunaly, this sorry state of affairs in by no means only a Japanese phenomenon, However, in Japan the situation contrasts with the all-too-understanding treatment that the government and authorities receive in the printed quality media – and the good manners that Japanese society is generally famous for.

It is everyone's guess how much the Japanese audience reads between the lines and understands that the quality media feels a need to go to extremes to protect smooth cooperation with the authorities. In Japan it does not raise too many questions if the government bans an access to a newspaper or television channel after the politicians rightly or wrongly believe that their message was not conveyed to the public in the favorable manner. Instead of defending the champions of free speech the rest of media will usually report these incidents by implicitly or explicitly questioning the professionalism and manners of the troublemakers rather than analysing whether the politicians deserved the less favorable treatment.

When the Japanese politicians suddenly are facing the Western media practices they often are genuinely surprised at the hostility and the first reaction usually is to blame the media as misunderstanding or mistranslating the politician's statement. The Japanese politicians have also been slow to realize that their statements in Japanese are closely followed abroad, especially when there is any international connection, and that making a statement that attracts a universal condemnation hardly ever counts as a good career move. A good example is Ôsaka Mayor and Japan Restoration Party co-leader Hashimoto Tôru, who badly miscalculated the domestic and international reaction to his statements on "comfort women" and prostitution in May 2013. Similarly, Prime Minister Abe's statements on history that account to airbrushing of the inconvenient historical episodes have largely been received with disbelief and astonishment abroad: especially the Japanese traditional friends find it difficult to understand how it serves any Japanese policy goals to deny the colonial wrongdoings of Japan. However, the domestic media has not focused on the lack of sophistication in Abe's history interpretations and the domestic media has largely been supportive of Abe and his Abenomics, instead.

On the contrary, Hashimoto, the populist politician and a challenger of the existing political system, had built his political career on his controversial statements on most everything and his ideas comfort women were already well known before he became worldfamous with his latest statements. At the time when he entered national politics he was often dubbed 'the most popular politician in Japan' and it probably was difficult for him to understand that populist politics is a very risky field and the image of outspokenness can easily turn into one of a loose cannon.

For a substantial share of the Japanese public it apparently was fine that Hashimoto as a Mayor demonstrated his leadership and belief in the 'public good' by such strange policies as requiring civil servants to disclose if they had tattoos and after seeing the lists telling that civil servants have no right to have tattoos and those who did should resign. Hashimoto also told the newly-appointed ward mayors of Ōsaka that civil servants cannot expect to have personal privacy or fundamental human rights while working for the public. All these controversial statements and policies have a pattern and it seems that many citizens were just happy to see that there was one politician who was not mincing his words and who was treating the civil servants in the same way that many private corporations were treating their employees. Making fun of human rights, harassing civil servants or trade unions, talking about Japan needing own nuclear weapons or insulting foreigners one group or nation at the time may work in the local politics of Ôsaka for a while, but most Japanese people realize that these are not very good ideas for national policy, as latest election results indicate.

However, Hashimoto has also demonstrated a very good awareness of his own human rights when he successfully battled against the (liberal) Asahi media house. The case also illuminates rather peculiar understanding about the freedom of press and how politicians can decide which aspects about their past become public knowledge. In October 2012 Shûkan Asahi (weekly magazine published by Asahi Shimbun) revealed that Hashimoto's father came from the *Burakumin* outcaste people and was affiliated with Yakuza, had a criminal record and committed suicide when Hashimoto was in elementary school. A third-party Press and Human Rights Committee was involved and it concluded that the Asahi Shimbun Company had "reinforced discrimination" and "was denying Hashimoto's integrity as a human being on the basis of his origin". As a result of this controversy Asahi Shimbun President resigned and there were a many personnel changes in the editorial department (Asahi Shimbun 13 November, 2012). The issue was not whether the story was true or not, but whether Hashimoto's human rights and some kind of code of conduct had been violated. It seems that for many the most sensitive issue had been that in the title of the article Hashimoto was called by his father's surname Hashishita written in *katakana* (usually reserved for foreigners, while Hashishita literally means "under the bridge" and is associated with the Burakunin and their living quarters), which surely is not a friendly thing to do. Hashimoto's mother had changed the name of the family, precisely to distance them from all Burakumin and Yakuza connections. Even people who do not share Hashimoto's political thinking may symphatize with Hashimoto's mother's attempt to protect her children.

However, the incident left it open whether Asahi Shimbun was reprimanded for its lack of courtesy and respect or for telling inconvenient facts about Hashimoto's family background. It does not help much that Asahi Shimbun adopted the usual way out of such situation: profuse apologies and strict punishments to everyone involved. We will never know how Asahi Shimbun should have acted to publish the story and continue discussion about Hashimoto's policies. So, in Japan it is fine for Hashimoto as a Mayor to deny a civil servant the right to continue working on the basis that someone may associate any small hidden tattoo with Yakuza connection while it is unforgivable for the media to reveal that the same Mayor's father had a real Yakuza background and a criminal record. It is also known that Hashimoto was raised by his mother and did not have much to do with his father, but surely Hashimoto is familiar with the history of his parents and, therefore, that history becomes relevant when Hashimoto's actions touch such issues as organized crime or the *Burakumin* issues, both of which are major issues in the city of Ôsaka. Furthermore, the pieces of information that Shûkan Asahi printed, and much more, had already been published elsewhere repeatedly by less respected and reliable sources and the whole controversy may tell more about who can better control (local) politics and media. As a lawyer by training Hashimoto must know something about choosing the winning arguments.

Another recent example from Japan illustrates well how ill-prepared the Japanese politicians can be to work with foreign media that does not hesitate to tell a story when they see one. In that case the New York Times stood by its article where Tokyo Governor Inose Naoki, who is also the chairman of the eventually successful Tôkyô 2020 Olympic bid committee, was quoted as saying ill-thought remarks about Istanbul, one of Tôkyô's rivals. Inose reportedly said in a recorded interview to two NYT reporters, one of whom was Japanese-born, in the presence of his own translator, that "So, from time to time, like Brazil, I think it's good to have a venue for the first time. But Islamic countries, the only thing they share in common is Allah and they are fighting with each other, and they have classes." He was also quoted as saying, "I'm sure people in Turkey want to live long ... And if they want to live long, they should create a culture like what we have in Japan. There might be a lot of young people, but if they die young, it doesn't mean much". In the end of the interview Inose also touched the issue of the relative value and hospitality of different cultures and cities: "I don't mean to flatter, but London is in a developed country whose sense of hospitality is excellent," Inose told reporters. "Tokyo's is also excellent. But other cities, not so much" (see e.g. Mainichi Shimbun 2013a and the original New York Times article: Belson & Tabuchi 2013).

After having seen all this nonsense in a printed form and having heard that the statement may break the International Olympic Committee rules Inose argued that his meaning "was not accurately reflected in the article". The content of Inose's statement also reveals that the Mayor of the largest city in the world with a former professional career in journalism and history can be so ignorant of foreign cultures and the basic rules for internationally acceptable behavior or what "hospitality" includes elsewhere. Of course, the strange remarks surely had an impact on the secretive voting of IOC members and while Tôkyô in the end was able to win the right to host the Olympics by wide margin the Mayor's comments raised ugly questions whether the Muslims in particular would be welcome and whether some people in Japan (and in the IOC) treat people differently according to the level of welfare and GDP in their countries.

The real teaching of the episode is that in Japan such an article would never have been published as no major newspaper would have wanted to cut its access to the Tôkyô Governor or cause harm to the Tôkyô Olympics bid. It is also interesting that the Japanese media reported the controversy between the Tôkyô Mayor and the New York Times mostly in a very short form by taking out a few words rather than analyzing whole sentences or explaining how the various statements would be interpreted abroad. Furthermore, there was no serious discussion about Inose's international comparisons and his ideas about the Japanese social model. No one in an eminent position in Japan has seriously challenged the ability of Mayor Inose to continue in the position of Mayor and the chairman of the Tôkyô 2020 bid committee. The episode was quickly forgotten in Japan and the domestic media has continued to inform the public about the positive reaction abroad to the Japanese bid, at the time when the foreign media has also been reporting far more accurately about the specific complaints raised in the IOC evaluation reports about all the rival bids and about the strengths and weaknesses of all three presentations in Lausanne in July 2013. Therefore, the Japanese public never heard in detail what kind of reception the representatives of the Istanbul and Madrid bid committees received. Most importantly, the Japanese public never had a change to hear any critical and informative analysis of the secretive workings of the IOC and what kind of issues and lobbying are likely to influence the decision-making of the IOC and, therefore, what kind of chance Japan actually had in getting the Olympics. The Japanese media coverage of the process resembles the nationalistic Japanese international sports coverage where the focus is mostly on the success of the Japanese athletes.

Japan may even not be the worst society in East Asia when it comes to nationalism and orchestrated national pride spoiling the spirit of sportsmanship: both the Seoul and Beijing Olympics were presented to the home audience as a means to show to the rest of the world the economic progress of these societies. Of course, the Tôkyô Olympics in 1964 are still presented in Japanese school books as the time when Japan demonstrated to the rest of the world how modern and developed it had become and how the Tôkyô Olympics gave the Japanese people high-speed Shinkansen trains. Interestingly Mayor Inose also touched the issue of suitably developed host cities and his idea of hospitality being equal to material wealth and development. Also in the IOC presentation in Lausanne Japan focused on the financial capabilities of Japan, public safety and the well-functioning infrastructure in Japan. In short, the 2020 bid would be a kind of rerun of the 1963 Olympics. Meanwhile, the Madrid bid is focusing on the possibility to organize Olympics without spending much money on them in a time when Spanish economy is going through difficult adjustments. Interestingly also the IOC President Jacques Rogge early on showed understanding to the Madrid bid by telling that "very little must be built. Much of the existing infrastructure is already in place. It will here and there need some refurbishment and upgrading, but they don't expect to have a big budget in terms of needing to add all the infrastructure. It's a bit like Atlanta. Atlanta did not have to build a lot. They had to build a big stadium, the rest was the utilization of existing facilities" (Hula 2011). Of course, the failed Madrid bid demonstrated that the IOC President did not single-handedly pick up the venue for the 2020 Olympics. However, it seems that it has not crossed anyone's mind in East Asia that the idea of trying to impress other people with newly acquired wealth can easily be seen more as a weakness than strength and may tell much about the challenges that the IOC faces in the future. Real hospitality in the context of the Olympics surely includes the principle that people of all nationalities are treated as equals.

Japan may continue to have a public sports policy that excels in public infrastructure construction, but China and South Korea have developed state-run sports regimes that have produced a steady supply of sports champions and good news to fill media. Especially in China this seems to include that young talents are separated from their families and shut up in closed training schools from a young age and they receive little education in anything else than sports. For every champion there are many more total losers (see e.g. Ransom & MacNeill 2012). Everywhere in East Asia, including Japan, there is strong evidence of systematic physical violence being an integral part of top sports. In Japan, where the sports associations tend to have more autonomy and less direct relationship with the state (and support from the state), the athletes have occasionally challenged the rationale of violence and discipline, but it seems that there are many people also in Japan who think that being an athlete requires total obedience to the coaches and anyone who happens to be in control.

To seek a comparison from the European past, perhaps the idea of *panem et circenses* (bread and games) has been around for a long time and it was used as a metaphor for a superficial means of appeasement. The Roman rulers knew well that the citizens, high and low, had lost the old values of civic virtue and public life. Sports, horse races and gladiators were suitable distractions to keep the masses satisfied and give them the champions and losers that they wanted. Judging from the long evidence, state and sports do not mix well. As for the Olympics, perhaps, there is a time for reflection whether the Olympic movement in its current form serves its purpose and whether the practice does more harm than good. A quick look at the current Olympic Charter reveals that the actual Olympics have very little to do with the stated mission and ideals of the movement (see International Olympic Committee 2011).

The example from international sports demonstrates the problems of combining the public and individual interests and can also be used to illustrate the role of cultural traditions and differences in the ways that sports are understood and made subject of public policies and propaganda/chauvinism in different societies. The Greek Olympic Games were always organized in the same venue in Olympia of Elis in honor of Zeus. The site was also the home to the Pheidias masterpiece statue of Zeus, which was known as one of the "Seven Wonders of the World". The point was very much to celebrate the common Greek cultural heritage. However, during the Roman time the participation was opened to all Roman citizens and the institution was "globalized". The Olympic Games were finally banned in 393 A.D. by the Christian Emperor, Theodosius I, when the Byzantine Empire had already adopted a very different kind of universalistic agenda and the pagan origins of the Olympic Games provided a good reason to discontinue the tradition. However, the at the heart of the Empire in Constantinople the Byzantine rulers repeatedly proved to be unable to control the mob, which used the Hippodrome races as an excuse to vent their frustration publicly and run amok – or worse – turn to politics.

CONCLUSION

This chapter has juggled and transcended the boundaries of academic disciplines in order to find explanations to developments in East Asia. A fitting conclusion for this chapter is to state that there are no such traditions in East Asia that would permanently put East Asian societies to very different courses of development. Traditions and culture do matter a lot, but they should be seen more as an opportunity than a destiny or curse. This chapter has also shown examples how people, most notably politicy makers, are masters of manipulating others and skilfully hijacking any crisis situation to bolster their old preferred agendas. This does not mean that those agendas are necessarily wrong. Since both Japan and Korea are democratic societies with free elections and contested politics it is easy to pass the responsibility of political developments to people. People are masters of their destiny and they deserve the leaders and policies that they have received. This conclusion is very much elsewhere in the world, as well.

In terms of international relations, East Asia also provides good examples that it is very difficult to live harmoniously with the neighbouring people or choose favourite neighbours. The next realisation is that the neighbouring people are remarkably similar, after all. In the Internet era it has become increasingly popular to refer to the world as the global village (or global theatre). However, in terms of culture, traditions and common experiences of life, people everywhere have inhabited the same village. Becoming aware of this communality should make people appreciate the diversity and divisions all the more.

REFERENCES

Asahi Shimbun. (2012, November 13). Panel: Shukan Asahi story on Osaka mayor adds to discrimination. *The Asahi Shimbun. Asia and Japan Watch.* Retrieved from http://ajw.asahi.com/article/behind_news/social_affairs/AJ201211130108

Asquith, P. J. (2002). Editor's preface and introduction. In *Imanishi Kinji: A Japanese view of nature: The world of living things*. London: Routledge.

Barthes, R. (1982). *The empire of signs*. New York: Hill & Wang.

Beck, U. (1998). The challenge of world risk society. *Korea Journal, 38*(4), 196–206.

Belson, K., & Tabuchi, H. (2013, April 26). In promoting his city for 2020 games, Tokyo's bid chairman tweaks others. *New York Times*. Retrieved from http://www.nytimes.com/2013/04/27/sports/in-praising-its-olympic-bid-tokyo-tweaks-the-others.html?pagewanted=all&_r=0

BirdLife International. (2000). *Threatened birds of the world*. Barcelona: Lynx Edicions.

Brazil, M. (1991). *The birds of Japan*. Washington, DC: Smithsonian Institution Press.

Castells, M., & Himanen, P. (2002). *The information society and welfare state: The Finnish model*. Oxford, UK: Oxford University Press. doi:10.1093/acprof:oso/9780199256990.001.0001

Covell, A. C. (1988). *Folk art and magic: Shamanism in Korea*. Seoul: Hollym.

Fenellosa, E. F. (1912). *Epochs of Chinese and Japanese art: An outline history of East Asiatic design*. Berkeley, CA: Stone Bridge Classics.

Fuller, E. (2000). *Extinct birds*. Oxford, UK: Oxford University Press.

Green, M. (2003). *Japan's reluctant realism: Foreign policy challenges in an era of uncertain power*. New York: Palgrave Macmillan.

Gries, P. H. (2004). *China's new nationalism: Pride, politics, and diplomacy*. Berkeley, CA: University of California Press.

Han, S.-J. (1998). The Korean path to modernization and risk society. *Korea Journal*, *38*(1), 5–27.

Hanley, S. B. (1997). *Everyday things in premodern Japan: The hidden legacy of material culture*. Berkeley, CA: University of California Press.

Hatanaka, K. (1986). Tôyôga no fuhenteki shisô o motomete. In *Nihonga: Zairyô to hyôgen*. Tôkyô: Bijutsu Shuppansha.

Hempel, H.-P. (1987). *Heidegger und Zen*. Frankfurt, Germany: Athenäum Verlag.

Heng, Y.-K. (2010). Mirror, mirror on the wall, who is the softest of them all? Evaluating Japanese and Chinese strategies in the 'soft' power competition era. *International Relations of the Asia-Pacific*, *10*(2), 275–304. doi:10.1093/irap/lcp023

Hughes, C. W. (2004). *Japan's security agenda: Military, economic & environmental dimensions*. Boulder, CO: Lynne Rienner Publishers.

Hula, E. (2011, September 26). IOC president on 2020 bids, Arab spring, cutting Olympic sports. *Around the Rings*. Retrieved from http://aroundtherings.com/articles/view.aspx?id=37990

Imanishi, K. (2002). *A Japanese view of nature: The world of living things*. London: Routledge.

International Olympic Committee. (2011). *Olympic charter: In force as from 8 July 2011*. International Olympic Committee. Retrieved from http://www.olympic.org/Documents/olympic_charter_en.pdf

Kataoka, M. (2012). Japan, the chaotic, and Aida Makoto. In *Aida Makoto: Tensai de gomen nasai: Monument for nothing*. Tôkyô: Mori Art Museum.

Katzenstein, P. J. (1996). *Cultural norms and national security: Police and military in postwar Japan*. Ithaca, NY: Cornell University Press.

Kim, C. (2003). *Korean shamanism: The cultural paradox*. Aldershot, UK: Ashgate.

Kim, D. H. (1998). Rush-to growth, economic crisis, limping modernization, and a dual-risk society. *Korea Journal*, *38*(1), 28–45.

Kim, J. W. (1998). Korea, land of environmental risk. *Korea Journal*, *38*(1), 220–240.

Lee, C. (1999). Modernity, legality, and power in Korea under Japanese rule. In G.-W. Shin, & M. Robinson (Eds.), *Colonial modernity in Korea*. Cambridge, MA: Harvard University Press.

Lee, S. E. (1983). *Reflections of reality in Japanese art*. Cleveland, OH: Cleveland Museum of Art and Indiana University Press.

Mainichi Shimbun. (2013a, May 1). Tokyo Olympic bid committee chief says Inose's remarks could infringe on IOC rules. *Mainichi Shimbun*. Retrieved from http://mainichi.jp/english/english/newsselect/news/20130501p2a00m0na002000c.html

Mainichi Shimbun. (2013b, May 28). Kûru-japan: Nihon ryôri de shôbu. *Mainichi Shimbun*. Retrieved from http://mainichi.jp/select/news/20130529k0000m040065000c.html

Merviö, M. (1988). *Harmony in the political tradition of Japan*. Tampere, Finland: University of Tampere.

Merviö, M. (1991). Harmony and conflict in the Japanese political tradition. In *Perspectives on Japan and Korea: Nordic proceedings in Asian studies*. Copenhagen: Nordic Institute for Asian Studies.

Merviö, M. (2001). *Construction of meanings for 'water' in Japanese culture and politics*. Paper presented at the International Water History Association (IWHA). Bergen, Norway.

Nye, J. S. (2004). *Soft power: The means to success in world politics*. New York: Public Affairs. doi:10.1111/j.1540-5842.2004.00673.x

Ransom, I., & MacNeill, R. (2012, August 9). Medals obscure cost of China's state-run sports regime. *Reuters*. Retrieved from http://uk.reuters.com/article/2012/08/09/uk-oly-chn-state-idUKBRE8781EC20120809

Samuels, R. J. (2013). *3.11: Disaster and change in Japan*. New York: Cornell University Press. doi:10.1353/jjs.2013.0016

Shimizu, I. (2013). Kinsei kindai manga ryakushi. In *Nihon no zushô manga*. Tôkyô: Pai Intânashonaru.

Steele, M. W. (2000). The history of the Tama River: Water and rocks in modern Japanese economic growth. *Asian Cultural Studies*, *26*, 39–50.

Thomas, J. A. (2001). *Reconfiguring modernity: Concepts of nature in Japanese political ideology*. Berkeley, CA: University of California Press.

Totman, C. (2004). Pre-industrial Korea and Japan in environmental perspective. In *Handbook of oriental studies* (Vol. 11). Boston: Brill.

Treat, J. W. (1996). Introduction. Japanese studies into cultural studies. In J. W. Treat (Ed.), *Contemporary Japan and popular culture*. Honolulu, HI: University of Hawai'i Press.

Tsuji, N. (2005). *Nihon bijutsu no rekishi: Jômon kara manga-anime made*. Tôkyô: Tôkyô Daigaku Shuppankai.

Umesao, T. (2003). *An ecological view of history: Japanese civilization in the world context*. Melbourne, Australia: Trans Pacific Press.

Wahlstedt, P. (2004). Elämme turvallisuusharhassa. *Suomen Luonto*, *4*, 50–51.

Warner, L. (1952). *The enduring art of Japan*. New York: Grove Press.

White House. (2003). *Speech of President Bush, September 7, 2003*. Retrieved from http://www.whitehouse.gov/news/releases/2003/09/20030907-1.html

KEY TERMS AND DEFINITIONS

Alternative Narratives of History: According to R.G. Collingwood history is an art, as it requires creativity and imagination. R. G. Collingwood was also a historian, archaeologist, sailor, artist, and musician and he understood well how much historical imagination was needed to recreate within his own mind the thoughts that make the narrative full, make it a story, history. After Collingwood there have been still many historians, many of whom have all but given up the attempt to truthfully understand and explain the past and present, not just record a few isolated facts. History is not simple, there are always conflicting accounts and alternative approaches. The narratives in the end are always interpretations, chosen among alternatives and destined to live together with other narratives.

Art: Life is short and art is long; art makes life worth living and moves within the realm of aesthetic experiences that are make humans human. Aristotle's ideas about the artistic representation (mimesis) opened the gates for still ongoing debate on the essence and limits of art.

Culture: Latin *cultura* (cultivation, growth) refers to the cultivation of plants or in a more abstract sense to the cultivation of human minds and spirits. Refined understanding is needed to appreciate culture, but that undestanding is often in short supply. A famous quote is: "Whenever I hear of culture... I release the safety catch of my Browning!" (Schlageter, Act 1, Scene 1, a Nazi play by Hanns Johst, 1933).

Japan: An archipelago of more than 6 800 islands (some of which are contested by Russia, China, Taiwan and Koreas). Earlier cultural contacts and influences connect with Korean and Chinese cultures while the Meiji political program transformed and modernized Japan by using Western models. Cultural traditions put to shame most others in the world.

Japanese Biodiversity: About 620 bird species have been recorded in Japan. Japanese macaques are the northernmost-living non-human primates and have been proved to be very intelligent. The other about 130 mammal species include, for instance, the extinct Japanese sea lion, likely extinct Japanese river otter and Amami black rabbit, the representative of ancient rabbits.

Korea: Peninsula between far larger and aggressive neighbours. "Korea" refers originally to the Kingdom of Goguryeo (mostly in current Noth Korea), while most ideas and traditions about anything Korean were formed during the long Joseon (Choson) Dynasty (1392-1897). After traumatic experiences of Japanese colonialism and civil war Korea has been divided between North and South, communism and non-communism, democratization and the Kims.

Korean Tigers: Among the animals important for Korean culture is the Korean tiger, which usually is claimed to become extinct during the Japanese colonial period. However, genetic samples indicate that Korean tiger has the same genetic origins as the Siberian (Amur) tiger and, therefore, the Korean tiger is still alive, but not in wild – in Korea. Meanwhile, magpies, the traditional partner of tigers, are doing just fine.

Olympic Games: Series of athletic competitions, religious rites and artistic events organized in honour of Zeus in Elis, Olympia every four years, or Olympiad from 776 B.C. to 394 A.D. The victors received wreaths of laurel leaves. After the Greek war of independence (1821) there were several attempts to revive the games, the most important being the games that were held in Athens in 1859, 1870 and 1875 after Evangelos Zappas, a wealthy Greek-Romanian had provided money to build a venue in Athens to organize permanently games there. However, the non-Greeks founded the International Olympic Committee in 1894 and after the Athens Olympics of 1896 the non-Greek leaders of the IOC soon hijacked the agenda and the Olympic games quickly started to drift away from their Greek origins. The modern Olympic games are strongly associated with such problems as political boycotts, doping, bribery and acts of terrorism.

Tradition: A tradition is a belief or behavior passed down within a group or society with symbolic meaning or special significance with real or assumed origins in the past. The English term is based on the Latin *traderer* (transmit) while, for instance, the Japanese term *dentô* encompasses very similar meanings and associations. Traditions are very important in every field of culture, arts, politics and society as they very much define how people see themselves, their past and future. Moreover, traditions pass over the experiences and wisdom of past generations and often are also used or manipulated to restrict the freedom to do and see things differently. In social arena tradition often is seen as a contrast to modernity, while in political science tradition is often seen as the bedfellow of conservatism. However, according to Hans-Georg Gadamer one can never escape from one's tradition and this does not mean he is insisting we endorse all traditions writ large. Gadamer is not espousing a conservative approach to tradition that blindly affirms the whole of a tradition and leaves one without recourse to critique it. His point is that in as much as tradition serves as the condition of one's knowledge, the background that instigates all inquiry, one can never start from a tradition-free place.

Chapter 2
On the Genealogy of Public and Private:
Beyond Market and State to the World of Pluralism

Jari Vuori
University of Eastern Finland, Finland

Marika Kylänen
University of Eastern Finland, Finland & Warwick Business School, UK

ABSTRACT

Since the late 1990s, the literature of public-private management and publicness have increased, but the genealogy of public-private in a frame of pluralistic definitions has not been studied. This study focuses on ascertaining how the nature and operations of public-private relations influence discursive practices in public-private management, organization, and policy studies. The literature review produced thousands of abstracts (N=2242), but only few articles (N=39) from 22 highly ranked journals (2000-2010). Despite the research of public-private management, it seems that a surprisingly small number of researchers have recognized that the public/private sphere provides a particularly useful approach to evolve organization, management, and policy studies. The only exceptions seem to be anchored by citizenship and especially individualism, "personalized public services." The authors also found that researchers did not integrate disciplinary traditions in their approaches and link them to different public/private arenas: public in organizations, private in organizations, public in social life, and private in social life. They conclude that the new trends in public-private organizing and management will remain an enigma unless the following is asked: how can the arenas of public/private counteract the effects of themselves?

DOI: 10.4018/978-1-4666-5031-2.ch002

INTRODUCTION

Recent decades have witnessed an attempt to replace the power of public policy implementation with such emerging topics as citizen participation embedded in new ways of organizing public services (e.g. public and private partnerships, deliberative democracy, co-production etc.). Nevertheless, it seems that public-private management and policy studies have been more concerned with introducing the efficiency of private organizations into public organizations than with the idea of direct democracy. At the same time, the effect of private organizations on productivity has been inconsistent (Boardman & Vining, 2010; Rainey & Chun, 2007, 80; Daft, 2004). However, a few studies have speculated that unnecessary duplication might be motivated by the wrong question: "are public and private organizations fundamentally alike in all important respects?" (Allison, 1992). This study therefore focuses on ascertaining how the nature and operations of public-private relations influence discursive practices in public-private management, organization and policy studies. In particular, we argue that the new trends in public-private organizing will remain an enigma unless we ask the following: have we ever defined "public" and "private" in studies of organizations, policymaking and social life?

Although this question may sound naive; it can no longer be ignored. In particular, criticism of privatization has been based on experiences from the developing countries (see e.g. Weizsäcker, Young & Finger, 2006), but neoliberals have declared periodically that welfare states are in crisis (see e.g. King & Ross, 2010). Nevertheless, in developed countries the political implications or fiascos of promoting a greater role for the private sector in the delivery of public services have been ignored or even concealed (Flinders 2010, p.115). Accordingly, the distinction between public and private organizations, services or actions in general is currently conceptually indefinite, but definitely included in the policy agenda in every society. In other words, there appears to be surprisingly little actual theoretical variety in terms of epistemological and ontological search for new original methodological approaches in public /private research.

Naturally, in practice, attempts have been made to use public-private partnerships (PPP) to solve the risks of ageing societies manifest in the heavy tax burden on working people and also by contracting out public services. Theoretically, Ulrich Beck's and Anthony Gidden's suggestion for a state/market distinction (a formulation of public-private) has been the Third Way in which the main risks and burden of caring for old people falls on themselves as well as on organizations. In other words, people are encouraged or even required to participate in the risk society as full members of its community (Beck, 1992, Giddens, 2000, King & Ross 2010, p.54) This citizen participation or freedom of choice is still available to those with a 'voice': poorer people are more likely to prefer the public domain than affluent people, who opt for private health care because they can afford it (cf. Hirschman, 1970). However, these examples reveal nothing about what "public" and "private" refer to in these different contexts. Although intellectual justification for public-private partnerships is provided by Third Way politics that allegedly move beyond the old alternatives of the market and state distinction (Skelcher 2007, p.350) the public and private definitions are anchored in partnerships. For example, if "individualization within the family" is part of the strategy to maintain the family as a group in Japan (Kataoka 2012, p.13), does it refer to the social construction of Japanese individual behavior" embedded in both the public and private sphere? In other words, if, from the moment that defined public and private, space is completely covered, do they arrive at the point of mutually defining themselves in the sense that the public domain extends only as far as the start of the private sphere? (cf. Bobbio, 1992, p.2, Somers, 2008, p.208). If markets, states, political cultures, and civil societies have become natural entities, we have reason to explore alternative conceptual frames in order to define the concepts of public and private in different cultural and policy domains as an ideal of the good life. In a nutshell, what is the ontology and etymology of public and private? Have men ever defined public or private sphere? What are the key criticisms of the public/private dichotomy? Can we ever overcome the grand dichotomy of western thought?

FROM DICHOTOMOUS DEFINITIONS TO THE WORLD OF PLURALISM

The starting point for a genealogy of public and private has to consider what we mean by 'public and 'private'. Naturally, numerous attempted definitions for public and private have been proposed, embedded in sectors, management, organization, and policy issues (see e.g. Parsons, 1995, Rainey & Chun, 2007, Billis, 2011). These definitions have essentially been based on a tension between what is held to be 'public' and what 'private' in a dichotomous sense. Therefore, these definitions are likely to be inherently misleading, because "the procrustean dualism of their categories will tend to blank out important phenomena" (Weintraub 1997, p.15). In addition, the definitions are often deliberately vague. For example "The development …between state and private actors gives rise to the phenomena of hybridity. This refers to an organization that has both public and private orientations" (Skelcher, 2007, p.348). But what is a hybrid organization? According to the Oxford English Dictionary, its etymology derives from the Latin word hybrid, meaning the "offspring of a tame sow and a wild boar", "child of a freeman and slave", and so forth. The term most common refers simply to a combination of the two highly different organizations, A and B. The combination generates mutually constructed disparate networks that cannot be replicated by single organizations. In a metaphorical sense, hybrid organizations can be seen as any offspring resulting from the mating of two genetically distinct species (Vuori, 2013). Thus, an organization, hybrid or PPP, that has both a public and a private orientation, does not give enough information about the key concepts public, private, or hybrid.

Why, therefore, should citizen participation, willingness to be involved in decision-making in organizations and services, not be ignored in the future studies of public-private management? The main reason for this is that the concepts of public and private serve as a point of entry to many of the key issues of policy, of ethical decisions and of the ordering of everyday life (Benn & Gaus 1983, pp.3-27 Weintraub 1997, pp.1-42; Parsons, 1995, p.3). Nevertheless, in public policy, the public is constituted through a plurality of perspectives aggregated to everyone, the commonwealth (Dewey 1946, p.16); whereas the private is constituted in particular by distinguishing between different parts of the totality, the well-being of individuals or the group of which they are a part (Saxonhouse, 1983, p.365; Parsons, 1995, p.3).

We attribute the elusiveness of the distinction between public and private largely to the fact that there is no distinction. In addition, the definitions of public or private are set by government action or business, but obviously they cannot capture the overall pattern of public and private social life in a society. For example, even if the conventional emphasis on direct public spending ignores other forms of public interventions and individuals voluntarily provide social benefits, researchers define public and private social welfare as a boundary problem (cf. Adema & Whiteford, 2010). Therefore, we agree with Habermas (1989, p.26), Weintraub (1997, p.15) and Savas (2000, p.5) that the "public" realm, politics and services cannot be reduced to the state, and the "private" realm of social life outside the state and governance is not the same as 'private'.

In brief, for us the public-private distinction is not a boundary problem, because public is not only related to expressive and political values and the basic rights related to vital needs, nor is private necessarily related to more instrumental, economic and necessity values than public values (cf. Dewey, 1946; Arendt, 1954, 1958; Parsons & Shils, 1951, p. 166.). Hence, private values are not always opposed to collectivist values of the public interest such as equality. Needless to say, many authors have tried to encapsulate the core values regarding "private organizations" and "public organizations" (Goss, 2003; Beck- Jørgensen & Bozeman, 2006; Van der Wal, Huberts, van den Heuvel, & Kolthoff, 2006). Van der Wal, Huberts, van den Heuvel, & Kolthoff (2006) found that in government and business, the core public values are social justice, impartiality, and transparency, and while the core private values are sustainability, profitability, and collegiality. However, the task of formulating clear boundaries between public and private values has proven enormously complex.

If public is not defined to be synonymous with public interest, and private with economic individualism, how should these concepts be defined in order to reveal their pluralistic contents? Why cannot exact definitions be found in the fields of management, social, or health sciences research? First, partnerships, hybrids, or even New Public Governance can be easily interpreted more by policy language-game playing than evidence-based management or policy science, because the definitions of public and private have not been interdisciplinary analyzed and synthesized. Secondly, the etymology of the definitions used in public-private management should be counterbalanced with the definitions used in sociology or other sciences. In order to reveal the scientific pluralism of public and private, we need to explore how public/private interdisciplinary counteracts its own effect. For example, researchers of sociology and history (see for example Steinberger, 1999, Bailey, 2000) frame the public/private distinction differently than do policy and management scientists, but in social life the public/private action in embedded in numerous disciplines rather than only one. Thirdly, we need a more systematic interdisciplinary analysis of public and private in different culture and policy domains, because exact definitions cannot be found in the different fields until we know what parts of the definitions are overlapping.

AIMS AND APPROACH

In a methodological sense, researchers who explore the genealogy of public and private concepts, write the history of these concepts. Thus, "the first problem which a historian of ideas has to face is, just what am I writing the history of?"(Boas 1969, 3), is also the key question for these studies. In Figure 1 we describe the research design for our exploration in order to frame scientific pluralism. Basically, pluralism, as we define it, accepts no single account of the arenas as the ideal, because Figure 1 itself functions in a plurality of ways. Our approach presupposes that the overlapping manifestations of arenas A, B, C, and D of public /private life and actions constantly generate pluralistic entities embedded in different cultural and policy domains. Depending on the culture(s) and public policy of country the arenas generate numerous configurations of public/private realms.

However, our critical analyses rather exploit the idea of an integrative literature review (see Torraco, 2005) than identify only cited works and authors of the published research into public/private in organizations and social life (cf. Marsilio, Cappellero & Cuccurullo, 2011). According to Torraco (2005, p. 356), "the integrative literature review is a form of research that reviews, critiques, and synthesizes representative literature on a topic in an integrated way such that new frameworks and perspectives on the topic are generated". The integrative literature review provides us with a critical tool to understand why knowledge production outside disciplines is no longer the search for basic research, but takes place in contexts of application – science of public /private issues is characterized by transdisciplinarity (Weingart, 2010, p. 12). For this reason,

Figure 1. Research design for the genealogy of public/private pluralism

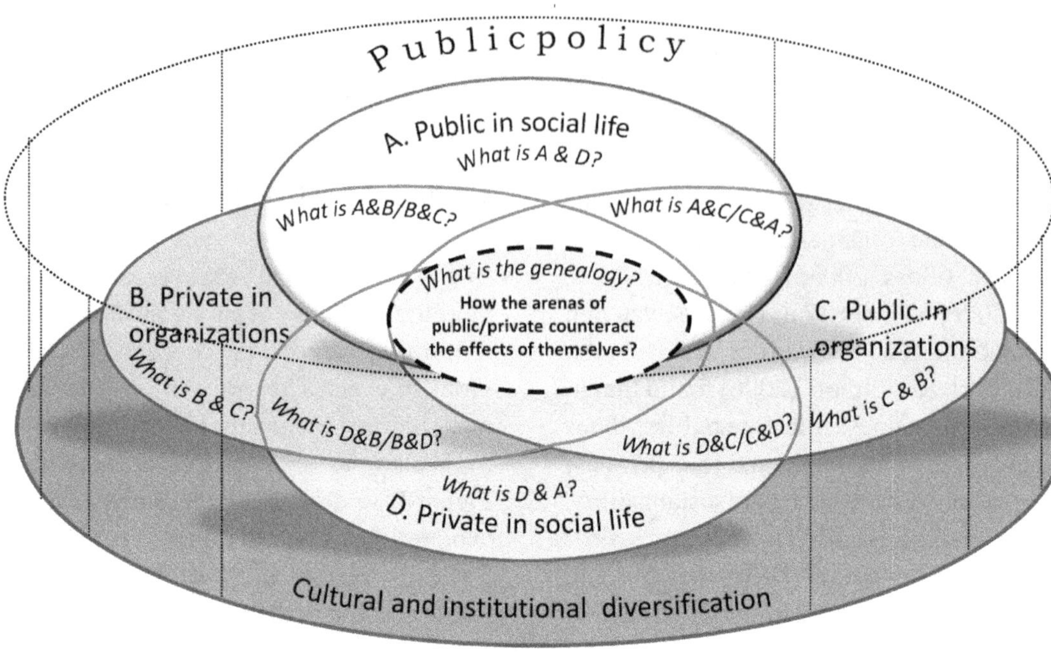

there will always be scholars who conceive of for instance public and private partnerships as a "language game" (cf. Hodge & Greeve 2007, p. 546).

The idea of this study is therefore to focus upon the conceptual boundaries of the four arenas AB, AC, DB and DC in order to explore the integrative features of the literature of public /private in general. In particular, our approach is consciously anchored by public and private social life, because citizens' behavior is assumed to construct the institutions of public and private action (e.g. organizations). Needless to say, in totalitarian or mass societies the configurations of CA, BD, CD and BC would easily dominate the discussion of the principles of welfare society. However, we believe that in risk societies "irresponsible ethics" presents itself in new forms of market and state. In other words, we live in societies with multiple choices for a good life in which we are no longer governed by the classical idea of public, social or health policy. Naturally, in this study, we cannot analyze all the arenas and their configurations (cf. AC & BC, AC & B, BC & A etc.). All the public /private arenas of actions are between the fundamental layers of all societies: publicness and privateness manifested in policies and cultural behavior. Therefore, we explore answers to the following questions: If and when the arenas of A, B, C, and D counteract themselves, what are the main critiques of the public-private dichotomy in arenas B and C ? To be more specific, are public/private management, organization and policy studies (arenas B and C) anchored by citizenship (arena A) or individualism (arena D) and what constitutes the potential intellectual structure these configurations in the public /private research field?

EXPLORING EMERGING TOPICS IN THE FRAME OF PUBLIC AND PRIVATE IN SOCIAL LIFE

In our analysis we intend to address two general kinds of topics—mature topics and new, emerging topics (cf. Torraco, 2005). Accordingly, the mature topic is related to the genealogy of public and private in social life in general, whereas an emerging topic is embedded in the new forms of public and private organizing from the citizen / state or citizen/provider relationship.

The analysis was conducted on the basis of the following criteria. First, our analysis was anchored by the public sphere as an area in social life where citizens come together to identify societal problems and needs that influence political action (Figure 1, arena A). The keywords were public, public sphere, citizenship, participation, political involvement, direct democracy and services. Secondly, the explorations were done in the frame of the private sphere, a certain sector of societal life in which an individual enjoys a degree of authority, unhampered by interventions from governmental or other institutions (Figure 1, arena B). The keywords were private, private sphere, privacy, freedom of choice, self-determination, personalization and services. Thirdly, the emerging topics also needed to have links to public organizations (arena B) and private organizations (arena C).

Despite the research of public-private management, it seems that a surprisingly small number of researchers have recognized that the public/private sphere provides a particularly useful approach to evolve organization, management, and policy studies. Fourthly, the emerging topics were expected to be related to public/private service delivery. We anticipated that these four criteria would identify people as citizens (arena A) and individuals (arena D), and their relation to public and private services (arena B and C).

The data included only articles from leading peer-reviewed journals in the fields of policy, management, and organization sciences during the years 2000-2010. The other fields were precluded for the purpose of exploring how much the interdisciplinary approaches of public and private sphere applied in the fields of policy, management and organization sciences. The time period for the analysis was selected for the following reasons. First, at the beginning of the 1990's governments began to create complex partnerships between government and the private sector in order to reduce the size of government (see Hodge et al. 2010). Secondly, at the beginning of the 2000's in health sciences there was a huge increase in the number of studies on evidence-based patient choice, informed decision-making and consumer involvement and consumerism, and lately on shared decision-making in social and healthcare – citizens as patients were becoming, and were expected to become, more autonomous and to take responsibility for their health and health care (see e.g. Coulter, 2002; Edwards & Elwyn 2009). Thirdly, during the past decade, it seems that politicians also highlighted the importance of direct democracy and used hybrid organizations for the implementation of public policy functions in order to reduce the cost of labor, because most public work is highly labor-intensive. Finally, because we presumed that the emerging topics were relatively new, it was likely that our review would produce a preliminary conceptualization in the frame of our research design (Figure 1) in any case. For these reasons, it would be interesting to know to what extent studies and new emerging topics in the fields of policy, management, and organization sciences address these themes with a view, for example to understanding policy failures.

Naturally, literature reviews can be organized in various ways so long as authors follow accepted conventions for reporting how the study was conducted (Torraco, 2005). In this review, the selection of the journals was done on the basis of the Association of Business School (ABS) Academic Journal Quality Guide that is mainly used in the United Kingdom. According to Harvey and co-workers (2010) ABS is a hybrid based partly upon peer review, partly upon statistical information relating to citation, and partly upon editorial judgments following from the detailed evaluation of many hundreds of publications over a long period. In the 2010 edition, the guide classifies 823 (100%) journals into four categories (grades 1 to 4*) in which category of 4* recognizes the quality of those journals ranked as 'top' class journals in at least seven out of ten international listings consulted. Only 22 (2.7%) journals were in the world elite category 4* and all journals 72 (8.7%) graded 4, whether included in the world elite or not, published the most original and best executed studies. As top journals in their field, these journals have high submission rates, low acceptance rates and papers are rigorously refereed.

As a first step, on the basis of our research design (Figure 1), we selected 205 (25%) journals from the six subject fields:

- Ethics and governance from 16 journals (2%)
- General management, 31 journals (4%)
- Organization studies, 28 journals (3%)
- Public sector management, 33 journals,(4%)
- Sector studies, 37 journals, (5%)
- Social sciences, 60 journals, (7%)

As a second step, we selected from these those 27(69%) journals in categories 4 and 4*:

- General management, 7(23%)
- Organization studies, 4(14%)
- Public sector management, 3 (9%)
- Sector studies, 1 (3%)
- Social sciences, 12 (20%)

Our basic assumption was that only original and dependable studies about new topics are published in these subject fields. Interestingly, over 60% of all the ABS journals in these subfields are in categories 4 and 4*. Thus, the publications in these journals are expected to be good representatives of top quality publications in general.

However, as a third step, we excluded the journals if they were not at all related to our criteria or included journals with grade 3 if their scope and aims were closely related to our criteria. In the subfield public sector management we included Public Administration: An International Quarterly, because of its scope and other journals in categories 4 and 4* were almost all American. In the subfield sector studies we excluded the journal for Transportation Research Part B: Methodological, because of its scope, and replaced it with the Non-Profit and Voluntary Sector Quarterly and Journal of Service Research, because their scope borders on public /private sectors and services. In the subfield social science we excluded the following journals, because their scope was not related to our criteria: Journal of Economic Geography, Economic History Review, Economic Geography, Environment and Planning A, Environment and Planning D: Society and Space, Research Policy and Risk Analysis: An International Journal. Our third step produced the following final list of subfields (including 22 journals):

- General management, 7
- Organization studies, 4
- Public sector management, 4, 3 with grade 4 and 1 with grade 3.
- Sector studies, 2 with grade 3.
- Social sciences, 5

In the frame of the private/public management these five subfields two categories could be formed in which the first two fields (1and 2) are located in our research design in arena B. and subfield 3 in arena C. and subfields 4 and 5 both A and B. The fourth step was the initial selection of articles on the basis of abstracts related our criteria.

FINDINGS

As we expected, we found thousands of abstracts (N=2242), but only few articles (N=39) from these 22 journals (see Table 1). We found that researchers did not cite the literature from other disciplines (e.g. Habermas and the public sphere) in these articles. In other words, they did not integrate disciplinary traditions in their approaches and link them to our arenas in the research design (Figure 1). In addition, we found that the definitions of public/private and the other keywords were used imprecisely. In particular, the literature review readily confirms (Table 1) that there are quite many publications using the keywords, but no organization, management or policy studies had integrated disciplinary traditions in order to increase interdisciplinary learning about the public and the private sphere. For example, we found numerous articles in one of the top management journals (4*), The Academy of Management Journal, but most these discusses how to link management theory and public policy research, bridging the gap between management and policy research or public-private partnerships. These studies are mainly located in our research design in arena BC, in which researchers discuss how private management can contribute to public policy and management (see e.g. D'Aunno, 2005). Only few researchers suggested that public policy issues should be more embedded in the theory development of private management (see e.g.Hitt 2005; Hitt, Beamish, Jackson & Mathieu, 2009) or even suggested that private and public interests could not be fully understood if conceived of independently (Kochan, Guillen, Hunter & O´Mahoney, 2009; Mahoney, McGahan & Pitelis, 2009). Naturally, in some of these journals (e.g. Human Relations) studies applied Habermas and Bourdieu's frameworks, but there were no specific discussions of public and private realms in these journals.

However, in the current literature the definition for private organization has been taken for granted: private refers to private ownership. On the other hand, publicness refers quite often to political and economic authority, but how these definitions are embedded on the citizens' behavior remains an open question. Namely, public authority is quite often measured by only analyzing how citizens obey the norms and rules of their society. However, these analyses are not very plausible, because the definition of privacy may manifest itself in the claim of individuals, groups, or institutions to determine for themselves when, how, and to what extent information about them is communicated to others.

Nevertheless, for now, it seems that at least one emerging topic about personalized public services seems to integrate public and private services in terms of citizen collective behavior and individual responsibility, not vice versa.

DISCUSSION: PERSONALIZED PUBLIC SERVICES—A NEW CONTRACT FOR CITIZEN, STATE AND MARKET?

In the information society, the public authority (e.g. the police) cannot wield power over citizens, who are not willing to co-produce. On the contrary, in social life the metamorphosis of public authority can be seen more or less in reforms to personalize public services toward a new state/citizen contract (cf. Needham 2006; Needham 2010; Needham, 2011). For example, in the UK politicians made a commitment at the end of 2004 'to change the National Health Service into a personalized health service for each individual'. In addition, politicians have been offering state-led tailor-made solutions and support for 'problem families" in many European countries for years. Therefore, the new literature at the interface of public/private action can named "personalized public services" with a strong emphasis on allowing citizens as service users to 'self-direct or self-manage' their needs (Needham, 2011). The literature of "personalizing public services" has different key concepts in different contexts. In general, it is related to the literature of direct democracy in which citizens decide (e.g. vote, eDemoracy) on policy initiatives directly (cf. participatory and deliberative democracy). In the parlance of public and private, public sphere represents a kind of blend of public and private in civil society.

Nevertheless, the literature of personalizing public services embraces such terms as service

Table 1. The literature review of 22 high ranked journals

Review / Journals	No. of Abstracts N=2242	No. of Articles N=39	Findings and Comments
General Management	n=238	n=3	General management studies do not focus on the boundary problem of public/ private management and services.
Academy of Management Review	29	1	The studies take public and private goods for granted and focus upon relationship between corporate and public policy. One study highlights corporate in a frame of individual's private sphere and active participation in society.
Academy of Management Journal	22	1	The studies and essays focus on the relationship between corporate and public policy. One study analyses employees' voices in public services.
Administrative Science Quarterly	117	1	The only study that was very close to the idea of public/ private in social life was about how a social organization has been able to avoid the consequences of an oligarchic leadership structure.
Journal of Management	26	0	Most of the keywords produced zero articles (e.g. public sphere, private sphere, personalization, services).Abstracts were found with the keywords privatizing services and political involvement, but none of the articles were selected for analysis, because they were based on the taken for granted definitions of a public/private dichotomy and ignoring comparative perspective.
Journal of Management Studies	15	0	The only the keywords abstracts included were public and private management or sector. All 15 publications ignored e.g. issues of public and private in social life. None of the articles were selected for analysis, because they were based on the taken for granted definitions of a public/private dichotomy.
Harvard Business Review	17	0	Most of the keywords produced zero articles (e.g. public sphere, private sphere, personalization, services).Abstracts were found with the keywords privatizing services and political involvement, but none of the articles were selected for analysis, because they were based on the taken for granted definitions of a public/private dichotomy and ignoring comparative perspective.
British Journal of Management	12	0	The only keywords the abstracts included were public and private service or sector. All 12 publications ignored e.g. issues of public and private in social life. None of the articles were selected for analysis, because they were based on the taken for granted definitions of a public/private dichotomy.
Organisation Studies	n=360	n=5	Organization studies do not focus on the boundary problem of public/private management and services.
Organization Science	10	2	One study explored the problems of information privacy in a cross-cultural and corporate context and another focused on the benefits of an interdisciplinary approach: private and public interests cannot be fully understood if they are conceived of independently.
Organization Studies	101	1	Almost all the abstracts ignored the public/ private dichotomy. One of the selected abstracts focused on the issue of a gendered division of private and public sphere in life.
The Leadership Quarterly	9	0	There was one special issue on leadership in the public sector, but none of the abstracts contrasted or compared public/private issues.
Human Relations	240	2	Naturally, because of the scope of the journal, the keyword participation was found in many abstracts, but only two articles were selected for analysis. One of the studies on the boundary problem of public /private was related the findings that suggest accounts by scholars and practitioners overstate the differences between the two groups of managers. One of the studies defined public according to the sociology of Bourdieu. The study found that the definition of 'the public' is the subject of a vigorous struggle at the symbolic level.

continued on following page

Table 1. Continued

Review / Journals	No. of Abstracts N=2242	No. of Articles N=39	Findings and Comments
Public Sector Management	n=606	n=25	Some of public sector management studies (approx. 4%) focused on the boundary problem of public/private management and services.
Journal of Public Administration: Research and Theory	313	11	One of the articles explored definitions for cross-sectoral partnerships. The results suggest that the prospects of public service improvement may depend on the sectoral choice that organizations make. One study looked specifically at the nature of public-private linkages in the frame of implementation. In addition, the one study was interested in whether satisfaction with services influences the likelihood that citizens will correctly identify a provider as a nonprofit or governmental agency. However, the rest of the selected articles did not explicitly question the dichotomy of public /private organization or services.
The Milbank Quarterly	23	1	Only one article concentrated on ownership structure, but did not discuss the boundary problem of public/private organizations. None of the other articles were selected for analysis, because they were based on the taken for granted definitions of a public/private dichotomy.
Public Administration Review	52	4	One of the articles tried to demonstrate how the recent businesslike reforms have led to the erosion of such publicness, but the article does not discuss the boundary problem at all. However, some articles questioned the boundaries interestingly: To whom are these hybrids accountable? How well is the public interest being protected against the interests of private parties? Are government sponsored enterprises alternatively form of government? Even if citizens are formal "owners" of the state, will ownership remain a symbolic banner for the governance and public administration?
Public Administration: An International Quarterly	218	9	Most of the selected articles focused on citizens' participation, self-service, and choices, neighborhood governance or co-production of services. In particular, the some selected articles focused on the boundary problem of public/private services from public and private social life point of view. For example one theme of personalizing the welfare state manifested itself in "putting people first" in a frame of user driven tailoring of services to the individual. In brief, the emerging topic was 'personalization' in public services.
Sector Studies	n=14	n=1	Sector studies do not focus on the boundary problem of public/private management and services.
Journal of Service Research	12	0	Most of the keywords produced zero articles (e.g. public sphere, private sphere, personalization, services). None of the other articles were selected for analysis, because they were based on the taken for granted definitions of a public/private dichotomy.
Non-Profit and Voluntary Sector Quarterly	2	1	Most of the keywords produced zero articles (e.g. public sphere, private sphere, personalization, services). One article tries to fill gaps that currently exist between research on the governance of nonprofit organizations and research on public governance and focuses on how nonprofit governance research can benefit from insights in the public governance literature. However, it did not explicitly question the dichotomy of public /private organization or services.
Social Sciences	n=1024	n=5	The studies of social sciences do not focus on the boundary problem of public/private management and services
American Journal of Sociology	2	0	Most of the keywords produced zero articles (e.g. public sphere, private sphere, personalization, services). None of the other articles were selected for analysis, because they were based on the taken for granted definitions of a public/private dichotomy.
American Sociological Review	6	1	Only the keywords public and private produced findings, but most of the other articles were not selected for analysis, because they were based on the taken for granted definitions of a public/private dichotomy. Only one articles focused the shifting boundaries between the public and private spheres in advanced capitalist societies through an examination of grassroots lobbying firms. The study concluded that the increasing formal organization of civil society has supported the development of a field of organizations that subsidize participation.

continued on following page

Table 1. Continued

Journals \ Review	No. of Abstracts N=2242	No. of Articles N=39	Findings and Comments
Social Science and Medicine	986	4	Most of the keywords produced zero articles (e.g. public sphere, private sphere, personalization, services).However, selected articles highlighted that 1) it is important to study the quality of the relationship between public and private and the meaning of both terms, 2) public involvement is the potential to sustain a compact between state and citizens, 3) clients, in rural situations requires a re-focusing of research beyond the for- versus non-profit dichotomy and 4) both private and public choices are needed for a successful reform effort.
Annual Review of Sociology	20	0	All the keywords produced zero articles (e.g. public sphere, private sphere, personalization, services). None of the other articles were selected for analysis, because they were based on the taken for granted definitions of a public/private dichotomy.
Sociology of Health and Illness	10	0	All the keywords produced zero articles (e.g. public sphere, private sphere, personalization, services). None of the other articles were selected for analysis, because they were based on the taken for granted definitions of a public/private dichotomy.

user, client, customer, consumer and expert by experience, but a scientific nature of them in a scientific sense this may extend to a wide range of interdisciplinary intellectual arenas (cf. Figure 1) Naturally, like McLaughlin (2009, 1106), we can argue that the 'service user' mandate in policy reforms comes from both the consumerist tradition of the 1990s and the democratic tradition of developing participation to ensure the suitability of services. In practice, historically practitioners, managers, and researchers have attached different labels to the ambiguous relationship between citizen and state or citizen and service providers in the 1970's., 1980's, 1990's: client, customer, service user, consumer and co-production (cf. Dunston, Lee, Boud, Brodie, & Chiarella, 2009; Edwards & Elwyn 2009; Dent, Fallon, Wendt, Vuori, Puhor, de Pietro & Silva, 2011). It seems that the tendency for renaming and debate will continue under the umbrella of personalized public services (Needham, 2011). If future generations of practitioners, researchers, and managers do not find renaming irritating, a generative epistemological foundation for understanding the genealogy of public/private cannot be established. In other words, they can only integrate the epistemological foundation of terms if they identify the scientific roots of these terms and their overlapping features in different disciplines (cf. Figure 1) Thus, the question "How can researchers come to integrate disciplinary traditions (cf. arenas in Figure 1), and what cognitive demands does interdisciplinary learning impose on them and their academic endeavors needs to be taken very seriously (cf. Mansilla 2010, p. 289).

The inadequacy of epistemological foundations of terms manifests itself in the paradoxes of terms in practical applications. First, the discourse of consumer underlines the assumptive? ideology in which the citizen as customer is inherently rational and hence always right, but according to many studies for example patients' input is not taken seriously because it is not based on scientific evidence (van den Bovenkamp 2010, p.42). In other words, when the conceptualizations of consumerism have developed more in the business studies of customer management than in health sciences, there has not been enough integrative reconstruction of the expanding and diversified knowledge produced by the different disciplines. Secondly, the impact of the cognitive perspectives of managers and practitioners upon the applications is tremendous. Thus, all these terms contain assumptive worlds and fail to effectively and accurately reflect the nature of the citizen/ service provider relationship (McLaughlin 2009, p.1114). Besides, each of these terms always has advantages and disadvantages in relation to something. For example, in Netherlands, van den Bovenkamp (2010, p.167) found several advantages and disadvantages of Dutch government policy related to patient organizations:

The advantages include:

- public accountability is ensured through checks on public spending;
- patient participation has proven to be a successful steering mechanism;
- patient organizations are given the opportunity to influence decision-making;
- participation can have an empowering effect on those who participate; and
- the policy can prevent undue influence from the pharmaceuticals industry.

The disadvantages include:

- the goals of patient organizations are being replaced;
- patient organizations' hands are being tied;
- patient organizations have been turned into policy and strategy followers;
- professionalization has resulted in a loss of empowerment; and
- patient organizations are being put to instrumental use.

Thirdly, in the disadvantages, "the goals of patient organizations are being replaced" refers the very common emerging problem in defining the boundaries of public and private organizations at the policy level (cf. Figure 1 arenas B & C.). Namely, if patient organizations are said to be taking over the responsibility of public authorities, what they are expected to take and what have they taken and what will likely complementary and necessary action by citizens' patient organizations lose in society? In other words, citizen involvement motivated by the social and political sciences may produce the ubiquitous hybrid organizations in which the accountability and responsiveness become very problematic. As Billis (2010, p.12) notes, the complex nature of financing, planning, and delivering welfare organizations has produced 'the abominable hybrids' that do not have explicit clarity of accountability either to the state or civil society. Thus, we argue that the dysfunctions of hybridity cannot be identified until we have studied how the arenas of public/private counteract their own effects. However, it is highly deceptive to believe that he illustrations of personalization as 24-7 call centers, booked appointments and timely access to standardized services will facilitate the identification, because it is practical and does not reveal integrative layers of different disciplines. Rather we need to even anchor the need for public and private services by the citizen life-cycle, every each of us have multiple aspects to our identities and are likely to require services at some stage in our lifecycle (McLaughlin, 2009, cf. Morone, 2000; Kylänen, Vuori, Allen, 2012).

In addition, above terms are unable identify experts by non-experiences and other distinct populations. Therefore, the emerging topics can be such as co-production might have been defined in the other field of studies (e.g. Hyde & Davies, 1994, cf. Figure 1 arena B & C) or they have highlighted more citizens activity as service users than analyzed those who exit, withdraw from the relationship (cf. Hirschman, 1970). In order to avoid these paradoxes and integrate a coherent interdisciplinary conceptualization, researchers should build intellectual process about the implications of the terms in every disciplinary arena (Figure 1, A, B, C, and D) and build an intellectual process within the boundaries of disciplines (Figure 1. A & B, B & A). In their reinterpretation of public and private dimensions in social life, they especially need to pay attention what discipline dominates and has dominated the genealogy of the terms.

Theoretically, the literature of personalizing the public services implicitly exploits the work of Hannah Arendt (1958) by constructing "the Third Way" in which transdisciplinarity does justice to differences between disciplines in order to improve the responsiveness of services. According to Habermas (1989, p. 30), the public sphere mediates between the private sphere (cf. Figure 1., arena D.) and the "sphere of public authority" (cf. Figure 1, arena A & C). However, the "sphere of public authority" was embedded in the state and public organizations, or the realm of the ruling class.

The discussion of 'public sphere' in private organizations may well pave the way for a potential new definition of private in social life in such a way that the private owners of organizations do not need to own all their actions in concrete terms (cf. contracting out). As Calhoun (2007, p.80) says, the very distinction between public and private took on new meaning in the early modern era when the separation of family finances from business finances was introduced, the Weberian story of modernization as rationalization got started.

Traditionally, the literature anchored by publicness, political, and economic authority seems to ignore the literature on "direct democracy" and "personalizing the public services" as potential integrative anchors of the publications in arenas B and C. Interestingly, the literature on direct democracy and personalizing the public services would strengthen their theoretical basis with a holistic conceptualization and synthesis of the literature at the core of the public/private distinction in social life (Weintraub & Kumar 1997; Benn & Gaus 1983; Sommers, 2008; Bailey, 2002; Crouch, 2011). However, it is easy to see that the literature of direct democracy has developed more on the basis of collective action (cf. markets or institutional state) than communities. The scholars and researchers of this branch come from policy, public management and organization sciences (cf. Bozeman 2007; Cho & Rainey, 2007; Perry & Hondeghem, 2009), whereas the researchers of "personalizing the public services" represent the whole panoply of social and health sciences. Hence there is a risk that the arenas of public and private organizations (B and C, Figure 1) counteract their effects, but researchers cannot recognize them, because they ignore the arenas A. and D. They therefore cannot identify the overlapping concepts in different arenas. In other words they still ignore the following ontological question from a transdisciplinary point of view: How in the different arenas of public /private (A, B, C and D) have the relationships between the public and private been constructed? How do these constructions counteract their own effects?

CONCLUSION: ANALYZING THE PAST TO PREPARE FOR THE FUTURE

The purpose of this article was to explore the genealogy of public and private from an interdisciplinary and pluralistic point of view. In particular, we were interested in public/private management, organization, and policy studies anchored by public and private in social life. Our literature review was designed (Figure 1) primarily to uncover how the arenas of public and private (B,C and A,D) counteract their own effects. The literature review should examine the literature with a particular lens defined by the article's objectives (Torraco, 2005). In our literature review we explored the emerging topics through the lens of the genealogy of public and private in social life. In particular, our analysis was guided by the citizen/state contract and personalized public services. However, because these topics are relatively new and no comprehensive review of the literature has so far been presented, our review is more a preliminary conceptualization of the topic by using research design (Figure 1) However, our analysis shows that the public/private studies have not been anchored by the public/private sphere in leading peer-review journals in the fields of policy, management and organization sciences during the years 2000-2011. Hence, we conclude that at least in this admittedly selected sample for the literature review indicate that public/private management, organization and policy scientists has not applied the pluralistic and multidisciplinary contents of public/private terminology in their studies. In other words, management, organization and policy studies are not exploited the approaches embedded in the arenas of public and private in social life.

In a nutshell, the main critiques of the public-private dichotomy in arenas B and C are decidedly related to imprecise and state/market driven definitions. The only exception in which arenas B and C (public/private management, organization, and policy studies) seem to be anchored by A (e.g. citizenship) and especially D (e.g. individualism) is the emerging topic "personalized public services". This topic is the rejection of the conventional wisdom that public services should serve the 'average citizen' and constitutes the potential pluralistic and intellectual configuration in the public /private research field. In concrete terms, personalized health budgets, learning for schoolchildren, self-directed support in social care recognize users' expertise in relation to their own needs, which may come into conflict with professional accounts of expertise as Needham (2010, p. 137) points out. In order to describe more specifically what a new intellectual structure the topic personalized services provides, we need to ask how the topic is constructed in different times and spaces in history and how it is related to such concepts as participation, co-production, shared decision-making etc.

In principle, researchers widely agree that the best literature review produces a firm foundation for advancing knowledge in an integrative sense as well. Apparently, the literature review is expected to facilitate theory development and impose interdisciplinary learning. As Watson & Webster (2002, xii) put it: close areas where a plethora of research exists, and uncover areas where research is needed. Nevertheless building strong interdisciplinary research agendas by engaging such "boundary concepts" as public and private requires radical changes in the approaches and the epistemological foundations of research. In practice, even if changes are clearly indicated, researchers are admittedly condemned to use orthodox canons of scientific reasoning and evidence with the different conventional concepts of research arenas A, B, C and D (Figure 1).In addition, for many science policy reasons, the majority of researchers would rather rewrite the existing literature than challenge it in order to avoid the crusade of paradigms.

The present study only examined the configurations of the fundamental layers of public/private social life in management, organization, and policy studies. Consequently, it does not provide adequate evidence of how the arenas of public and private counteract their own effects. Thus, although the findings suggest that citizen or individual anchored definitions of public and private in management, organization, and policy studies are mainly ignored, several limitations in this review should be mentioned. First, the journals consulted were selected on the basis of ABS, but the results might have been different if the review had been done through a search of selected databases (e.g. the Social Science Citation Index, The Web of Science etc.). However, in this study we chose the ABS journals because we expected them to cover the research object in the research design. Second, in order to support interdisciplinary learning, the researchers from arenas A, B, C and D need to do the conceptual structuring of the review. Thus the terminology of other disciplines as regards public/private also needs to be reviewed. Third, in particular, the researchers did not pay enough attention to the epistemological anchor of their analysis. In other words, the results would have been more insightful if public or private sphere had been defined more accurately. Finally, because the study focused on short periods of time, the review of the articles is inadequate for providing a "thick description" of the genealogy of public/private as a grand dichotomy of the western world. Besides, a researcher who challenges the existing science policy as a paradigm crusader may not succeed in getting his paper published in a high-quality journal. Thus, we believe that it is impossible to describe the genealogy in one study because of the number of the configurations of research arenas.

In future research, reviews should also include the other configurations of the arenas described in the research design. In addition, more research should be undertaken to ascertain the advantages of a generative epistemological foundation for the study of interdisciplinary "bridges" of public and private in management, organization, and policy studies. First, this presupposes the interdisciplinary learning process of the researchers and scholars in different research arenas A,B,C and D in which they "integrate insights and modes of thinking from two or more disciplines or established fields, to advance their fundamental or practical understanding of a subject than stands beyond the scope of a single discipline" (Mansilla 2010, p. 289). Secondly, in concrete terms, for this interdisciplinary learning process we need to identify good theories as "bridges" between different research arenas. Both the different epistemic viewpoints and distinguished scholars' values as peer-review gatekeepers need to be balanced in order to serve the different anchors of the public/private research (cf. Huutoniemi, 2010). For example, Somers (2008, p. 279-288) provides a potential historical reconstruction of the expanding and more diversified knowledge of public and private in social life on the basis of the great dichotomies of Anglo-American citizenship theory. We suggest that researchers of policy, organization, and management studies should introduce more of these approaches in their future studies. In particular, in order to reform the public/private research of organizational and social life, new pluralistic and unbiased sociological and historical approaches need to be introduced. Thus, the following research questions need to be taken more seriously: does collectivism/egalitarianism really promote less public value than hierarchism in societies? Can the forms of direct democracy produce more public value than organized welfare societies? In particular, we conclude that the new trends in public-private organizing and management will remain an enigma unless we ask the following how the arenas of public/private counteract the effects of themselves?

ACKNOWLEDGMENT

We are grateful to the anonymous referees for their insightful comments and the Editor for his advice and encouragement.

This work was supported by the Academy of Finland, Research Council for Culture and Society. Project title: Comparing Citizens' Choice and Public Involvement: The Meaning of Public and Non-public Provider especially in Social- and Healthcare [grant number no: 0134467]. Vuori, J. Head of the PubPri research group, University of Eastern Finland, 2002- [project leader 2010 -2013].

REFERENCES

Adema, W., & Whiteford, P. (2010). Public and private social welfare. In *The Oxford handbook of the welfare state* (pp. 121–138). Oxford, UK: Oxford University Press. doi:10.1093/oxfordhb/9780199579396.003.0008

Allison, G. (1992). Public and private management: Are they fundamentally alike in all unimportant aspects? In J. Shafritz, & A. Hyde (Eds.), *Classics of public administration* (pp. 371–395). Belmont, CA: Wadsworth.

Arendt, H. (1958). *The human condition*. Chicago: The University of Chicago Press.

Bailey, J. (2000). Some meanings of 'the private' in sociological thought. *Sociology*, *34*(3), 381–401.

Beck, U. (1992). *Risk society: Towards a new modernity*. London, UK: Sage Publications.

Beck Jørgensen, T., & Bozeman, B. (2007). The public values universe: An inventory. *Administration & Society*, *39*(3), 354–381. doi:10.1177/0095399707300703

Benn & Gaus. (1983). The public and the private: The concepts and action. In *Public and private in social life* (pp. 3–27). New York: St Martin's Press.

Billis, D. (Ed.). (2010). *Hybrid organizations and the third sector: Challenges for practice, theory and policy*. London, UK: Palgrave MacMillan.

Boardman, A. E., & Vining, A. R. (2010). Assessing the economic worth of public-private partnerships. In G. A. Hodge, G. Greve, & A. E. Boardman (Eds.), *The international handbook on public private partnerships*. London, UK: Edward-Elgar. doi:10.4337/9781849804691.00016

Boas, G. (1969). *History of ideas*. New York: Charles Scribner's Sons.

Bobbio, N. (1992). *Democracy and dictatorship: The nature and limits of state power*. Minneapolis, MN: University of Minnesota Press.

Bozeman, B. (2007). *Public values and public interest: Counterbalancing economic individualism*. Washington, DC: Georgetown University Press.

Calhoun, C. (2007). *Nations matter: Culture, history and the cosmopolitan dream*. London: Routledge.

Coulter, A. (2002). *The autonomous patient: Ending paternalism in medical care*. London, UK: Nuttfield Trust.

Crouch, C. (2011). *The strange non-death of neoliberalism*. Cambridge, UK: Polity Press.

D'Aunno, T. (2005). Management scholars and public policy: A bridge too far? *Academy of Management Journal*, *48*(6), 949–951. doi:10.5465/AMJ.2005.19573093

Daft, R. L. (2004). *Organization theory and design*. Cincinnati, OH: South-Western Publishing.

Dent, M., Fallon, C., Wendt, C., Vuori, J., Puhor, M., de Pietro, C., & Silva, S. (2011). Medicine and user involvement within European healthcare: A typology for European comparative research. *International Journal of Clinical Practice*, *65*(12), 1218–1220. doi:10.1111/j.1742-1241.2011.02803.x PMID:22093529

Dewey, J. (1946). *Public and its problems: An essay in political inquiry*. New York: Henry Holt & Co.

Dunston, R., Lee, A., Boud, D., Brodie, P., & Chiarella, M. (2009). Co-production and health system reform – From re-imagining to re-making. *Australian Journal of Public Administration*, *68*(1), 39–52. doi:10.1111/j.1467-8500.2008.00608.x

Edwards, A., & Elwyn, G. (Eds.). (2009). *Shared decision-making in health care: Achieving evidence-based patient choice*. Oxford, UK: Oxford University Press.

Flinders, M. (2010). Splintered logic and political debate. In *The international handbook on public private partnerships*. London, UK: Edward-Elgar. doi:10.4337/9781849804691.00014

Gaus, B. (1983). Public and private interests in liberal political economy, old and new. In *The public and private in social life*. New York: St. Martin's Press.

Giddens, A. (2000). *The third way and its critics*. Cambridge, UK: Polity Press.

Goss, R. P. (2003). What ethical conduct expectations do legislators have for the career bureaucracy? *Public Integrity*, *5*(2), 93–112.

Habermas, J. (1989). *The structural transformation of the public sphere: An inquiry into a category of bourgeois society*. Cambridge, MA: MIT Press.

Hirschman, A. O. (1970). *Exit, voice and loyalty: Responses to decline in firms, organisations and states*. Cambridge, MA: Harvard University Press.

Hitt, M. A. (2005). Management theory and research: Potential contribution to public policy and public organizations. *Academy of Management Journal, 48*(6), 963–966. doi:10.5465/AMJ.2005.19573098

Hitt, M. A., Beamish, P. W., Jakson, S. E., & Mathieu, J. E. (2007). Building theoretical and empirical bridges across levels: Multilevel research in management. *Academy of Management Journal, 50*(6), 1385–1399. doi:10.5465/AMJ.2007.28166219

Hodge, G. A., & Greeve, G. (2007). Public-private partnerships: An international performance review. *Public Administration Review, 67*(3), 545–585. doi:10.1111/j.1540-6210.2007.00736.x

Hodge, G. A., Greve, G., & Boardman, A. E. (Eds.). (2010). *The international handbook on public private partnerships*. London, UK: Edward-Elgar. doi:10.4337/9781849804691

Huutoniemi, K. (2010). Evaluating interdisciplinary research. In *The Oxford handbook of interdisciplinarity*. Oxford, UK: Oxford University Press.

Hyde, P., & Davies, H. T. O. (2004). Service design, culture and performance: Collusion and co-production in health care. *Human Relations, 57*(11), 1407–1426. doi:10.1177/0018726704049415

Kataoka, Y. (2012). Japanese individualized family as a form of risk protection and adaption to rural life. *International Journal of Public and Private Healthcare Management and Economics, 2*(3), 17–26. doi:10.4018/ijpphme.2012070101

King, D., & Ross, F. (2010). Critics and beyond. In *The Oxford handbook of the welfare state* (pp. 45–60). Oxford, UK: Oxford University Press. doi:10.1093/oxfordhb/9780199579396.003.0004

Kochan, T. A., Guillen, M.F., & Hunter, L.W., & O'Mahoney. (2009). Introduction to the special research forum—Public policy and management research: Finding the common ground. *Academy of Management Journal, 52*(6), 1088–1100. doi:10.5465/AMJ.2009.47084646

Kylänen, M., Vuori, J., & Allen, P. (2012). Exploring theory for citizens' preferences in health policy: The contribution of health policy cultures to understanding the roles of public and private health service providers. *International Journal of Public and Private Healthcare Management and Economics, 2*(2), 38–57. doi:10.4018/ijpphme.2012040103

Mahoney, J. T., McGahan, A. M., & Pitelis, C. N. (2009). The interdependence of private and public interests. *Organization Science, 20*, 1034–1052. doi:10.1287/orsc.1090.0472

Mansilla, V. B. (2010). Learning to synthesize: The development of interdisciplinary understanding. In *The Oxford handbook of interdisciplinarity (pp-288-306)*. Oxford, UK: Oxford University Press.

Marsilio, M., Cappellero, G., & Cuccurullo, C. (2011). The intellectual structure of research into ppps. a bibliometric analysis. *Public Management Review, 13*(6), 736–782. doi:10.1080/14719037.2010.539112

McLaughlin, H. (2009). What's in a name: 'Client', 'patient', 'customer', 'consumer', 'expert by experience', 'service user'—What's next? *British Journal of Social Work, 39*(6), 1101–1117. doi:10.1093/bjsw/bcm155

Morone, J. A. (2000). Citizens or shoppers? Solidarity under siege. *Journal of Health Politics, Policy and Law, 25*(5), 959–968. doi:10.1215/03616878-25-5-959 PMID:11068741

Needham, C. (2006). Customer care and the public service ethos. *Public Administration, 84*(4), 845–860. doi:10.1111/j.1467-9299.2006.00615.x

Needham, C. (2010). Debate: Personalized public services – A new state/citizen contract? *Public Money & Management*, *30*(3), 136–138. doi:10.1080/09540961003794246

Needham, C. (2011). *Personalizing public services: Understanding the personalisation narrative*. Bristol, UK: The Policy Press.

Newman, J., & Kuhlmann, E. (2007). Consumers enter the political stage? The modernization of health care in Britain and Germany. *Journal of European Social Policy*, *17*(1), 99–111. doi:10.1177/0958928707075191

Parsons, T., & Shiels, E. (Eds.). (1951). *Toward general theory of action*. Cambridge, MA: Harvard University Press.

Parsons, W. (1995). *Public policy: An introduction to the theory and practice of policy analysis*. Northampton, MA: Edward Elgar Publishing.

Perry, J. L., & Hondeghem, A. (2009). *Motivation in public management: The call of public service*. Oxford, UK: Oxford University Press.

Rainey, H. G., & Chun, Y. H. (2007). Public and private management compared. In *The oxford Handbook of public management* (pp. 72–102). Oxford, UK: Oxford University Press. doi:10.1093/oxfordhb/9780199226443.003.0005

Roberts, N. C. (2008). *The age of direct citizenship participation*. New York: M.E. Sharpe.

Savas, E. S. (2000). *Privatization and public private partnerships*. New York: Chatman.

Saxonhouse, A. W. (1983). Classical Greek conceptions of public and private. In *Public and private in social life* (pp. 363–384). New York: St. Martin's Press.

Skelcher, C. (2007). Public-private partnerships and hybridity. In *The Oxford handbook of public management* (pp. 317–370). Oxford, UK: Oxford University Press. doi:10.1093/oxfordhb/9780199226443.003.0016

Somers, M. R. (2008). *Genealogies of citizenship: Markets, statelessness, and the right to have rights*. Cambridge, UK: Cambridge University Press. doi:10.1146/annurev.lawsocsci.2.081805.105847

Steinberger, P. (1999). Public and private. *Political Studies*, *47*(2), 292–313. doi:10.1111/1467-9248.00201

(1997). Theory and politics of the public/private distinction. InWeintraub, J., & Kumar, K. (Eds.), *Public and private in thought and practice: Perspectives on a grand dichotomy* (pp. 1–42). Chicago: The University of Chicago Press.

Torraco, R. J. (2005). Writing integrative literature reviews: Guidelines and examples. *Human Resource Development Review*, *4*(3), 356–367. doi:10.1177/1534484305278283

Van den Bovenkamp, H. M. (2010). *The limits of patient power: Examining active citizenship in Dutch health care*. Rotterdam, The Netherlands: Optima Grafische Communicatie.

van der Wal, Z., Huberts, L. W. J. C., van den Heuvel, J. H. J., & Kolthoff, E. W. (2006). Central values of government and business: Differences, similarities and conflicts. *Public Administration Quarterly*, *30*(3), 314–364.

Vuori, J. (2013). Citizen participation embedded in public, private and hybrid organizations. *International Journal of Public and Private Healthcare Management and Economics*, *3*(1), xi–xiii.

Webster, J., & Watson, R. T. (2002). Analyzing the past to prepare for the future: Writing a literature review. *Management Information Systems Quarterly*, *26*(2), xiii–xxiii.

Weingart, P. (2010). A short history of knowledge formations. In *The Oxford handbook of interdisciplinarity* (pp. 3–14). Oxford, UK: Oxford University Press.

Weizsäcker von. E.U., Young, O.R., & Finger, M. (Eds.). (2006). Limits to privatization: How to avoid too much of a good thing. London, UK: Earthscan.

ADDITIONAL READING

Aleksander, J.A., Weiner, B.J., Succi, M. (2000). Community accountability among hospitals affiliated with health care systems.*The Milbank Quarterly. A Journal of Public Health and Health Care Policy*78(2), 157-184

Amirkhanyan, A. A. (2007). The smart-seller challenge: exploring the determinants of privatizing public nursing homes. *Journal of Public Administration: Research and Theory*, *17*(3), 501–527. doi:10.1093/jopart/mul009

Blair, R. (2002). Policy tools and implementation networks: understanding state enterprise zone partnerships. *Journal of Public Administration: Research and Theory*, *12*(2), 161–190. doi:10.1093/oxfordjournals.jpart.a003528

Blomgren, M., & Sunden, E. (2008). Constructing a European healthcare market: the private healthcare company Capio and the strategic aspect of the drive for transparency. *Social Science & Medicine*, *67*(10), 1512–1520. doi:10.1016/j.socscimed.2008.06.035 PMID:18703262

Bradley, E. W. (2001). Public-Sector Work Motivation: A Review of the Current Literature and a Revised Conceptual Model. *Journal of Public Administration: Research and Theory*, *11*(4), 559–586. doi:10.1093/oxfordjournals.jpart.a003515

Contandriopoulos, D., Denis, J.-L., & Langley, A. (2004). Defining the 'public' in a public healthcare system. *Human Relations*, *57*(12), 1573–15. doi:10.1177/0018726704049990

Cornwall, A., & Shankland, A. (2008). Engaging citizens: Lessons from building Brazil's national health system. *Social Science & Medicine*, *66*(10), 2173–2184. doi:10.1016/j.socscimed.2008.01.038 PMID:18336976

Cutler, T., Waine, B., & Brehony, K. (2007). New epoch of individualization? Problems with the 'personalization' of public sector services. *Public Administration*, *85*(3), 847–855. doi:10.1111/j.1467-9299.2007.00672.x

Denhardt, R. B., & Denhardt, J. V. (2000). The new public service: serving rather than steering. *Public Administration Review*, *60*(6), 549–559. doi:10.1111/0033-3352.00117

Essers, C., & Benschop, Y. (2007). Enterprising identities: Female entrepreneurs of Moroccan or Turkish origin in the Netherlands. *Organization Studies*, *28*(1), 49–69. doi:10.1177/0170840607068256

Feeney, M. K. (2008). Sector-Perceptions among state-level public managers. *Journal of Public Administration: Research and Theory*, *18*(3), 465–494. doi:10.1093/jopart/mum025

Fotaki, M. (2006). Patient choice in healthcare in England and Sweden: from quasi-market and back to market? A comparative analysis of failure in unlearning. *Public Administration*, *85*(4), 1059–1075. doi:10.1111/j.1467-9299.2007.00682.x

Frumkin, P. K., & Mark, T. (2001). Strategic Positioning and the Financing of Nonprofit Organizations: Is Efficiency Rewarded in the Contributions Marketplace? *Public Administration Review*, *61*(3), 266–275. doi:10.1111/0033-3352.00029

Glaser, M. A., Denhardt, J. V., & Hamilton, L. K. (2002). Communty vs. self-interest: citizen perceptions of schools as civic investments. *Journal of Public Administration: Research and Theory*, *12*(1), 103–127. doi:10.1093/oxfordjournals.jpart.a003518

Harrison, S. (2009). Co-optation, commodification and the medical model: governing UK medicine since 1991. *Public Administration*, *87*(2), 184–197. doi:10.1111/j.1467-9299.2009.01752.x

Houston, J. D. (2000). Public-service motivation: A Multivariate test. *Journal of Public Administration: Research and Theory*, *10*(4), 713–728. doi:10.1093/oxfordjournals.jpart.a024288

Houston, J. D. (2006). Walking the walk of public service motivation: public employees and charitable gifts of time, blood, and money. *Journal of Public Administration: Research and Theory*, *16*(1), 67–86. doi:10.1093/jopart/mui028

Kelly, J. (2007). Reforming public services in the UK: bringing in the third sector. *Public Administration*, *85*(4), 1003–1022. doi:10.1111/j.1467-9299.2007.00680.x

Lowndes, V., & Sullivan, H. (2008). How low can you go? Rationales and challenges for neighbourhood governance. *Public Administration*, *86*(1), 53–74. doi:10.1111/j.1467-9299.2007.00696.x

Mahoney, J. T., McGahan, A. M., & Pitelis, N. C. (2009). The Interdependence of Private and Public Interests. *Organization Science*, *20*, 1034–1052. doi:10.1287/orsc.1090.0472

Mardsen, D. (2006). Individual employee voice and performance management in public services. *Academy of Management Proceedings*, *1*, 1–6.

Matten, D., & Crane, A. (2005). Corporate citizenship: toward an extended theoretical conceptualization Academy of Management Review January, 30(1), 166-179.

Milberg, S. J., Smith, H. J., & Burke, S. J. (2000). Information privacy: corporate management and national regulation. *Organization Science*, *11*(1), 35–57. doi:10.1287/orsc.11.1.35.12567

Moe, R. C. (2001). The emerging federal quasi government: issues of management and accountability. *Public Administration Review*, *61*(3), 290–312. doi:10.1111/0033-3352.00031

Morrell, K. (2009). Governance and the public good. *Public Administration*, *87*(3), 538–556. doi:10.1111/j.1467-9299.2009.01756.x

Needham, C. (2006). Customer care and the public service ethos. *Public Administration*, *84*(4), 845–860. doi:10.1111/j.1467-9299.2006.00615.x

Needham, C. (2009). Policing with a smile: narratives of consumerism in new labour's criminal justice policy. *Public Administration*, *87*(1), 97–116. doi:10.1111/j.1467-9299.2008.01744.x

Nutt, P. (2006). Public and private sector decision-making practices. *Journal of Public Administration: Research and Theory*, *16*(2), 289–318. doi:10.1093/jopart/mui041

Osterman, P. (2006). Overcoming oligarchy: culture and agency in social movement organizations. *Administrative Science Quarterly*, *51*(4), 622–649.

Palmer, N., & Mills, A. (2005). Contracts in the real world: Case studies from Southern Africa. *Social Science & Medicine*, *60*(11), 2505–2514. doi:10.1016/j.socscimed.2004.11.030 PMID:15814176

Pandey, S., & Kingsley, G. (2000). Examining red tape in public and private organizations:altarnative explanitations from a social psychological model. *Journal of Public Administration: Research and Theory*, *10*(4), 779–800. doi:10.1093/oxfordjournals.jpart.a024291

Parkinson, J. (2004). Why deliberate? The encounter between deliberation and new public managers. *Public Administration*, *82*(2), 377–395. doi:10.1111/j.0033-3298.2004.00399.x

Pendleton, A. (2003). Does privatization create a 'new breed' of managers? A study of the UK railway industry. *Human Relations*, *56*(1), 85–111. doi:10.1177/0018726703056001451

Rainey, H. G., & Bozeman, B. (2000). Comparing public and private organizations: empirical research and the power of the a priori. *Journal of Public Administration: Research and Theory*, *10*(2), 447–470. doi:10.1093/oxfordjournals.jpart.a024276

Skinner, M. W., & Rosenberg, M. W. (2006). Managing competition in the countryside: Non-profit and for-profit perceptions of long-term care in rural Ontario. *Social Science & Medicine*, *63*(11), 2864–2876. doi:10.1016/j.socscimed.2006.07.028 PMID:16959392

Stone, M. M., & Ostower, F. (2007). Acting in the public interest? Another look at research on nonprofit governance. *Nonprofit and Voluntary Sector Quarterly*, *36*(3), 416–438. doi:10.1177/0899764006296049

Van Slyke, D. M., & Roch, C. H. (2004). Whatdo they do, and whom do they hold accountable? Citizens in the government-nonprofit contracting relationship. *Journal of Public Administration: Research and Theory*, *14*(2), 191–209. doi:10.1093/jopart/muh013

Vigoda, E. (2002). From responsiveness to collaboration: governance citizens and the next generation of public administration. *Public Administration Review*, *62*(5), 527–540. doi:10.1111/1540-6210.00235

Walker, E. T. (2009). Privatizing participation: civic change and the organizational dynamics of grassroots lobbying firms. *American Sociological Review*, *74*(1), 83–105. doi:10.1177/000312240907400105

KEY TERMS AND DEFINITIONS

Genealogy: The study of public/private ontology and the tracing of their etymology and history.

Management: How services are delivered, organized and governed.

Personalization Services: How public and private services are tailored more closely to their users.

Pluralaralism: An methodology which does not accept any dichotomous definitions of public and private account as the ideal but which itself functions a plurality of ways.

Preference: If we do not really know what we prefer, we must construct our preferences as the situation arises in a certain cultural context – choosing between two culturally constructed services, products etc.

Private Sphere: The types of private organization and individualism in political and cultural sense. Private sphere is a certain sector of societal life in which an individual enjoys a degree of authority, unhampered by interventions from governmental or other institutions.

Public Sphere: The types of public organization and collectivism in political and cultural sense. Public sphere an area in social life where citizens come together to identify societal problems and needs that influence political action.

Section 2

Family Institution and the Spectrum of Public and Private Spheres

This section focuses on the family institution in the East Asian context and proceeds to analyze family-related policies and social issues in different societies in the region. Family is the basic institution of any society, but in the East Asian context, it has played and continues to play a particularly important role in social development, often adopting roles that elsewhere belong to other social actors and institutions. Furthermore, in reference to public and private spheres, the family institution in the East Asian context provides a good chance to test how these spheres interact and how East Asian models are evolving.

Chapter 3
The Impact of Global Financial Crises on the Family in Taiwan

Lih-Rong Wang
National Taiwan University, Taiwan

Fen-ling Chen
National Taipei University, Taiwan

ABSTRACT

Family plays an unusually important role in Taiwanese society, and this chapter analyzes the consequences of global financial crises on the family in Taiwan. With its export-oriented economy, Taiwan is vulnerable to global vacillations. In the periods from 1997 to 2004 and from 2008 to the 2009, Taiwan experienced mass unemployment and family suffering. This chapter deals with the effects of the economic recession on family finances and family attitudes involved. The study shows how the anxiety affected the willingness of people to have children and/or support their parents. Furthermore, the victims of financial crises had a greater awareness of the necessity of providing intergenerational support, but they also wanted to have fewer children. The data clearly presents that economic hardship changes the traditional generational contract as well.

INTRODUCTION

With its export-oriented economy, Taiwan is much vulnerable to global vacillations. In the periods from 1997 to 2004 and from 2008 to the 2009, Taiwan experienced mass unemployment and family sufferings. This paper deals with the effects of the economic recession on family finances and family attitudes involved.

According to survey data conducted by the Social Policy Research Center at National Taiwan University, 2008 and 2009 separately, named SQSQ survey in Taiwan, most Taiwanese citizens' biggest worry is financial insecurity at the time

DOI: 10.4018/978-1-4666-5031-2.ch003

of financial tsunami. Their anxiety in turn affects their willingness to have children or/and values of support their parents. The data show that victims of financial crises have a greater awareness of the necessity of providing intergenerational support, but they want to have fewer children. The data clearly present that economic hardship changes the traditional generational contract as well.

In addition, the responsiveness of family policy in Taiwan tends to be lag behind this social and economic change. Although here are new social policies such as national pension scheme and child allowance responsive to the social and economic stress, the tremendous change of family values after financial tsunami should be attended by the government locally and internationally.

BACKGROUND

Taiwan's economy has been strong in recent decades. Since the 1960s, Taiwan has developed labor-intensive export-orientated industries. In the 1970s, transnational corporations transferred production processes of electronic industries to Taiwan. Taiwan became a home to the OEMs (original equipment manufacturers) of many famous companies in developed countries (Tuan, 1992, p. 55). In the 1990s, a buyer-driven global commodity chain was established: companies in Taiwan receive orders for merchandise from developed countries, which subcontract to China or other countries in Southeast Asia. The merchandise was then shipped to the developed countries directly (Gereffi, 1999). After four decades of

Table 1. GNP per capita/economic growth rate (1998- June 2009) (US$)

Year	Economic Growth Rate (%)	Average GNP	GNP per Capita
1998	4.55	12,773	11,552
1999	5.75	13,737	12,324
2000	5.77	14,721	13,090
2001	-2.17	13,348	11,692
2002	4.64	13,604	11,914
2003	3.50	14,012	12,242
2004	6.15	15,156	13,252
2005	4.16	16, 113	14,075
2006	4.80	16,532	14,455
2007	5.70	17,299	15,122
2008	0.06	17, 542	15,153
Q1	6.25	4,705	4,137
Q2	4.56	4,372	3,766
Q3	-1.05	4,444	3,824
Q4	-8.61	4,021	3,426
2009(f)	-4.04	16, 280	13,974
Q1 (r)	-10,13	4, 061	3,510
Q2 (p)	-7.54	3,871	3,314

development, Taiwan achieved the position of an important economic entity: in 2004, it was the third-highest foreign reserve country and received the fourth-highest ranking in competitive performance.

Taiwan's economic growth was not affected a lot by the economic crisis of 1998 but the massive earthquake of 21st September, 1999 in Jiji, Nantou County, had a huge impact on the society and also economic growth. The death toll was about 2500 people and more than 100.000 people lost their homes. The economic growth rate was -2.17%. This case demonstrates well that a natural disaster can be a big role in influencing the economic development of the society, far more than external shocks created by regional or global economic crises or fluctuations. Meanwhile, in the first and second quarters of 2008, Taiwan's economic growth rate maintained its strengths with the economic growth rate staying between 4% to 6%. However, from the third and fourth quarters 2008, Taiwan could not escape from the impacts of global financial tsunami. Serious negative growth reached to -8.41% in the fourth quarter and -1.05% in the third quarter. In fact, things got even worse in the first quarter of 2009, and the negative economic growth rate reached the peak, -10.13%. And fortunately, during the second quarter of 2009, Taiwanese economy started to improve with the economic growth of -7.54%. (see Table 1)

By further comparing the Taiwan situation with other countries /societies in Asia, in 2008, Taiwan economic growth rate only reached 0.06% (the previous year being 5.70%), which was only marginally better than Japan with its -0.7% while China could sustain its great economic growth 9.0% even during that difficult year. (see Table 2)

Table 2. Economic growth rates in Asian countries (Regions) (1998-June 2009) (%)

Year	Taiwan	South Korea	Singapore	Hong Kong	Japan	Mainland China
1998	4.55	-6.9	-1.4	-6.0	-2.0	7.8
1999	5.75	9.5	7.2	2.6	-0.1	7.6
2000	5.77	8.5	10.1	8.0	2.9	8.4
2001	-2.17	4.0	-2.4	0.5	0.2	8.3
2002	4.64	7.2	4.2	1.8	0.3	9.1
2003	3.50	2.8	3.5	3.0	1.4	10.0
2004	6.15	4.6	9.0	8.5	2.7	10.1
2005	4.16	4.0	7.3	7.1	1.9	10.4
2006	4.8	5.2	8.4	7.0	2.0	11.6
2007	5.70	5.1	7.8	6.4	2.3	13.0
2008	0.06	2.2	1.1	2.4	-0.7	9.0
Q1	6.25	5.5	6.7	7.3	1.3	10.6
Q2	4.56	4.3	2.5	4.1	0.6	10.1
Q3	-1.05	3.1	0.0	1.5	-0.3	9.0
Q4	-8.61	-3.4	-4.2	-2.6	-4.3	6.8
2009(f)	-4.04	-1.9	-4.5	-2.9	-6.5	+8.0
Q1 (r)	-10.13	-4.2	-9.5	-7.8	-8.7	+6.1
Q2 (p)	-7.54	-2.5	-3.5	-3.8	-6.4	+7.9

Source: DABS, 2009

Taiwan's export strategy has its weaknesses and risks, particularly due to its vulnerability to global economic fluctuations. The economic insecurity of its citizens has increased significantly under the new global economy, as a result of the relocation of enterprises, the volatility of the financial market, the need to upgrade skills, and the global recessions.

In recent years, Taiwan has experienced two waves of mass unemployment. From 1997 to 2004, industrial restructuring and the relocation of enterprises led to a large number of factory closures. Many industries moved their capital and equipment to the mainland China due to wage increases in Taiwan. The most recent peak was primarily the result of the 2008 to 2009 global recession.

As Taiwan's economy is very dependent on the American market, the global recession caused many companies in Taiwan to reduce production drastically or stop their production entirely. Many workers were dismissed or assigned unpaid leave, and investors experienced major losses, as well. In the past, Taiwan had maintained a very low unemployment rate: before the mid-1990s, it was around 2%. In 2004, however, it reached a peak of 5.17%, which was surpassed in March 2009, with a peak of 5.82%. Both peaks created anxiety on the part of the Taiwanese government and citizens. The rise in the unemployment rate forced the Taiwanese government to improve its employment services and social security system. In the past, the government had been reluctant to intervene in matters that were traditionally considered the responsibility of the family. (see Figures 1 and 2)

Low Income Families Increasing

The percentage of low income families increased dramatically after the financial tsunami, particularly after the year of 2008 and during the first half of 2009. The low income population has been identified on the basis of relative poor indicators calculated though the standardized formula, and that proportion increased more than one percent in the year of 2009. The effect is a somewhat late response to the serious global financial crisis in the preceding year 2008. (see Table 3)

The Numbers of the Poor and Near-Poor Are Increasing

Compared with 1998, the total disposable income for the household in 2008 decreased (from NT$310,865 to NT$303,517) although the total household income increased (from NT$1,254,611 to NT$1,508,926) among the lowest 20% income population. (see Table 4)

Disparity between High and Low Income Families Widening

Income disparity between top 20% and lowest 20% groups was even worse. In 1998, there was about 5 times difference, but in 2008 it had been increased to about 6 times after the transfer payment was counted. If government transfer payment is not included, the disparity amount the richest people and the poorest people reached a 7.73 times difference. (see Tables 5 and 6)

Financial crises affect not only employment and income but also social networks and cultural institutions. Although most people tend to view the global economic crises as simply economic crises, the secondary effects may be much broader (Anderson, 2009). In this chapter, we next explore the extent to which family finances have been affected by the economic recessions and examine whether the change in household income affects people's attitudes towards the family. Finally, we review the policies the government has introduced to deal with the problems related to global economic crises.

Figure 1. Unemployment rate (1998-2009)

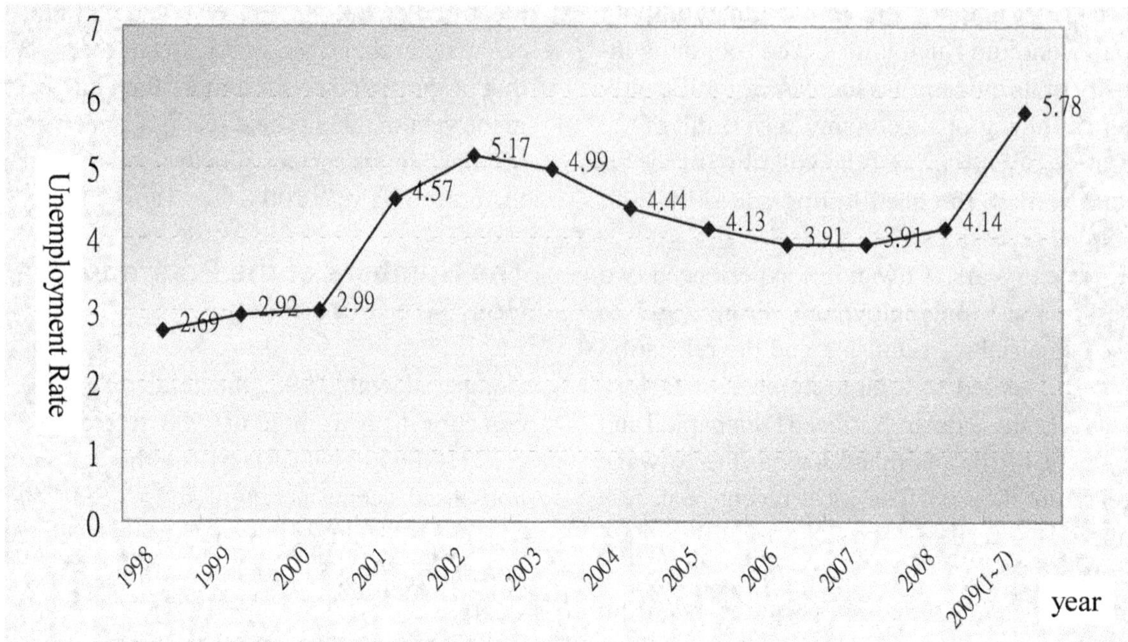

Figure 2. Unemployment rate (2007-2009)

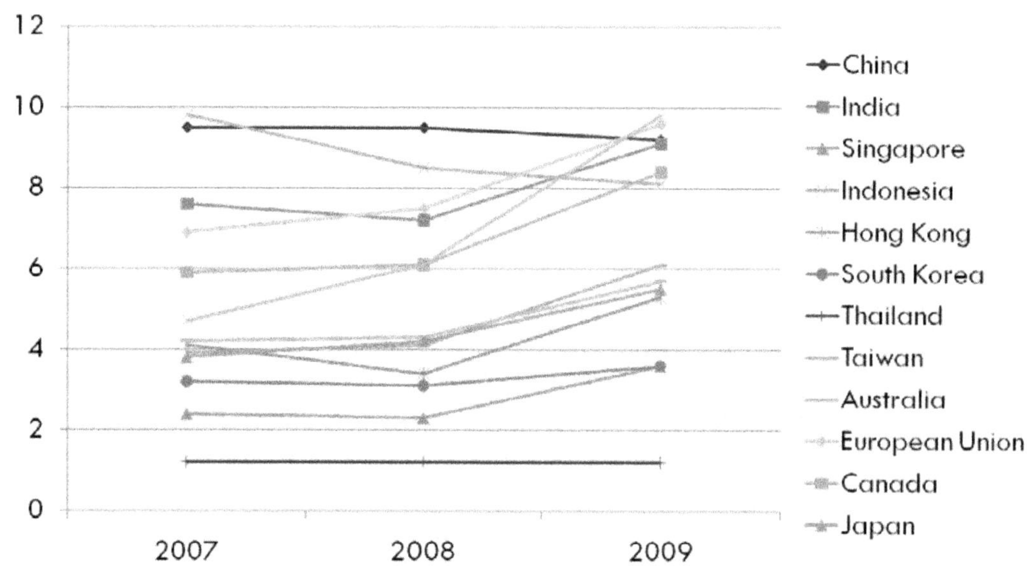

Table 3. The number of low income families (1998-June 2009)

Year	Household number		Population	
	total	As % of total household (%)	total	As % of total population (%)
1999	58,310	0.89	136,691	0.62
2000	66,467	0.99	156,134	0.70
2001	67,191	0.99	162,699	0.73
2002	70,417	1.02	171,200	0.76
2003	76,406	1.08	187,875	0.83
2004	82,783	1.15	204,216	0.90
2005	84,823	1.16	211,292	0.93
2006	89,900	1.22	218,166	0.95
2007	90,682	1.21	220,990	0.96
2008	93,032	1.22	223,697	0.97
Q1	83,709	1.11	199,841	0.87
Q2	87,664	1.16	209,945	0.91
Q3	90,525	1.19	217,400	0.94
Q4	93,032	1.22	223,697	0.97
2009	99,359	1.29	241,237	1.05
Q1	93,059	1.21	223,934	0.97
Q2	99,359	1.29	241,237	1.05

Table 4. Household income and consumption (1998~2008)

Total Household	Year	Total average	Every 20% of disposable income household				
			1 (lowest)	2	3	4	5 (highest)
Total household (household)	1998	6,273,056	1,254,611	1,254,611	1,254,611	1,254,611	1,254,611
	2007	7,414,281	1,482,856	1,482,856	1,482,856	1,482,856	1,482,856
	2008	7,544,629	1,508,926	1,508,926	1,508,926	1,508,926	1,508,926
Per household person (person)	1998	3.77	2.13	3.47	4.12	4.38	4.77
	2007	3.38	1.93	2.94	3.65	4.07	4.32
	2008	3.35	1.88	2.91	3.62	4.06	4.29
Disposable income (N.T. dollar)	1998	873,175	310,865	560,766	765,375	1,014,770	1,714,097
	2007	923,874	312,145	571,128	799,418	1,069,885	1,866,791
	2008	913,687	303,517	564,893	796,225	1,068,804	1,834,994
Consumption expenditure (N.T. dollar)	1998	646,343	288,889	496,500	632,744	763,930	1,049,654
	2007	716,094	313,309	530,417	699,698	868,505	1,168,540
	2008	705,413	309,419	522,744	687,699	849,967	1,157,234
saving (N.T. dollar)	1998	226,831	21,976	64,267	132,630	250,840	664,443
	2007	207,780	-1,164	40,711	99,720	201,380	698,251
	2008	208,274	-5,902	42,149	108,526	218,837	677,760
Saving rate (%)	1998	25.98	7.07	11.46	17.33	24.72	38.76
	2007	22.49	-	7.13	12.47	18.82	37.40
	2008	22.79	-	7.46	13.63	20.47	36.94

Table 5. Effect of government transfer on household income distribution

Year	Proportion before transfer payment (A)	Effect of income redistribution			Effective proportion (A)+(B)
		From government transfer payment	To government transfer payment	Total (B)	
1991	5.31	-0.24	-0.10	-0.34	4.97
1992	5.56	-0.23	-0.09	-0.32	5.24
1993	5.76	-0.26	-0.08	-0.34	5.43
1994	5.79	-0.30	-0.11	-0.41	5.38
1995	5.93	-0.50	-0.09	-0.59	5.34
1996	6.19	-0.69	-0.12	-0.81	5.38
1997	6.25	-0.72	-0.12	-0.84	5.41
1998	6.49	-0.84	-0.14	-0.98	5.51
1999	6.47	-0.82	-0.15	-0.97	5.50
2000	6.57	-0.88	-0.14	-1.02	5.55
2001	7.67	-1.13	-0.15	-1.28	6.39
2002	7.47	-1.18	-0.13	-1.31	6.16
2003	7.32	-1.12	-0.13	-1.25	6.07
2004	7.41	-1.24	-0.15	-1.39	6.03
2005	7.45	-1.26	-0.15	-1.41	6.04
2006	7.45	-1.30	-0.15	-1.45	6.01
2007	7.52	-1.40	-0.14	-1.54	5.98
2008	7.73	-1.53	-0.16	-1.69	6.05

SOCIAL IMPACT: DOMESTIC VIOLENCE INCREASING

The effect of increased unemployment rate to the family violence has been apparent. The features reflected from the data include:

- Total violence includes domestic violence, children abuse, elderly abuse, sexual assault.
- Pearson correlation = 0.68**
- There is clear correlation between domestic violence and unemployment rate.

The family/ intimate violence signifies that family emotional resources can be exhausted and profoundly affected by substantial changes in family economic resources. Violence might be a way of dealing with stress rising from unemployment. (see Figure 3)

METHOD

This study uses the data from two surveys conducted by the Social Policy Research Centre, National Taiwan University (NTUSPRC), in 2008 and 2009. The respondents were asked to evaluate the changes of their quality of life as a result of the 1997 Asian financial crisis and the 2008 global recession. The first survey dealt with the long-term impact of an economic recession, and the second focused on short-term effects. We first examined the answers of the respondents to determine the extent to which families were affected by the two periods of economic hardships. In order to determine whether there had been significant changes in the family structure, we reviewed the respondent's views on filial piety, the ideal number of children, the effects of living with parents, and the responsibility for the care for aged parents. More specifically, we analyzed the difference in

Table 6. Disparity between high and low income families widening, compared in Asia

	Taiwan			Japan		South Korea		Singapore		United State	
year	top 20% / low 20%	Gini	Proportion before transfer payment	top 20% / low 20%	Gini	top 20% to low 20%	Gini	top 20% / low 20%	Gini	top 20% /low 20%	Gini
1991	4.97	0.308	5.31	4.71	-	…	0.29	…	…	…	…
1992	5.24	0.312	5.56	4.64	-	…	0.28	…	…	…	…
1993	5.43	0.315	5.76	4.63	-	…	0.28	…	…	9.10	0.40
1994	5.38	0.318	5.79	4.62	-	…	0.28	…	…	8.61	0.36
1995	5.34	0.317	5.93	4.72	-	…	0.28	13.8	0.45	8.48	0.36
1996	5.38	0.317	6.19	4.76	-	…	0.29	…	…	8.75	0.37
1997	5.41	0.320	6.25	4.78	-	…	0.28	13.6	0.44	9.50	0.38
1998	5.51	0.324	6.49	4.62	-	5.45	0.32	14.6	0.45	9.70	0.38
1999	5.50	0.325	6.47	4.85	-	5.52	0.32	17.9	0.47	9.89	0.41
2000	5.55	0.326	6.57	4.74	-	5.28	0.32	20.9	0.49	10.15	0.41
2001	6.39	0.350	7.67	4.68	-	5.39	0.32	19.5	0.49	10.44	0.41
2002	6.16	0.345	7.47	6.36	-	5.16	0.31	25.4	0.51	10.20	0.41
2003	6.07	0.343	7.32	6.11	-	5.18	0.31	28.1	0.51	9.83	0.39
2004	6.03	0.338	7.41	6.04	-	5.22	0.31	29.6	0.52	9.59	0.40
2005	6.04	0.340	7.45	5.97	-	5.43	0.31	31.9	0.52	10.70	0.42
2006	6.01	0.339	7.45	6.24	-	5.38	0.31	-	-	11.14	0.42
2007	5.98	0.340	7.52	6.39	-	5.44	0.31	-	-	-	-
2008	6.05	0.341	7.73		-						

Figure 3. Total violence and unemployment in Taipei

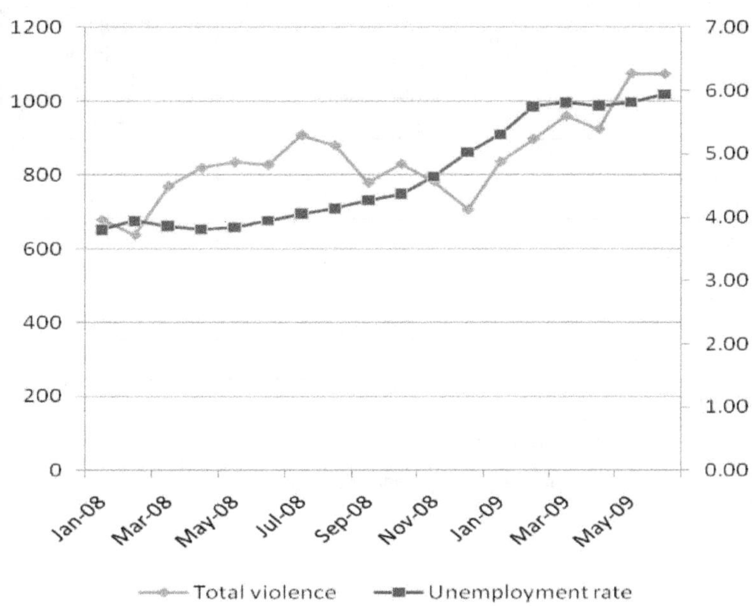

attitudes between people who had suffered from a reduction in income and those who had not.

The two-wave survey data used in this study was collected by the Gallup Market Research Corp., Taiwan, and commissioned by NTUSPRC in 2008 and 2009. The respondents were Taiwanese citizens aged 20 or older from 23 cities and counties. This survey used the quota sampling method. The first survey resulted in 1,607 completed questionnaires; the second, with 1,221. The analysis of data was conducted with SPSS.

RESULTS

The Impact of the Financial Stress on the Family

The surveys reveal that many families were affected by two economic downturns, particularly the second. More than half of the respondents (54%) reported loss of income as a result of the 2008 recession and 24% stated that at least one person in their family had experienced job loss or bankruptcy. The economic crisis led to family crises: 6.1% of the respondents experienced family dissolution (through divorce or separation) and 14.3% reported more family arguments and violence during the 2008 recession. Children's accesses to educational resources were greatly reduced: 12.9% of respondents withdrew their children from after-school programs to cut costs (see Table 7). Many seniors were required to leave their nursing homes. Overall, dependent family members are more threatened by social exclusion during or after financial crises.

The respondents in the two surveys were divided into three income levels, based on Taiwan's taxation levels. Table 8 shows that the incomes in Taiwan have shrunk as a result of the recession, especially personal income. Fewer respondents qualified for the "high income" category, while more were identified as "low income." During 2008 financial crisis, many people in Taiwan lost their jobs or were forced to take "unpaid leave," resulting in a significant drop in personal income. Though other family members may shoulder the financial responsibility after a job loss, the general finances of the family as a whole are diminished.

Table 7. Family problems caused by economic stress (%)

Family Situation	1997 Asian Financial Crisis	2008 Global Recession
1. Property loss	42.1	47.0
2. Reduced income	38.5	54.0
3. Debt/credit problems	14.0	12.7
4. Job loss or business bankruptcy	15.8	24.0
5. Family dissolution	7.3	6.1
6. Family violence or increased discord	---	14.3
7. Health problems due to economic problems	10.3	9.6
8. Suicide or mental illness due to economic problems	7.0	7.0
9. Inability to access medical treatment due to economic problems	---	5.2
10. Inability to afford children's after-school programs due to economic problems	---	12.9

Note: ---means no such attributes in the survey.

Table 8. Changes in personal and family income (%)

	Personal		Family	
	1997 Asian Financial Crisis	2008 Global Recession	1997 Asian Financial Crisis	2008 Global Recession
High income	15.2	8.0	11.5	5.9
Medium income	55.4	56.3	46.9	51.1
Low income	29.4	35.6	41.6	43.0

Note: Personal income: low = NT$0–19,999, medium = NT$20,000–59,999, and high = NT$60,000 and over. Family income: low = NT$0–59,999, medium = NT$60,000–149,999, and high = NT$150,000 and over.

Figure 4. Full time worker in Taiwan's labor market in 2008 and 2009

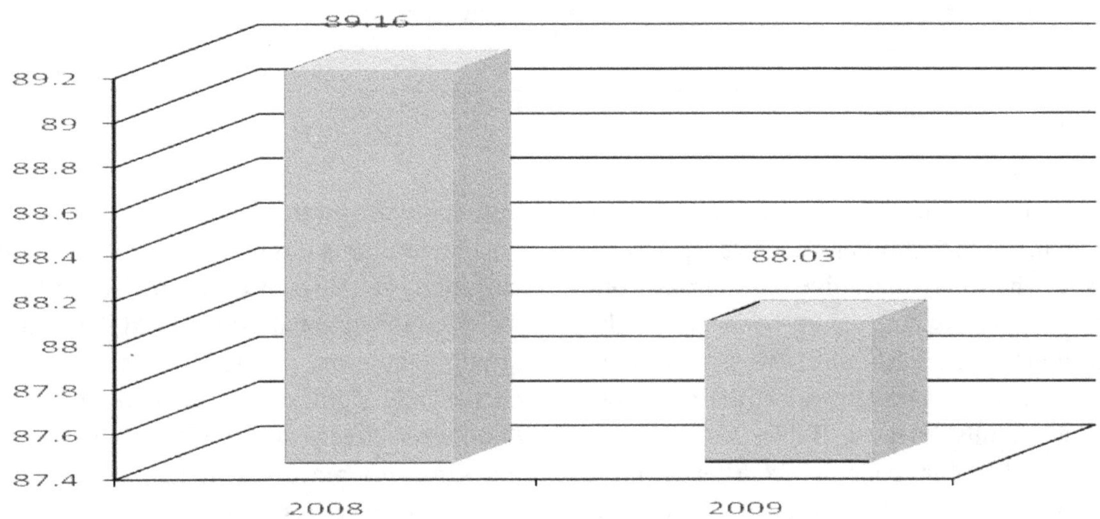

The Number of Low Income Family in Economic Recession

The number of low income families increasing gradually but there was a substantially larger increase between 2008 to 2009, with 2.2% up to 2.9%. That signifies an almost 33% increase in terms of low income household rate.

By looking into the number of low income population, it was gradually increasing since 1998 but there was a dramatic increase between 2008 and 2009. The increase percentage is about 8.2% (from 0.97% to 1.05%).

Income Loss

The survey conducted by NTUSPRC this summer shows the monthly income in average declines 14%, from NT$ 43,290 in 2008 to NT$37,130 in 2009. (see Figure 4)

According to Confucian teachings, the family is the core of society. The eldest son is responsible for the care of his family and parents. Confucianism also requires children to obey their parents. Neo-Confucianism is considered a key element of the shared heritage of East Asia (Shin & Shaw, 2003). Goodman et al (1998) conclude that Neo-Confucianism is the primary reason for

Table 9. Most important values for Taiwanese

	Highest in importance		Second in importance	
	1997 Asian Financial Crisis	2008 Global Recession	1997 Asian Financial Crisis	2008 Global Recession
Health	68.6	57.7	14.9	21.6
Stable economy	19.5	28.0	48.5	41.1
Stable job	2.5	6.2	6.1	12.5
Intimate love	2.7	2.9	11.3	7.5
Children's success	2.1	1.6	8.8	8.7
Religion	2.0	0.8	1.7	1.8
Leisure	1.5	0.9	4.5	3.8
Good friends	0.9	0.8	3.6	1.6
Stable politics	---	0.6	---	1.0
Other	0.3	0.5	0.6	0.3

Note: ---means no such attributes in the survey.

East Asian economic success, due to its focus on education, strong family ties, benevolent paternalism, social harmony, discipline, and a strong work ethic. However, when the respondents in the Social Policy Research Center surveys were asked about their most important value, their answers were not family-oriented. Table 9 shows that "health" and "stable economy" were the two most important values: "children's success" and "intimate love" ranked fourth and fifth, respectively. During times of financial hardship, a stable income gains importance and other social values seem less pressing.

Care Provision

When the respondents were asked who they wanted to live with when they were old, the majority answered with their partners as a couple (61.2% in 2008 survey and 64.8% in 2009). In the 2009 survey, 15% of respondents wanted to live with their most compatible child and 7.6% wanted to live with their eldest son. If (the affected group), and those whose incomes were unaffected and even increased (the unaffected group)— it appears that the affected group is more inclined to rely on their children in their old age, while the unaffected group was more inclined to continue as an elderly couple (see Table 10). The differences between the affected group's and the unaffected group's preferred arrangements for old age are statistically significant. When we analyzed the long-term effects of the 1990s financial crisis, the same differences emerged.

The respondents were also asked what living arrangements they would prefer when they are old and unable to take care of themselves. One-half said they would like their partners to take care of them, 15.2% were willing to stay at free nursing homes, and 11% hoped that their eldest son would provide care (see Table 11). Statistical analysis showed that these reported attitudes towards elder care were significantly influenced by income. More people in the affected group would like to stay in a free nursing home, although, according to Taiwanese tradition, such a fate is shameful because it is seen as an abandonment on the part of the child. The survey measuring the effect of the 1990s financial crisis showed that the affected group was more inclined to choose the free nursing home or the care of their eldest son when they reached that stage of life. Parents

Table 10. Living arrangements during old age (%)

Year 2009	Affected group	Unaffected group	Average
Living with one's partner as a couple	59.1	62.8	61.2
Living with one's eldest son	6.4	6.2	6.3
Living with a son who is not the eldest	1.6	1.2	1.4
Living with a daughter	2.1	4.0	3.2
Living with a child one likes	19.8	14.7	16.9
Living with friends	6.6	5.9	6.2
Other	4.4	5.2	4.9
P-value			0.048*

Table 11. Attitudes towards arrangements when in need of care (%)

Year 2009	Affected group	Unaffected group	Average
Care given by partner	44.9	55.5	50.2
Care given by the eldest son's family	9.7	12.5	11.1
Care given by the families of other sons	4.7	5.3	5.0
Care given by the daughter's family	3.9	3.7	3.8
Home care with hired help	8.5	7.1	7.8
Residence in a free nursing home	20.0	10.4	15.2
Residence in a paid nursing home	8.2	5.6	6.9
P-value			0.000*

who were vulnerable to the economic recessions revealed more traditional attitudes towards sons' contributions to parents' care. Parents who lost their income in middle age and were therefore unable to support their children in the traditional manner, however, may have felt ashamed to ask their children repay them: the respondents in the affected group had less hope of receiving inter-generational help and expressed willingness to stay in a free nursing home.

Attitudes towards Number of Children in Economic Recession

As we noted, Taiwan's fertility rate is among the lowest ones in the world. Why are the Taiwanese reluctant to have children? When the respondents were asked this question, their most common response was insufficient finances: 61.5% said that "raising children requires a lot of money." The unstable economy was the second most popular response: 45.1% stated that "the current financial situation was unstable." The instability of the social environment was also a cause for concern: 37.1% were "worried about the children's future," and 25.4% felt that "the social and political environment was not suitable for children." The increased demands due to the rise in the number of women entering the workforce was a less popular reason: 26.3% of respondents considered that "difficulties dealing with the balance of the family and work life" led to a reluctance to have children, and only 12.2% felt that children would damage the quality of married life and hinder self-achievement.

Table 12. Number of expected children, by family events

Family events, 2009	Has experienced	Has not experienced	T value
1. Property loss	2.02	2.29	-4.327***
2. Reduced income	2.02	2.33	-4.914***
3. Debt/credit problems	1.99	2.19	-2.077*
4. Job loss or business bankruptcy	2.02	2.21	-2.525*
5. Family dissolution	1.95	2.18	-1.715
6. Family violence or increased discord	2.18	2.16	0.287
7. Health problems due to economic problems	2.14	2.16	-0.250
8. Suicide or mental illness due to economic problems	2.05	2.17	-0.987
9. Inability to access medical treatment due to economic problems	2.30	2.15	1.021
10. Inability to afford children's after-school programs due to economic problems	2.10	2.17	-0.902

***P<0.001;**P<0.05;*P<0.01

Note: T-test results of other family events are not significant.

Worries about finances also affected the respondents' view of the ideal number of children. As Table 12 shows, people who experienced financial or job loss expected to have fewer children than people who were unscathed by the financial crises. Other types of family events did not have a significant impact on the respondents' expectations of their number of children. Therefore, we assume that the unstable economy under globalization has exacerbated the Taiwanese tendency towards fewer children.

Filial Piety

Although the Taiwanese seem to have changed their attitudes towards children and elder care, the majority still believes in the core value of the family—filial piety. In the 2009 survey, 57.7% of the respondents maintained that the best option for elder care is care provided by children; only 13.1% opposed this traditional view. There were no significant gender, age, or educational differences to account for this disparity.

The survey also asked whether children who were suffering financially should take care of their parents. One-third (33.3%) of the respondents believed that financially strapped children should still take care of their elderly parents; 51.9% thought that children should do their best to fulfill their intergenerational responsibilities if possible; and 14.8% maintained that it is not necessary for children to take care of their elderly parents. A higher percentage of the affected group felt that children did not need to act as caregivers (19.7%). The difference between the affected group and unaffected group was statistically significant in both surveys (p value = 0.003, 0.033). Gender, age, education, and other family events had no significant effect on the degree of filial piety.

CONCLUSION

The family in Taiwan is facing a crisis. The unstable economic has become a source of worry for most Taiwanese and has affected couples' willingness to have children. Traditionally, Taiwanese parents provide extensive financial support for their children, particularly their sons, paying their education fees, buying them a house when they marry, taking care of their small children, helping them start businesses, and bequeathing them all their property when they die. In return, parents expect their children to take care of them when they are old and regularly hold memorial ceremonies after their death. This exchange has been called the "generational contract" (Chen, 2000). This contract has been weakened, however, by financial crises, which have robbed parents of the ability to support their children. Some children have grown up in poverty and will be unable to support their parents.

Many scholars have concluded that the family structure has fundamentally changed in Taiwan and that the elderly will not receive sufficient care (Frankenberg et al, 2002; Zeng et al, 2006; Hsueh, 2008). However, Yang et al (2008) found that the family structure has not changed significantly in the last twenty years. Most households in Taiwan contain three generations. Hu (2001) has examined the changes in elder care from the perspective of intergenerational exchange. He found that the extent of parents' property affects children's willingness to provide care. Children are less willing to take care of aged parents who have no valuable property to bequeath to them. In our survey, we found that Taiwanese people who were victims of financial downturns had higher expectations of intergenerational support. Paradoxically, the affected group wanted fewer children, though they hoped to rely on their children in later years.

The unstable economy, which has forced many families to acquire a second income, may be one of the most important reasons for the drop of the birth rate in Taiwanese society. Little child-care support from the government exacerbates this situation. The traditional Taiwanese family structure and reliance on intergenerational support may be altered by new conditions. It is fortunate that most people in Taiwan still maintain the value of filial piety even in times of economic uncertainty.

REFERENCES

Anderson, R. (2009). Social tsunami: Cultural and structural factors in the emergence of welfare. *Social Policy and Administration*, *37*(4), 3.

Chen, F. L. (2000). *Working women and state policies in Taiwan: A study of political economy*. London: Palgrave Publishers. doi:10.1057/9780230508873

Department of Household Registration Affairs. (2009). *Fertility rate for women.* Retrieved from http://www.ris.gov.tw/

Department of Household Registration Affairs, Ministry of the Interior. (2009). *Statistics - household registration statistics.* Retrieved from http://www.ris.gov.tw/version96/stpeqr_01_04.html

Directorate-General of Budget, Accounting and Statistics, Executive Yuan. (1994-2009). *Family income and expenditure survey.* Retrieved from http://win.dgbas.gov.tw/fies/result.asp

Directorate-General of Budget, Accounting and Statistics, Executive Yuan. (2009). *Conditions statistical bulletin.* Retrieved from http://www.dgbas.gov.tw/public/Data/012616104771.pdf

Frankenberg, E., Chan, A., & Ofstedal, M. B. (2002). Stability and change in living arrangement in Indonesia, Singapore and Taiwan, 1993–99. *Population Studies*, *56*(2), 201–213. doi:10.1080/00324720215928

Gereffi, G. (1999). International trade and industrial upgrading in the apparel commodity chain. *Journal of International Economics*, *48*(1), 37–70. doi:10.1016/S0022-1996(98)00075-0

Goodman, R., White, G., & Kwon, H. J. (1998). *The east Asian welfare model.* London: Routledge.

Holliday, I. (2000). Productivist welfare capitalism: Social policy in east Asia. *Comparative Political Studies*, *48*, 706–723. doi:10.1111/1467-9248.00279

Hsueh, C. T. (2008). Taiwan family living patterns change and the elderly: Current status and future. *Community Development Journal*, *121*, 47–56.

Hu, K. W. (2001). *Family values, resources and intergenerational support in Taiwan*. Taipei, Taiwan: Academia Sinica.

Kwon, H. J. (2002). The Korean welfare state: Development and reform agenda. In C. Aspalter (Ed.), *Discovering the welfare state in east Asia*. Westport, CT: Praeger.

Labor Affairs Council. (2009). *Labour statistics*. Retrieved from http://www.cla.gov.tw/cgi-bin/siteMaker/SM_theme?page=41d35566

Ministry of the Interior. (2008). *Interior statistical yearbook*. Retrieved from http://sowf.moi.gov.tw/stat/year/list.htm

Ministry of the Interior. (2009). *Internal statistical bulletin*. Retrieved from http://www.moi.gov.tw/stat/

Ministry of the Interior. (2009). *2009 total population*. Retrieved from http://www.moi.gov.tw/news_detail.aspx

Shin, C. S., & Shaw, I. (2003). Social policy in South Korea: Cultural and structural factors in the emergence of welfare. *Social Policy and Administration*, *37*(4), 328–341. doi:10.1111/1467-9515.00343

Tuan, C. P. (1992). *The economy in Taiwan after the war*. Taipei, Taiwan: Jen-Chien Publications.

Yang, C. L., Chen, K. C., & Li, T. C. (2008). Changes in family structure in nearly two decades: Social changes in Taiwan during 1985 – 2005. *In Proceedings of 11th Symposium on Taiwan Social Change Survey Plans*. Taipei, Taiwan: Institute of Sociology, Academia Sinica.

Zeng, L. Y., Chang, C. O., & Chen, S. M. (2006). Choose the elderly living arrangements– Discussion of intergenerational relations. *Journal of Housing Studies*, *15*(2), 45–64.

KEY TERMS AND DEFINITIONS

Anxiety: A state of mind often classified as a disorder that is associated with nervousness, fear, apprehension, and worrying.

Confucianism: Is an ethical and philosophical system developed from the teachings of the Chinese philosopher Confucius (Kŏng Fūzĭ, or K'ung-fu-tzu, literally "Master Kong", 551–479 B.C. While the original Confucianism is deeply humanist in its nature, the tradition has later mixed in particular with Legalism, Buddhism and Daoism. The so called Neo-Confucianism from the Tang Dynasty developed the Confucian tradition toward more rationalist and secular direction (rejecting many aspects of more mystical Chinese traditions). As a result, Confucianism attained a position of basic social teaching in China (and some neighboring countries) for centuries.

Family Finances: The financial resources controlled by the family. The management of these resources varies greatly according to the power relations and changing circumstances within individual family units.

Family: Group of humans or animals. In human context, a family (from Latin: *familia*) is a group of people affiliated by blood ties (or by recognized birth with supposed blood ties), affinity (by marriage or similar social arrangement), or co-residence/shared consumption (definition often used by tax and other authorities).

Financial Crisis: Term applied broadly to a variety of situations in which some financial assets suddenly lose a large part of their nominal value.

Intergenerational Support: Takes usually place within families. This support is often closely connected with the norms and values concerning filial and parental responsibilities.

Taiwan: The Republic of China, a state in East Asia with multiparty democracy. The Republic of China governs the island of Taiwan and some smaller islands and following the Chinese civil war its government has claimed sovereignty over all of China and continuity to the Republic of China that was established in 1912 and which relocated its government to Taiwan at the end of the civil war. Meanwhile, the government of the People's Republic of China regards Taiwan as its 23rd province.

Unemployment: Joblessness, which occurs when people are without work and actively seeking work.

Values: Can be defined as preferences concerning appropriate courses of action or outcomes. As such, values reflect a person's sense of right and wrong or what "ought" to be. Types of values include ethical/moral, ideological/doctrinal, social and aesthetic values.

Chapter 4
Protective Factors in Family Relationships

Ann Buchanan
University of Oxford, UK

ABSTRACT

This chapter analyzes the importance of protective factors in family relationships. In Confucian societies, where services for older people may be limited, intergenerational family relationships are crucial in providing care for the elderly. Confucian societies are better at recognizing the protective influence of the family, but scholars from these areas suggest that the culture may be changing. As the "One child" norm extends (not only in China) across many Asian societies, the challenges for young people in supporting their parents and grandparents may become overwhelming. This chapter suggests that at every stage of the life cycle, some families will need state support in order to carry out their protective role in mitigating the risks experienced by both the young and the old. A state/family partnership approach is likely to be more acceptable, more effective, and more economic than state care alone.

己所不欲，勿施於人。

"What you do not wish for yourself, do not do to others."

—Confucius, Analects XV.24

DOI: 10.4018/978-1-4666-5031-2.ch004

INTRODUCTION

Professor Sir Michael Rutter, the distinguished UK child psychiatrist, was one of the first to highlight that although there are many risk factors associated with poor child outcomes, there are also 'protective' factors, which can mitigate the risks. Rutter's ideas, together with those of Bronfenbrenner (1979) who highlighted the importance of the wider ecology on children's development, have been at the core of the research at the Centre for Research into Parenting and Children in Oxford for over 20 years. This paper will focus on one domain of the Ecological framework: protective factors in family relationships. It will discuss the new brain research that shows that positive relationships in the early years have a measurable impact on the child's cognitive and emotional development. It will show how fathers have an important role to play and how their involvement is associated with positive outcomes for children both in the short and long term. It will also discuss the role of grandparents and the measureable benefits to young people as a result of their involvement. Finally, it will hypothesise that relationships with the wider family may also support better child outcomes.

In Confucian societies, where services for older people may be limited, intergenerational family relationships are crucial in providing care for the elderly. Confucian societies are better at recognising the protective influence of the family, but scholars from these areas, suggest that the culture may be changing. As the 'One child' norm extends (not only in China) but across many Asian societies, the challenges for young people in supporting their parents and grandparents may become overwhelming. This article suggests that as every stage of the life cycle, some families will need state support in order to carry out their protective role in mitigating the risks experienced by both the young and the old. A state/family partnership approach is likely to be more acceptable, more effective and more economic than state care alone.

This study focuses on 'protective factors' in family relationships. In the West with the growth of unmarried parenthood; increase in divorce, growth in single households, it is no wonder newspapers are using the statistics to claim the Western family is dead (Harry Wallop 2009).

For those brought up in Confucian tradition, the value and importance of the family is ingrained in their very psyche. In thinking about family relationships the above quote from Confucius is perhaps appropriate. Despite, the changes in family life in the West, the 'family', however reconstituted, remains one of the most powerful agents of influence in young people's lives. Although the coming of the Welfare State has brought enormous benefits, particularly to those are the margins of society, there has been a tendency, often seen in British social workers, to ignore the strengths of the family. The argument in this paper is that the best outcomes for vulnerable families are when the state works *in partnership* with families at risk. Children, we need to remember, are our economic future and for both humanitarian and economic reasons it makes sense to invest in children maximizing the potential of those who may be socially excluded (Buchanan and Rotkirch 2013). Only in situations of 'significant risk' of harm to a child is it right to separate a child from his family.

RISK AND PROTECTION AND THE CHILD'S ECOLOGY

Professor Sir Michael Rutter, the distinguished child psychiatrist, highlighted that although there are many risk factors associated with poor child outcomes, there are also 'protective' factors, which can mitigate the risks and promote 'resilience'. Environments for those at risk can be artificially created to compensate for the risks. Children who are exposed to a variety of adverse experiences in the early years can suffer long-term damage or negative psychological outcomes. Yet, studies have demonstrated a diversity of responses to events, even within similar environments and conditions (Rutter 1989). Outcomes vary because individuals differ in terms of their susceptibility to risk and because there may be protective mechanisms, which reduce risk (Rutter 1985). The hopeful news is that many problems are not irreversible and negative outcomes are dependent on whether risk experiences are intensified or ameliorated by subsequent experiences. Improvements in the child's economic situation can have a significant impact across a number of intellectual indicators, including IQ (Kolvin, Miller, Scott, Gatzanie & Fleeting 1990). Similarly, negative childhood experiences may be ameliorated by economic security and supportive relationships in adulthood (Quinton & Rutter 1985).

Linked into Rutter's idea of risk and protective mechanisms are those of Bronfenbrenner (Bronfenbrenner 1979). This theory looks at a child's development within the context of the system of relationships that form his or her environment. Bronfenbrenner's theory defines complex "layers" of environment, each having an effect on a child's development. Basically, there are four layers or 'domains' each with their own risk and protective factors. First there is *the Child* and his/her genetics; secondly there is *the Family*; thirdly there is the *School/Community* and finally there is the *Wider environment*. The final domain is often the focus for Social Policy interventions to ameliorate the impacts, for example of structural inequalities such as severe poverty, discrimination.

This chapter will focus on one domain of the Ecological framework: protective factors in family relationships. It will take a life course perspective starting with pre-birth and the Early Years, childhood, adulthood and old age.

PREGNANCY AND THE FIRST THREE YEARS

Every since Bowlby, we have been well trained on the importance of 'attachment' and how a baby bonds with his/her primary caregiver in the early months. This relationship is crucial to the child's subsequent development (Bowlby 1969). Research showed us that children who were more or less attached in the early years had very different patterns in later life (Ainsworth, Blehar, Waters & Wall 1978). However in the last two decades, we now know that early care giving relationships can have both a psychological and *physical impact* for better or worse.

Work by Rutter on the children rescued from the Romanian orphanages opened our eyes (Rutter 1998). There was a vague assumption that given a move to a nurturing environment, effective attachment and love, babies would recover from their early deprivation. Rutter, however, showed that it all depended on the amount of time the infant stayed in the institution. Those removed to loving adoptive parents before they were 6 months did just fine... but those who had languished in the orphanages for more than 18 months had ongoing cognitive and other difficulties despite their loving and nurturing adoptive parents.

But perhaps, the more dramatic finding was that summarised in the more recent paper by Perry (Perry 2002).

As Perry (2002) noted:

Abuse studies from the author's laboratory.... point to the need for children ...to have both stable emotional attachments with, and touch from, primary adult caregivers and sponteneous interactions with peers. If these connnections are lacking, brain development both of caring behaviour and cognitive capactities is damaged in a lasting fashion.

A key mechanism is that essential neural systems do not develop without the necessary experiences. In essence, the brain is like a formatted computer disk that needs information in order to operate. The neural systems which allow us to think, feel and act are the product of an interactive dynamic process. The brain *is most sensitive* to experience in infancy and childhood. At birth, the brain is incomplete. The child's inherited potential is designed to work in an environment. The brain has sensitive periods and although this may be marginally different for each child, the most sensitive period is around birth and during the first three years.

The implications of this are profound. In the development of socio-emotional functioning, early life nurturing appears to be critical. If this is absent for the first three years of life and then a child is adopted and begins to receive attention, love and nurturing, the positive experiences may not be sufficient to overcome the lack of development/ damage to the brain. (Perry, 2002)

One of the problems is that such neglect is difficult to see.. there are no broken bones.

If we put the recent findings in layman's terms there appears to be three mechanisms leading to lack of brain development or brain damage in the Early Years:

1. With lack of parental/carer interaction, there is a lack of neural network development. The vital links across the network of the brain are not developed. The brain needs information to help it organise itself into a completely functioning system. '*Use it or lose it*' is an axiom mentioned by Perry.
2. Chronic stress, in the case of abuse, over-stimulates an infant's brain stem and the child develops an *over-active adrenaline* system. Such a child will display increased aggression, impulsivity, and violence later in life because the brainstem floods the body with adrenaline and other stress hormones at inappropriate and frequent times.
3. With high stress, high levels of cortisol are generated that can cause brain cells to die and reduce the connections between the cells in certain areas of the brain, harming the vital brain circuits (Shonkoff & Phillips, 2000). The result – a violent, impulsive, emotionally unattached child.

Those at risk are likely to be those living in deprivation with chronic family problems such as mental health, drug and child abuse.

WHAT CAN BE DONE IN THE EARLY YEARS BY WORKING IN PARTNERSHIP WITH FAMILIES?

Family Nurse Partnership

In England and Wales extensive trials are underway on the US programme: the Nurse Family Partnership – here it has been renamed The Family Nurse Partnership (FNP). More than 30 years of rigorous research in the US has shown significant benefits for vulnerable young families in the short, medium and long term across a wide range of child and family outcomes (Department of Health). Health visitors, or nurses, visit families from the birth of a child up to, in some cases until the child is five years old. In some cases the visits will start before the baby is born. They offer parents a range of social support and advice about childcare.

Community Programmes: 0-5 Years – Sure Start/Family Centres

Many of these centres have now become family centres in Britain. The first 524 Sure Start local programmes (SSLPs) were established between 1999 and 2003. They were aimed at families with children up to the age of four living in disadvantaged areas. The aim was to bring together early education, childcare, health services and crucially *family support* to promote the physical, intellectual and social development of babies and children. Although the early research evidence was mixed, more recent studies have shown improved child outcomes.

Families with Multiple Needs

One of the most challenging groups are those families with multiple needs/risks. Often these families suffer mental health problems, may be abusing drugs as well as presenting child protection concerns. There are now agencies that undertake to support these families 'from cradle to grave'. One of these projects in the UK is run by the charity Family Action and is called Building Bridges, that is they work across all ages and across the child protection/ parentalmental health divide. Local authorities across the UK commission the charity to undertake the work. There is now good evidence that their work is effective (Family Action Building Bridges evaluation 2011).

Pre-School Provision for Under 5's

Although the ages 0-3 are the most crucial years, children from age 2 plus may be placed in some sort of pre-school provision, especially when their mothers are working.

In the UK Professor Kathy Sylva, and a large team conclusively demonstrated the positive effects of high quality pre-school provision on children's intellectual and cognitive development. Pre-school education, for children over three, they concluded, could play an important part in combating social exclusion and promoting inclusion by offering disadvantaged children, in particular, a better start to primary school (Sammons, Elliot, Sylva, Melhuish, Siraj-Blatchford, & Taggart 2004).

DOES THE INVOLVEMENT OF FATHERS MAKE A DIFFERENCE?

In the past, the role of fathers has been dramatically underrepresented in the research literature on family relationships and child development.

Ann Buchanan and colleagues undertook two major studies demonstrating the protective role fathers have on child well-being (Buchanan and Flouri 2005). The first study used longitudinal data from the National Child Development Study (NCDS). An 'involved' father, as defined in this research, was a father who read to his child, took outings with his child, was interested in his child's education and took a role equal to mother in managing his child. He may or may not live with the child's mother, and he may or may not be the biological father to the child. There were some strong findings:

- Early father involvement with a child was associated with continuing involvement with that child throughout childhood and adolescence. Generally once fathers were '*involved*' they remained involved with that child throughout childhood. In a sense they became 'bonded' to that child. At different ages, fathers related to their children in different ways, but the underlying concept of father involvement was a continuous one.
- Father involvement was associated with good parent-child relationships in adolescence and also with later satisfactory partnerships in adult life. Good father-child relations were associated with an absence of emotional and behavioural difficulties in the young adolescent and greater academic motivation. Teenagers felt close to their fathers when their fathers were involved with them as they were growing up. When the children grew up those who have felt close to their fathers in adolescence were more likely to have satisfactory adult marital relationships.
- Children with involved fathers were less likely to be in trouble with the police Boys in particular were less likely to be in trouble with the police where they had 'involved' fathers. However, we must also remember research by Farrington that showed boys with chronically antisocial fathers were more likely to be delinquent (Farrington et al. 2001).
- Father involvement protected children in separated families against later mental health problems Involvement of the father or a father figure had a significantly protec-

tive role against psychological problems in adolescents in families where parents had separated. This finding was independent of whether mothers were also involved.

- Father involvement was strongly related to children's later educational attainment Father involvement at age 7 and mother involvement at age 7 significantly and independently predict higher educational attainment by age 20 and this applied to both girls and boys.
- Early father involvement protected against an adult experience of homelessness in sons of manual workers. As might be expected absence of partners in women, and psychological distress and large families in men were the key predictors of welfare dependency. However, both father and mother involvement in families of manual workers was highly protective against an adult experience of homelessness in their sons.

Because the children in NCDS were born in 1958, Buchanan undertook a second study of over 2000 children in secondary schools in 2005 to see if things had changed. The results from this study were also positive. But qualitative research showed that the involvement of low and middle-income fathers, was often quite superficial and their main role was to respond to problems as they arose by 'being there' (Welsh, Buchanan, Flouri & Lewis 2004). Even so, this minimal role was protective. In contrast, better educated fathers were more 'hands on'.

Here we must remember other research by Buchanan and her team on the parents and children going through the divorce court (Bream & Buchanan 2003). Where there was family ongoing conflict over the residence and contact arrangements this could have a major negative impact on child well-being and possibly negate any good of father involvement.

So how can we Increase Father Involvement?

Since our research and that undertaken by others, there has been a major focus on involving fathers in maternity wards, the early years, school meetings and in a range of other ways. Much of this work has been lead by The Fatherhood Institute (http://www.fatherhoodinstitute.org). The message is that once fathers become involved, they are likely to stay involved and this has positive benefits for the child

THE PROTECTIVE ROLE OF GRANDPARENT INVOLVEMENT

With changing families, increased life expectancy, growing numbers of dual-worker households, and higher rates of family breakdown, it was noted that grandparents appeared to be playing an increasing role in their grandchildren's lives. Buchanan and the team at the Centre for Research into Parenting and Children decided to investigate this further. The resulting study by Buchanan and colleagues (Attar-Schwartz et al. 2009), focused on the view of adolescents aged 11-16. It was assumed that adolescents busying themselves with their own relationships would have little to do with their grandparents. The results however were surprising.

1. **Extent of involvement:** More than 80 per cent of the young people saw their grandparents regularly. Almost a third of maternal grandmothers provided regular caretaking, while another 40 per cent did so occasionally.
2. **Most grandparents gave regular financial support or other assistance.** In addition, there was considerable involvement in sharing young people's interests and activities, and talking about future plans.
3. They were also involved in helping to solve problems, and taking part in school activities.

What Made Involvement Likely?

1. The child's age, living in a less deprived area, frequent contact, and good grandparent health and closeness to the grandchildren, are all factors influencing involvement.
2. Proximity was not necessarily important, as young people used modern technology to communicate.
3. Parents acted as 'gatekeepers' to grandparent involvement. Grandchildren felt grandparents became closer when they undertook some traditional parenting tasks.

Child Well-Being

1. Previous research in the UK and US has shown that grandparents with heavy grandchild commitments can be severely depressed, with impact on children, and that adolescents become less close to them as they get older.
2. In this study, grandparent's active involvement was significantly associated with better-adjusted adolescents. In particular, taking part in grandchildren's hobbies and interests was associated significantly with fewer emotional, behaviour and peer problems.

For those of you from Confucian societies it will seem odd that in the UK grandparents have no rights to see their grandchildren if parents deny them access. This study, however, has been quite influential, although the law has not changed to permit grandparents greater rights over their grandchildren, all political parties are now recognising the importance of intergenerational relationships. It was interesting that in this study young people spoke out strongly as they felt it was *their right* to remain in contact with their grandparents.

What can be done to Increase Grandparent Involvement?

Joan Hunt at Oxford has undertaken considerable research researching the benefits and limitations of kinship care (Lutman, Hunt and Waterhouse 2009; Hunt 2008; Hunt, Waterhouse, Lutman 2008; Waterhouse, Hunt, Lutman 2008). In less extreme situations, state interventions could consider how intergenerational relationships can be maintained – for example by housing elderly close to families, helping with telecommunication and transport costs etc.

THE POSSIBLE VALUE OF INVOLVEMENT FROM THE WIDER FAMILY

Further work is planned at the Centre to explore possible benefits from wider family relationships. Among proposed studies, is one on the importance of sibling relationships. Today in the UK, if a Court rules that it may never be safe for a child to live with their parents, most children will be placed in foster families or may be put up for adoption.. When this happens, many are separated from their siblings. It is possible, however, that these decisions may have unintended long-term consequences. Earlier research by Buchanan showed that in adult life, families were the first port of call when they needed help (Buchanan & Ten Brinke 1997). However, children, who had been in public care, did not call on their families. The act of protecting them as children meant that as adults they did not have family support they might need. The author will be exploring this further in her next project.

WHAT HAPPENS WHEN WE GET OLD?

Research by Finch and Masson has shown that earlier intergenerational relationships are important in deciding what is the 'proper thing to do' when faced with an elderly relative who needs care (Finch and Masson 1993). Where a good relationship had been established with children and grandchildren in earlier times, the children and grandchildren were more helpful in providing care. Of course, in Confucian Societies the duty to care for elderly members of your family is generally felt to be nonnegotiable. In post-war Japan, however, social changes have transformed people's attitudes and more people are seeing elderly dependence on children as less desirable. In Taiwan as the country's fertility rate has dropped dramatically (since 2005, two adults are only producing one child), the idea of sending elderly parents to an institutions has become more acceptable (Wang 2011). Whereas in 1985, 91.6% felt this was very wrong only 46.5% considered it so in 2005. In Japan there is evidence that the elderly are now more reluctant to accept financial support from their children. In Hong Kong in a major review of the literature on Filial Piety (Ting 2009) they note that socio-demographic changes make it increasingly difficult for families to take care of elderly members and these changes had fundamentally altered the relationships between adult children and their parents. As the world comes together, perhaps Confucian societies too, will have to develop state organisations to work in partnership in caring for their elderly. But the other side to the story is that where grandparents are involved in caring for their grandchildren, these grandchildren, once adult, may be more inclined to support their ageing relatives.

CONCLUSION

Positive family relationships are perhaps, the most important 'protective' factors in mitigating risks at every age. This paper suggests that as every stage of the life cycle, some families will need state support in order to carry out their protective role in mitigating the risks experienced by both the young and the old. Except where there are major child protection concerns, a state/family partnership approach is likely to be more acceptable, more effective and more economic than residential state care. Families need to be kept involved. In old age families may be more willing to help, if they have been helped by family members, when they were young.

REFERENCES

Ainsworth, M., Blehar, M. C., Waters, E., & Wall, S. (1978). *Patterns of attachment: A psychological study of the strange situation.* Hillsdale, NJ: Erlbaum.

Attar Schwartz, S., Tan, J.-P., & Buchanan, A. (2009). Adolescents' perspectives on relationships with grandparents: The contribution of adolescent, grandparent, and parent–grandparent relationship variables. *Children and Youth Services Review, 31*(9), 1057–1066. doi:10.1016/j.childyouth.2009.05.007

Bowlby, J. (1969). *Attachment and loss.* New York: Basic Books.

Bream, V., & Buchanan, A. (2003). Distress among children whose separated or divorced parents cannot agree arrangements for them. *British Journal of Social Work, 33*, 227–238. doi:10.1093/bjsw/33.2.227

Bronfenbrenner, U. (1979). *The ecology of human development.* Cambridge, MA: Harvard University Press.

Buchanan, A., & Flouri, E. (2005). *Father Involvement and outcomes in adolescence and adulthood*. Retrieved on 29 October, 2012 from http://www.esrc.ac.uk/my-esrc/grants/R000223309/outputs/Read/3871fa69-89d7-4d32-9ad2-c5d04d5974f5

Buchanan, A., & Rotkirch, A. (2013). *Fertility rates and population decline: No time for children?* London, UK: Palgrave Macmillan. doi:10.1057/9781137030399

Buchanan, A., & Ten Brinke, J.-A. (1997). *What happened when they were grown up? Outcomes from parenting experiences*. York, UK: Joseph Rowntree Foundation.

Department of Health. (n.d.). *The family nurse partnership programme*. Retrieved on 29 October, 2012 from http://www.dh.gov.uk/en/Publicationsandstatistics/Publications/PublicationsPolicyAndGuidance/DH_118530

Family Action Building Bridges Evaluation. (2011). *Summary report*. Retrieved on 29 October, 2012 from www.family-action.org.uk/uploads/documents/Building%20Bridges%20Summary%20Evaluation.pdf

Farrington, D., et al. (2001). *Family influences on delinquency*. Retrieved on 29 October, 2012 from samples.jbpub.com/.../60564_CH10_Springer.pdf

Fatherhood Institute. (n.d.). Retrieved on 29 October 2012 from http://www.fatherhoodinstitute.org/

Finch, J., & Masson, J. (1993). *Negotiating family responsibilities*. London: Routledge.

Hunt, J. (2008). *Family and friends care*. Research in Practice.

Hunt, J., Waterhouse, S., & Lutman, E. (2008). *Keeping them in the family: Children placed in kinship care through care proceedings*. London: BAAF.

Kolvin, I., Miller, F. J. W., Scott, D. M., Gatzanie, S. R. M., & Fleeting, M. (1990). *Continuities of deprivation? The Newcastle 1000 family study*. Aldershot, UK: Avebury.

Lutman, E., Hunt, J., & Waterhouse, S. (2009). Placement stability for children in kinship care: A long term follow up of children placed in kinship care through care proceedings. *Adoption & Fostering*, *33*(3), 28–39. doi:10.1177/030857590903300304

Perry, B. D. (2002). Childhood experience and the expression of genetic potential: What childhood neglect tells us about nature and nurture. *Brain and Mind*, *3*, 79–100. doi:10.1023/A:1016557824657

Quinton, D., & Rutter, M. (1985). Parenting behaviour of mothers raised in care. In R. Nicol (Ed.), *Longitudinal studies in child psychology and psychiatry* (pp. 157–201). Chichester, UK: Wiley.

Rutter, M. (1985). Intergenerational continuities and discontinuities in serious parenting difficulties. In D. Cicchetti (Ed.), *Child maltreatment*. Cambridge, UK: Cambridge University Press.

Rutter, M. (1989). Pathways from childhood to adult life. *Journal of Child Psychology and Psychiatry, and Allied Disciplines*, *30*, 23–61. doi:10.1111/j.1469-7610.1989.tb00768.x PMID:2647779

Rutter, M. (1998). Developmental catch-up, and deficit, following adoption after severe global early privation. *Journal of Child Psychology and Psychiatry, and Allied Disciplines*, *39*(4), 465–476. doi:10.1017/S0021963098002236 PMID:9599775

Sammons, P., Elliot, K., Sylva, K., & Melhuish, M., Siraj-Blatchford, & Taggart, B. (2004). The impact of pre-school on young children's cognitive attainments at entry to reception. *British Educational Research Journal*, *30*(5), 691–712. doi:10.1080/0141192042000234656

Shonkoff, J. P., & Phillips, D. A. (Eds.). (2000). From *neurons to neighborhoods*: The *science of early childhood development.* National Academies Press. Retrieved on 29 October, 2012 from http://www.nap.edu/catalog/9824.html

Ting, K.-F. (2009). *A review on the literature on filial piety*. Central Policy Unity, Government of Hong Kong. Retrieved on 29 October, 2012 from http://www.cpu.gov.hk/chs/documents/new/press/Filial%20Piety%20Literature.pdf

Wallop, H. (2009). Death of the traditional family. *Daily Telegraph.* Retrieved on 29 October, 2012 from http://www.telegraph.co.uk/family/5160857/Death-of-the-traditional-family.html

Wang, K. (2011). Child care and elder arrangements in Taiwan. *Journal of Comparative Social Welfare*, *27*(2), 165–174. doi:10.1080/17486831.2011.567021

Waterhouse, S., Hunt, J., & Lutman, E. (2008, May). Keeping them in the family: Neglected and abused children placed with family or friends carers through care proceedings. *Family Law (Chichester)*.

Welsh, E., Buchanan, A., Flouri, E., & Lewis, J. (2004). 'Involved' fathering and child well-being: Fathers' involvement with secondary school age children. *National Children's Bureau for the Rowntree Foundation Parenting in Practice Series*. Retrieved on 29 October, 2012 from http://www.jrf.org.uk/publications/fathers-involvement-with-their-secondary-school-aged-children

KEY TERMS AND DEFINITIONS

Child Psychiatry: Branch of psychiatry that specializes in the study, diagnosis, treatment, and prevention of psychopathological disorders of children, adolescents, and their families.

Family Relationships: Relationships taking place within the family institution.

Filial Piety: In Confucian philosophy, filial piety (Chinese: *xiào*) is a virtue of respect for one's parents and ancestors. In more general terms filial piety includes the ideal that good conduct inside and outside the home brings a good name to one's parents and ancestors.

Life Cycle: From cradle to grave; from creation to disposal. Human life cycle includes different stages, which show certain patterns within different social groups and cultures.

Protective Factors: Conditions in families and communities that, when present, increase the health and well-being.

Well-Being: A general term for the condition of an individual or group, for example their social, economic, psychological, spiritual or medical state.

Chapter 5
Globalization and Transformation of Care in Japan

Reiko Ogawa
Kyûshû University, Japan

ABSTRACT

This chapter deals with the situation of family and care work in Japan, and, in particular, the Conjunction between Family, Care Work, and Immigration in Japan. The chapter is aimed to elucidate the complex interplay between family and care work from both paid and unpaid work. Furthermore, Japan currently does not have an immigration policy that would include social integration policies. Since the care needs cannot be met solely by the families or the domestic labor market, globalization of care will become a salient trend for a foreseeable future. Moreover, the chapter proceeds to analyze the globalization thesis within the Japanese context. According to the author, one should be able to see the convergence of welfare states in many countries, but as in the case of Japan, the process of globalization is not linear but contingent. Instead, what one has seen is a dialectical process of how the domestic factors are differently shaping the well-being of the people within their own institutional histories and strategies.

1. INTRODUCTION

Japan is known to be one of the most advanced economies in the world but the structural change since the 1990s has brought poverty, inequality and social exclusion to the everyday lives of the people. The term 'social inclusion' originated from the European Council first appeared in the policy agenda in Japan in 2000 (Ôsawa, 2007, p. 21). The term 'unequal society' (*kakusa shakai*) was chosen as a 'vogue word' in 2006. A book titled 'anti poverty' (*han hinkon*) was published by Iwanami Shoten in 2008.

The structural change from industrial to post industrial society was further accelerated by the demographic change of population ageing and the

DOI: 10.4018/978-1-4666-5031-2.ch005

state is restricted in responding to these changes when there is an ever growing need for social protection. The residual nature of Japanese welfare state has long being dependent on companies and families as the two main sources of welfare service provider. Insofar as the two institutions were stable and resourceful, individuals were provided with either formal or informal safety net. However, the two institutions started to deteriorate as the company encountered fierce competition in the global capital market demanding deregulation and flexibility, and the family became more individualized and diverse.

The growing polarization, inequality and unemployment that are taking place in Japan closely echoes with similar trends in USA and Western Europe where the welfare states have come under serious pressure (Castells, 2000; Swank, 2002). Scholars have argued that the international capital mobility has significantly deregulated the working conditions, reduced taxation, removed protection mechanisms and weakened the welfare state to undertake redistribution (Beck, 2000). The globalization thesis undertakes causal analysis to perceive the globalization as a cause of the retrenchment of the welfare state. However, the others argue that globalization should not be treated as a monolithic phenomenon and has to be disentangled with the other political, demographic and social trends (Yeates, 2007, p. 642; Swank, ibid). They emphasize the particular importance of national institutions which are detrimental in mediating how globalization would affect the national politics and the larger social change.

Instead of adapting a causal analysis between globalization and welfare state, McGrew (1992, p. 74) has emphasized that the process of globalization is "dialectical in nature and unevenly experienced across time and space". Similarly, Giddens (1990) acknowledges that the dialectical process does not bring change in a uniform direction but produces contradictory tendencies. One of the contradictory tendencies that I would like to apply in this paper is the binary opposition of "universalization" verses "particularization" (Harvey, 1989). This refers to the universal tendencies that globalization produces and the specific strategies that the state adapts according to its own institutions, capacities and social norms. Instead of the causal analysis between globalization and social policy, to understand globalization as a contingent and dialectical process allows us to see how different factors are shaping the social welfare provision today.

In this chapter, I would like to elaborate the changes that took place in Japan in the past two decades revolving around the field of long term care and examine the globalization thesis. It maps the four terrains; employment, family, long term care insurance and entry of migrants and examine the factors that shape the changes. First, I will outline the theoretical foundations of the scholarly works on globalization and social policy. Secondly, I will elaborate the changing structure in employment and family and how it affects the status of long-term care. Thirdly, I will outline the introduction of Long Term Care Insurance responding to the population ageing. Finally, the entry of migrant nurses and caregivers under the Economic Partnership Agreement (EPA) will be discussed together with the challenges. I argue that the impact of globalization is not linear but dialectical representing universal trends as well as specific particularities due to the ways in which national institutions respond to the challenges.

2. GLOBALIZATION AND SOCIAL POLICY

Discussions on globalization and the intensification of interconnectedness and interdependencies has now become one of the central concerns of the social science analysis. Globalization has been analyzed from a plethora of approaches including economic, political and socio-cultural dimensions and a wide divergence of positions including criticism of 'anti-globalization movements' to the optimism of 'neo-liberal' ideologies. Even though far from reaching a consensus, globalization studies challenges the social science notion to perceive nation state as a container of the society as it is increasingly becoming difficult to ignore the transnational mobilities of capital, goods, information, images, ideas and people.

However, in the contemporary discussion, social policy is largely confined within the nation state framework without taking into account the influence of international institutions and globalizing forces. In the standard definition, 'social policy' has been defined as:

[A] deliberate intervention by the state to redistribute resources amongst its citizens so as to achieve a welfare objective (Baldock, Mannin and Vickerstaff, 2007).

This is not surprising as social policy deals with the reproduction of a social system embodied within the nation state, aims to protect its members from different risks and meet their needs in their life course. Most of the social policy studies enshrine their analysis within the national context even though one of the driving forces for the structural change that the social policy has to take into account is the effect of globalization.

Attempts have been made to disentangle the multiple and contested ways in which globalization intersects with social policy. Situated in the historical context, the welfare state has been developed during the nineteenth and twentieth century in industrialized countries under the international trade and monetary systems of Bretton Woods. The Keynesian welfare state was conceived with active state intervention by stimulating growth and realizing full employment through international trade.

Yeates (2001) point out that there are different ways in which welfare state and globalization intersect, influence and negotiate with each other. She elaborates that there are three approaches to discuss the relationship between globalization and social policy. First is to look into the ways in which globalization impacts the welfare states. This approach perceives the erosion of the autonomy of the national government to conduct universal redistribution programs and realize full employment as the competition in the global capital market intensifies and market principles dominate the public sphere. The strategies that the TNCs will adapt include deregulating the working condition, increase unemployment and tax avoidance in order to maximize the productivity, and remove social protection to maintain the competitiveness. This 'race to the bottom' includes relocation of production sites and increase in flexible forms of employment.

For example, Beck (2000, p. 1) writes:

The premise of the welfare state and pension system, of income support, local government and infrastructure policies, the power of organized labor, industry-wide free collective bargaining, state expenditure, the fiscal system and 'fair taxation' – all this melts under the withering sun of globalization and becomes susceptible to (demands for) political moulding.

Globalization is seen as an external force penetrating and eroding the national welfare system and the state is left without the countervailing power. Beck further argues that globalization is creating "capitalism without work" and the project of modernity that is based on the historical association of market economy, welfare state and democracy is destined to break down (ibid, p. 8). Yeates (2007, p. 641) responds that this view is deeply problematic as it overestimates the power of the capital and underestimates the capacity of states and suggests the importance of domestic factors.

The second approach is to see social policy as a contributing factor to globalization. This approach situates the nation state as a central actor which performs a critical role in mitigating the structural changes brought by globalization. Taking into account the social and political institutions, state ideologies, and demographic features countries may respond in a very different way to similar kinds of pressures. For example, Gøsta Esping-Andersen (1996) emphasizes the continued importance of national institutions and traditions, which allows the welfare states to produce different policy measures to achieve the same objectives. Swank echoes with this view and argues that the globalization thesis has to operate in the institutionally defined context of "pluralist systems of interest representation, exclusive electoral institutions, and politics of historically embedded decentralization of policy-making authority" (2002, p. 279).

The third approach is to look into the globalization of social policy processes. This approach sees the transnational dimensions of social policy that is influenced by the different actors at the supranational level. The international arena has become a sphere where not only the government but also other actors such as civil society participate and advocate their vision for their well being. As more countries are adapting liberal market economies and integrated into the global capital market, the autonomy of the nation state to design its own policy becomes restricted. Instead global institutions such as World Bank, IMF, European Commission or non-governmental organizations shape the social policy of the country (Yeates, 2001, p. 28-29). Zimmerman et al. (2006, p. 24) resonates with this view that especially in the developing countries multilateral organizations have a strong power in determining the nature of care provisions. She states that for the developing countries, outside interventions are not new but globalization has significantly increased the legitimacy of multilateral organizations to expand its role in policy making.

While the impact of globalization has to be taken into account, we need to consider several points. First, state is not a monolithic entity and the way globalization manifests itself in the domestic sphere does not always displays a universal character. Secondly, globalization cannot account for all the causes for the erosion of the welfare state and there are other domestic forces at work such as the demographic change. Thirdly, globalization may not necessarily result in deterioration of the welfare state but bring new opportunities in an unexpected way, which may or may not be a solution to the crisis of the welfare state. In the following sections, I will elaborate the globalization effect and how it manifest itself in Japan shifting between the two poles of 'universal' and 'particular'.

3. CHANGING STRUCTURES OF EMPLOYMENT AND FAMILY

Japan's post war welfare regime emerged out of the rapid economic development under the industrial society. It was based on the male breadwinner model, which was guaranteed with lifelong employment and ensured with decent income under the Fordist mass production system. The company provided all the necessary benefits for their employees and their families and entering a society was considered to be synonymous to enter into the company. The male who obtained the full membership in the company had a strong sense of belonging and loyalty so work was always prioritized over family life. The clear gender division of labor was established and the reproductive work including care work was relegated to the domestic sphere of women. Still, the salary for male workers increased steadily as they grow old so the family's desire for material needs according to their life course, such as purchasing a house or the educational cost for children, were fulfilled. This employment security allowed the people to plan their life stage and have control in their life course.

However, when the production model shifted from Fordism to post Fordism, the male breadwinner lifelong employment model which was the foundation of the society became replaced by the post industrial model characterized by 'flexibility' and 'informalization'. In Japan, the benchmark for this shift took place in the 1990s when the major sectors shifted from manufacturing to IT and finance (Oguma, 2012). In 1994, the number of employment in the service sector overrode the employment in the manufacturing sector. The economic bubble collapsed in early 1990s and increasing off shore production of the companies to overseas seeking for cheap labor resulted in decrease in white color jobs. The lifelong employment system, which used to be one of the strength of "Japanese management" became a burden when the global competition intensified and the companies started to fire their employees for the sake of their survival.

In 1995, Japan Business Federation presented a policy paper proposing to categorize the workers into three groups: long term workers provided with sufficient training; highly skilled expertise employed according to the needs of the company; and flexible workers (Nihon Keieisha Dantai Renmei, 1995). The state endorsed this categorization and labor laws were amended several times after mid 1990s. By late 1990s, the number of permanent male workers in companies with more than 500 employees decreased from 8.06 million in 1999 to 6.93 million in 2007 (Miyamoto, 2011, p. 135).

The economic downturn was also reflected in the increase in suicide ratio, which drastically went up after 1998. From 1978 to 1997, the suicide ratio was stable between 20,000~25,000 per year but in 1998 it suddenly jumped up to 32,000 and it remained above 30,000 per year till 2012. In 1998, among those who committed suicide, 70% was male and more than 80% were in their middle age or above (Cabinet Office, 2012). The male bread winner model was challenged not only by the increasing number of women's entry into the labor market but also more and more male became employed as non permanent workers who work on contract bases or part time bases with less salary and benefits.

In 2012, the number of those who are not permanently employed was increased to more than 20 million for the first time in the past 20 years, which signifies 38.2% of the total of employees (Statistics Bureau, 2012, p. 56-7). Similarly, the number of those who live on welfare also reached 16 million households, which became the highest since 1955 (National Institute of Population and Social Security Research, 2013). Those who are out of work and out of family are left to live a 'bare life' (Agamben, 1998) of uncertainty. More than half of the non-permanent workers are household heads, who are forced to live precarious life full of risks (Miyamoto, 2011, p. 136). Due to increasing competition and relaxation of the labor laws, sometimes the companies did not provide for the health and unemployment insurance and the workers are deprived of their basic social safety net.

The working condition of non permanent workers is far from the 'decent work' in the definition of ILO with an income of less than 2~3 million yen sometimes ending up on streets when they lose the jobs and cannot pay for the rent (Yûasa, 2008). According to the ILO, decent work includes opportunities for work that is productive and delivers a fair income, security in the workplace and social protection for families, better prospects for personal development and social integration, freedom for people to express their concerns, organize and participate in the decisions that affect their lives and equality of opportunity and treatment for all women and men, ILO, 2013). Yûasa, an advocate for the anti poverty movement named the situation where the workers are deprived of their basic safety net 'a slide society' *(suberidai shakai)*. This indicates that once you lose your job, you will immediately slide down to the bottom of the society (Yûasa, ibid).

Those who are permanent are also pressured to follow the demand of the company in fear of losing their jobs. Following the European Union's policy on social inclusion, poverty and inequality became a social issue in a country, which has the third largest economy in the world. Stable and secure employment, which once was an integral

Figure 1. Number of marriage and divorce

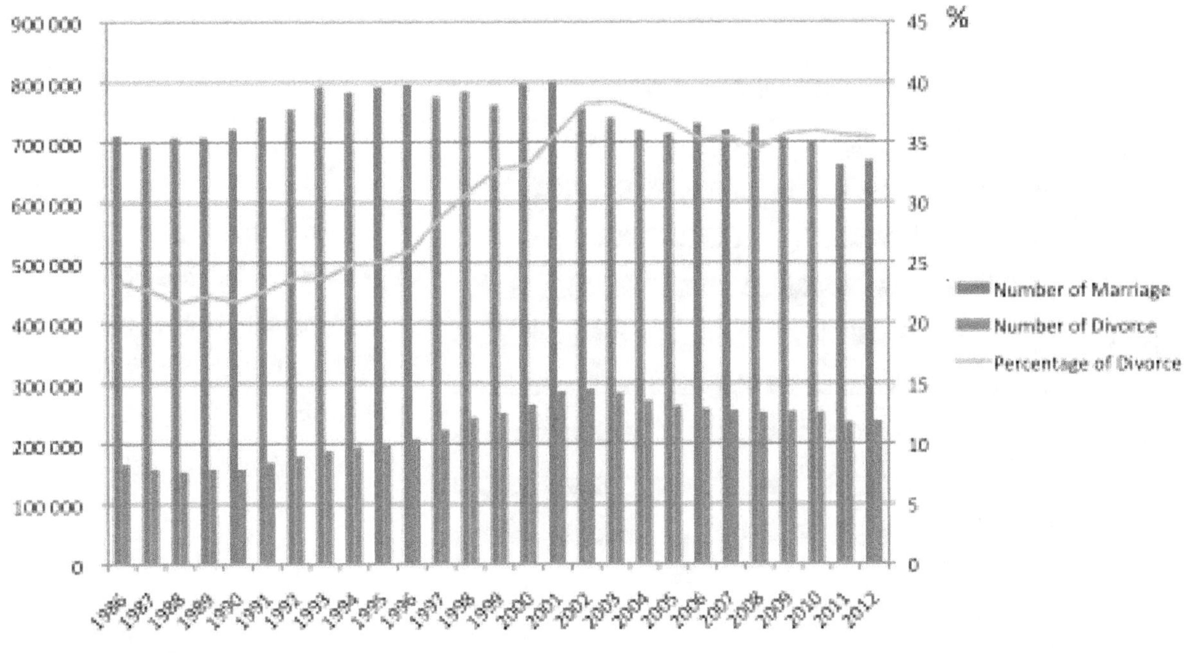

Source: MHLW, 1998~2012.

part of the social welfare deteriorated drastically putting males, females and children into risk.

While the employment system based on the male breadwinner model was challenged, family, which is another important institution for Japan's social welfare also faced a major transformation. Just like the families in any other developed countries, the families in Japan became much smaller in size and the form became diversified. In 1986, the average number of family members in a household was 3.22 and by 2012 it gradually dropped to 2.57 (MHLW, 2012). Coinciding with the increase in suicide ratio, the divorce ratio also started to increase in mid 1990s (Figure 1), which resulted in a large number of impoverished single parent families. Shockingly, the degree of poverty became widespread to the extent that a number of deaths have been caused by starvation in the midst of an affluent society like Japan.

In May 2013, a 28 years old mother and a three-year old child were found dead in an apartment in Ôsaka. The mother was working until December 2012 but divorced with her husband and did not even inform her parents of their whereabouts. There was no food in the room except for salt and the note was left in the room written by the mother to her son 'I'm sorry that I could not feed you fully'. The son did not have anything in the stomach so there is a possibility that he has starved to death. This tragic case clearly reflects the deterioration of the two main institutions of employment and family and no support was provided to her either from the community or from the government (Asahi Shimbun, 2013; Yomiuri Shimbun, 2013; Nihon Keizai Shimbun, 2013a).

This decreasing capacity of the company and family to ensure stable social life profoundly affects the provisions for long term care. In terms of living arrangements, Figure 2 illustrates the decreasing number of three generation households

Figure 2. Living arrangements of the elderly

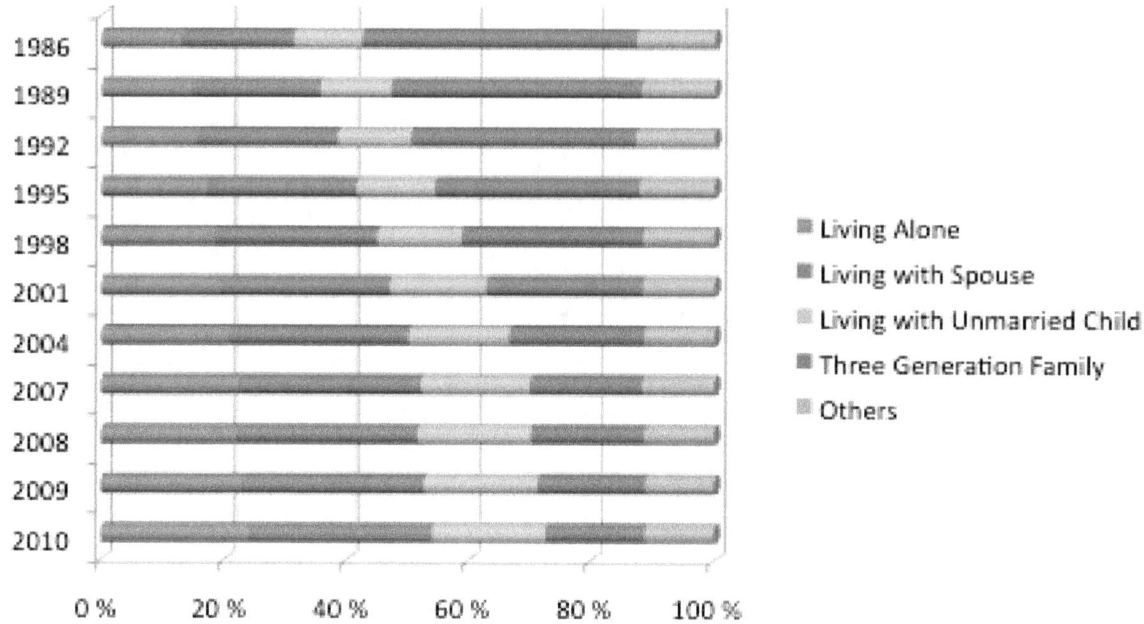

Source: MHLW, 2012.

Figure 3. Who are the caregivers?

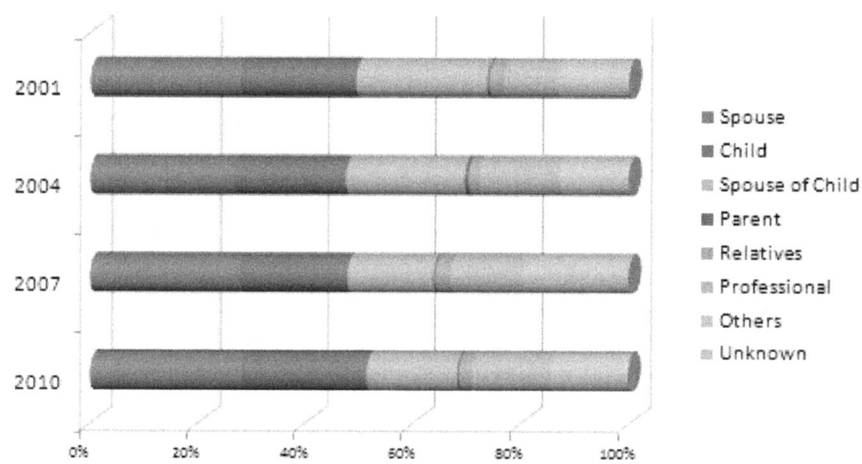

Source: MHLW, 2012.

and increasing number of single household or elderly couple living by themselves.

Figure 3 explains the composition of the family caregivers.

Among the family caregivers, 30.6% were male and 69.4% were female (MHLW, 2010) indicating the strong gender bias in care work. In a super aging society, the family caregivers are also aging so it is common for those who are in their 70s to provide care for their parents in their 90s or the wife in her late 80s is providing care for her husband in his 90s. More than 50% of the family caregivers are above 60 years old (Statistics Bureau, 2012:70). The growing number of dementia patients worsens this situation. A woman in her mid 50s had to resign from work in a trading company in order to care for her mother who had a dementia. She has been caring for her mother for the past eight years but when she saw the people coming back from work during rush hours at the station she felt depressed and felt like she is not contributing to the society. One day, she shouted at her mother to go to the toilet but her dementia mother after all wet in her pants replied calmly 'I didn't do anything'. Then she slapped her mother's face shouting 'stop it!' (Nihon Keizai Shimbun, 2013b). In the past five years, 487,000 people left their jobs in order to care for their family among which 389,000 were women (Statistics Bureau, 2013:72).

As the family size becomes smaller, the caregivers are burdened both physically and mentally. In 2006, Elderly Abuse Prevention and Support towards Family Caregivers Law came into effect. In a survey on elderly abuse published in 2007 states that 84.4% of the elderly abuse was conducted by the family member who is living together with the elderly. Abuse was done by son (38.5%), husband (14.7%), daughter (14.5%) and daughter-in-law (10.7%) etc (MHLW, 2007).

In the same year, reported cases of elderly abuse by family caregivers were 13,273 while abuse in care facilities was 62 cases (MHLW, 2009). In another survey conducted in 2003, the top five cause of elderly abuse in a multiple choice answer was: the personal character of the family caregiver (50.1%), personal character of the elderly (38.5%), relationship between the elderly and the family caregiver (48.0%), tired to provide care (37.2%), and problems due to dementia (37.0%) (Iryô Keizai Kenkyû et al., 2003). This indicates the importance of outsider intervention to prevent abuse so that both the elderly and the family caregiver will not be isolated from the society. As the aging population increased and life expectancy became longer it became no longer possible for the family alone to shoulder the care responsibility and the reproductive work had to be outsourced to some extent. The deteriorating labor conditions, smaller and diverse patterns of family life and privatization of care services all resemble the universalism of globalization. Taylor-Gooby (1997, p. 171) writes:

[E]conomic globalization, labor market flexibility, more complex patterns of family life and the dissolution of traditional class structures require a new welfare settlement. (...) Welfare states are all driven in the same direction by the imperatives of international competition.

As Beck (2000, p. 8) predicts, in the age of globalization the economic development does not increase jobs but results in unemployment and poverty and the nation state is caught between the growing competition in the world economy and individualization of its members. To some extent Japan is following this universal trail.

4. LONG TERM CARE INSURANCE

While striving for economic growth, Figure 4 shows that Japan has become the top runner in the population ageing among numerous OECD countries. The post war economic prosperity brought an improvement in sanitation and nutrition as well as high quality medical care and as a result the longevity of Japanese has marked 79.44

Figure 4. Ratio of population over 65

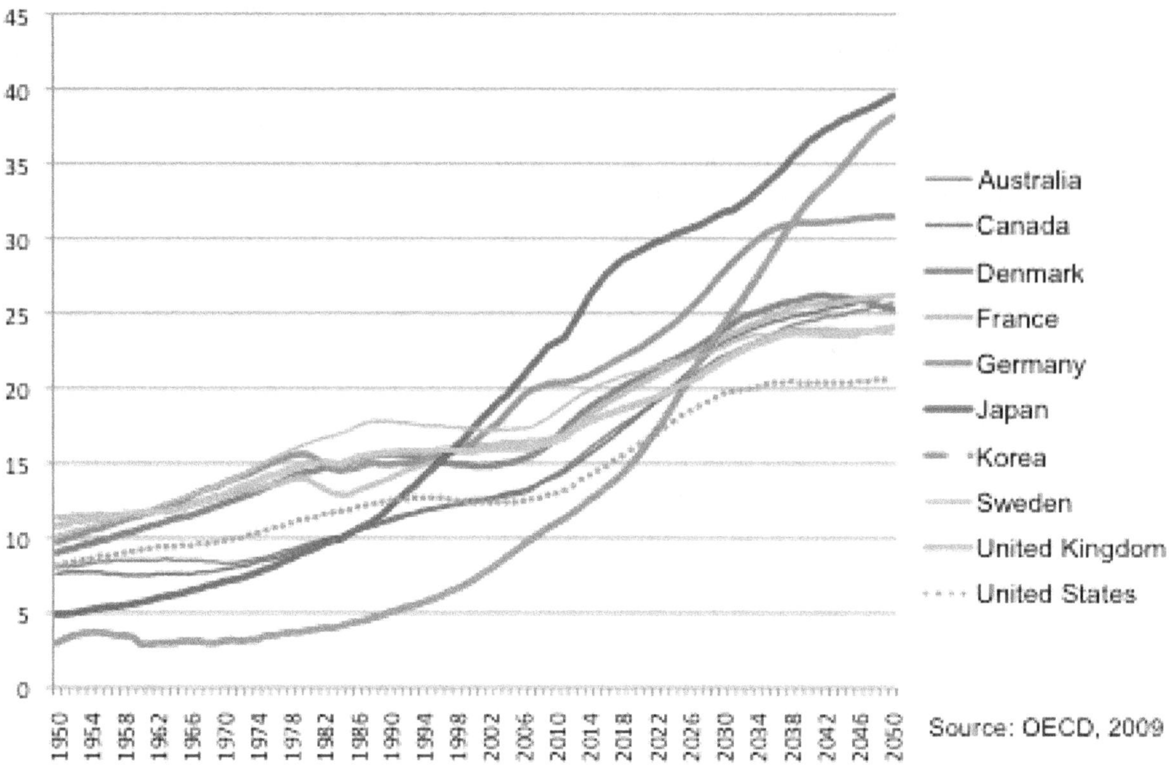

for men and 85.90 for women (MHWL, 2011b). However, this victory of the social policy, which brought the world longest life expectancy drastically changed the demographic structure when the fertility rate started to fall. In 1950, the TFR was 3.0 and dropped below the replacement level of 2.0 in 1975, and in 2011 it became 1.39 (MHLW, 1998~2012) (Figure 5).

The number of babies born was 2.09 million in 1973 but has dropped to roughly half of 1.07 million in 2010 (National Institute of Population and Social Security Research, 2012).

Due to the low fertility rate, the population of Japan will shrink from the current status of 128 million to 86 million in 2060 a drastic decrease of less than 70%. While the total population started to decrease, the shrinking part is the productive age population (Figure 6).

From 2010 to 2060, the population between 0 to 14 years old is expected to shrink drastically from 16.8 million to 7.9 million, the productive age population (15-64 years old) will also shrink from 81.7 million to 44.1 million while the elderly population (above 65 years old) will continue to grow from 29.4 million to 34.6 million (National Institute of Population and Social Security Research, 2012). The elderly population is growing far more rapidly than the younger generation, which can be seen in the changes in the household composition (Figure 7). This demographic change is becoming to be felt as a tremendous risk in sustaining the quality of life, which Japan has started to enjoy only after the rapid economic development.

Considering the unprecedented speed of aging, elder care was paid special attention and in 2000, Long Term Care Insurance (LTCI) was enacted aiming to 'socialize' care. The introduction of LTCI was aimed to shift the unpaid work of care undertaken predominantly by women to the paid

Figure 5. Changes in the total fertility rate

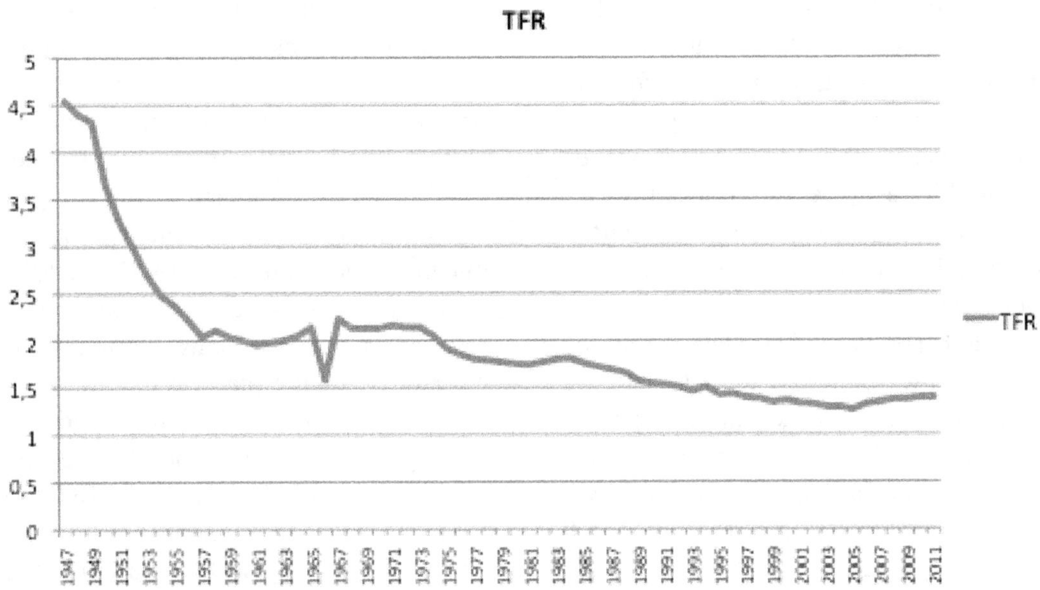

Source: MHWL, 1998~2012

Figure 6. Population prospects in Japan

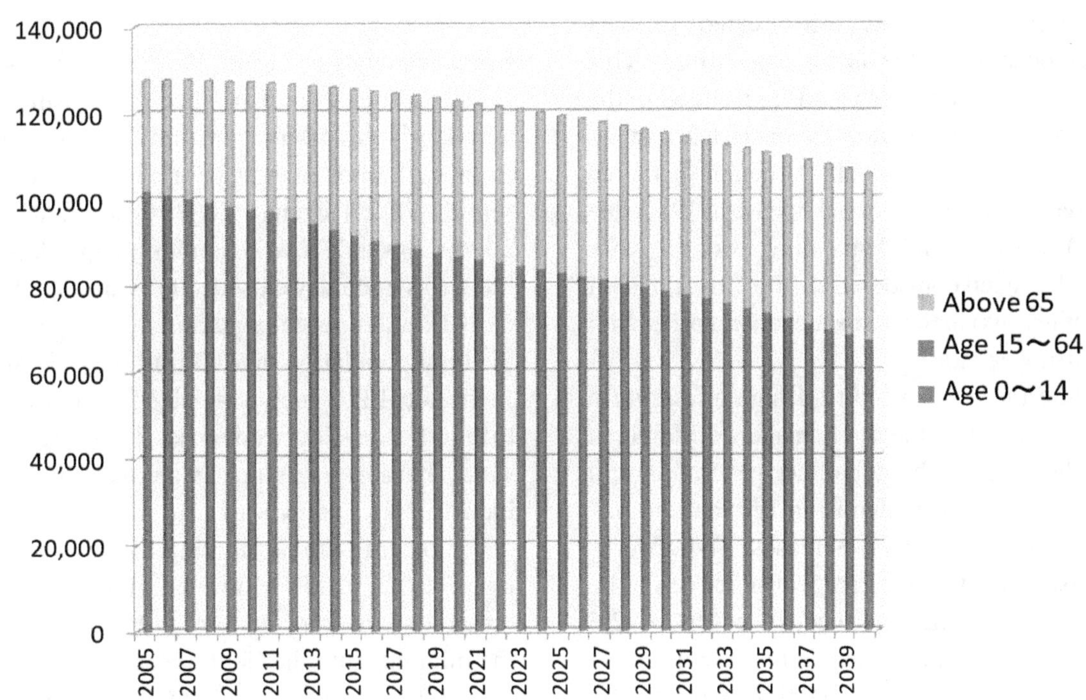

Source: National Institute of Population and Social Security Research, 2012

work, which can be purchased in the market. The system was intended to assist the independent living of the elderly and be able to choose whatever support they need. LTCI took the form of insurance and not tax to ensure the right of the elderly in purchasing the service and it opened the market to different types of service providers such as private sector, co-operatives and NPOs so that the elderly can choose the services according to their needs.

As expected, the care market expanded rapidly allowing the private business to enter into the field of long term care. Quickly the government expenditure on LTCI increased to more than double in ten years. In 2000 the spending was 3.6 trillion yen but in 2012 it jumped up to 8.9 trillion yen reflecting the actual need for care and the inability of the families to provide care. The number of care receivers under LTCI also expanded more than twice from 2.18 million in 2000 to 5.33 million in 2012 (MHLW, 2013a) and the government tightened its control by limiting the assessment on who ought to be cared to restrict the skyrocketing of the social expenditure[1]. This cut back in the social expenditure resulted in the low salary of the workers and soon the labor shortage was beginning to be felt. Although "certified caregiver" became a national license in 1987, due to the low salary and demanding work the work of care has been considered as 3D (dirty, difficult and dangerous) in the domestic labor market with high turnover ratio[2].

While there is a need to design a long-term plan to secure both the funding and workforce, in 2025 the post war baby boomer generation will reach 75 years old which is an age that the risk of becoming dependent increases. The government estimates that the care workforce has to be expanded for 1.5 times and need to secure 2.3 ~2.5 million workers and the expenditure will further increase to 21 trillion yen (MHLW, 2013a, b).

The state initiative to ensure long term care has been fundamentally challenged not so much from the globalization forces but more from the domestic condition of population ageing. Although the LTCI has been established, how to sustain it with the shrinking productive population is a major challenge. The measure that have been proposed is, 1) to promote preventive measures so that elderly will not become dependent and 2) to increase the salary of the caregivers and develop a career path for them so that the work of care becomes attractive (MHLW, 2013a). The former strategy is needed in order to promote healthy ageing and many promotion activities are already taking place at the grass root level. However, within the backdrop of deteriorating employment and stagnation of the economy the latter strategy may not look plausible. To avoid the risk for the government to become bankrupt or the risk of the elderly to be left without care there has to be some alternative measures.

5. ENTRY OF MIGRANTS INTO THE CARE WORKFORCE

In many countries in the West, Middle East and Asia NIES, care work has been increasingly undertaken by migrants constituting a gender and racialized labor market (Ehrenreich and Hochschild, 2002; Parrenas, 2003; Oishi, 2005; Lan, 2006; Constable, 2007). For long, Japan has been known as a country closed to migrants. At the end of 2012, the foreign population is 1.6 percent of the total population or 2.03 million (Ministry of Justice, 2013), which is much smaller compared to the other developed countries. In fact, Hollifield states that Japan remains an anomaly among the industrialized nations to achieve the economic development without inviting the migrant work force (1992, p. 15). However, globalization has brought an unexpected opportunity to introduce the migrants into the field of care.

Just like many other liberal democratic countries, Japan supports liberal market economy and participated in the multilateral agreement of GATT and WTO. After the failure of the multilateral

Figure 7. Change in the household structure

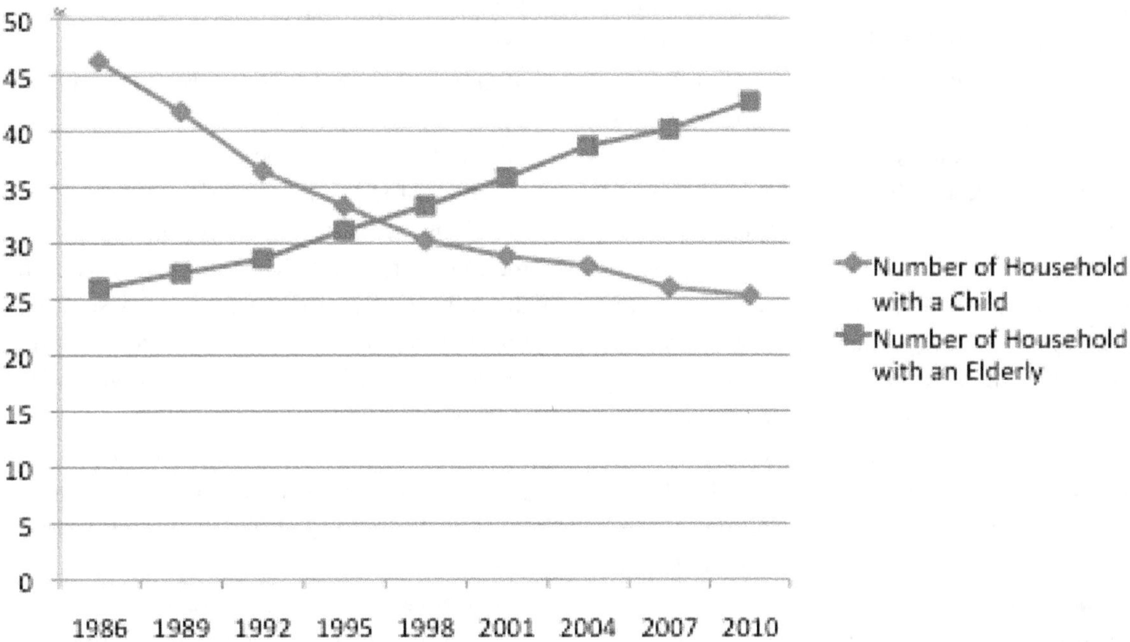

Source: MHLW, 2012

negotiations of Doha Round, many countries turned into bilateral agreements such as Economic Partnership Agreements (EPA) or Free Trade Agreements (FTA). In 2002, Japan entered into the first EPA with Singapore, a country which has no conflict of interest over agricultural products. In 2003, the negotiations with the Philippines have started where the Philippines government proposed the acceptance of nurses, caregivers, nannies and domestic helpers (Asato, 2007, p. 33). Philippines have institutionalized migration in the 1970s under the Marcos Regime and have become one of the largest suppliers of migrants to North America, Europe, Asia NIES and Middle East. Filipino nurses are trained under the American curriculum installed during the colonial period and the Filipino caregiver program is accredited by the government agency (Choy, 2003, Hugo, 2009).

The Japanese government set up a working group to discuss this issue and they concluded that in order not to jeopardize the agreement there is no way but to accept the migrants (Iguchi, 2005; Asato, ibid). The demographic change and population ageing was certainly in the minds of the policy makers (Watanabe, 2008). However, in line with the Japanese Immigration Law, which accepts only the occupations that are considered 'skilled', and due to the lobbying of certain groups, the nurses and caregivers are accepted but not the nannies and domestic helper[3]. The Japan-Philippines EPA was signed in September 2006 and ratified in October 2008. The EPA with Indonesia followed the same arrangement and was signed in 2007 and approved by the Japanese Diet in May 2008. The EPA with Vietnam was signed in December 2008[4]. These three countries included the provision of Movement of Natural Persons in the agreement, which allows the nurses and caregivers to work in Japan.

In the process of negotiation, Japan Nursing Association (JNA) made a counter proposal stipulating that 1) foreign nurses should pass the Japanese national license exam in order to work as a nurse in Japan; 2) foreign nurses should have a good language proficiency in order to provide safe nursing care; 3) foreign nurses should be employed under the same working condition as Japanese nurse; and 4) there will be no mutual recognition of the license (2006). As a professional organization, JNA tried to protect their professionalism and to avoid the deterioration of the already demanding working condition of nurses. This proposal shaped the condition of the migrant nurses and caregivers who work in Japan. In order to ensure safe care, the migrants are given free language training before they start working and the hospitals and care facilities are mandated to support the study of the migrants so that they can pass the national exam of nursing and care-giving within a limited period of time[5].

The migrants are treated as 'candidates' until they pass the exam so the nurse candidates are paid equal salary to the nurse assistants and the caregiver candidates are paid equal to those Japanese staff at the equivalent level. The migrants are covered under the labor standard law and other laws and in some cases receive benefits such as housing allowance. From 2008 to 2012, 629 migrant nurses and 933 migrant caregivers from Indonesia and the Philippines have arrived in Japan (JICWELS, 2013a). Figures 8 and 9 demonstrate the number of entries, number of successful candidates and the number who are still working in Japan as of June 2013 (JICWELS, ibid).

In order to protect the domestic labor market, the official government position, especially the Ministry of Health, Labor and Welfare (MHLW) towards acceptance of the migrants is that this is in line with the EPA so it is not meant to supplement the shortage of care workforce, thus an 'exception' (MHLW, 2011c). This makes a sharp contrast with countries such as Taiwan, which hosts approximately 200,000 migrant caregivers, a number that has increased five times in the past 15 years (CLA, 2013). The migrant caregivers from Indonesia, Philippines and Vietnam provide 60% of the most affordable long-term care predominantly in private homes (Wang, 2010). In many countries, migrants are integral part of the care workforce. Considering the high speed of population ageing than any other countries there seems to be no reason for Japan not to accept the migrants. However, Japan is very reluctant to accept migrant care workers as part of the immigration policy or labor policy. The government especially the MHLW and the professional organizations are making it conditional, if not against the entry of migrants. These institutions has shaped the migration regime of caregivers so that there will not be an influx of 'cheap labors' who will replace the native workers or downgrade their working condition.

The entry of EPA migrants are also quite different in the way the other migrants are accepted ranging from English teachers, sex workers or *Nikkeijin* (descendants of Japanese from Latin America) who are working in a far more vulnerable condition (Yoder, 2011). The Japanese nurses are well organized with a strong political voice, which shaped the migration regime of the migrant nurses and caregivers. The JNA's counter proposal under the flagship 'to maintain the security in the medical field' has allowed the migrants to be employed at the same condition as Japanese but created other problems which will be mentioned later.

According to our research[6], migrants are well received in hospitals and care facilities (Ogawa, 2012). In a survey to the care facilities which accepted the first batch of Indonesian caregivers in 2009, despite of the language and cultural differences, 89.5% replied "applicable" or "somewhat applicable" that the "workplace became revitalized". Also, 78.9% replied "applicable" or "somewhat applicable" that Indonesian migrant caregivers "motivated the Japanese staff to understand different cultures". Interestingly, more than half even replied that the "elderly became more lively". In an interview to more than 20 care facilities, the migrant caregivers are popular among the elderly, the family and the staff because they are kind, gentle and good at communication.

One director of the care facility says that the migrant caregivers have the heart for care so she

Figure 8. Number of Indonesian caregivers

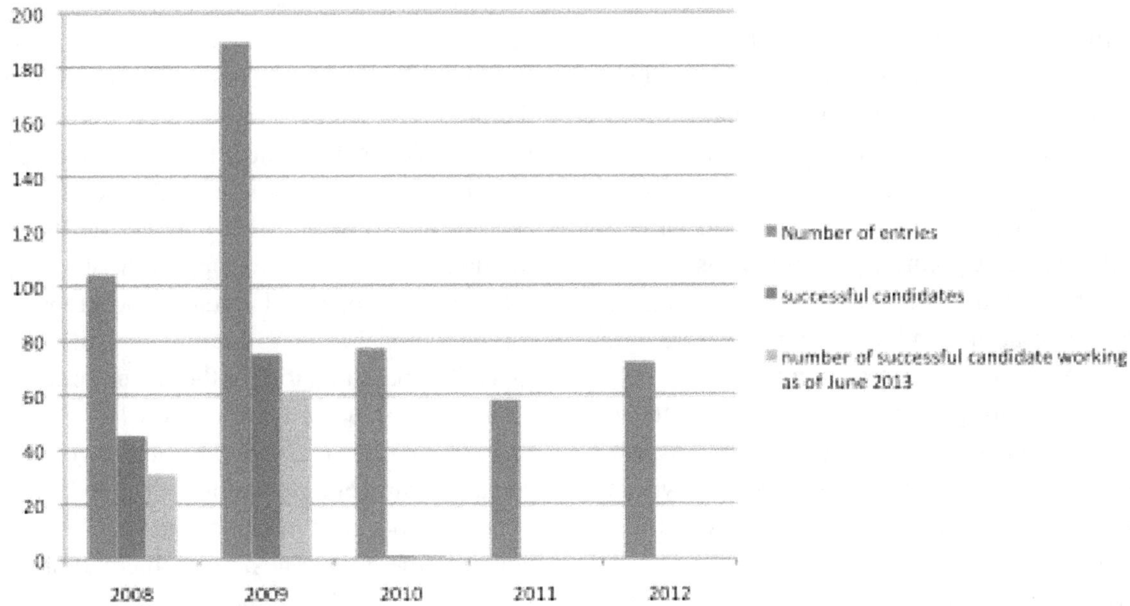

Source: JICWELS, 2013a

Note: The caregivers can take the exam only after three years of working experience.

Figure 9. Number of Filipino caregivers

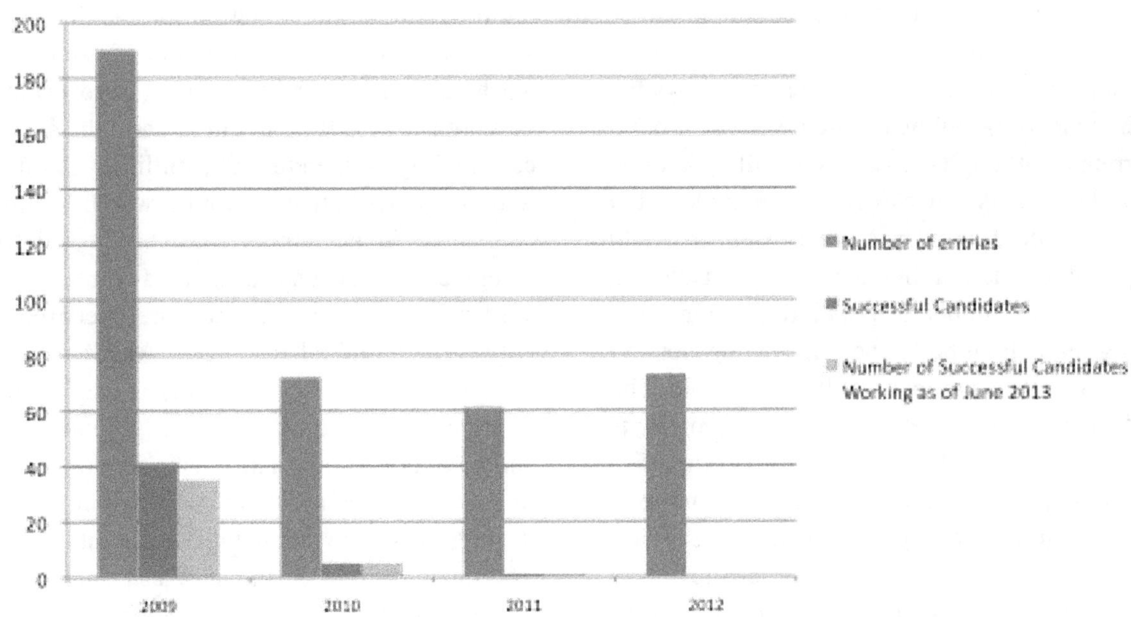

Source: JICWELS, 2013a

does not have to teach how to relate to the elderly. Japanese younger generation who no longer live with their grandparents are not used to the elderly so they have to be trained from A to Z including how to talk with a person on a wheel chair, how to keep eye contact, what to say before transfer etc.[7]

Another director who hired five Japanese high school graduates a couple of years ago lament that the Japanese younger generation has a lot of problem including committing suicide, drugs or having love affairs and don't come to work etc. and all of them resigned after a while. He says the work of care-giving is not possible for those who are not matured enough as a person. He now employs an Indonesian migrant caregiver whom he trusts and feels that it is too risky to employ a Japanese young generation[8].

These interviews testify the emotional aspect of care as a labor. Himmelweit (2007) and Glenn (2000) argue that two components are important for care work: caring for (physical care) and caring about (psychological care) so it is not just about providing physical care such as assisting in their daily livings but it is also about the development of relationships. Ironically, "being Japanese" or "being able to speak perfect Japanese" does not necessarily make one a good caregiver while language and cultural differences are always the main concern of public debate revolving around migrants. Although the state is unwilling to open up the labor market in fear of rising unemployment rate one would wonder to what extent it would be possible to maintain the position considering the growing number of population ageing, the young generations preference in selecting jobs and increasing transnational mobility of people. The EPA opened up a new possibility for the migrants to enter into the field of care, which may otherwise did not happen. Although negligible in number, the migrants effectively deconstructed the notion that 'Japanese have to be cared by Japanese' and performed the potential to provide quality care.

However, in order to mitigate the shortage of care workforce, the migration scheme under the EPA has at least two problems from the point of view of sustainability. First is the cost for both the care facility and the state and second is the long-term settlement of the migrants. The care facilities have to pay approximately 600,000 yen, which includes the agency fees, part of language training and administrative costs aside from the salaries (JICWELS, 2013b). Moreover, the care facilities are mandated to support the study of the migrants in Japanese language and preparation for the national exam to become a certified caregiver. The passing ratio for the Japanese certified caregivers for the past five years is 48%~63% and the examination includes 13 subjects including social welfare, elderly welfare, disabled welfare, rehabilitation, psychology of the elderly and disabled, home economics, medicine and skills in long term care. The candidates have to tackle 120 questions in 210 minutes, which means less than two minutes for one question. This is extremely difficult for the migrants who are not native in Japanese and the government has extended the time for the exam for 1.5 times to increase the chances of passing.

According to our research[9], the care facilities are providing support within the facility by the senior staff or outsource it to outside schools or teachers with some subsidy from the government (Tsubota et al. 2012). In either case, the average care facility is spending 2.2 million yen during four years (Tsubota et al. ibid.), which is almost equivalent of an annual salary of a full time caregiver. This cost has been felt as a tremendous burden and the care facilities are overstretched within their limited resources. Answering to a question, whether they would like to employ more migrant nurses and caregivers, 54% replied 'yes' and 46% replied 'no'. The reason for not wanting to continue to employ was 'not sure until when the migrants will work in the care facility' (15%), 'too much burden on the staff in terms of time and mental stress (to provide support so that the migrants will pass the exam)' (13%), and 'too costly' (13%) (Tsubota et al. ibid.).

From 2006~2011, the state has been spending 4.3 billion yen for the education of the migrants (Ministry of Internal Affairs and Communication, 2013) but Figures 8 and 9 informs us that the passing ratio is limited and even fewer migrants are staying for work. The calculation of the state is not to see the cost and the benefit of the migration component of EPA alone but to review the overall cost and benefit of the free trade with the Philippines and Indonesia. In this respect, the migration project under EPA is still oriented under the parameters of Japan's social welfare policy to prioritize economic growth, which has not been changed since the Meiji period (Goodman and Peng, 1996:201). The discrepancy is that those who largely benefit from free trade between Southeast Asian countries are not those who are investing on the education of the migrants which makes the care facilities reluctant to accept further migrants even though the individual capacity and personality of the migrants are satisfactory.

Secondly, as Figures 8 and 9 indicates not all the migrants are willing to stay and continue to work in Japan. Some have left without taking the exam as they found it to be too difficult. As of June 2013, among 629 migrant nurses and 896 migrant caregivers, 231 nurses and 138 caregivers have already left the country (JICWELS, 2013a). There is no systematic research on the returnees and the reason includes family problem, marriage, no prospect for passing the exam, migrating to Canada, depression, harassment at workplace[10] etc. Compared to migration regimes in other countries, migration under EPA is mediated by the government agencies requiring no placement fees on the side of the migrants. Although they are restricted in their mobility such as changing employers compared to Japanese workers, in principle they are free labors to exercise their agencies.

Considering these two risks, the potential for the migrants to mitigate the shortage of care workforce is very slim unless MHLW will admit the shortage of care workforce and take measures to revise the migration scheme.

6. CONCLUSION

The globalization thesis emphasizes the causal relationship between the erosion of the welfare state and the impacts of globalization. This chapter examined four terrains revolved around long-term care in Japan. The structural change in employment and family clearly showed the universal character of post-industrial societies with the commonalities elsewhere. However, the introduction of LTCI and the entry of migrants under the EPA arrangements were shaped by the particularities of the national institutions and conditions. LTCI was largely driven from the demographic change aiming to provide universal long-term care through the insurance system at the time when the structural change was taking place. Even though LTCI has been encountered by the major challenge in how to finance and secure the care workforce, once the state has made the commitment, the retrenchment will become a political issue. The entry of migrants under EPA, which can only happen with the strong influence of global institutions to promote free trade was mediated by national institutions which shaped the ways in which migration regime was established. In order to protect the labor market, the Japan Nursing Association together with the Ministry of Health, Welfare and Labor ensured that the migrants are employed as the same working condition as Japanese and mandated them to pass the national exam. As a result, the employment cost went up while the benefit went down for the employers and the prospect of having the migrants to mitigate the shortage of the care workforce is blurred.

To attest to the globalization thesis, we should be able to see the convergence of welfare states in many countries but as in the case of Japan the process of globalization is not linear but contingent. Instead, what we have seen is a dialectical process of how the domestic factors are differently shaping the well being of the people within its own institutional histories and strategies.

REFERENCES

Agamben, G. (1998). *Homo sacer: Sovereign power and bare life*. Stanford, CA: Stanford University Press.

Asahi Shimbun (2013, 14 June).

Asato, W. (2007). Nippi keizai renkei kyôtei to gaikokujin kangoshi, kaigo rôdôsha no ukeire. In *Kaigo kaji rôdôsha no kokusai idô* [International Movement of Caregivers and Domestic Workers]. Tôkyô: Nihon Hyôronsha.

Baldock, J., Manning, N., & Vickerstaff, S. (Eds.). (2007). *Social policy* (3rd ed.). Oxford, UK: Oxford University Press.

Beck, U. (2000). *What is globalization?* Cambridge, UK: Polity Press.

Cabinet Office. (2012). *Heisei 24 nen jisatsu no tôkei.* [Statistics on Suicide, year 24 Heisei]. Retrieved from http://www8.cao.go.jp/jisatsutaisaku/toukei/

Castells, M. (2000). *End of millennium* (2nd ed.). Oxford, UK: Blackwell Publishing.

Choy, C. C. (2003). *Empire of care*. Manila: Ateneo de Manila Press.

Constable, N. (2007). *Maid to order in Hong Kong*. New York: Cornell University Press.

Council of Labor Affairs. (2013). *Foreign workers statistics*. Retrieved from http://www.cla.gov.tw/cgi-bin/siteMaker/SM_theme?page=49c05774

Ehrenreich & Hochschild (Ed.). (2002). *Global women: Nannies, maids, and sex workers in the new economy*. New York: Holt.

Esping-Andersen, G. (1996). Positive-sum solutions in a world of trade-offs? In *Welfare state in transition: National adaptations in global economies*. London: Sage Publications. doi:10.4135/9781446216941.n9

Giddens, A. (1990). *The consequence of modernity*. Cambridge, UK: Polity Press.

Glenn, E. N. (2000). Creating a caring society. *Contemporary Sociology*, *29*(1), 84–94. doi:10.2307/2654934

Goodman, R., & Peng, I. (1996). The east Asian welfare states: Peripatetic learning, adaptive change, and nation building. In G. Esping-Andersen (Ed.), *Welfare state in transition: National adaptations in global economies*. London: Sage Publications. doi:10.4135/9781446216941.n7

Harvey, D. (1989). *The condition of post modernity*. Oxford, UK: Blackwell.

Himmelweit, S. (2007). The prospects for caring: Economic theory and policy analysis. *Cambridge Journal of Economics*, *31*(4), 581–599. doi:10.1093/cje/bem011

Hollifield, J. F. (1992). *Immigrants, markets, and states: The political economy of postwar Europe*. Cambridge, MA: Harvard University Press.

Hugo, G. (2009). Care worker migration, Australia and development. *Population Space and Place*, *15*, 189–203. doi:10.1002/psp.534

Iguchi, Y. (2005, February 15). Shôshika nihon ni senryaku hitsuyô. [Need for Strategy in Low Fertility Rate Japan]. *Asahi Shimbun*.

International Labor Organization (ILO). (2013). *Decent work*. Retrieved from http://www.ilo.org/global/topics/decent-work/lang--en/index.htm

Iryô Keizai Kenkyû. (2003). *Kateinai ni okeru kôreisha gyakutai ni kansuru chôsa*. [Survey on elderly abuse at home]. Retrieved from www.ihep.jp/publications/report/search.php?dl=170&i=1

Japan Nursing Association. (2006). *Nippi EPA firipin-jin kangoshi no ukeire ni kansuru nihon kango kyôkai no kenkai.* [Japan Nursing Association's Position on Acceptance of Filipino Nurses under the Japan-Philippines EPA]. Retrieved from http://www.nurse.or.jp/home/opinion/newsrelease/2006pdf/20060912.pdf

JICWELS. (2013a). *Keizai renkei kyôtei ni motozuku gaikokujin kangoshi/ kaigo fukushishi kôhôsha to no genjô.* [Current Situation of Foreign Nurse and Caregiver Candidates under the Economic Partnership Agreement]. Unpublished.

JICWELS. (2013b). *Heisei 26 nendo ukeire tebiki kaigo fukushishi course.* [2013 Guide for Acceptance of Caregivers]. Retrieved from http://www.jicwels.or.jp/files/H26E4BB8BE8ADB7E-6898BE5BC95E3818D_2.pdf

Lan, P. C. (2006). *Global cinderellas: Migrant domestics and new rich employers in Taiwan.* Durham, NC: Duke University Press. doi:10.1215/9780822387787

McGrew, A. (1992). A global society? In *Modernity and its futures.* Cambridge, UK: Polity Press in Association with Open University.

Ministry of Health Labor and Welfare (MHLW). (2007). *Heisei 18 nendo kôreisha gyakutai no boshi, kôreisha no yogôsha ni taisuru shien to ni kansuru hôritsu ni motozuku taiô jyokyô ni kansuru chôsa kekka* (kakutei ban). [2006 = Heisei 18 survey result for the law on elderly abuse prevention and support towards family care givers]. Retrieved from http://www.mhlw.go.jp/houdou/2007/12/h1219-1.html

Ministry of Health Labor and Welfare (MHLW). (2009). *Kôreisha gyakutai boshi taisaku ni tsuite.* [Elderly abuse prevention measures]. Retrieved from http://www.mhlw.go.jp/houdou/2007/12/h1219-1.html

Ministry of Health Labor and Welfare (MHLW). (2010). *Kokumin seikatsu kiso chôsa no gaikyô.* [Survey on the Life of the People]. Retrieved from http://www.mhlw.go.jp/toukei/saikin/hw/k-tyosa/k-tyosa10/index.html

Ministry of Health Labor and Welfare (MHLW). (2011). *Keizai renkei kyôtei ni motozuku gaikokujin kangoshi kaigo fukushishi kôhôsha no ukeire to ni tsuite.* [Acceptance of Foreign Nurse and Caregiver Candidates under the Economic Partnership Agreement]. Retrieved from http://www.mhlw.go.jp/bunya/koyou/other22/index.html

Ministry of Health Labor and Welfare (MHLW). (2012). *Kokumin seikatsu kiso chôsa no gaikyô.* [Survey on the Life of the People]. Retrieved from http://www.mhlw.go.jp/toukei/saikin/hw/k-tyosa/k-tyosa12/index.html

Ministry of Health Labor and Welfare (MHLW). (2013a). *Kaigo hoken seido o torimaku jyôkyô.* [Situations of the Long Term Care System]. Retrieved from http://www.mhlw.go.jp/stf/shingi/2r98520000031zxr-att/2r9852000003202m.pdf

Ministry of Health Labor and Welfare (MHLW). (2013b). *Kaigo jinzai no kakuhô kankei.* [Securing Care Workforce]. Retrieved from http://www.mhlw.go.jp/stf/shingi/2r98520000033t43-att/2r98520000033t98.pdf

Ministry of Health Labor and Welfare (MHLW). (1998~2012). *Jinkô dôtai tôkei.* [Statistics on Population Dynamics]. Retrieved from http://www.mhlw.go.jp/toukei/list/81-1a.html

Ministry of Internal Affairs and Communication. (2013). *Gaikokujin no ukeire taisaku ni taisuru gyôsei hyôka/ kanshi.* [Public Sector Evaluation regarding Acceptance of Foreigners]. Retrieved from http://www.soumu.go.jp/menu_news/s-news/73055.html

Ministry of Justice. (2013). *Heisei 24 nen matsu genzai ni okeru zairyû gaikokujinsû ni tsuite.* [Number of Foreign Residents at the end of 2012 = Heisei 24]. Retrieved from http://www.moj.go.jp/nyuukokukanri/kouhou/nyuukokukanri04_00030.html

Miyamoto, T. (2011). Hataraku koto no seijigaku. [Politics of Labor] In *Hataraku*. Tôkyô: Fûkôsha.

National Institute of Population and Social Security Research. (2012). *Nihon no shôrai suikei jinkô.* [Future Population Projection of Japan]. Retrieved from http://www.ipss.go.jp/syoushika/tohkei/newest04/gh2401.pdf

National Institute of Population and Social Security Research. (2013). *Seikatsu hogo ni kansuru kôteki tôkei data ichiran.* [Data on Social Security System]. Retrieved from http://www.ipss.go.jp/s-info/j/seiho/seiho.asp

Nihon Keieisha Dantai Renmei. (1995). *Shinjidai no nihonteki keiei* [Japanese Management in the New Era]. Tokyo: Nihon Keieisha Dantai Renmei.

Nihon Keizai Shimbun (2013a, 28 May).

Nihon Keizai Shimbun (2013b, 20 March).

OECD. (2009). *Factbook.* Retrieved from http://www.oecd-ilibrary.org/economics/oecd-factbook-2009/population-aged-65-and-over_factbook-2009-table4-en

Ogawa, R. (2012). Globalization of care and the context of reception in Japan. *Southeast Asian Studies*, *49*(4), 570–593.

Oguma, E. (2012). *Shakai o kaeru niha* [To Change a Society]. Tôkyô: Kôdansha Gendai Shinsho.

Oishi, N. (2005). *Women in motion: Globalization, state policies and labor migration in Asia.* Stanford, CA: Stanford University Press.

Ôsawa, M. (2008). *Gendai nihon no seikatsu hosho shizutemu* [Contemporary Social Security System in Japan]. Tôkyô: Iwanami Shoten.

Parrenas, R. S. (2003). *Servants of globalization.* Manila: Ateneo de Manila University Press.

Statistics Bureau (Sômushô). (2010). *Rôdôryoku chôsa.* [Labor Survey]. Retrieved from http://www.stat.go.jp/data/roudou/tsushin/pdf/no02.pdf

Statistics Bureau (Sômushô). (2012). *Shûgyô kôzô kihon chôsa, kekka no gaiyô.* [Survey on Labor Force: An Overview]. Retrieved from http://www.stat.go.jp/data/shugyou/2012/pdf/kgaiyou.pdf

Swank, D. (2002). *Global capital, political institutions, and policy change in developed welfare states.* Cambridge, UK: Cambridge University Press. doi:10.1017/CBO9780511613371

Taylor-Gooby, P. (1997). In defense of second-best theory: State, class and capital in social policy. *Journal of Social Policy*, *26*(2), 171–192. doi:10.1017/S0047279497004996

Tsubota, K., Ogawa, R., Ôno, S., & Hirano, Y. (2012). *Gaikokujin kaigo fukushishi kôhôsha ukeire ankêto kekka.* [Results of the Questionnaire Survey on Acceptance of Foreign Care Workers]. Unpublished.

Wang, F. T. (2010). Globalization of care in Taiwan: From undutiful daughter-in-law to cold-blooded migrant killer. In *Transnational migration from southeast Asia to east Asia and the transformation of reproductive labor: Comparative study between Korea, Taiwan and Japan.* Paper presented at the Kitakyushu Forum on Asian Women (KFAW). Tokyo, Japan.

Watanabe, Y. (Ed.). (2008). *Kaisetsu FTA/EPA kôshô* [Commentary FTA/EPA Negotiations]. Tôkyô: Nihon Keizai Hyôronsha.

Yeates, N. (2001). *Globalization & social policy.* London: Sage Publications.

Yeates, N. (2007). Globalization and social policy. In J. Baldock, N. Manning, & S. Vickerstaff (Eds.), *Social policy* (3rd ed.). Oxford, UK: Oxford University Press.

Yoder, R. S. (2011). *Deviance and inequality in Japan: Japanese youth and foreign migrants*. Bristol, UK: The Polity Press. doi:10.1332/policypress/9781847428325.003.0001

Yomiuri Shimbun (2013, 31 May).

Yûasa, M. (2008). *Han hinkon* [Anti poverty]. Tôkyô: Iwanami Shinsho.

Zimmerman, M. K., Litt, J. S., & Bose, C. E. (2006). *Global dimensions of gender and carework*. Stanford, CA: Stanford University Press.

ENDNOTES

1 In 2002, the Advisory Committee on Economy and Finance [Keizai Zaisei Shimon Kaigi] published a report to restrict the social expenditure for five years from 2003 to 2008. The benefits of the LTCI were cut back in 2003 and 2006.

2 The average salary for male caregiver working in the institutions is 231,000 yen while the other sector's average is 362,000 yen. The average salary for female caregiver working in the institutions is 211,000 yen, while the other sectors will pay 249,000 yen. (MHLW, 2013b).

3 Interview with officials of the Ministry of Foreign Affairs, July 3, 2011.

4 The nurses and caregivers from Vietnam are expected to arrive after 2014.

5 Three years for nurses and four years for caregivers. This is because the caregiver exam requires three year of working experience in order to qualify for taking the exam.

6 The quantitative research was conducted under "A Global Sociological Study on Japan's Opening of Its Labor Market in the Field of Care and Nursing" (Representative: Shun Ôno) and the collaborative team members were Shun Ôno, Yûko Hirano, Yoshichika Kawaguchi, Kiyoshi Adachi, Takeo Ogawa and Reiko Ogawa. This has been funded by Kyûshû University Interdisciplinary Programs in Education and Projects in Research Development.

7 Interviewed on April 30, 2009.

8 Interviewed on November 10, 2013.

9 The questionnaire was distributed in January, 2012 to 264 care facilities which accepted the migrants under EPA. The response rate was 33%. The collaborative members were Kunio Tsubota, Yûko Hirano, Shun Ôno and Reiko Ogawa.

10 From the interviews on various occasions in Japan, Indonesia and the Philippines.

Chapter 6
Foreign Aid and Family at Risk:
Role of Foreign Aid to Myanmar

Kana Takamatsu
International Christian University, Japan

ABSTRACT

This chapter examines how the foreign aid policy should and should have supported families facing risks by using the case study of Myanmar. The chapter starts by addressing the issue of poverty, which continues to be the gravest risk in the developing countries, and how family could be the cause of poverty as well as the solution of poverty in foreign aid policy discussion. The situation of poverty and migration as a risk management tool are then examined in the second section of the chapter. Interviews with migrant workers in Thailand and Japan were conducted. Finally, there is a discussion about the developments of Myanmar and how the foreign aid and international community has inadequately responded to the democratization of Myanmar and to the needs of its people.

1. INTRODUCTION

Changing the size and capacity of family, increasing instability of labor market and globalization, new social risks have emerged. How we should manage new social risks? International Social Security Association (ISSA) mentions that new social risks require the state to have a new family policy targeting parents who provides child care and pursues a full professional career (ISSA website (A)). It tries to manage risks by supporting family. ISSA also considers developing countries faces different risks and indicates "a better articulation of formal social security policies with the traditional family and community-based model could attenuate some of these problems" (ISSA website (A)).

DOI: 10.4018/978-1-4666-5031-2.ch006

Table 1. Situation of poverty

Countries	Population in Multidimensional Poverty Headcount (%), 2000-2010	Population below PPP $ 1.25 a day(%) 2000-2009
Very High Human Development	2.7 (9)	0.2 (9)
High Human Development	2.4 (22)	2.6 (29)
Medium Human Development	19.4 (37)	17.6 (34)
Low Human Development	61 (40)	47.3 (39)

Source: UNDP (2011) Human Development Report

What are the risks in developing countries? Poverty has been the key foreign aid policy issue for a long time. In the Millennium Assembly in 2000, UN member states adopted the United Nations Millennium Declaration. This declaration is "the basis for a 'road map'-the Millennium Development Goals (MDGs)" (Sumner and Tribe, 2008, p. 23), and these are committed by the international community. The MDGs aim to eradicate poverty through eight goals with time-bound targets should be achieved by 2015 (UN Millennium Project, 2005, p. 1, 281-293). These eight goals are developed by the pre-existing agendas which were proposed by the international conferences and summits in the 1990s (Feeny and Clarke, 2009, p. 3). The Millennium Development Report 2012 shows "the proportion of people living on less than $1.25 a day fell from 47 per cent in 1990 to 24 per cent in 2008—a reduction from over 2 billion to less than 1.4 billion" (UN, 2012: 4). This report addressed the progress of income level poverty; however, poverty means more complex and diverse situation.

The "Multidimensional Poverty Index" (MPI) is implemented in UNDP's Human Development Report (HDR) since 2010. This index describes the deprivations of most disadvantaged population by three dimensions such as health, education and living standards (UNDP, 2010, p. 5). The HDR 2011 shows that the population below PPP $ 1.25 a day of low human development countries is 47.3%, even though the population in multidimensional poverty 2000-2010 of those is 61% headcount (UNDP, 2011, p. 143-245). Accordingly, poverty eradication is still the most important internationally committed agenda, and it requests more efforts. (see Table 1)

Foreign aid agenda has been targeting poverty. Many poverty eradication programs/projects in developing countries have been targeting family to manage risks reinforcing poverty situation. One of the concerns is family size. Estimation shows, "the average poverty incidence in 45 countries would have fallen by one third if the crude birth rate had fallen by an additional 5 per 1,000 in the 1980s" (UNFPA, 2012, p. 17). UNFPA indicates rapid population growth is a threat to poverty reduction, and "family planning program" creates the opportunity for women to join the labor force, which provides resources to family and improve family living standards (UNFPA, 2008).

In addition, Mokomane indicates that changes in family structure are one of the factors to poverty and family poverty in particular beyond economic factors in many developing countries (Mokomane, 2012, p. 11). Various socio-economic factors shape family. One of the strong impacts on family is migration trend and it changes the situation of family. For example, remittances given by migrant family members affect the socio-demographic characteristics of the family members as well as the standard of living in Philippines (Semyonov and Gorodzeisky, 2008, p. 627). Furthermore, family policy also changes family structure like China where one child policy shapes the sex ratio and old age dependency ratio (Hesketh and Lu, 2005, p. 1172-1174). ISSA indicates the universal phenomenon of the ageing society and its rapid pace in the developing countries. It estimates 79 per cent of the world's elderly people will be living in the developing world by the 2050, rising proportion of women in employment (over half of the developed countries, around 40 per cent in the developing countries), and social exclusion as a universal social phenomenon and these facts require to change social policy and its system (ISSA Website (B)). The UN expert meeting of the Department for Economic and Social Affairs notes wide variation of family recognition and necessity to have context specific research to identify the policies for supporting families (UNDESA, 2011).

How family has tried to manage poverty in developing countries? How the foreign aid policy should and should have supported family at risks? This chapter aims to examine family and risks in the foreign aid context by using the case study of Myanmar. The reason to take Myanmar as a case study is their current transitional situation. Recent political shift towards "democracy" calls attentions from the international community to invest and support their economic development, and foreign aid policy of Myanmar will be developed. However its transitional changes, Myanmar was isolated and designated as Least Development Country over last 20 years. Management of risks in a family should be re-examined for re-considering foreign aid policy. The first part of this chapter examines the poverty and risk management in Myanmar. The second half of the chapter examines the family, risks and the foreign aid policy.

2. POVERTY, MIGRATION AND RISK MANAGEMENT

Myanmar has included into the list of LDCs (the Least Developed Countries) since 1987, and Myanmar is one of the poorest and weakest nations in the world, and Myanmar faces various socio-economic development issues. Myanmar is so called CLMV countries (Cambodia, Laos, Myanmar and Vietnam) that are late developing ASEAN countries. Poverty eradication has been a crucial topic for foreign aid as well as country's development policy. Furthermore, minimizing the

Figure 1. GNI growth (annual 1%) (Source: World Bank "World Development Indicators")

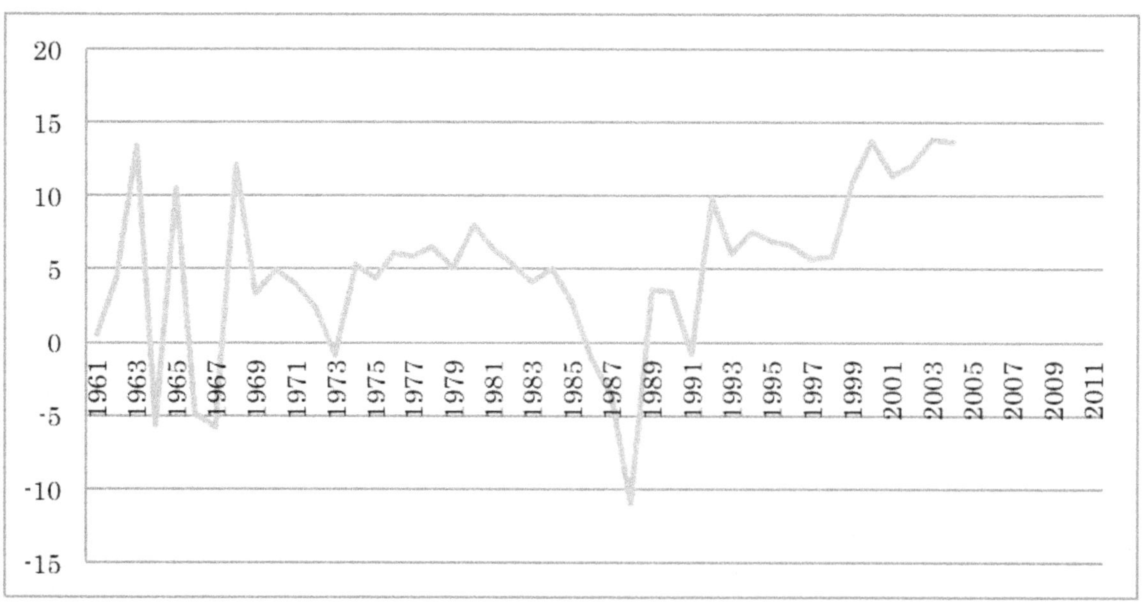

Figure 2. Net migration (Source: World Bank "World Development Indicators")

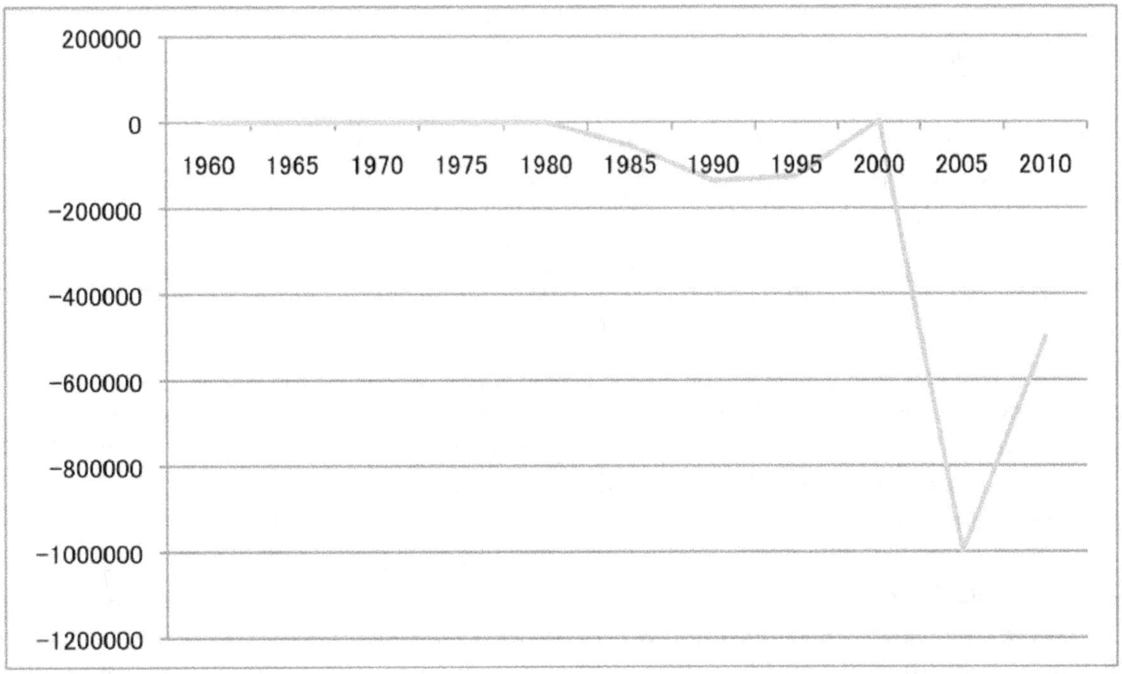

economic disparities with neighboring countries is strongly requested by other ASEAN members.

The growth rate (annual %) of GNI shows unstable situation, but it is relatively high after 1999 compared to the earlier time. The decrease in 1988 was caused by the democratic uprising and the dislocated economy in the situation. (see Figure 1)

Nevertheless, poverty is still the serious issue in Myanmar. In addition, the headcount of the population in "Multidimensional Poverty" by UNDP which shows the percentage of the population with a weighted deprivation score of at least 33 percent is 31.8%, and "Intensity of Deprivation" which shows the average percentage of deprivation experienced by people in multidimensional poverty is 48.3% (UNDP, 2011, p. 144). President Thein Sein said recently that the rural development and poverty alleviation are still the most important tasks of Myanmar government (The Nation, June 28, 2013).

Newspaper reports the situation around 2009 when people severely survived the poverty and being migrant workers is a hope to overcome their situation (Asahi shimbun, 6 June, 2009). The Net Migration stands for the total number of immigrants minus the annual number of emigrants shows negative in Myanmar. (see Figure 2)

Net migration shows international migration trend. There are no data available for internal migration, but the interview research which will indicate the following part of this chapter shows that poverty situation in a rural area motivates people to migrate. Obviously, migration shapes the size of family and intra family relations.

3. FAMILY AND MIGRATION FROM MYANMAR

Migration is one of strategies to overcome the poverty situation. How family members decide

Table 2. Profile of interviews

	Interviews in Thailand	Interviews in Japan
Year	2009	2010-on going
Place of the interview	Samut Sakorn Province	Japan (mainly Kanto area)
Number of Interviewees	14 (9 female, 5 male)	22 (8 female, 14 male)
Legal Status of Entry point	Irregular migrant-13 With working visa-1	Irregular migrant -22
Place of origin	Rural area of Myanmar (both border area and inland area)	Urban area of Myanmar (mostly from Yangon)

Source: Interviews by author

migration and how they manage the risks to reinforce poverty.

An economic disparity between Myanmar and neighboring countries is the factor behind the migration. People are searching a job opportunity which is unavailable inside of the country.

The foreign companies originating from developed countries absorb local workers in relatively better employment conditions than local companies in Samut Sakorn Province, Thailand, although foreign company relocate bases for production to developing countries to get cheaper labor than in their home countries. Therefore, weaker and smaller local companies need to search workers from neighboring countries with lower standards of wages and no legal status.

In response to push and pull factors of migration, the smuggling network has been developing. For example, in 2009, people were arrested and charged with smuggling people from Myanmar into Japan for the purpose of illegal labor. These people were central figures in the "illegal labor business" for supplying cheap labor. These people smuggle people wanting to work in Japan by ship for about 1.5 million yen, plus an introduction fee from small- to medium-sized business owners of about 50,000 yen, which is deducted from their 200,000 yen wages (Mainichi Shimbun, 7 July, 2009 afternoon edition).

This section examines and discusses the relation between the family and risks through the interview research to Myanmar migrant workers will be analyzed. Life history interviews were conducted since 2009 in two locations. One was conducted in Thailand, and another was conducted in Japan. (see Table 2)

Research area in Thailand is Samut Sakhorn Province which is located in 30km from Bangkok. Major industry in the province is the fish processing industry, which relies on "cheap labor". Formerly, the industry in the province was sustained by workers from Isan area (northeast Thailand), but now the majority of workers are migrant workers. Especially, the small scale fish processing factories relies heavily on migrant workers, largely from Myanmar.

Behind the migration, people experienced serious poverty in rural areas in Myanmar. Interviews with migrant workers highlighted the seriousness of poverty and the breakdown of livelihood. Every day living in farming villages that failed to deliver sufficient food, poor medical conditions and financial difficulties where falling ill immediately the loss of family members. The vulnerable situations where the loss and illness of family members were the reasons of migration. It is practically impossible for people from rural areas of Myanmar to obtain passports required to establish their identities, and people without education or skills have little prospect of getting visas. Under these circumstances, the migration to support their livelihood naturally has to be irregular. Those who migrate paid exorbitant fees to agents and try to cross borders, but the safety of this migration process is far from guaranteed.

From the interview in Thailand, serious poverty motivates people to migrate, and migration was the decision of the family rather than individuals.

The life in Myanmar was living from hand to mouth. I sold the vegetables, and I made a handicraft article for sale, but life was not stable one. I had no idea about my income in home town because I had to buy food immediately I got some money. (female-40's, interviewed in Thailand)

My family had a problem to sustain everyday life and borrowed money from villagers...... Migration was the strong advice of mother. Mother knew the agent of other villages and she arranged everything......(Female-20's, interviewed in Thailand)

There was the strong advice of my mother. I did not want to come, but my mother contacted an agent and decided to go. My mother borrowed 15,000 baht from the neighborhood and paid in the agent. It paid back by my remittance. (Female-20's, interviewed in Thailand)

From the interviews, it is showed that many migrant workers contributed to improve the welfare of the family.

Younger sister was able to complete 10th grade by remittance (female-20's, interviewed in Thailand)

My mother could have medications for her ill. (Female-30's, in Thailand)

My family could get a house. (Male-30's, interviewed in Thailand)

My family could have regular food. (Female-20's, interviewed in Thailand)

However, some contribution to their family was identified, most of them are unable to send money home regularly due to the low and unstable income in Thailand. In addition, their life course change makes new issues. All interviewees stay Thailand for quite a long period of time. Shortest one stays 4 years and longest one stay 14 years. 12 interviewees met their partners and married in Thailand. Creation of a new family makes them to less motivated to send money home since their living expenses increased by having children.

All interviewees in Japan are applying for refugee status at the time. It should be noted that there were regular and irregular workers when they entered Japan, but various reasons faced after the arrival made them apply for refugee status. It is not easy to receive refugee status in Japan, and their living situation is hard because they do not have legal status to stay Japan. They cannot receive permission to work, and they cannot receive national health insurance" (Asahi Shimbun, 30 March, 2009) (Asahi Shimbun, 29 August, 2009). The risk of being forcibly deported was abolished in the 2005 reform of immigration law, but the labor restrictions became strict. It has been pointed out that people are being placed in an economically and mentally unnerving situation while their refugee application is being review (Mainichi Shimbun, 14 February, 2008).

From the interview in Japan, motivation of migration is for contributing to the family. Some of them have a strong motivation to support family in Myanmar.

I came to Japan in order to send money to my father. My father passed away while I am in Japan. Now I am sending the money to my father's sister who is in ill (female-40's, interviewed in Japan).

There is little job availability in Myanmar. Even if, there is a job, the salary obtained there is not enough to help family. That is why I wished to go abroad (female-20's, interviewed in Japan)

In Myanmar, a family's bonds are stronger than Japan. It will not be easy to make a decision which lives in a foreign country by one person without meeting a family (female-20s, interviewed in Japan).

All interviewee came to Japan for economic purposes, and all of them are detained as "illegal" workers. Most of them joined the anti-government activities in Japan which motivated them to apply refugee status. Some of them knew the refugee application in the detention facility. All of them are having very difficult life in Japan, and they were not able to send money home. All travel expenses to Japan were made by their family and relatives, thus they feel so sorry for their family not to send money home. In addition, most of the interviewees have higher educational attainment. Thus, they feel so much stress to engage in low paid jobs in Japan without work permission.

Interview research shows that migrant workers have implicit and explicit pressures from their family. What does family mean for people in Myanmar? There is not much literature focusing on family in Myanmar, but we can get an idea from gender roles in the family.

Myanmar National Committee for Women's Affairs (MNCWA) published research on gender situation in Myanmar in 2001. MNCWA is the national machinery for gender equality established in July 1996. This research included gender situation in various areas such as household, education, health, violence against women, employment and decision-making and women's role in a family. This research indicated that the most significant role of women is being a good mother as to foster excellent citizen in the future, and traditionally women are and prefer to spend time in the well-being of the family as a tradition (MNCWA, 2001). It is not sure if this idea is widely shared by people, however, the military regime grasp the family image as such family is the unit of society where mother is taking a care role, and father, though it was not mentioned by MNCWA, is taking responsibility for income.

Findings show that there is serious poverty in rural areas in Myanmar behind the migration, and life in a rural area of Myanmar is indeed fraught with deprivation and fear. Migration is the strategy of survival in rural poor family. Role and obligation to contribute to family was strong for people from a rural area. Myanmar migrant in Japan also had a feeling to contribute to their family; however, it is feeling rather than obligation compared with those migrated to Thailand. Poverty condition shapes and changes even the relation within the family. People to Japan from urban areas, their living situation is better than rural areas, however their migration was also motivated by economic reasons. Family managed travel expenses by borrowing money from relatives. The families tried to manage the risks of poverty, but they could not solve the problem. (see Figures 3, 4, 5, and 6)

4. RISKS AND THE INTERNATIONAL COMMUNITY

Family was the function to reduce the risk of poverty, but the family was not easily functioning well. Myanmar's case shows that migration was not always so suitable choice for risk management. What is requested to foreign aid?

Of course, question is raised that international assistances is whether effective to improve people's life or not. There is a strong image of foreign aid that it only revitalizes macro-economic development, but, in fact, many community based assistances by foreign aid have been implementing. Naqvi addresses economic growth, equity and poverty reduction are the "irreducible" set of the policy objective in the new Development Paradigm (Naqvi, 2010, p. 334). Indeed, most of the UN agencies, exclude monetary and financial institutions so-called "Bretton Woods" institutions, the support of people have been more focused theme of foreign aid policy since 1990. In 1990, the UNDP launched the first "Human Development

Figure 3. Mortality rate, under -5 (per 1000 live births) (Source: World Bank "World Development Indicators")

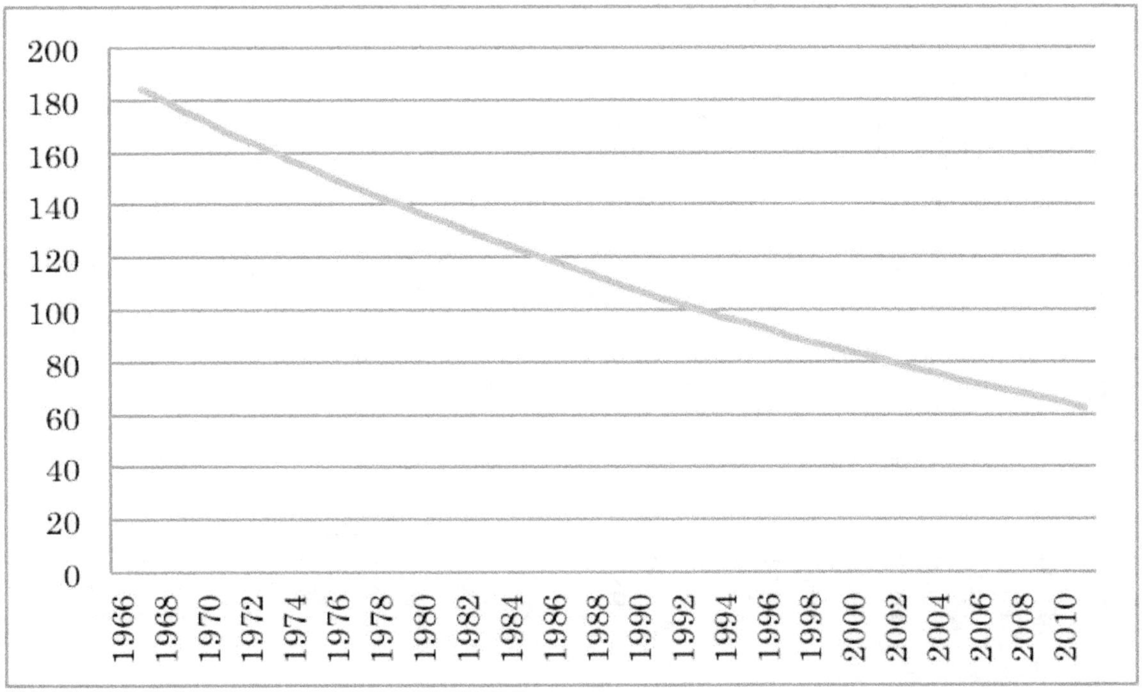

Figure 4. Life Expectancy at Birth (Source: World Bank "World Development Indicators")

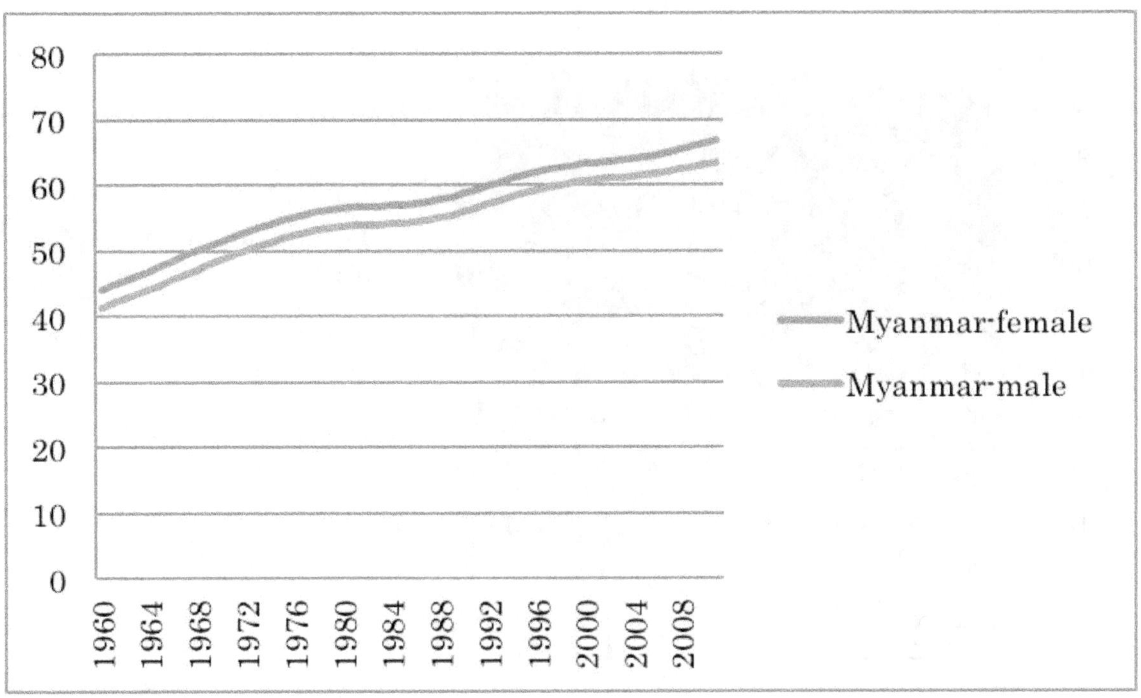

Figure 5. Fertility rate, total (births per woman) (Source: World Bank "World Development Indicators")

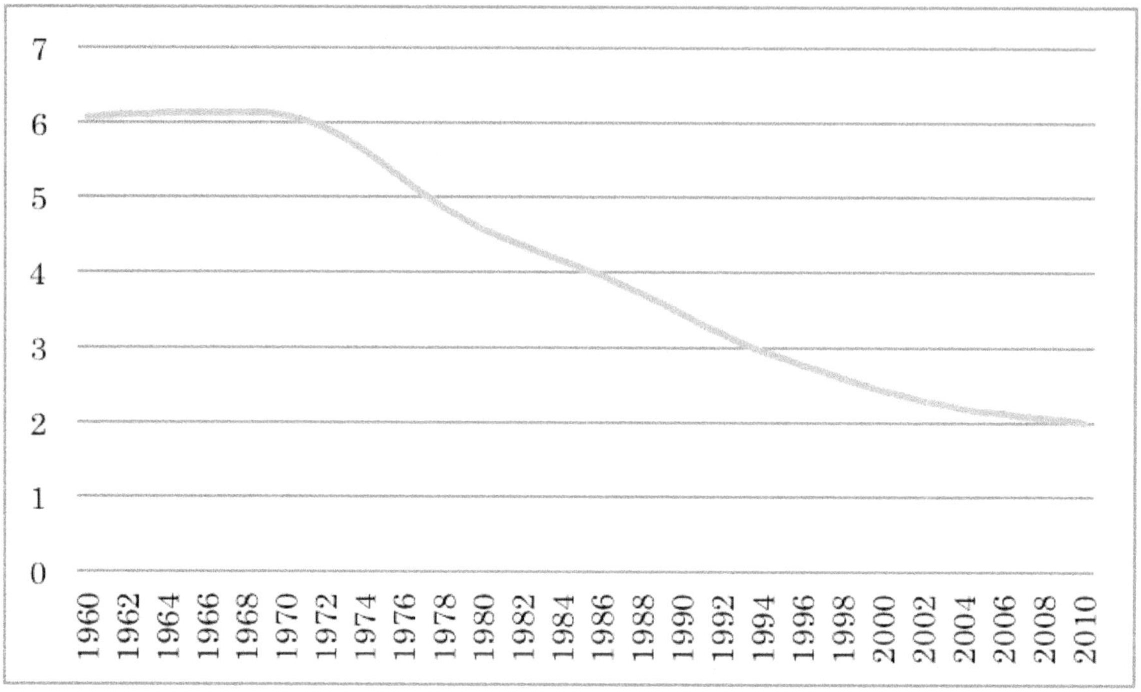

Figure 6. Population Structure -Myanmar (Source: World Bank "World Development Indicators")

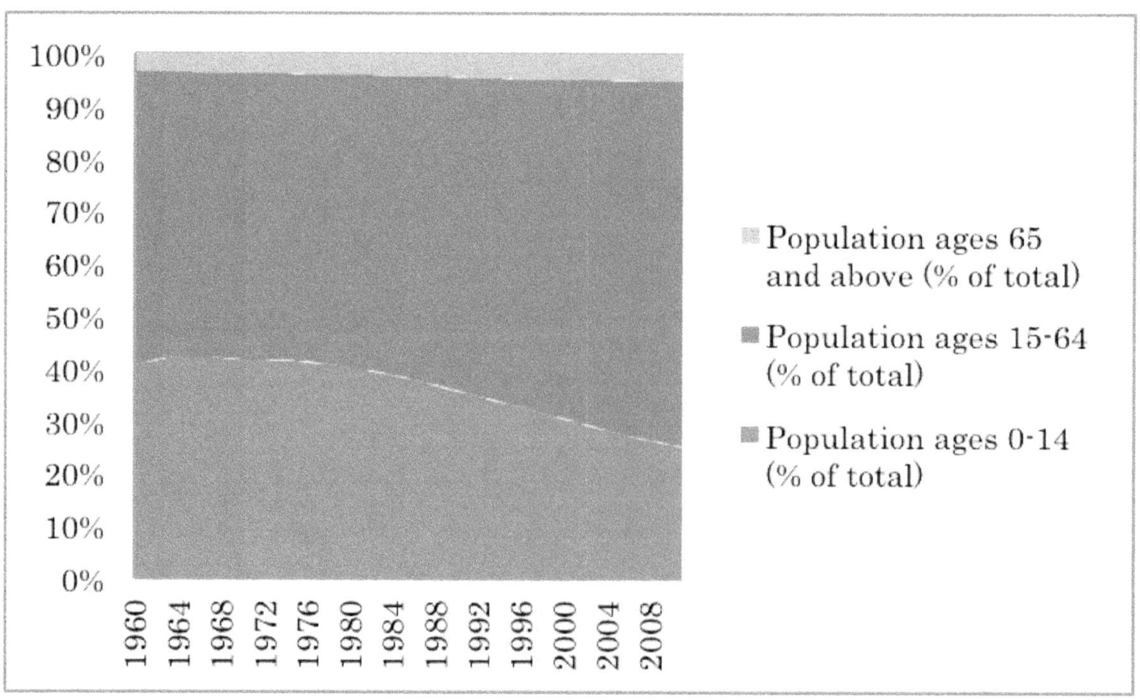

Figure 7. Total Net ODA (constant price: 2010 USD millions) Source: DAC Database

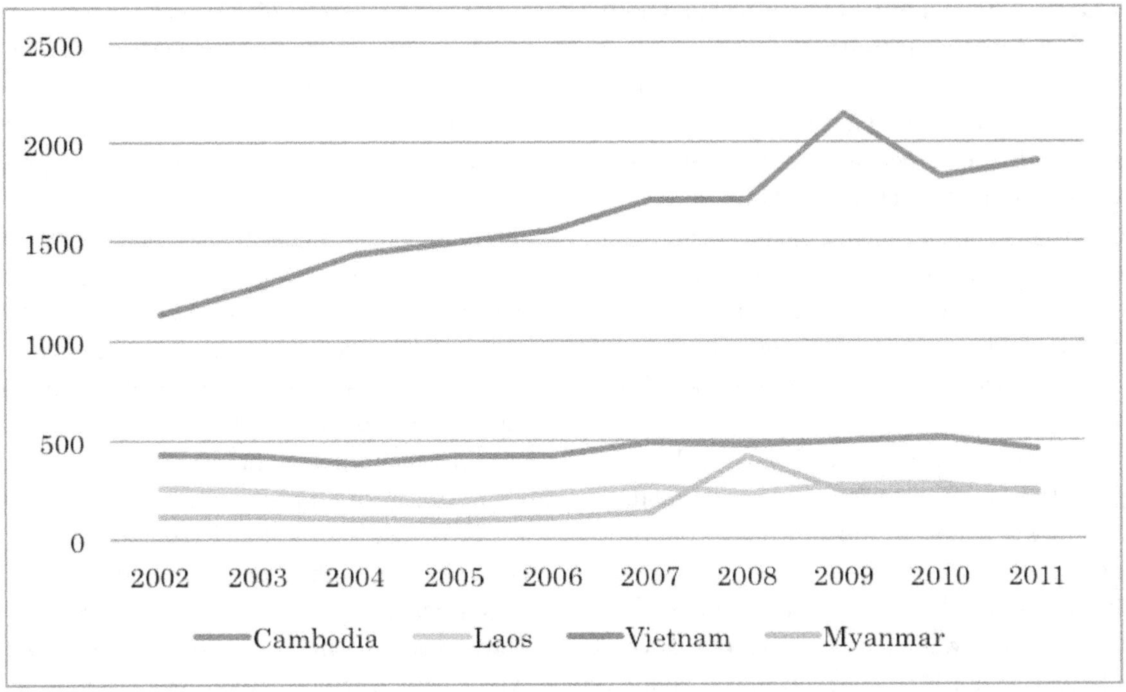

Report" and the concept of human development was used which is the opposed concept of economic development that uses economic growth as an indicator (UNDP, 1990). Additionally, the 1994 Human Development Report focused the concept of human security. Moreover, the concept of "social exclusion" at the World Summit for Social Development in 1995 was a turning point from which foreign aid policies started to become more focused marginalized and socially excluded individuals and groups.

Thus, foreign aid policy has more approached most disadvantaged populations, equity and individuals especially since mid-1990s. According to the aims and purposes of the foreign aid, poor family is one of the target groups. How did the international community react to Myanmar? Foreign aid changed the situation of many poor families through community development in Myanmar; however change of the policy environment was not achieved (Pedersen, 2006, p. 289). It is true that much of the foreign aid was delivered through highly limited period of the time, very limited of the amount, and uncoordinated projects which are not part of the Myanmar's national development plan or strategy. Comparing the amount of foreign aid to other so-called "CLMV" countries, this is the smallest amount. Humanitarian assistance to the cyclone victims in 2008 increased the amount of foreign aid.

One of the reasons of limited aid is due to the policy of recipient side. Myanmar government had restricted the activities of bilateral and multilateral aid agencies as well as NGOs. For example, Myanmar government did not easily accept the humanitarian assistance from other nations when the heavy cyclone struck Myanmar and killed more than 130,000 people in May 2008, and thus most of donor countries and agencies could start their humanitarian assistance only 2 weeks after the disaster.

Of course, problem is not only from the recipient side of foreign aid, but also from the execution side. Though Myanmar faces serious conditions and the development issues indicated in, donors tend not to deliver substantial aid to them until there are a disaster and policy changes.

Yet foreign aid to Myanmar was so limited, trend of foreign aid has paid more attentions to individuals in need. There is the policy discussion of foreign aid to "fragile states". "Fragile states" is the term used for countries facing particularly severe development challenges, such as weak institutional capacity, poor governance, political instability, and frequently on-going violence or the legacy effects of past severe conflict (IDA 2007, p. 2).

It is assumed that there had been the obstacle to provide foreign aid towards "fragile states" because donor countries and the agency could not expect the positive effect and good cost-benefit.

International Development Association's (IDA) selected Myanmar as a fragile state. Myanmar is described as the least developed country (LDC) and is a country which is weak not only in the economic situation but which also has healthcare, education, social equality and various other sectors.

A factsheet published by the OECD in 2007 examines ODA flows to fragile states, listing countries requiring monitoring and responses under four categories (OECD, 2007, p. 2). First category is "countries receiving less aid than would be predicted given their high levels of need, compared to countries with similar policy and institutional performance ratings", second category is "countries with high levels of need and weak governance or low capacity", third category is "countries with improving aid levels", and fourth category is "countries with access to a limited number of donors" (OECD, 2007, p. 2). Myanmar was categorized in the second category. Needs for foreign aid assistances were recognized in Myanmar; however, the increase in the amount of assistance may not be justified due to its weak governance, and low government capacity.

This clearly shows that the decision of execution of foreign aid is based on political concerns rather than need of the people, or perhaps, the international community strongly supposed that the greatest need of the Myanmar people is democratization, and assistance should be restricted to the minimum level possible. Undemocratic nature of the military regime caused poverty, but poverty eradication was not received much attention. The international community has been focused on democratization, rather than poverty situation and other development issues of Myanmar. UN appointed the special rapporteur on the situation of human rights in Myanmar since 1992. UN issued the press statement so many times for expressing concern of human rights issue, house arrest of Daw Aung San Suu Kyi, and political prisoners.

Thus, the international community's strong concern over Myanmar was mainly consisting of political and human rights issues. There were unmotivated to provide assistance to countries where human rights violation existed, and the major opinion was that we should minimize assistance. Consequently Myanmar was controlled by the military regime, foreign aid to Myanmar has been suspended or limited for a long time by most of the donor countries.

Moreover, it should be noted that activities of non-governmental organization were limited in Myanmar due to the restriction by the military regime. Thus, the supports by both local and international NGOs were also limited. People in Myanmar have to find a way to overcome the poverty situation with limited formal supports from internal and the international community.

But the issue is not only the absence or limit of supports individuals from outside of the country but also is the given the specific policy. The problems such as the undemocratic nature of the military regime, the forced labor issue, and the problem of the house arrest of Aung San Suu Kyi until 2010 caused deepening antagonism with the international community, especially EU and US, and they imposed sanctions against Myanmar until recently.

According to US Department of the Treasury, the president issues the Executive Orders on May 1997, July 2003, October 2007 and April 2008 in order to prohibit defined activities (US Department of the Treasury website). These orders include such as blocking of property of higher officials of SPDC and Myanmar government, prohibiting the importation of products of Myanmar, prohibiting the exportation or re-exportation of financial services to Myanmar, and prohibiting new investment in Myanmar by US persons (after May 1997).

EU imposed the restriction since 1996 and made several renewing and strengthening on it afterward. According to the Council Regulation (EC) No 194/2008 adopted on 25 February 2008, imposed measures were, for example, such as an arms embargo, bans on technical and financial assistance related to military activities, freezing of funds and economic resources of government personals, prohibition of financial loans/credits of government owned enterprises (EU, 2008).

Khin Zaw Win argues "it is undeniable that those advocating sanctions are willing to condone the ensuring hardship upon the people as a "necessary price for democracy"" (Khin Zaw Win, 2007, p. 281). It seems that sanctions gave more negative impact on people rather than the military regime. US sanction against Myanmar does not work well, rather it weakened the economy by limiting trade, investment and foreign aid (Sachs, 2004). Kudo examines the impact of US sanction on the garment industry in Myanmar, and finding shows fewer influences by U.S. sanctions both in the military regime and the majority of the population however ordinary people receive more impact than regime (Kudo, 2008, p. 1016). Seekins also address that US sanction against Myanmar caused hardship for ordinary people rather than military regime (Seekins, 2005, p. 450-452). The poverty is caused by the military regime, but also the policy by the international community influenced to people.

Analysis may give various factors behind the ineffective economic sanctions to the military regime. One of the factors is a failing coherent action of the international community towards Myanmar. For example, Chinese government has been developing close diplomatic ties with Myanmar's government. It was very observable in 2007 when the military government violently crackdown on protesters, the UN Security Council failed to pass a resolution but was only able to issue a president's statement expressing strong regret due to China and Russia vetoed the proposed draft resolution (The International Herald Tribune, September 28, 2007).

Sanctions have not proven to be an effective tool for changing the governments like Myanmar, and to a certain extent, sanctions may increase poverty. Thus, the international community needs to reconsider using economic sanctions as a tool.

5. CONCLUSION

This chapter examines how the foreign aid policy should and should have supported families facing risks by using the case study of Myanmar.

The chapter starts by addressing the issue of poverty, which continues to be the gravest risk in the developing countries, and family could be the cause of poverty as well as the solution of poverty in foreign aid policy discussion. The situation of poverty and migration as a risk management tool are examined in the second section of the chapter. People became migrant workers in order to survive poverty, and migration was the only hope to overcome the situation. Interviews to migrant workers in Thailand and Japan were conducted. Interview result showed in the third section addressed the serious poverty situation especially in a rural area, and migrant workers were strongly expected to send money home however they could not manage remittance well due to the difficult living situation in the new place. This fact was the annoyance of migrant workers since family members prepared the money for migration. In addition, their no or weak legal status gave new risks.

Section four examined how foreign aid replied those situations. However the policy discussion of foreign aid showed more focus on people and socially excluded people and groups, the actual provision of foreign aid was restricted by national interests and international relations. The lack of service provision by foreign aid could not play a crucial role to support people. Additionally, the economic sanctions given by the international community made people's life more severe one. Thus, people were motivated to migrate to manage the family risks. As it has been thus far, the greatest concern of the international community is the democratization of Myanmar. Ending the military regime and the release of Daw Aung San Suu Kyi, the symbol of democratization was focused, and ordinary people's life in Myanmar was not equally concerned. Difficult situation people faced was understood as a cost of democratization, and that the situation was expected to motivate changing the political situation. Examination of Myanmar case shows the discrepancy between what has been discussed and focused in foreign aid and what were actually replied.

In 2010, Daw Aung San Suu Kyi, a symbol of democracy of the country was finally freed from the house arrest constantly continued since 1989, and she has been taken a seat in parliament. The recent military regime's reforms are considered the shift to build democratic country. In response to this reform, various countries change their policy towards Myanmar. US eased some sanctions (The New York Times, April 5, 2012). In April 2012, EU suspended sanctions against Myanmar for one year with conditionality only if country prohibits on arms sales (The Guardian, April 24, 2012). 26 countries and five international organizations agreed to support Myanmar with its reform efforts in the meeting initiated by the government of Japan in October 2012 (The Japan Times, 14 October, 2012). "The impoverished but the resource-rich country is being seen as South-east Asia's next investment darling" (The Straits Times (Singapore), May 23, 2013).

Previous years, political reforms including the release of Daw Aung San Suu Kyi and political prisoners, and the hold of elections were realized. Nevertheless it is still difficult to understand that this reform is democratization what the international community means. As several newspaper article shows, this election was "neither free nor fair" (The Nations, November 11, 2010), and election was managed for the military backed party by the military regime to keep their power (The New York Times, November 10, 2010). This election was held while remaining under house arrest of Daw Aung San Suu Kyi, thus many criticisms were given to the election.

The international community changes their policy to Myanmar after the release of Daw Aung San Suu Kyi, but it should be questioned that Myanmar is on the right track of the democratization process. For example, the ethnic minorities in Myanmar still face serious human rights violations. Newspaper reported "the Muslim Rohingya people have been denied citizenship and are severely mistreated in the western state of Rakhine, where the local government recently restricted Rohingya family size to two children" (The International Herald Tribune, June 1, 2013).

The international community changes their policy to Myanmar. Foreign aid policies also shift to economic development and investment from the indifferent policy. Foreign aid has not been successfully addressing the issue of risk and family in Myanmar. It is assumed that socio-economic change will create new social risks. People centered foreign aid policy to Myanmar should be actively considered.

REFERENCES

Asahi Shimbun. (2009a, March 30). Myanmar people with no work permits or insurance fall through the cracks, illegally working refugees/ Ibaraki prefecture. *Asahi Shimbun.*

Asahi Shimbun. (2009b, August 29). Rohingya people/minorities escape persecution and hard life Tatebayashi, Gunma. *Asahi Shimbun.*

Asahi Shimbun. (2009c, June 6). Economic growth with unaccompanied actual situation. *Asahi Shimbun.*

EU. (2008). *Council regulation (EC) no 194/2008 of 25 February 2008 renewing and strengthening the restrictive measures in respect of Burma/ Myanmar and repealing Regulation (EC) No 817/2006*. Retrieved from http://eur-lex.europa.eu/LexUriServ/LexUriServ.do?uri=OJ:L:2008:066:0001:0087:EN:PDF

Fenny, S., & Clarke, M. (2009). *The millennium development goals and beyond – International assistance to the Asia-Pacific*. Hampshire, UK: Palgrave Macmillan.

Hesketh, T., Lu, L., & Zhu, W. (2005). The effect of China's one-child family policy after 25 years. *The New England Journal of Medicine*, *353*(11), 1171–1176. PMID:16162890

IDA. (2007). *Operational policy and country services (OPCS) and resource, mobilization department (FRM), operational approaches and financing in fragile states, June 2007*. Retrieved from http://siteresouces.worldbank.org/IDA/Resources/IDA15FragileStates.pdf

International Herald Tribune. (2007, September 28). China blocks UN effort to condemn Myanmar. *The International Herald Tribune.*

International Herald Tribune. (2013, June 1). Terror in Myanmar. *The International Herald Tribune.*

Kudo, T. (2008). The impact of U.S. sanctions on the Myanmar garment industry. *Asian Survey*, *48*(6).

Mainichi Shimbun. (2008, February 14). Tokyo kenbunroku: Visit unrecognized Myanmar refugee mother and child living in Japan/Tokyo. *Mainichi Shimbun.*

Mainichi Shimbun. (2009, July 7). Former diet member secretary running the show? Denies charges of smuggling people at 1.5M yen/person and introducing them to small business. *Mainichi Shimbun.*

Ministry of Foreign Affairs website Japan's ODA Data by Country. (n.d.). Retrieved from http://www.mofa.go.jp/policy/oda/data/pdfs/myanmar.pdf

MNCWA. (2001). *Gender statistics in Myanmar*. Yangon, Myarmar: MNCWA.

Mokomane, Z. (2012). *Anti-poverty family-focused policies in developing countries, department of economic and social affairs, division for social policy and development, family-oriented policies for poverty reduction, work-family balance and international solidarity*. Retrieved from http://www.un.org/esa/socdev/family/docs/WorkFamilyBalanceandIntergenerationalSolidarity.pdf

Naqvi, S. N. H. (2010). *The evolution of development policy: A reinterpretation*. Oxford, UK: Oxford University Press.

Nation (Thailand). (2010, November 11). Not free or fair. *Nation (New York, N.Y.).*

Nation (Thailand). (2013, June 28). Thein Sein calls for action against poverty. *Nation (New York, N.Y.).*

New York Times. (2010, November 10). In Myanmar, opposition concedes defeat in vote. *New York Times.*

New York Times. (2012, April 5). U.S. moves toward normalizing relations with Myanmar. *New York Times.*

OECD. (2007). *Ensuring fragile states are not left behind*. Retrieved from http://www.oecd.org/dataoecd/34/24/40090369.pdf

OECD. (2011). Executive summary. In *Doing better for families*. Paris: OECD Publishing.

Pedersen, M. B. (2006). A comprehensive international approach to political and economic development in Burma/Myanmar. In T. Wilson (Ed.), *Myanmar's long road to national recongiliation*. Singapore: ISEAS Publications.

Roycee, A. (2008). *Burma in turmoil*. New York: Nova Science Publishers.

Sachs, J. (2004, July 27). Myanmar: Sanctions won't work. *The Financial Times*.

Semyonov, M., & Gorodzeisky, A. (2008). Labor migration, remittances and economic well-being of households in the Philippines. *Population Research and Policy Review*, *27*(5), 619–637.

Straits Times (Singapore). (2013, May 23). Myanmar economy set to grow 6.75%: IMF, gas production, investment to lead expansion, up from 6.5% last year. *Straits Times*.

Sumner, A., & Tribe, M. (2008). *International development studies-Theories and methods in research and practice*. London: Sage Publication.

The Guardian. (2012, April 24). EU lifts Burma sanctions for one year to support reform. *The Guardian*.

The Japan Times. (2012, October 14). Aiding Myanmar's reforms (opinion). *The Japan Times*.

UN. (2012). *The millennium development report 2012*. New York: UN.

UN Millennium Project. (2005). *Investing in development - A practical plan to achieve the millennium development goals*. London: Earthscan.

UNDESA. (2011). *Summary of the proceedings assessing family policies: Confronting family poverty and social exclusion & ensuring work-family balance*. New York: United Nations Expert Group Meeting.

UNDP. (1990). *Human development report 1990 concept and measurement of human development*. UNDP.

UNDP. (2010). *Human development report*. New York: Palgrave Macmillan.

UNDP. (2011). *Human development report*. New York: Palgrave Macmillan.

UNDP. (2011). *Human development report*. New York: Palgrave Macmillan.

UNFPA. (2008). *Family planning and poverty reduction: Fact sheet 2008*. Retrieved from http://www.unfpa.org/rh/planning/mediakit/docs/sheet4.pdf

UNFPA. (2012). *Impacts of population dynamics, reproductive health and gender on poverty*. New York: UNFPA.

US Department of the Treasury Website. (n.d.). *An overview of the Burmese sanctions regulations title 31 part 537 of the U.S. code of federal regulations*. Retrieved from http://www.treasury.gov/resource-center/sanctions/Documents/burma.pdf

ISSA Website (n.d.a). *Family policies*. Retrieved from http://www.issa.int/Topics/Family-policies

ISSA Website (n.d.b). *Technical seminar on family policies - Family policies in the face of changes in family structures and the evolving socio-economic context*. Retrieved from http://www.issa.int/News-Events/Events/Technical-Seminar-on-Family-Policies-Family-policies-in-the-face-of-changes-in-family-structures-and-the-evolving-socio-economic-context

OECD-DAC Website. (n.d.). *DAC list of ODA recipients*. Retrieved from http://www.oecd.org/dac/aidstatistics/48858205.pdf

UNDESA Website (n.d.). *Tackling family poverty*. Retrieved from http://www.un.org/en/development/desa/news/policy/tackling-family-poverty.html

UNRISD Website. (n.d.). *Social policy and development*. Retrieved from http://www.unrisd.org/80256B3C005BB128/(httpProgrammeAreas)/BFA13785EC135F568025718B003C5FA7?OpenDocument

Win, K. Z. (2007). Reality check on the sanctions policy against Myanmar. In *Myanmar state, society and ethnicity*. Singapore: ISEAS Publishing.

Chapter 7
An Analysis of Contemporary Japanese Rural Families:
The Changing Balance between Individual Freedom and Responsibility for Unity of the Family

Yoshimi Kataoka
Shimane University, Japan

ABSTRACT

Many Japanese researchers have suggested that both Japanese and Western societies are experiencing individualization of the family; whether or not this is the case in Japanese rural farming villages remains unclear. The purpose of this chapter is to investigate this question using a case study. The research involves interviews of families living in rural areas within the Shimane Prefecture, each engaged in agriculture, forestry, and/or fishery. The emerging picture is that it is increasingly difficult to find traditional Ie in rural farming villages today. For the rural farming family, individual freedom is important. However, respecting individuals seems to occur for the purposes of maintaining unity of the family as a group rather than for the purpose of individual self-realization. Therefore, emphasizing individual freedom does not mean conflict among family members (i.e., enforcement of competition with other family members or compromises by them).

DOI: 10.4018/978-1-4666-5031-2.ch007

1. INTRODUCTION

Beck and his colleagues argue that the individualization of the family during the second modernity is now taking place in Western societies (Beck & Beck-Gernsheim, 2001). Since the rise of modernization, people have pursued freedom. The pursuit of freedom (e.g., freedom from kinship in marriage and family life, and freedom to choose an occupation) resulted in the "isolated (autonomous) nuclear family." Nevertheless, in nuclear families, there have still been contradictions, such as dependence and authority. For example, children must depend upon their parents and, as a result, parents possess power over their children. Today, societies have entered into second modernity, in which the pursuit of freedom has reached a new phase. Nuclear families are unstable, which has adversely affected dependence and authority in the family unit (Beck, 1998). Family has become a risky undertaking in which individuals must maintain their autonomy in order to choose his/her family life.

Japan also experienced the spread of the nuclear family through industrialization following World War II. However, as many researchers suggested, nuclear families have declined in Japan since the 1990s. Furthermore, Japanese families have diversified. There has been an increase in the numbers of women in the workforce, a trend for remaining single, and a tendency toward having fewer children, resulting in nuclear families being but one option. In addition, researchers have reported that Japanese society is experiencing the individualization of family (Yamada, 2004). Thus, a new approach to family in which it is regarded as a lifestyle based on individual independent choices was proposed (Nonoyama, 2007).

However, these discussions fundamentally refer to urban families; families in rural areas of Japan appear to have a different style of family life. The *Ie* system was abolished and the model of the nuclear family was introduced in Japan following World War II, however, rural village residents regarded *Ie* as essential. *Ie* refers to the patriarchal lineal family system in which the first-born son exclusively succeeds to the family property (a house and farming land) and the family's lineage from generation to generation. The head of the family has authority over the other family members within the *Ie* family paradigm and must represent them to the village community. The village community consisted of the unions of various *Ie* groups, in order for *Ie* to be maintained based on cooperation with other *Ie* groups (Hosoya, 1993). Furthermore, there is still an emphasis on the traditional *Ie* system in rural areas of Japan. When a family makes a decision, the *yome* (daughter-in-law) is given some input. Also the local traditions and customs create difficulties for residents (Mitsuoka, 1996: Watanabe, 2002; Nagano, 2004; Hosoya, 2005). Many Japanese today, therefore, perceive that life in rural farming villages involves having less freedom than in urban areas since the rural family system and territorial connections maintain that individuals' duties to the family and local groups are more important than individual freedom.

Although many Japanese researchers have suggested that both Japanese and Western societies are experiencing individualization of the family, whether or not this is the case in Japanese rural farming villages remains unclear. The purpose of this article is to investigate this question using a case study.

2. JAPANESE RURAL FAMILIES

According to Kizaemon Aruga, in traditional rural farming neighborhoods, the *Ie* system functioned to protect the livelihoods of individuals. Aruga proposed that, during periods in which it was difficult for individuals to obtain economic independence and the social security system was insufficient, survival was dependent upon people living together based on the assets accumulated by their family ancestors. If a family exhausted inherited assets, members would soon face danger to their livelihood. Thus, all members of the family were obliged to maintain the family assets, and were held responsible for their assets. Additionally, family assets were insufficient to satisfy the needs of all family members. As a result, inequality among members was unavoidable in terms of distribution of assets (Aruga, 1972). Therefore, conditions suppressed the individual freedom of members.

In this sense, we can say that the *Ie* family was the principle uniting a (stem) family, securing the livelihood of family members, and assigning them responsibilities. Post-war Japan legally abolished the *Ie* system, resulting in an increase in economic affluence. Principles that were not found in the *Ie* system, such as affection, childrearing, a purpose in life, and others, became factors that maintained a family unit (Yamada, 2005). Still, the *Ie* system did not necessarily lose its influence in rural Japan as a major principle of uniting and maintaining a family. Masatoshi Ôuchi, observing the women of farming families, provided the following explanation: While many males of farming families had non-farming jobs and became part-time farmers amid the post-war economic expansion, many females, occupying lower statuses within the *Ie* family unit, remained bound to the family following the war. They, therefore, worked on farms in place of their husbands, cared for aged family members, and did many other things to maintain the *Ie* system (Ôuchi, 2004). As such, *Ie* has survived in rural Japan.

During the last decade or so, however, the situation has remained unchanged. The Basic Plan for Gender Equality, set up by the Japanese Government in 2000, called for an improvement of the social statuses of farming family women. The Plan emphasized "independence of individuals" for both women and men of rural areas, for which independence would allow them to autonomously make decisions, and design and materialize their own life courses; this was succeeded by the Second and Third Basic Plan for Gender Equality in 2005 and 2010, respectively. Recently, Japan's Ministry of Agriculture, Forestry and Fisheries, has recommended that farmers sign a "household management agreement," with a view to reforming *Ie* customs, which has been an obstacle to the establishment of individual freedom (The Ministry of Agriculture, Forestry and Fisheries, 1998; Gojô, 2003).

Needless to say, this has been requested by the government and some assert that many farmers themselves have not changed, which is evident by the fact that many women of farming families continue to work hard labor positions, but have not obtained higher social statuses (Watanabe, 2002; Nagano, 2004). However, a study exists indicating the possibility that entrepreneurship, which has been gradually spreading among farming family women, can help with gaining independence (Iwasaki, 1995). In addition, some studies have argued that a growing number of farming family women engaged in non-farming occupations are bringing significant changes to the traditional roles of women in farming neighborhoods, as well as to the *Ie* system (Tsuru, 2003; Ôuchi, 2004).

Several earlier studies have shown a rise in the number of part-time farming families, whose members are engaged in non-farming occupations as well, and has resulted in increased individuality. Akihiko Hasegawa discussed "separate-living stem families," in which parents, children, and their spouses live separately while sharing the same household, based on survey results obtained during the 1970s and 1980s. The parents, children, and spouses make decisions and act separately in terms of farming, meals, budgeting, and so on, unlike the traditional, patriarchal *Ie* system. Hasegawa calls the separate-living stem family an "individual-oriented family" (Hasegawa, 1993). Still, this particular kind of an individual-oriented family consists of two nuclear families, centered on the two couples, not the individuals. Further studies, however, have confirmed that life in farming families tends to be increasingly individualized. Among them, Sonoko Kumagai found that rural families were becoming places in which greater diversity of lifestyles coexisted together. Within a rural family, Kumagai witnessed diversification in terms of gender and generations based on life space, time, and household budgets (Kumagai, 1991, 1996). These studies suggested the emergence of farming families in which each member was seeking to enjoy his/her individual lifestyle.

3. INDIVIDUAL FREEDOM AND UNITY OF THE FAMILY

Previous studies have suggested that individual freedom is gradually emphasized, including in Japanese rural farming families. However, as the pursuit of individual freedom progresses, the question of whether rural families experiencing individualization are at risk of dissolution arises. A 2006 analysis of survey data obtained from a rural area in the Shimane prefecture in Japan included residents aged 20 and above. The results of the analysis suggested that, in the case of rural farming families, an emphasis on the unity of the family might result in consideration for each family member's freedom (Kataoka and Fukino, 2007).

The questionnaire included items on the participant's attitudes toward family relationships. Respondents were asked to indicate their level of agreement with each item on a five-point scale. Higher points indicated greater agreement with the statement (from 1 to 5 points) and a factor analysis was conducted based on scores. As a result, three factors with eigenvalues from one and above were abstracted.

Factor 1 is strongly related to items emphasizing solidarity of the family, fairness among family members, and joining community activities in units of the family. This factor seems to be related to maintaining unity of the family, so we have termed it "emphasizing unity of the family." Factor 2 is associated with items such as understanding each family member's feelings, emphasizing a strong bond among family members, and respecting each family member as an individual. This factor is related to consideration for each family member to strengthen the emotional ties, so we have termed it "respecting the individual freedom." Factor 3 is related to items such as allowing each family member freedom, pushing through self-assertiveness, giving private things priority over the family matters, and permitting divorce. Although this factor emphasizes individual freedom, similar to factor 2, this seems to be related to individualization in the second modernity, so we regard this as "individualization."

Based on factor analysis results, we created the following three variables: "emphasizing unity of the family," "respecting the individual freedom," and "individualization." We focused on the relationship between these variables and compared them to the rural farming family and the non-rural non-farming family. In this data, "non-rural" does not necessarily mean "urban"; the non-rural non-farming family is a family of non-farmers living somewhere that is not considered farmland.

Figure 1 shows the result of path analysis to examine the difference in the relationship among variables between the rural farming family and the non-rural non-farming family. It suggests a significant effect from "emphasizing unity of the family" to "respecting individual freedom." There is also a significant difference between the causal coefficient of the rural farming family and that of the non-rural non-farming family (the test of the difference between parameters was statistically significant: $z=-3.098$, $p<.01$). The relationship between "emphasizing unity of the family" and "respecting individual freedom" in the rural farming family is stronger than that of the non-rural non-farming family. This suggests that in the rural farming family, there may be a causal relationship in which regarding the unity of the family as important results in respecting the freedom of individual family members. Even in rural areas in which traditional *Ie* is still prevalent, individual freedom is considered important. Furthermore,

Figure 1. Path Analysis using family relationship variables (Simultaneous Analysis of Several Groups)

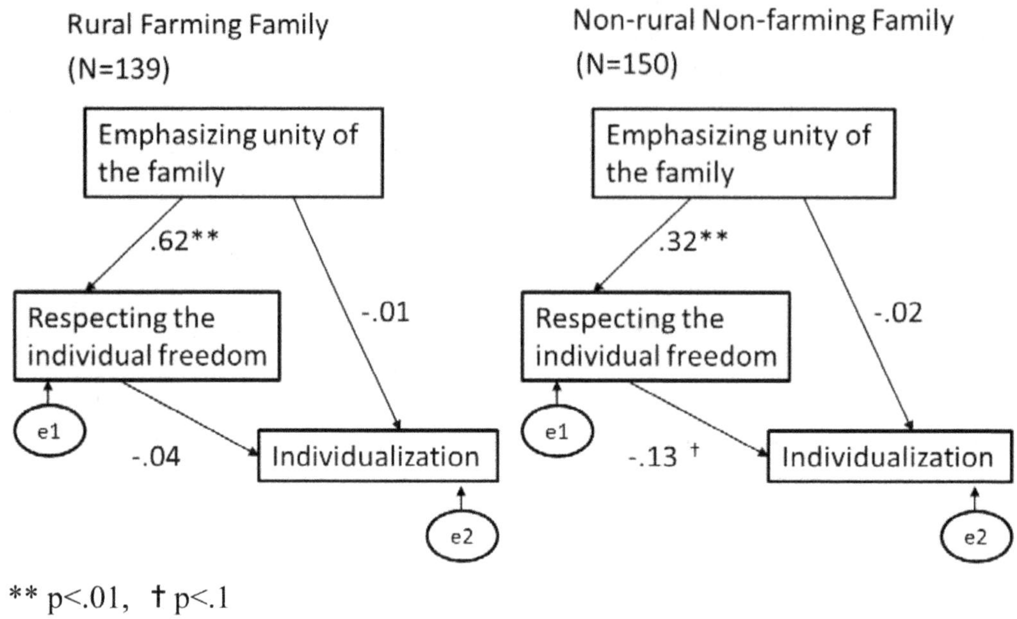

there is no conflict between respecting individual freedom and emphasizing unity of the family.

The following sections will verify these hypotheses by investigating a case study of rural families.

4. CASE STUDY

4.1 Data

Are rural Japanese families experiencing change from *Ie*? How does the relationship between individuality and family groups occur? To discuss these points, we will investigate the cases obtained from interviews.

The interviews involved 11 families living in rural areas within the Shimane Prefecture, each engaged in agriculture, forestry, and/or fishery.[1] The Prefecture's government, in its 1999 "Basic Regulations for Vitalization of Hilly and Mountainous Areas of Shimane Prefecture," defined as "hilly and mountainous areas" those "in need of further development in terms of industrial promotion, securing of employment opportunities and of healthcare, medical, and welfare services, as well as other social activities, since currently they are falling behind the other areas with respect to these." In more specific terms, the Prefectural Government specifies as a "hilly or mountainous area" any area that meets the following conditions: 1) The area has been specified as a "depopulated area" in accordance with Japan's "Special Law for Independence of Depopulated Areas," 2) the area has been specified as a "Designated Rural Village" as defined by the "Specified Rural Village Law," 3) the area has been specified as a "remote area" in accordance with the "Act on the Special Financial Measures for Total Improvement of Public Facilities of Remote Areas," and 4) the area is as disadvantaged as the other areas covered by the three requirements above (to be designated by the Prefecture's Governor) (Shimane Prefecture Government, 2006).[2] Based on this definition, the majority of the Shimane

Prefecture, with the exception of places as the central part of the City of Matsue, is "hilly or mountainous areas." The interviews referred to herein were conducted solely with families living in hilly and mountainous areas. Thus, this paper refers to those hilly and mountainous areas as "rural farming villages."

The families chosen for the interviews included those running a family farm, those who relocated to a farming village after living in an urban area for some time, and those farming families who have signed a "household management agreement." The purpose for choosing a variety of families was to include those farming families who have immigrated into the mountainous areas away from urban living, as well as those who have signed a "household management agreement," both of which are groups that have been gradually increasing in number, in addition to traditional farming families in which farming has been succeeded generationally. A high range of choice is considered necessary in order to discuss the trends and future outlook of modern farming families. In selecting the families to interview, the author obtained generous cooperation from "Furusato Shimane Teijû Zaidan" (literally, "Hometown Shimane Settlement Foundation"), "Shimane-ken Kawamoto Nôrin Shinkô Center" ("Shimane Prefecture Kawamoto Promotion Center of Agriculture and Forestry"), the local government of the Town of Okinoshima, and others. The interviews were conducted between August 2005 and January 2006.

In each interview, the interviewer presented the topics to talk about based on a checklist (which included questions on the interviewee's occupation, family, neighborhood, life values, and so on) and allowed the interviewee to speak freely. In addition, we made an effort to interview two or more members of each family. Each interview took an average of three hours. This paper will refer to the typical findings among all interviewees.

4.2 Respecting Individual Freedom

The interviewee Mr. C (aged in his late 30s) previously lived in a major city and worked as a prison guard in the Kansai District, but began to feel highly stressed one year prior to the interview and wished to retire. He consulted his wife (aged in her early 30s), who found a fishing job in Shimane Prefecture via the Internet, and he decided to pursue the fishing position. The couple moved to Shimane Prefecture; they do not have children.

Following the move, his wife joined a hospital as a nurse, a position for which she occasionally works night shifts. Both husband and wife now have to work since Mr. C currently earns only around two-thirds of his past income. After settling in Shimane, the couple began sharing chores; Mr. C is responsible for laundry and dinner preparation when his wife works during the day.

Mr. C and his wife live in a rented single-family house located in a farming area a short distance from the fishing harbor. Despite the difficulty of finding a single-family house for rent in the area, the wife requested this type of accommodation and Mr. C continued searching until he found the appropriate property.

The consideration shown to his wife by Mr. C was due to two main reasons: 1) the decline of his income, and 2) his concern for his wife's mental health, as he felt she might have difficulty adapting to her new neighborhood. As for Mr. C himself, he says that he laughed more, began working out at a local gym, and felt more emotional ease since moving to Shimane Prefecture. His wife, however, seems to be occupied with her work. In fact, one month after the couple moved and she commenced her new position, she felt highly stressed and was hospitalized for eczema that covered her body. Moreover, Mr. C reported that she still occasionally feels sadness to the point of tears due to missing her old life. The husband described his concern for her, saying, "It was my decision to settle down here. And now, my wife is experiencing a hard time here… You know, I have no right to say some strong words to her. Anyway, we are still newcomers here. We try to adapt for a little longer, and if it doesn't work out, then we'll think again."

Mr. F's family is known as a "U-turn family" in Japanese (settling in one's birthplace, after working elsewhere for a period of time). This family consists of Mr. F (late 40s), his wife (early 40s), their daughter (a high school student), and their son (a junior high school student). When Mr. F decided to resign from his position of seven years, he chose his birthplace, Shimane, as the location for his new career. His wife was working as a visiting caretaker to people requiring in-home care, and trying to obtain a license as a second-class care-taking helper; as a result, she was unable to relocate to Shimane immediately. Mr. F obtained a job in Shimane in the forestry industry and moved there with his children; his wife followed five months later. Since settling, Mr. F has been the secretary general of a non-profit organization working for environment protection and neighborhood fellowship, in addition to working at his new position in forestry. Mr. F's wife was once involved in activities to create and provide opportunities for life-long learning students to publish the achievements of their learning and other activities; she was also responsible for related publicity activities. Though she can no longer be involved in those activities given the location of Shimane, she still participates in them around once a year. Thus, both the husband and wife have been active in social activities. The two, though they have respect for each other's activities, are not involved in each other's activities. However, they pay membership fees to each other's activity groups and occasionally join special events.

The husband and wife socialize with their neighbors separately. As he grew up in Shimane, Mr. F has old friends in the area. He and his lower secondary school graduate often have reunion gatherings, involving taking trips and other activities together. Thus, he maintains strong relationships with his neighbors. Meanwhile, the wife states, "I've got no intention to join in my husband's circles of friends. I have my own. I simply do not care much."

In the cases of Mr. C and Mr. F, the move to Shimane, whether returning to a birthplace and a completely new area, the husband chose to move to a new place and commence a new career. Their wives agreed and cooperated with their husbands to do so, however, this does not necessarily mean that the wives sacrificed their aspirations. Regarding Mr. F's wife, Mr. F helped her with her decision to work in care-taking and engagement in social activities. As for Mr. C's wife, her husband is making an effort to understand her needs.

Regarding other cases of families that relocated to Shimane, the move was the husband's decision, and the wife respected this decision; this was unanimous among all the cases surveyed. However, unlike the wives of Mr. C and Mr. F, whose wives were involved in activities individually without their husbands, in some instances the wives simply followed their husband in choice of activities. It is important to note that even in such cases, the wives did not mimic their husbands. For instance, Ms. D (early 30s) followed her husband (late 30s) to Shimane, saying, "Well, some people might think I do not make my own decisions. Yet, I honestly prefer to set the course of my life along with my husband's." In other words, out of her own will and intention, she chose to share her husband's decision and decided to follow him. Therefore, they relocated to Shimane, settled there, and opened a pear farm.

Another new Shimane resident, Ms. E (early 40s) respected her husband's (late 40s) decision to move there to run a farm and willingly joined him. She said, "I have big thing to achieve in my life. I just wanted to raise my kids (two sons: an elementary school student and a junior high school student), and this place (Shimane) has been a good place to do it, I think. I have nothing to regret, and hope I never will." In this case, though Ms. E wife does not have individual goals beyond her family, her remark above, "I have nothing to regret, and hope I never will" suggests that she that she believes that she has chosen her lifestyle. As we see in these cases, even in cases in which the wife appears to follow her husband, she has freely chosen her lifestyle and made the decision to relocate willingly.

Elsewhere, Ms. K's family (husband in his late 50s, wife in her late 40s, residing with their third daughter in her early 20s, and their second and third sons who are junior high school students) is running a livestock farm and a construction business succeeded from her husband's parents. When the husband's mother passed away, he claimed it was due to medical errors made by the hospital and filed a lawsuit. His case against the general hospital in a small town was, as he described it, "like fighting against the whole town." Furthermore, he said that, "I had no hope to win any money from the hospital. I just did it out of my sense of justice." Respecting his sense of justice, his wife fought along with him until the case ended. Approximately five months before the court announced its decision, the husband's father suffered a stroke, resulting in the requirement for regular care. Formerly a medical nurse, Ms. K cared for him from her home for thirteen years, including the family in this endeavor. At that time, she tended to the farm's cattle before breakfast, prepared breakfast for her family, prepared lunch boxes for the employees of her husband's construction firm, and assisted with the firm's paperwork during the day. She also used a combine harvester to collect rice in the paddy that was part of the family's farm, when necessary. In short, she was responsible for countless jobs.

Today, Ms. K is not as energetic as she once was, and her husband gets up early each morning to prepare breakfast. Also inspired by the stroke of her father-in-law, the wife founded a group of paid volunteers who visit aged people living alone to assist with household chores, and so on, as well as a group of unpaid volunteers who recycle used clothes and other objects. Concerning those activities, through which she feels she has found meaning in her life, her husband assists her with them while taking care of her health, though he himself does not join the volunteers. He says he is very grateful to his wife, who has carried on the livestock farm and worked so hard for the family over the years. Being a member of the town's parliament, the husband ascribes much of his election success to her as well, saying, "Without my wife, I would never have made a parliament member."

Ms. K always understood her husband's intentions and cooperated. In return, he respects her involvement with voluntary activities. Moreover, he does not intend to force the family business onto his children as successors. His wife is aware of each person's individuality. She does not like it when her neighbors call her "Mr. K's wife." Regarding her children, she is careful not to make comparisons between her second and third sons, who are twins. Also, she never refers to her older children as "bro" or "sis," which is a common practice in Japanese families. Instead, she refers to each of her children by his/her name because, "every one of them is a person."

In the case of Mr. I (late 40s), who runs a dairy farm with his wife (early 40s) and second son (late 20s), Mr. I's second son reported that there was no room for individual freedom, since they were keenly aware of their responsibilities to the family business. However, Mr. I is responsible for management of the business while the son works in the field. Thus, each has his own discretion in his own domain. The son stated that, "So, I just want my dad to do what he should, and I do mine. You might not believe this, but it's actually easy, since nobody blames me at work."

In the case of Mr. H, whose family (consisting of Mr. H in his late 40s, his wife in her early 40s, his mother in her early 70s, and their two daughters who are elementary school students) has succeeded a farm and signed a household management agreement, he is currently solely responsible for the rice and livestock farms. Though his ambition is to run them along with his family, his mother is elderly and unable to be involved in farm work. His wife, the daughter of an urban company employee, has little interest in farming. Rather, the wife hopes to concentrate on household chores and raising her children.

Five years prior to the interview, however, following a recommendation from the local government, the family members signed a household management agreement, defining the roles of each family member. The wife agreed to take care of the farm's accounting; pleased that his wife was willing to be involved in the business, Mr. H took her to an accounting class. Later, Mr. H reported that "She gave it up. She said she was unable to understand, she found double-entry book-keeping system too tough for her. She cannot tell which money goes to what. I explained the fertilizer expense is for fertilizers. Still, she was not able to follow me. She had no knowledge of farming at all. She even mistook fertilizers for some agrichemicals." Mr. H then became responsible for the accounting as well, with his wife returning to her position as home maker. With regard to the household management agreement, Mr. H commented, "Well, the agreement is nothing more than a list of wishes."

In the case of Mr. H, the wife tried to cooperate with her husband's wishes to run the farm with her, which is why she offered to take over accounting duties. Though her attempt failed, Mr. H continued to respect his wife's choice to remain a home maker.

Mr. G's family, who operates a dairy farm, also signed a household management agreement. This family (consisting of Mr. G in his late 50s, his wife in her late 50s, their first son in his late 20s, the first son's wife in her early 20s, the first son's baby, and Mr. G's second son in his late 20s) has implemented a system in which each member of the family is involved with the farming business, including Mr. G's wife and his son's wife; they each receive compensation in the form of salary. Thus, this family regards individual economy as important.

In most of the families interviewed, free will decisions made by each member of a family are respected. We should emphasize those cases in which each family member maintained his/her own will and choices independently (and sometimes in contradiction to others) while respecting the other members' decisions. In those cases, a single member's intention did not sacrifice the other members' hopes and/or choices.

4.3 Responsibility for Management of the Family

Among the interviewed families, several members discussed their responsibilities to the other members of the family and/or the family group. For example, Mr. F and his wife, stressing the family members' shared responsibilities, referred to their family members as "companions living together" and stated, "After my kids have grown up, I'll have to take care of my parents." They also described that the respective members of their family shared household chores responsibly.

The family of Mr. F, following his return to Shimane and subsequent career changes, lived on a low-budget and maintained busy schedule. Stimulated by this change, all members of the family became aware of the need to share roles in their family life. In this particular family, the wife returned home later than the husband. Each member had their respective role to play within the family. The husband prepared dinner, while the daughter prepared lunches for herself and her father. They also implemented a family rule in which members collected dried laundry, among other jobs. These rules began following their move to Shimane. Living on a lower budget than they were previously accustomed to, the family reported that they could not afford to depend on each other to take care of their the chores. In addition, the children did not receive an allowance unless their chores were completed. The children did not attend cram school in an attempt to save money.

The wife stated her beliefs about family, saying, "Mmm – a family? We are not very family-like and do not fit into the word, I suppose. In short, I guess a family is a group of people living together. So, well, if someone living together with you is not your kin, it doesn't matter. If you are just living together with some people in, say, a dorm, you are still a family." On the same topic, the husband replied, "Well – what is it anyway, I wonder. For the time being, I have to take care of my kids. Then, after they grow up, I'll have to take care of my parents. Those generational relationships involve the most problems, I think." Thus, Mr. and Mrs. F were aware of their individual responsibilities to their family.

In some of the families, we saw some members intentionally trying to enhance their family unity and group awareness, in order to alleviate the psychological stress that family members felt in the new environment of Shimane. For example, Mr. C's wife felt massive stress following relocation and her health deteriorated. Mr. C perceived this as an issue that affected the whole family and supported his wife throughout. At a socializing meeting for new residents to Shimane, he became friends with other couples of similar ages. Though he had fellowship with only the husbands of some of those couples, he hoped to introduce his wife to them at some point in an effort to help her make new friends. As Mr. C is a fisherman, he leaves early each morning, while his wife sometimes works nights at a hospital. Thus, the two maintain different timetables, and have little time with each other during the week. To make up for this, Mr. C stated that he spent all of his days off with his wife, and the couple had more occasions to spend their free time together than before.

At the same time, those families running a family business together were also evidently aware of the family as a group. Mrs. K's family, for instance, successfully expanded their livestock farm, thanks in part to her commitment, with its number of cows and oxen rising from about 10 initially to approximately 50 today. Recently, with Mr. K being a member of their town's parliament, the farm was run mainly by Mrs. K and their third daughter (aged 23) with some help from their sons, lower secondary school students at the time.

Mr. C and Ms. K believed that, out of gratitude to their wives who kindly respected their life choices, they had a duty to respect their wives' choices in return. In any of those cases, the members were well aware of their responsibility to keep their family members united and to maintain the life of their family units.

Another interviewee involved in a family-run dairy farm, Mr. I, commented about his family, "No doubt they are important to me. Yet, if you speak of freedom, well, I have no freedom in the strict sense of the word. If I had it, I would move to an uninhabited island and settle down there alone. In reality, now two are engaged (in the management of my business), we both have to respect and understand each other." Commenting on the family's farm business, his second son spoke of his views, saying, "Hope and ambitions – I'd say they are just fancy dreams. We cannot live on hope and ambitions alone." Both Mr. I and the second son seemed to be aware of their responsibilities in terms of business management, respecting each other as business partners.

Regarding another family running a dairy farm, Mr. G's family signed a household management agreement. The general manager of the farm, Mr. G described his disbelief in unrestricted demand for individual freedom, saying, "As a farm manager, I see some discrepancy between my business and the outside world's calls for a gender-free society, household management agreements, and the likes... Some people seem to be mistaking freedom for something else – though we do need to have freedom. Yet some fail to see the line between freedom and rights and selfishness, desires, and so on." He emphasized the importance of family unity, "If each member of a family went his or her own way as he or she wanted to, nothing would be accomplished."

In Mr. H's family, who runs family farms of livestock and paddy rice, the husband aspired to run the farms together with his family, though this did not come to fruition. Ms. E's husband, who settled down in Shimane and ran a farm, said that the farm work allowed him to show his children how he worked and further enabled him to have more time with his family. These farm-running families show us that a family business promotes awareness of the importance of unity of the family group.

We found some cases in which families consider themselves a closely-knit group while socializing locally. Though Mr. and Mrs. F were actively involved in the activities of the local neighborhood community circle, there was no pressure for the family to join them given that the family lived in a rented house. This is because people in the community tend to view those living in rented accommodation merely as temporary residents, such as public school teachers, rather than as fixtures in the community. Still, though the wife does not enjoy these activities, she reported that she "works hard in them" because she believes "[These activities are] part of the requirements as we live here, sort of… once we have settled in here, we've got to do them." Regarding local events and activities, Mrs. H said, "There are times I hate to do them, honestly. Still, troublesome as they are, they are recreational activities of the neighborhood. So, I have to join them and help them become fun." For this couple, neighborhood events are somehow compulsory, and they are only involved in a few major events each year, such as seasonal festivals, athletic meetings, and the summer *obon* (a Buddhist festival to welcome back the spirits of the dead) ceremony. Both Mr. F and Mr. H, as well as their wives, consider neighborhood events and activities to be compulsory. As they and their families live in these communities, they consider events and activities to be part of their responsibilities to the local community, with either the couple or the whole family joining them to socialize. Mrs. D's family also said that there were many occasions of a local event involving the whole family. For example, an athletic meeting of an elementary school often includes the neighborhood adults.

Thus, the cases surveyed have allowed us to assess the degree to which family members were aware of the unity of the family as a group. Individuals deemed their families to be highly important given that families offered support during the transition from urban to rural living and/or they were able to work together in a family business, not only to make a living but also to add deeper meaning to their lives. Another factor was the neighborhood, where people socialized with each other in terms of the family group.

There, there is evidence that for individuals living in rural farming villages, the family is considered highly important as means of living and adapting to a new community. As a result, they possess a sense of responsibility for maintaining unity of the family. We assume that the exact meaning of adaptation differs between immigrant families that have moved into a rural farming village and those that have lived in such a village for generations. However, the fact is that an individual has to be aware that he or she is living in a farming village and must adapt to life in that community.

5. DISCUSSION

The sense of responsibility likely arises because each individual member of a family recognizes that his or her family was an indispensable means for adaptation to life in a rural farming village. We recall a discussion by Aruga (1972) which asserted that people in rural farming villages had responsibilities and obligations to maintain *Ie* given that *Ie* functioned to protect an individual member's life. However, *Ie* enforced each member to be submissive to the patriarchal authority. However, the present case study suggests that respecting each member's freedom is part of the integral efforts to protect the family as a group that is an integral part of their living and adaptation.

As mentioned previously, the Japanese government has recently facilitated the spread of modern values and norms, such as respecting individual freedom, to rural farming villages. They assume that individual freedom must be restrained in a rural farming village because of an emphasis on the unity of the family group and *Ie* union (combination of families in the community). However, the present case study suggests that the importance of unity of the family may cause respect to individuals. This supports the results of path analyses, shown in Figure 1. Thus, the propriety of the government policy to the rural farming village requires further examination.

It is difficult to find traditional *Ie* in rural farming villages today. For the rural farming family, individual freedom is important. However, respecting individuals seems to occur for the purposes of maintaining unity of the family as a group rather than for the purpose of individual self-realization. Therefore, emphasizing individual freedom does not mean conflict among family members, i.e., enforcement of competition with other family members or compromises by them.

One's preference or opinion about family life is often made as a sacrifice to other family members. Even so, in rural farming families, family members' cooperation to maintain the unity of the family is given the highest priority and individuals will then consider each other's freedom. As such, it is suggested that respecting individuals in rural farming families stresses allowance of the other family members' freedom rather than one's own freedom. As a result, there may be few, if any, complaints or conflicts between members. Yamada explained that love concealed the existence of enforcement or restraint in the Japanese modern (nuclear) family (Yamada, 2004). Responsibility for maintenance of the family as a means of adaptation to rural life may have the same function as love for the modern family.

With regard to this point, "Japanese groupism," as discussed by Eshun Hamaguchi, is worthy of consideration. According to Hamaguchi, Japanese groupism does not mean that individualism and autonomy are hidden within the group. Thus, it is not the principles of totalitarian domination that opposes individualism. It aims at a symbiosis between the individual and the group, and emphasizes the harmony among group members (Hamaguchi, 1982). In other words, it stresses the fact that each person's needs are fulfilled through his or her group, so that there is no conflict between the individual and the group. Although Hamaguchi suggests that Japanese groupism has been deeply rooted in Japanese rural areas as a tradition, the present study cannot conclude whether this was the case before the abolition of *Ie*. We have found that, at least in the contemporary Japanese rural farming villages, the individual freedom of each family member is respected because unity of the family is an important factor to the adaption of rural farming life.

REFERENCES

Aruga, K. (1972). *Ie*. Tôkyô: Shibundô.

Beck, U. (1998). *Democracy without enemies* (M. Ritter, Trans.). London: Blackwell Publishers.

Beck, U., & Beck-Gernsheim, E. (2001). *Individualization: Institutionalized individualism and its social and political consequences*. London: Sage Publications.

Beck, U., & Beck-Gernsheim, E. (2004). Families in a runaway world. In *The Blackwell companion to the sociology of families*. London: Blackwell Publishing.

Gojô, M. (2003). *Kazoku keiei kyôtei no tenkai* [Development of Family Management Agreements]. Tôkyô: Yûhikaku.

Hamaguchi, E. (1982). Nihonteki shûdanshugi to wa nanika. [What is Japanese Groupism?] In *Sono shinka o tou* [Japanese Groupism]. Tôkyô: Yûhikaku.

Hasegawa, A. (1993). *Nôson no kazoku to chiiki shakai: Sono ronri to kadai* [Families and Local Community of a Farming Village: Their Logic and Problems]. Tôkyô: Ochanomizu Shobô.

Hosoya, T. (1993). Nômin seikatsu ni okeru ko to shûdan. [Individual and Group in the Farmer's life] In *Nômin seikatsu ni okeru ko to shûdan* (pp. 403–445). Tôkyô: Ochanomizu Shobô.

Hosoya, T. (2005). Ie to nihon shakai, saikô. [Rethinking 'Ie' and the Japanese Society]. *Shakaigaku hyôron, 56*(1), 2–15.

Iwasaki, Y. (1995). Nôson ni okeru josei kigyô no igi to hokosei: Nôson no josei kigyô jittai chôsa o tsûjite. [Significance and Orientations of Female Entrepreneurs in Farming Villages: Through Fact Surveys of Female Entrepreneurs in Farming Villages]. *Nenpô Sonraku Shakai Kenkyû, 31*, 169–190.

Kataoka, Y., & Fukino, T. (2007). Nôson kazoku ni okeru ketsugô patân ni kansuru sûryôteki bunseki: shimaneken chûsankanchiiki de no chôsa deta o mochiite. [A Quantitative Analysis of the Binding Patterns in the Rural Family: Using Survey Data from the Hilly and Mountainous Areas of Shimane Prefecture]. *Shakai Bunka Ronshû, 4*, 31–39.

Kumagai, S. (1991). Gendai nihon nôson no kazoku. [Families in Japanese Farming Villages Today]. *Japanese Journal of Family Sociology, 3*, 28–40. doi:10.4234/jjoffamilysociology.3.28

Kumagai, S. (1996). Nôgyô kazoku ni okeru kojinka. [Individualization in Farming Families] In *Ima kazoku ni nani ga okotte irunoka* [What Is Happening to Families Now?]. Kyôto: Mineruva.

Ministry of Agriculture. Forestry and Fisheries of Japan. (1998). Kazoku keiei kyôtei suishin no tebiki. [Guide to Promotion of Family Management Agreements]. Tokyo: The Rural Women Empowerment and Life Improvement Association.

Mitsuoka, K. (1996). *Nôson kazoku no kekkon-nan to kôreisha mondai* [Difficulty of Finding Spouses and Aging Population Problems of Farming Village Families]. Kyôto: Mineruva.

Nagano, Y. (2004). *Gendai nihon no noson kazoku to noson shakai: Nôson josei no 'ko' no jiritsuka o megutte* [Farming Families and Society of Japan Today: with Focus on Independence of the 'Individuality' of Farming Village Women]. Tôkyô: Waseda Daigaku Shuppankai.

Nonoyama Hisaya. (2007). *Gendai kazoku no paradaimu kakushin* [Paradigm change for the modern family in Japan]. Tôkyô: Tôkyô Daigaku Shuppankai.

Ôuchi, M. (2004). Life course no tayôka to 'ie' seido. [Diversification of Life Courses and the 'Ie' System]. *Nenpô Sonraku Shakai Kenkyû, 39*, 97–132.

Shimane Prefecture. (2006). *Shimane-ken no chu-sankan chiiki no teigi*. [Definitions of Hilly and Mountainous Areas of Shimane Prefecture]. Retrieved from http://www2.pref.shimane.jp/teiju/mrteigi/index.html

Tsuru, R. (2003). Nôson ni okeru 'ie' no henyô: Nagasaki-ken ikishima no jirei kara. [Transformation of 'Ie' in a Farming Village: Based on Cases at Ikishima, Nagasaki Prefecture]. *Kibi Kokusai Daigaku Shakai Gakubu Kenkyû Kiyô, 13*, 73–88.

Watanabe, M. (2002). Kazoku nôgyô keiei ni okeru josei no katari ni miru rôdô to jendâ. [Labour and Gender Observed in Talks by Women Engaged in a Family-run Farm]. *Japanese Journal of Family Sociology, 14*(1), 21–32. doi:10.4234/jjoffamilysociology.14.21

Yamada, M. (2004). Kazoku no kojinka. [Individualization in Family]. *Shakaigaku Hyoron, 54*(4), 341–354. doi:10.4057/jsr.54.341

Yamada, M. (2005). *Meisosuru: Sengo kazoku moderu no keisei to hôkai* [Families in a Runaway World: Formation and Collapse of the Post-war Model of Family]. Tôkyô: Yuhikaku.

KEY TERMS AND DEFINITIONS

Case Study: A descriptive, exploratory or explanatory analysis of a selected case, the criteria used for selection becoming an important part of the study.

Contemporary Japan: Present Japan; contemporary history is often defined to be that part of history, which is still in living memory. For some people living memory is very short, indeed, and they certainly would restrict contemporary period to the latest developments which they still happen to remember while for many older members of our society contemporary period easily extends about 80 years back in history. In the Japanese case there are many alternatives to choose a convenient definition of "contemporary". One choice would be to use regnal periods and years *(gengô)* used in official documents in many academic studies such as Taishô, Shôwa or Heisei Period (which started respectively in 1912, 1926 and 1989 with the enthronement of new Emperors). Post-war era was once a convenient way to define "contemporary", but the longer the peace prevails the less there are people around with fresh memories of the whole period. If one decides to study, for instance, the contemporary Japanese fashion or technology it makes sense to focus on more recent developments than when studying the contemporary Japanese family institution.

"Ie": Japanese term for household. It can refer either to the physical home and family estate or, more often, to one's family lineage. The Japanese family registration law requires all families to record detailed information about all changes concerning the *ie* to official family registers *(koseki)* kept by the municipal authorities of the original physical household estate and assign one person as the household head (98 percent of household heads being currently male, the rest consisting, for instance, of families with foreign husband who is not allowed to be registered as a regular member of *ie* or have a new family register). The family register reflects the traditional thinking that the eldest son *(chônan)* inherits the family household property and is required to live with together with his parents and take care of them with his wife. The current family registration law serves to support gendered roles in Japan and is vigilantly protected especially by the conservative politicians.

Individual Freedom: Based on philosophies, such as liberalism, anarchism and existentialism, emphasizing the moral worth and independence of the individual. The liberalist political agenda introduced individual rights and freedoms to most modern societies and their legal systems and was much concerned especially with political freedom and freedom of economic transactions. Since the idea of individual freedoms is strongly based on the idea of individualism, it is always up to the individual him/herself to pursue independence and self-realization while the state and social groups should respect the individual freedoms.

Individualization: The consequence of social changes in late modernity in which individuals are increasingly required to construct their own lives.

Japanese Rural Families: Families living in non-urban areas in Japan (as defined by Japanese statistical conventions).

ENDNOTES

1 The survey was carried out on 2,000 people of 20 years and over who lived in Unnan City, Shimane Prefecture. Unnan City is designated as a hilly and mountainous area by "Basic Regulations for Vitalization of Hilly and Mountainous Areas of Shimane Prefecture." The number of valid cases was 1,079.

2 The terms we have used that have been defined by the national government of Japan include "hilly agricultural areas" (hilly towns and villages between flat and mountainous lands, with the forest ratio between 50% and 80%, and much of the cultivated area consisting of slopes) and "mountainous agricultural areas" (towns and villages with the forest ratio at 80% or above and the cultivated area ratio less than 10%), as defined in governmental statistics of agriculture and forestry.

Chapter 8

Teenage Pregnancy and its Support System in Korea:
Transition from "Abortion or Adoption" to "Childbirth and Childrearing"

Naoko Sôma
Yokohama National University, Japan

Jiyoon Park
Tôyô University, Japan

Sun-Hee Baek
Seoul Theological University, Korea

Akemi Morita
Tôyô University, Japan

ABSTRACT

While family structure continues to diversify in Korean society, society's rejection of unmarried mothers continues to be a strong obstacle. However, Korean teenage mothers increasingly are deciding to raise their own children and live their daily lives in communities that hold biases and express rejection towards them. At present, the Single-Parent Family Support Act is central to the development of support policies for unmarried mothers, but as pointed out in this study, it is important to implement detailed, individualized, comprehensive, and continual assistance, not limited to those who opt for childrearing but also towards all unmarried mothers who opt for adoption. While raising one's own child, it is important to provide long-term and continual support and support that helps the recipient foresee how she can step her way up to independence, rather than short-term and sporadic handouts.

DOI: 10.4018/978-1-4666-5031-2.ch008

1. INTRODUCTION

Aims of this Research

Viewing the international situation, in Europe and America some time has passed since the increase in teenage single mother households emerged as a social problem. Although not to the extent of Europe or America, East Asia, in particular Japan and Korea are now showing an increase in the birthrate among teenagers. Korea, even more than Japan, sees the rapid decrease in its birthrate as a critical problem, and the problems arising from "teenage pregnancies, childbirth and childrearing," have been overlooked in the countermeasures dealing with the declining birthrate. The problems of "teenage pregnancies, childbirth and childrearing," however, are involved further with issues concerning poverty among women and children, the provision of education for women extended to mothers, employment, and child development. Thus, it can be assumed that in the near future it will be increasingly necessary to develop policies to meet them.

Until recently, the major portion of cases in Korea involving pregnancies and births among unmarried mothers have been resolved by either choosing "not to give birth (abortion)" or "delivering the child but not raising it (giving the child up for adoption)." In Korean society, where enthusiasm for education is high, the stigma placed on teenagers who choose to become parents rather than live up to social expectations that assume they ought to be receiving an education is strong, more so than in Japan. Even before the option to "go the full term of pregnancy but not raise the child (choosing adoption)" was available, there was no choice except "not to give birth/unable to give birth (abortion)," and it has been pointed out that the number of teenage abortions is greater than official statistics have indicated.

While the situation in which "not to give birth/unable to give birth (abortion)" and "delivering the child but not raising it (giving the child up for adoption)" were the common choices, in recent years there is an increase in teenage parents who have chosen to "give birth and raise" their own children, leading to claims that a great change is seen in the behaviour of Korean teenagers concerning childbirth and rearing. A question can be raised as to why in recent years Korean teenage parents choosing to "give birth and raise" their own children have increased. In conjunction, one needs to ask what the primary factors in the background of this change are.

To explain the change, it becomes necessary to address the multifaceted aspects of the changes occurring around teenage parents, namely, (1) institutional changes in areas such as welfare policies, (2) change in social consciousness towards what is considered stigma, and (3) the consciousness and social relationships of the teenage parents themselves. The aim of this article is to gain an understanding of the actual conditions of teenage parents through the use of qualitative investigation, and to examine the situation brought about by institutional reforms involving teenage parents, giving special attention to the activities in private organisations that have provided major support, and the characteristics of this change involving teenage parents in recent years.

Review of the Literature Concerning Teenage Pregnancy and Parenting

Influence of Teenage Pregnancy on Social-Economic Consequences

Berthoud and Robson (2001) compared teenage pregnancies in 13 EU nations using the European Community Household Panel (ECHP). This research examined the consequences for women, who gave birth for the first time in their teens and twenties, and their families. Although variations existed between each country, they found that for all of the EU (excepting Sweden) the circumstances for women who had given birth in their teens were relatively worse in comparison to women

Table 1. Five outcomes: Teenage mothers compared with women whose first child was born in their twenties(%)

	15 to 19	20 to 29	Ratio
Less than upper secondary education	67	34	2.0
Without partner	23	19	1.2
Not working (inactive or unemployed)	59	41	1.4
Neither woman nor partner is working	26	8	3.3
Household income below bottom quintile	45	21	2.1

Source:Berthoud and Robson (2001: 4)

who had done the same in their twenties. Also, the percentage of their partners not cohabiting with them was slightly higher in their teens. The most striking difference was concerning employment, with approximately 60% of women bearing children in their teens not engaged in work, and the percentage of women who had given birth a child in their teens and their partners both being unemployed was three times higher. Furthermore, concerning education for those becoming parents in their teens, the ratio of women having secondary education or less was high, and also the poverty rate among teenage mothers was double that of mothers in their twenties (Berthoud and Robson 2001: 3-4). Poverty rate, in particular, is a generally accepted standard of evaluation that indicates the disadvantages people have, and the Netherlands scored the highest with 81% of teenage parent households living below poverty line. This was a strikingly high percentage within the EU (Berthoud and Robson 2001: 43-44). (see Table 1)

In Japan, investigation into the conditions of teenage parents is limited, but reference can be made to the Tokyo Council of Social Welfare, Division of Childcare Investigation Committee's survey made in 2002. According to the survey, fathers were absent from approximately half of the families with teenage mothers raising children, support from the child's grandparents was of great importance, and the majority of mothers were employed in unstable job conditions.

European countries have amassed quantitative investigative research on the effect of teenage pregnancies on social and economic factors. Although results differ between particular studies concerned with the influence of teenage pregnancies on income, employment, and educational achievement, they do show correlation of teenage pregnancies with educational achievement (especially secondary education) and duration of education, as well as wages and work experience. There are also studies that point to results showing a negative influence (Arai 2009: 80-83).

Increasing Research on Teenage Parenthood in Korea

Research on teenage parenthood in Korea, has been conducted by raising issues including "unmarried mothers (single mothers)," "unmarried adolescent mothers," and "unmarried student mothers." Research focusing on unmarried (single) mothers has been active since 2000, and of special note is that in the last half of the first decade the Korean government and government research institutions have been at the centre of research activity. Furthermore, this has taken concrete shape by appearing in the legislation process. Policy research concerning Korean single mothers and how it has appeared in actual legislation can be pointed to in the following four primary factors. First, there has been much effort on the part of organizations and movements concerned with single mothers to develop public discourse on the problems single mothers face. Second, there has been a shift in the social perception of single mothers. Third, policy proposals have been put forward based on investigative research of the actual conditions of these mothers by the government and government funded research institutions. And fourth, there is a rising concern shown towards the children of single mothers in relation with the problem of Korea's declining birthrate.

Of the member countries of the Organisation for Economic Co-operation and Development (OECD), the ratio of children borne by single mothers to the total number of childbirths is the lowest, and the proportion of adolescent single mothers is also not high. Therefore, the problem of adolescent single mothers had not been given a closer look. With the concern shown for single mothers, however, the media has produced dramas and documentary programmes focusing on them, and they have been receiving rising attention. Looking at recent trends in the research, there are studies concerning single mothers that take into consideration adolescent single mothers, but work is appearing that focuses solely on adolescent mothers. It can be assumed that the issues associated with adolescent mothers will again be given social attention in relation with the other problem in Korean society, which is concern for the human rights of adolescents in schools.

Adolescent Single Mothers in the Context of Research on Single Motherhood

Studies concerning the conditions of single mothers have been conducted by the following organisations and institutions: Ministry of Health and Welfare, Ministry of Gender Equality and Family, Korean Women's Development Institute (KWDI), Korea Institute for Health and Social Affairs (KIHASA). Research related to adolescent single mothers has been carried out by, Eun Hye-Mi (1999), Bae Young-Mi (2001), Do Mi-Hyang and Jeon Eun-Mi (2001), Hong Seung-Hye et al. (2007), Kim Yu-sin and Kim Eun-Yeong (2008), Jae Seok-Bong et al. (2008), concerning social perception and attitudes towards single mothers reference can be made to, Kim Hye-Young and Ahn Sang-Soo et al. (2009), Kim Hye-Young et al. (2009), and there is a study on single mothers and child rearing by Kim Yu-Gyeong et al. (2006). Other research focusing on actual policy development for single mothers can be found in Ho Nam-Sun et al. (2005), Lee Mi-Jeong et al. (2009), and Lee Mi-Jeong et al. (2010).

Because the number of adolescent single mothers is low, interest had been low. Since the year 2000, however, surveys concerning the conditions of adolescent single mothers were implemented. Two representative studies are, "A Study of Securing Rights for Adolescent Single Mothers to Receive Education" implemented by the National Human Rights Commission in 2007 (Hong Seung-Hye et al. 2007), and "Conditions of Student Single Mothers" Ministry of Education, Science, and Technology in 2008 (Jae Seok-Bong et al. 2008).

The 2009 "Study for the Social Integration of Single Mothers and Fathers" (Kim Hye-Young and Sun Bo-Young et al., 2009) marks the full-scale effort to outline ways for social integration. It was conducted with the cooperation of nationwide single mothers' facilities, and was a comprehensive investigation targeting single mothers covering the circumstances for becoming single mothers, their psychological and emotional changes, reasons for the decisions to raise or put their children up for adoption, the difficulties faced in their decision making, changes in the relationships with the unmarried fathers, and future planning and needs for supporting policies.

This investigation found that 54% of the single mothers surveyed answered they were raising their children or intended to do so; confirming that the needs for child rearing among single mothers is gradually increasing. In decreasing order, the major source of income for these women came from support received from family, social welfare facilities, government subsidies, earnings of the unmarried fathers, and the families of the unmarried fathers. The study indicated that a high percentage of these young women had experienced second or subsequent pregnancies, and a high number of these women, when asked as to their motives for entering sexual relations, answered they and their partners "loved each other," but a significant portion answered they had "not intended to / did not want to" become pregnant, emphasizing the importance of sex education. Another point that needing to be addressed is that 90% of single mothers claimed they were subjected to serious difficulties resulting from social prejudices and discrimination.

Although there are various needs for policies to assist these single mothers in achieving independence, in particular the indication is clear that needs differ depending on whether they choose to put their children up for adoption, or decide to keep their children and raise them themselves. For those choosing to keep their children the most acute problem they face is economic, and if they do not choose to rear their children the most important concern is returning to school or receiving support in finding employment. Even for single mothers choosing to raise their children, the needs demanded of policies vary according to the stages of childcare, such as postpartum care and support in taking care of a growing child. In relation to surveying single mother policy, the study also addressed the difficulties encountered by single mother facilities in accepting women and the general administration, and drew attention to problems ranging from the barriers set by the conditions placed on recipients of basic national welfare benefits, restrictions on medical services, and insufficient support for procuring housing.

It also stated that the percentage of young teenagers was increasing, but that there was a lack of support for their education. It was found that there were many cases where these young women abandoned their studies, and some were actually induced to drop out of school. In discussing these problems, the author claimed they were the reasons for these women falling into poverty and measures were necessary to alleviate the situation. While the measures proposed for adult single mothers were subsidies for living costs and childcare, assistance in finding housing, and active support for achieving independence and occupational training, in the cases of adolescent single mothers greater support was needed in overcoming emotional anxiety, academic and career counselling and offering opportunities to pursue education, along with subsidizing living and childcare costs. By focusing on single mothers, this study, along with providing an understanding of their actual situation presents fundamental data necessary for developing policies, and is significant because its perspective is to facilitate social integration of teenage parents through a systematic approach.

In 2010, the KWDI in cooperation with the Korean Unwed Mothers Support Network (KUMSN) conducted research focusing on single mothers and their childrearing and reported their findings in "Improvement of Welfare Support Services to Single Mothers and Childrearing" (Lee Mi-Jeong et al. 2010). The study introduces government related assistance services offering support for single mothers involved in childcare, such as facilities for single mothers raising children, welfare benefits, housing assistance, loans for welfare funding, financial help during childcare changeover phases, administrative assistance for single mother and father institutions, and enterprises involved in helping adolescent single parents achieve independence, along with describing the experiences of single mothers and their childrearing who receive these government assisted services. This 2010 survey introduces the recent data concerning living conditions of single mothers and their childrearing, and offers focused analysis of their income levels and expenses, provision of financial support available before and after giving birth, and the childcare responsibilities of unmarried fathers.

Based on this survey, it proposes the following criteria for policy creation to help single mothers involved in childrearing to achieve independence. They are: (1) the necessity for separate policies that address the different needs of teenage and adult single mothers, (2) prohibit discriminatory practices towards single mothers in workplaces, (3) install active support measures to vitalize self-help groups for single mothers raising children, (4) improvement of services offered at mother-child facilities (single mothers' facilities), (5) improvement of human care services by social welfare civil servants, (6) expansion of mother-child protection facilities (mother and child nurseries) with new structural models, (7) placing stronger emphasis on the responsibilities of unmarried fathers, (8) raising childcare subsidies to 100 thousand won (KRW), and (9) collecting statistical data concerning single mothers raising children. Concerning teenage single mothers in particular, it claims that "teenage and adult single mothers should not be considered a group sharing the same characteristics, because there are great differences between them in regards to the understanding of childrearing, institutional dependence, and educational and employment background." Policies for adult single mothers should be oriented towards rehabilitating careers interrupted by social prejudice, and providing infant childcare support. In contrast, it proposes that policies for teenage single mothers should be more focused on assistance for continued education, sex education, and offering counselling for planning and attaining lifetime goals. Despite claims made by part of the media that the percentage of teenage single mothers is increasing, the study could not verify the claim as fact, but the reason it gives for such a claim to be made was most likely due to the fact that social discourse concerning teenage single mothers had grown and media coverage had become more frequent, leading to a greater consciousness of this controversial problem.

Research Concerning Adolescent Single Mothers

The 2007 study of adolescent single mothers surveyed 63 adolescent mothers and people related to them (Hong Seung-Hye et al., 2007). Some of the major results of the study are as follows. After these adolescents became pregnant, many gave as the reason for deciding for themselves to discontinue their education to be a fear of having others find out, and some stated they had been pressured to drop out of school. The fact that these mothers had been induced to leave school is claimed by the study to be a problem infringing on an individual's right to education and a violation of human rights. After giving birth, these adolescents did express their desire to recontinue their education with answers, in order of frequency, such as "wanting to graduate from high school," "because of social bias placing high value on educational background," "wanting to study," and "for a better future." The study's report made it clear that the survey results pointed to the need for implementing a wider variety of educational structuring in order for these girls to continue their education, find solutions to financial problems and child rearing, and transformation of negative social attitudes. This report concludes with proposals to enable adolescent single mothers to continue their education while raising their children by assisting them with living costs, childcare subsidies, nursery and school tuition, and establish a support system coordinating the various resources of social communities that would include twenty-four hour childcare facilities.

The 2008 study by the Ministry of Education, Science, and Technology, "Conditions of Student Single Mothers" (Jae Seok-Bong et al. 2008) is a survey of sociopsychological, economic, educational, and welfare needs of adult and student single mothers entered into the care of single mother facilities. It also implemented a study of social attitudes towards student single mothers by surveying members of their peer group, parental

Table 2. Educational welfare measures for student single mothers

Areas		Short Term Measures	Long Term Measures
Schools	Prevention	Prevent school dropout, realize sex education, vitalize peer-to-peer advising activity, create school atmosphere for healthy male-female relations, incorporate instruction for guardians on juvenile sex education.	Reinforce human rights and gender equality education, reinforce birth control education, continued effort preventing harmful elements for juveniles entering school surroundings
Schools	Solutions	Counselling for student single mothers, counselling for guardians of student single mothers, report exact situation of incidents of female student pregnancies (student mothers), remove disadvantages for student single mothers.	Establish American 4T type schools, implement hospital facilities in schools, "Wee Project" (creation of school safety network)
Communities	Prevention	Change attitudes towards student single mothers, host abortion prevention campaigns.	Healthy thought on sex promoted in community centres develop guardian education programmes for the effective instruction of children.
Communities	Solutions	Mobilize CYS-Net (community juvenile integration support group system), programmes to enhance self-respect of student single mothers, offer customized programmes assisting achievement of independence.	Mentoring systems for women university students, enactment of bylaws for single mothers, increase of single mother facilities (group homes), support for single mother families.
National Government	Prevention	Install a publicity ambassador to promote student single mother prevention, utilize mass media (TV, Press, Internet)	Develop effective birth control and sex education programmes, develop marriage preparation programmes (MPP) for proper intimate relations, develop programmes for guardian instruction to promote healthy family relations and family life.
National Government	Solutions	Implement tutoring system to dispatch teachers to single mother facilities, utilize community education and welfare related centres, establish alternative models for education, provide support for educational needs of student single mothers, deregulate restrictions enabling student single mothers to transfer to correspondence high schools, include legislation for student single mothers in education welfare enactment regulations.	Legislate a single body of law for single mothers, enact regulations concerning responsibilities of unmarried fathers, accredit home schooling for single mothers living at home.

Source: Jae Seok-Bong et al. (2008)

guardians, and teachers. The result of the study revealed that in many cases the pregnancy was not reported to the respective schools, and responses included complaints concerning negative social attitudes experienced after adolescents became pregnant, the necessity for crisis counselling, and fears regarding discontinuing education. These adolescents expressed their great need for education, but stated that there were obstructions to re-entering school or transferring to another school, and difficulties faced by the loss of confidence in their ability to study after having to stop attending school. The expectations held toward government support voiced by school age single mothers were, "financial support in order to accomplish educational goals and raise children," "measures to continue education," and "efforts to resolve social prejudice towards single mothers." Another aspect clarified by the study concerned the reasons student single mothers gave for their sexual relations. Compared to past studies that indicated sexual relations were spontaneous, many of the answers obtained by those interviewed indicated that their sexual relationships were entered into "naturally because of a love-based relation," indicating a change in the nature of intimate relationships. The outcome of the above mentioned relationships can be supported by the fact that many cases involved unmarried fathers who were friends of the girls. Although the percentage of single mothers who had received sex education was high, they did express dissatisfaction with its content. Responses of the unmarried fathers after being confronted with the reality of pregnancy showed the largest number suggesting the child be given up for adoption after birth, followed by many indicating a desire to raise the child together with the mother after birth, and only a low percentage expressed their desire to break off relations because of the pregnancy. Based on the results attained from the survey on the conditions of single mothers, the report proposes the following policy measures. These proposals, presented in Table 2, call for very concrete measures.

In the background of this increased effort to research and develop policies for single mothers is the situation created by a decreasing birthrate in Korea. Found in many of the recent studies on single motherhood is the importance of placing relevance on policy measures implemented for a society faced with a declining birthrate and single mother support.

For example, the authors of a recent study (Kim Hye-Young et al, 2009) stressed "regardless of the situation and the decisions that need to be made, the next generation is a valuable resource for Korean society, and from this perspective a decision to bestow proper recognition of a birth, or to deny a child its birth and nurturing on grounds of legal authority based on whether a parent has a spouse or not, is an attitude concerned only with supply and demand that refuses to accept the changes in the Korean social environment such as a decreasing birthrate."

The Ministry of Health and Welfare and Korea Institute for Health and Social Affairs (KIHASA) together published a 2010 policy paper on "Critical Issues for Research Promoted in the Next Five Years on Low Birthrate and Aging Society," and it contains measures for single mothers (Lee Sam-Sik et al, 2010). As part of its major policy commitment, the following proposals should be noted. (1) If it is necessary for a single mother to receive special care concerning room and board, she is to be provided this through a group home (single mother and child in a communal household) for two years (with a possible extension for a period of no more than one year) at no cost for accommodation, and which is also provided with employment, childcare, human development education, and counselling and guidance services. (2) For single mothers and fathers not staying in a facility and living in a local community, in 2009 the government, through single mother and father support centres, started to provide educational instruction on pre- and post-natal health management, financial and legal knowledge, and preparation for achieving independence, and also defrayment of medical costs generated from emergencies during childbirth and rearing, provision of daily necessities, and services supervised through self-help groups in building networks and information access. (3) For adolescent single mothers and fathers and single parents, the Ministry of Gender Equality and Family announced in 2010 its intention to set in motion a "Support Project for Adolescent Single Parents Seeking Independence." This means policies for single mothers in Korea can be categorized in three domains, namely, care for single mothers in facilities, support for single mothers and fathers living on their own, and support given to adolescent single mothers and fathers, and we can confirm here that the latter, support for adolescent parents, has found sound grounding in mainstream policies.

In local governments, also, concern has risen for single mothers and investigation into their conditions and policy development studies has been undertaken. As an example, in Gyeonggi Province one can see how the initial investigative studies on conditions have led up to actual policy making. In 2010, the Gyeonggi-do Family and Women's Research Institute conducted a survey study of resident single mothers raising children in Gyeonggi-do (Soh Hye-Jung et al. 2010) and it has made policy proposals based on the findings (Soh Hye-Jung 2011). Although the survey lacks an actual concrete investigation of adolescent single mothers, it did point out that adolescent single parents are also "faced with the difficulties

Table 3. Gyeonggi Province support for adolescent single parent independence (Dec. 2010)

Support Type	Below 100% of Minimum Living Costs (1)	Below 150% of Minimum Living Costs	2010 Budget
Adolescent single parent independence	For 300 single adolescent parents under 25 years of age *Designated alternative educational institute: Instruction fees, class tuition support *Education and training for employment		46 million won (100% coverage by Province)
Living/Childcare expenses	Eligible for national basic livelihood assistance	*Childcare expenses 100,000 won/month (Low income single parent family 50,000 won/month +Added support 50,000 won/month) *Child medical fees 24,000 won/month (Medical insurance or bank deposit)	Childcare cost: 370 million won Child medical expenses: 161 million won
Skill development	Support for certification exams (for high school or lower level dropouts): Deposited to institute account directly.		1,961 million won
Household account for asset formation (2)	Household asset support (50,000 won/month limit)	Household Asset Support (200,000 won/month limit)	1,535 million won

If paternity and family tests are desired, support is provided (400,000wonper household)
Notes:(1) For household of 2, minimum living cost is 858,747 won (100%), 1,288,120 won (150%)
(2) Household Asset building support is provided for those registered in 2010.
Source: Soh Hye-Jung (2011: 6)

experienced by adult single parents who suffer from poverty and childcare and are burdened with housework, along with interruption of their education, inadequate occupational training leading to a lack of capability to achieve independence" (Soh Hye-Jung 2011). Gyeonggi Province is promoting measures to assist adolescent single parents to achieve independence by implementing family-friendly policies that favor adolescent single parents who do not abandon efforts to raise their children or put their children up for adoption in order to facilitate the creation of home environments suitable for childcare. Table 3 shows the content of these policies, but it should be noted that not only are young single parents under the age of 25 provided with alternative school education and occupational instruction and training, they are also given assistance with childcare and medical costs, certification examinations, and monetary help to open a household account for asset formation. Along with educational efforts that meet the character of problems faced by teenage single mothers, great emphasis is placed on the point of investing in the future.

The research led by the KWDI in the last half of the 2000s has been greatly influenced by the KUMSN (http://www.kumsn.org). This organisation was established in 2007 by Dr. Richard Boas, and opened its Korean office in 2008. Since then it has helped support research by KWDI. KUMSN together with KWDI has given direct and indirect support to studies, such as the "Korean Public Opinion Survey on Unwed Mothers and Their Children" (2009), "Reviewing Issues on Unwed Mothers' Welfare in Korea" (2009), "Improving Attitudes towards Unwed Mothers and Promoting Support" (2009) and "How to Improve Government Welfare Services for Low-Income Unwed Mothers in Korea" (2010). In addition, it independently prepares its own material and devotes much effort to improving social consciousness. It is activities such as these that are influential in generating the present research.

Gyeonggi Province[1] and Seoul have also enacted student rights bylaws that include the assurance of the right to education for pregnant adolescents, and it is most likely that in the near future issues surrounding single mothers will enter the dimension of education and once again become a point of social controversy. (see Table 4)

Definitions of Concepts Concerning Teenage Parents

Problems concerning Korean teenage parents have the characteristic of being formulated within the larger conception of "unmarried mothers." In Korea, a "teenage parent" refers to both families with parents who become pregnant, give birth and are rearing children while they are still in their teens, and unmarried mothers who are teenagers. However, in this case as well, the age category of "unmarried teenage mothers" differs according to the focus of particular investigative studies. Studies conducted by Jae Seok-Bong et al. (2008), focus on "unmarried student mothers" and they fall within the age group of girls over 13 to under 18, and in comparison by KWDI includes all "under 24" in its studies. Research concerns focus much more on unmarried teenage mothers in comparison to teenage parent families.

The concept of "unwed" or "unmarried" mothers has been defined according to the various perspectives found in specific historical and social situations. In Korea, the meaning of "unmarried mother" is a woman who either becomes pregnant or gives birth when not legally married and is raising her child after childbirth (Single-Parent Family Support Act Article 4 Section 1, South Gyeongsang Provincial Bylaw for Unwed Mother Support Article 4, Jae Seok-Bong et al., 2008: 37). Understood in its broadest meaning, "unmarried" includes the state of premarital pregnancy and/or childbirth, induced abortions and separation, divorce, having a child by someone unrelated to a deceased spouse (Ministry of Health, Welfare 1999), but a pregnant woman not going through with childbirth is excluded from this category. Therefore, in Korea it is very difficult to determine the percentage of unmarried pregnancies or the total number of mothers of unmarried mothers groups (Kim Hye-Young et al. 2009: iv).

Also, there are the concepts "unmarried student mother" and "unmarried adolescent mother." Jae Seok-Bong et al. (2008) defines "unmarried student mother" as legally being unmarried at the time of pregnancy or childbirth and being a student over the age of 13 and under 18. In this case, to the category of "unmarried mother" the criteria of adolescence and being a student are added. In the case of KWDI research, age divisions are drawn at "under 19," "ages 20-24," "ages 25-29" and "over 30," and based on the Youth Basic Law that defines an adolescent as a person between the ages of 9 to 24, "unmarried adolescent mothers" are women under the age of 24 (Kim Hye-Yeon et al. 2009: 38).

In Korea, age distinctions vary accordingly to different laws, in the Youth Basic Law adolescents are defined as being over the age of 9 and under 24; the Juvenile Sexual Protection Law includes all male and females under the age of 19; Juvenile Law considers anyone under the age of 19 as a child; and the Child Welfare Act defines the child as anyone under the age of 18. Recently, the Ministry of Health and Welfare is in the process of integrating child welfare and adolescent welfare, and the Reform Proposal for the Child Welfare Act, which lays the basis for the preparation of the integration, defines an adolescent as being over the age of 13 and under the age of 18 (Jae Seok-Bong et al., 2008: 39).

Table 4. Policies for the support of Korean adolescent single mothers (As of 2011)

Project Title	Content and Type of Support
Initial crisis support	*At the time of childbirth, during the period of rearing or when emergencies arise, hospital expenses for childbirth, medical fees for the child, necessary everyday expenses for milk, nappies, etc. *Mental support provided by counselling to single mothers and fathers. *Self-help groups, education, and cultural experience programmes.
Support for low income single parent and child to receive child financial support from father	*Support for legal action claims in obtaining paternity recognition of the child from unmarried father, free legal aid, and paternity test fees. *Support to receive financial support for childrearing
Child *dolbomi* (baby and child sitting) support	*Child *dolbomi*offers temporary baby and child sitting and nursing services while parent needs to leave home, after daytime nursery, play activities, etc. *School *dolbomi*offers learning instruction for schoolchildren including after school assistance, checking homework, preparation and review of schoolwork, help prepare things needed at school, etc. *Facility dispatch *dolbomi*assists in the safety of children looked after in groups at community centres.
Dream start	*Family support. Eligible age from 0 to 12 for children and families in the low income group, recipient families of basic welfare and next level have priority.
Adolescent single parent certification training expenses	*1.54 million won support per household (Training institution registration fees and study material expenses)
High school education support for adolescent single parents	*High school education support for a high school student single parent in selected adolescent single parents as a target of the independence support (single parent under the age of 25), actual school tuition is defrayed.
Child school tuition support	*Free schooling for children under 5 years, exemption of all school fees *Schooling fee support for children ages 3 to 4according to income levels *Support for day school expenses
Loans for low income single parents	*Maximum amount of loan per person: Housing loan (50 million won), Uninsured loan (12 million won), Insured loan 20 million won. *Fixed annual interest 3% *5 years amortization
Single-mother, single-father household health insurance support	*Local resident household registrants receive 10 to 30% deduction from monthly health care insurance payments according to levels of additional income and equity.
Infant medical check-up	*Monthly check-ups (vision and hearing included) and treatment, group health examinations (height, weight, skull size, etc.), Type 2 to 3 health education and development evaluation and counselling (4th month not included) *Reduced fees for mother and foetus health examination and sonic examination to insure safe childbirth, and services to prepare environment for smooth delivery.
Medical provisions recuperation expenses	*Type 1 and Type 2 recipients *Illness, accident, childbirth, etc. medical coverage.
Medical provision pre-delivery examination fee support	*Eligible medical provision recipients who have had pregnancy confirmed. *All Type 1 and Type 2 recipients eligible for 200,000 won *From the day following registration at city, county, and ward offices until 15 days after delivery due date.
Low income single parent family housing support	*Local governments set aside public housing under their jurisdiction in accordance to zoning criteria, and give priority to low income single parent families to rent.

Source: Ministry of Gender Equality and Family Website "withmom"
http://withmom.mogef.go.kr/supportpolicies/singleParentFamily.do(2012/04/26)

Table 5. Number of deliveries by age (number(%))

Age	2002	2003	2004	2005	2006	2007
19	2,911 (0.63)	2,277 (0.48)	2,034 (0.44)	1,622 (0.38)	1,444 (0.33)	2,336 (0.49)
19~24	38,266 (8.28)	33,932 (7.2)	30,315 (6.59)	24,193 (5.69)	21,299 (4.87)	26,152 (5.45)
25~29	201,106(43.54)	195,189(41.4)	176,660(38.41)	155,002(36.46)	151,888(34.75)	166,129(34.61)
30~34	175,651(38.03)	188,945(40.07)	193,733(42.12)	183,700(43.21)	192,199(43.97)	212,730(44.32)
35~39	36,011 (7.8)	39,618 (8.4)	43,581(9.47)	46,029(10.83)	53,147(12.16)	65,091(13.56)
40~44	5,551 (1.2)	5,634 (1.19)	5,648 (1.23)	5,714 (1.34)	6,019 (1.38)	7,224 (1.51)
Over 45	253 (0.05)	279 (0.06)	280 (0.06)	275 (0.06)	277 (0.06)	301 (0.06)
Others	2,179 (0.47)	5,612 (1.19)	7,734 (1.68)	8,646 (2.03)	10,823(2.48)	2 (0)
A:total number of delivery	461,928 (100)	471,486 (100)	459,985 (100)	425,181 (100)	437,096 (100)	479,965 (100)
B:total number of baby	492,111	490,543	472,761	435,031	448,153	493,189
B-A	30,183	19,057	12,776	9,850	11,057	13,224

Source: Lee Mi-Jeong et al. (2009: 85)

Table 6. Birth rate of two age groups (per 1,000) and total fertility rate

	1996	2000	2005	2006	2007	2008
Birth Rate of 15~19 (age)	3.3	2.5	2.1	2.2	2.2	1.7
Birth Rate of 20~24 (age)	58.8	38.8	17.8	17.6	19.5	18.2
Total Fertility Rate	1.58	1.47	1.08	1.12	1.25	1.19

Source: Ministry of Health, Welfare and Family Affairs (2009)

2. STATISTICS CONCERNING THE CONDITIONS OF TEENAGE PARENTS

Number of Deliveries

The question is how many teenage parents are there? First let us have a look at the number of deliveries and percentages of childbirths according to age. In 2007, there were 2,336 deliveries by women under the age of 19, and between the ages of 19 to 29 there were 26,152 (Table 5). The percentages of childbirths (per thousand people) show a significant change from the year 1996 and 2007. The childbirth among teenagers fell from 3.3 to 1.7, and in the early 20s the percentage fell from 58.8 to 18.2, revealing a severe decline in the birthrate (Table 6).

The Situation Understood through Data Collected from Welfare Facilities

Concerning unmarried mothers, it is possible to grasp their numbers by the number of children placed with adopting families recorded by domestic adoption organisations, or studies on the administrations of nationwide unmarried mothers' facilities and the records of women entering and leaving. There are limitations to the above method of data collection, because these only include the situations of unmarried mothers' facility administrations receiving government support. In fact, the "White Paper on Health, Welfare and Family Affairs," prepared by the Ministry of Health, Welfare and Family Affairs, reports a total of 25 unmarried mothers' facilities in the entire nation, but according to the "Survey of Unmarried Student Mothers" (Jae Seok-Bong et al., 2008), it is claimed that there are 46, and included in this number are group homes (communal facilities for unmarried mothers and children) or facilities that are not under government supervision, such as *shintô* that are run independently (most are managed by religious groups).

In order to understand the situation by examining facilities, it is possible to (1) study the records produced by domestic adoption organisations concerning the number of unmarried mothers by looking at the number of children adopted, and (2) referring to the administrative studies of unmarried mothers' facilities and noting the number of women entering and leaving, but there is a limit to this because it is only possible to grasp the administrative situation in government-supported unmarried mothers' facilities.

According to the recent sample survey of 2009, which was done to 43 unmarried mothers' facilities in Korea and to receive answers from 571 unmarried mothers, the percentage of unmarried teenage mothers *of all unmarried mothers in welfare facilities* is 30.6%. Their education level is that the percentage of junior high school graduates is 25.7% and that of high school students including those who withdraw from school temporarily and drop out is 52.6%. Regarding their plan of childrearing, the percentage of those who plan to choose adoption is 50.3%, that of those who *want to* keep their baby is 22.6%, and that of those who are keeping their child is 27.0% (Kim Hye-Young and Sun Bo-Young et al., 2009: 39, 41, 51).

3. KOREAN "ADOLESCENT SINGLE PARENT" RECOGNITION IN POLICY OBJECTIVES AND ITS FACTORS

Development of "Single Parent Family Support" in Family Policy

Korean single parent family support has been developed along the axis of the Single-Parent Family Support Act (the equivalent of Japan's Mother and Child and Widows Welfare Act) and the National Basic Living Security Act (equivalent to Japan's Livelihood Protection Act).

In terms of financial subsidies, childcare support similar to the child allowance in Japan is distributed according to the regulations set by the Single-Parent Family Support Act. Central to economic support is (1) nursery school tuition support (Infant Nursery Act and Early Childhood Education Promotion Act), (2) childrearing cost support, (3) living cost support, and (4) housing cost support, (Single-Parent Family Support Act, National Basic Living Security Act). Social services offered include, (1) single parent family welfare facilities (single mother and childcare facilities), (2) counselling (single parent family support centre, or healthy family support centre), (3) occupational training, and (4) legal advice and support in procuring child support costs from former spouses (Single-Parent Family Support Act, National Basic Living Security Act).

Present Situation of "Adolescent Single Parents" as a Sub-Category of Support

The Single Parent Family Support Act was enacted on January 18, 2008. Its purpose is defined in Article 1 as, "to contribute to the stabilization of living and to the promotion of welfare of single-parent families by supporting them to lead a healthy and civilized life." "The state and local governments shall take the responsibility of promoting welfare of single-parent families"

(Article 2 Section 1), and "[a]ll the nationals shall cooperate in promoting welfare of single-parent families" (Section 2). Furthermore, it clarifies that "[t]he mother and child or the father and child of a single-parent family shall endeavor to achieve self-support and elevate the standard of living by making the most of their asset, work capability, etc." (Article 3).

Also in 2008, the eligibility of recipients of single parent family childcare cost assistance was expanded to include children under the age of eight, and with the restructuring of government organisations, single parent family welfare services were transferred from the Ministry of Gender Equality and Family to the Ministry of Health and Welfare.

Furthermore, in 2009 eligibility of recipients of single parent family childcare cost assistance was expanded to include children under age ten, and coordinating organisations to administer support for unmarried mothers, fathers and their children were opened in six locations.

From 2010, the term "adolescent single parent" became a clearly defined policy category and was institutionalized. In the same year eligibility of recipients of single parent family childcare cost assistance was expanded to include children under age twelve. Also, with the reform of the Single-Parent Family Support Act enactment regulations, among the single parent family welfare facilities, the period for protective residence in group homes was extended (from 1 year to 2 years), and in the temporary care facilities the residence period was similarly extended (from 3 months to 6 months). At the same time, during government restructuring single parent family welfare services were transferred from the Ministry of Health, Welfare and Family Affairs to the Ministry of Gender Equality and Family. This ushered in further expansion of government enterprises, such as support for achieving independence among adolescent single parents initiated (April), childcare support and independence assistance for adolescent single parents under the age of 25 (for those receiving the minimum living cost of 150%), childcare and medical financial assistance, tuition grants for certificate study and examinations, monetary help to open a household account for asset formation, the construction of a computerized system for supporting adolescent single parents to achieve independence, surveys for determining the situation of childcare by unmarried mothers and their independence, homepage construction for the support of unmarried mothers, and the implementation of services to improve social awareness towards unmarried mothers (oriented towards local government employees).

In 2011, expansion of support for adolescent single parents in achieving independence was seen. Adjustments were made to the ceiling for childcare costs (100,000 won to 150,000 won per month), and high school tuition cost defrayment and independence incentive benefits (at 100,000 won per month) were newly implemented (child medical expense defrayment and the new account establishment for asset formation was discontinued). (see Table 7)

Looking at the number of single parent family welfare facilities, a change is observed with the increase of unmarried mother-child facilities and unmarried mother-child group homes (see Tables 8 and 9).

Recognition of "Adolescent Single Parents" as Policy Objectives and Rapid Institutional Development in Korea

Seen historically, Korea's institutional development related to single parents can be divided into the three consecutive stages summarized below. The first stage corresponds to the period from the end of WWII until the 1990s. During this time a woman who had missed her chance for an abortion entered a facility outside of her home region where she would give birth, but had no other option but to give the child up for adoption. It was also the time when government policies

Table 7. Adolescent single parent support program

Category	2010	2011 Revision Proposal
Adolescent single parent childcare subsidy	(Revision) *Application 15 days or earlier: 100% *Application 15 days or later: 50% (To existing low income family childcare recipient of 50,000 won, additional 50,000 won/month provided)	*Regardless of application date full subsidy for that month is paid *Monthly subsidy: 150,000 won (To existing low income family childcare recipient of 50,000 won, additional 100,000 won/month provided)
Adolescent single parent childcare support (discontinued)	(Newly implemented)	* Full monthly amount is paid to recipient for the month support is discontinued.
Adolescent single parent independence incentive	(Newly implemented)	*Adolescent single parent receiving national public livelihood assistance eligible for 10,000 won/month conditional to active efforts to gain independence.
Child medical coverage	(Revision) *Application 15 days or earlier: 100% *Application 15 days or later: 50%	Support discontinued
Adolescent single parent asset formation account support	(Revision)	*Only adolescent single parent families that applied in 2010 received support for deposits. *From 2011 no applicants accepted.
Adolescent single parent certificate instruction tuition	(Revision) *Annual support ceiling of 1,155,000 won	*Annual support ceiling of 1,540,000 won
Adolescent single parent high school tuition	(Newly implemented)	*Support for low income (150% below minimum cost of living) adolescent single parent (recipient of public livelihood assistance ineligible)
Adolescent single parent household designation	(Revision) *A three generation household is designated as an adolescent single parent household if the grandchild's single parent is under 25 yrs.	Removed
Age eligibility for adolescent single parent support	(Revision) *Support started from 1985	*Support started from 1986
Response to unlawful receipt of adolescent single parent childcare and other support	(Revision) *Violating recipient is required to return total or part of amount from the month payments were started.	*If unlawful receipt and violator's designation is higher than eligibility, all support is discontinued from the month of violation. *If adolescent single parent, eligibility is maintained and receives amount of readjusted support.

Source:Ministry of Gender Equality and Family(2011: 5)

were aimed at curbing the population, and was promoting overseas adoptions.

The second stage lasted until the latter half of the 2000s. The decline in birthrate progressed, and as Korea's economic power increased it became one of the developed nations in Asia. The government's adoption policies received criticism internally as an "overseas adoption superpower." At this time, solidarity grew among the concerned parties (the establishment of KUMSN) and the awareness of the mothers themselves was seen to change gradually. Support efforts in the private sector grew, and it was at this time that institutional formation needed to spur the country towards becoming a welfare state started to take shape. As already mentioned above, around 2009

Table 8. The number of welfare facilities for single parents by year

	2004	2005	2006	2007	2008	2009	2010
total	79	85	95	100	107	118	121
Mother-child support facility	40	40	41	41	41	41	41
Father-child support facility	-	-	-	1	1	1	1
Mother-child self-reliance support facilities	4	4	4	4	3	3	3
Mother-child temporary support facility	14	14	14	14	14	16	15
Unmarried mother-child facilities	12	18	20	25	27	32	32
Unmarried mother-child group home	9	9	16	15	19	23	24
Unmarried mother group home	-	-	-	-	2	1	1
Mother-child group home	-	-	-	-	-	1	2
Father-child group home	-	-	-	-	-	-	2

Source:Ministry of Gender Equality and Family(2011: 15)

studies related to the conditions of single parents increased, indicating the rising social awareness of the problems.

The third stage began in 2010 with the categorization of "adolescent single parents" as a policy target, and given special provision as recipients needing to be supported. "Single parents" themselves have increasingly become part of welfare policy and as a sub-category of "single parents" concrete objectification of "adolescent single parents" is now a reality. Networks of the persons concerned have gained solidarity with private organisations involved with assistant activities and concrete welfare practices have grown increasingly deeper roots in local communities. These movements provided the impetus for national institutional expansion. In particular, for "adolescent single parents" the issues are not simply to achieve independence through employment, but are seeking better forms of support based on the perspective for "a guarantee of rights to receive education."

4. TEENAGE PARENTS AND ANALYSIS OF THE ACTUALITIES OF SUPPORT PRACTICE: FROM THE SURVEY INTERVIEWS

According to what factors do "adolescent single parents" opt for and make a decision on adoption or raising the child by themselves? What kinds of support and social relations exist in the background to this? In this section, we will shed light on the realities of adolescent single parents and the actualities of support based on a qualitative survey.

Survey Method

A total of 12 adolescent single parents were interviewed in 2009 and 2011. In the first survey (hereafter known as the "2009 survey") separate interviews with a total of nine mother-child households living in Seoul were conducted between August 10 and 17, 2009. The nine persons interviewed in the 2009 survey consisted of 1) one mother still pregnant at the time of the interview and three mothers who had already given birth, all four being interviewed at the "A unmarried mothers' facility" in A City, 2) one mother residing at

Table 9. Welfare facilities for single parents(December 31, 2010)

	Number	Resident eligibility	Support period (extendible period)	Admission capacity(households)
Mother-child support facility (母子保護施設)	41	Low income single mother raising child under 18 years, without housing.	Three years (Two years)	1,052
Father-child support facility (父子保護施設)	1	Low income single father raising child under 18 years, without housing.	Three years (Two years)	20
Mother-child self-reliance support facilities (母子自立施設)	3	Low income single mother raising child under 18 years, without housing, who has left single mother care facility and is preparing to establish an independent single mother household.	Three years (Two years)	41
Mother-child temporary support facility (母子一時保護施設)	15	For mothers and children who are victims of a spouse's violence and who face risk to proper childrearing and harm to mother.	Six months (Six months)	460
Unmarried mother-child facilities (未婚母子施設)	32	For pregnant unmarried women and for mothers 6 months after childbirth who are in need of protective support.	One year (Six months)	767
Unmarried mother-child group home (未婚母子共同生活家庭)	24	Unmarried mother raising infant under 2 years in need of protective support.	Two years (One year)	205
Unmarried mother group home (未婚母共同生活家庭)	1	Unmarried mother not rearing child after childbirth in need of protective support.	Two years (Six months)	10
Mother-child group home (母子共同生活家庭)	2	Single mother family unable to live self-sufficiently, to prepare for independence through temporary group living and homemaking.	Two years (One year)	40
Father-child group home (父子共同生活家庭)	2	Single father family unable to live self-sufficiently, to prepare for independence through temporary group living and homemaking.	Two years (One year)	15

Source: Ministry of Gender Equality and Family(2011: 15)

Table 10. Subjects by adoption or raising the child (Our 2009 Survey)

Subjects Opting for Adoption	Subjects Opting for Raising by Themselves
Ms. A: 15 years (14 years at time of birth) Gave birth at an unmarried mothers' facility No contact with the child's father In preparation to undergo screening for independence Family of origin nonexistent due to death of parents Due to leave facility after passing screening	Ms. D: 18 years (17 years at time of birth) Gave birth at an unmarried mothers' facility No contact with the child's father No particular plans for the future Has the understanding of family of origin (mother) Determined to raise child but situation is unstable
Ms. B: 17 years (17 years at time of birth) Planned to give birth at an unmarried mothers' facility No contact with the child's father Decided to opt for adoption at birth Family of origin are opposed to upbringing Will return to her family after giving birth	Ms. E: 18 years (17 years at time of birth) Gave birth at an unmarried mothers' facility Has contact with (and the understanding of) the child's father Now preparing for qualification as an assistant nurse No contact with family of origin (left home when becoming pregnant) Wishes to make use of the group home due to economic reasons
Ms. C: 24 years (18 years at time of birth) Gave birth at an unmarried mothers' facility No contact with the child's father Was hesitant, but opted for adoption Is in contact with the family of origin Later married, gave birth and is now raising the child. Wishes to meet the child that was adopted	Ms. F: 23 years (20 years at time of birth) Gave birth at a regional unmarried mothers' facility No contact with the child's father Made use of the group home Lives in a rented room Refuses contact with the family of origin Now preparing for qualification as an assistant nurse Uses a kindergarten Is now applying for public livelihood assistance
	Ms. G: 24 years (21 years at time of birth) Gave birth at an unmarried mothers' facility Child's father now on military service (frequent contact) Made use of the group home Now residing with the child at a mother-child facility Family of origin give mental support Now preparing for qualification as an assistant nurse Will receive public livelihood assistance Uses a kindergarten
	Ms. H: 23 years (22 years at time of birth) Gave birth at an unmarried mothers' facility No contact with the child's father Now living at the group home Preparing for independence through qualifications, etc. Has the understanding of the family of origin Is receiving public livelihood assistance Is worried about housing after leaving the group home
	Ms. I: 20 years (19 years at the time of birth) Gave birth at an unmarried mothers' facility No contact with the child's father Family of origin (mother) is cooperative Is living at an group home Feels social prejudice Now applying to live at a mother-child facility

Source: Author's data.

an "intermediary home (group home)" operated by the same organisation that runs the "A unmarried mothers' facility," 3) one mother residing at an "group home" operated by a different organisation, 4) two mothers living in communities after having given birth in a facility, and 5) one mother who had given birth at the "B unmarried mothers' facility" in A City (Table 10).

The second survey (hereafter known as the "2011 survey") was carried out on May 7 and July 29, 2011. Interviews were conducted with two mothers who had already given birth at the "A unmarried mothers' facility," and two mothers (of which one was a continuing subject who had been interviewed in August 2009) who were residing at the "group home" and preparing to live independently after opting to raise their children by themselves (Table 11).

Support System at the A Unmarried Mothers' Facility

Of the unmarried mother-child facilities in Korea, 66.7% are religion-affiliated (Jae Seok-Bong et al. 2008). An unmarried mothers' facility (the "A unmarried mothers' facility") operated by a "religion-affiliated management organisation," the most common management form in Korea, was selected for this survey.

The purpose of the "A unmarried mothers' facility" is to provide medical, educational, consultation and other welfare services in accordance with the needs of the users (mothers), who are placed in a position of social exclusion and experience difficulties due to an unwanted pregnancy. In addition, services such as employment after leaving the facility, study, support for independence and education are also provided through the operation of an "group home" in which mothers who opt for raising the child can achieve independence.

Since the facility is located close to A Station, it is easy for people from the regions to use. As the operating organisation has also had roots in this area for many years, it is assumed that the facility has good links with the community. From the viewpoint of the form of management, the support whereby a mother can move to a "group home" from an "unmarried mother-child facility" run by a private entity is the most common form of management for unmarried mothers' facilities in Korea, and therefore gives us a good overview of the activities of unmarried mothers' support facilities in the whole country. As a policy of the management of the facility, the adoption system and the childrearing system are both explained on entering the facility. In recent years, emphasis is being placed on providing services to aid the unmarried mother and her child to achieve social independence, thus implementing model services for the future.

Overview of the Facility

The facility was established to provide social protection and support services to women in need of protection. It was approved as a women's welfare facility in 1950s to provide a rest home for unmarried mothers concerned about the negative perceptions and prejudice of society before and after childbirth, as well as the necessary medical services for childbirth. In addition, through diverse consultation programmes including technical education, liberal arts education and emotional education, the facility also has the purpose of achieving full reintegration with society by regaining psychological peace of mind, seeking the causes of becoming an unmarried mother and preventative education.

Organization of the Facility

Unmarried mother-child facility is for support when childbirth by unmarried mothers; mothers who have not submitted a notification of marriage. Use of the facility is for one year, which may be extended for a further six months. Many users live in the facility up to about 100 days following childbirth, after which this may be extended according to the wishes of the user herself. However, with regard to a mother and child in compelling circumstances, a further extension is possible on the judgement of the facility, and the provision of welfare services that only privately-operated facilities can provide is also possible.

Table 11. Subjects who opted for raising the child (Our 2011 Survey)

[1] Continuing survey subject from the 2009 survey
Ms. D: 20 years Has found employment after passing the high school accreditation examination Has moved to a group home operated by the "A unmarried mothers' facility" The child is attending kindergarten while the mother works The mother of the family of origin gives understanding but no support Is also receiving support from an NGO Is making use of systems such as Ministry of Employment and Labor programmes Has anxieties about childrearing but does not regret opting for raising the child by herself
[2] New survey subjects
Ms. J: 21 years (20 years at time of birth) After dropping out of high school was unemployed when becoming pregnant Entered a childbirth facility when 8 months pregnant on recommendation of an acquaintance Child's father is a salesperson three years older than Ms. J (In prison when notified of the pregnancy) Family of origin gives understanding but no support Was uncertain whether to opt for adoption or raising the child, but decided on raising by herself after entering the facility Has obtained a qualification as a barista Working as a barista at a café run by the childbirth facility
Ms. K: 22 years (22 years at time of birth) Gave birth at an unmarried mothers' childbirth facility No contact with the child's father (who is now living in a factory dormitory) Gave birth after the second pregnancy with the child's father (the first pregnancy was aborted) Has the understanding of the family of origin (Ms. K's older brother is living with the family as an unmarried father) Is making use of the state mother's card (mainly in the healthcare centre) Wishes to find work using Chinese
Ms. L: 17 years (17 years at time of birth) Was living at a childcare institution prior to pregnancy No contact with the family of origin since primary school (family's whereabouts are known) Possible to contact the child's father (now preparing to enter military service) Wishes to live in the group home Seeking employment (is undergoing an aptitude test) Working part time at a café run by the childbirth facility

Source: Author's data.

Main contents provided by the facility: Psychological treatment services, general education (handicraft, reading, etc.), career education services (qualifications in computing, etc.), special programmes (outdoor camping, bazaars, etc.) are provided for all mothers. In addition, to support mothers who opt for raising the child after childbirth, material support (provision of nappies, milk, pushchairs, etc.), support for independence (obtaining qualifications, etc.), educational programmes (parenting education, education in economic concepts, etc.), community linkage programmes (introduction to facilities that can be used for reintegration into society) are also carried out.

Group home for mothers opting for raising the child was established in late 2000s to provide support for independence for mothers who opt to raise their children. These mothers are increasing in number each year. This is a facility that can be used free of charge by mothers who are raising an infant of less than two years of age. However, since this is a group home, the condition for users is that they must be a mother and child who are capable of communal living. The home may be used for one year, but this can be extended for a further year according to need.

Main contents provided by the home: Support for childrearing costs (pocket money for the mother, costs for clothes for mother and child, etc.); support for children's supplies (nappies, milk, etc.); education for independence and employment linkages in accordance with the characteristics of the user; career, parenting, daily life consultation and so on are carried out.

Support for Unmarried Mothers "Opting for Raising the Child" by the A Unmarried Mothers' Facility

At present, in order to support the independence of the annually increasing adolescent single mothers "opting for raising the child," general welfare support to link mothers with the community, such as support from the mother of the family home,[2] a qualification incentive system,[3] introduction of the state housing savings system,[4] and operation of the unmarried mothers' independence shop[5] are being carried out in addition to the previous support for independence. In particular, the café, which has the purpose of providing support for independence of unmarried mothers, is a multipurpose shop that sells clothes and miscellaneous goods as well as being a place where mothers who have obtained qualifications as a barista, now very popular with young people, or in breadmaking are able to become independent by gaining experience through practice.

In addition to the previous support for obtaining qualifications or certificates, these are valuable support programmes for provision of stable employment that comprehends the situation of unmarried mothers from the viewpoint of providing places to work, and to gain economic stability and social experience. Besides these programmes, it is also planned to operate commissioned schools for unmarried mothers who were not able to complete schooling, establish a kindergarten (a crèche facility) inside the group home, and provide a place where mothers can feel safe and secure at night and at weekends.

Case Analysis

What factors lead to the opting for and deciding upon adoption or raising the child? What kinds of support and social relations exist in the background to this? The following factors can be found by our case analysis from the interviews.

The Existence of Familiar Role Models

We can discuss things with other mothers that we cannot talk to the staff about. (Ms. E)

My mother who has already brought up her children gave me advice. (Ms. H)

In Ms. G's case, a staff member had become a role model.

Not only can we consult with them on careers and education, but also talk with them as people more experienced in life and get advice about childrearing. (Ms. G)

There are mothers who gave birth before me, and that's useful because we get all kinds of information from them. (Ms. I)

The Existence of Familiar Supporters

I decided to opt for raising the child when I saw a mother younger than myself making great efforts.

Accessible State Support (Free Childbirth Fees, Receipt of Public Livelihood Assistance, Ability to Use Kindergartens)

Although mothers find it hard to get education, there is a kindergarten available here and we can get information about qualifications. (Ms. E)

Employment consultancy staff from the Ministry of Labor also comes here to talk to us. (Ms. G)

I am receiving money from the state single parent support and the under-24 single parent support... ...I am saving money in the pass book from the government. (Ms. J)

I am using the Ministry of Employment and Labor's programme... ...I am using the kindergarten. (Ms. D)

Even though they were quite expensive, I received my child's inoculations and my vitamin pills free of charge. (Ms. K)

Special Support Available from the Childbirth Facility (Daily Necessities, Preparation for Qualifications, etc.)

When I get anxious about childrearing, there is a maternity nurse I can talk to, and this is very useful. (Ms. G)

I am getting information about supporters and about what to do after leaving the facility from a university teacher who comes here every week to give parenting education. (Ms. I)

I found employment through the childbirth facility. (Ms. D)

I was employed at the café run by the childbirth facility. (Ms. J and Ms. L)

I participated in a special programme run by this facility where you read books and receive savings. (Ms. K and Ms. L)

When I feel psychologically unstable, the psychology treatment doctor comes to the group home for a consultation. (Ms. J)

When you are in the facility, you can get full support for basic living and information. (Ms. K)

Easily Obtainable Information on Support and Its Availability

The staff member in charge of education at the facility gives me information on a priority basis. (Ms. G)

When I have problems with childrearing, the facility staff give me information about other NGOs. (Ms. D)

If I have problems, the facility staff immediately give me useful information. (Ms. J)

Being here, we can even get information that we need after we leave the facility. (Ms. K)

Nothing to do with the Family of Origin or the Child's Father

In the case of Ms. D, she decided "to give birth without contacting the father because I was unsure about him."

In the case of Ms. E, she is continuing to contact her family of origin and the child's father, but has decided to stay in the facility "until we are financially stable rather than be together right away, because we would not be economically stable."

In the case of Ms. I, she has good relations with her family, who "come to see her five times a week, but" did not tell them about the time of the birth because the relationship with her family has nothing to do with the raising her child.

I want to be independent through my own strength and with no relation to the child's father or my family. (Ms. H)

At first, my family of origin were opposed, but now they understand... [but] ...I do not receive any support from them. (Ms. D, Ms. J, and Ms. K)

The child's father knows about the existence of the child, but has not contacted me. (Ms. J, Ms. K)

The child's father is quite self-centred and contacts me from time to time when he remembers... ... When he gets another girlfriend he stops contacting me. (Ms. L)

Discussion

The following points can be raised from the data collected during the interviews presented above.

First, although it is a basic understanding, when an unmarried teenage mother makes the decision to rear her child, is significantly important that she have a strong will to raise her "own child."

The second point is that the relationship between the children and their fathers or members of their parents' families of origin is not very strong. Establishing contact with fathers itself was not carried out in many of the cases, and the mothers had not approached the fathers of their children to demand financial responsibility. Even if contact was possible at the time of the interviews, reasons such as "men cannot be trusted" were offered and the mothers had no plans to raise their children together with the fathers. Also, in the background to this decision to continue as a single parent is the fact that if they "became a couple they would not be able to receive support." Furthermore, the presence of a mother's family of origin did provide "moral support" when rearing her child, but it was not always the case that the existence of her family of origin was considered when she made the decision to give birth and commit herself to raising the child. After the child was born, however, mothers realized that having the support of their families was reassuring when they were involved in "child rearing." In the interviews with those offering assistance, it was revealed that "80% of the families of unmarried mothers were divorced and living in poverty, causing conflict with the parents resulting in the girls running away from home and becoming independent early," leading to a conclusion that relationships with families of origin were weak. If relationships with families existed, it was claimed they did provide moral support. This too was verified by support workers interviewed, who stated that the particular circumstances of unmarried teenage mothers caused them to "have anxieties, regardless of whether they were raising their children or putting them up for adoption." Because of their strong sense of "anxiety," one can infer that unmarried teenage mothers seek "moral support" from their families.

The third point is that the personnel working for the unmarried mothers' facilities where the mothers give birth to their children also provide the support received during child rearing. The government-provided support such as welfare assistance and free nursery care is utilized, or its provision expected when the time comes.

The fourth point is that from this study an understanding was gained concerning the conditions unmarried teenage mothers were faced with in achieving independence and economic security. As they proceeded to live in the residences provided, (1) unmarried mother-child facilities, (2) group homes, and then (3) welfare facilities for mothers and their children, or rented housing in their communities, at each stage they are faced with different conditions for attaining those goals. Furthermore, their movements through (1) unmarried mothers' facilities, (2) group homes, and finally into (3) welfare facilities for mothers and children, mark the stages for them in improving their condition, and the cases that received the various forms of support from government institutions and facilities proved to be in the most stable childrearing environments. Even if these mothers felt anxiety towards childrearing while still in a facility for childbirth, such as unmarried mothers' facilities, when they receive continued support through to the next stage in the group homes, it is possible for them to settle down and rear their children.

Although there are individual differences, as shown above, receiving housing support, welfare assistance, occupational certification, and benefits such as nursery services for their children, suggests that long-term support in stages improves the child rearing environment and chances for the mothers to achieve independence.

The role of the group homes in particular proves to be of great significance. After childbirth in the unmarried mothers' facilities, rather than moving directly into regular rented housing in the community, for single mothers who decide to rear their children the group homes where they receive continued support are favorably described by the residents, who express opinions such as, "When one has no knowledge of raising a child, the other mothers can be asked for advice," and "We have separate rooms, but we live cooperatively, so it is possible to look after each others' children." According to the superintendent of the "A unmarried mothers' facility," "if a young mother has a strong resolve to raise her child, then we encourage her to move from the facility to a group home, where they can set their sights on the goal of becoming independent." The actual number of group homes, however, is insufficient. The same superintendent stated, "One hundred women enter the unmarried mothers' facilities, but only five can take advantage of the group home," emphasizing the necessity for an increase in the number of these homes.

The above illustrates the present situation, in which there is an insufficient number of places for unmarried teenage mothers to receive support for improving their conditions. It is the offering of support enabling these young single mothers to upgrade their living conditions that will open the gate for them to enter society as independent individuals.

5. CONCLUSION

While in Korean society family structure continues to diversify, stigma against unmarried mothers continues to be a strong obstacle. In the concluding statement of Rejection of Diverse Families in Neighborhood Communities (52nd Women's Forum 2009) it was verified that unmarried single mother families were still receiving the highest degree of social rejection among "divorced families," "families of remarriage," and "marriage immigrants." The low tolerance towards childbirth and rearing by unmarried mothers still remains in Korean society.

It is in this Korean society where teenage mothers have "decided to raise their own children" and live their daily lives in communities that hold "biases" and express "rejection" towards them. Of mothers who "choose to put their children up for adoption," if there is economic support, 37.7% desire to raise their own children (Ministry of Gender Equality and Family 2005), but if social tolerance towards diverse family structures were to rise it can be assumed that the proportion of parents desiring to raise their children will also increase.

At present, the Single-Parent Family Support Act is central to the development of support policies for unmarried mothers, but as pointed out in this study, it is important to implement detailed, individualized, comprehensive and continual assistance. Not limited to those who opt for "childrearing," but also towards all unmarried mothers who opted for "adoption," while raising one's "own child" it is important to provide long-term and continual support, and support that helps the recipient foresee how she can step her way up to independence, rather than short-term and sporadic handouts. As the foundation for these types of assistance, it is necessary to restructure society based on the principle of the "socialization of childcare" so that society as a whole protects mothers and their growing children with tolerance while offering them help to seek independence.

REFERENCES

An, S. et al. (1984). *Study on single mothers in Korea. Korean Women's Development Institute*. KWDI. [in Korean]

Arai, L. (2009). *Teenage pregnancy: The making and unmaking of a problem*. Bristol, UK: Polity Press.

Bae, Y. (2001). A study on the temperament and MBTI personality type of unmarried adolescent mothers. [in Korean]. *Journal of the Korea Academy of Psychological Type*, *8*(3), 45–70.

Berthoud, R., & Robson, K. (2001). *The outcome of teenage motherhood in Europe* (Innocenti Working Paper No.86). Florence, Italy: UNICEF.

Do, M., & Jeon, E. (2001). Research on issues and welfare policy for teenage single mothers. [in Korean]. *Youth Welfare*, *3*(2), 1–11.

Eun, H. (1999). Teen pregnancy & childbirth: Trends and alternatives. [in Korean]. *Journal of the Korean Society of Child Welfare*, *8*, 161–186.

Ho, N. et al. (2005). *Study on comprehensive policy for single mother and father*. Ministry of Gender Equality and Family. [in Korean]

Hong, S. et al. (2007). *A study of securing rights for adolescent single mothers to receive education*. National Human Rights Commission. [in Korean]

Jae, S. et al. (2008). *Survey of student single mothers. Ministry of Education, Science, and Technology*. MEST. [in Korean]

Kim, H. (2008). Where should single parent policy go? In Conditions and controversy over single mothers. Korean Women's Development Institute (KWDI). [in Korean].

Kim, H. et al. (2009). *Korean public opinion survey on unwed mothers and their children. Korean Women's Development Institute*. KWDI. [in Korean]

Kim, H., & Ahn, S. et al. (2009). *Korean attitudes toward unmarried parents and adoption: Improving attitudes towards unwed mothers and promoting support. Korean Women's Development Institute*. KWDI. [in Korean]

Kim, H., & Son, B. et al. (2009). *Unwed mother's life world and policy agenda. Korean Women's Development Institute*. KWDI. [in Korean]

Kim, Y. et al. (2006). *Study on social support for childbirth and childcare of single mothers. Korea Institute for Health and Social Affairs*. KIHASA. [in Korean]

Kim, Y., & Kim, E. (2008). *Life and future of adolescent single mothers*. Nuipun Women Support Centre. [in Korean]

Korean Unwed Mothers Support Network (KUMSN). (n.d.). Retrieved from http://www.kumsn.org

Lee, M. (2008). The reality of ignoring single mothers in Korea. In Conditions and controversy over single mothers. Korean Women's Development Institute (KWDI). [in Korean].

Lee, M. et al. (2009). *Reviewing issues on unwed mothers' welfare in Korea: Intercountry adoption, related statistics, and welfare policies in developed countries. Korean Women's Development Institute*. KWDI. [in Korean]

Lee, M. et al. (2010). *How to improve government welfare services for low-income unwed mothers in Korea. Korean Women's Development Institute*. KWDI. [in Korean]

Lee, S. et al. (2010). *Critical issues for research promoted in the next five years on low birthrate and aging society. Ministry of Health and Welfare, and Korea Institute for Health and Social Affairs*. KIHASA. [in Korean]

Ministry of Gender Equality and Family. (2005). *Guide for single parent policies*. Author. [in Korean]

Ministry of Gender Equality and Family. (2011). *Guide for single parent policies*. Author. [in Korean]

Ministry of Gender Equality and Family Website with Mom. (n.d.). Retrieved from http://withmom.mogef.go.kr/supportpolicies/singleParentFamily.doc

Ministry of Health. Welfare and Family Affairs. (2008). *White paper on health, welfare and family affairs 2007*. Seoul, South Korea: Ministry of Health, Welfare and Family Affairs. [in Korean]

Ministry of Health. Welfare and Family Affairs. (2009). *White paper on children and adolescents 2009*. Author. [in Korean]

Soh, H. (2011). *Policy proposal: Support programs of development of children of single mother and father parents*. Gyeonggi-do Family and Women's Research Institute. [in Korean]

Soh, H. et al. (2010). *Survey on single mother and father and policy research*. Gyeonggi-do Family and Women's Research Institute. [in Korean]

Sôma, N., & Park, J. (2007). Korean single mother policy. In Life styles and welfare policies of single mothers: Comparative study of Japan, the U.S., Denmark and Korea. Kyôto, Japan: Minerva. [in Japanese].

Tokyo Council of Social Welfare, Division of Childcare Investigation Committee. (2002). *Report on the study of mothers who gave birth as teenagers, childrearing and childcare support*. Author. [in Japanese]

Youn, M., & Lee, J. (2003). Characteristics of teenage unwed mothers in Korea. [in Korean]. *Korean Journal of Child Studies*, *23*(3), 149–169.

KEY TERMS AND DEFINITIONS

Pregnancy: The fertilization and development of one or more offspring, known as an embryo or fetus, in a female's uterus.

Single-Parent Family Support Act: Korean law instrumental in new family-policy.

Teenager: A person aged from puberty to maturity.

ENDNOTES

1 Seongnam city also started maternity expenses assistance for pregnant adolescents under the age of 18 (Jan. 6, 2012). According to Seongnam city in the past the city had provided support to pay for medical costs related to pregnancy and maternity expenses for adolescents under age 18, limited to those residents in single mothers' facilities. From this year restrictions had been eased and the assistance was extended to young pregnant girls living at home. The amount was 100,000 won/day and the highest total receivable was 1.2 million won.

2 Support from the mother of the family home is a programme whose purpose is to provide a place for the unmarried mother after leaving the facility that has a function similar to the family home in the community. For unmarried mothers who may be experiencing problems with forming a relationship with the family of origin, this programme links the unmarried mother and child household with a home in the community where the mother wishes to live. Often, the home that becomes the family home is that of the head teacher of the community's kindergarten.

3 The qualification incentive system is a provision of cash from the A unmarried mothers' facility as funds for stabilizing daily life for mothers who pass the qualifications (for instance in the beautician field, medical, or high school accreditation) that they have aimed for. The purpose of the incentive system is to raise the awareness of setting objectives. The system provides support for independence so that the mother can reach final attainment of the desired objective, since many mothers abandon objectives before reaching the goal.

4 The housing savings system is a state system that has the purpose of expediting the solution to the housing problem by providing the same amount of money from the state that an individual has saved in order to solve the low-income group housing problem. The "A unmarried mothers' facility" has introduced this system for all unmarried mothers in order to solve the housing problem, the greatest problem faced in becoming independent, and to raise the awareness of unmarried mothers regarding independence.

5 A shop selling refreshments, clothes and recycled goods opened as an independence shop for unmarried mothers by the A unmarried mothers' facility. Unmarried mothers work in the shop, which has monthly sales of about 10 million won. At present, 15 mothers are employed at the shop in positions such as baristas, confectionary makers and salespersons. This shop was opened and is being supported jointly by the representative of the KUMSN, the ward office of Seodaemun, in which the A unmarried mothers' facility is located, and the A unmarried mothers' facility.

Chapter 9
Difficulties in Work-Family Reconciliation in Taiwan

Pei-Yuen Tsai
Yuan Ze University, Taiwan

ABSTRACT

In order to extend the understandings of work-family reconciliation patterns and following problems in Taiwan, this chapter reviews the development of employment and childcare trends in Taiwan to show how these changing phenomena affect Taiwanese families and contribute to families' difficulties in work-family reconciliation. This chapter includes three main sections. The first section demonstrates the changes of household structure and employment in Taiwan. The second section focuses on childcare arrangements to demonstrate Taiwanese families' decisions between work and childcare. Finally, there is a concluding section to sum up the implications of these phenomena.

INTRODUCTION

In many countries, there have been noticeable changes in female employment and family structure in recent decades. These changes bring many new challenges to welfare systems and one of the significant issues is how to help families to reconcile work and family responsibilities (OECD, 2007). Some scholars have identified difficulties in work-family reconciliation as one of the new social risks that contemporary welfare states have to deal with (Bonoli, 2006; Taylor-Gooby, 2004). However, given the diverse circumstances and welfare institutions around the world, it is debatable to what extent the patterns of these difficulties are similar in different countries. Under the influences of various welfare institutions and cultures, similar challenges may be translated into very different problems (Taylor-Gooby, 2004).

In order to extend the understandings of work-family reconciliation patterns and following problems in Taiwan, this article reviews the development of employment and childcare trends in Taiwan to show how these changing phenomena affect Taiwanese families and contribute to families'

DOI: 10.4018/978-1-4666-5031-2.ch009

difficulties in work-family reconciliation. This article draws upon official datasets to explore these issues including Women's Marriage, Fertility and Employment Survey (WMFES) and Manpower Utilization Survey (MUS). In addition to official datasets, this article also draws on statistical data from government agencies to provide an overview of changing employment and childcare patterns in Taiwan. Moreover, in order to compare the patterns of Taiwan and other countries, this research also employs statistical data from international organisations and related publications and literature for a international comparison. This article includes three main parts. The first section demonstrates the changes of household structure and employment in Taiwan. The second part focuses on childcare arrangements to demonstrate Taiwanese families' decisions between work and childcare. Finally, there will be a concluding section to sum up the implications of these phenomena.

EMPLOYMENT PATTERNS

There have been dramatic changes in terms of families' employment patterns in recent years. These changes contribute to the potential difficulties of families in dealing with work and family responsibilities. The following sections will demonstrate important employment characteristics in Taiwan and the implications of these characteristics on work-family reconciliation.

General Trends in Female Labour Market Participation

In the past several decades, the development of female employment in Taiwan displays an upward trend but the pace appears relatively slow compared to OECD countries (OECD, 2007). Figure 1 shows that the overall labour market participation rate in Taiwan was very stable in the past 30 years. It was kept at about 60% and there was

Figure 1. Labour market participation rate in Taiwan (1980-2012) (Source: National Statistics, 2013)

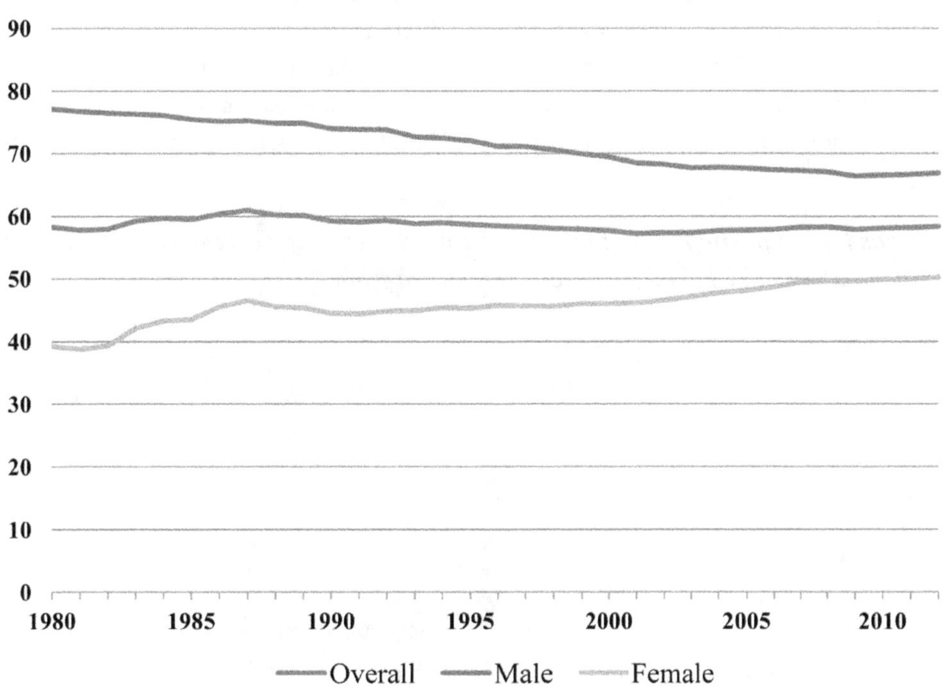

no significant change between 1980 and 2012. Despite the steadiness of overall labour market participation rate, there has been a considerable change in terms of the composition of gender. The female labour market participation rate has risen about 10% from 40% in 1980 to 50% in 2012. In contrast, the male labour market participation rate has decreased from 77% to 67% during the same period.

The relatively low female labour market participation in Taiwan could partly result from difficulties in work-family balance. If families are unable to cope with work and family responsibility simultaneously, this may reduce women's opportunities and incentives to enter the labour market. In order to understand the influence of work-family balance difficulties on female's employment behaviours in Taiwan, this article draws on the data of the MUS to explore this issue. For those aged 20-49 who did not participate in the labour market, the MUS asks a question: 'If the working conditions such as pay, working location, time, environments match your expectations, are you willing to work?', According to the result of this survey in 2012, about 92% of men and 95% of women were still not willing to work. Among those who responded not willing to enter the labour market, Figure 2 shows their reasons and care responsibility is an important one. According to this data, overall about 36% of them said it was because of the need to take care of family members. 41% were because of study and 15% responded that because the family income had been enough. It shows that care responsibility is an important constraint for many people to work. Moreover, there is a large difference between men and women. About 49% of women did not enter the labour market due to the need to care for family members, whereas only 2.3% of men were for this reason. In addition, 1.5% of women responded not willing to work due to marriage or childbirth (Figure 2).

Household Employment Structure

When examining the composition of female employment by marriage status, the increase of female employment rate in Taiwan in the past 30 years was mostly contributed by the increase of married or cohabited women (Table 1). Among married or cohabited women, both the employment rates of women with and without children increased. The increase of women with children under 6 appeared to be faster than women without children under 6. This increase intensifies the potential conflicts between work and family responsibilities.

Figure 2. Reasons for not participating in the labour market even if working conditions match expectations by sex (aged 20-49 in 2012) (%) (Source: calculated from the MUS)

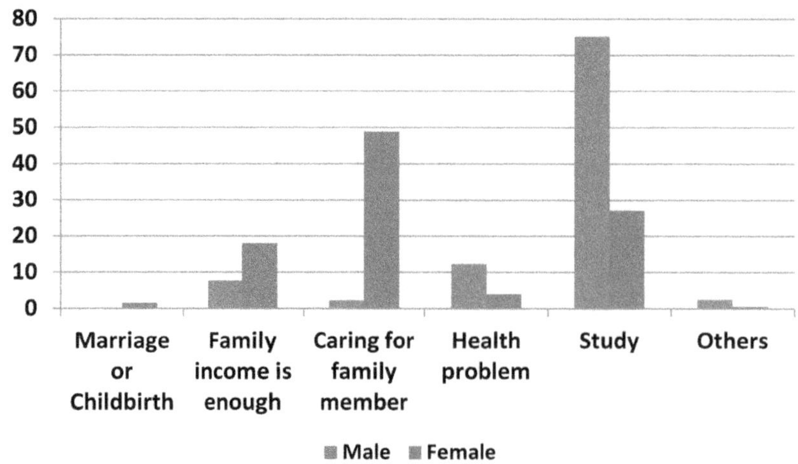

Table 1. Employment rate of women aged 20-49 by marriage status and children's age (1982-2012) (%)

	Single		Married or Cohabited	
			Without Children under 6	With Children under 6
1982	75.1	35.7	41.4	29.1
1992	73.4	50.6	54.9	42.8
2002	65.3	57.0	59.4	52.1
2012	69.0	63.2	65.1	58.0

Source: Calculated from the MUS.

With the increase in employment rate of married women, the percentage of dual earner households also increased in the past 30 years. This transformation of household employment structure shows that there are more families encountering the issue of work-family balance in Taiwan than 30 years ago. Table 2 shows the household employment structure by earners. It shows a dramatic increase of dual earner households and the decline of male sole earner households. Among the women aged 20-49, 57% of families were male sole earner households in 1980, whereas only 38% of families were dual earner households. However, the number of dual earner families grew very fast in the past 30 years. In contrast, male sole earner households kept declining. The percentage of dual earner households has reached 60% which was almost twice the number of male sole earner households in 2010. As a result, for women aged 20-49 which is the main age of childbearing, dual earner households have become the mainstream during the 2000s, whereas the traditional male breadwinner family has dramatically eroded.

Working Hours

The increase of dual earner households brings the potential risk of difficulties in balancing work and family responsibilities, particularly childcare for young children. However, as Lewis and Campbell (2009) have pointed out, the change of male breadwinner model varies by countries. Even if dual earner households have become the mainstream of families, the types and working hours of jobs still matter. In several European countries such as Austria, Germany, and the Netherlands, they show a growing number of male full-time and female part-time families with children. However, the case of Taiwan shows a quite different pattern. Part-time employment is not a prevalent phenomenon for women in Taiwan. The family employment structure in Taiwan is closer to a dual full-time earner model rather than one-and-a-half earner model (i.e. one full-time earner and one part-time earner in the household). Therefore, the work-family balance problems in Taiwan could be different from those countries with a large percentage of women in part-time employment.

Table 2. Household employment structure (women aged 20-49)(%)

	Dual Earner Household	Male Sole Earner	Female Sole Earner	Both are Not Working
1980	37.5	57.3	2.0	3.2
1990	47.9	46.9	2.4	2.9
2000	53.4	39.3	3.2	4.1
2010	60.1	31.6	4.7	3.6

Source: Calculated from the WMFES.

In general there is a considerable percentage of women working part-time to reconcile work and family responsibilities, although there are large variations (Lewis & Campbell, 2009). On average, about 25% of all women and one-third of employed mothers take part-time employment in OECD countries. The incidence of part-time employment is higher for women than men in these countries and the gaps between men and women in part-time employment are quite large (OECD, 2007, 2009). However, the working hours of females in Taiwan show a very different pattern. The percentages of workers working part-time in Taiwan are very low for both males and females. Compared to the average of OECD and EU countries, there are only a small number of women working part-time in Taiwan. For international comparison, this chapter adopts the definition of part-time employment used by the OECD. Part-time employment is defined as working less than 30 hours per week in one's main job (OECD, 2009: 268). Based on this definition, the percentage of women in part-time employment as a proportion of total employment in Taiwan was only 4.3% in 2008. This rate was basically similar to men's percentage in part-time employment (Figure 3). Moreover, the part-time employment pattern in Taiwan did not show much difference between different marriage statuses. The percentage of part-time employment of single women was 3.8% and the percentage of married women was 4.3% in 2008. The percentage for single men was 4.1% and married man was 4.2% (calculated from the MUS in 2008).

This shows that working part-time was not a prevalent way to reconcile work and family responsibilities in Taiwan. The difficulties of work-family balance in Taiwan cannot be correctly appreciated if only looking at employment rate and labour force participation rate. The assessment of work-family balance problem should take working hours into consideration. When examining the pattern of working time, it will be found that the working hours of mothers in Taiwan are longer than in most industrialised countries. Based on European Social Survey data and the MUS in Taiwan, the working hour patterns of women with children aged 0-6 can be compared. The working hours of mothers in Taiwan are concentrated on either longer than 34 hours or 0 hour. In Taiwan, 41% of mothers with children aged 0-6 did not work at all. This rate was higher than in Germany, Sweden, and the UK (Table 3). However, there were also 58% of women working more than 34

Figure 3. Part-time employment as a percentage of total employment in 2008 (Source: data of Taiwan calculated from the MUS; OECD, 2009)

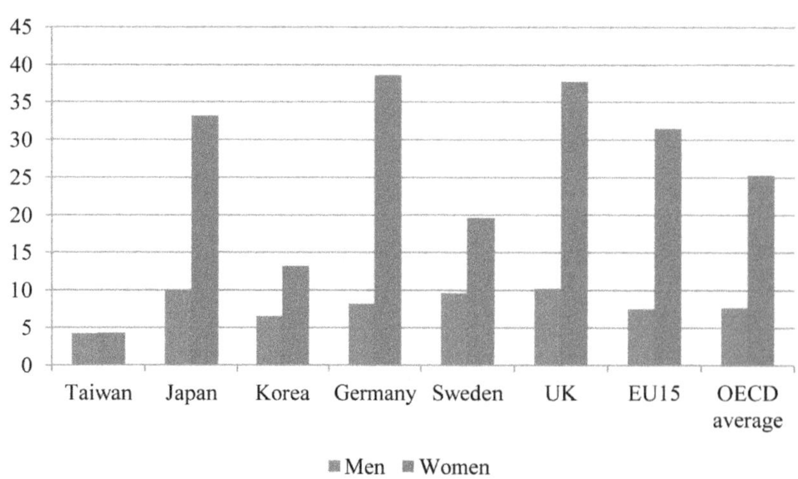

Table 3. Working hour structure of mothers with children aged under 6 (2004-2006)[1](%)

	0	1-19	20-34	35 and Above
Taiwan	40.5	0.6	1.3	57.6
Germany	38.0	24.9	17.0	20.1
UK	31.0	25.4	20.2	23.4
Sweden	12.8	0.9	26.6	59.6

Source: data of Taiwan calculated from the MUS; Lewis and Campbell (2009).

hours per week. This percentage was only slightly lower than that of Sweden (60%). In contrast, the percentage of those working between 1-34 hours was only 1.9%. This is much lower than in many European countries. Therefore, the impact of young children on mothers' employment in Taiwan is mainly on employment status rather than on working hours. Most mothers with children under 6 in Taiwan do not reconcile work and family responsibilities through reducing part of working time. Moreover, the working hours of full-time mother workers in Taiwan are particularly long. Figure 4 shows that 23% of mothers with children aged 0-15 in Taiwan worked more than 46 hours per week. This percentage was much higher than that in Germany, Sweden, and the UK.

Household Working Time Structure

Table 4 shows the comparison of working time structure of households with children aged 0-15 between Taiwan and several European countries. Among all the households with children aged 0-15, dual full-time employment household structure was the most prevalent form in Taiwan. About 56% of families are dual full-time employment families. In contrast, the percentage of male full-

Figure 4. Percentage of mothers with children aged 0-15 working more than 46 hours per week in 2006 (Source: data of Taiwan calculated from the MUS; Lewis and Campbell, 2009)

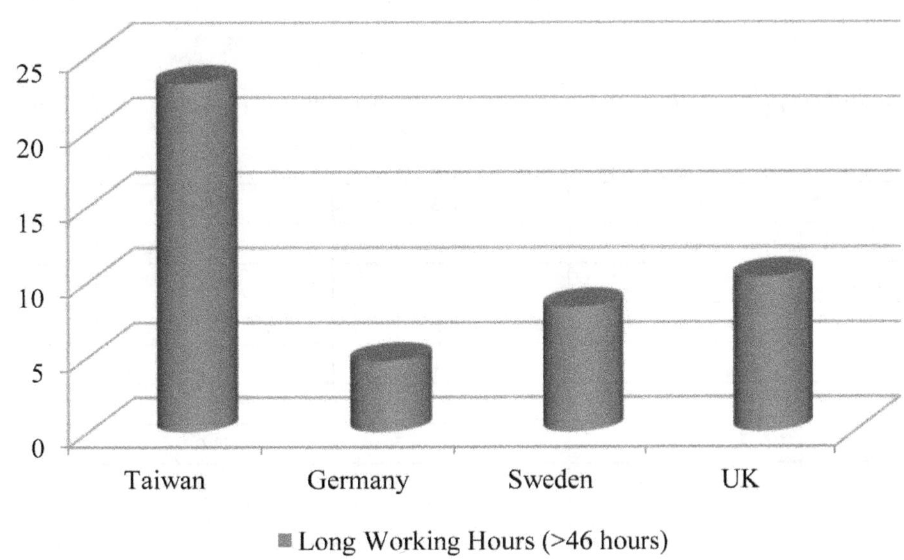

Table 4. Household employment structure by types of employment and working hours (partnered adults with child aged 0-15, 2004-2006)(%)

	Male Full-Time +Female Full-Time	Male Full-Time + Female Long Part-Time	Male Full-Time +Female Short Part-Time	Male Sole Earner	Other
Taiwan	55.7	1.8	0.6	32.3	9.6
Germany	19.1	17.4	15.6	33.7	14.2
Sweden	53.8	24.8	1.8	12.2	7.5
UK	19.6	22.0	14.2	25.5	18.7

Source: data of Taiwan calculated from the WMFES in 2006; Lewis and Campbell (2009).

time/female part-time households in Taiwan was much lower than in other European countries. Mothers in Taiwan either work full-time or do not work at all. Therefore, most of the families are either male breadwinner households or dual full-time earner households.

Career Interruption

The strong dual full-time employment structure in Taiwan to some extent also increases the difficulties in take work and family responsibilities at the same time. Although the employment rate of married women has increased in the past decades, more working women have to face the interruption of their career due to their family responsibilities. This WMFES investigated the employment status of female employees before and after marriage and their reasons to withdraw from the labour market. For all the women aged 20-49 who worked before getting married, the percentage of women who kept working without any break had slightly declined between 1979 and 2010 (taking maternity or parental leave is not regarded as break in this survey). About 60% of these working women in Taiwan still experienced career interruption for some reasons (Table 5).

When examining the pattern of career interruption specifically, the withdrawal of employment can be divided into two types: temporary and permanent. The 'permanent withdrawal' is defined as those who have ever withdrawn from the labour

Table 5. Career interruption pattern of women who have working experiences before marriage (aged 20-49)(%)

	1979	1993	2000	2010
Without break	**45.6**	**41.3**	**40.0**	**42.1**
Permanent withdrawal	**46.7**	**40.5**	**37.4**	**29.6**
Marriage	30.3	25.1	22.8	14.7
Childbirth	10.0	11.4	9.7	8.6
Other	6.4	4.0	4.9	6.3
Temporary withdrawal	**7.6**	**18.2**	**22.6**	**28.3**
Marriage	3.3	7.8	10.8	13.6
Childbirth	2.7	8.4	9.6	9.7
Other	1.6	2.0	2.2	5.0

Source: Calculated from the WMFES.

market and have never returned to employment so far. 'Temporary withdrawal' is defined as those who have ever quit the labour market for some reasons but have returned to work (including those who have returned to work but then quit again). However, it should be noted that permanent employment withdrawal may not really be permanent. Due to the limitation of the timing of the survey, this data can only show respondents' current employment experiences. Therefore, respondents could return to work in the future and then their permanent employment withdrawal could become temporary employment withdrawal. In any case, temporary employment withdrawal could result in loss of income for a period, whereas permanent employment withdrawal could make the women entirely leave the labour market.

Table 5 shows that the proportion of permanent withdrawal has steadily declined since 1979. This result is accordant with the increase of employment rate of married women. However, there are significant changes in temporary employment withdrawal. More women leave the labour market for a period due to marriage or childbirth. This to some extent shows the transformation of work-family balance difficulties of working women in Taiwan. The pattern of work-family balance difficulties appears to transform from career termination to career interruption.

CHILDCARE PATTERNS

With the increase in female labour market participation, particularly married women, many Taiwanese families have to make arrangements on childcare. Different from many countries, part-time employment is not prevalent for female workers in Taiwan. Therefore, many dual full-time employment families with young children need to turn to other resources. In this process, there are two important issues that could affect the level of difficulties in work-family reconciliation: availability of childcare provision and the expenses for childcare. With different needs of children at different ages, the childcare arrangements for children aged under 3 years old and aged 3-6 years old are quite different. The following sections will in turn demonstrate the childcare patterns of children at different ages in Taiwan.

Children Aged 3 Years and Under

In response to the increasing pressures in dealing with work and childcare responsibilities, the childcare arrangements for children under 3 in Taiwan showed a change in the past decades. Families with children under 3 generally take two main strategies to deal with this problem. Firstly, there is increasing reliance on children's grandparents to take care of children. Existing literature on East Asian welfare systems has suggested that family is an important source to meet the demand of childcare (Gough, 2004; Jacobs, 1998; Jones, 1993; Kwon, 1997). The data of WMFES also accords with this depiction. However, the main carer was shifted from children's parents to their grandparents. For dual earner families, about 33% of children under 3 were cared for by their parents in 1990. This rate has dropped to 22% in 2000 and 12% in 2010. In contrast to the decrease parents as the main carer, the percentage of grandparents as the main carer has grown from 51% in 1990 to 65% in 2010 (Table 6).

Table 6. Main carer of children aged 0-3 in dual earner families (%)

	1990	2000	2010
Family	**85.0**	**82.3**	**79.5**
Parents	33.1	21.7	12.1
Grandparents	50.8	58.3	64.8
Other Relatives	1.1	2.3	2.6
Market	**15.0**	**17.7**	**20.4**
Childminders and nannies	14.8	16.0	17.8
Migrant care workers	0.0	0.7	0.7
Private childcare facilities	0.2	1.0	1.9
State	**0.0**	**0.0**	**0.2**
Public childcare facilities	0.0	0.0	0.2

Source: Calculated from the WMFES.

Secondly, the use of market services increased. There was an increase in using childminders, nannies, migrant care workers, and private childcare facilities as the main child carer. In 1990, only 15% of dual earner families used market services to take care for their children under 3. This rate has increased to 20% in 2010. Childminders are the main market solution for parents whose children are under 3. The percentage of using childminders or nannies has increased from 15% to 18% between 1990 and 2010.

When examining the changes of childcare provider based on the division between the family (including parents, grandparents, and relatives), the market (including childminders, nannies, migrant care workers, and private childcare facilities), and the state (public childcare facilities), the role of the family in childcare for children under 3 was still the most important. Although there was a slight decline, there are still more than 80% of dual earner families relying on families to care for children under 3. With regard to the state, the provision from the state for children under 3 is still very limited. In contrast, the role of the market has been strengthened. Nevertheless, family day care services are still more important than centre-based childcare. Overall, the provision of childcare for children under 3 was mostly transferred from children's parents to grandparents and partly to childminders.

The strong reliance on family members to provide childcare to some extent reflects the high costs of childcare for children under 3. For dual earner families with children aged under 3 years old, childminders are the main market services in Taiwan. However, the childcare costs are very expensive for parents. According to the WMFES in 2010, the median daytime childcare cost of childminders for families with children under 3 was 15,000 NTD per month. Compared to the expenses of childminders, the median income of dual earner families with children under 3 in 2010 was 63,000 NTD and the median income of mother was 28,000. As a result, the childminder fees could take about 24% of household income and 54% of mother's income for one child. The median number of children of these families was 2. Hence, if these families have two children under 3 years old at the same time, the childcare costs could almost double. Such expensive childcare costs are a very heavy financial burden for many families with young children. (see Table 7)

With such high costs, the patterns of using childminder services also show a large variance between different income groups. Among all the dual earner households with children under 3 years old, only 6% of the households at the lowest 20% income level use childminder services in 2010. In contrast, 33% of the dual earner households at top 20% income level use childminder services to meet the needs of childcare. (see Figure 5)

In terms of the source of childcare, most of the childcare provision for children under 3 in Taiwan rely on the family and the market. Figure 6 shows that overall about 80% of dual earner families have to rely on their families to meet the demands of childcare. However, there were large variances between different income groups. For the dual earner income families with lowest 20% income, 93% of childcare provision was provided by the family, whereas the reliance on family decreased to 65% for the highest 20% income families.

To sum up, the data shows that expensive childcare fees are an important source of difficulties in work-family reconciliation for Taiwanese families. If parents cannot afford the expensive

Table 7. Median childcare costs and median income of dual earner households with children under 3 in 2010 (NTD)

Childminder Expenses	15,000
Household Income	63,000
Mother's Income	28,000

Source: calculated from the WMFES.

Figure 5. Pattern of using childminder service for dual earner households with children under 3 by percentile group of household income in 2010 (Source: Calculated from the WMFES)

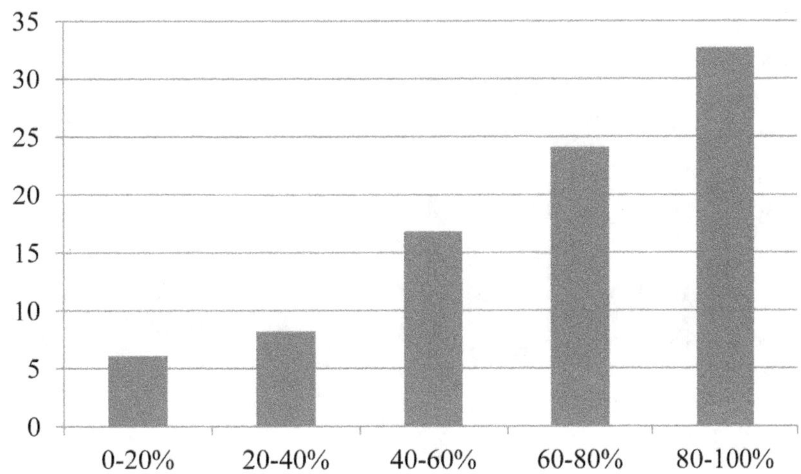

Figure 6. Source of childcare for dual earner households with children under 3 by percentile group of household income, 2010

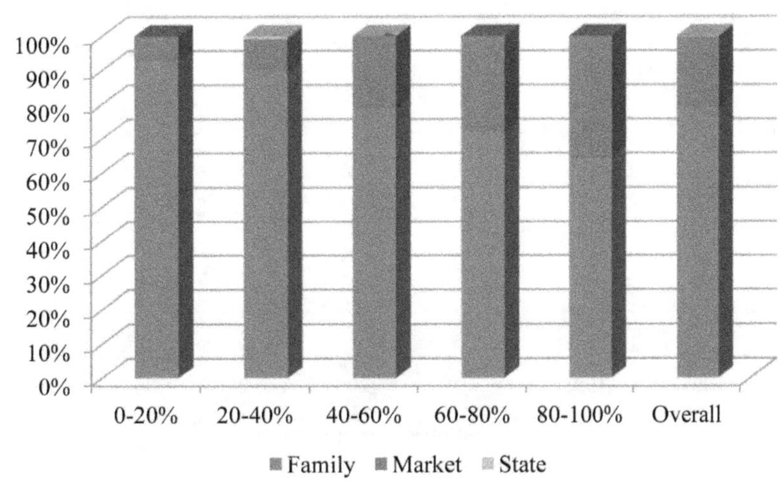

childcare costs, many of them have to turn to other family members (mostly children's grandparents) to care for their children. Moreover, the expensive childcare costs also contribute to the segregation in the measures to address the childcare demands between different income groups. In general higher income families seem to have more choices between the family and the market in balancing their work and family balance responsibilities than lower income families.

Children Aged 3-6 Years Old

For children aged 3-6 years old, there are more children cared for in institutional Early Childhood Education and Care (ECEC) services. Nevertheless, these services are highly marketised and privatised (Lin, 2006; Wang & Lai, 1997; Wang & Sun, 2003; Wu, 2006). Due to the insufficient provision of public ECEC facilities in Taiwan, the number of private facilities shows a dramatic

Figure 7. Percentages of public and private ECEC facilities (Source: calculated from Child Welfare Bureau, 2013; Ministry of Education, 2013)

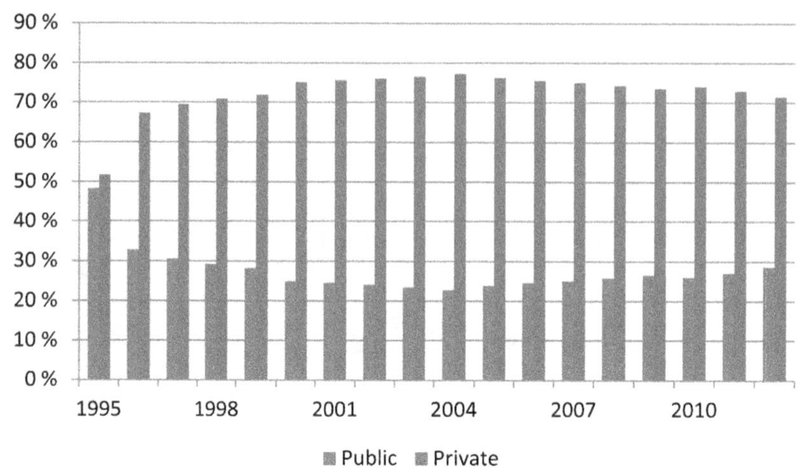

Figure 8. Percentages of children in public and private ECEC facilities (Source: calculated from Child Welfare Bureau, 2013; Ministry of Education, 2013)

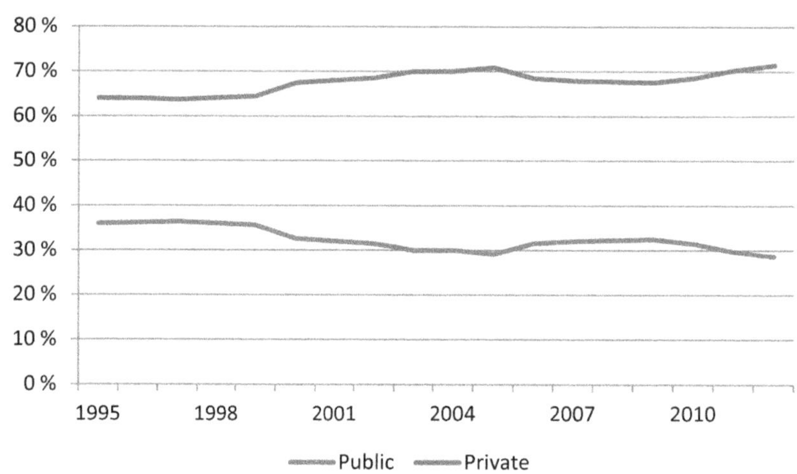

expansion in the 1980s and the 1990s. During the 2000s, about 70% of ECEC facilities are private facilities and more than one-third of children are cared for in these private facilities (Figure 7 and Figure 8).

In general private ECEC facilities are more expensive than public ECEC facilities and this also increased families' financial burden in childcare. Chiu and Liu's research (2012) has suggested that the average expenses of private ECEC services are about 9,000 NTD and the average expenses of public ECEC services are 4,000 NTD (including registration fees and monthly fees). Nevertheless, according to parents' responses, the prices these parents can comfortably afford are only about 6,000 NTD and 3,600 NTD for private and public ECEC facility users. For public childcare facility users, the gap between the real price and parents' expectation seems relatively narrow. However, the gap for private ECEC facilities is about 33% of the average expenses. This heavy financial burden also increases parents' difficulties in using market ECEC services to reconcile work and family responsibilities.

CONCLUSION

Under different context and institutional arrangements, the difficulties in work-family reconciliation may show in different ways. This article has examined several important aspects of employment and childcare patterns in Taiwan. The increase of female employment in Taiwan in recent decades was mostly from the increasing labour market participation of married women. Therefore, the conflicts between work and family responsibilities are increasingly intensified even if the total female employment rate seems not particularly high. Based on these findings, the difficulties in work-family reconciliation in Taiwan is materialised in several ways.

Firstly, family responsibilities hinder many female from employment. In Taiwan, almost 50% of female non-labour force can be explained by care for family members. Therefore, the relatively low female labour market participation in Taiwan to some extent results from serious difficulties in reconciling work and family responsibilities.

Secondly, the tendency towards full-time employment and long working hours increases the difficulties of Taiwanese families in reconciling work and family life. Contrary to the position in some European countries such as Germany, Sweden, or the UK, the female employment pattern in Taiwan shows a strong orientation towards full-time employment. Only small numbers of women take part-time employment as a way to reconcile work and childcare responsibilities. As a result, the employment behaviours of married women in Taiwan show a polarisation. They either take full-time employment or do not work at all. This tendency also shows in the dual development of the household employment structure in Taiwan. The percentage of dual full-time earner households is increasing and this has become the mainstream family structure. However, male breadwinner families are still quite entrenched. The tendency of females to stay in full-time employment may help to reduce the risk of falling into atypical employment and lower pay. Nevertheless, it also increases the conflict between work and family responsibilities and this problem is exacerbated by the very long working hours of women in Taiwan. The working hours of mothers in Taiwan are much longer than in many European countries.

Thirdly, for those women who have been already in employment, one of their difficulties in work-family balance reconciliation shows in the interruption of their careers. Although there have been more married women entering the labour market in recent decades, many women still have to leave the labour market after marriage or childbirth to fulfil their family responsibilities. In this sense, the difficulties of work-family balance for working women in Taiwan are being transformed from career termination to career interruption, and this could affect their income and welfare entitlement.

Fourthly, the expensive childcare costs in Taiwan increase the difficulties in work-family balance reconciliation for parents. With the privatisation and marketization of ECEC services in previous decades, the state only provides very limited childcare provision. Hence, dual earner households have to look for other resources to deal with the problem of childcare. For children under 3 years old, the family is still the most important source of childcare but the provision has been largely transferred from parents to grandparents. For children aged 3-6, private facilities are the most important source to provide ECEC services. Nevertheless, the expensive childcare fees lead to the segregation between different income groups. Families with higher income are more likely to use market services to meet their childcare demands, whereas low income groups still have to rely on their family support. Therefore, work-family balance difficulties appear severer for dual earner families with lower income.

REFERENCES

Bonoli, G. (2006). New social risks and the politics of post-industrial social policies. In *The politics of post-industrial welfare states: Adapting post-war welfare states to new social risks*. London: Routledge.

Child Welfare Bureau. (2013). *Childcare service statistics*. Retrieved from http://www.cbi.gov.tw/CBI_2/internet/main/index.aspx

Chiu, C.-P., & Liu, C.-L. (2012). *A study on childcare insitutions in Taiwan*. Taipei: Research, Development and Evaluation Commission, Executive Yuan. [in Chinese]

Gough, I. (2004). East Asia: The limits of productivist regimes. In *Insecurity and welfare regimes in Asia, Africa and Latin America: Social policy in development contexts*. Cambridge, UK: Cambridge University Press. doi:10.1017/CBO9780511720239.007

Jacobs, D. (1998). Social welfare systems in east Asia: A comparative analysis including private welfare. *CASEpaper*.

Jones, C. (1993). The Pacific challenge: Confucian welfare states. In *New perspectives on the welfare state in Europe*. London: Routledge.

Kwon, H.-J. (1997). Beyond European welfare regimes: Comparative perspectives on east Asian welfare systems. *Journal of Social Policy*, *26*(4), 467–484. doi:10.1017/S004727949700514X

Lewis, J., & Campbell, M. (2009). The policymaking context: Behaviour and attitudes. In *Work-family balance, gender and policy*. Cheltenham, UK: Edward Elgar. doi:10.4337/9781848447400.00008

Lin, W.-I. (2006). *Social welfare in Taiwan: Historical experiences and institutional analysis*. Taipei, Taiwan: Wu-Nan. [in Chinese]

Ministry of Education. (2013). *Number of schools, teachers, staff, classes, students, and graduates between 1950 and 2012*. Retrieved from http://www.edu.tw/pages/detail.aspx?Node=4075&Page=20046&Index=5&WID=31d75a44-efff-4c44-a075-15a9eb7aecdf

National Statistics. (2013). *Labor force statistical tables*. Retrieved from http://eng.stat.gov.tw/ct.asp?xItem=12683&ctNode=1609&mp=5

OECD. (2007). *Babies and bosses - Reconciling work and family life: A synthesis of findings for OECD countries*. Paris: OECD.

OECD. (2009). *OECD employment outlook 2009: Tackling the job crisis*. Paris: OECD.

Taylor-Gooby, P. (2004). New risks and social change. In *New risks, new welfare: The transformation of the European welfare state*. Oxford, UK: Oxford University Press. doi:10.1093/019926726X.003.0001

Wang, S.-I., & Lai, S.-Y. (1997). The predicament of childcare and role of the state in Taiwan. In *Women, state, and care*. Taipei, Taiwan: Fembooks. [in Chinese]

Wang, S.-Y., & Sun, M.-W. (2003). The role of the state in the childcare policy. [in Chinese]. *National Policy Quarterly*, *2*(4), 147–174.

Wu, S.-C. (2006). Current childcare services in Taiwan. In *Childcare services*. Taipei, Taiwan: Psychological Publishing. [in Chinese]

KEY TERMS AND DEFINITIONS

Childminder: A person who looks after children, especially those whose parents are working.

New Social Risk: Risks related to the de-industrialisation and tertiarisation of employment, women's entry into the labour market, the increasing instability of the family structure and processes linked to the privatisation of the welfare state. In short, the discourse on new social risks reflects social and political changes that have occurred in recent years especially in Western Europe, but which have significance also elsewhere.

Work-Family Reconciliation: The reconciliation between work, private and family life.

ENDNOTES

[1] 2006 data for Taiwan.

Chapter 10
The Social Risk of Low Fertility in Taiwan

Pei-Yuen Tsai
Yuan Ze University, Taiwan

ABSTRACT

This chapter examines the low fertility phenomenon in Taiwan and argues that the low fertility problem can be identified as a type of new social risk. Existing studies on new social risks tend to focus on the social risks that have negative influences on individuals but ignore those that have more negative influences on the whole society, such as the low fertility problem. This chapter illustrates how the Taiwanese government recognizes low fertility as a social risk and how such recognition facilitated the recent development of policies that support families and children.

INTRODUCTION

This chapter examines the low fertility phenomenon in Taiwan and argues that the low fertility problem can be identified as a type of new social risk. Existing studies on new social risks tend to focus on the social risks that have negative influences on individuals but ignore those that have more negative influences on the whole society than individuals, such as low fertility problem. This chapter illustrates how the Taiwanese government recognises low fertility as a social risk and how such recognition facilitated the recent development of policies that support families and children.

DOI: 10.4018/978-1-4666-5031-2.ch010

Managing social risks is one of the important goals of social policies (Esping-Andersen, 1999). Nevertheless, it appears that social risks have shown significant changes in the past decades. During the period after Second World War, the main social risks were recognised as interruptions of employment due to retirement, unemployment, disability, sickness, and widowhood (Taylor-Gooby, 2004). However, with the changes of social, economic, and demographic circumstances, many scholars have pointed out that there has been a dramatic change in social risk structure in post-industrial society (Bonoli, 2007; Esping-Andersen, 1999; Huber & Stephens, 2006; Taylor-Gooby, 2004).

Although many countries have faced similar trends of post-industrial transitions and challenges, the social risks and problems in every welfare system are not necessarily identical. Since social risks derive from idiosyncratic national contexts with distinct institutions, political structures, and policy discourses, these post-industrial challenges could be translated into different problems in different backgrounds (Pierson, 2001; Prior & Sykes, 2001; Taylor-Gooby, 2004). Under different institutional arrangements, some welfare systems may be more vulnerable to some post-industrial changes. Therefore, the pattern of new social risks in different countries could be very different. Moreover, the identification of social risks could involve a process of social construction and interpretation between many different policy actors in the society (Cox, 2001; Mehta, 2011). Thus, in the circumstances with very different compositions of policy actors and perspectives, the types and extent of social risks or problems recognised by policy makers could be accordingly very different.

This diverse social risk structure in different contexts elicits two questions. Firstly, although some scholars such as Taylor-Gooby (2004) and Bonoli (2006) have indicated several types of new social risks in post-industrial society, the concept, definition, and consequences of these new social risks are mostly originated from the studies on Western welfare states (Aust & Bonker, 2004; Bonoli, 2006; Huber & Stephens, 2006; Larsen & Taylor-Gooby, 2004; Taylor-Gooby, 2004; Timonen, 2004). Given the diversities in social, economic, political, and demographic structure between different countries, it is debatable whether the welfare systems outside the Western welfare states share the same new social risks. Apart from the types of new social risks indicated in existing literature, do these countries outside the Western world have other type of new social risks? In order to gain a more extensive comprehension of new social risks and corresponding policies, it is crucial to examine prominent problems in other societies to explore this issue. As low fertility is a very serious issue in many East Asian countries including Taiwan, this chapter attempts to take Taiwan as a case to examine whether low fertility problem in Taiwan can be identified as a type of new social risks.

Secondly, previous new social risk studies tend to focus on the influences of new social risks on some individuals or social groups. These studies indicated that there are some groups who are more exposed to the threats of new social risks, such as working women, families with young children, young people, and low-skilled workers. Although these groups may have more incentives to promote new policies that address new social risks, in general their capacity to influence policy making tends to be lower. Thus, the pressures of the government to formulate new policies to address new social risks are accordingly lower (Bonoli, 2006). Nevertheless, the development of new social risk policies seems not always to reflect the political power of new social risk groups. Taking the development of work-family balance policies in Taiwan as an example, the state intervention in childcare and leave policies in Taiwan has shown significant reinforcement in the past ten years (Tsai, 2011b). However, the political power of the direct beneficiaries of these policies such as working women or families with children did not really show a dramatic increase during this period. In this case, how can policy analysts explain the changes of these work-family balance policies?

The aim of this chapter is to address these two research questions. First, can low fertility be identified as a new social risk in the context of Taiwan? Second, given that the political power of new social risk groups (including working women and families with young children) in Taiwan did not show significant changes, why did work-family balance policies in Taiwan still show quick development in the last decade? In order to explore the two issues, this chapter will firstly examine the fertility phenomenon in Taiwan. The second half will illustrate how the general public and policy actors in Taiwan understand and interpret the low fertility phenomenon. Finally, the chapter will return to the discussions on the two research questions.

SEARCHING FOR 'NEW' NEW SOCIAL RISK?

With the transition from industrial society to post-industrial society in many countries, some scholars have suggested the concept of 'new social risks' to distinguish the difference of social risks between the two different stages (Esping-Andersen, 1999; Taylor-Gooby, 2004). According to Talylor-Gooby's definition, the term 'new social risks' refers to the risks which people encounter in their lives resulting from the transition to a post-industrial society (Taylor-Gooby, 2004, p. 3). Based on this definition, Taylor-Gooby (2004) identified a few types of new social risks which include difficulties in balancing work and family life and changing labour market risks. Changing labour markets risks can be further divided into three types: risks in entering the labour market, difficulties in maintaining stable, secure, and well-paid employment and associated social security entitlement, and problems in getting proper training in a flexible labour market.

In a similar approach, Bonoli (2005) also elaborated new social risks more specifically in five categories. Bonoli's classification of new social risks includes reconciliation between work and family life, lone parenthood, having a frail relative, possessing low or obsolete skills, and insufficient social security coverage. Essentially Bonoli's classification of new social risks is similar to Taylor-Gooby's typology (Bonoli, 2005; Taylor-Gooby, 2004).

Slightly different from their approach, Huber and Stephens (2006) adopted the notion of poverty to conceptualise social risks. They define new social risks as the increasing possibility of social groups at risk in falling into poverty due to demographic, economic, and social structure changes. In their analysis, working-age population, lone mothers, and children are new social risk groups whereas elderly people are regarded as old social risk groups.

Summing up these definitions and classifications, broadly speaking, there are several common features of new social risks. Firstly, these new social risks are 'new'. These social risks were marginal in the post-war period but they are typical in contemporary post-industrial society. Secondly, new social risks are not shared by all the people. They tend to concentrate on some vulnerable groups such as young people, families with young children, working women, and low-skill or low-education workers. Thirdly, the needs of new social risk groups are not sufficiently met by post-war welfare states (Bonoli, 2005, 2006; Huber & Stephens, 2006).

Although the concept of new social risks provides some insights in understanding the changes of social pressures and problems, there are some limitations to this concept. Firstly, although many scholars generally agree that new social risks refer to the social risks which emerge in post-industrial societies, it appears that there is a lack of consensus on clear definitions and criteria of post-industrial society. According to their illustrations, post-industrial transitions do not only refer to the changes from manufacturing to service employment. It also includes the changes of family structure, female employment, demographic changes, and so on. However, the transformation of these phenomena is not all the same in every country. This makes the concept of post-industrial society and new social risks vague and unclear. In societies with different levels and patterns of post-industrial transition, these societies could also have different types of new social risks (Tsai, 2011a).

Secondly, in addition to the different level of post-industrial changes, the institutions are also diverse in every country. For instance, according to Bonoli's classification of new social risks, it includes the insufficiency of social security coverage to meet the demands of new social risks (Bonoli, 2006). However, the social welfare and social security systems in every country are not the same. Therefore, even if these countries encounter similar challenges, the social risks and social problems in these countries still could be quite different, not to mention the post-industrial challenges for these countries may be very different as well. As Huber and Stephens (2006) have suggested, the debate on old and new welfare states overlooks the diversities between different welfare regimes. With the dissimilar types of welfare regimes and institutions, the risk structure could be also different. Therefore, the concept of new social risks is not always identical in different contexts.

Thirdly, the recognition of social risks is not constant. As Esping-Andersen (1999) has suggested, there are three reasons why 'individual risks' become 'social risks'. Firstly, when individual risks lead to collective consequences, these risks will be regarded as social risks. Secondly, if the control of individual risks is beyond individual's capacity, these risks could be de-individualised and shared by the society. Finally, some individual risks are socialised just because the society believes these risks need serious public consideration. Based on these criteria, new social risks could be any risk which policy makers or the society recognise as an important problem to address. Hence, the concept and implications of new social risks could vary according to the contexts and the understandings of policy makers.

From the review of existing studies on new social risks, it can be found that new social risks are not necessarily a fixed idea or concept. The definition or concept of new social risks could be highly affected by a specific background of a society. Therefore, in societies with very different social, political, economic, and demographic structures, the social risks recognised by policy makers could be very different. As a result, there could be more types of new social risks apart from existing classifications. Accordingly, with different ideas and understandings of new social risks, the politics of new social risks may display different political cleavage, policy dynamics, and policy discourse. Hence, the patterns of policy development also could show very different results.

In order to explore new types of new social risks, this chapter attempts to examine the low fertility phenomenon in Taiwan. As one of the East Asian welfare systems, the institutional arrangements, social circumstances, political structure, level of economic development, and demographic structure all show very different characteristics from those in Western welfare states (Aspalter, 2001; Goodman, White, & Kwon, 1998; Gough, 2004; Holliday, 2000; Walker & Wong, 2005). Hence, the social risk structure in Taiwan could be very different from that in Western societies. Since low fertility issue is a very prominent issue in Taiwan in recent years and Taiwan has become the country with the lowest fertility rate in the world in 2010 and 2011 (Department of Household Registration Affairs, 2012; OECD, 2012). This chapter attempts to examine the low fertility issue in Taiwan and examine whether this phenomenon can be identified as a type of new social risk and how it influences the development of new social risk policies in Taiwan.

This research mainly adopts descriptive statistics and documentary analysis to illustrate the lower fertility issue in Taiwan. Firstly, this chapter uses the data of government statistics and the data of 'Survey of Social Development Trends' (a large-scale government survey in Taiwan) to show the fertility phenomenon in Taiwan. With the demonstration of the descriptive statistical data, it can show the seriousness of this problem in Taiwan. Secondly, this research adopts documentary analysis to show the public concern towards low fertility. The analysis of policy documents can help to understand how policy makers in Taiwan recognise and interpret the low fertility issue, and how these understandings contributed to policy changes.

THE DECLINE OF FERTILITY RATE IN TAIWAN

The fast decline of fertility rate has become a prominent issue in Taiwan. In the past 30 years, the total fertility rate has dropped from 2.5 in 1981 to 0.9 in 2010 (Figure 1). Although the rate in 2011 showed a slight increase to 1.1, it was still much lower compared to many countries.

Compared to OECD countries, the pace of fertility decline in Taiwan was much faster than many OECD countries. It dropped from 1.4 in 2001 to 0.9 in 2010. In 2010, the fertility rate in Taiwan (0.9) was only about half of the OECD average (1.7). Even if in the comparison between East Asian countries, which tend to have lower fertility rates in general, the fertility rate in Taiwan was still lower than Japan (1.4) and Korea (1.2) in 2010 (Table 1).

With the lowest fertility rate around the world, the concern for fertility has become an urgent issue for the Taiwanese government. The decline of fertility could have significant implications and impacts on the labour supply and financial sustainability of welfare systems in the future (OECD, 2007). According to the estimation of Council for Economic Planning and Development in Taiwan, with the decline of fertility rate and increase of the elderly, the dependency ratio in Taiwan will start to increase from 2015 and it could reach 104% in 2060. This development could have significant influences on the economic development of Taiwan (Department of Manpower Planning, 2010). If this trend continues, it will also lead to heavy care burden for the working population in the following 50 years (Table 2).

With regard to the reasons which constrain fertility behaviours, the Survey of Social Development Trends in 2006 investigated the factors which affect Taiwanese people's decisions in giving birth

Figure 1. Total fertility rate in Taiwan (1981-2011) (Source: Department of Household Registration Affairs, 2012)

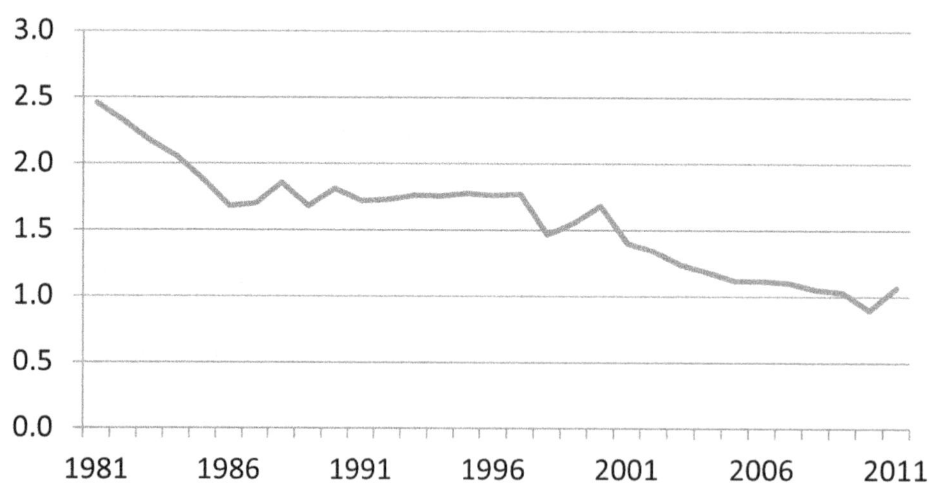

Table 1. Total fertility rate (2001-2010)

	2001	2002	2003	2004	2005	2006	2007	2008	2009	2010
Taiwan	1.4	1.3	1.2	1.2	1.1	1.1	1.1	1.1	1.0	0.9
Finland	1.7	1.7	1.8	1.8	1.8	1.8	1.8	1.9	1.9	1.9
France	1.9	1.9	1.9	1.9	1.9	2.0	2.0	2.0	2.0	2.0
Germany	1.4	1.3	1.3	1.4	1.3	1.3	1.4	1.4	1.4	1.4
Japan	1.3	1.3	1.3	1.3	1.3	1.3	1.3	1.4	1.4	1.4
Korea	1.3	1.2	1.2	1.2	1.1	1.1	1.3	1.2	1.2	1.2
Sweden	1.6	1.7	1.7	1.8	1.8	1.9	1.9	1.9	1.9	2.0
UK	1.6	1.6	1.7	1.8	1.8	1.8	1.9	2.0	1.9	2.0
US	2.0	2.0	2.0	2.1	2.1	2.1	2.1	2.1	2.0	1.9
OECD-34	1.6	1.6	1.6	1.7	1.7	1.7	1.7	1.8	1.7	1.7

Source: Department of Household Registration Affairs (2012); OECD (2012).

Table 2. Population structure estimation in Taiwan (2005-2006)

	Population Age Structure (%)			Dependency Ratio (1)+(3) / (2) (%)
	0-14 years (1)	15-64 years (2)	65 years and Above (3)	
2005	18.7	71.6	9.7	39.7
2010	15.6	73.6	10.7	35.7
2015	13.0	74.4	12.6	34.4
2025	11.0	68.7	20.3	45.6
2030	10.7	64.9	24.4	54.1
2060	9.4	48.9	41.6	104.3

Source: Council for Economic Planning and Development (2011).

to children. The result (Figure 2) shows that among those aged 15-49 who do not want to have children, financial pressures were the most important concern (25%). Moreover, 23% reported that they had doubts towards the prospect of the society. In addition, 17% of them were worried about the difficulties in caring for and educating children. There were also 2% who thought that having children could affect their career development. This demonstrates that financial pressures and care responsibilities were two important reasons why the fertility rate in Taiwan was so low. Moreover, a high percentage of people did not have confidence towards the future of the society.

Overall, the data shows that the low fertility problem is very serious in Taiwan. Encountering many difficulties and constraints, many people were not willing to have children. Such a trend could threaten the sustainability of the economic development and welfare system in Taiwan and thus it arouses the concern of the government and the general public.

POLICY MAKERS' CONCERN FOR LOW FERTILITY

With the concern for the future of economic development and sustainability of the welfare system in Taiwan, low fertility has been recognised as an important social issue by policy makers in Taiwan. This concern can be found in politicians'

Figure 2. Main reason for not having children in 2006 (aged 15-49)(%) (Source: Calculated from the Survey of Social Development Trends)

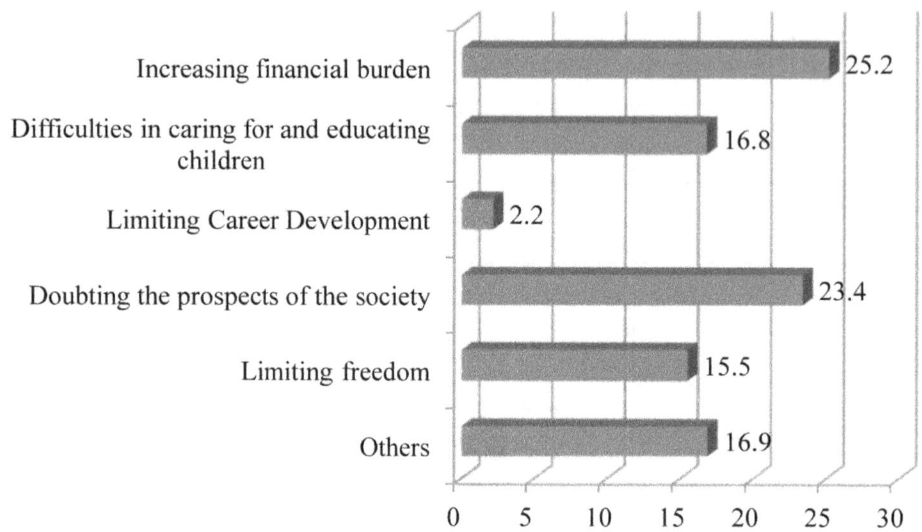

discourse and policy statements. The worries for low fertility also facilitated the development of childcare and leave policies in Taiwan.

The problem of low fertility has been emphasised by politicians and this shows that this issue has aroused high level of public attention in political arena. One of the evident examples is the discourse of the president. In 2011, the president of Taiwan, Ma Ying-Jeou, expressed his concern for low fertility and pointed out that this problem should be taken as an important issue equivalent to national security. Moreover, the president ordered the Council for Economic Planning and Development (CEPD) to formulate corresponding policies to address the low fertility problem (Lo, 2011). To some extent this demonstrates that the problem of low fertility has drawn high attention of politicians and they have realised that this problem cannot be addressed only by individuals and families. Instead, the government has recognised the imperative to tackle this problem with state intervention.

The worries for low fertility also showed in important government meetings. In 2006, the Taiwanese government organised a national conference, the National Conference on Taiwan's Economic Sustainable Development, and invited many influential people including politicians, public officials, entrepreneurs, scholars, and leaders of social groups to discuss the most important pressing social issues in Taiwan and seek for corresponding policies. In this national conference, low fertility was taken as one of the most prominent social security issues in the conference agenda (Secretary of the National Conference on Taiwan's Economic Sustainable Development, 2008a, 2008b). Moreover, several policy recommendations such as the reform of childcare policies and parental leave policies were made by the participants of this conference in order to cease the trend of the declining fertility (Secretary of the National Conference on Taiwan's Economic Sustainable Development, 2008a; Tsai, 2012). These policy recommendations were later adopted and implemented by the government (Ministry of the Interior, Ministry of Education, Council of Labor Affairs, & Department of Health, 2006). This also shows the public concern for the low fertility issue. There has been a general agreement that the low fertility problem is an important social security issue and the government should formulate policies to address this problem.

In addition to government conferences and meetings, the government also implemented population policy reforms to respond to the demographic challenges including the decline of fertility rate and ageing population. The Taiwanese government amended the 'Population Policy Guidelines' in 2006 and 2011 (Executive Yuan, 2011; Ministry of the Interior, 2011). In the introduction section of the 2011 Population Policy Guidelines, it particularly emphasised that Taiwan is one of the countries with the lowest fertility rate in the world and the fertility change in Taiwan is faster than in Western countries. This will bring severe challenges to national development in the future. For this reason, the government should formulate corresponding policies to address this problem (Executive Yuan, 2011).

Apart from the general policy guidelines, the Taiwanese government also formulate specific policies to target at the problem of low fertility. The government published the 'Population Policy White Paper' in 2008 and later revised it in 2011 (Ministry of the Interior, 2011). The goal of this Population Policy White Paper is to address three prominent population issues: declining fertility, ageing population, and immigration. In this policy white paper, the Taiwan government again emphasised low fertility rate as an urgent social problem. In order to deal with this problem, the government would implement policy changes in 7 areas: 'Strengthen the childcare system for families', 'Provide financial support for families with children', 'Create a family-friendly working environment', 'Improve maternity and parental leave arrangements', 'Enhance health care for childbirth', 'Reinforce child protection system', and 'Improve marriage opportunities and promote the value of children as public goods' (Ministry of the Interior, 2008). This shows how the public worries about low fertility contributed to the development of policies that support families.

These examples demonstrate that the general public and the government in Taiwan have identified low fertility as a pressing problem. Moreover, many policy actors and the government also recognised that it requires the intervention of the government to tackle this problem. Therefore, many new policies were formulated and implemented in the past ten years to enhance the support for families and encourage families to have children.

LOW FERTILITY AS A SOCIAL RISK

This chapter has examined the low fertility phenomenon in Taiwan, how the Taiwanese government and policy makers interpreted this issue, and how they responded to this problem. It shows that the Taiwanese government has recognised the low fertility problem as a social risk and it acknowledged the imperative for state intervention to deal this problem. This understanding facilitated the formulation of more new policies to support families to have children.

According to Esping-Andersen (1999), individual risks could become social risks for several reasons, such as when individual's fates have common effects on the society, when the risks are beyond individual's control, or when the society recognises the needs for public consideration. In these cases, individual risks will need to be socialised and they need collective actions to tackle these risks. The low fertility problem in Taiwan fits into all the three cases. Firstly, many individuals' decisions of not having children could threaten the sustainability of economic development and the welfare system so it could lead to common negative effects. Secondly, an increase in the fertility rate of the whole society cannot be done by only a small number of individuals so it is beyond individuals' control and needs some collective actions or policies to deal with it. Thirdly, it has been officially recognised as a pressing issue by the government and this can be confirmed in many government meetings and policy documents, such as the conclusions of the National Conference on

Taiwan's Economic Sustainable Development, Population Policy Guidelines, and Population Policy White Paper. Therefore, the low fertility rate should be identified as a type of new social risk in the context of Taiwan.

Existing literature on new social risks tends to focus on the effects of social risks on individual's life (Bonoli, 2006; Taylor-Gooby, 2004). However, these studies ignored the social risks which have more impacts on the public instead of individuals. Low fertility is this type of social risk that has been ignored. According to Taylor-Gooby's definition (2004, p. 3), new social risks are those problems which individuals may face during the transition from industrial to post-industrial society. However, some new challenges in post-industrial societies like the low fertility may not have direct negative impacts on individual's life, but they could have significant influences on collective welfare and then indirectly affect people's life. This type of problems also needs the actions of governments to address them but they were missing in the new social risk discussions. Therefore, this chapter argues that apart from those social risks that have negative impacts on individuals, the discussion of social risks should include those social risks that have negative on whole the society but not necessarily have direct negative influences on individuals.

Incorporating this kind of collective social risks is particularly important for understanding the development of new social risk policies. Previous new social risk studies tend to focus on the influences of new social risks on individuals or some social groups. Based on such a tendency, some studies assumed that there are some groups who are more vulnerable to new social risks and these groups may have more incentives to promote new policies which address the new social risks. However, these groups tend to have lower political power in general and thus they usually find it difficult to promote policies that address new social risks (Bonoli, 2006).

This assumption may be very correct and useful in explaining the development of new social risk policies in many cases. Nevertheless, such an understanding of the politics of new social risk policies may encounter difficulties in explaining why some new social risk policies still can develop even if the political power of new social risk groups is not particularly strong. Drawing on the case of Taiwan, the Taiwanese government still implemented many policy changes to help families to reconcile work and family responsibilities (these policies are usually identified as policies addressing new social risks), even if the political power of working women and families with children (usually identified as new social risk groups) is not particularly strong. The explanation of such a development needs to take the influences of low fertility into account. When Taiwan faces the post-industrial challenges, the data shows that the fertility rate in Taiwan declined much faster than in many other countries in recent 10 years. With this dramatic demographic change, the general public and the Taiwanese government recognised the imperative to address the problem of low fertility, and this understanding facilitated the development of work-family balance policies because policy makers believed that these policies could raise fertility rate. From the diagnosis in government policy documents, it shows that the Taiwanese government believed that difficulties in work-family reconciliation are an important factor that leads to low fertility. If families can better reconcile work and family responsibilities, they may have more incentives to have children. This understanding of and concern for low fertility contributed to the development of new policies that support families to reconcile work and family responsibilities. Without taking low fertility into account, it will be difficult to explain these policy changes in Taiwan. In the context of Taiwan, low fertility is an important social risk recognised by the government and it indeed facilitated the changes of some family policies such as childcare and parental leave policies. Therefore, this chapter suggests that the studies on new social risks or the development of corresponding policies should take this type of social risk into account.

REFERENCES

Aspalter, C. (2001). *Conservative welfare state systems in east Asia*. Westport, CT: Praeger.

Aust, A., & Bonker, F. (2004). New social risks in a comparative welfare state: The case of Germany. In P. Taylor-Gooby (Ed.), *New risks, new welfare: The transformation of the European welfare state*. Oxford, UK: Oxford University Press. doi:10.1093/019926726X.003.0002

Bonoli, G. (2005). The politics of the new social policies: Providing coverage against new social risks in mature welfare states. *Policy and Politics, 33*, 431–449. doi:10.1332/0305573054325765

Bonoli, G. (2006). New social risks and the politics of post-industrial social policies. In K. Armingeon, & G. Bonoli (Eds.), *The politics of post-industrial welfare states: Adapting post-war welfare states to new social risks*. London: Routledge.

Bonoli, G. (2007). Time matters: Postindustrialization, new social risks, and welfare state adaptation in advanced industrial democracies. *Comparative Political Studies*, *40*(5), 495–520. doi:10.1177/0010414005285755

Council for Economic Planning and Development. (2011). *Human resource and social welfare*. Retrieved May 10, 2011, from http://www.cepd.gov.tw/m1.aspx?sNo=0012631

Cox, R. H. (2001). The social construction of an imperative: Why welfare reform happened in Denmark and The Netherlands but not in Germany. *World Politics*, *53*(3). doi:10.1353/wp.2001.0008 PMID:17595731

Department of Household Registration Affairs. (2012). *Total fertility rate*. Retrieved Oct 20, 2012, from http://sowf.moi.gov.tw/stat/year/y02-04.xls

Department of Manpower Planning. (2010). 2010-2060 Taiwanese population estimation. *Taiwan Economic Forum, 8*(9), 66-70.

Esping-Andersen, G. (1999). *Social foundations of postindustrial economies*. Oxford, UK: Oxford University Press. doi:10.1093/0198742002.001.0001

Executive Yuan. (2011). *Population policy guidelines*. Author.

Goodman, R., White, G., & Kwon, H.-J. (1998). *The east Asian welfare model: Welfare orientalism and the state*. London: Routledge.

Gough, I. (2004). East Asia: The limits of productivist regimes. In I. Gough, & G. Wood (Eds.), *Insecurity and welfare regimes in Asia, Africa and Latin America: Social policy in development contexts*. Cambridge, UK: Cambridge University Press. doi:10.1017/CBO9780511720239.007

Holliday, I. (2000). Productivist welfare capitalism: Social policy in east Asia. *Political Studies, 48*(4), 706–723. doi:10.1111/1467-9248.00279

Huber, E., & Stephens, J. D. (2006). Combatting old and new social risks. In K. Armingeon, & G. Bonoli (Eds.), *The politics of post-industrial welfare states: Adapting post-war welfare states to new social risks*. London: Routledge.

Larsen, T. P., & Taylor-Gooby, P. (2004). New risks at the EU level: A spillover from open market policies. In P. Taylor-Gooby (Ed.), *New risks, new welfare: The transformation of the European welfare state*. Oxford, UK: Oxford University Press. doi:10.1093/019926726X.003.0008

Lo, I.-C. (2011). Ma ying-jeou: Low fertility has become a national security problem. *World Journal*. Retrieved from http://www.worldjournal.com/pages/full_news/push?article-%E9%A6%AC%E8%8B%B1%E4%B9%9D%EF%BC%9A%E5%B0%91%E5%AD%90%E5%8C%96%E6%88%90%E5%9C%8B%E5%AE%89%E5%95%8F%E9%A1%8C+&id=10942140&instance=noon

Mehta, J. (2011). The varied roles of ideas in politics: From whether to how. In D. Béland, & R. H. Cox (Eds.), *Ideas and politics in social science research*. Oxford, UK: Oxford University Press.

Ministry of the Interior. Ministry of Education, Council of Labor Affairs, & Department of Health. (2006). 2015 economic development visions-The three-year implementation scheme of the great warmth social welfare package: Stage one (2007-2009). Author.

Ministry of the Interior. (2008). *Population policy white paper: Strategies towards declining fertility, ageing population, and immigration problems*. Taipei, Taiwan: Ministry of the Interior.

Ministry of the Interior. (2011). *A century retrospect and prospect of population policy*. Taipei, Taiwan: Ministry of the Interior.

OECD. (2007). *Babies and bosses - Reconciling work and family life: A synthesis of findings for OECD countries*. Paris: OECD.

OECD. (2012). *OECD family database*. Retrieved Oct 20, 2012, from http://www.oecd.org/els/familiesandchildren/42293894.xls

Pierson, P. (2001). Post-industrial pressures on the mature welfare states. In P. Pierson (Ed.), *The new politics of the welfare state*. Oxford, UK: Oxford University Press. doi:10.1093/0198297564.003.0004

Prior, P. M., & Sykes, R. (2001). Globalization and the European welfare states: Evaluating the theories and evidence. In R. Sykes, B. Palier, & P. M. Prior (Eds.), *Globalization and European welfare states: Challenges and change*. Basingstoke, UK: Palgrave.

Secretary of the National Conference on Taiwan's Economic Sustainable Development. (2008a). *The minute of the national conference on Taiwan's economic sustainable development: Part 1*. Taipei, Taiwan: Council for Economic Planning and Development.

Secretary of the National Conference on Taiwan's Economic Sustainable Development. (2008b). *The minute of the national conference on Taiwan's economic sustainable development: Part 2*. Taipei, Taiwan: Council for Economic Planning and Development.

Taylor-Gooby, P. (2004). New risks and social change. In P. Taylor-Gooby (Ed.), *New risks, new welfare: The transformation of the European welfare state*. Oxford, UK: Oxford University Press. doi:10.1093/019926726X.003.0001

Timonen, V. (2004). New risks: Are they still new for the Nordic welfare states? In P. Taylor-Gooby (Ed.), *New risks, new welfare: The transformation of the European welfare state*. Oxford, UK: Oxford University Press. doi:10.1093/019926726X.003.0004

Tsai, P.-Y. (2011a). The transformation of social risks and adaptation of welfare institutions in Europe. In B. Li (Ed.), *European and American welfare systems: Challenges, reforms and constraints*. Beijing: China Social Press.

Tsai, P.-Y. (2011b). *The transformation of work-family balance policies in Taiwan*. Paper presented at the The 8th EASP International Conference. Social Policy in East Asia and Beyond: Rethinking Social Policy Strategies in Times of Uncertainty. Hong Kong.

Tsai, P.-Y. (2012). The transformation of leave policies for work-family balance in Taiwan. *Asian Women*, *28*(2), 27–54.

Walker, A., & Wong, C.-K. (2005). Introduction: East Asian welfare regimes. In A. Walker, & C.-K. Wong (Eds.), *East Asian welfare regimes in transition: From Confucianism to globalisation*. Bristol, UK: Policy.

KEY TERMS AND DEFINITIONS

Low Fertility: In a society, the sub-replacement fertility (at a level below about 2.1 children born per woman) will in the absence of immigration lead to decrease in population. The total global fertility rate per woman is about 2.3. Most countries with sub-replacement fertility still have growing populations due to immigration and increases in life-expectancy, while some countries with the combination of sub-replacement fertility and emigration/ low levels of immigration have experienced population decline. These countries include Russia, Ukraine, Lithuania and Japan.

Post-Industrial Society: Originally in the 1970s a concept in sociology describing a certain stage of society's development when the service sector generated more wealth than the manufacturing sector of the economy. The changes in production and lifestyles were accompanied by profound changes in culture, creativity and technology. The discourse on post-industrial society paved way to the concept of post-modern society.

Section 3

Health and Care Sector and the Spectrum of Public and Private Spheres

In this section, the book tackles the health and care-related issues and policies. In fact, health and care-related issues often inhibit the grey area between the private and public spheres. Furthermore, families are still very much involved in these issues, as the East Asian examples clearly demonstrate.

Chapter 11
Utilization of Primary Health Services in Hong Kong:
Inequality, Risk, and Public–Private Interaction

Raymond K. H. Chan
City University of Hong Kong, Hong Kong

Kang Hu
Southwestern University of Finance and Economics, China

ABSTRACT

This chapter analyzes the issue of primary health care utilization in Hong Kong and introduces the case of Hong Kong where a special division between public and private sectors has developed in the field of primary health services. The chapter argues that in the foreseeable future, it is likely that the division of health care between the public and private sector will be maintained. In recent years, more and more individuals and families have purchased private health insurance so as to gain more options. The idea of universal health insurance was rejected by the public in recent consultations; the current alternative is government-regulated private insurance. Although private primary health services will continue as usual in the near future, public primary health services should be maintained or even expanded. Given the costliness of private services (especially specialist services), it is recommended that more resources should be invested in corresponding public health services.

DOI: 10.4018/978-1-4666-5031-2.ch011

INTRODUCTION

In the area of health care, Hong Kong has shown favourable indicators and positive development in the past decades. The provision of low-cost universal health services has served as a safety net, though the quality of these services is sometimes doubtful and there is still a reliance on supplemental private treatments. Still, health care in Hong Kong receives its share of criticism, not only because of its overall quality but also because of its accessibility and affordability. There is a clear division of labor between the public and private providers: the former deals with most secondary and tertiary health-care services, while the latter concentrates on primary health care. Since 2000, the government, which strongly supports greater private sector contribution (though it recognizes the necessity of public health provision), has sought to promote a better connection between the two sectors and, more particularly, more efficient utilization of private sector services.

Since the private services are profit-driven and the public services are heavily subsidized by the government, there are significant differences in the fees charged by the two types of providers. However, private health services remain competitive by offering shorter waiting times, easier to be accessible by having the clinics operated in the local communities, and arguably better service quality, to those who can afford that.

The aim of this chapter is to examine the utilization of primary health services by Hong Kong residents in order to determine their accessibility and affordability. Two surveys, conducted in 2009 and 2013, reveal that Hong Kong citizens, on the whole, are satisfied with their utilization of primary health services, as well as with their perceived health status. The findings also confirm that certain demographic and economic background variables are significant predictors of utilization. In this chapter, we will see that inequalities in primary health-care services are increasingly evident across social classes, mostly due to economic factors. Hong Kong has a long history of supporting private primary care. While better synchronization between public and private health-care sectors may improve the situation, any reform must address the plight of those who cannot afford private services. This is particularly important because income disparities in Hong Kong are widening, and redistributive measures are limited due to the conservative taxation system and the small scale of welfare provision.

HEALTH STATUS IN HONG KONG

In terms of health indicators, Hong Kong has attained a level comparable to other advanced economies and recorded consistent improvement in the past few decades. In 2012, life expectancies were 80.7 and 86.9 for men and women, respectively, compared to 67.8 and 75.3 in 1971. Infant mortality and maternal mortality rates were 1.5 and 2.2, respectively, in 2012, compared to 18.4 and 14.2 in 1971. As Table 1 illustrates, there have been very favourable developments in recent years (Census and Statistics Department, 2012b).

These achievements were made possible by government investment in health, as well as adequate private funding of both public and private health services. The Hong Kong government invested in the public health infrastructure, supporting general and specialized clinics, as well as hospitals. The government spent HK$ 34,182 million[1] on health services in 2001/02 and HK$ 45,181 million in 2011/12—an increase of 32.2% (Census and Statistics Department, 2012b). From 1989/90 to 2009/10, the percentage of the GDP devoted to health expenditure rose from 3.6% to 5.2% (Food and Health Bureau, n.d.). Still, 5.2% does not compare well with the percentages of other Asian advanced economies and is even less impressive when compared to all other advanced economies (see Table 2).

In Hong Kong, the share of private expenditure to the total health expenditure is significant. The share of private health expenditure was 45.5% in 2000 and has steadily increased, reaching 50.6%

Table 1. Health indicators, 1971–2012

	1971	1976	1981	1986	1991	1996	2001	2006	2012
Infant mortality rate	18.4	14.3	9.7	7.7	6.5	4.0	2.7	1.8	1.5
Maternal mortality rate	14.2	18.21	7.99	2.76	5.68	3.09	2.03	1.53	2.2
Crude death rate	5.0	5.1	4.8	4.7	5.0	5.0	5.0	5.5	6.1
Life expectancy									
Male	67.8	69.6	72.3	74.1	75.2	76.7	78.4	79.4	80.7
Female	75.3	76.2	78.5	79.4	80.7	82.7	84.6	85.5	86.9

Source: Census and Statistics Department, 2012a.

Table 2. Total expenditure on health, 2000–2010

	2000	2002	2004	2006	2008	2010
Total Expenditure on Health as % of GDP						
Hong Kong*	5.1	5.3	5.5	4.9	4.7	5.2
Japan	7.6	7.9	8.0	8.2	8.6	--
Singapore	2.4	2.9	3.4	3.3	3.6	4.0
South Korea	4.5	4.9	5.3	6.0	6.5	7.1
Taiwan	5.5	6.0	6.2	6.3	6.5	6.5
France	10.1	10.6	11.0	11.1	11.0	11.6
Sweden	8.2	9.2	9.1	8.9	9.2	9.6
United Kingdom	7.0	7.6	8.0	8.5	8.8	9.6
Canada	8.8	9.6	9.8	10.0	10.3	11.4
Private Share Expenditure on Health as % of Total Expenditure on Health						
Hong Kong*	45.5	43.1	42.3	47.7	50.8	50.6
Japan	19.2	18.7	19.3	20.6	19.2	--
Singapore	48.6	62.8	69.3	69.9	68.1	63.7
South Korea	51.4	46.3	47.4	44.7	44.1	41.8
Taiwan	40.0	39.6	41.1	42.7	42.8	43.0
France	20.6	20.3	21.2	21.3	23.3	23.0
Sweden	15.1	18.6	18.6	18.9	18.5	19.0
United Kingdom	21.2	20.4	18.8	18.7	17.5	16.8
Canada	29.6	30.5	29.8	30.2	29.5	28.9

Note: Figures for Hong Kong refer to financial years (i.e., the 12 months preceding 31 March of the year). The 2010 figures, then, refer to the period from April 2009 to March 2010.

Source: Food and Health Bureau, n.d.

in 2010. Only Singapore has a higher percentage (see Table 2). This illustrates the significant role played by the private consumption of health services.

Still, in terms of secondary and tertiary care, private health-care providers offer much less than public ones. For example, in 2011 there were 27,041 hospital beds under the Hospital Authority's management compared to 4,190 beds in the private sector (Census and Statistics Department, 2012b) (see Table 3). In 2010, private hospitals admitted 381,554 patients, which represented

Table 3. Public and private provision of hospital beds

	2001	2011
Public hospital beds (secondary care)	29,243	27,041
Public nursing homes (tertiary care)	1,971	4,190
Private hospital beds (secondary care)	2,903	4,098

Source: Census and Statistics Department, 2012b.

approximately 21% of the total admissions that year. Generally speaking, about 80 per cent of the health expenditure for secondary and tertiary health care is from public funding (Hong Kong Government, 2012b). There is evidence, though, that the private sector share is growing: though the number of hospital beds it provides is still relatively small, it did increase by 41.2% from 2001 to 2011. The main reason for this increase was the sudden demand for obstetric services due to the influx of Mainland women who wished to have their babies in Hong Kong.

Private health services have concentrated on primary health care, which is usually provided by small clinics operated by one medical practitioner or a small group. If we use expenditure as an indicator, in 2009/10, hospital services accounted for approximately 70% of public health expenditure. In contrast, hospital care expenditure only accounted for 18% of the private health expenditure. Nevertheless, private expenditure in hospital care has recorded a substantial increase from mid-2000s, very likely due to the sudden increase of obstetric services (Table 4).

Statistics also show that the share of health expenditure from out-of-pocket payments and private insurance steadily increased in the 2000s (Table 5).

The private sector share of primary health services was also tracked by doctor consultation surveys conducted by Census and Statistics Department. In the most recent survey in 2012, 67.5% of the respondents who had consulted medical practitioners during the preceding fourteen days had consulted private practitioners. Only 31.8% had consulted a practitioner from public outpatient clinics. Nevertheless, a comparison with a 1996 survey shows that the percentage of people consulting private medical practitioners has been decreasing which could be possibly explained by the worsening economic condition from 2000s (see Table 6).

Table 4. Hospital care expenditure by sectors

	% of Public Expenditure	% of Private Expenditure
1989/90	58.4	8.5
1991/92	65.6	9.2
1993/94	66.7	9.2
1995/96	68.7	9.3
1997/98	69.8	9.0
1999/2000	70.3	9.3
2001/02	71.1	10.1
2003/04	72.1	11.4
2005/06	72.1	13.2
2007/08	72.0	15.6
2009/10	69.2	18.0

Source: Food and Health Bureau, n.d.

Of course, this does not mean that public health care plays a negligible or shrinking role in the provision of primary health services. As the figures in Table 6 show, its share has increased in recent years. Because public health facilities charge much lower fees than private ones, they attract many patients (Table 7), particularly from lower-income groups.

In summary, the Hong Kong health service system is characterised by a division of labour between the private and public health sectors: the former focuses on primary health-care services. Out-of-pocket payments are the main source of

Table 5. Total health expenditure by selected sources (HK$ million)

	Government	% of Total	Employer-Provided Group insurance	% of Total	Private Household Out-of-Pocket Expenditure	% of Total	Private Insurance	% of Total
1989/90	7,749	39.8	2,049	10.4	9,212	46.9	263	1.3
1991/92	13,393	45.6	2,724	9.3	12,554	42.7	361	1.2
1993/94	18,657	64.1	3,652	9.3	15,948	40.1	480	1.2
1995/96	25,316	49.4	4,622	9.0	18,989	37.0	1,336	2.6
1997/98	31,671	50.9	5,782	9.3	21,952	35.3	1,961	3.2
1999/2000	35,997	54.5	5,733	8.7	21,359	32.3	2,374	3.6
2001/02	39,152	56.9	5,388	7.8	21,006	30.5	2,721	4.0
2003/04	39,889	57.7	5,073	7.3	20,367	29.5	3,079	4.5
2005/06	36,934	52.3	5,359	7.6	23,712	33.6	3,663	5.2
2007/08	38,828	49.2	6,162	7.8	27,440	34.8	4,721	6.0
2009/10	43,823	49.4	6,595	7.4	30,961	34.9	6,041	6.8

Source: Food and Health Bureau, n.d.

Table 6. Percentage distribution of consultations made by type of practitioner consulted

	Public sector	Private sector	Others
1996	23.2	76.8	--
2001	18.9	81.2	--
2002	23.9	76.1	--
2006	28.2	71.2	--
2008	29.4	69.6	1.0
2009	28.3	70.7	1.0
2012	31.8	67.5	0.7

Source: Surveys of doctors' consultations with Hong Kong Residents conducted by the Census and Statistics Department in various years.

payment to the private providers, followed by private insurance. While government funding is still crucial for the health service system, the role of the private health sector cannot be ignored. The ability to avail oneself of private health services, particularly for primary care, contributes to the maintenance of good health (Chan and Hu, 2012).

PRIMARY HEALTH SERVICES IN HONG KONG: THE PRIVATE-PUBLIC PARTNERSHIP

Public health services, especially for secondary and tertiary care, have received more attention, as well as the lion's share of government funding, in recent years (Chan, 2011). Nevertheless, in the last decade, there has been growing recognition of the importance of primary health services in the overall health system. Primary health care is the first step in the health-care process.

In 2005, the Health and Medical Development Advisory Committee issued a discussion paper regarding an increase in primary care services and the strengthening of the collaboration between

Table 7. Outpatient services provided by public sector, 2000–2010

Public primary health services	2000	2003	2005	2007	2009	2011
Hospital Authority						
General out-patient attendances	813,013	3,297,989	5,211,682	4,774,703	4,703,732	4,933,794
Specialist out-patient attendances (clinical)	5,697,507	5,490,046	5,804,970	5,817,147	6,124,699	6,684,152
Family medicine specialist clinic attendances	74,760	189,506	174,552	204,321	267,633	281,014
Accident and emergency attendances	2,423,079	1,911,508	2,049,129	2,073,443	2,200,540	2,202,456
Department of Health						
General outpatient services	6,546,033	3,124,661	712,988	670,706	683,679	639,739
Other outpatient services	7,244,084	7,050,484	6,998,348	6,576,295	6,477,286	6,307,697

Note: The significant decrease in the number of visits for general outpatient services was mainly due to the phased transfer of public general outpatient clinics from the Department of Health to the Hospital Authority from September 2001 to July 2003.

Sources: Census and Statistics Department, 2006, Tables 13.12 & 13.13; 2011, Tables 13.11 & 13.12.

the public and private sectors. The government followed up with a consultation document—'Your Health, Your Life'—in 2008, which reiterated its commitment to enhance primary health-care services in order to reduce the burden put on the secondary and tertiary services, which the government mainly funds (Hong Kong Government, 2008). Both documents argue that more effective use of the private sector to promote primary health services is essential. In 2010, other health reforms were proposed: the general direction of the reforms was to strengthen the core public health-care system, which would be complemented by a competitive private sector that would be available to a greater number of citizens. There should also be measures to enable more people to be able to consume private health services (Hong Kong Government, 2010). The emphasis on collaboration between the private and public sectors—the so-called public-private partnership (PPP) model—has been well received. So far, the main strategy has been to provide subsidies to those patients who receive needed health services from the private sector. This reduces the pressure on public health services and, at the same time, better utilizes the private health services. In the past few years, the Hospital Authority has launched several such initiatives:

1. **The Cataract Surgery Programme (Initiated in February 2008):** Participating patients receive subsidies (HK$ 5,000) for cataract surgery performed by private ophthalmologists. The patient is required to make an additional payment of not more than HK$ 8,000. By March 2013, of the 67,707 eligible patients, 18,439 had engaged the services of 107 ophthalmologists and more than 13,900 had completed the surgery. This substantially reduced the wait time. For surgeries performed in public health facilities, as the average wait times range from seven months (Hong Kong West Cluster) to 21 months (New Territories West Cluster).[2]
2. **General Outpatient Services:** The general outpatient PPP project was implemented in

Tin Shui Wai, a typical low-income community, in June 2008 and was expanded in 2010. Patients dealing with chronic diseases whose health is stable but who require long-term follow-up care are invited to join the programme. Their health service needs are met by private medical practitioners in the vicinity. The patients receive a subsidy from the Hospital Authority to cover extra costs, so that they pay the same fees for their consultation and drugs as those charged by public health services. The scheme also covers medical tests and diagnostic services. By the end of 2011, ten private doctors and 1,618 patients had enrolled in the programme.

3. **The Public-Private Chronic Disease Management Shared Care Programme:** A pilot of this program was introduced in the Sha Tin and Tai Po districts of the New Territories East Cluster of the Hospital Authority in March 2010 and was subsequently extended to the entire Hong Kong East Cluster in September 2010. The programme offers chronic disease patients partial subsidies to allow them to have follow-up consultations with private practice doctors.
4. **The Haemodialysis Public-Private Partnership Programme:** Launched in March 2010, this programme allows eligible patients with end-stage renal diseases to have their services delivered by private haemodialysis providers.

The government has also introduced a number of vaccination schemes for children and the elderly through PPP. Its aim is to provide easily accessible subsidized services that will prevent the spread of infectious diseases. Another important policy—the Elderly Health Care Voucher Scheme—was introduced in 2009. During the pilot project for the scheme, seniors over the age of 70 were provided with five HK$ 50 health-care vouchers per year, as a partial subsidy for private health-care services if they chose to use them and thus reduce the burden on public primary health services. By the end of 2011, 3,066 private health service providers had joined this scheme and more than 387,000 eligible seniors (57%) have claimed the vouchers. The scheme was extended and expanded in 2012 so that each eligible senior now receives ten HK$ 50 health vouchers per year. Due to high demand, the pilot scheme became a full-time programme and the total value of the vouchers per senior rose again—from HK$ 500 to HK$ 1,000 per year (ie., from ten to 20 vouchers)—in 2013. The government also allows up to HK$ 3,000 of unspent vouchers to be carried forward to the next year.

It could be argued that primary health-care services have received increasing attention in the overall government health service strategic plan. There are concerns, however, that the fact that these services are provided predominantly by the private sector limits their accessibility and affordability.

The public primary health services also have been criticized for long wait times and inconvenient locations. According to the Hospital Authority, the median waiting period for new patients seeking specialist services for the period from April to December 2011 could be as long as 101 weeks (in the case of routine cases seeking orthopaedics services in the Kowloon East region).[3] In 2013, longest waiting times (the 90th percentile) for ear, nose and throat specialists for routine cases ranged from 33 weeks in New Territories West Cluster to 151 weeks in the Kowloon East Cluster. The Hospital Authority has introduced triage measures in order to provide priority services to those who are classified as 'urgent' or 'semi-urgent' cases. In the case of orthopaedics services in the Kowloon East region, the wait times were reduced to one week for urgent cases and seven weeks for semi-urgent.

The problem of affordability is mainly confined to the private sector. The Hospital Authority's mission is to provide services that are affordable to lower-income groups. The current charges are

HK$ 45 for general outpatient visits, HK$ 100 for the first visit with a specialist (and HK$ 60 thereafter), and HK$ 100 for a visit to the accident and emergency unit. Prescriptions are HK$ 10. Those receiving social security have these charges waived, and those who do not receive social security but still cannot afford these services can apply to have the charges waived after means testing. It is generally held that public primary health services are affordable.

Higher costs are typical of the private sector. A 2010 survey conducted by the Hong Kong Medical Association found that the median charge for a regular clinic consultation was HK$ 200 and the median charge for a specialist consultation was HK$ 575 per visit (though follow-ups were lower: HK$ 100 and HK$ 300 for general practitioners and specialists, respectively. In the period between 2006 and 2010, there was an increase of 11.1% and 15.0% in general and specialist consultation fees, respectively. The average rate of increase per year was not particularly high but was higher than the overall inflation rate of 8.8%.

The fact that the cost for specialist services is much higher in the private sector than in the public may explain the increase in the demand for public specialist outpatient services in recent years (see Table 7). As Hong Kong has experienced successive economic challenges since late 1990s, which have limited income growth, lower-income groups are particularly sensitive to fee hikes. It is natural that people have serious concerns about the fees charged in the private sector. Defending the sector's interest, the Hong Kong Medical Association has argued against any kind of public intervention in fee setting.

Inequality in the utilization of health services, even in highly developed countries heavily subsidized by state, is not rare. Utilization of, or access to, health services is commonly understood as the ability to obtain needed health-related services (Kirby and Kaneda, 2005). In practice, it is usually measured by determining how many individuals have unmet medical needs, experience delays in getting medical care, and have a reliable source of medical care or by simply counting the number of physician visits (Hall et al., 2008). The effect of better utilization of health services on health status is obvious. Other things being equal, better access to affordable health services promotes individuals' health.

Given the importance of this issue, considerable research had been devoted to identifying the determinants of inequality in the utilization of health services. One well-documented determinant is socio-economic status (SES) (Kirby and Kaneda, 2005; Kirby, Taliaferro and Zuvekas, 2006). Studies commonly adopted income, education and occupation as the indicators of SES (Goodridge et al., 2012). These three indicators, as Fujishiro et al. (2010) note, reflect the two aspects of SES—resources and status. Income and education indicate the volume of resources and imply status, while occupation, through its prestige in a particular social context, is an explicit indicator of one's social status. Occupation is a valid indicator, especially in Hong Kong, as a significant percentage of private health services are paid for by company health insurance benefits (see Table 5).

The health services provision in Hong Kong, like many other developed economies, is mostly financed by the government. In the sphere of primary health services, great efforts have been made to increase access to affordable private health services through subsidization. Nevertheless, there are no limits on the charges made by private medical practitioners. Given the increasingly important role to be played by primary health-care services in the overall health services system and current concerns about utilization (its accessibility and affordability), it is timely to examine primary health services, a subject that has received relatively little attention. This type of study will provide us with additional information on primary health services utilization and its associated problems in Hong Kong.

THE STUDY

Data for this comparative analysis are drawn from two social quality surveys conducted in Hong Kong in late 2009 and 2013. Access to two similar surveys provides richer data to verify hypotheses and support arguments. A comparison of the two surveys' findings can also provide us with insight into the impact of changing socio-economic trends on utilization of primary health services and health assessment in Hong Kong during this four-year period. For the 2009 survey, samples were drawn by a quota sampling method from various districts in Hong Kong. Voluntary respondents were invited to complete a self-administered questionnaire with close-ended question. Altogether, there were 681 valid samples in this survey. For the 2013 survey, the study collected data from 1,075 respondents through a random household telephone survey. The response rate was 37.8%.

Utilization of Primary Health Services

We selected three similar indicators to measure satisfaction in the utilization of primary health services (UPHS) in the two surveys. The higher the score, the better the appraisal of UPHS in its accessibility (distance and waiting time) and affordability. The ranges of the UPHS indicators in the two datasets were different: those in 2009 dataset ranged from 1 to 3, while those in 2013 dataset ranged from 1 to 4. As shown in Table 8, 77.4% of 2013 respondents considered the distance to clinic and hospital was not an issue. This rate was quite close to the finding in 2009: 79.9% of respondents said they have 'no difficulty' with the distance to the clinic or hospital (Table 9).

Regarding the issue of wait times, 52% of the 2013 respondents agreed that wait times were 'too long', while only 36.9% of the 2009 respondents felt this way. More than half (53.8%) of the 2013 respondents considered medical costs an issue compared to only 31.6% of 2009 respondents.

As well as comparing percentages, we used a 0 to 100 scale to formulate a standardized mean (the higher the score, the more positive the evaluation) to facilitate comparisons of the 2009 and 2013 findings. On the basis of the standardized mean, we can see that respondents in the 2013 survey were barely satisfied with primary health services (standard mean = 51.74). Of the three indicators, the only one that did not seem to pose a problem was distance to the health services. Comparing the two survey results, it is easy to conclude that overall evaluation of UPHS is declining (the overall standardized mean = 51.74 and 82.42 in 2013 and 2009, respectively) (see Tables 8 and 9).

Table 8. Descriptive statistics of 2013 UPHS

Items	Percentage				Mean (SD)	Standardized Mean (SD)	N
	1. Totally Agree	2. Somewhat Agree	3. Somewhat Disagree	4. Totally Disagree			
1. Too far away from clinic / hospital	8.6	14	51.9	25.5	2.94 (.86)	**64.72 (28.65)**	934
2. Too much waiting time	21.8	30.2	34.5	13.5	2.40 (.97)	**46.59 (32.40)**	934
3. Medical cost too expensive	23.2	30.6	37.5	8.7	2.32 (.92)	**43.91 (30.82)**	934
Overall (3 indicators)	Alpha=.535				2.55 (.66)	**51.74 (22.07)**	935

Table 9. Descriptive statistics of 2009 UPHS

Items	Percentage			Mean (SD)	Std. Mean (SD)	N
	1. Very Difficult	2. Some Difficulty	3. No Difficulty			
1. Distance to clinic/hospital /medical centre	2.3	17.8	79.9	2.78 (.470)	**88.79 (23.51)**	642
2. Waiting time for arranging an appointment	8.7	28.2	63	2.54 (.651)	**77.15 (32.54)**	641
3. Medical costs	5.4	26.2	68.4	2.63 (.585)	**81.47 (29.25)**	645
Overall (3 indicators)	Alpha=.644			2.65 (.447)	**82.42 (22.33)**	650

Self-Perceived Health Condition

In both surveys, the respondents' health satisfaction was measured by a single indicator. In the 2009 survey, they were asked to rate their satisfaction with their health status, and in the 2013 survey, they were asked to rate their health condition. Though the wording is slightly different, the meaning is the same.

In the 2013 survey, the respondents were asked to rate their health condition on a scale ranging from 1 to 5, where 1 indicates 'very poor' and 5, 'excellent'. On average, the respondents reported good health (mean = 3.52, S.D. = .823). In the 2009 survey, the respondents were asked to rate their satisfaction with their health status on a scale ranging from 1 to 10, where 1 indicates 'very unsatisfactory' and 10, 'very satisfactory'. The respondents also exhibited a good level of satisfaction; their score (mean = 6.88, S.D. =1.544) was above the scale midpoint. Judging by the standardized mean scores, the variation in overall health condition was very small across the two waves of the survey, though the 2013 score was slightly lower than the 2009 one (Table 10).

Inequality of Utilization of Primary Health Services

We chose seven socio-economic background variables for both surveys: gender, age, marital status, children, education, occupation, and social stratum. For the social stratum variable, we used self-perceived 'income' stratum in the 2009 survey and self-perceived 'social' stratum in the 2012 survey. The residents of Hong Kong consider income the main criterion in the definition of social stratum, so terms 'income stratum' and 'social stratum' have similar, though not identical meanings, which are still comparable.

Regression analysis was adopted to provide further insight into the relationship between background variables and UPHS. In the first model, only the effects of demographic back-

Table 10. Self-rated health conditions, 2009 and 2013

	Min	Max	Mean (SD)	Standardized Mean (SD)	N
2009 – self-rated health satisfaction	1 (very unsatisfactory)	10 (very satisfactory)	6.88 (1.544)	65.33 (17.16)	681
2013 – self-rated health condition	1 (very poor)	5 (excellent)	3.52 (.823)	62.92 (20.57)	1059

ground variables on UPHS were examined. In the second model, in addition to the demographic variables, three SES indicators were included in the regression model: education, occupation and self-perceived income/social stratum. These indicators were entered in the second model, as analyzing in such a way would make clear that whether the impacts of these demographic background variables on UPHS were due to these additional variables.

Table 11. Multiple regression analysis: Predicting UPHS, 2013 survey

	Dependent Variable: UPHS (2013)	
	Model 1	**Model 2**
Gender (male=0)	-.013	.014
Age(21 to 30=0)		
20 or younger	.004	.060
31 to 40	-.052	-.090*
41 to 50	-.129*	-.119*
51 to 60	-.026	.013
61 or older	-.030	.086
Marital status (unmarried=0)	.066	.029
Children (no=0)	-.170**	-.017
Education (primary=0)		
Secondary		.040
Post-secondary		.264**
Occupation (managers & professionals=0)		
Unemployed		-.189**
Clerk		-.009
Service workers		-.050
Plant workers		-.008
Elementary workers		-.040
Social stratum (lower=0)		
Middle		.093**
Upper		.105**
R^2	3.4%	12.4%
F (sig.)	3.814 (.000)	7.270 (.000)
N	888	

Note: *p<.05, **p<.01.

In the 2013 survey, the first model indicates that gender and marital status did not exhibit a statistically significant effect on UPHS (Table 11). However, people with children and middle-aged people had lower levels of UPHS. The results of the second model show that the three SES indicators are all predictors of UPHS. People with post-secondary education have higher levels of UPHS than those with a primary education. The unemployed exhibit lower levels of UPHS than the employed. Still, the variations in UPHS among occupations are negligible after controlling for background variables. People in a higher social stratum exhibit higher levels of UPHS. In addition, the results show that the impact of having children on UPHS was negligible after SES variables were added to the model. This finding suggests that the higher levels of UPHS among people without children might be due to their better socio-economic status. However, middle-aged people still exhibit lower levels of UPHS, even after controlling for the three indicators of SES.

In the 2009 survey, the first model indicates that gender, age, and marital status do not exhibit a statistically significant effect on UPHS (Table 12). Like the 2013 survey, the 2009 survey found that those who had children have a lower level of UPHS than their counterparts. In the second model, with economic background variables added to the analysis, the results show that income stratum is a robust predictor of UPHS; people in the middle- and upper-income strata exhibit a higher level of UPHS than those in the lower stratum. This also corresponds to the 2013 survey. However, education and occupation show no statistically significant effect on UPHS. The results show that the effects of having children are not sustained after controlling for the three SES indicators. Again, this finding suggests that the higher levels of UPHS among people without children might be due to their higher income.

Table 12. Multiple regression analysis: Predicting UPHS, 2009 survey

	Dependent Variable: UPHS (2009)	
	Model 1	Model 2
Gender (male=0)	-.028	-.023
Age(21 to 30=0)		
20 or younger	.034	.077
31 to 40	-.060	-.061
41 to 50	.001	.016
51 to 60	-.041	-.016
61 or older	-.081	-.043
Marital status (unmarried=0)	.131	.075
Children (no=0)	-.172*	-.090
Education (primary=0)		
Secondary		-.005
Post-secondary		.023
Occupation (managers & professionals=0)		
Unemployed		-.056
Clerk		.028
Service workers		-.012
Plant workers		-.008
Elementary occupation		-.058
income stratum (lower=0)		
Middle		.244**
Upper		.166**
R^2	2.9%	8.9%
F (sig.)	2.323 (.018)	3.599 (.000)
N	641	

Note: *p<.05, **p<.01.

Table 13. Multiple regression analysis: Predicting self-rated health condition, 2013 survey

	Dependent variable: self-rated health condition		
	Model 1 (Beta)	Model 2 (Beta)	Model 3 (beta)
Gender (male=0)	-.112**	-.093**	-.094**
Age(21 to 30=0)			
20 or younger	-.118**	-.132**	-.138**
31 to 40	-.080	-.123**	-.114**
41 to 50	-.207**	-.192**	-.180**
51 to 60	-.283**	-.275**	-.276**
61 or older	-.459**	-.387**	-.396**
Marital status (unmarried=0)	.126**	.097*	.094*
Children (no=0)	-.083	-.040	-.038
Education (primary=0)			
Secondary		.094*	.090*
Post-secondary		.092	.066
Occupation (managers & professionals=0)			
Unemployed		-.125*	-.106*
Clerk		-.051	-.050
Service workers		-.085*	-.080
Plant workers		.046	.047
Elementary workers		-.079*	-.075*
Social stratum (lower=0)			
Middle		.171**	.162**
Upper		.183**	.172**
UPHS (2013)			.100**
R^2	15.8%	22.9%	23.8%
F (sig.)	20.511 (.000)	15.153 (.000)	15.012 (.000)
N	886		

Note: *p<.05, **p<.01.

Utilization of Primary Health Services and Self-Rated Health Condition

To show the effects of UPHS on health, multiple regression analysis was adopted, in which some key background variables were controlled (Tables 13 and 14). In the first model, four demographic variables were entered, including gender, age, marital status, and children. In the second model, three SES indicators were added: education, occupation, and self-perceived social stratum. In the third model, the key predictor—UPHS—was introduced.

In the 2013 survey, the results of the first model show that gender, age, and marital status are predictors of health condition. Male and unmarried people have poorer health than their re-

Table 14. Multiple regression analysis: Predicting self-rated health condition, 2009 survey

	Dependent Variable: Self-Rated Health Satisfaction		
	Model 1 (Beta)	**Model 2 (Beta)**	**Model 3 (Beta)**
Gender (male=0)	-.076	-.051	-.049
Age (21 to 30=0)			
20 or younger	-.109**	-.053	-.059
31 to 40	-.065	-.060	-.055
41 to 50	-.113	-.078	-.079
51 to 60	-.251**	-.212**	-.211**
61 or older	-.130**	-.087	-.083
Marital status (unmarried=0)	.070	.033	.027
Children (no=0)	.018	.076	.083
Education (primary=0)			
Secondary		.009	.009
Post-secondary		.070	.068
Occupation (managers & professionals=0)			
Unemployed		-.134*	-.130*
Clerk		-.072	-.075
Service workers		-.003	-.002
Plant workers		-.015	-.015
Elementary workers		-.072	-.067
Social stratum (lower=0)			
Middle		.125**	.105*
Upper		.046	.032
UPHS (2009)			.080*
R^2	4.9%	8.3%	8.9%
F (sig.)	4.054 (.000)	3.303 (.000)	3.356 (.000)
N		641	

Note: *p<.05, **p<.01.

spective counterparts. The 21 to 30 age cohort has the best health of any age group. The difference in the health conditions of people with children and those without children is not statistically significant. The results of the second model show that the three SES indicators are all predictors of health. These SES indicators explain an additional 7.1% of variances in health condition. People with primary education suffer from poorer health. Those with a managerial or professional position have better health than service workers, unskilled workers, and the unemployed. People in the lower social strata have poorer health. Gender, age and marital status remain predictors of health after controlling for the SES indicators. The results of the third model show that UPHS has a positive effect on health (beta = .100, p<.01), even after controlling for socio-demographic and SES variables (Table 13).

In the 2009 survey, the results of the first model show that gender, marital status and children have no statistically significant effect on health. In both the 2009 and 2013 surveys, the 21 to 30 age cohort were more healthy than other age groups. The results of the 2009 and 2013 surveys differ, however, in the second model, which shows the impact of SES indicators on health. In 2009, education did not have a statistically significant effect on health condition. In terms of occupation, the unemployed had a poorer health than people with an occupation, but variations across occupations were not apparent. In terms of self-perceived income stratum, people in the lower stratum had poorer health than people in middle stratum, but the variation between the lower stratum and higher stratum was not obvious. The results of the third model reveal that UPHS has a positive effect of health condition (beta = .080, p < .05), even after controlling for demographic and SES variables—a finding that was repeated in the 2013 survey (Table 14).

Public-Private Interaction and Utilization of Primary Health Services

Three observations can be drawn based on the two waves of the survey. First, for the most part, utilization of primary health services in Hong

Kong society is satisfactory (though the 2013 result is marginally satisfactory). The surveys also suggest that self-perceived health and health satisfaction are not areas of concern. Nevertheless, a comparison between the standardized mean scores of UPHS in the two surveys shows a declining situation. Second, the analysis reveals that better utilization of primary health services would contribute to individual's health satisfaction and condition. Third, the study showed that demographic variables have an impact on self-rated health and economic background variables are also significant predictors (especially in the 2013 survey). If self-rated social or income stratum is a good proxy of economic condition, the surveys show that those who are better off and have higher occupational status enjoy better UPHS and health. This clearly demonstrates an inequality, in terms of utilization of primary health services as well as self-rated health.

The study found that certain social groups merit special attention: seniors, the unemployed and those belong to a lower self-perceived social or income stratum. In the 2013 survey, women also recorded a lower level of self-rated health. Statistical analysis confirms that those who are not well off are less likely to utilize primary health services suffered more As a result of the current wave of health reform, which emphasizes the role of private sector and its partnership with the public sector, these economically less privileged groups might be forced to turn to private sector services. Though our findings do not directly bear on the success of the PPP initiatives, the relatively poor 2013 UPHS score requires us to examine this reform carefully in the context of the 'uncertain' socio-economic conditions that have persisted since 2009. The sense of uncertainty and at-risk could be more powerful in predicting one's perception.

Macro-economic indicators showed that Hong Kong has experienced stable economic growth since the 2009 survey, with the unemployment rate contained at an acceptable level. Both median household incomes and individual incomes have shown positive growth. The minimum wage, which offers protection to low-income workers, was implemented in May 2011. All poverty indicators show signs of an improving economy as well (Table 15). Given this relatively positive scenario, one would assume that people would be more likely to be able to spend their money and access private primary health services. Nevertheless, residents of Hong Kong people seem reluctant to do so; they have not overcome the sense of the uncertainty and risk. The government, which has

Table 15. Unemployment and poverty indicators, 1997–2011

		Social Assistance		Poverty Rate Measured by 50% of the Median Household Income	
Year	Unemployment Rate	Total Claimants	% of Total Population	No. of Persons in Low-Income Households	% of Persons in Low-Income Households
1997	2.3	282,623	4.3	1,130	17.2
2001	5.1	397,468	5.9	1,150	17.7
2003	7.9	522,456	7.7	1,140	17.6
2005	5.6	539,963	7.9	1,140	17.4
2007	4.0	496,922	7.3	1,180	17.7
2008	3.5	475,625	6.8	1,170	17.6
2009	5.3	482,001	6.9	1,190	17.7
2010	4.3	466,006	6.6	1,210	17.9
2011	3.4	443,322	6.2	1,151	17.1

Sources: Census and Statistics Department, 2010, 2012d; Hong Kong Council of Social Services, 2012.

proposed a cautious and stringent budget, shares this uncertainty. It is not surprising: Hong Kong has experienced unprecedented economic fluctuation since 1997, with a series of economic crises (including the Asian financial crisis in 1997, the IT bubble burst in 2000, the SARS crisis in 2003, and the global financial crisis in 2008). A sense of uncertainty has been deeply implanted, leading to a more pessimistic orientation.

Statistics also show that those with lower incomes benefit less from the positive economic development (Table 16). Although, on the whole, there was income growth for each income decile group from 2001 to 2011, detailed analysis shows that those in the lower decile groups experienced less income growth than those in the higher decile groups. The Gini coefficient has remained at a high level. Recently, lower-, and even middle-, income groups are complaining about the increases in inflation (2.4%, 5.3%, and 4.1% in 2010, 2011, and 2012, respectively) and property

Table 16. Median monthly household income of economically active households, 2001– 2011

Income Decile Group	2001	2006	2011
1st (lowest)	6,000	5,500	7,000
2nd	10,000	9,000	10,240
3rd	12,600	12,000	14,250
4th	15,830	15,000	18,000
5th	19,600	18,210	22,000
6th	23,000	22,000	27,000
7th	28,410	27,000	33,000
8th	35,000	34,000	41,400
9th	47,250	45,750	57,000
10th	85,000	82,500	103,100
Overall	21,000	20,000	24,500
Gini coefficient			
Original	0.525	0.533	0.537
Post-tax	0.515	0.521	0.521
Post-tax post social transfer	0.470	0.475	0.475

Source: Census and Statistic Department, 2012c.

prices (private housing price indices increased from 150.9 in 2010 to 206.2 in 2012), which have swallowed up any increases in income. Many Hong Kong residents, therefore, remain uncertain, risk-averse, and pessimistic when managing their budget.

Health expenses have become a sensitive topic in the past few years, due to a series of public consultations on health finance reform, as well as the steady increase in the private health-care costs. While those with lower incomes are able (or forced) to rely on the public sector, the middle class, which is looking for an alternative to public health services, is even more worried about future medical costs. The recent PPP reforms subsidize those who can afford to pay the additional costs involved in opting for private primary health services. Theoretically, this should be a welcome development. However, it does not apply to those who cannot afford to avail themselves or choose not to for various reasons. The small scale of the current PPP coverage also means that most of the money for private primary health services still comes from non-government sources. Statistics have shown that most of the income (and hence, profits) for private primary health services come from out-of-pocket payments (including purchased private health insurance). These income and profits also rely on health insurance provided by employers (see Table 5). Reforms promoting private sector participation may actually consolidate the inequalities in health care in Hong Kong.

Most primary health-care services are provided by private medical practitioners, who charge fees according to the free market. Because Hong Kong strongly upholds participation in a free market, it would be politically unacceptable for private medical practitioners to have their prices set by the government.

After the economic upheavals of recent years, the Hong Kong government has learnt its lesson: the concept of risk has been entrenched in the government policy (Chan, 2006, 2009). To tackle risk and uncertainty, a more cautious and stringent public expenditure policy has been adopted and families have been encouraged to be prudent in managing their affairs. In an effort to contain public expenditure, and promote individual and family responsibility, reliance on the free market for service provision is a natural option in Hong Kong.

It would be unfair to argue that individuals and families are reluctant to assume the responsibility for their health care (Chan, 2010). The residents of Hong Kong still believe that they have the main responsibility to manage family-related risks. As we have noted, however, the experience of recent decades have made their attitude more cautious and risk-averse. They expect the government to continue its investment in public health services. They may not object to PPP, but they do not want to pursue it at the expense of the public health services, provided at a lower and fixed cost. Illness is an 'inevitable accident', and the cost is difficult to estimate. Private health services have been repeatedly criticized for their lack of transparency in fees. The public health service represents a safety valve for all Hong Kong residents.

Given that health services are essential for every citizen in a society, equity in the utilization—measured in terms of accessibility and affordability—is of the utmost importance. Adequate health services 'ought to be allocated on the basis of need and not willingness or ability to pay' (Doorslaer, Masseria and Koolman, 2006, p. 177). The matter for debate concerns the respective roles of the public and private sectors in satisfying these needs. The current division between the public and private sectors in the provision of primary, secondary, and tertiary care services seems reasonable: the more costly secondary and tertiary care services are heavily subsidized and hence affordable for most people.

An alternative is the further expansion of the public health provision, particularly in primary care. This is theoretically possible, but practically it is not feasible for at least three reasons: the strong private health sector might oppose it, which will threaten its survival; there is a limited supply of health-care professionals, particularly those willing to work in the public sector; and there would be an increasing burden on health funding, which the government may not be willing to commit (Chan, 2011). The current effort to establish a PPP model is acceptable as an alternative to divert some of the demands on public services, as long as patient participation is voluntary. We do not object the better utilization of private sector health services, as long as the subsidization is an aid to those can afford this option.

In the foreseeable future, it is likely that the division of health care between the public and private sector will be maintained. In recent years, more and more individuals and families have purchased private health insurance so as to gain more options. The idea of universal health insurance was rejected by the public in recent consultations; the current alternative is government-regulated private insurance. Again, this option is useful only to those who can afford the insurance. Such developments will promote private health services, especially in the areas of primary health services and less costly hospital treatments. When the cost becomes prohibitive, even with insurance, public health services remain the alternative.

Although private primary health services will continue as usual in the near future, public primary health services should be maintained or even expanded. Given the costliness of private services (especially specialist services), it is recommended that more resources should be invested in corresponding public health services. Any effort to promote PPP should not preclude the responsibility to provide public services. The low-cost public health services are particularly crucial for those with low incomes who have faced great uncertainty and risk in recent years. The 2013 survey findings alert us that low-income groups, seniors and women have suffered disproportionately in the past few years. Improving their income and their buying power through subsidization in the current PPP model is one alternative.

REFERENCES

Census and Statistic Department. (2012c). *2011 population census household income distribution in Hong Kong*. Hong Kong: Census and Statistics Department.

Census and Statistics Department. (2006). *Hong Kong annual digest of statistics, 2006*. Hong Kong: Census and Statistics Department.

Census and Statistics Department. (2010). *Feature article: Statistics on comprehensive social security assistance scheme, 1999 to 2009*. Hong Kong: Hong Kong SAR Government Census and Statistics Department.

Census and Statistics Department. (2012a). *Hong Kong life tables 2006-2041*. Hong Kong: Census and Statistics Department.

Census and Statistics Department. (2012b). *Hong Kong annual digest of statistics, 2012*. Hong Kong: Census and Statistics Department.

Census and Statistics Department. (2012d). *Feature article: Statistics on comprehensive social security assistance scheme, 2001 to 2011*. Hong Kong: Hong Kong SAR Government Census and Statistics Department.

Chan, R. K. H. (2006). Risk and its management in post-financial crisis Hong Kong. *Social Policy and Administration*, *40*(2), 215–229. doi:10.1111/j.1467-9515.2006.00485.x

Chan, R. K. H. (2009). Risk discourse and politics: Restructuring welfare in Hong Kong. *Critical Social Policy*, *29*(1), 24–52. doi:10.1177/0261018308098393

Chan, R. K. H. (2010). Managing family risk in Hong Kong: How and why. In *Risk and public policy in east Asia*. Aldershot, UK: Ashgate.

Chan, R. K. H. (2011). The politics of health finance reform in Hong Kong. *International Journal of Public and Private Healthcare Management and Economics*, *1*(2), 17–25. doi:10.4018/ijpphme.2011040102

Chan, R. K. H., & Hu, K. (2011). Primary health services utilization and inequality: The emerging symbiotic public/private model in Hong Kong. *Journal of Public and Private Healthcare Management and Economics*, *1*(4), 1–13.

Doorslaer, E. V., Masseria, C., & Koolman, X. (2006). Inequalities in access to medical care by income in developed countries. *Canadian Medical Association Journal*, *174*(2), 177–183. doi:10.1503/cmaj.050584 PMID:16415462

Food and Health Bureau. (n.d.). *Hong Kong's domestic health account (HKDHA) – Estimate of domestic health expenditure, 1989/90 – 2009/10*. Retrieved from http://www.fhb.gov.hk/statistics/en/dha.htm

Fujishiro, K., Xu, J., & Gong, F. (2010). What does 'occupation' represent as an indicator of socioeconomic status? Exploring occupational prestige and health. *Social Science & Medicine*, *71*(12), 2100–2107. doi:10.1016/j.socscimed.2010.09.026 PMID:21041009

Goodridge, D., Hawranik, P., Duncan, V., & Turner, H. (2012). Socioeconomic disparities in home health care service access and utilization: A scoping review. *International Journal of Nursing Studies*. doi:10.1016/j.ijnurstu.2012.01.002 PMID:22300550

Hall, A. G., Lemak, C. H., Steingraber, H., & Schaffer, S. (2008). Expanding the definition of access: It isn't just about health insurance. *Journal of Health Care for the Poor and Underserved*, *19*(2), 625–638. doi:10.1353/hpu.0.0011 PMID:18469432

Hong Kong Council of Social Services. (2012). *Poverty in figures (2001-2011)*. Hong Kong: Hong Kong Council of Social Services.

Hong Kong Government. (2008). *Your health, your life: Report on the first stage public consultation on healthcare reform*. Hong Kong: Hong Kong Government Printer.

Hong Kong Government. (2010). *My health, my choice: Healthcare reform second stage public consultation*. Hong Kong: Hong Kong Government Printer.

Hong Kong Government. (2011). *Hong Kong annual report, 2010*. Hong Kong: Hong Kong Government Printer.

Hong Kong Medical Association. (2010). *Report of doctors' fees survey, 2010*. Hong Kong: Hong Kong Medical Association.

Kirby, J. B., & Kaneda, T. (2005). Neighborhood socioeconomic disadvantage and access to health care. *Journal of Health and Social Behavior*, *46*(1), 15–31. doi:10.1177/002214650504600103 PMID:15869118

Kirby, J. B., Taliaferro, G., & Zuvekas, S. H. (2006). Explaining racial and ethnic disparities in health care. *Medical Care*, *44*(5Suppl), I64–I72. PMID:16625066

KEY TERMS AND DEFINITIONS

Cost: In terms of production, the value of money that has been used up to produce something, and hence is not available for use anymore. In business, the cost may be one of acquisition, in which case the amount of money expended to acquire it is counted as cost. External costs are the costs that people other than the buyer are forced to pay as a result of the transaction, while social costs are the costs that people other than the buyer are forced to pay as a result of the transaction.

Healthcare Inequality: Differences in the quality of health and health care across different populations. This may include differences in the presence of disease, health outcomes, or access to health care across racial, ethnic, sexual orientation or socioeconomic groups.

ENDNOTES

1 Exchange rate is HK 7.75 to USD 1.

2 The current public health services, both in-patient and outpatient, provided by Hospital Authority are organized into seven clusters, based on their geographical proximity.

3 Waiting time varied across regions due to supply and demand. For example, for orthopaedics, the median waiting time for routine cases was only 15 weeks for Hong Kong West region in the period from April to December, 2011. This has been criticized as resources misallocation within the Hospital Authority, meaning lesser manpower being allocated to those cluster with greater demand.

Chapter 12
Policies and Politics:
The Alternatives and Limitations of Health Finance Reform in Hong Kong

Raymond K. H. Chan
City University of Hong Kong, Hong Kong

ABSTRACT

Since the late 1950s, Hong Kong's public health services have increased. They are mainly funded by taxes, supplemented by minimal user fees. In the late 1980s, the government recognized the limitations of this financing model and has subsequently proposed alternative methods of funding. Their proposals have been rejected by various stakeholders, who represent different, and even conflicting, values and interests. This chapter describes the development of health services and the debates that have surrounded health financing since the late 1980s. It shows that the health finance debate in Hong Kong is not a simple issue that can be tackled by rational planning; instead, it is a complex consequence of welfare politics in an increasingly mobilized society.

INTRODUCTION

The earliest public health services in Hong Kong were mainly devoted to combating communicable diseases. As the government was largely unresponsive to demands for further services, the gap in provision was filled by traditional Chinese medical practitioners and hospitals operated by local philanthropic organizations. It was not until the late 1950s that the government expanded its role and investment in health care.

During the past five decades, a system of service provision has developed with a clear division of labour: the private sector oversees primary health care, and the public sector is responsible for the more expensive secondary and tertiary health care services. In terms of financing, the private sector is mainly funded by user fees, and the public sector by taxes.

DOI: 10.4018/978-1-4666-5031-2.ch012

From the 1990s onwards, there has been a heavier reliance on public health services in Hong Kong, due to improvements in these services and to the increasing number of people without the funds for private care. The burden of financing these services will soon become even heavier due to the aging population. Facing these challenges, the government has repeatedly called for health finance reforms. However, all its proposals, with the exception of a medical fee increase, have been met with strong resistance, and no decisions have been reached. In the process, conflicts have arisen among various stakeholders and social classes, though all agree that some type of reform is necessary.

This paper describes the development and characteristics of public health services in Hong Kong since the 1960s, various proposals for health care reform, and key conflicts among stakeholders. It will be shown that efforts for reform have been impeded by the welfare politics of this increasingly mobilized society.

THE DEVELOPMENT OF PUBLIC HEALTH SERVICES IN HONG KONG

The first long-term plan for the development of health services was initiated in 1957. Since that time, the government has played an increasing role in health services provision. In the 1960s, government financing was primarily devoted to the construction of clinics and hospitals. According to the White Paper "Development of Medical Services in Hong Kong",(1964) the government planned to construct a network of clinics, supplemented by specialists and hospital facilities, that would be operated by the government or by government-assisted voluntary organizations (Chan, 1996, p. 98). The document also laid down the principle that users were required to pay only a nominal fee for this universal public health service (Chau & Yu, 2003).

In 1974, the White Paper "Further Development of Medical and Health Services in Hong Kong" was endorsed. Its major objectives were to improve the hospital bed to population ratio and to establish a network in which regional hospitals and clinics combined forces with the private sector to provide primary health care. The fees charged for public health services were kept low. For example, in 1980, the charge for out-patient treatment was HK$ 3 and for in-patient treatment, HK$ 5 per day. In the 1980s, public health services continued to expand: there was a 17.5% increase in the number of government hospital beds during the decade. In the mid-1980s, however, cost efficiency became a priority. The government stated that,

The lesson of public health services all over the world is that increased expenditure does not necessarily translate into higher standards. What is really important is the way the money is used and how well the facilities are managed (Hong Kong Government, 1989, p. 14).

"The Delivery of Medical Services in Hospitals", also known as the Scott Report was published in 1985 (W.D. Scott Pty Company, 1985). It focused on health services administration, cost-recovery, and cost-containment. Improving the management of limited resources was a key issue in the 1990s. The Hospital Authority was formally established in December 1990, with the aim of maintaining the quality of services without increasing state investment.

While new forms of health financing were being explored, the easiest option—to increase user fees—was adopted. It was hoped that such policies could help to improve the Hospital Authority revenue and reduced demand on public health services (such as the accident and emergency services). In 1992, the out-patient fee was raised to HK$ 21 and the in-patient ward fee to HK$ 43. These rates are now HK$ 45 and $100, respectively. Though the increase seems dramatic, it is consistent with the growth in the general income level (e.g., the median household income was HK$ 1,425 in 1976, and HK$ 18,100 in the third quarter of 2010).

While the government concentrated in hospitals and clinics construction plan, the private sector continued to concentrate on primary health-care provision offered in small, individually owned clinics (in the past decade, there has been an increase in health-management organizations and group-practice clinics). The fees charged by these clinics are determined by the market and are not subject to government regulation. Most users pay for their treatment, though some are covered by health insurance that is either independently purchased or provided as part of an employee benefit package.

The health system in Hong Kong is based on a "dual medical economy" in which "the government has been significantly involved in both the funding and provision of health services mainly through tax financing, whereas the private sector operates in a loosely organized manner as individual clinics that dominate the ambulatory care sector" (Yeung & Chan, 2006, p. 436). In 2005, private doctors provided 76% of the primary care services, and the Hospital Authority was responsible for 92.8% of secondary and tertiary care services. In 2009, the public share of secondary and tertiary health-care expenses was 82% and the ratio of private to public hospital beds was 1:7.1. There is clearly a distinct division of labour between the two sectors.

There was no significant progress in health finance reform in the 1990s, and in the last decade health care has become further complicated by three factors: a series of financial crises beginning in the late 1990s, higher costs prompted by a rapidly aging population and outbreaks of infectious diseases (e.g., Avian Flu, SARS), and public outrage on the part of low-income earners and the middle class, who complain of the compound burden of financing health care through user fees and extra taxes. There is widespread recognition of the need to reform the health finance system.

Public health expenditure has steadily increased in the past four decades. It soared from HK$ 252 million in 1970/71 to HK$ 9,290 million in 1990/91 when the Hospital Authority was established, and by 2008/09 had grown to HK$ 36,706 million. Although the Hospital Authority intended to ensure more efficient use of financial resources, government funding increased almost four-fold from 1991/92 to 2010 (from HK$ 8,562 million in 1991/92 to HK$ 33,098 million).

Approximately 90% of public health expenditure goes to the Hospital Authority, which has no other significant source of income. Government subsidies accounted for 92.8% of the Hospital Authority's budget in 2001 and 90.6% in 2010. The second-largest source of income for the Hospital Authority is user fees. Despite increases in these fees in the last decade, they still accounted for only 7.5% of the budget in 2010 (see Table 1).

Total health expenditure, including both public and private, increased 381.7% in the period between 1989 and 2007. Government expenditure rose 482.9%, and user fees increased by 287.4%. The contribution of private insurance agencies to health expenditure increased 16-fold during this period, reflecting the growing popularity of this means of managing health risks among those who can afford it (see Table 2).

The share of private insurance in total health expenditure has increased steadily, from 1.3% in 1989/90 to 5.6% in 2006/07. The government maintains the largest share (rising from 39.4% in 1989/90 to 57.6% in 2003/04, but dropping to 49.9% in 2006/07). The total share occupied by insurance (including employer provided and private) remained stable, with 11.9% in 1989/90 and 13.0% in 2006/07. Nevertheless, share of employer-provided insurance decreased whereas the share of private insurance increased significantly. User fees, which accounted for 46.8% of total health expenditure in 1989/90, decreased to 35.2% in 2006/07. Nevertheless, Wagstaff (2005) maintains that the share of user fees is catastrophically high in comparing to other East Asian countries. In 2006/07, the share between public and private sector was roughly equal, though the public sector share was the single largest source, and took care the majority of the more expensive secondary and tertiary health services. (see Table 3).

Table 1. Hospital authority account, 2000–2010 (HK$ m)

Year	Total Income	Government Subsidy	User Fees Collected
2001	30,336	28,159	754
2002	31,474	30,138	782
2003	31,325	29,977	849
2004	31,858	30,039	1,243
2005	30,267	28,417	1,386
2006	30,130	28,019	1,628
2007	30,680	28,041	1,987
2008	32,976	29,915	2,296
2009	35,106	31,915	2,527
2010	36,544	33,098	2,726

Source: Hospital Authority Annual Report, *various years*

Table 2. Total health expenditure at current market price, 1989/90–2006/07 (HK$ m)

Fiscal Year	Total Health Expenditure	Government	Employer-Provided Group Medical Benefits	Private Insurance	Private Household Out-of-Pocket Expenditure
1989/90	19,659	7,749	2,075	263	9,202
1990/91	23,788	10,016	2,375	306	10,716
1991/92	29,382	13,394	2,755	361	12,537
1992/93	34,173	15,844	3,204	419	14,332
1993/94	39,486	18,658	3,695	480	15,910
1994/95	44,823	21,582	4,177	716	17,618
1995/96	51,288	25,316	4,680	1,336	18,963
1996/97	56,854	28,653	5,338	1,641	20,557
1997/98	62,231	31,671	5,841	1,941	21,888
1998/99	66,273	35,800	6,010	2,188	21,347
1999/00	65,929	35,997	5,745	2,374	21,214
2000/01	67,290	37,028	5,546	2,541	21,619
2001/02	68,687	39,152	5,396	2,721	20,847
2002/03	67,105	38,526	5,203	2,935	19,839
2003/04	69,214	39,889	5,115	3,079	20,443
2004/05	68,263	37,094	5,150	3,284	22,114
2005/06	70,643	36,930	5,395	3,663	23,753
2006/07	75,048	37,417	5,573	4,213	26,451
Increase (%)	381.7	482.9	268.6	1601.9	287.4

Source: Food & Health Bureau, *date unknown*

Table 3. Distribution of health expenditure by sectors, 1989/90–2006/07 (%)

Fiscal Year	Government	Employer-Provided Group Medical Benefits	Private Insurance	Private Household Out-of-Pocket Expenditure
1989/90	39.4	10.6	1.3	46.8
1990/91	42.1	10.0	1.3	45.1
1991/92	45.6	9.4	1.2	42.7
1992/93	46.4	9.4	1.3	41.9
1993/94	47.3	9.4	1.2	40.3
1994/95	48.1	9.3	1.6	39.3
1995/96	49.4	9.1	2.6	37.0
1996/97	50.4	9.4	2.9	36.2
1997/98	50.9	9.4	3.1	35.2
1998/99	54.0	9.1	3.3	32.2
1999/00	54.6	8.7	3.6	32.2
2000/01	55.0	8.2	3.8	32.1
2001/02	57.0	7.9	4.0	30.4
2002/03	57.4	7.8	4.4	29.6
2003/04	57.6	7.4	4.4	29.5
2004/05	54.3	7.5	4.8	32.4
2005/06	52.3	7.6	5.2	33.6
2006/07	49.9	7.4	5.6	35.2

Note: There are other sources of revenue, such as service providers' funds, corporation contributions, non-profit institution contributions, and non-patient-care-related revenue. Nevertheless, the total share of these items small (2.8% of the total in 2006/07).

Source: Adapted from Food & Health Bureau, *date unknown*

As Leung et al. have noted, when public health services rely on tax revenue, the burden of financing is shouldered by the well-to-do and the poor benefit, thus creating a net redistribution of resources from rich to poor (2008, p. 3). O'Donnell et al. similarly observe that the Hong Kong has the most progressively financed and strongly pro-poor system of the Asian countries compared (2007; 2008).

The situation in Hong Kong is clear: total health expenditure is steadily increasing; an growing share of public expenditure is devoted to health services; relying solely on better resource management will not solve the problem; and, for taxpayers, the set-up is not equitable—contribution does not equal consumption. The increasingly heavy reliance on public expenditure, without alternative funding sources, has become unsustainable, especially since the current tax-funded system has become the target of criticism.

HEALTH FINANCE REFORM

Financing health services was a concern even in the 1980s. During a Legislative Council debate in March 1984, Dr. Henrietta Ip suggested a medical insurance scheme where "able-bodied" citizens would pay a minimum premium and a modification of the current subsidy policy to achieve better value for money (Chan, 1996, p. 234). That year the government announced a plan to review the hospital services and commissioned the W. D. Scott Pty Co. from Australia to conduct the review. The Scott Report (W.D. Pty. Company, 1995) proposed the establishment of an independent Hospital Authority and an increase in hospital charges to improve cost recovery. The Provisional Hospital Authority was established in 1988 and was formally recognized as the Hospital Authority in December 1990.

The Provisional Hospital Authority proposed to set the cost-recovery level at 15 to 20%. In 1990, faced with accusations of unfair treatment of low-income families, the Secretary of Health and Welfare repeatedly declared that "no one will be denied adequate medical services because they cannot afford it. This is a policy statement, and policy statements do not change" (Chan, 1996, p. 241). This assurance held true in the following two decades: the principles of universality and low user fees have been maintained.

In 1993, the government published *Towards Better Health*, (1993) a position paper that suggested fee increases, but the proposal was met with strong resistance and was not adopted. In 1997, the government commissioned a team of experts from Harvard University to conduct a vigorous review of the health-care and finance systems. The resultant report "Improving Hong Kong's Health Care System – Why and For Whom?" was submitted to the government in 1999. The team proposed two schemes to tackle rising health costs: the Health Security Plan (HSP) and the Savings Accounts for Long-Term Care (Medisage). The HSP was conceived as a contributory pay-as-you-go scheme funded by employers and employees, which contributes to in- and out-patient treatments in both public and private facilities. Employers and employees would also contribute to Medisage, a mandatory long-term care insurance policy. The government would provide support to the elderly, poor, and unemployed who could not afford to contribute.

The public, however, disliked the compulsory redistribution associated with medical insurance. The budget for such schemes was also questioned by many stakeholders (e.g., Lau & Yu, 1999). The government decided to conduct another round of consultations, which resulted in the publication of "Lifelong Investment in Health" in 2000. This document offered the public more options: the maintenance of the government-funded model, an increase of fees and charges, or the establishment of individual health protection accounts for acute care after the age of 65. Again, the plan did not receive general support: the public remained hesitant to adopt a health insurance scheme. Critics of these plans have argued that changes are not necessary, and that similar results could be obtained by better rationalization of resources, more attention to health prevention, and a more progressive taxation system.

The Report, "Final Report: A Study of the Health Care Financing and Feasibility of a Medical Savings Scheme in Hong Kong" was published in 2004. The government concluded that the general public did not support compulsory contributory saving schemes, particularly younger adults. Even if such schemes were endorsed, the contributory level would have to be very low, given the consequences of the economic recession in 2003. The government chose not to pursue actions that would cause public discontent (Yu, 2006). Instead, further consultation and prolonged discussion were proposed in order to keep the agenda alive.

The document "Building a Healthy Tomorrow" was published in 2005, reviewed Hong Kong's health system, with special attention to health financing. It was followed in 2008 by another position paper, "Your Health, Your Life", which solicited the public's views on reforms to the health system and its response to five methods of health financing: mandatory social health insurance, user fees, medical savings accounts, voluntary private health insurance, and personal health care reserves (combining mandatory savings and insurance).

After long consultation and discussion, *My Health My Choice: Healthcare Reform Second Stage Public Consultation* was published in 2010.

The government realized that the public, while recognizing the need for reform, had reservations about mandatory schemes and preferred voluntary, individual health insurance schemes. It has decided to pursue the Voluntary Health Protection Scheme (HPS) —a government-regulated but privately operated scheme. A sum of HK$ 50 billion will be allocated for subsidizing HPS subscribers. It is important to note that the government has made it clear that, given its voluntary nature, the HPS cannot tackle long-term health-care financing problems and can only offer supplementary funding for more effective use of private health services.

Twenty years of consultation and public discussion have resulted in the adoption, perhaps temporarily, of a limited voluntary private insurance scheme. The sustainability of Hong Kong's public health system remains in doubt.

HEALTH FINANCE AND WELFARE POLITICS

The current health-care system, as noted, is pro-poor, with a strong orientation towards equitable treatment. Leung et al. argue that it is even more marked in pro-poor in terms of redistribution than in the social insurance systems adopted, for example in South Korea and Taiwan (2008, p. 3). The document, "Your Health, Your Life", provides a good summary of the debates surrounding health-care reform. These debates have not been restricted to methods of calculating benefits or contributions; they have also focused on the values represented by various finance options as outlined below (Food & Welfare Bureau, 2008, p. 44):

1. **Individual vs. Communal:** As the current tax-funded health system has already addressed low-income needs, the public is reluctant to adopt an additional burden of social insurance by pooling resources and risks (which translates into additional taxes for those better off).
2. **Risk-Pooling vs. Saving:** Most people felt their savings might not be adequate to cope with their medical expenses, but those with high incomes expressed stronger support for voluntary or mandatory health insurance, whereas those with low incomes tended to support the current tax-funded system.
3. **Voluntary vs. Mandatory:** There is a general bias against any mandatory scheme; voluntary options, such as voluntary health insurance and, to a lesser extent, user fee increases are preferred.
4. **Equity vs. Two-Tier System:** While those who have taken up greater tax burden and can afford the payment are demanding better quality health services for them, low-income groups are concerned that they will not be granted equal access if there is any change to the current system.

Roberts (2006) rightly notes that societal values are the ultimate determinant of health systems, and in Hong Kong, concerns about equity—in terms of service consumption (i.e., equal access to all) and service financing—have played an important role in decisions about health care. Yeung and Chan (2006) have observed that the current system separates the users from the payers – with those who are paying (the tax) mainly consuming private sector services, which will easily engender a feeling of antagonism between the payer and the uses. The system is supported by taxes paid by those who belong to the narrow tax base in Hong Kong (high tax exemptions allow a large portion of the working population to avoid taxation).

The past decades of health financing in Hong Kong have created a strong vested interest in users who have been only required to pay low fees and have been exempt from taxation. It is not surprising that the strongest resistance to change originated in low-income groups. Beginning in the early 2000s, however, the middle class, debilitated by the financial crisis, resented the obligation to pay more tax or compelled to contribute to social health insurance scheme to finance the health care system (Chan, 2009).

The government too is always keen to enact reforms that will reduce the financial burden of health care and deter the growth of a dependency culture. Still, it is unlikely that it will risk the political gamble of introducing social insurance schemes that, despite their reasonableness, will certainly be unpopular among all social classes (Yu, 2006). Both the government and the public are trapped in a dilemma: they recognize the need to change but are resistant to take up the burden of change. The current end result—the voluntary private insurance scheme—represents the lowest common denominator. Critics is already there arguing that this scheme will prove ineffective and have urged the government to do something different.

As Cheung notes, the government's failure to provide solutions is not only due to its lack of clear policy but also to the decline of its power and the lack of social cohesion in an increasingly differentiated and politicized environment. Political consultations and negotiations have been undertaken in the uncertain arena of partisan politics and political mobilization (2009, pp.10–11).

CONCLUSION

The issue of health financing cannot be solved simply by performing financial calculations and assuming that stakeholders will take up assigned positions and responsibilities. The citizens of Hong Kong have become increasingly skeptical about their government and are motivated to challenge its policies. The debates of the last twenty years clearly illustrate that the conflicts are based on opposing values. A change of the system will reflect a change of values, and a corresponding reassignment of risk responsibility among different social classes.

The technical plans of bureaucrats can no longer adequately address the welfare politics and value conflicts that have plagued health-care finance. The current situation is the lowest common denominator and does not represent a long-term or adequate solution. The government has clearly stated that it can only provide supplementary funding. As Sidorenko and Butler note, voluntary private health insurance might fail to protect the most disadvantaged (2007, p. 48).

Voluntary private health insurance might be able to reduce the public finance burden slightly, by enabling the insured to meet their needs with private health services. Nevertheless, given the aging population of Hong Kong, the increases in life expectancy, and the high costs of secondary and tertiary health care, the history of procrastination must come to an end. During the wait for the government to assume a leading role in determining health, consultations have created a platform for various stakeholders. The next move belongs to these stakeholders: to make realistic compromises to achieve a better solution.

REFERENCES

Chan, R. K. H. (1996). *Welfare in newly-industrialised society: The construction of the welfare state in Hong Kong*. Aldershot, UK: Avebury.

Chan, R. K. H. (2009). Risk discourse and politics: Restructuring welfare in Hong Kong. *Critical Social Policy*, *29*(1), 24–52. doi:10.1177/0261018308098393

Chau, R. C. M., & Yu, W. K. (2003). Marketisation and residualisation – Recent reforms in the medical financing system in Hong Kong. *Social Policy and Society*, *2*(3), 199–207. doi:10.1017/S1474746403001222

Cheung, A. B. L. (2009). *Governance in Hong Kong: In search of identity, legitimacy and trust*. Hong Kong: Hong Kong Institute of Education. doi:10.5353/th_b4675579

Food & Health Bureau. (n.d.). *Domestic health accounts (1989/90 – 2006/07)*. Retrieved July 21, 2013 from http://www.fhb.gov.hk/statistics/en/dha/dha_summary_report.htm#C

Food and Health Bureau. (2008). *Your health your life: Report on first stage public consultation on healthcare reform*. Hong Kong: Government Printer.

Food and Health Bureau. (2010). *My health my choice: Healthcare reform second stage public consultation*. Hong Kong: Government Printer.

Harvard Team. (1999). *Improving Hong Kong's health care system – Why and for whom?* Hong Kong: Government Printer.

Health, Welfare and Food Bureau. (2004). *Final report: A study on health care financing and feasibility of a medical savings scheme in Hong Kong*. Hong Kong: Government Printer.

Hong Kong, S. A. R. Government. (2000). Lifelong investment in health: A consultation document on health care reform. Hong Kong: Government Printer.

Hong Kong, S. A. R. Government. (2005). Building a healthy tomorrow: Discussion paper on the future service delivery model for our health care system. Hong Kong: Government Printer.

Hong Kong Government. (1964). *Development of medical services in Hong Kong*. Hong Kong: Government Printer.

Hong Kong Government. (1974). *Further development of medical and health services in Hong Kong*. Hong Kong: Government Printer.

Hong Kong Government. (1989). *Hong Kong annual report, 1989*. Hong Kong: Government Printer.

Hong Kong Government. (1993). *Towards better health: A consultation document*. Hong Kong: Government Printer.

Lau, K. K., & Yu, S. S. (1999). *The proposal of the harvard expert team and its comparison with other health finance models*. Hong Kong: Research and Library Section, Legislative Council Secretariat.

Leung, G. M., Tina, K. Y. K., & O'Donnell, O. (2009). Redistribution or horizontal equity in Hong Kong's mixed public-private health system: A policy conundrum. *Health Economics*, *18*(1), 37–54. doi:10.1002/hec.1342 PMID:18264997

ODonnell, O., van Doorslaer, E., Rannan-Eliya, R. P., Somanathan, A., Adhikari, S. R., Harbianto, D., … Zhao, Y. (2007). The incidence of public spending on health care: Comparative evidence from Asia. *The World Bank Economic Review*, *21*(1), 93–123. doi:10.1093/wber/lhl009

ODonnell, O., van Doorslaer, E., Rannan-Eliya R. P., Somanathan, A., Adhikari, S. R., Akkazieva, B., … Zhao, Y. (2008). Who pays for health care in Asia? *Journal of Health Economics*, *27*(2), 460–475. doi:10.1016/j.jhealeco.2007.08.005 PMID:18179832

Roberts, M. (2006). Philosophy, ethics and societal values in health system reform. In G. M. Leung, & J. Bacon-Shone (Eds.), *Hong Kong's health system: Reflections, perspectives and visions* (pp. 27–40). Hong Kong: Hong Kong University Press.

Scott Pty, W. D. Company. (1985). The delivery of medical services in hospitals. Hong Kong: Government Printer.

Sidorenko, A. A., & Butler, J. R. G. (2007). Financing health insurance in Asia Pacific countries. *Asian-Pacific Economic Literature*, *21*(1), 34–54. doi:10.1111/j.1467-8411.2007.00191.x

Wagstaff, A. (2005). *Health systems in east Asia: What can developing countries learn from Japan and the Asian tigers?* (World Bank Policy Research Working Paper 3790). Washington, DC: World Bank.

Yeung, R., & Chan, W. S. (2006). Health financing in Hong Kong: The current status. In G. M. Leung, & J. Bacon-Shone (Eds.), *Hong Kong's health system: Reflections, perspectives and visions* (pp. 435–446). Hong Kong: Hong Kong University Press.

Yu, W. K. (2006). The reforms of health care finance in Hong Kong and urban China: A mixed attitude to social welfare. *Critical Social Policy*, *26*(4), 843–864. doi:10.1177/0261018306068478

KEY TERMS AND DEFINITIONS

Debate: A method of interactive and representational argument.

Financing Model: An abstract representation that is meant to correspond to a real world financial situation.

Rational Planning: The process of realizing a problem, establishing and evaluating planning criteria, creating alternatives, implementing alternatives, and monitoring progress of the alternatives.

Chapter 13
Meeting the Care Needs of Older People:
Long-Term Care Practice in England, The Netherlands, and Taiwan

Henglien Lisa Chen
University of Sussex, UK

ABSTRACT

To address the risks to families of the availability of care for their older family members, this chapter explores the impact of different care systems on the way that relevant care actors contribute to the long-term care of older people. It focuses on how front-line professionals and formal/informal carers meet the needs of older people who are frail and disabled, since caring for older people has become one of the potential family risks in East Asia and many industrial countries in the West for a number of reasons. On the one hand, the rise in life expectancy and multiple disabilities means the number of older people requiring long-term care has increased. On the other hand, the decreased younger population with increased female employment calls into question the continued availability of family carers and requires support from public and formal carers to help them to care for their older family members for as long as possible.

DOI: 10.4018/978-1-4666-5031-2.ch013

INTRODUCTION

To address the risks to families of the availability of care for their older family members, this chapter explores the impact of different care systems on the way that relevant care actors contribute to the long-term care of older people. It focuses on how front-line professionals and formal/informal carers meet the needs of older people who are frail and disabled since caring for older people has become one of the potential family risks in East Asia and many industrial countries in the West for a number of reasons. On the one hand, the rise in life expectancy and multiple disabilities means the number of older people requiring long-term care has increased. On the other hand, the decreased younger population with increased female employment calls into question the continued availability of family carers and requires support from public and formal carers to help them to care for their older family members for as long as possible (Moss and Cameron, 2002). Although the special issue focuses on East Asia, the paper draws on a study in England, the Netherlands and Taiwan to include a wide range of readers from East and West. One of the main reasons to include the three countries is that in East Asia, e.g. Taiwan, the responsibility of care for older people is no longer sustainable by the family alone. In contrast, Western society, such as England and the Netherlands, has shifted caring responsibilities from the public to individuals and families to meet the increasing demand of ageing care. As a result, the difference between the challenges of ageing care in the three countries has closed somewhat.

Generally, meeting the care needs of frail and disabled older people required identifying their needs through assessment and providing care support through relevant formal and informal care actors, such as care professionals, service providers, hands-on care workers and family carers. With regard to the objective measurement of care needs for older people, the key principle of social policies in England, the Netherlands and Taiwan were similar. Based on the theories of human need of Maslow (1943) and Doyal and Gough (1991), firstly, one of the factors that make older people require long-term care is that they lose their ability to be able to meet the six senses of human needs themselves - a sense of security; a sense of belonging; a sense of continuity; a sense of security; a sense of achievement; and a sense of significance (Maslow, 1943) - and require help to do so. Policy has to make sure that these are taken into account in the minimal standards of long-term care provision. Secondly, the ideology of a service must have as an objective that older people need not only to survive but also to have some quality of life (Doyal and Gough, 1991).

However, the way of meeting the needs of older people are complex in practice. The thresholds of public funding support in meeting needs of older people in long-term care were different between the countries. Various English reports have indicated the focus on those with the highest demand on basic need – i.e. wash, dress, food. - and the lowest incomes (DH, 1997a). Similarly, in Taiwan where focused on those with lowest incomes, but the majority older people's needs have been met by their family or self-funding. In contrast, the Dutch public support threshold is comparably more generous, which not only includes what the other two countries provide, but also the satisfaction of higher ranked needs and guidance, such as supporting and activating/advising (Schrijvers *et al.,* 2001).

How much care support should be provided is an issue in all three countries but is associated with their historical welfare development and care culture. In the case of England, Langan (1998) and the latest Dilnot Report (Dilnot, 2011) highlighted the way in which historical budget and allocation restrictions have affected the outcome of assessment. This means that there is a great variation in the amount of service support within the country. Although there is a lack of literature on this issue, in Taiwan, it is widely acknowledged that there are great variations in assessing public funding entitlement because of a lack of central and local guidelines. The Netherlands is the only country of the three which actively addresses service inequality by centralising objective assessment criteria and independent professional mechanisms (i.e. The Regional Assessment Board (RIO)) carried out since 1997/8 (Ex *et al.*, 2004).

In both England and the Netherlands, there are formal timescales for the process of assessment, with decisions required after a maximum of six weeks (Ministry of Health, 1997; Schrijvers *et al.*, 2001; DH, 2004). A number of English research studies have shown that the face-to-face work of assessors with service users has declined in the past ten years (Levin and Webb, 1997; Audit Commission, 1999; Weinberg *et al.*, 2003; Samuel, 2005). Rushing the judgment would be likely to result in the offer of a single, often basic, support service (Fuller and Tulle-Winton, 1996; DH, 1997a). The Commission for Social Care Inspection (2004) conducted research into the impact of the English Delayed Discharge Reimbursement Scheme (HCHC, 2002) and expressed similar concerns. It found that a third of older people needing care were moved with too little consideration directly to a care home from hospital. Efficiency and effectiveness of care assessment and care support arrangements are high on the policy agenda in England and the Netherlands, and to some degree in Taiwan. However, the quality of life of older people cannot simplify be quantitative. Indeed, much of the research into the care for older people has focused on physical functioning, while mental and social-health measures have rarely been examined (Stawbridge *et al.*, 2002; Chang, 1997). Thus, there is a substantial literature that challenges the oversimplification of needs identification (e.g. Warren, 1990; Glendinning, 1992; Ungerson, 1997). It can be argued that when we examine the ways in which needs are meet in welfare systems, there is an over-emphasis on objective, professional, physical and medical definitions but not enough on the subjective views and experiences of participants and consumers.

Twigg (1997) for example, in her work on care provision, addressed the often-overlooked consequences of policy concerning the privacy and dignity of service users in care. It is evident from English studies that what older service users want in their care are professionals and carers who are able to develop and maintain a direct personal relationship, who listen and respect service users as individuals (Harding and Beresford, 1996; Godfrey, 2000; Little, 2002; Scottish Executive, 2006). Older people's perspective on the care they received is indeed important in this study and has been addressed elsewhere (see Chen, 2007). Both Phillips (2000) and Boyle (2003) further suggest that, when addressing the issues of care, the breadth of factors such as the capacity and abilities of the carers should also be recognised. This paper argues that, in order to increase the capacity and ability of caring professionals, formal carers and families, they also have to experience Maslow's six senses themselves (Nolan, 1997; Davies *et al.*, 1999; Nolan *et al.*, 2001). In 1999-2001 Jörg *et al.* (2006) carried out a survey, in the Netherlands, of 214 assessors across RIO organisations and concluded that only clearly motivated assessors were willing to support their service users' wishes. Wang (2002) suggested care actors who adopted a 'do-gooder role' (i.e. trying to be kind by acquiescing to their clients' every need) found it difficult to retain a professional distance. An increasing amount of research has been focused on informal/family carers around the areas of: a) employment and financial well-being (e.g. Glendinning, 1992; Baldwin, 1995; Carers National Association, 1999; Knijn, 2004); b) gender issues of female carers (Baldwin and Twigg, 1991; Knijn and Kremer, 1997; Lewis, 2002; Lister, 2003) and c) welfare support for informal carers (e.g. Knijn, 2001; Pickard, 2001, 2004; Ungerson, 1997, 2000, 2004).

In spite of this increasing recognition and research focus on informal carers, the wellbeing of formal carers and professionals has been largely ignored. It can therefore be argued that the volume of care workers and professionals might shrink unless better conditions can be created to stimulate them to continue providing care/services.

This chapter, therefore, explores how different care systems identify the care needs of older people. To what extent did the relevant front-line care professional and in/formal carers influence the quality of care older people received? To what extent did the caring role affect the lives of the frontline care professionals and in/formal carers?

COMPARATIVE METHODOLOGY

The research which this chapter draw was part of a qualitative cross-national study exploring the quality of life and care offered within LTC for older people through snowball method of sampling by centring on the views and experiences of older people and radiating out to their carers, professionals, local administrators, service providers, civil servants and voluntary agency officials who had held care provision responsibilities. To minimise variation in the comparative research, the service users were female, aged over 60, from the majority ethnic group, and receiving formal care support. Women were chosen to reflect on the demographic trend in the countries studied where women's propensity to live longer than men and thus their increased likelihood of needing long-term care are higher. In addition, suburban locations were chosen because neither cities nor rural areas are typical of the industrial countries studied. To maximise the range of service users in this research, five in each country received community care; two in each country received nursing care; and two received residential care in England and Taiwan. Additionally, three (including the one resident in the care hotel) received residential care in the Netherlands. The service users were approached through a local authority in England and service providers and general public in the Netherlands and service providers in Taiwan. Multiple research ethics approval was obtained according to the requirements of the countries studied. All potential participants received an information sheet and invitation letter, and those responding positively were contacted by the researcher. Twenty eight clusters with a total of 143 participants (see Table 1) were included. It is to note that migrant care workers were only involved in Taiwan because while research had conducted between 2004 and 2005, policy had been focus on qualified professionals in England and the Netherlands (Stone and Wiener, 2001). It is notable an increase awareness on the issue of migrant care workers has developed in the two countries (see Williams, 2010; van Hooren, 2012; Shutes, 2013). Nevertheless, the study provided with current debates about welfare in the light of economic pressures on long-term care of older people.

Table 1. Research participants

Participants	Number of Participants			
	England	Netherlands	Taiwan	Total
Older people	9	10	9	28
Informal carers	6	1	3	10
Low-level care workers	5	9	9	23
Health and social care professionals	11	8	11	30
Service providers	10	7	8	25
Local administrators	4	4	6	14
Civil servants, senior officials of national NGOs	3	4	6	13
Total	48	43	52	143

Comparability is restricted by the different scale and structure of each care system. The numbers of participants varied according to the nature and scale of the support network for the older people studied and the government and NGO structures at national and local levels. For example, the number of participants at national level and local administrators in the study (see Table 1) reflected the English care system's level of public responsibility, with fewer departments and NGOs in comparison with the other two countries. The snowball method of sampling in this study reflected some characteristic of care arrangement as well as care cultural differences. For instance, the number of care-workers was lesser in England in comparison with the two countries due to some care-workers was care for more than one older people studied. Access to informal carers was not always possible in England and the Netherlands, because some Dutch and English older people studied saw themselves as being independent when receiving formal support and therefore as not being dependent on their families. In Taiwan, some older people saw the research involvement as a burden for their family/informal carer, many of whom are working full-time. As result, the dissimilar number of interviewees within each interview group across the countries reflected on the structure of care system in some way and care culture in others. Nonetheless, the study included views of a wide range of people within long-term care system on issues of long-term care.

Participants were interviewed for between half and one hour, and were asked to describe their role and experience around service resources, the power and autonomy of older people, partnership working and the social inclusion of older people. Seven semi-structured interview schedules were used to match the different types of knowledge and expertise in each participant group. Although the interviews tackled a number of issues, this paper focuses only on data concerning meeting the care needs of older people.

Interviews were recorded and transcribed in full in the language of origin and English. Transcripts were scrutinised to identify emergent themes; these, combined with the main research questions, were used to develop an initial coding frame. Two-layers of comparative analysis were employed in this study: the first focuses on each interview group across the countries studied, and then analyses the themes shared by all of the groups across the three countries. The former layer provided fewer samples to manage each time, thereby allowing careful scrutiny of data at the first stage of the overall analysis and the prevention of some issues from being overlooked as they might have been if only a single layer had been used. In addition, multiple organising approaches in each layer analysis were applied by using multiple data analysis tools (i.e. Microsoft Word, Microsoft Excel and MindMap software) to minimise the potential for information to go missing (Crabtree and Miller, 1992) and by applying Becker's 'sequential' methodology in the systematic coding and analysis of the interviews, and some thematic characteristics emerged (Becker and Bryman, 2004). The methodological challenges of cross-national research have been further explored elsewhere (Chen, 2012).

FINDINGS

Macro and Meso Perspective of Care Needs: Civil Servants, NGOs Senior Officials and Local Administrators

The participants at the macro and meso levels claimed that, at national level, healthcare had been a higher priority than social care in the English system. The Director of Social Services in the English county interviewed argued that current healthcare policy had prioritised the reduction of hospital waiting lists, and that came into conflict with other policies such as client-centred care. Furthermore, there had been a very long tradition of minimum care support in England, particularly if it felt that families were able to step in. The Poor Law principle of less eligibility had still not been entirely eradicated. Most English interviewees at the macro and meso levels (5/7) suggested that the care system was subject to the availability of local resources and provided a 'safety net' of care, implying a selective welfare approach:

The amount of service they get will depend again on their dependency levels, their frailty and so on... And a lot of it is, who decided at what point in there, you know, history, what they needed, as it were, what was the assessment of need, what was available locally and so on, so people with equivalent levels of need might end up in different services (Senior official, Commission for Social Care Inspection, England).

Similarly, the Dutch interviewees at the macro and meso levels acknowledged that healthcare had dominated in their system. However, all of the Dutch participants at the national level expressed a clearer ethical obligation by the state to deliver high quality care. The state expected the care system to offer support to 'citizens' to improve their 'social participation', to achieve 'normalisation' and to obtain an 'equal right' to a decent quality of life.

In both Taiwanese and English cases, the supply of care was particularly dependent on the availability of resources. In England, there were disparities at the local authority level which led to different service entitlement thresholds. In Taiwan, the supply of care was dependent on the availability of family resources. It was also the Taiwanese aim to stimulate employment through care provision:

The government hopes it can provide affordable welfare for those older people who are financially disadvantaged. For those older people who are able to afford it, there will be a service available to help them to buy care services. It is our aim to develop both [the] welfare and the care market (Civil servant, Council of Economic Planning and Development, Taiwan).

Nearly all of the Taiwanese participants at the macro and meso levels (10/12) argued that the economy-oriented perspective might have a significant impact on the quality of care provision. Moreover, the limitation of what families can provide, within a fragmented system of state support, must be a matter of concern.

Needs Assessment in Practice: The Views of Professionals

Methods of assessment had a strong influence on the support which individuals were entitled to receive. Each country's assessment mechanism and process reflected the outcome of needs identification and the entitlement to services amongst older people. Needs identification could be defined in two parts – assessment for public funding purposes and assessment by service providers. England was the only country of the three where the assessors and budget holders were under the same authority. It is hardly surprising that English local authorities had such a strong influence on assessing needs in practice. High dependency needs, available family resources as well as funding availability were the keys to the assessment. The availability of resources restricted the assessor's autonomy significantly as most of their recommendations had to be approved by the Resource Allocation Panels (RAPs) within the local authority:

Your assessments are presented to a funding panel [RAP] which is examining those assessments and deciding whether or not to accept the recommendations (Social worker-8, England).

Many English professionals (8/11) shared the concern that resources-led services assessment had been interpreted as aiming to fit the service users into criteria, available service resources in particular, rather than to make an objective judgement which addressed the needs of individuals.

To meet the demand of care, [We assess clients] by rationing, by gate keeping, by spreading the jam very thinly, by applying the criteria more rigorously and by other routes, i.e. funding panels. This is something that forms a regular pattern within this part of social services when we get to a part of the financial year when the resources are getting low, then restrictions are applied, criteria alter (Social worker-1, England).

It doesn't matter whether that person meets these [needs] criteria, if there's no service available, that person does not meet these criteria [for care services] (Social worker-5, England).

This seemed to result in some difficulties for many English assessors (8/11). As one of the participants argued, it was difficult and rather lacking in objectivity to be an assessor and then gate-keep the very resources you were assessing for.

By contrast, assessment of needs in both the Netherlands and Taiwan was more or less independent and separate from the agencies that provided public funding. The assessors from the regional assessment agencies (RIO) in the Netherlands and healthcare professionals in Taiwan carried out assessments and identified care needs. Based on the assessment, the budget holder (the insurance company in the Netherlands and the local authority in Taiwan) had the obligation to arrange for services to be funded. The advantage of such a structure was that identification of care needs could be more objective.

The strength is that if there's a need for care, you can get it (Social worker-3, the Netherlands).

'Objective' needs identification was relatively strong in the Dutch system from this study. Firstly, the organisation of assessment was independent from local and national resource allocation. Secondly, nearly all of the assessors (7/8) said that a second opinion was usually sought when there was a disagreement between the client and the assessor. Thirdly, a uniform assessment tool was used across the country. However, more than half of the Dutch assessors (5/8) were concerned that the standard assessment tool did not reflect every individual's care needs.

The Dutch government, however, was moving in the direction of Taiwanese practice where, in order to speed up the process, assessment had been introduced with little face-face contact. Most of the Dutch assessors (6/8) were opposed to this, as less time spent on an individual client might prevent an adequate assessment outcome. The Taiwanese assessor claimed it was the only way to work in a big geographical area with a limited amount of time. In most cases, they only saw the older people once and the rest of the contact was by telephone or letters. The English assessors studied maintained strong face-to-face contact with their clients, family and relevant professionals and agencies throughout the assessment process. However, the frequency of personal contact had also declined:

At the moment, for each service user, we spend 2-3 hours visiting but several days, not hours, sitting in front of the computer to complete the paper work of their assessment (Social worker-4, England).

Most assessments were carried out by social workers and health professionals in Taiwan and the Netherlands; and by assessors, senior carers or nursing professionals in England. Assessors who worked for the service providers interviewed in

Taiwan (10) and the Netherlands (3) worked in a multi-disciplinary organisation and carried out the needs assessment based on their own professional field:

The nurse is the focus for the medical treatment of the clients, the nutritionist is the focus for the nutritional needs of clients and I am the focus for their daily wellbeing and provide them the emotional support. When the older people are first admitted into the care home, I work with them to deal with any financial problems and apply for financial support from the government, private sector or voluntary sector when necessary (Residential home social worker, Taiwan).

In Taiwan, assessors commented on the strong family influence on needs identification:

Families have a very strong influence in the assessment. Some families would force us to provide certain care which is not of much benefit to the client (Physiotherapist, Taiwan).

In practice, needs identification was often far more complicated. We have seen in all countries that assessments are undertaken following the same principles. The assessors look at the older person's physical health, mental health, mobility and ability to self-care. However, the thresholds and the services provided vary from country to country. In addition, three quarters of the assessors interviewed across the countries had to address the difficulty of meeting the expectations not only of the older people themselves but also of their families, other professionals and service providers. This shows that the power and autonomy of various actors was influential in determining the needs of, and care supports for, older people (an issue which is discussed in Author's own, 2007).

Meeting Needs: Care Provision

Following the needs assessment, the service providers, and formal and informal carers in particular, were central to providing care.

Service Providers

This paper looks at people's day-to-day experiences under the care provision. Part of day-to-day experiences was not only about basic care provision – personal care, but also about the experiences or opportunity to retain some forms of independence. A basic knowledge of needs was evidenced in interviews with English service providers, nearly half of whom (4 out of 10) visualised the principle of long-term care needs as primarily a matter of basic day-to-day living tasks:

My little pet flowers that were dying. But, she's [home carer] been told she mustn't help in the garden. She's only here for personal care, they say (Older people-6, England).

We're just there to see to the day-to-day living ... personal care, shopping, helping with laundry, cleaning, that sort of thing (Home care manager, England).

In England, the formal carers were focused on trying to get the job done and meeting people's basic needs. It was pretty stressful for the service users too, because they couldn't expect anything more sophisticated.

Many of the service providers interpreted promoting the independence of older people as meaning providing less care:

[Ms Munro[1]] is very independent, but if you do a lot for her, she'll let you do it. So you do have to

be very careful, because if you made her tea every day, she'd never make her tea again. You do have to push the independence really, say to her, come on, get yourself dressed, come on get yourself a cup of tea (Extra care housing manager, England).

While English care providers tried not to help with what the older people could do by themselves, Dutch providers focused on client-centred care provision to meet individuals' care needs and promote their independence:

To meet [an] individual's needs... [clients] need time to talk, to do the washing, not quick, quick, quick, but slowly and waiting and resting, and then again... what we always do was to get to learn about these clients, and to see what's important, and think about how to do it... and I can't tell you what that is, because everyone is different (Home care manager, the Netherlands).

The above quote also shows that the Dutch ideology of 'normalisation' was not only about individuals having equal rights, but individuals having the right to their own normal routines. The interpretation of promoting independence of older people from the English and Dutch sample also reflect the differences of care culture and training opportunities of the care workforce. These issues all relate to the differences in values reflected by the different welfare regimes in English and Dutch societies.

In the open care market of Taiwan, care providers were competitive in providing low cost (3/8) or the full range of care (5/8) to attract potential clients:

It's more economic to have a live-in carer to take care of the older people, which cost them 20,000 Taiwanese dollars [684 US dollars] a month in their own home [compared with] admitting them into a care home which will cost them much more (Foreign care agencies manager, Taiwan).

We do not provide personal care but healthcare, treatment, rehabilitation and social care to the clients. We have our own transport for older people to attend our hospital for rehabilitation (Nursing home manager, Taiwan).

Nearly all of the service providers (7/8) viewed the care service as primarily for the families:

We are helping the family to take care of their elderly (Residential home manager, Taiwan).

Formal Care

The interviews with service users and formal carers across the countries revealed that the care, which the formal carers provided, varied depending on the individual needs of the older people and also the quality of the carers. For people who lived in their own home, a wide range of support with a variety of carers providing specific tasks could be found in Dutch homecare services. For example, Ms Flipsen received formal care to assist her with personal matters by a home care assistant and two hours per week house cleaning provided by a domestic carer. There was also a volunteering hot meal delivery service available for Ms Boersbroek daily during the week. In addition, the home carers of Ms Boersbroek and Ms Flipsen said there were also nursing staff within home care support to provide healthcare for them. The Dutch personal budget (PGB) made it possible for Ms Duijts to employ a single carer to provide support involving personal, health and domestic care assistance. In contrast, in England, Ms Becker received only personal care. House cleaning services were seen as housewifery rather than care and were unlikely to be available unless the person was very dependent. Formal care in Taiwan provided flexibility and single care support to meet the needs of older people in the community, especially through foreign carers who provided 24-hour care in all respects. Taiwanese home care support was more likely to be provided by the same carers to assist older people, such as Ms Bai and Fu with personal care, domestic tasks, shopping, meal preparation and basic health needs such as daily blood pressure measurement and massage. Live-in carers in Taiwan provided all the care support for older people as well as the families who live in the same household.

For older people who lived in residential/nursing homes, in the Netherlands, there were many nurses providing personal and health care and volunteers providing feeding assistance and social/recreational activities. In contrast, care assistants provided personal care primarily and some degrees of healthcare in England. In Taiwan, it was the carers in the care home who were primarily responsible for providing personal care to meet the older people's daily needs. As in the Netherlands, volunteers were used in the care home setting to meet the social and recreational needs of older people.

In short, all the formal carers in each of the three countries provided personal care to the older people. Essential personal care needs were seen as universal basic human needs. However, the Dutch had a more comprehensive professional care arrangement within a unified service, the Taiwanese were more likely to be able to provide one single carer to meet an older person's complicated needs, and English care support was primarily focused on personal care tasks.

A number of the older people studied received both formal care from professionals and informal care from relatives; for instance Mrs Bames lived in her own home and received home care from the statutory services while her daughter provided emotional support and performed a number of domiciliary tasks. We have already seen that the care carried out by the informal care in the three countries was influenced by issues such as kinship. For formal carers also, care was not only associated with manual caring tasks. They tended to bring their personal experiences into the job. Old age and caring were closely related to every one's life and influenced many people deeply. Issues of daily care could reflect on one's life experience universally:

...we should provide care with passion and love and care for them just like our parents. Because one day, when we need to be cared for, we also want to have care with love and emotional support (Residential carer, Taiwan).

I can empathise with the people I go to because they've got the same problems that my mum and dad have got. So I try and treat them like I treat my mum and dad (Home carer, England).

Imagine if my mother was in bed here with a broken hip for a week without the correct help, then I should be very angry. I should not agree with the situation (Nursing carer, the Netherlands).

To maintain older people's daily routine and individual expectations, however, was the greatest challenge to formal carers in the three countries. Nearly half of the Dutch (4/9) and Taiwanese (4/9), and one English formal carer had difficulty meeting older people's individual daily routine and care expectations. To satisfy older people's individual preferences and habits was a great challenge to carers.

Informal Care

There was little doubt that most older people, whatever kind of formal care they received, also received support from their families. The small numbers of informal carers in this research project (6, 1 and 3 in England, the Netherlands and Taiwan respectively) is noteworthy. Most of the informal carers across the countries (8/10) started to provide care for their elderly relatives far earlier (more than 5 years on average) than formal services. There was little doubt that formal care support reduced but did not replace the physical work and responsibilities of informal carers. Although Taiwanese informal carers had less physical care involvement with older relatives who received live-in care, they provided a similarly large amount of psychological and emotional support for their elderly as they did in the other two countries. In all three countries, informal carers also organised doctor appointments and visiting relatives. Those who had assistance from live-in carers in Taiwan, nevertheless, assisted their elderly relatives with managing financial matters and medication, arranging hospital appointments and supervising the foreign carer regularly. Two Taiwanese and most English and Dutch informal carers who received support from homecare services performed similar care tasks to those who received live-in carer support. It was difficult to quantify the amount of caring which informal carers undertook in all three countries, because, even when there were times when informal carers did not need to provide hands-on care, there were other tasks relating to older people's overall wellbeing that had to be performed. In addition, alertness was constantly required of informal carers for needs that were difficult to foresee:

It is difficult to say how long care takes, because, it's not just her that we look after. We look after her garden and house as well. It all takes time (Daughter, England).

There are 24 hours a day and of those 24 hours, I spend a few hours in bed, and the rest of the day I am looking after her. From the minute I get up till the minute I go to bed (Husband, the Netherlands).

24 hours a day, 7 days a week. Because I am afraid of her having a fall and need to supervise her all the time (Granddaughter-in-law, Taiwan).

The complexity of informal care was often underestimated. For instance, providing care was not a natural task as such, but required learning. However, in the interview with assessors and formal carers, there was only one Taiwanese home carer and one English health professional who admitted they had given training and advice to informal carers on family care provision. This suggests that family carers have been left alone to face the care situation, a task that can be particularly difficult for male carers:

Cooking! Well I learned how, it wasn't exactly my profession after all (Husband, the Netherlands).

It was very difficult to start with but you pick up how to do the care day-by-day by trying different ways of doing things with [mum] (Son, Taiwan).

Meeting psychological needs could be far more demanding and challenging than physical care work. Nearly all of the English informal carers (4/6) expressed the great challenge in emotional/psychological support for the people they cared for and for themselves as carers:

Doing the job, it's okay. It is when she is depressed and you have to cheer her up. I think that is the most horrible thing to do, when she keeps saying, I've got this wrong with me and that wrong with me. I say, well, look, we all have pains and that, and we have to learn to live with it (Daughter-in-law, England).

Surviving I think really is the most difficult task just simply surviving, carrying on with a way of life that is not obvious what anybody wants so you know that in itself is a difficult task (Son, England).

There were constant debates about safety and independence during care provision. When disagreements occurred between the older person and their informal carer, it could make relationships difficult:

Everything has to be her way and if I do it a different way, she gets quite annoyed. I don't like those flowers like that and that's how she talks to you and I just have to bite my tongue you know and think you silly, old devil. Otherwise it would upset me (Daughter, England).

CONCLUSION

This paper demonstrates the various care actors that are involved with addressing family risk in the availability of care for their older family members. Although cross-national qualitative comparisons can be problematic as the dataset is relatively small and therefore not generalisable, some important findings have emerged. Objective needs-measurement was the policy in all three countries. In practice, however, the policy implementation is complex which impacts on the everyday life of front-line care professionals and in/formal carers. The amount of support from informal carers remains extensive and difficult to estimate in all three countries. This study suggests that official training was not commonly available to family carers in any of the three countries. Informal carers struggled to find out how to provide appropriate care. Adapting to the individual's routine and normality was of great concern to the formal carers studied in the Netherlands and Taiwan but not so much in England, and this might be the result of its selective support care system. This study has also shown that care goes beyond objective and physical tasks. A personal and emotional element to care is universal and unavoidable. For formal and informal carers, mental support for older people was far more of a challenge than physical work. This was even more so when dealing with someone who was a member of one's own family. Formal carers in the three countries related their own personal experience of care provision. Professionals across the board also found facing clients' personal and emotional needs unavoidable.

It was also suggested that in order to provide quality care, the well-being of carers and professionals was of significance. Informal carers, formal carers and professionals in this study showed less satisfaction with their caring roles in England than in Taiwan followed by the Netherlands. There was evidence of unmanageable workloads for professionals in England and Taiwan and to some degree the Netherlands. All three countries showed a tendency for less direct professional contact with service users. This had an impact on the outcome of needs assessment and caused job dissatisfaction. If we take this into account, the Dutch older people studied were the most satisfied with their lives in terms of the living environment, the extent of accessibility to social intervention, participation and feelings of loneliness. Taiwan came second and England came a distant third (see author's own, 2007), we may conclude that the Dutch system delivered a better outcome in terms of older people's welfare, and the welfare of their informal carers, formal carers and professionals, the Taiwanese came second and the English third.

The striking findings from this study are: first, needs assessment is far from satisfactory and insufficiently client-centred in England and Taiwan. Both countries ought to re-examine service-user involvement. Second, there is little doubt that older people's needs are complex and assessment often involves consultation with a number of parties. Policy makers should consider that the dangers of limiting the assessment time for individuals may result in inadequate assessment and service outcome. Similarly, care is not only about tasks but is strongly related to personal perceptions. Time for carers and professionals to spend with individual older people is significant in providing humane care. Third, care for older people could not be met by single care actor alone. Research should be increasingly directed to the development of explicit policies and methods to support professionals and carers. Helping informal carers extend their ability to carry out their role may improve their well-being as carers and reduce the demand for formal care services.

REFERENCES

Audit Commission. (1999). *Children in mind: Child and adolescent mental health services.* London: Audit Commission.

Baldwin, S. (1995). Love and money: The financial consequences of caring for an older relative. In I. Allen, & E. Perkind (Eds.), *The future of family care for older people.* London: HMSO.

Baldwin, S., & Twigg, J. (1991). Women and community care – Reflections of a debate. In M. Maclean, & D. Groves (Eds.), *Women's issues in social policy.* London: Routledge.

Becker, S., & Bryman, A. (Eds.). (2004). *Understanding research for social policy and practice: Themes, methods and approaches.* Bristol, UK: The Policy Press.

Boyle, G. (2003). *The promotion of quality of life in long-term acre policy.* Paper presented at ESPAnet Conference. New York, NY.

Carers National Association. (1999). *Welfare to work: Carers and employment project evaluation report.* London: Carers National Association.

Chang, T. (1997). Taiwan's 1995 health care reform. [in Chinese]. *Health Policy (Amsterdam), 39,* 225–239. doi:10.1016/S0168-8510(96)00877-9

Chen, H. L. (2007). Power and autonomy of older people in long-term care: Cross-national comparison and learning. *Social Policy Report, 19,* 177–203.

Chen, H. L. (2012). Cross-national qualitative research into the long-term care of older people: Some reflections on method and methodology. *European Journal of Social Work.* doi:10.1080/13691457.2012.708903

Commission for Social Care Inspection (CSCI). (2004). *Leaving hospital – The price of delays.* London: Commission for Social Care Inspection.

Crabtree, B. F., & Miller, W. L. (1992). *Doing qualitative research.* Thousand Oaks, CA: Sage.

Davies, S., Nolan, M. R., Brown, J., & Wilson, F. (1999). *Dignity on the ward: Promoting excellence in care.* London: Help the Aged.

Department of Health (DH). (1997). *The cornerstone of care: Inspection of care planning for older people, CI(97)21.* London: Department of Health.

Department of Health (DH). (2004). *SSI performance assessment 2004: Operating policies.* London: Department of Health.

Dilnot, A. (2011). *Fair care funding: The report of the commission on funding of care and support.* London: The Independent Commission on Funding of Care and Support.

Doyal, L., & Gough, I. (1991). *A theory of human need.* Basingstoke, UK: Macmillan.

Ex, C., Gorter, K., & Jansen, U. (2004). Providing integrated health and social care for older persons in The Netherlands. In K. Leichsenring, & A. M. Alaszewski (Eds.), *Providing integrated health and social care for older persons.* Aldershot, UK: Ashgate.

Fuller, R., & Tulle-Winton, E. (1996). Specialism, genericism and others: Does it make a difference? A study of social work service to elderly people. *British Journal of Social Work, 26,* 679–698. doi:10.1093/oxfordjournals.bjsw.a011141

Glendinning, C. (1992). *The costs of informal care: Looking inside the household.* London: HMSO.

Godfrey, A. (2000). What impact does training have on the care received by older people in residential homes? *Social Work Education, 19*(1), 55–65. doi:10.1080/026154700114658

Harding, E., & Beresfords, P. (1996). *The standards we expect: What service users and carers want from social services workers.* London: National Institute of Social Workers.

House of Commons Health Committee (HCHC). (2002). *Delayed discharges, third report session 2001-2, vol 1, HC 617-1*. London: The Stationary Office.

Jörg, F., Borgers, N., Schrijvers, A. J. P., & Hox, J. J. (2006). *Variation in long-term care needs assessor's willingness to support client's requests for admission to a residential home: A vignette study*. London: Sage Publications.

Knijn, T. (2001). Care work: Innovations in The Netherlands. In M. Daly (Ed.), *Care work: The quest for security*. Geneva: International Labour Office.

Knijn, T. (2004). Challenges and risks of individualisation in The Netherlands. *Social Policy and Society*, *3*(1), 57–65. doi:10.1017/S1474746403001490

Knijn, T., & Kremer, M. (1997). Gender and the caring dimension of welfare states: Towards inclusive citizenship. *Social Politics*, *4*(3), 328–361. doi:10.1093/oxfordjournals.sp.a034270

Langan, M. (1998). *Welfare: Needs, rights and risks*. London: Routledge.

Levin, E., & Webb, S. (1997). *Social wok and community care: Changing roles and tasks*. London: National Institute of Social Work.

Lewis, J. (2002). Gender and welfare state change. *European Societies*, *4*(4), 331–357. doi:10.1080/1461669022000022324

Lister, R. (2003). *Citizenship: Feminist perspectives*. Basingstoke, UK: Macmillan.

Little, M. (2002). *Improving older people's services: Policy into practice, the second phase of inspections into older people's services*. London: Department of Health.

Maslow, A. (1943). A theory of human motivation. *Psychological Review*, *50*(4), 370–396. doi:10.1037/h0054346

Ministry of Health. (1997). *Zorgindicatiebesluit* (White paper). The Hague, The Netherlands: Author.

Moss, P., & Cameron, C. (2002). *Care work in Europe: Current understandings and future directions—WP6 care work and the care workforce—Report on stage one and state-of-the-art review*. London: Thomas Coram Research Unit, Institute of Education, University of London.

Nolan, B., & Whelan, C. T. (1997). Measuring poverty using income and deprivation indicators: Alternative approaches. *Journal of European Social Policy*, *6*, 225–240.

Nolan, M. R., Davies, S., & Grant, G. (Eds.). (2001). *Working with older people and their families: Key issues in policy and practice*. Buckingham, UK: Open University Press.

Phillips, D. R. (2000). Ageing in the Asia-Pacific region: Issues, policies and future trends. In D. R. Phillips (Ed.), *Ageing in the Asia-Pacific region: Issues, policies and future trends*. New York: Routledge. doi:10.4324/9780203463086

Pickard, L. (2001). Care break or carer-blind? Policy for informal carers in the UK. *Social Policy and Administration*, *35*(4), 441–458. doi:10.1111/1467-9515.00244

Pickard, L. (2004). *The effectiveness and cost effectiveness of support and services to informal carers of older people*. London: Audit Commission.

Samuel, M. (2005, December 15). Profession becoming less focused on clients and more on paper work. *Community Care*.

Schrijvers, A. J. P., Jedeloo, S., Jorg, F., & Hoogerduin, J. G. (2001). *Rio, the youngest child grows*. Utrecht, The Netherlands: Julius Centre. [in Dutch]

Scottish Executive. (2006). *Changing lives: Report of the recommendation made by the 21st century social work review group for the future of social services in Scotland*. Edinburgh, UK: Scottish Executive.

Shutes, I. (2013). Long-term care and migrant labour in the UK. In Europe's immigration challenge: Reconciling work, welfare and mobility. London: I.B.Tauris.

Stone, R., & Wiener, J. (2001). *Who will care for us? Addressing the long-term care workforce crisis*. Washington, DC: The Urban Institute and the American Association of Homes and Services for the Aging.

Strawbridge, W. J., Wallhagen, M. I., & Cohen, R. D. (2002). Successful aging and well-being: Self rated compared with Rowe and Kahn. *The Gerontologist*, *42*, 727–733. doi:10.1093/geront/42.6.727 PMID:12451153

Twigg, J. (1997). Deconstructing the social bath: Help with bathing at home for older and disable people. *Journal of Social Policy*, *26*(2), 211–232. doi:10.1017/S0047279497004960

Ungerson, C. (1997). Social politics and commodification of care. *Social Politics*, *4*(3), 362–381. doi:10.1093/sp/4.3.362

Ungerson, C. (2000). *Care work: Gender, labour and the welfare state*. London: Routledge.

Ungerson, C. (2004). Whose empowerment and independence? A cross-national perspective on cash for care schemes. *Ageing and Society*, *24*, 189–212. doi:10.1017/S0144686X03001508

Van Hooren, F. (2012). Varieties of migrant care work, comparing patterns of migrant labour in social care. *Journal of European Social Policy*, *22*(2), 133–147. doi:10.1177/0958928711433654

Wang, F. T. Y. (2002). Contesting identity of Taiwanese home-care workers: Worker, daughter, and do-gooder? *Journal of Aging Studies*, *16*, 37–55. doi:10.1016/S0890-4065(01)00033-0

Warren, L. (1990). We're home helps because we care: The experiences of home helps caring for elderly people. In P. Abbott, & G. Payne (Eds.), *New directions in the sociology of health*. Baskingstroke, UK: Falmer.

Weinberg, A., Williamson, J., Challis, D., & Hughes, J. (2003). What do care managers do? A study of working practice in older people's services. *British Journal of Social Work*, *33*, 901–919. doi:10.1093/bjsw/33.7.901

Williams, F. (2010). Themes and concepts in migration, gender and care. *Social Policy and Society*, *9*(3), 385–396. doi:10.1017/S1474746410000102

KEY TERMS AND DEFINITIONS

Caregiver or Carer: An unpaid person, often relative or friend, who is helping person who is in need of care.

Formal Carer: A person with formal recognition and regular pay encaged in care work. The official title may be, for instance, Personal Care Attendant.

Informal Carer: Person doing care work without a formal recognition and regular pay. The use of term emphasizes the lack of formal status.

ENDNOTES

1 The names used in this chapter are pseudonyms.

Section 4

Risk Society and the Spectrum of Public and Private Spheres

This section deals with modern societies dealing with contemporary social issues and social risks. While societies have modernized and people have become aware of the risks and global connectedness of the modern global society, the particular modes of "risk societies" are rather varied, reflecting various cultural and social traditions.

Chapter 14
Using Social Quality as a Framework for Analyzing Social Development in Taiwan

Lih-Rong Wang
National Taiwan University, Taiwan

Yun-Tung Wang
National Taiwan University, Taiwan

Peishan Yang
National Taiwan University, Taiwan

ABSTRACT

This research applies social quality framework to analyze the current social development of Taiwan by utilizing the governmental database as a secondary dataset and using meta-analysis as a further check in data collection. This study found that the social development of current Taiwanese society keeps progressing along with requirements and indicators of social quality. Among them, Taiwan's performance of social development within the dimension of social economic security attains the best results. Furthermore, in the fields of social inclusion and social empowerment dimensions, the indicators show much progress. However, the biggest room for further improvement and development clearly is in social cohesion.

BACKGROUND

In 1997, the Amsterdam Declaration, supported by over 1,000 social scientists from throughout Europe, urged the nations of the European Union to develop their individual societies with the concept of social quality (SQ). The main purpose was to denounce a purely economic development model and to promote a comprehensive model that encompasses not only economic development, but social justice, equity and solidarity. Societies should allow each citizen full opportunities to 'participate in the social and economic life of their communities and to do so under conditions which enhance their well-being, their individual potential and the welfare of their communities.' (Amsterdam Declaration, 1997) Though this important document primarily addressed the European countries at that time, it caught the attention of Asian scholars as well (Ku, 2001). Later

DOI: 10.4018/978-1-4666-5031-2.ch014

on, the European Foundation on Social Quality further developed the social quality approach from a 'vision for Europe' to a more global vision. Asian social scientists and researchers became new partners of social quality research. In March 2007, the 2nd Asia Social Quality Conference was held in Taipei, Taiwan, as initiated by the Social Policy Research Center, National Taiwan University. Since the conference's conclusion, a social quality team in Taiwan has been working on social quality development. In addition, other Asia Social Quality teams working in cooperation with European Social Quality Teams include those in Japan, Korea, Thailand, and Hong Kong.

Taiwan's participation in the development of Social Quality Indicators was motivated by the hope to fill the gap between social quality as evidenced by existing data and social policies. Through applying the social quality framework, scholars from Taiwan intended to find deeper theoretical underpinnings for social welfare policy and practice.

Throughout Taiwan's recent history, the development of social welfare has been secondary to economic and political development. From inauguration of the Constitution in 1947 until the present time, social welfare in Taiwan has been used to counterbalance the effects of capitalist market economy commodification, and to answer calls for more democracy and social rights (Ku, 2001; Lin, 2006). Democratic politics has improved, marked by the abolition of the Military Curfew Law in 1987 and the victory of the oppositional Democratic Progressive Party (DPP) in the 2000 and 2004 presidential elections. Under both the Kuomintang (KMT) and the DPP governance the rationale for social welfare has remained to stabilize political power and economic prosperity by way of basic social security and minimal social assistance. Levels of social provision have been quite low, compared to many developed countries. For example, the total tax revenues, as a percentage of GDP (not including social security contribution) in 2009, were only 12.3% in Taiwan, but 22.9% in Germany, 25.7% in France, and 27.6% in Great Britain (Ministry of Finance, 2012).

Ancient Chinese doctrines have clearly laid out a hierarchical life path for ordinary men. That is, to first focus on personal development, and then if any capacity left, to use it to manage his family, and then if any capacity left, to use it to benefit his country, and finally, then if still any capacity left, to use it to benefit the world. That is, the social comes after the affirmation of the individual and the family. The more intimate social systems or communities always come before the more remote ones. A famous Chinese philosopher, Hsio-Tung Fei, had presented the theory of particularistic ties in 1947. Fei (1947) pointed out that in a Chinese society, people need particularistic ties to relate to each other. More discussions on the welfare of the family and the community are needed in order to help the Taiwanese individuals find their particularistic ties to relate to the society. We found that while applying social quality as a framework for analyzing social development, the European social quality indicators may require some modification in order to incorporate the hierarchical values embedded in Chinese culture.

USING THE SOCIAL QUALITY AS A FRAMEWORK OF CONCEPTUALIZATION

Basic Concern of Social Quality

The concept of social quality was developed in the mid-1990s in Europe. Social quality was defined as a comprehensive conception of the quality of people's daily lives; it is a function of the constant tension between individual self-realization and participation in the various collective identities that constitute everyday life within a social context. In addition, social quality was proposed as a goal, not only of social policy, but also of economic, environmental and other relevant policies for ensuring human well being and happiness (European Foundation of Social Quality, 2006; Ogawa, 2006). Beck et al. (1997) characterized social quality into 'vertical' and 'horizontal' tensions and produced a quadrant cell with four conditional factors: socio-economic security, social cohesion, social inclusion, and social empowerment. Socio-economic security is the extent to which people have resources over time, including five domains: financial resources, housing and environment, health and care, work, and education. Social cohesion is the extent to which social relations, based on identities, values, and norms, are shared. Four domains are included: trust, other integrative norms and values, social networks, and identity. Social inclusion is the extent to which people have access to and are integrated into the different institutions and social relations that constitute everyday life, including four domains: citizenship rights, labor market, services (public and private), and social networks. Social empowerment is the extent to which social relations enhance the personal capacities of individuals and their ability to act, including four domains: knowledge base, labor market, openness and supportiveness of institutions, and personal relations. Each domain included several mutually related sub-domains. In addition, each sub-domain included several indicators.

The four conditional factors include 95 indicators, 24 in socio-economic security, 20 in social cohesion, 27 in social inclusion, and 24 in social empowerment (van der Maesen &Walker, 2005; Keizer & van der Maesen, 2003; Berman & Phillips, 2004; Walker & Wigfield, 2003; Herrmann, 2003).

Caution in Utilizing the Indicators of Social Quality

A few remarks need to be made before detailed discussion of the social quality takes off. Application of the European social quality framework to analyze Taiwan society requires open-mindedness on the part of authors and readers alike. Also, it is important to emphasize that this analysis is a process, not an end.

The social quality approach is one of many competing paradigms in the social policy arena in Taiwan. Besides the more traditional economic or political model, newer paradigms such as cultural pluralism or social development affect policy standards as well. Specialists in various professional fields creatively apply different paradigms to assert their influences. All together, as a result of competing paradigms and competing specialists, the actual pattern of social policies is a mosaic presenting a patch-like image or a hybrid of mixed ideological origins and departmentalized administration. Seeking a clear path of social quality may very likely be futile. As Ku (2001) tactically said, at this uncertain age, it is not as important to decide which paradigm to follow as it is to realize what insights each paradigm may provide to Taiwan society. Thus, this article does not intend to make any final evaluation of social quality in Taiwan. Rather, the authors try to explore the social development of current Taiwan society by using social quality as a tool, as well as a framework.

In addition, social quality is a relatively new policy framework in Taiwan. The data regarding social quality indicators may not be available, or they may have never been composed together systematically. A question remains whether or not the 95 social indicators developed in Europe to measure social quality remain valid in the Taiwanese context, and do the indicators measure similar concepts in Taiwan as they do in Europe? For example, 'proportion of hidden families in one household' is a highly confusing indicator for Taiwanese society. It is not uncommon to have multiple families living in one household in Taiwan. In addition, what the term of 'family' implies in Europe might be different from the meaning of this term in Taiwan. For example, some people may register themselves as one household for the benefits of tax deduction, social assistance, or to get into certain educational districts, but they do not actually live in the same household. Thus, from a measurement point of view, the exploration of the meanings of the 95 indicators is crucial for constructing Taiwan's social quality framework and very important for making a valid comparison between Europe and Asia.

As stated above, the concept of social quality is relatively new in Taiwan. Other concepts such as quality of life or social indicators are more readily applied to analyze the conditions of the individuals or the society. However, quality of life is more individually based and subjective. Social indicators, on the other hand, do not aim to measure the quality of the society (Wang, 2007). Therefore, this study intends to use the more objective and comprehensive social quality approach to investigate and explore the nature and basic trends of social development in Taiwan.

Based on the preceding literatures and discussion, this study intended to specifically answer the four following research questions:

1. How is the reality of social economic security in Taiwan from SQ perspective?
2. How is the situation of social cohesion in Taiwan from SQ perspective?
3. How is the status of social inclusion in Taiwan from SQ perspective?
4. How is the profile of social empowerment in Taiwan from SQ perspective?

METHODS

This study used the secondary data analysis and meta-analysis of existing literature and data sources. The major data sources include 'Household Survey Statistics in Taiwan',' Survey of Social Developmental Trend',' Quarterly National Economic Trends', 'Employment and Unemployment Statistics', 'Survey of Employee's Salary', 'Social Indicators', and 'Economic Statistics Indicators' from Directorate General of Budget, Accounting and Statistics (2000, 2003, 2007, 2009, 2011, 2012a,b,c), 'Labor Statistics' from Council of Labor Affairs (2007a,b, 2009), 'Report of the Survey of Living Situation', 'Monthly Bulletin of the registered residence', and 'Monthly Bulletin of the Statistics' from Ministry of Interior (2006, 2010, 2011a, 2012), and some databases from Ministry of Finance (2012), Department of Health (2010), Ministry of Education (2010), and Research, Development and Evaluation Commission, Executive Yuan (2012). The authors searched official reports or database released by the government for SQ indicators similar to those developed in the European Union (EU). The reason why most data were from official reports or databases is due to their better reliability and validity.

RESULTS

The Reality of Socio-Economic Security

Among the four conditional factors of SQ, the data of socio-economic security is more comprehensive, based on its secondary dataset. Among the 24 socio-economic security indicators developed in EU, official data are available for 16 indicators. After decades of economic and social welfare development, the socio-economic security in Taiwan is fairly competitive, though there still remains a lot of room for improvement in equality.

First, the total incomes of individuals and households have continuously increased in 1990s[1] (Directorate General of Budget, Accounting and Statistics, 2009). However, between 2000 and 2008, during the change in ruling party to DPP[2], Taiwan did not deal well with the ensuing economic stagnation. The economic growth rate (-2.2% in 2001 to 4.7% in 2006) became relatively weak in comparison to nearby Asian countries/areas such as Hong Kong (0.6% in 2001 to 6.9% in 2006), Singapore (-2.4% in 2001 to 7.9% in 2006) and South Korea (3.8% in 2001 to 5.0% in 2006) (Directorate General of Budget, Accounting and Statistics, 2007). Both the per capita GDP and the average disposable income per household have remained unchanged from 2000 to 2005[3] (Directorate General of Budget, Accounting and Statistics, 2007). Due to the downturn in the economic situation and widespreading scandals involving corruption, the KMT won the Presidential election in 2008. However, due to the global financial crisis beginning in 2008, economic stagnation continued. In evidence, the economic growth rates in 2009 among the Asian countries/ areas of Hong Kong, Singapore, South Korea, and Taiwan were -2.5%, -1.0%, 0.3%, -1.8%, (Directorate General of Budget, Accounting and Statistics, 2012).

Although economic growth does not necessarily equate to better socio-economic security, in today's global world, people tend to evaluate their quality of life in relation to general international indicators. While social standards often vary widely, economic indicators may have a more consensual basis. Furthermore, an economic standstill situation relative to other nearby Asian countries may bring about feelings of insecurity, especially in Taiwan where people believe in hard work and constant advancement and perceive that 'no progression is regression'.

In the sub-domain of income security, the proportion of people and the proportion of households below the poverty line have steadily increased. The proportion of people below the poverty line went from 0.54% in 1995 to 0.70% in 2000, and to 1.18% in 2010; the proportion of households below the poverty line went from 0.83% in 1995 to 0.99% in 2000, and to 1.41% in 2010 (Ministry of Interior, 2010). However, the poverty rate in Taiwan remains quite low in comparison to that of other countries[4], and the increasing poverty rate does not mean that there are more "poor" people in Taiwan in recent years. The major reason why the proportion keeps rising is that the Social Assistance Act keeps widening its definition of working persons and real estate. Moreover, the economically vulnerable people are not the ones below poverty line in Taiwan because, based on Social Assistance Act, those below the poverty line are eligible for 12 categories of social assistance. The most vulnerable people in Taiwan are the ones just above poverty line, the so-called 'near poor', because their disposable income is too low to support normal lives, yet too high to get assistance from public welfare system. As mentioned above, the total tax revenues, as a percentage of GDP in Taiwan, is quite low (only 12.3% in 2009). The government is conservative in exercising its power to redistribute income and wealth. People need to rely on themselves or their family. When people are faced with life risks, the social safety net in Taiwan is often not strong enough to catch them.

Another facet of income security is income distribution. In Taiwan, the ratio of disposable income of the highest 20% to that of the lowest 20% went up from 4.97 in 1991 to 6.39 in 2001, and then stayed between 5.98-6.34 until landing at 6.19 in 2010 (Directorate General of Budget, Accounting and Statistics, 2011). The major reason for this is that among the years studied, the economic growth rate was lowest in 2001 at -2.2%, which caused considerable unemployment[5] and a serious negative effect on households in the lowest and second lowest 20% disposable income bracket (Directorate General of Budget, Accounting and Statistics, 2011). The lowest and second lowest 20% average household disposable incomes went down 5.5% and 2.7% respectively from 2000 to 2005. However, the consumer price index (CPI) went up 3.5% over the same period. This caused deterioration in financial situation for people in the lower end of the income spectrum over this period.

In the domain of 'housing and environment', the indicators of 'proportion of people who have certainty of keeping their home' (78.46% in 1990 to 84.90% in 2010) and 'number of square meters per household member' (27.44 in 1991 to 43.56 in 2010) can reveal that the housing security and housing conditions have been improved (Directorate General of Budget, Accounting and

Statistics, 2000, 2011; Ministry of Interior, 2006). Meanwhile, the indicator of 'people affected by criminal offences per 10,000 inhabitants' (118.38 in 2003 to 128.23 in 2009) shows that social environmental condition and personal safety still have room to improve (Directorate General of Budget, Accounting and Statistics, 2009; Ministry of Interior, 2010).

In the domain of 'health and care', the indicator of 'proportion of people covered by compulsory/voluntary health insurance' (89.54% in 1995 to 99.62% in 2010) reflects the significant effect of National Health Insurance in Taiwan to ensure the minimal health status for all (Bureau of National Health Insurance, 2011). In addition, the indicator of the 'number of medical doctors per 10,000 inhabitants' (15.10 in 1992 to 23.56 in 2009) signaled the increased access to medical care (Department of Health, 2010).

Education is another great achievement in Taiwan. The indicator of 'proportion of students leaving education without finishing compulsory education (early school leavers)' revealed that very few students leave schools while receiving the nine years of compulsory education in Taiwan (from 0.24% in 1995 to 0.20% in 2009) (Ministry of Education, 2010). This also contributes to a stable and secure Taiwan society.

In general, among the 16 available socio-economic security indicators, six are stably progressing, and only one is backslidden. That is to say, socio-economic security in Taiwan has developed quite well in almost every facet, especially in health and education. However, due to the minimal level of social assistance and unequal provision of social security, the socio-economic security in Taiwan is not as good as it looks. It needs special policy intervention to deal with the recent larger differences between the rich and the poor and the vulnerable life situation of the near poor.

The contextual meaning of the socio-economic indicators in Taiwan is that human capital investment is highly emphasized and individuals and families are expected to be self-reliant. Social safety net is scarce and designed only for the extremely poor (about 1% of total population). When the economy is good and unemployment rate is lower, people's socio-economic situation is better, and when the economy is in stagnation, many people may fall into life risks. Thus, immediate family members are required by law to support each other.

The Reality of Social Cohesion

Generally speaking, quality of social cohesion is not as progressive as the other three conditional factors of social quality in Taiwan (Lin et al., 2010). Official data are available for only 4 indicators in Taiwan out of 20 social cohesion indicators developed in EU (20.0%). This may mean that the concept of social cohesion is still under-developed in Taiwan. At the same time, it also provides great help in developing future social policy in Taiwan.

First, we contemplated on one variable derived from the concept of social cohesion --national identity. Here in Taiwan national identity seems more confusing than constructive under the concept of social cohesion. Although Taiwan has its own military, diplomacy, and the President, the status of the national identity is very uncertain in many respects. Since its loss of UN membership in 1971, Taiwan has faced tremendous difficulties in claiming its own national identity in the international arena. Complicated international politics are beyond the control of normal Taiwanese people, but it affects our daily life and work significantly. Taiwan also suffers from the strained relationship with China. Thus far, both sides are in constant struggle to maintain a peaceful balance, though the balance may be contested at any time. Historical residue, such as the Constitution that started in 1947 in Mainland China[6], causes confusion of the current Taiwan identity. Constant ideological debates and party politics have made Taiwan's society highly fractured. Every time an election comes, this issue of national identity will be staged again, and the society will be stirred up. The level of social cohesion in Taiwan will not rise easily until the people in Taiwan, together with the people in China and the rest of the international world, find a resolution to this identity issue.

In the domain of trust, a 2003 survey in Taiwan showed the extent to which people believed most people can be trusted was 56.7% (Directorate General of Budget, Accounting and Statistics, 2003). In addition, in the domain of 'other integrative norms and values', volunteers as a proportion of total population increased year by year (5.05% in 1988 to 14.50% in 2003), but the numbers of volunteering hours per week were still very low (1.69 in 1996, 2.08 in 2001, and 1.62 in 2006) (Directorate General of Budget, Accounting and Statistics, 2003, 2009). One possible reason for the increase of the number of volunteers is that the bureaus of education of some local governments, such as Taipei City Government, stipulate that senior high school students have to do 8 hours of voluntary service before graduation. Therefore, whether the social cohesion in Taiwan is improving or not cannot accurately be assessed from this indicator alone and more research and data are needed. As one positive indicator, the amount of blood donation continued to increase (327.5 million cc in 1994 to 627.5 million cc in 2010) and the rate of blood donation was 7.62% in 2010 (Taiwan Blood Foundation, 2010; Directorate General of Budget, Accounting and Statistics, 2009).

In the domain of social networks, the proportion of people joining social organizations/clubs in Taiwan has remained low (36.85% in 1999 to 28.11% in 2003) (Directorate General of Budget, Accounting and Statistics, 2003). 'No available time' is the major reason why people do not join social organizations/clubs in Taiwan (Directorate General of Budget, Accounting and Statistics, 2003). Possible reasons for this are that people in Taiwan spend a lot of time maintaining their immediate family networks and many of those who are employed work a lot of overtime, which leaves little time to join social organizations.

From the prior illustrations, among these 4 available social cohesion indicators, 1 is stably progressing and 1 is backslidden. In Taiwan, social cohesion has the most indicators missing (80%) among the four conditional factors, notably in the domains of identity, tolerance, and social contract. Why are they missing? The authors have found the concept of social cohesion contains many norms and assumptions that are not resonant in Taiwan. For example, the concept of tolerance is a tricky one. Many Taiwanese people will describe themselves as quite tolerant but the concept may refer more to family and interpersonal relationships rather than broader social relationships. Little measurement was done to explore family and interpersonal cohesion as it might interfere with privacy. The high intensity of family interaction may result in less time spared for other social organizations. Again, family plays a major role in social contracting, but since family is an informal system, there is usually no apparent formal contracting.

Geography and history may have also caused the differences between the European and Taiwanese concepts of social cohesion. There are many countries in Europe and people have easier contacts with different ethnic and linguistic people. But Taiwan is an island, let alone facing many difficulties in the international arena. People in Taiwan are mostly homogeneous. Foreigners have come and ruled Taiwan in the past history, but they were all gone with very few left in Taiwan. Only recently, with the growing trend of international marriage, there have become a significant number of foreign spouses and their children residing in Taiwan and facing issues of social cohesion. Economic and cultural globalization further highlights the similarities and differences among various countries and ethnicities. Therefore, it is expected that as Taiwan is getting more absorbed into the global world, the concept of social cohesion will definitely call for further development.

Social Inclusion

Official data are available for 11 indicators in Taiwan among the 27 social inclusion indicators developed in EU (40.7%). In the domain of citizenship rights, most people (98.2%) living in Taiwan are permanent residents (Directorate General of Budget, Accounting and Statistics, 2000). Based on the Immigration Act, a person can obtain Taiwan citizenship if he/she has been born in Taiwan or lives here continuously for at least 5 years. There were 469,518 registered foreign spouses in Taiwan from Jan. 1987 to Sep. 2012. Among these, 92.93% were female, and 67.4% were from Mainland China. However, the naturalization rates of foreign spouses from Mainland China and other countries/areas are quite different. The naturalization rate of foreign spouses from Mainland China is only 33.15% until Sep. 2012 much lower than 65.70% of those from other countries/areas (Ministry of Interior, 2012). The major reason is that foreign spouses from Mainland China are regulated by laws different from the usual Immigration Act due the special relationship between Taiwan and Mainland China. Therefore, it is much harder for foreign spouses from Mainland China to be naturalized than those from other countries/areas.

In addition, the proportion of the population having the rights to vote in presidential elections in Taiwan has continued to increase (67.16% in 1996, 69.86% in 2000, 73.12% in 2004, 75.56% in 2008, and 77.88% in 2012) and the proportion of the population who exercises that right is high (76.04% in 1996, 82.69% in 2000, 80.28% in 2004, 76.33% in 2008, and 74.38% in 2012) (Central Election Council, 2012). These data may mean that democracy in Taiwan is continually developing and citizenship rights have progressed well.

In a sub-domain of social rights, the female labor force participation rate continued to increase from 44.4% in 1991 to 50.0% in 2011 (Directorate General of Budget, Accounting and Statistics, 2012b). Meanwhile, women's pay as a proportion of men's pay also increased from 66.20% in 1991 to 84.75% in 2009 (Directorate General of Budget, Accounting and Statistics, 2012c). These data revealed that women are being successfully integrated to the labor market.

In the domain of the labor market, the two peaks of unemployment rates were 5.17% in 2002 and 5.21% in 2010 (Council of Labor Affairs, 2007a; Directorate General of Budget, Accounting and Statistics, 2012b). Furthermore, although the long-term unemployment[7] rate went up from 9.9% in 1996 to 21.0% in 2003, it then decreased to 16.4% in 2011 (Directorate General of Budget, Accounting and Statistics, 2012b). The reason why the unemployment rate and long-term unemployment rate went up from the 1990s to 2000s is quite similar to the reason why the overall economy was weakened in Taiwan as described previously. To eradicate this, the government has tried various measures to promote employment, especially for the vulnerable groups, such as Public Service Employment Program, Multi-categorical Employment Program (including economic and social patterns), and Wage Subsidy for Employer to Hire Higher-aged Workers. As a result, the unemployment rate continuously went down from 2002 to 2006. However, the effects of these noted measures on the unemployment rate might be relatively short-termed. Whether these measures will be effective in the long run needs to be monitored and evaluated later.

In the domain of services, the coverage of health services (98.8% in 2011) and education (net primary/secondary/higher education enrollment rate: 98.0%/95.4%/65.0% in 2009) is very high, indicating that almost everybody can acquire health services and receive compulsory or higher education in Taiwan (Bureau of National Health Insurance, 2012; Directorate General of Budget, Accounting and Statistics, 2009; Ministry of Education, 2010). However, in the domain of social networks, the proportion in regular contact with neighbors went down from 42.31% in 1999 to 37.21% in 2003 (Directorate General of Budget,

Accounting and Statistics, 2003). This may have happened not only due to changes in family and neighborhood structures, but also the changes in communication patterns found in an active Internet and high-tech society.

On the whole, the preceding data clearly indicated that social inclusion in Taiwan has been progressing; among these 11 available social inclusion indicators, 4 are stably progressing and only 1 is backslidden.

Moreover, as mentioned above, Taiwan is a relatively homogeneous society, so people are generally included in traditional family and other informal social networks. As democracy improves, citizenship rights are progressing steadily. Since the work ethic is strong, promoting labor market participation and keeping the unemployment rate as low as possible have remained high policy priority. Health and educational services are easily accessible. However, recent social changes pose challenges to the traditional mechanisms for social inclusion. Family and neighborhood interaction has weakened, which leaves some people not attended to. To mend this defect, efforts are made to foster social networks beyond personal and family levels, such as community care for the aged and disabled citizens. National security issues complicate immigration and naturalization laws and regulations. Disparity in health and educational resources and qualities may threaten the hard-earned accomplishments in these two areas. Fortunately, recent policy debates have been directed towards more right-based social policy. A greater emphasis on the concept of social inclusion at this time in Taiwan will resonate well with this right-based policy direction.

Social Empowerment

Official data are available for 9 indicators in Taiwan among the 24 social empowerment indicators developed in EU (37.5%). With regards to social empowerment, this study found some indications of improvement and also some of setbacks. It seems rather difficult for the authors to evaluate the implications of such findings.

In the domain of knowledge base, the ratio of the population who are literate went up from 93.17% in 1992 to 98.17% in 2011 in Taiwan, possibly due to continuous high educational expenditure (Ministry of Interior, 2012). In addition, the proportion of the population with access to the Internet increased rapidly from 0.2% in 1992 to 77.4% in 2011 (Research, Development and Evaluation Commission, Executive Yuan, 2012). These two indicators show that the knowledge base in Taiwan is good and keeps increasing.

However, in the domain of the labor market, the percentage of laborers who are the members of a trade union went down from 34.3% in 1991 to 29.1% in 2009 (Council of Labor Affairs, 2007a; Council of Labor Affairs, 2009). Also, the percentage of the labor force covered by a collective agreement went down from 6.59% in 2003 to 1.76% in 2006 (Council of Labor Affairs, 2007b). In addition, the percentage of employed labor force receiving work-based training went up from 1991 to 2001, and then dramatically went down by 2006 (0.32% in 1991, 0.47% in 2001, and 0.20% in 2006) (Council of Labor Affairs, 2007a). These facts show that empowerment of laborers is unstable and underdeveloped in Taiwan.

In the domain of openness and supportiveness of institutions, Taiwanese people can start to vote for the President in Taiwan since 1996. In addition, referendums were initiated in Taiwan in 2004. Moreover, the proportion of marches and demonstrations banned (including "not allowed" and "not applied") declined from 29.36% in 1993 to 7.54% in 2010 (Ministry of Interior, 2010). These reveal that Taiwan continues to be open to the mass demonstrations. It is good for Taiwanese people that they can present and demonstrate their opinions to the government. However, if the responsiveness of the government to the requests were not addressed, it would be hard to say whether the people are in fact empowered or they are actually pacified.

In general, the preceding data indicate that social inclusion in Taiwan has been marginally progressing in that, among these 9 available social empowerment indicators, 4 are stably progressing and 2 are backslidden.

Empowerment is defined by the enhancement of personal capacities of individuals and their choices of action as supported by institutions and human relations. It is also considered as the cornerstone of the other three conditional factors. Education and the recent information and high-tech revolution have improved the personal capacities of Taiwanese people. The democratic process continues to enlighten all the citizens about their values and power. However, collective empowerment, such as trade unions, mass movement and community organizations, needs further development. Empowerment is a long process. Knowing one's power is one thing, using it is another, and collaborating with others in making a better society is yet another. In the framework of social quality, it is important to delineate clearly such different stages of the empowerment process.

DISCUSSION

Based on the preceding analysis, this study found that the social development of current Taiwan society from a social quality perspective is basically progressing. In addition, Taiwan society fared best in social economic security. Social inclusion and social empowerment were also clearly improved and progressive. However, significant room for further improvement and development is seen in social cohesion.

Countries exist in different stages of social development. This study presents a lot of findings that can provide both the European networks and the Asian colleagues for thought. The gaps shown between the European standards and the Taiwan scenario may be due to the unsuccessful social development in some social quality factors in Taiwan, but they may also be due to the unsatisfactory compatibility of the instrument. The most important gap is that, in the Taiwan scenario, there needs to be more emphasis on family and immediate communities, and more SQ indicators to measure the extent of such informal support networks in maintaining a high level of social quality.

The major contribution of this study is that this is the first study to use a comprehensive social quality framework to examine the social development of current Taiwan society. It provides Taiwanese policy makers and researchers with a more overall policy framework and valuable information to help them understand what are the most important things to do in the near future. It also helps the policy development, dialogues, and comparisons among international partners.

The major limitation of this study is its sole use of official reports and databases to perform secondary data analysis and meta-analysis. Though this study offers better reliability and validity, we could only find 40 similar social quality indicators in Taiwan out of the 95 developed in EU. Therefore, we suggest that future researchers try to use more sources, reports, and databases to find additional available SQ indicators in performing analyses.

This article proposes that policy makers and researchers in Taiwan may work more closely with the European Foundation on Social Quality and other colleagues in Asia by continuing research and actual efforts to embody the social quality approach in specific policy fields. The authors also suggest that the measurement issues in the current social quality framework need to be seriously discussed in the future to facilitate its application within and outside of Europe.

REFERENCES

Amsterdam Declaration. (1997). *Amsterdam declaration on the social quality of Europe*. Retrieved on 22 July 2013, from http://www.socialquality.org/site/index.html

Beck, W., van der Maesen, L., & Walker, A. (Eds.). (1997). *The social quality of Europe*. Dordrecht, The Netherlands: Kluwer Law International.

Berman, Y., & Phillips, D. (2004). *Social quality and the conditional factor of social cohesion: 3rd draft*.

Bureau of National Health Insurance. Taiwan. (2012). *Immediate statistics*. Retrieved on 22 July 2013, from http://www.doh.gov.tw/statistic/data

Central Election Council, Taiwan. (2012). Retrieved on 22 July 2013, from http://web.cec.gov.tw/files/11-1000-1642-1.php

Council of Labor Affairs. Taiwan. (2007a). *Monthly bulletin of labor statistics*. Retrieved on 22 July 2013, from http://statdb.cla.gov.tw/html/mon/26080.htm

Council of Labor Affairs. Taiwan. (2007b). *Yearbook of labor statistics*. Retrieved on 22 July 2013, from http://statdb.cla.gov.tw/html/year/year96/rptmenuyear.htm

Council of Labor Affairs. Taiwan. (2009). *Yearbook of labor statistics*. Retrieved on 22 July 2013, from http://statdb.cla.gov.tw/html/year/year96/rptmenuyear.htm

Department of Health, Taiwan. (2010). Retrieved on 22 July 2013, from http://www.doh.gov.tw/statistic/data/

Directorate General of Budget, Accounting and Statistics, Taiwan. (2000). *Household survey statistics in Taiwan*. Retrieved on 22 July 2013, from http://www.stat.gov.tw/public/Data/411716314171.rtf

Directorate General of Budget, Accounting and Statistics, Taiwan. (2003). *Survey of social developmental trend 2003*. Retrieved on 22 July 2013, from http://www.dgbas.gov.tw/public/Attachment/4112911545171.xls

Directorate General of Budget, Accounting and Statistics, Taiwan. (2007). *Quarterly national economic trends, Vol. 117*. Retrieved on 22 July 2013, http://eng.stat.gov.tw/public/Attachment/761310155271.xls

Directorate General of Budget, Accounting and Statistics, Taiwan. (2009). *Social indicators 2009*. Retrieved on 22 July 2013, from http://eng.stat.gov.tw/public/data/dgbas03/bs2/socialindicator

Directorate General of Budget, Accounting and Statistics, Taiwan. (2011). *Social indicators 2011*. Retrieved November 17, 2012, http://www.dgbas.gov.tw/public/Attachment/28111192871.pdf

Directorate General of Budget, Accounting and Statistics, Taiwan. (2012a). *Economic statistics indicators*. Retrieved on 22 July 2013, from http://2k3dmz2.moea.gov.tw/gnweb/Indicator/wFrmIndicator.aspx

Directorate General of Budget, Accounting and Statistics, Taiwan. (2012b). *Employment and unemployment statistics*. Retrieved on 22 July 2013, from http://www.stat.gov.tw/ct.asp?xItem=17144&ctNode=517

Directorate General of Budget, Accounting and Statistics, Taiwan. (2012c). *Survey of employee's salary*. Retrieved on 22 July 2013, from http://www.stat.gov.tw/ct.asp?xItem=1135&ctNode=525

European Foundation of Social Quality. (2006). *Introduction to the theory of social quality*. Retrieved on 22 July 2013, from http://www.socialquality.nl/site/index.html

Fei, H. T. (1947). *On particularistic ties*. Hong Kong: Phoenix Publishing Company.

Herrmann, P. (2003). *Social quality and the conditional factor of social empowerment: 3rd draft*. Amsterdam, The Netherlands: EFSQ.

Keizer, M., & van der Maesen, L. (2003). *Social quality and the conditional factor of socio-economic security: 3rd draft working paper*. Amsterdam: EFSQ.

Ku, Y. W. (2001). An uncertain age—A balancing act of international social welfare development. In G. Chan, & Y. W. Ku (Eds.), *The new thoughts of social welfare policy*. Taipei, Taiwan: Laureate Books.

Lin, C. Y., Wang, Y. T., & Shi, S. J. (2010). The features of social cohesion in Taiwan: A social quality perspective. *Journal of State and Society*, *8*, 47–98.

Lin, W. Y. (2006). *Social welfare in Taiwan*. Taipei, Taiwan: Wu-Nan Book Co., Ltd.

Ministry of Education. Taiwan. (2010). *Important educational statistics*. Retrieved on 22 July 2013, from http://140.111.34.69/EDU_WEB/EDU_MGT/STATISTICS/EDU7220001/overview/brief-htm/index.htm?open

Ministry of Finance. Taiwan. (2012). *Total tax revenues as percentage of GDP of key countries (not including social security contribution)*. Retrieved November 17, 2012 from http://eng.stat.gov.tw/public/data/dgbas03/bs1/handbook/other/p6-23c.xls

Ministry of Interior. Taiwan. (2006). *Report of the survey of living situation*. Retrieved on 22 July 2013, from http://www.cpami.gov.tw/pwi/ph/ph_14.php

Ministry of Interior. Taiwan. (2010). *Monthly bulletin of the statistics*. Retrieved on 22 July 2013, from http://www.moi.gov.tw/stat/

Ministry of Interior. Taiwan. (2011a). *Monthly bulletin of the registered residence*. Retrieved on 22 July 2013, from http://www.ris.gov.tw/ch4/static/st1-9-95.xls

Ministry of Interior. Taiwan. (2011b). *Social assistance act*. Retrieved on 22 July 2013, from http://law.moj.gov.tw/LawClass/LawAll.aspx?PCode=D0050078

Ministry of Interior. Taiwan. (2012). *Monthly bulletin of the statistics*. Retrieved on 22 July 2013, from http://www.moi.gov.tw/stat/

Ogawa, T. (2006). The concept of social quality and its implications for social well-being and aging policy in Asia and the pacific—Developing a social quality approach in Asian types of civil society and its implications for 3S developments. Paper presented in Social Policy Research Workshop--Social Economic Security in Later Life in National Taiwan University. Taipei, Taiwan.

Research, Development and Evaluation Commission, Executive Yuan, Taiwan. (2012). *2011 survey on individual/household digital opportunity*. Retrieved on 22 July 2013 from http://www.rdec.gov.tw/public/Attachment/222114532071.pdf

Taiwan Blood Foundation. (2010). *Yearbook*. Retrieved on 22 July 2013, from http://www.blood.org.tw/index.php?action=sas&PId=28

van der Maesen, L., & Walker, A. (2005). Indicators of social quality: Outcomes of the European scientific network. *European Journal of Social Quality*, *5*, 8–24. doi:10.3167/146179105780337431

Walker, A., & Wigfield, A. (2003). *Social quality and the conditional factor of social inclusion: 3rd draft*. Amsterdam, The Netherlands: EFSQ.

Wang, Y. T. (2007). *Social quality in Taiwan*. Paper presented in the Second Asian Conference on Social Quality and Sustainable Welfare Societies in National Taiwan University. Taipei, Taiwan.

KEY TERMS AND DEFINITIONS

Identity: Whatever makes an entity definable and recognizable. People typically have multiple identities, which are more or less subject to change.

Social Cohesion: The members of a given group are inclined to participate readily and to stay with the group.

Social Development: Changes in the structure and framework of society.

Social Empowerment: Increasing the spiritual, political, social, educational, gender, or economic strength of individuals and communities.

Social Network: A social structure made up of a set of social actors (such as individuals or organizations) and a set of the dyadic ties between these actors.

Social Quality: A term used for assessing social and economic progress. It aims to measure the extent to which communities can participate in social, political and economic life under conditions which enhance both individual and community well-being.

ENDNOTES

1 Per capita GDP went up from US$9,008 in 1991 to US$14,519 in 2000. Average disposable income per household went up from NT$587,242 in 1991 to NT$891,445 in 2000. In 1991–2000, $US1=$NT28.4 averagely around.

2 The first change in ruling party in Taiwan occurred in 2000.

3 Per capita GDP almost kept same from US$14,519 in 2000 to US$15,271 in 2005. Average disposable income per household almost kept same from NT$891,445 in 2000 to NT$894,574 in 2005. In 2000–2005, $US1=$NT33.3 averagely around.

4 In Taiwan, the definition of a low-income household was originally based upon the criteria of "60% of the average annual household expenditure as the upper limit of the annual household income of all residents", as well as "certain amounts of market prices of movable property and real estate as the upper limit of assets"; these will differ for different areas. However, from July 2011, the first criterion was changed to "60% of the medium of household disposable annual income of all residents as the upper limit of the household income of all residents". In Taiwan, the proportion of low-income household residents was about 1% these years (Ministry of Interior, 2011b).

5 In 2001, the unemployment rate was 4.57%, which is the third highest unemployment rate before 2008 in Taiwan.

6 In 1949, the original central government (Republic of China, ROC) in Mainland China moved to Taiwan because it lost the Civil War. In the meantime, the new central government (People Republic of China, PRC) in Mainland China was founded.

7 The definition of long-term unemployment is that a person has been continuously unemployed for over 12 months.

Chapter 15
Fiji:
Violence against Women – Identifying and Combating Structural Discrimination that Furthers Sexual and Gender-Based Violence (SGBV)

Hansdeep Singh
International Center for Advocates Against Discrimination (ICAAD), USA

Jaspreet Singh
International Center for Advocates Against Discrimination (ICAAD), USA

Marjory D. Fields
Beldock Levine & Hoffman LLP, USA

ABSTRACT

Fiji is a very interesting case for studying the bridges between private and public spheres and social and cultural background. Despite its idyllic setting and concentration of resources, Fiji has one of the highest rates of violence against women, outside of conflict zones, in the world. The state, legal system, and society have simply failed to protect the women against different forms of violence and discrimination. The lack of parliamentary democratic process certainly has contributed to the deplorable situation. After analyzing the roots of the problem, the authors introduce comprehensive policy recommendations to help rectify the situation. The problems in Fiji are rather extreme, and there is a lot to learn for everyone about the weakness of state and institutions to perform some of their most fundamental functions.

DOI: 10.4018/978-1-4666-5031-2.ch015

Figure 1. ICAAD global presence

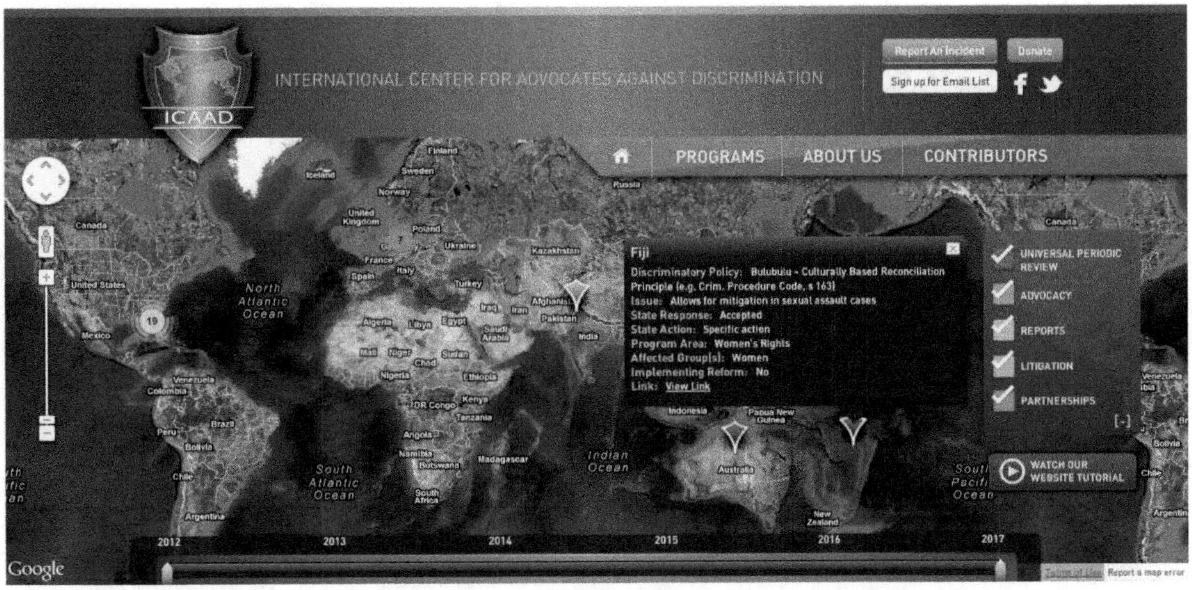

INTRODUCTION

Fiji is a study in contradiction. Fiji's idyllic scenery and beaches make it a hub for tourism. Its central location in the South Pacific makes it a busy trade route. Also, it houses United Nations (U.N.) agencies working on the rule of law and gender equality. Yet, despite its idyllic setting and concentration of resources, Fiji has one of the highest rates of violence against women, outside of conflict zones, in the world.

Fiji is a party to the Convention on the Elimination of Discrimination Against Women (CEDAW) and the Convention on the Rights of the Child (CRC), which means it has ratified those treaties. In the absence of domestic legislation to protect women from violence and proper enforcement of existing laws and policies, women and girls suffer sexual and gender based violence (SGBV) at high rates.

From 2010-2011 the Fijian Women's Crisis Center (FWCC) conducted a two-year national survey of women and found that 64% of women faced physical or sexual violence by an intimate partner (Press Release, *Violence Against Women in Fiji Touches all Aspect of Women's Lives, Survey Finds*, The Jet; Jan. 31, 2013) The survey was run over two years and included more than three thousand women in the study). These conditions are not unique to Fiji but are pervasive throughout the Pacific Island Countries (PICs) where cultural practices and patriarchal systems supersede universal human rights norms. (see Figure 1)

Attorneys at the International Center for Advocates Against Discrimination (ICAAD) have represented Fijian women seeking asylum in the United States. In four asylum cases before the federal appellate courts, ICAAD Attorneys showed the continuing risk of SGBV if the petitioners were not granted asylum or withholding of removal. These cases revealed the discriminatory treatment women confront in Fiji and demonstrated that the structural defects in the criminal and civil justice systems are barriers to equality, safety, and redress for survivors of SGBV [*Rashika v. Holder* (Indo-Fijian Women in Fiji lack a system of support and have a greater than 10% chance of facing SGBV. Therefore, have a reasonable fear of future

Figure 2. Department of Public Health and Primary Care - Fiji School of Medicine

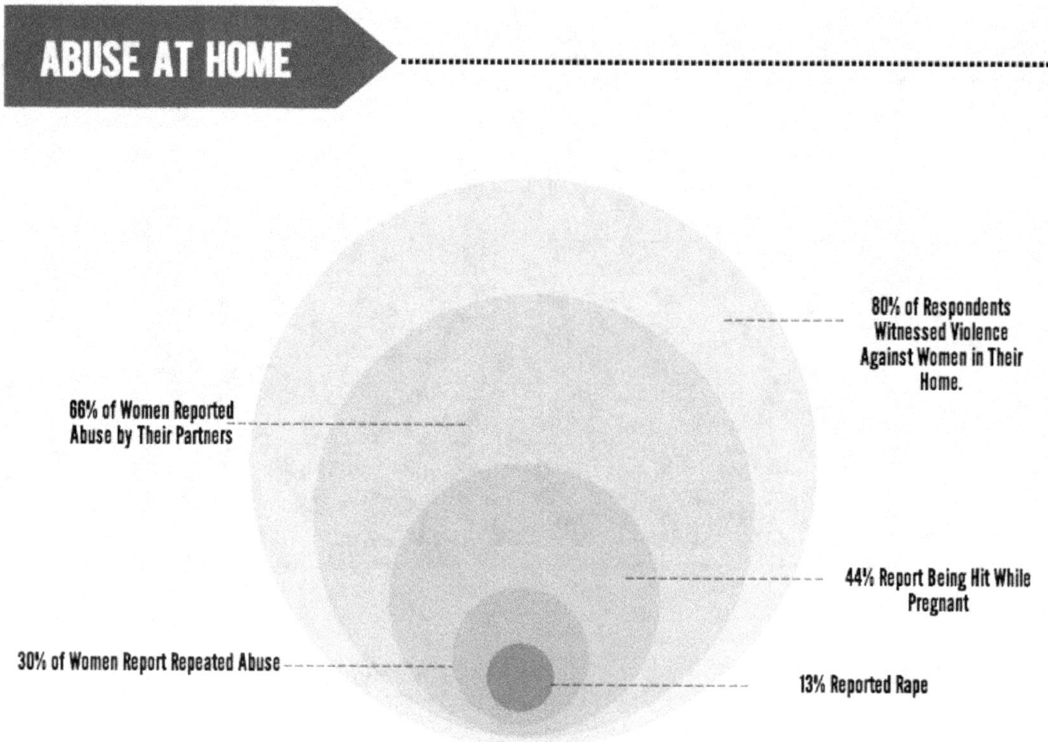

persecution even if they have not faced past persecution.), *Veliamma v. DHS* (granted withholding of removal), *Rattan Singh v. Holder* (pending), *Nijjar v. Holder* (pending)]. This chapter describes the legal conditions in Fiji that allow SGBV to permeate every level of society while identifying solutions to uproot structural discrimination against women in Fiji. (see Figure 2)

1. GOVERNMENT AND SOCIAL STRUCTURES

A. Violence against Women

In the last three decades, Fiji has suffered four political coups (United Nations Population Fund, 2008) [hereinafter "UNFPA"], The current military dictator took power in 2009. He removed all independent government officials and judges, and replaced them with military officers and civilian allies. The Government operates under a continuing 'State of Emergency' decreed in April 2009 (Amnesty International, *Fiji: Submission to the UN Universal Periodic Review*, 3 (Feb. 2010) [hereinafter "Amnesty UPR"]. This Government abrogated the national democratic Constitution of 1997 and uses violence, torture, and arbitrary detention. The government bans all political meetings, denies government opponents the right to travel outside the country, censors the press, forbids courts to rule on the validity of the government coup that took place in 2006-07, and excludes foreign journalists from entering the country. Furthermore, Fiji's Human Rights Commission has been suspended from the International Coordinating Committee for National

Human Rights Institutions and the Asia Pacific Forum for lacking sufficient independence (Id).

Collaborative efforts to protect women from violence through legislation have been stalled because of the lack of parliamentary democratic process (see *generally* Fiji Women's Rights Movement (FWRM) (2010) [hereinafter "FWRM"]; Fiji Women's Crisis Centre (FWCC) (2010) [hereinafter "FWCC"]; Lechuga Foundation and Sexual Rights Initiative (LFSRI) (2010) [hereinafter "LF-SRI"]. Each NGO presented consistent criticisms of government repression, violations of human, political, and economic rights, and in particular state accepted violence against women). Unfortunately, PICs, including Fiji, value "communal cohesiveness" over a woman's right to safety and redress from SGBV (Fenton 1998). Institutional violence against women is supported by societal tolerance of violence against women. Survivors are blamed for causing family instability and law enforcement keeps SGBV cases out of the courts. This pattern and practice of discrimination against women arguably makes Fiji culpable for femicide. Femicide is defined as State tolerance for the failure of public officials to protect women from violence and discrimination by government and private actors (Human Rights Council 2012).

International organizations confirm that violence against women in Fiji is pervasive. The government has repressed women's advocacy non-governmental organizations (NGOs) and their leaders (FWCC, *supra* note 6, at 2). The United Nations Population Fund (UNFPA) found that, "[v] iolence and the threat or fear of violence forms a part of many women's daily realities in Fiji. A range of social, economic, political, and cultural factors combine to create an environment where women are particularly vulnerable to abuse" (UNFPA, *supra* note 3, at 6-7). Furthermore, UNFPA found that "cultural, ethnic and religious fundamentalism is on the rise in Fiji. This promotes conservative ideas and negative myths about women and their rights" (*Id.* at 8). For example, some traditional leaders are attempting to restrict women to their homes. Survivors who seek to enforce their rights are accused of causing families to breakdown for reporting domestic violence or sexual abuse (id.). The Assessment foreshadowed the 2009 Christian crime crusade during which police raped and tortured sex workers and "compel[ed] women survivors of violence to reconcile with their violent husbands." (Amnesty International, CEDAW 2010; hereinafter "Amnesty CEDAW").

Amidst a breakdown of the rule of law, the military dictatorship has made public assurances at the international stage that it seeks to affirmatively address violence against women by implementing three decrees (Fiji News Mar. 7, 2013). However, the dictatorship's assurances to address violence against women suffer from a fatal flaw: the failure to actually implement any laws and policies through a parliamentary democratic process aimed at protecting women (Coalition of Women's NGOs for the CEDAW Shadow Report, 2009; hereinafter "Coalition Shadow Report").

Furthermore, the assurances given by the military are undermined by the Special Rapporteur on VAW whose Report states:

A key characteristic of militarisation is the increased power given to the military to violate human rights under the guise of national security....... In many cases, militarisation becomes extremism, allowing no space for any dissent. Women activists who had been vocal about the coup in Fiji, for instance, were taken up to the military camp; some of them forced to run around the ground at the barracks, made to lie face down on the ground and lick the boots of the military officers while other women had their hair cut to humiliate them..... (Id. at 10).

Under the Due Diligence standard crafted by the CEDAW Committee, in its general recommendation No. 19 (1992) on violence against women, it confirmed that "[u]nder general international

Figure 3. Recommendations: Government recommendations[1]

- Create an Inter Agency Taskforce on Violence against Women;
- Institutionalize gender equality training, including, government ministries tasked with representing women's rights and civil society;
- Data collection systems need to be strengthened and data disaggregated by sex, area (rural, urban), race/ethnicity, religion, age, sexual orientation;
- Institute workplace policies against sexual harassment with complaint and enforcement tracking mechanisms;
- Support NGOs that offer legal literacy and human rights training about women's rights;
- Develop SGBV guidelines for the Ministry of Health (MOH);
- Establish and fund shelters for women and girls who are survivors of gender based violence;
- The Fiji Human Rights Commission should ensure compliance with the Paris Principles.

law and specific human rights covenants, States may … be responsible for private acts if they fail to act with due diligence to prevent violations of rights or to investigate and punish acts of violence, and for providing compensation." Committee on the Elimination of Discrimination against Women (CEDAW) 1992; hereinafter "CEDAW Recommendation). (see Figure 3)

B. Legislation and Domestic Policies that Address Violence against Women

Over the last two decades, the Fijian government has failed in its attempts to address SGBV from a law enforcement and legislative perspective. Some of the affirmative steps the Fijian government has taken over of the last two decades to address SGBV include:

- Creating the *Sexual Offences Unit (SOU) within Law Enforcement in 1995*;
- Instituting the *"No Drop Policy" for Police Officers in 1995*;
- Passing the *Family Law Act in 2003*;
- Passing four decrees in 2009 making it easier to prosecute sexual violence offences in response to CEDAW recommendations in 2008;
- *Issuing the Domestic Violence Decree of 2009.*

Legislation

The passage of the Family Law Act of 2003, which created a no-fault basis for divorce, restraining or protection orders, and a Family Division of the High Court, serves as a model for PICs. This comprehensive legislation was developed in consultation with women's rights organizations. The purpose of this act has not been achieved because of the "reluctance among police and enforcement officials to understand and enforce the legislation." (United Nations Development Fund for Women 2010; hereinafter "UNIFEM").

Unlike the Family Law Act, the Domestic Violence Decree of 2009 was put in place with "little or no" consultation with women's rights organizations (Amnesty UPR, *supra* note 4, at 7). The Decree provides greater protection for domestic violence survivors, clarifies the duties of law enforcement, allows for restraining orders, and seeks to implement CEDAW, CRC, and related conventions. After promulgation of the Decree, a government press release criticized the coordinator of the Fiji Women's Crisis Centre for disputing the genuineness of the government's claim to protect women from domestic violence (Sera 2009).

The Decree suffered a similar fate as the Family Law Act. The Government consistently prosecuted cases under the Crimes Decree of February 10, 2010 rather than the Domestic Violence Decree of 2009 (*State v S.T* [2011] FJHC 135; HAD002.2011 (4 March 2011) ("This is rather an unfortunate state of affairs. The Domestic Violence Decree came into effect on 6 September 2010. But it seems to me that there is a lack of commitment to enforce the law by the law enforcement officers"). The Crimes Decree does not specifically address violence against women (Amnesty CEDAW, *supra* note 13, at 10). All assaults against women were charged as crimes of "common assault" with brief or suspended sentences imposed in those cases (Id). Moreover, the courts in many instances granted bail and but did not grant restraining orders to protect the women from the accused or convicted offenders.

The failure to implement the Decree is demonstrated in judicial decisions. In *State v. S.T.* [2011], the High Court Appellate Jurisdiction noted the lack of commitment by law enforcement officers to implement the provisions of the Decree. The decision stated:

"[j]udicial experience has shown that [women] do not have equal bargaining power as their spouses. They are forced to reconcile in domestic violence cases because of cultural and social constraints placed on them. The Domestic Violence Decree is designed to take away those constraints and to empower them to live a life without violence" (State v S.T [2011] FJHC 135; HAD002.2011; 4 March 2011).

Law Enforcement Policy

Progressive laws and policies are undermined by law enforcement, which tolerates SGBV and ignores the complaints of women. Furthermore, law enforcement lacks resources and training (Australia: Refugee Review Tribunal 2010; hereinafter "Refugee Tribunal"). Bribery and corruption also play a significant role in the failure to respond to SGBV matters (Id.). Thus, rape and domestic violence are underreported to the police (Id.). For example, the Sexual Offence Units (SOUs) created specifically to build expertise to address SGBV, are "largely under-resourced and are usually inundated with cases" and police lack the required sensitivity towards victims of sexual abuse. Moreover, SOUs don't investigate individual cases they only deal with the victims (Coalition Shadow Report, *supra* note 15, at 28 Box. 2). And finally, there are only three SOUs for the entire country (Id.).

The police and prosecutors are charged with implementing the "No-Drop Policy," which requires cases of domestic violence to be investigated by the police and if criminal charges are brought, the case can't be dropped because the parties of have reconciled. This policy extends to both domestic violence and rape, (Coalition Shadow Report, *supra* at 33; Refugee Tribunal, *supra* note 25, at 3), but does not extend to relationships outside marriage or to the LGBT community (UNIFEM, *supra* note 18, at 20 (No-Drop Policy "states that violence against heterosexual adults who are living together as husband and wife (or previously lived together) will be fully investigated . . ."). Although there is anecdotal evidence of improving prosecution rates, (*Id.* at 19) law enforcement remains predisposed to keep SGBV cases out of courts (*Id.* at 19-20).

Cultural practices such as *bulubulu* (a custom for reconciling differences) provide justification for the police to drop SGBV cases. In Fijian culture, *bulubulu* is an essential part of traditional village life. Disputes were settled with the offer of a whale's tooth (*tabua*), a gift or compensation, and asking for forgiveness (Engle Merry 2004). There is social pressure to accept this apology because the historic outcome of accepting *bulubulu* was to break the cycle of vengeance. The offer is directed to the senior male member of the family, but not the victim. (Engle Merry 2006). As the population has begun to move from rural to urban locations, however, the "custom itself is being redefined" (Id. at 18).

Traditionally, *bulubulu* did not apply to domestic violence and sexual assault cases, but rather, to resolve tribal disputes peacefully (*Id.* at 127). Conservative Christian religious tradi-

Figure 4. Recommendations: Law enforcement recommendations

- Training of Police Officers regarding SGBV within the Fiji Police Academy needs to be a continuous part of the curriculum;
- SGBV Police Units should be adequately resourced;
- Consistent disciplinary action against police officers should be applied when necessary;
- Police should monitor the pattern and practice of SGBV to identify particularly vulnerable populations;

tions and nationalistic pride, however, perpetuate cultural norms and shape the attitudes of police towards women. Thus, police officers continue to promote reconciliation in domestic violence and rape cases (FWCC, *supra* note 6, at 5; Coalition Shadow Report, *supra* note 15, at 34). Even with improved laws, judicial oversight, and specialized law enforcement divisions there is a failure to implement policies to combat SGBV.

2. STRUCTURAL DISCRIMINATION EMBEDDED IN THE LEGAL SYSTEM

The Special Rapporteur on violence against women, Rashida Manjoo, describes violence against women as intersecting circles comprised of: "structural, institutional, interpersonal, and individual factors" (HRC, *supra* note 8, at ¶ 17 ("The structural factors include macro level social, economic and political systems; institutional factors include formal and informal social networks and institutions; interpersonal factors include personal relationships between partners, among family members and within the community; and individual factors include personality and individual capacities to respond to violence"). Structural discrimination includes laws, societal norms, cultural values, and government structures that mask discrimination and impede the social, cultural, economic, or political rights of vulnerable communities. The resulting structural discrimination creates social inequality amongst groups and leads to further stigmatization of already marginalized groups. Structural discrimination manifests in multi-faceted ways (see Figure 4). ICAAD has identified five salient forms of structural discrimination:

- **Social Exclusion:** One result of social exclusion are societal and cultural norms that favor assimilation rather than integration for all members of society. Social exclusion leads to the "othering" of individuals and communities that do not conform to prevailing norms. Additionally, certain communities are shunned merely for who they are.
- **Formal Equality/Equality Per Se:** Formal equality results from facially neutral laws, policies, or case-law that reflect majoritarian sentiment and lead to disparate treatment or have a disparate impact on specific communities.
- **Denial or Suppression of Identity:** The State views the distinctive identity of specific communities with suspicion or fear and uses majoritarian influence or legal means to mandate conformity.
- **Failure to Protect:** Countries have an international (if not also a domestic) obligation to protect communities from violence perpetrated by government officials or private persons. When the institutions that exist to protect vulnerable communities from violence fail, the State bears the responsibility for these failures.
- **Cultural Norms:** Deeply embedded traditions that permeate all spheres of life and may explicitly be integrated into the differ-

> ent branches of government. Even if there is no government sanction of these traditions, for example traditions that further patriarchal or caste based ideology, the government is still unwilling or unable to enforce laws that seek to remove these discriminatory barriers.

Analysis of the social, cultural, and political context of Fiji, exposes "patterns of structural discrimination and inequality that continue to form part of the reality of women's lives" (*Id.* at ¶ 18). To illuminate systemic patterns of violence, the Special Rapporteur stressed the importance of disaggregated data that included: "race, ethnicity, education, sexual orientation and economic status . . . ." (*Id.)*

In Fiji, structurally discriminatory practices are multi-layered. They are embedded in: culture, legislation (or lack thereof), law enforcement's failure to enforce laws, judicial opinions, and the failure to implement directly applicable international human rights norms.

A. Structural Discrimination in Legislation and Recommendations to Close the Gap[2]

For the rule of law to be functional in a state, domestic laws must incorporate principles of international human rights law. Legislation provides guidance for public policy, informs the citizenry of their rights, and provides mechanisms for redress when rights are violated. When uprooting structural discrimination, however, new laws or strengthening legislation are insufficient without enforcement.

To have the intended results, laws must be: 1) developed through collaboration between government and civil society; 2) published and disseminated broadly, with the opportunity for public comment; 3) include mechanisms for transparency, implementation, and accountability (right to redress or punishment for state actors); and 4) have social support, legal advocacy, and judicial adherence.

Although, comprehensive legislation is essential, it can be undermined by case law. As seen in Fijian case law citing *bulubulu* (reconciliation) (The International Center for Advocates Against Discrimination (ICAAD) 2013, hereinafter "ICAAD"), judge-made law has had a corrosive effect on legislation and Decrees against SGVB (*see eg*. Gertner, 2012: 109-124). For example, in the 2011 case of *Raisoqoni v State*, High Court of Fiji Appellate Jurisdiction, the judge found that although *bulubulu* could not be used to escape custodial sentences, it could be used as a form of mitigation in sentencing (*Raisoqoni v State* [2011] FJHC 32; HAA004.2011 (7 February 2011) "Under the new law, domestic violence offences are not reconcilable and therefore there is no discretion given to the courts to encourage reconciliation. However, if the victim freely reconciles with her partner and gives evidence of that effect, reconciliation is a factor that ought to be taken into account in sentencing the offender."). Although the Criminal Procedure Decree 2009 clearly states that the promotion of reconciliation "does not apply to offences of domestic violence," (Criminal Procedure Decree 2009, Div. 4, section 154; 6) that has not stopped courts from promoting reconciliation or reducing the sentence of perpetrators when reconciliation has taken place (*See generally* ICAAD, *supra* note 43; Coalition Shadow Report, *supra* note 15, at 34-35).

For the section below, we have heavily relied on The United Nations Department of Economic and Social Affairs: Division for the Advancement of Women guidelines which includes recommendations that would eliminate structural discrimination embedded in legislation either through amendment or clarification (UNESA, *supra* note 42, at 26). It is also important to note that the Fijian government passed numerous Decrees in 2009 (Pacific Islands Legal Information Institute (PacLII, 2009) that seek to replace prior legislation. Many of the Decrees are progressive and address some of the structural issues that further SGBV but they cannot be seen as permanent solutions unless codified in law through a parliamentary democracy. Therefore, for purposes of this paper, if legislation prior to 2009 contributes to furthering SGBV, it will be recognized as a gap in the law even if a recent Decree may fill that gap.

Crimes Decree: Need for Clear, Consistent, and Complete Definitions

- **Fijian criminal law defines rape narrowly** as penile-vaginal penetration only, does not provide minimum sentence for rape, and is not tiered based on aggravating factors (Penal Code Penal Code (Consolidated Acts 1985) [Cap 17], c. XVII, section 149, 150). However, the Crimes Decree 2009 includes additional elements of the crime common in the definition of rape: penetration no matter how slight; penetration with a penis, finger or foreign object, achieved by force, the threat of harm or death, and the threat to harm or kill others, or damage property, by one or more actors, aggravating factors that would affect sentencing terms (Crimes Decree 2009, The Offence of Rape, Part 12, section 207; 2).
- **Marital Rape:** (FWCC, *supra* note 6, at 3. "In a confidential submission to the Commission a representative of the Soqosoqo-ni-Marama of one rural village said that most of the members were victims of domestic violence and one reason that it is difficult for women to report is that a prevalent form of domestic violence is marital rape". UNFPA, *supra* note 3, at 16). There is no express exemption of husbands from prosecution for rape of their wives in the criminal or penal laws (Penal Code Penal Code (Consolidated Acts 1985) [CAP 17], c. XVII, section 149). There is however only one case of prosecution for marital rape that came before the Magistrate and High Court in searching the Pacific Islands Legal Information Institute (PacLII) database. (*Dutt v The State* [2006] FJCA 59; AAU0066.2005 (10 November 2006) ("It is high time that men should realise that there is no longer a rule of law (or any other form of rule) that a wife was deemed to have consented irrevocably to sexual intercourse with the husband and

Figure 5. U.N. Policy recommendation (UNESA, supra note 42, at 26.)

Legislation should:

- Define sexual assault as a violation of bodily integrity and sexual autonomy;
- Replace existing offences of rape and "indecent" assault with a broad offence of sexual assault graded based on harm;
- Provide for aggravating circumstances including, but not limited to, the age of the survivor, the relationship of the perpetrator and survivor, the use or threat of violence, the presence of multiple perpetrators, and grave physical or mental consequences of the attack on the victim;
- Remove any requirement that sexual assault be committed by force or violence, and any requirement of proof of penetration, and minimize secondary victimization of the complainant/ survivor in proceedings by enacting a definition of sexual assault that either;
    - Requires the existence of a "unequivocal and voluntary agreement" and requiring proof by the accused of steps taken to ascertain whether the complainant/survivor was consenting; or
    - Requires that the act take place in "coercive circumstances" and includes a broad range of coercive circumstances; and
- Specifically criminalize sexual assault within a relationship (i.e., "marital rape"), either by:
    - providing that sexual assault provisions apply "irrespective of the nature of the relationship" between the perpetrator and complainant; or
    - stating that "no marriage or other relationship shall constitute a defence to a charge of sexual assault under the legislation."

that therefore a husband could not be convicted of rape or attempted rape of his wife ..."). (see Figure 5)

Best Practices: *Canada's Criminal Code includes tiers for sexual assaults (section 271) that include: sexual assault with a weapon, threats to harm or kill a third party, or causing bodily harm (section 272), and aggravated sexual assault, wherein the perpetrator wounds, maims, disfigures or endangers the life of the complainant or others. (Section 273). (Id. at 27). Under the Namibian Combating Rape Act (2000), "marriage or other relationship" does not provide a defense for rape (Id.).*

Evidence Rules: Ensuring Gender Equality in Rule Making

- **Corroboration in Sexual Offence Cases**: In *State v. Balelala* (2004), the Court of Appeals found that requiring corroboration in sexual offence cases was discriminatory and violated Fiji's obligations to CEDAW (*Balelala v State* [2004] FJCA 49; AAU0003.2004S (11 November 2004) (holding "that the Rule [corroboration in sexual assault cases] is counterproductive, confusing and both discriminatory and demeaning of women"). Codifying judicial decisions into statute is not necessary for enforceability, however, we have consistently seen in Fijian judicial opinions significant variance in judicial opinions, often producing results that are inconsistent with higher court rulings (*See* ICAAD, *supra* note 43). The Criminal Procedure 2009 Decree does not require corroboration in sexual assault cases (Criminal Procedure Decree 2009, Div. 6, section 129). (see Figure 6)

Best Practice*: In another PIC, the Cook Islands Evidence Amendment Act (1986-87), evidence in sexual assault cases no longer require corroboration to obtain a conviction.*

- **Sexual History**: Cross-examination of the complainant regarding her sexual history is not codified in legislation, (Criminal Procedure Code, Consolidated Acts 1985 [CAP 21] 1978) although the Criminal Procedure Decree 2009 does prohibit the use of sexual history in criminal proceedings (Criminal Procedure Decree 2009, Div. 6, section 130). (see Figure 7)

Best Practice*: New South Wales, Australia, Section 293(2) of the Criminal Procedure Act (1986) states: "[e]vidence relating to the sexual reputation of the complainant is inadmissible." (Id. at 44. The "rape shield law" is in many jurisdictions, but it is weak because the sexual history of the*

Figure 6. U.N. Policy recommendation (UNESA, supra note 42, at 43.)

Legislation should abolish the cautionary warning/corroboration rule in regard to complainants in cases of sexual violence by either:

- Stating that "it shall be unlawful to require corroboration of the complainant's evidence";
- Creating an assumption of the complainant's credibility in sexual violence cases;
- Stating that "the credibility of a complainant in a sexual violence case is the same as the credibility of a complainant in any other criminal proceeding."

Figure 7. U.N. Policy recommendation (UNESA, supra note 42, at 43.)

Legislation should prevent introduction of the complainant's sexual history in both civil and criminal proceedings.

complainant is often allowed "in the interests of justice" when the defense requests).

Court System: Specialized Courts/ Procedures for Sexual Assault Cases

- **Delay in Processing Sexual Violence Cases**: UNFPA reported that sexual violence cases take up to 4 years (UNFPA, *supra* note 3, at 23, 31). Part of the delay is caused by the low priority given to sexual offence cases compared to other violent crimes. Delay results in many cases being concluded by reconciliation or suspended sentences because the complainants need conclusion of their cases for their peace of mind (*Id).*
- **Delay in the Reappointment of Magistrates and Judges**: Hindering the efficiency and functionality of the Court (FWCC, *supra* note 6, at 4) results in the devastating impact on survivors who often drop their claims rather than enduring a protracted court case.
- **Deliberate Delay Tactics by Defense Counsel** (UNFPA, *supra* note 3, at 31). (see Figure 8)

Best Practice*: Title V of the Organic Act on Integrated Protection Measures against Gender Violence (2004) in Spain and article 14 of the Maria da Penha Law (2006) in Brazil streamlines and centralizes court proceedings, reduces redundancy in witness and complainant testimony, and eliminates contradictory orders (Id. at 20).*

Sentencing: Consistency and Capturing the Gravity of the Crime

- **Sentencing Consistency:** (*Kadavu v State* [2001] FJHC 292; [2001] 1 FLR 180 (4 May 2001)

"I must say that Magistrates and Judges in this country appear to be severely disadvantaged in that there is not a central collection point for sentencing information from which to draw in times of need. It appears that sentencing offenders is simply a matter of an exercise of the discretion of each individual judicial person with little or no opportunity to establish a parity in sentencing. This is particularly disadvantageous to those judicial persons who preside in areas outside of the capital for they are often denied the opportunity of discussing the matters with their fellows to obtain a proper range of the "tariff" applicable to any one offence. Regrettably, when the courts pass sentences which vary significantly from one offender to another, notwithstanding there is similarity in the offences, it serves to create an impression in the general public that the court system is unjust. This further serves to create a lack of confidence and respect for the law with a consequential breakdown in discipline. This is a most unfortunate state of affairs. One hopes that all of us judicial persons combine to assist in formulating a simple system to assist, in particular, our fellows in the outlying areas." Id.

- **Sentencing Reductions**: Domestic violence is treated as simple or common assault (Coalition Shadow Report, *supra* note 15, at 33). Even with the Domestic

Figure 8. U.N. Policy recommendation (UNESA, supra note 42, at 19)

Legislation should:

- Provide for the creation of specialized courts or special court proceedings guaranteeing timely and efficient handling of cases of violence against women; and
- Ensure that officers assigned to specialized courts receive specialized training and that measures are in place to minimize stress and fatigue of such officers.

Violence Decree 2009, police and prosecutors charge domestic violence crimes under the Crimes Decree 2009. Moreover, courts have relied on "main income earner" or "sole bread winner" (*Maharaj v State* [2010] FJHC 467; HAA048.2010 (25 October 2010); *Prasad v State* [2004] FJHC 130; HAA0058.2004 (4 August 2004) (discussion on how this argument is often used by offenders but should not be accepted by courts) findings to shorten sentences after convictions (FWCC, *supra* note 6, at 2; Coalition Shadow Report, *supra* note 15, at 34). (see Figure 9)

Best Practice*: Sentencing guidelines contribute to consistency and predictability of sentencing in cases of VAW. One example is the United Kingdom's Sentencing Guidelines on the Sexual Offences Act (2003) (UNESA, supra note 42, at 51).*

- **Removal of Exceptions for Sentencing Reduction**: As covered previously, cultural practices like *bulubulu* (reconciliation) are still used as a form of mitigation during sentencing and perpetrators of SGBV rarely get custodial sentences. In conducting a survey of case law where *bulubulu* had taken place between the two parties, in almost 50% of the cases, judges reduced the sentence (*See* ICAAD, *supra* note 43. Research on Fijian case law was conducted on the Pacific Islands Legal Information Institute (PacLII) (http://www.paclii.org/) website. Over 100 cases were reviewed and 61 case studies produced). (see Figure 10)

Best Practice*: Turkey, Brazil, and Uruguay have amended their Penal Codes, which previously stipulated that sentence reductions were appropriate in cases of honor killings and where the perpetrator "married the survivor of sexual violence." (Id. at 51).*

Legal Representation: Access to Justice is the First Step in Combating SGBV

- **Absence of Free Legal Representation for Survivors**: Legal representation is necessary to properly file a claim and obtain legal remedies for safety, for example, a restraining or protection order; restitution for physical injuries and property damage; and payment of legal fees and medical bills. (see Figure 11)

Figure 9. U.N. Policy recommendation (UNESA, supra note 42, at 50; see also UNFPA, supra note 3, at 40)

Legislation should provide that:
- Sentences should be commensurate with the gravity of crimes of violence against women; and
- Sentencing guidelines should be developed to ensure consistency in sentencing outcomes.

Figure 10. U.N. Policy recommendation (UNESA, supra note 42, at 51)

Legislation should remove provisions that:
- Provide reduced penalties or exculpate perpetrators in cases of so-called honour crimes;
- Exculpate a perpetrator of violence if he subsequently marries the survivor; and
- Provide for the imposition of lesser penalties in cases involving particular "types" of women, such as sex workers or non-virgins;
- **[ICAAD Addition]** Provide reduced penalties in sexual assault cases, based on reconciliation principles, embedded in cultural practice.

Figure 11. U.N. Policy recommendation (UNESA, supra note 42, at 39)

Legislation should ensure that complainants/ survivors have the right to:

- Free legal aid in all legal proceedings, especially criminal proceedings, in order to ensure access to justice and avoid secondary victimization;
- Free court support, including the right to be accompanied and represented in court by a specialized complainants' service and/or intermediary, free of charge, and without prejudice to their case, and access to service centres in the courthouse to receive guidance and assistance in navigating the legal system; and
- Free access to a qualified and impartial interpreter and the translation of legal documents, where requested or required.

Figure 12. U.N. Policy recommendation (UNESA, supra note 42, at 27)

Legislation should:

- Criminalize sexual harassment;
- Recognize sexual harassment as a form of discrimination and a violation of women's human rights with health and safety consequences;
- Define sexual harassment as unwelcome sexually determined behaviour in both horizontal and vertical relationships, including in employment (including the informal employment sector), education, receipt of goods and services, sporting activities, and property transactions; and
- Provide that unwelcome sexually determined behaviour includes (whether directly or by implication) physical conduct and advances; a demand or request for sexual favours; sexually coloured remarks; displaying sexually explicit pictures, posters or graffiti; and any other unwelcome physical, verbal or non-verbal conduct of a sexual nature.

Best Practice*: Bulgaria's Law on Protection against Domestic Violence (2005) provides for free legal representation for survivors in protection order cases (Id).*

Article 21 of the Guatemalan *Law against Femicide and other Forms of Violence against Women* (2008) obligates the government to provide free legal services to victims/ survivors (*Id*).

Employment: Discrimination in the Workplace

- **Sexual Harassment: State and non-state actors must be held accountable.** Fiji has a National Policy on Sexual Harassment in the Workplace, which only applies to state actors. Also, the National Employment Centre Decree 2009 specifically states that employers are liable for harassing or failing to prevent harassment (National Employment Centre Decree 2009, Part 2, section 12-13). Both of these only cover sexual harassment as a civil offense (Coalition Shadow Report, *supra* note at 15, at 78). However, no formal legislation, passed through a parliamentary democracy, currently exists. A 2008 study found 1 in 3 women have been sexually harassed and is one of the leading forms of violence against women (*Id*. at 3). (see Figure 12)

Best Practice(s)*: Countries have begun to develop comprehensive anti-discrimination laws that also criminalize sexual harassment. "The Anti-Discrimination Act (1977) of the State of New South Wales, Australia, provides that sexual harassment is against the law when it takes place in employment; educational institutions; receipt of goods or services; renting or attempting to rent accommodation; buying or selling land; and sporting activities" (Id. at 28). Turkey's Penal Code criminalizes sexual harassment (Id).*

International Norms: Inclusion of Sexual and Gender Based Violence (SGBV)

- **Domestic implementation of CEDAW** principles is lacking. The government has not provided resources to effectively fulfill its commitment to international treaties it has ratified. However, courts have used international human rights principles in their judgments (Coalition Shadow Report, *supra* note 15, at 25-26).
- **International Criminal Law**: Widespread or systematic rapes of civilians constitute Crimes Against Humanity. Fiji is a party to the Rome Statute, (Rome Statute of the International Criminal Court, 2187 U.N.T.S. 90. The Rome Statute was adopted on July 17, 1998, and came into force on July 1, 2002. Fiji Ratified Rome Statute on Nov. 29, 1999), which gives the International Criminal Court (ICC) jurisdiction to prosecute grave crimes under international law if Fiji is unwilling or unable to prosecute those cases domestically.

Best Practice: *"Rome Statute provides the broadest statutory recognition of gender-based violence as a crime under international criminal law to date. In article 7(1)(g), the Rome Statute classifies "rape, sexual slavery, enforced prostitution, forced pregnancy, enforced sterilization, or any other form of sexual violence of comparable gravity" committed "as part of a widespread or systematic attack directed against any civilian population" as crimes against humanity." (UNESA, supra note 32, at 7).*

B. Cultural Norms Fostering SGBV in Fiji

Fijian women are treated unequally in every sector of private and public life. This discriminatory treatment arises from entrenched cultural, religious, and patriarchal traditions. The use of *bulubulu* (reconciliation) in sexual assault cases is an example of the denigration of women. Historically, *bulubulu* was used to resolve conflicts between tribes. It is now established in rape law and cited frequently by judges to mitigate sentences in sexual assault cases.

Bulubulu: Customary Norm in Fijian Culture

In Fijian culture, *bulubulu* - a custom for reconciling differences - is an essential part of traditional village life. Disputes were settled with the offer of a whale's tooth (*tabua*), a gift or compensation, and asking for forgiveness (Merry, *supra* note 34, at 9). There is social pressure to accept this apology because the historic outcome of accepting *bulubulu* was to break the cycle of vengeance. The offer is directed to the senior male member of the family, but generally not the victim (*Id.* at 123). As the population has begun to move from rural to urban locations, however, the "custom itself is being redefined" (*Id.* at 118).

Advocates from Fijian Women's Crisis Center (FWCC) argue that the current practice of *bulubulu* in violence against women cases is an affront to the traditional practice of *bulubulu* "because in the olden days, the punishment for the crime [of rape] under customary law was death." (Merry, *supra* note 35, at 126; Elizabeth Powell and Teuila Percival, *Fijian Pathways to the Prevention of Sexual Violence*, Pacific Health School of Population Health University of Auckland, 9; Oct. 2010). Over the past two decades, *bulubulu* has been manipulated by perpetrators of SGBV to: get sexual assault and domestic violence cases dropped by police officers, receive reduced court sentences, and deny redress to survivors of SGBV. Unfortunately, judges contribute to the misuse of *bulubulu* in SGBV cases because of their reliance on using the evidence of reconciliation to mitigate sentences. Judges have also expanded the applicability of *bulubulu* to sexual assaults and domestic violence in the Criminal Procedure Statute, even though the statue provides for reconciliation only in common assaults (Criminal Procedure Code (Consolidated Acts 1985) [CAP 21], section 163 ("In the case of any charge or charges brought under any of the provisions of subsection (1) of section 197 or of section 244 or of section 245 or of subsection (1) of section 324 of the Penal Code, the court may, in such cases which are substantially of a person or private nature and which are not aggravated in degree, promote reconciliation and encourage and facilitate the settlement in an amicable way of the proceedings, on terms of payment of compensation or on other terms approved by the court, and may thereupon order the proceedings to be stayed or terminated."), http://www.paclii.org/fj/legis/consol_act_OK/cpc190/).

In CEDAW's Concluding Observations on Fiji, the Committee noted:

The concept of one system of justice being relevant to all our communities, and being accessible and significant to all our people, is an important one to ensure that cultural norms in relation to justice take a subordinate place to the national justice system. This is particularly because culture has often driven gender biased attitudes towards women, with no right of redress in a culturally accepted justice model. Our experience is that gender equality has a better chance in a justice system which is sensitive to culture, but removed from patriarchal cultural norms (CEDAW Committee, Concluding Observations of the Committee on the Elimination of Discrimination against Women: Fiji, CEDAW/C/FJI/CO/4/Add.1, 5.14 (Aug. 2, 2012) [hereinafter "CEDAW Committee"].

Bulubulu: Legal System

In 1987, when indigenous Fijians sought to remove from power Indo-Fijians (who were brought to Fiji as agricultural workers by the British during colonial times), there was a "resurgence of interest in Fijian custom along with Fijian cultural nationalism." (*Id.* at 125). After 1987, it became problematic to criticize *bulubulu* as an alternative to the court system, and therefore, *bulubulu's* use in SGBV cases was sanctioned (*Id.* After women's rights organizations protested, including Fiji Women's Rights Movement (FWRM), there was support from the Chief Justice in strengthening sentencing guidelines, but what followed was only further regression). (see Figure 13)

In challenging this notion, former Solicitor General of Fiji, Mr. Maitaitoga, is quoted as saying:

Traditional means of reconciliation should not influence the sentencing of rapists.... I do not accept that the taukei (Indigenous Fijians) culture and traditions permit the use of the i bulubulu traditional as a means for a criminal to conveniently escape the fruit of his deeds ... The courts, police and all other law enforcement personnel dealing with rape, must not accept the pleading of traditional values and customs as a substitute for criminal sanctions (Fenton, supra note 7, at 4).

Nonetheless, *bulubulu* is strongly encouraged when the complaint is made for which arrest would be proper, at the charging stage (by not filing the case in court), and during sentencing (as a mitigating factor). Fiji Criminal Procedure Law

Figure 13. Recommendations: Informal justice mechanisms

- Strengthen community-based justice systems to protect women from violence;
- Ensure that customary courts are familiar with CEDAW's concept of equality so that their rulings are not discriminatory against women.

section 163 provides that judges and magistrates should encourage *bulubulu* in cases of "common assault" and assault causing bodily harm (Criminal Procedure Code (Consolidated Acts 1985) [CAP 21], section 163, http://www.paclii.org/fj/legis/consol_act_OK/cpc190/). Although domestic violence and sexual assaults are not included in the section 163 list of crimes, (Amnesty CEDAW, *supra* note 13, at 12; Criminal Procedure Code (Consolidated Acts 1985) [CAP 21], section 163, http://www.paclii.org/fj/legis/consol_act_OK/cpc190/) judges routinely mitigate sentences because those crimes are charged as common assault, under Penal Law section 244. The result is that Fijian women are reluctant to file complaints with the police and perpetrators of violence against women know that they can escape custodial sentences. According to Amnesty International, "[s]uch informal extrajudicial forms of settlement deny the victims recognition of the gravity of the offense[s] committed against her [sic] and foster a climate of impunity for the perpetrators" (Amnesty CEDAW, *supra* note 13, at 12).

Even with the progressive promulgation of the Domestic Violence Decree 2009, judges consistently try SGBV cases under the Crime Decree 2009. This can be seen through our case law survey analysis regarding *bulubulu's* use to mitigate sentences in sexual assault and domestic violence cases is in the Appendix (*See* ICAAD, *supra* note 43).

Case Law Survey: *Bulubulu* (Reconciliation)

In reviewing the Pacific Islands Legal Information Institute database, we narrowed our review to all cases (61) [Our initial search revealed over 100 cases, which we narrowed to 61 cases. Our review was limited to this database, which unfortunately does not contain every Fijian case at the various court levels] at the Magistrate, High Court, High Court (Appellate Jurisdiction), Court of Appeals, and Supreme Court level from 1977-2013 where *bulubulu* was considered as a mitigating factor in sexual assault and domestic violence cases.

The case law survey looked at 3 primary points:

- Was evidence of *bulubulu* in SGBV a factor in mitigating the defendant's sentence;
- Did the court award no custodial sentence or partially suspend a sentences where the perpetrator was found to have committed SGBV;
- Whether or not *bulubulu* was used to mitigate a sentence in that case, did the judge generally believe it was acceptable to do so in SGBV cases.

In 27 of 55 cases (6 were N/A for this point), or 49% of cases, judges used reconciliation as a factor in mitigating the sentence in domestic violence and sexual assault cases. In 30 of 59 cases, or 50.8% of case, judges gave no custodial sentences or partially suspended sentences in sexual assault and domestic violence cases. Interestingly, almost all the judges cited legislation that specifically prohibited the dismissing of SGBV cases because there was evidence of SGBV, yet, other factors like the defendant being a "first time offender," or "sole bread winner," led to outright suspension of sentences. And, finally, slightly more than half the judges who rendered decisions in these cases believed that it was acceptable to reduce a sentence based on evidence of reconciliation (ICAAD, *supra* note 43).

In breaking down the data, we found that after the Domestic Violence Decree 2009 went into effect, judges were more cognizant in their judicial opinions of not giving undue weight to reconciliation because of the power imbalance. Yet since 2010 Magistrate judges still used *bulubulu* to mitigate sentences in 77.7% of cases (14 of 18). In contrast, in all the High Court, Appellate

Jurisdiction cases (8; 1 N/A) where the appellant sought reduction of sentence based on reconciliation, not one case awarded a reduced sentence. A similar result was reached in all Court of Appeal (From 2005-2006, a study found that the Court of Appeals quashed or reduced sentences for SGBV in 95% of cases. CEDAW Committee, *supra* note 97, at 11) (3) cases. This brings into question the value of precedent and authority of the higher courts.

One example is the Supreme Court's refusal to reduce a sentence in a domestic violence case where the husband had "expressed remorse in Fijian style" (*Koro v Reginam* [1977] FJSC 161; Criminal Appeal 112 of 1977 (18 November 1977). The Court was clear, "[t]he responsibility for his conduct must rest upon the husband. If by reason of his crimes his family may be reduced to poverty the blame cannot be laid at the door of the Court which imprisons him" (*Id*). Even in 1977, the Supreme Court understood that there was a power imbalance in SGBV cases and that accountability (custodial sentences) was necessary to prevent husbands from having a license to harm women. Yet, this long-standing precedent continues to be ignored.

Despite the Assistant Minister of the Fiji Ministry for Women, Social Welfare and Poverty Alleviation's contention that *bulubulu* functions largely outside the legal system, (Merry, *supra* note 34, at 6) judges today continue to mitigate sentences for sexual assault and domestic violence cases based on *bulubulu,* as shown in our case law survey analysis. (see Figures 14 and 15)

Figure 14. The role of culture shaping judicial opinions

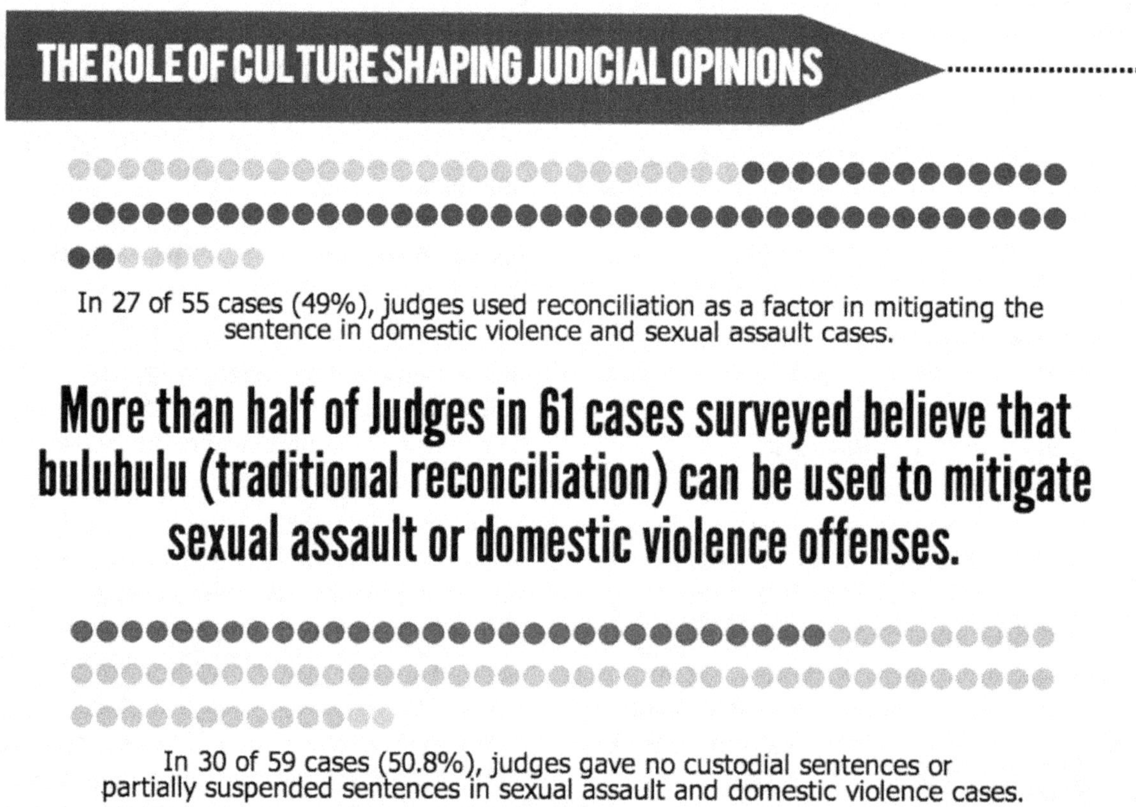

Figure 15. Recommendations: Legal recommendations

- Adopt a new constitution through a collaborative process involving the full participation of women and to fully restore the rule of law and the independence of the judiciary through re-establishment of the Judicial Service Commission;
- Implement training for judiciary, law enforcement, and health service providers on SGBV;
- Draft stand-alone anti-discrimination legislation that is inclusive of gender;
- Explicit acknowledgement that SGBV is a form of discrimination and breaches international law;
- Legislation reform on SGBV needs to be supported when parliamentary democracy returns;
- Avoid further traumatizing or stigmatizing of victims during the judicial process;
- Ensure victims of SGBV receive adequate medical and psycho-social support and safety;
- Customary laws must be harmonized with legislation on VAW and gender equality;
- Providing legal aid to all victims of SGBV;
- Ensure protections for sexual orientation are included in all relevant legislation.

3. FIJI'S OBLIGATIONS UNDER INTERNATIONAL LAW

A. International Instruments Fiji is Bound to Uphold

Fiji has ratified three human rights treaties: 1) The International Convention on the Elimination of all forms of Racial Discrimination (ICERD, 1973); 2) The Convention on the Elimination of All Forms of Discrimination Against Women (CEDAW, 1979); and 3) the Convention on the Rights of the Child (CRC, 1993). Each has a Committee that monitors the States' Parties' compliance with the provisions.

Fiji has not signed the optional protocols for both CRC and CEDAW. Although both conventions are binding on Fiji, the ratification of the optional protocols would grant the individual Committees jurisdiction to review complaints from groups and individuals. If a Committee has jurisdiction to review individual claims, a Committee can issue binding legal decision. Moreover, that decision informs national courts on application of that specific convention provision in domestic cases.

Fiji has ratified other international instruments that address violence against women:

- The United Nations Declaration on the Elimination of Violence Against Women (DEVAW) (1994);
- The Beijing Platform for Action (1995);
- The UN Declaration of Commitment on HIV/AIDS (UNGASS);
- The President's Cabinet approved the ratification of United Nations Convention against Transnational Organized Crime and the three optional protocols (two of which specifically address trafficking of persons). This was in 2011 There has been no formal ratification of this Convention since (UNFPA, *supra* note 3, at 21 ("This Declaration identifies measures to address violence against women and children, including domestic violence, as a strategy to combat HIV/AIDS").

Additionally, Fiji reports to UN Universal Periodic Review (UPR) process. The UPR mechanism brings together over 190+ UN Member States to voluntarily report on their human rights conditions and undergo a review where recommendations made from other Member States are accepted or rejected. Other UN treaty bodies, Special Rapporteurs, and NGOs can also participate in the process through the submission of reports.

In 2010, the Attorney General of Fiji, at the Review Conference for the Rome Statute in Kamapala, Uganda, asserted that the Crimes Decree of 2009 serves as implementing legislation (Statement by the Attorney General & Minister for Justice, *Review Conference of the Rome Statute of the International Criminal Court, Kamapal, Uganda*, 2-3; June 1, 2010). The legislation asserts, "any law which makes provision for the jurisdiction of the International Criminal Court shall not affect the primacy of Fiji's right to exercise its jurisdiction with respect to offences created by this Division (and any other law prescribing offences against humanity or war crimes) that are also crimes within the jurisdiction of the International Criminal Court" (Crimes Decree of 2009, Part 12, Div. 1, section 76; 3). Provisions for genocide and crimes against humanity are laid forth in the legislation, but there is no provision for war crimes.

Therefore, if it is argued that Fiji has the necessary implementing legislation in place to avoid ICC jurisdiction, Fiji must still show that it is willing to hold accountable perpetrators of international crimes. Here, it is arguable that the atrocities committed during the coup, including SGBV against women leaders and sex workers amounted to crimes against humanity, which is a widespread or systematic attack against a civilian population (Rome statute of the International Criminal Court, 2187 U.N.T.S. 90, Art. 7 (1)(g). The Rome Statute was adopted on July 17, 1998, and came into force on July 1, 2002. Fiji Ratified Rome Statute on Nov. 29, 1999).

B. Building an International Human Rights Framework

Fiji has not ratified the foundational human rights conventions: UN Declaration on Human Rights; International Covenant on Civil and Political Rights (ICCPR); International Covenant on Economic, Social and Cultural Rights (ICESCR); Convention Against Torture (CAT) and their accompanying Optional Protocols. What underscores Fiji's failure to protect women from violence is the lack of recognition of core international human rights treaties. PICs, including Fiji, have the lowest ratification rate of human rights treaties in the world (Jalal 2008).

There are practical reasons that PICs have the lowest rates of ratification. According to P. Imrana Jalal, a legal scholar on women's rights in the Pacific, the internal capacity and expertise that is required for participation, such as monitoring, reporting, implementation, and travel to New York or Geneva to engage with the Committees, is prohibitive for many PICs. Also, to fill the existing gap in capacity or expertise, some of the PICs hire external consultants to draft their reports for the treaties they have ratified, building little institutional knowledge and memory (Jalal 2006).

Fiji's previous Constitution allowed courts to cite international human rights treaties even without ratification, (Jalal, *supra* note 115, at 33) though this arises infrequently in SGBV cases. In one example, the Court of Appeals found the rule on corroboration of sexual assaults at trial was found to be a law of general and neutral applicability that had a disproportionate impact on women who were the main complainants, and therefore, was discriminatory under CEDAW's human rights framework (*Id.* at 34). In another example, a judge struck at the heart of the use of *bulubulu* as a means of reducing a sentence against a rapist. The magistrate commented:

"Women are your equal and therefore must not be discriminated on the basis of gender. Men should be aware of the provisions of CEDAW, which our country had ratified. Under the Convention the State shall ensure that all forms of discrimination against women must be eliminated at all costs. The courts shall be the watch-dog with the obligation" (Merry supra note 34, at 3-4).

Human rights treaties often conflict with customary norms, like *bulubulu*, *kustom*, and *f'a* that are prevalent in PICs (Jalal, *supra* note 115, at 34). Unfortunately, custom prevails and "[t]he power traditionally accorded to males in Fiji results in an unofficial sanctioning of sexual violence"

Figure 16. Recommendations: Ratification of international treaties

- International Covenant on Civil and Political Rights (ICCPR) and its Optional Protocols;
- Convention against Torture and Other Cruel, Inhuman and Degrading Treatment or Punishment (CAT) and its Optional Protocol;
- International Covenant on Social, Economic and Cultural Rights (ICESCR) and its Optional Protocol;
- Optional protocol for Convention on the Elimination of Discrimination Against Women (CEDAW);
- Optional protocol for the Convention for the Rights of the Child (CRC).

(UNFPA, *supra* note 3, at 19 ("This Declaration identifies measures to address violence against women and children, including domestic violence, as a strategy to combat HIV/AIDS"). Fiji National Research statistics show that 80% of survey respondents have witnessed SGBV at home. Thus, it is important that courts recognize this conflict and make decisions that are consistent with human rights norms. Implementing human rights norms, "improves the public standing of PICs and their governments and encourages a fairer and equitable system of aid, technical support and global justice." (see Figure 16)

Ultimately, the role of NGOs is crucial in advocating ratification and implementation of human rights treaties. Only by working with the relevant government agencies and creating a "well-organised, effective, strategic, and well-funded local" movement will the chances for ratification improve (Jalal, *supra* note 116, at 20).

Ms. Jalal, a women's rights scholar and regional expert for the PICs, presents a comprehensive list of how PICs can benefit from an international human rights framework:

- Providing the moral and legal framework for decolonization and independence from former PIC colonial powers (a key feature of the Universal Declaration on Human Rights (UDHR) and ICCPR);
- Providing a framework for democracy and elections for PIC constitutions and membership into the UN;
- Providing a legal framework of good governance;
- Enabling the majority of PICs to be perceived globally as functioning democracies respecting human rights (compare PIC records to that of Africa and South East Asia);
- Enabling the establishment of an independent judiciary;
- Encouraging overseas aid because PICs are able to demonstrate elected leadership and good governance;
- Providing aid and technical support conditioned upon combating child pornography, human trafficking, violence, and discrimination against women, or for other human rights infrastructure development needs. For example, in Fiji, the EU provided support for development projects, such as the building of bridges, because Fiji was able to demonstrate human rights compliance with article 96 of the Cotonou Agreement;
- Providing protection against the arbitrary use of power by the state in terms of the right to free movement, speech, fair trial, freedom from discrimination, free and fair elections, a just wage, protection against torture, and an independent judiciary;
- Ratification has . . . been a strong leverage for national improvements - for example, CRC being the catalyst for legislation against child pornography in PIC (Jalal, *supra* note 115, at 22).

4. DATA ON VIOLENCE AGAINST WOMEN REVEALS THE STATE'S FAILURE TO PROTECT

Data on SGBV is limited. Many organizations working in the PICs find that data collection is one of the largest gaps in the fight against SGBV. Statistics in this section come from a commissioned project by the Fijian Department of Public Health, national research on Domestic Violence by FWCC, and the Fiji Police Force.

According to the Fiji Police Force, from 2003-2007, 13% of all crimes reported were regarding domestic violence (Tuiketei et al 2010). According to the FWCC, "74% of female victims did not report violence to the police" (*Id.* at 18). This is a staggering statistic of domestic violence related crime. Many factors contribute to underreporting, including familial pressures to keep the incident private, religious clergy who insist on reconciliation, police who do not view SGBV as serious crime, and societal belief that violence is a "part of marriage" (UNIFEM, *supra* note 18, at 20). Hence, it is no surprise that 32% of women report violence after declining to have sex with their spouse (UNFPA, *supra* note 3, at 16). In cases of rape, the victim knows the perpetrator in 70% of the cases and that number rises to 94% in child sexual abuse cases (UNIFEM, *supra* note 18, at 3). (see Figure 17)

If data collection is to be robust on matters of SGBV, then inclusion of health professionals in

Figure 17. Department of Public Health and Primary Care - Fiji School of Medicine

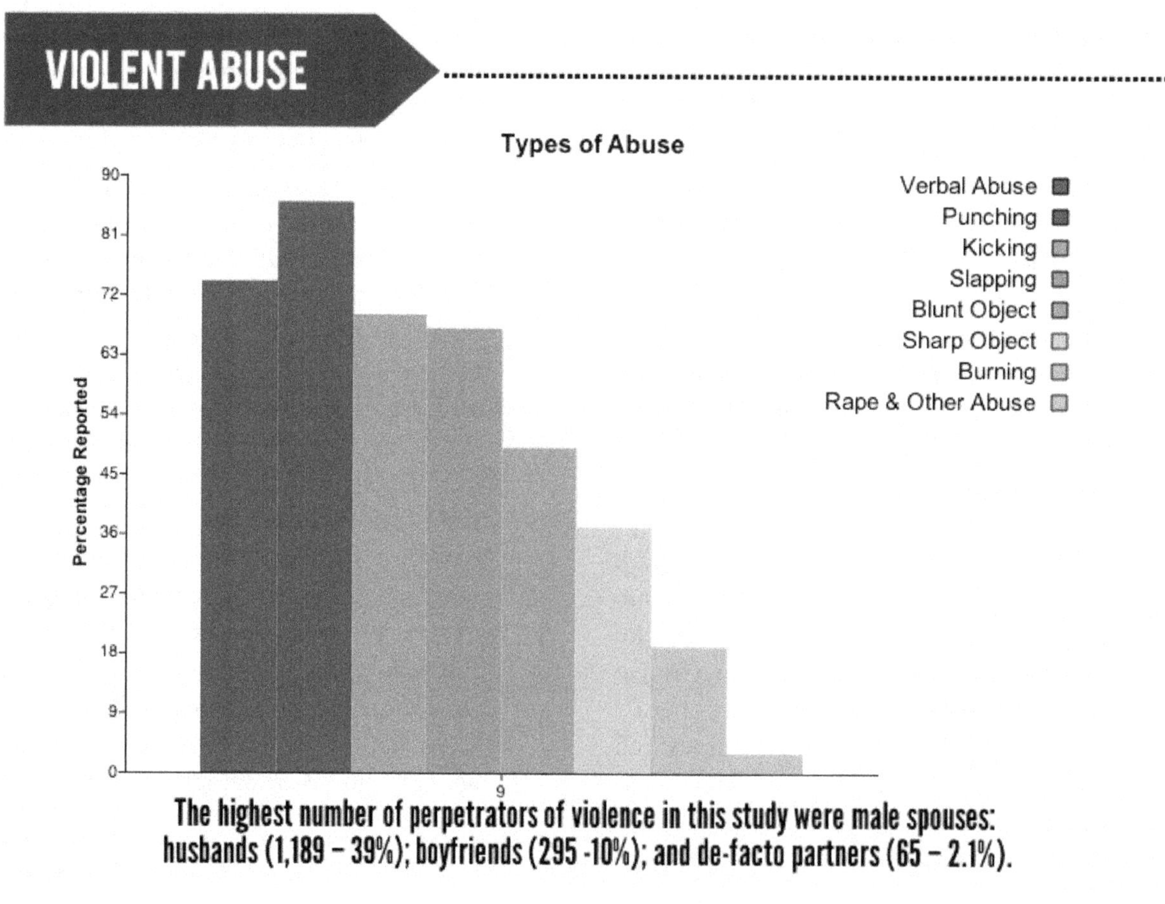

setting "standard procedures within the hospital system to ensure that cases of gender-based violence are responded to in the correct medico-legal manner, with appropriate empathy" (UNFPA, *supra* note 3, at 30) is essential. Currently, no standard procedure exists. The Public Health Department's commissioned study shows the value of being able to collect data on SGBV and the training of health professionals to document properly.

Violence directed at women has an economic cost that is disproportional to the economy of Fiji. The "Reserve Bank calculated the direct and indirect costs of violence [against women] in Fiji to be FJ$210.69-million per year, or 7% of GDP" (UNIFEM, *supra* note 18, at 3). This includes cost borne by victims and their families, welfare, law enforcement, and health care. What is absent is the cost of court resources to prosecute domestic violence and rape cases as well as opportunity costs (Coalition Shadow Report, *supra* note 15, at 10). (see Figures 18 and 19)

CONCLUSION

Acceptance of SGBV permeates all facets of Fijian life and government structures directly impeding the movement towards gender equality. Though some Fijian court decisions are progressive in response to addressing violence against women by citing CEDAW, for example, other decisions are sexist (Fenton, *supra* note 7, at 5). In authoring numerous opinions in sexual assault and do-

Figure 18. Department of Public Health and Primary Care - Fiji School of Medicine

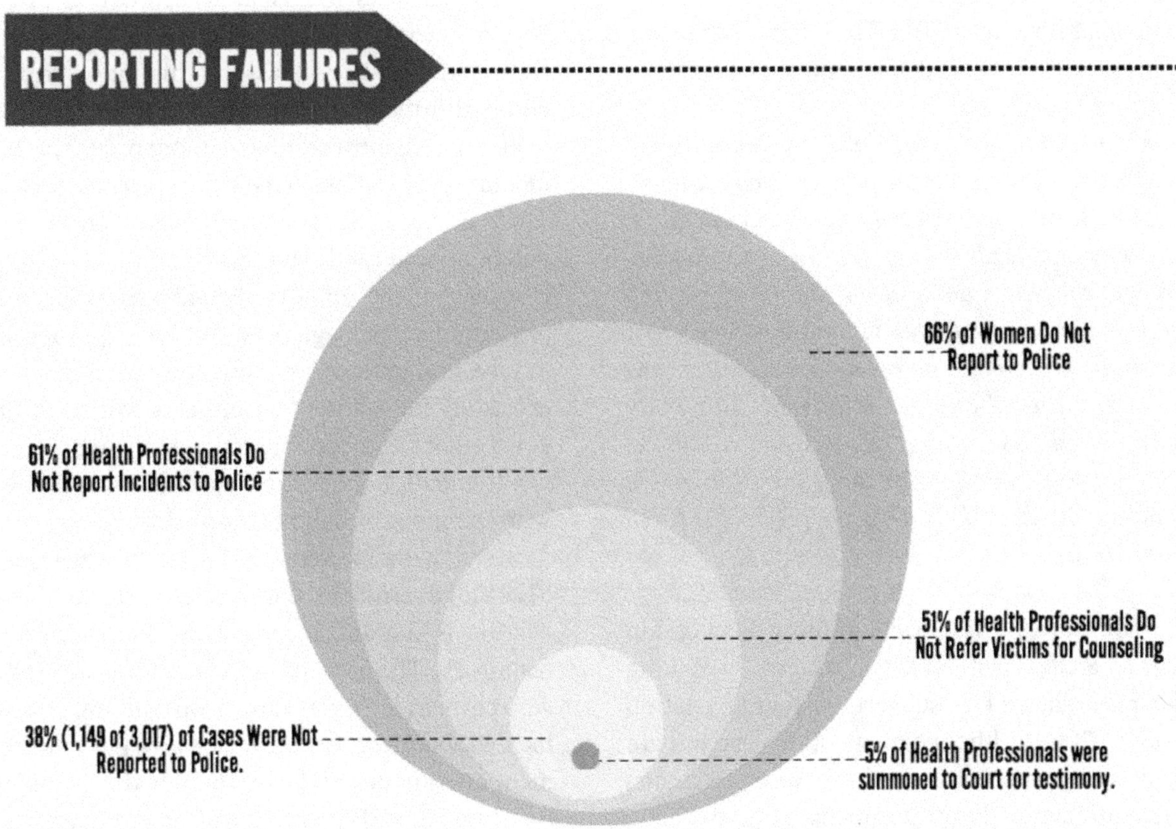

Figure 19. Recommendations: Health [Care] Recommendations

- Policies and protocols for handling SGBV must be introduced into the health system;
- VAW training needs to be compulsory within the Fiji School of Nursing and Medicine;
- Ensure that all rape survivors have access to timely post-exposure HIV prophylaxis;
- A "one stop shop" model for dealing with SGBV victims needs to be set up within the public health system to ensure speedy and proper handling of cases;
- Health services data collection system needs to record all victims of SGBV;
- Special attention needs to be given to support pregnant women living in violent situations;
- Develop a specialized counseling unit within health facilities where a counselor, social worker, religious personnel, and others can be available 24 hours/day;
- Strengthen referral networks with NGOs;
- Improve reporting of SGBV to the police, but without violating patient confidentiality and free choice in the decision regarding reporting to police;
- Strengthen curriculum on identifying and addressing SGBV injuries for health professionals;
- Conduct training on clinical management, medico-legal issues, evidence collection and storage, and counseling on SGBV;
- Conduct studies on SGBV reporting and recording cases anonymously at health facilities such as identification of cases, reporting of those cases, their treatment and follow up;
- Maintain timely and accurate records at the health facilities.

mestic violence cases, Judge Goudnar identifies the important role culture plays in Fiji, but also recognizes that culture cannot be used to subvert accountability. In a 2012 High Court decision, *Roligalevu v State*, Judge Goudnar states,

[i]n our country, we take pride in our customs and traditions. Customs and traditions should never be used to restrict access to justice. If anything, customs and traditions should be a medium to correct the harm done to the victim by making the offender accountable. Without accountability, relationships cannot be restored, no matter how much traditional apology is offered. This is an exceptional case where customs and traditions were exploited to suppress the truth. (Roligalevu v State [2012] FJHC 1092; HAC052.2011 (18 May 2012).

Additionally, the current military dictatorship has created a parallel legal system by issuing Decrees that seek to subvert existing legislation prior to 2009. Although many of the Decrees are progressive and seek to address women's rights, the legitimacy of these instruments is questionable. Without legislation that is crafted by a parliamentary democracy, the difficulty of addressing the structural defects in legislation become magnified.

One recommendation from Fijian women's rights organizations was an admonition to "[r]efrain from making further changes to laws relating to violence against women without proper parliamentary proceedings" (FWCC, *supra* note 6, at 4). There is some indication that a new Constitution will be adopted and elections will be held in 2014. However, if the military dictatorship delays the proceedings once again, would it be appropriate to take comprehensive steps towards amending or adding legislation that protects women if the government is amenable to such changes? This is a foundational question that must be resolved with the input of local organizations.

Even with Decrees that seek to ameliorate SGBV, government enforcement of such legislation is limited, inconsistent, and lacking in resources. The lack of accountability for those who perpetrate SGBV flows from cultural norms, like *bulubulu*, that have affected how law enforcement investigates SGBV cases, whether prosecutors litigate SGBV cases, and how judges craft

Figure 20. Recommendations: Prevention and education recommendations

- Gender equality and non-violent conflict resolution training needs to be introduced into the school curriculum at all levels;
- Schools should have a trained counselor available to assist students living in violent situations;
- Outline a National Action Plan for prevention of SGBV that recognizes the state's responsibility to respect, protect, and uphold human rights;
- Government programs aimed at shaping the attitudes of men and boys need to be strengthened and not reinforce gender stereotypes;
- Empower faith-based organizations and institutions to be champions against SGBV;
- Disseminate findings on VAW (i.e. Family Health and Safety studies);
- Focus on cultural traditions that perpetuate SGBV;
- Strengthen partnerships with churches, faith based organizations, and traditional chiefs;
- Encourage progressive, non-gender biased interpretations of religious texts;
- Mobilize resources of religious organizations to assist victims of SGBV (e.g. shelters);
- Challenge male assumptions about gender roles;
- Media campaign to increase men's awareness of laws on domestic violence;
- Cultivate high-level male champions on violence against women (e.g. Commissioners);
- Develop community-level male champions (e.g. village court magistrates);
- Integrate VAW into public and private initiatives (i.e. micro-finance, health, peace building, sexual harassment, disaster preparedness programs etc.);
- Using the WHO methodology to enhance data gathering;
- Gender-sensitive methodology should be used which respects confidentiality and women's human rights and does not jeopardize women's safety;
- Assess effectiveness of measures taken to prevent and redress VAW;
- Specific outreach by government and civil society to include particularly vulnerable women (e.g. rural areas, Indo-Fijian, H.I.V., disabled) is crucial.

judicial decisions and sentence perpetrators of SGBV. Until the Fijian government understands the gravity and destabilizing effect of SGBV on a society's well-being, consistency amongst all the various branches of government in combating SGBV will be lacking.

Civil society has played a tremendous role in bringing awareness to SGBV in Fiji. However, stronger partnerships with government and private-public partnerships will help to strengthen and disseminate the importance of combating SGBV. More importantly, consistent engagement at the international level is crucial in maintaining state accountability and building capacity and technical expertise to further Fiji's commitment to the rule of law. (see Figure 20)

ACKNOWLEDGMENT

This chapter was the first in a series of reports by the International Center for Advocates Against Discrimination (ICAAD) focusing on violence against women in the Pacific Island Countries. This chapter focused on Fiji. Subsequent reports, written in partnership with Manatt, Phelps, & Phillips, LLP and DLA Piper, will address violence against women in the remaining Pacific Island Countries.

SPECIAL THANKS

ICAAD would like to acknowledge the assistance provided by Navdeep Tucker, Esq., Ilana Ofgang, Esq., and Jaspreet Bansal, Esq., on assisting with research regarding Fijian case law.

REFERENCES

Amnesty International. (2010). *Fiji: Submission to the UN universal periodic review*. Retrieved from http://lib.ohchr.org/HRBodies/UPR/Documents/Session7/FJ/AI_UPR_FJI_S07_2010_Amnesty_International.pdf

Amnesty International. CEDAW. (2010). *Fiji: Submission to the committee on the elimination of discrimination against women 46th session*. Retrieved from http://www2.ohchr.org/english/bodies/cedaw/docs/ngos/AI_Fiji_Cedaw46.pdf

Australia: Refugee Review Tribunal. (2010). *Fiji: 1) Would an 18-year-old Indo Fijian woman, from Lautoka, be able to get protection from being harassed, abducted and raped by a young native Fijian male?* Retrieved from http://www.refworld.org/docid/4ccff48c2.html

Coalition of Women's NGOs for the CEDAW Shadow Report. (2009). *Shadow NGO report on Fiji's second, third and fourth combined periodic report to the committee on the elimination of discrimination against women*. Retrieved from http://lib.ohchr.org/HRBodies/UPR/Documents/Session7/FJ/FWRM_UPR_FJI_S07_2010_Fiji_WomensRightsMovement_annex1.pdf

Committee on the Elimination of Discrimination against Women (CEDAW). (1992). *General recommendation no. 19: Violence against women*. Retrieved from http://www.un.org/womenwatch/daw/cedaw/recommendations/recomm.htm#recom19

Criminal Procedure Code (Consolidated Acts 1985) [CAP 21]. (1978). Retrieved from http://www.paclii.org/fj/legis/consol_act_OK/cpc190/

Fiji News. (2013). Fiji's *steps towards protecting women and children*. Retrieved from http://www.fbc.com.fj/fiji/8634/fiji%E2%80%99s-steps-towards-protecting-women-and-children

Fiji Women's Crisis Centre (FWCC). (2010). *Submission to the United Nations periodic review on violence against women: Fiji* (2010). Retrieved from www.FWCC_UPR_FJI_507_2010

Fiji Women's Rights Movement (FWRM). (2010). *Submission to the United Nations universal periodic review on Fiji* (2010). Retrieved from www.FWRM_UPR_FJI_507_2010

Florence Fenton. (1998). *Ethnic diversity – Challenges for courts, Fiji law reform commission.* Retrieved from http://www.familycourt.gov.au/wps/wcm/resources/file/eba6c00346fcab8/FENTON.pdf

Human Rights Council. (2012). *Report of the special rapporteur on violence against women, its causes and consequences*. Retrieved from http://www.ohchr.org/Documents/Issues/Women/A.HRC.20.16_En.pdf

International Center for Advocates Against Discrimination (ICAAD). (2013). *The role of culture in shaping judicial opinions on domestic violence and sexual assault: Case law survey of bulubulu*. Retrieved from http://icaadglobal.org/mediaItem.php?id=158

(2006). *International Law into Local Justice, 123*. Chicago: The University of Chicago Press.

Jalal, P. I. (2006). *Pacific culture and human rights: Why Pacific island countries should ratify international human rights treaties. Pacific Regional Rights Resource Team*. RRRT/ UNDP.

Jalal, P.I. (2008). Legal protection against discrimination in Pacific island countries. *The Equal Rights Review, 2*(32).

JET. (2013, January 31). *Violence against women in Fiji touches all aspect of women's lives, survey finds*. Retrieved from http://thejetnewspaper.com/2013/01/31/violence-against-women-in-fiji-touches-all-aspect-of-womens-lives-survey-finds/

Lechuga Foundation and Sexual Rights Initiative (LFSRI). (2010). *Report on Fiji 7th round of the universal periodic review*. Retrieved from www. LF_SRI_UPR_FJU_507_2010

Merry, E. S. (2004). Tensions between global law and social justice. *CEDAW and the Problem of Rape in Fiji, 9*.

Merry, E. S. (2006). *Human rights and gender violence: Translating*. Pacific Islands Legal Information Institute (PacLII). Retrieved from http:// www.paclii.org/

Pacific Islands Legal Information Institute (PacLII). (2009). *Republic of Fiji decrees 2009*. Retrieved from http://www.paclii.org/fj/indices/ legis/Fiji%20-%20Decrees_2009.html

Powell, E., & Teuila Percival, T. (2010). *Fijian pathways to the prevention of sexual violence*. Paper presented at the Pacific Health School of Population Health University of Auckland. Auckland, New Zealand.

Raisoqoni v State [2011] FJHC 32, HAA004.2011. (2011, February 7). Retrieved from http://www. paclii.org/cgi-bin/disp.pl/fj/cases/FJHC/2011/32. html?stem=0&synonyms=0&query=raisoqo ni%20and%20v%20and%20state%20and%20 [2011]%20and%20fjhc%20and%2032%20 and%20haa004%20and%202011%20and%20 7%20and%20february%20and%202011

Sera, J. (2009). A-G defends domestic violence decree. *Fiji Sun*. Retrieved from http://www. fijisun.com.fj/2009/09/15/a-g-defends-domestic-violence-decree/

Tuiketei, T. et al. (2010). *Violence against women – A public health perspective*. Department of Public Health.

United Nations Department of Economic and Social Affairs. Division for the Advancement of Women. (2010). *Handbook for legislation on violence against women*. Retrieved from http:// www.un.org/womenwatch/daw/vaw/handbook/ Handbook%20for%20legislation%20on%20violence%20against%20women.pdf

United Nations Development Fund for Women. (2010, August). *Ending violence against women & girls: Evidence, data and knowledge in the Pacific island countries*. Retrieved from http:// www.undp.org.fj/pdf/unp/evaw.pdf

United Nations Population Fund. (2008). *An assessment of the state of violence against women in Fiji*. Author.

KEY TERMS AND DEFINITIONS

Coup or Coup d'état: The sudden deposition of a government, typically by the military.

Discrimination: The prejudicial and/or distinguishing treatment of an individual based on their actual or perceived membership in a certain group or category, in a way that is worse than the way people are usually treated.

Legal System: A system for interpreting and enforcing the laws. The system may be religious or secular in its nature, but in order to be called a system there must be certain predictability and coherence in the interpretation of laws. The developed legal systems are heavily based on the use of written laws and their interpretation.

Parliamentary Democratic Process: A state of democracy ensures that the processes by which power is acceded to, wielded and alternates allow for free political competition and are the product of open, free and non-discriminatory participation by the people, exercised in accordance with the rule of law, in both letter and spirit.

ENDNOTES

1 All recommendations throughout the chapter have been compiled and consolidated from the following sources: UNPFA, *supra* note 3, at 42-44; LFSIR, *supra* note 6, at 4-5; UNIFEM, *supra* note 18, at 32-33; AusAID Office of Development Effectiveness, Fiji Country Report (2008); *See* Tuiketei, *supra* note 124; *See* CEDAW, *supra* note 97; Amnesty CEDAW, *supra* note 13, at 14-15; Jalal, *supra* note 115.

2 The legislative recommendations throughout Part 2 of the chapter are taken directly from: United Nations Department of Economic and Social Affairs; 2010 [hereinafter UNESA]

Chapter 16
The Japanese Model of Risk Society:
Challenges to Japanese Public Policy

Mika Markus Merviö
Kibi International University, Japan

ABSTRACT

Japan, two years after the triple catastrophe of earthquake, tsunami, and Fukushima nuclear plant crisis, is only slowly wakening to the new reality of a new kind of reflexive relationship with nuclear power and, more generally, the use of modern technology and the social risks linked with modern life. In Japan, the idea that Japan's very own catastrophe is, instead, a global catastrophe has not really sunk in. Coping with the disasters may be the most urgent and visible task of the government, but the Japanese society can hardly wait to find solutions to many long-term policy choices. This chapter analyzes the Japanese model of risk society, the risk society discourse in Japan, and the challenges of risk society to Japanese public policy.

THE JAPANESE MODEL OF RISK SOCIETY *(NIHONGATA RISUKU SHAKAI)*

As a consequence of globalisation, all risk societies and regimes (using Ulrich Beck's term) are an integral part of the world system and include social risks ranging from economic risks to ecological ones. However, perceptions of these risks differ considerably between societies. Japan is usually seen to be a centralised state since the role of national government and especially the ministries has been so central. Furthermore, at first glance it may appear that things are very much under control in Japan and, therefore, there must be some public authority that is able to manage things so effectively. However, compared with most European countries the role of the Japanese state is quite weak when it comes to welfare so-

DOI: 10.4018/978-1-4666-5031-2.ch016

ciety and many other functions. In short, family and business corporations and increasingly also volunteer organisations take care of functions that the public sector prefers to neglect. Taxation remains at relatively low levels and it is politically very difficult to raise taxes, although most people in Japan know very well that sooner or later there will be increased taxation. While the Japanese state has used its power and financial resources without hesitation in some fields such as public construction it has conserved resources by making people face many social risks, such as most family-related risks and unemployment, the best way that they can. If people fall ill or face other individual problems Japanese society often has surprisingly little room for such values as social solidarity and compassion. On the other hand, there have been social practices that have served to soften the image of Japanese working life practices, such as the strong emphasis on lifelong employment and relatively small wage differences among employees, especially among the elite salarymen *(sararîman).*

The characteristics of the Japanese model of risk society are that the weak political leadership muddles along with the rest of the societies with globalisation and most sectors of the society need to adjust to the changed realities the best way they can. On the one hand Japanese society has its cultural values emphasising the merits of social harmony and virtues of intersubjective practices. However, conflicts have always existed openly or been managed under the facade of harmony and the new era of even weaker national governance, accelerated by the process of decentralisation (*chihô bunken*) has imposed individualisation on Japanese people from above (for more on *chihô bunken*, Shindô, 2002). This individualisation has already encompassed every corner of Japanese society and, for instance, in Yoshimi Kataoka's chapter in this book there is an analysis on the changed balance between individuals and families in very conservative rural areas in Japan. The stated objectives of decentralisation in Japan are related to enhancing citizens' participation and democratisation. However, the other part of the programme is to find local solutions to problems ranging from local economy to ageing society and environmental problems. However, the real motive for the national government to push through the change, regardless of which party has been in power, has been to stop the deterioration of the nation's fiscal state and reduce dependency on subsidies funnelled through the national budget. In the process the poorest regions are at risk of being left without current levels of help from the economically more prosperous regions.

Beck believed that we do not yet live in a risk society, but we also no longer live only within the distribution conflicts of a scarcity society (Beck, 1992, p. 20). For him the contemporary societies still live very much in state of 'not yet…but no longer' and naturally such a state of systemic switch or interregnum is by definition characterised by tensions between the old and the new. The current social tensions in Japan are very much in the realm of an old industrial society and often surprisingly traditional society (some less Japanophile people may use the term 'feudal') finding ways of distributing wealth. The declining economic fortunes of Japan together with waste, mismanagement and demographic trends are contributing to more socially unequal arrangements that herald the birth of the Japanese model of risk society.

Some Korean authors make references to the use of Confucian traditions to strengthen and legitimise state-led authoritarian development and to explain the contemporary Korean risk society (see e.g. Han, 1998, p. 5-27). Kim Dae Hwan creates a most original analytical tool of dual-risk approach to explain how both the insufficiency of modernisation and modernisation have created risks and dangers for Koreans. Another name for this Korean model of modernisation would be "rush-to" growth or limping modernisation (Kim Dae Hwan, 1998, p. 28-45). For me it appears that the dual-risk approach would also fit particularly well for Japan. In his comment on Kim's article Beck argues that the concept of "dual-risk society" enriches the analysis of Western societies, too, because what is a dominant aspect in the Korean context might be an additive aspect in many parts of the West as well (Beck, 1998a, p. 201). This is a very important point. For me a better term would be "multiple-risk societies", because in all societies there are multiple risk narratives and the whole idea of rigid classifications between traditional (pre-modern), modern and post-modern fit badly with most societies. It is even more so with dualistic classification of reflexivity either being there or being absent. In some other disciplines (than some branches of sociology) there has been far more sensitivity to traces of Eurocentrism, colonialism, racism, sexism and other forms of imposing one's own values on other cultures without finding out about all the multiple ways of constructing the world. For me Korea is a perfect example of a multiple risk society and Kim Dae Hwan's analysis merits compliments for raising the issue of the need to modify Beck's idea of singular-risk approach and uniform reflexivity with something else that would make more sense in the Korean case. Beck seems to miss the point if he thinks that there is only a difference of "dominant" and "additive" elements. Instead, there is a whole range of alternatives and mixes, which would make far more sense in a context of multiple risk society.

In some ways Kim Dae Hwan's dual-risk approach modified with multiple risk focus would make much sense in the Japanese context. Modernity in Japan did not mean that old traditions and narratives disappeared but that they continued their lives in different forms forming new hybrids (see e.g. Ooms, 1984, p. 27-61 and Ooms, 1985). One should also note that unlike China the Japanese Confucianists at the height of their influence, the Edo period, were usually just scholars and did not achieve the role of decision-makers and bureaucrats (McMullen, 1980, p. 276-282). In Japan the peasants, especially the wealthier members of this class, also actively selected those intellectual currents which appealed to them. In political transformations in early modern Japan the wealthy farmers *(gônô)* also played a very important role and their relatively good education and wide knowledge of different schools of thought helped them to prepare for this role. The development of the Japanese *kokugaku* school ("National learning", a school emphasising the study of national myths of Japan) especially owes much to the Japanese peasant class (see e.g., 1988, p. 23-39). Of course, the peasant class was far less influenced by the Chinese classics than the ruling elite of Japan and, instead, it is easy to understand why its interests were far more local or ethnocentric. The farmers made the majority of Japanese people until the 1950s. While the Japanese government especially through school education has promoted the view of national history writing where the ideals of the elite somehow became the ideals of whole nation, there is also a good reason to suspect that the Japanese peasant traditions and views continue to play far more important role than most Japanese and foreign researchers have believed.

In Korea, Confucianism in its different forms is a convenient way to explain how Korea is different from the West. However, Confucianism itself is a true monster of traditions, containing, transforming and mixing everything it once touches. For most contemporary Japanese the Confucian code of ethics is something from a different century and rather refers to Korea and China than Japan, and when applied to Japanese history, it never had an undisputed role and was only one of the intellectual currents – with clear class bias. Most contemporary Japanese intellectuals find very little use for any Confucian concepts and the persistence with which some Western scholars try to explain everything in East Asia by "Confucianism" (often without explicitly stating what they mean by the whole concept) is met with disbelief or frustration.

Perhaps the most influential Western work which has brought Japanese Confucianism to

Western academic discourses is that of Bellah (1985, original 1957) which presented Confucianism as a functional equivalent of Protestantism in Japanese society. In the foreword of the 1985 edition Bellah, who in the meantime had risen to rank among the most appreciated American sociologists, strongly criticises his work and analyses the reasons which made him write that way in 1957. Bellah admits that his framework had more to do with the American society of the 1950s that with that of Japan. Another example of Confucianisation of the Japanese past is Reischauer (1978, p. 214), according to whom in Japanese society "strong Confucian traits still lurk beneath the surface, such as the belief in the moral basis of government, the emphasis on interpersonal relations and loyalties, and the faith in education and hard work. Almost no one considers himself a Confucian today, but in a sense almost all Japanese are." Reischauer acknowledges that hardly any Japanese considers himself a Confucian but for some reason he claims to know better about the thought preferences of the Japanese, and that according to his definition of Confucianism, one could claim that there are plenty of people all around the world who are Confucian without knowing it.

Sometimes individual East Asian scholars or politicians (such as Lee Kuan Yew) are themselves guilty of producing the most simplistic generalisations on the role of Confucianism in the whole of East Asia. More elaborate interpretations of Japanese intellectual history have, instead of declaring Japan Confucian or Shintôist, analysed the history of the co-existence of these two traditions, and more, in Japan and how some conceptions, apparently of Confucian origin, seem to have survived under Shintôism as spiritual pillars of the nation, helping to maintain order in the state, in society, and within family (see e.g. Fukui, 1992, p. 203-205). Some Japanese scholars even say that the concept of *'on'* (kindness, goodness, favour) and its manifestations, for instance in volunteer work in Japan, can more closely be related to the Japanese Buddhist tradition than anything else (Soeda, 1994, p. 127-128).

In English language literature on Japanese society Ruth Benedict's *The Chrysanthemum and the Sword* (1946) seized to the concept of *'on'* and saw it as the core of the hierarchical structure of Japanese society and explained Japanese society in most Confucian terms in English. When the book is translated into Japanese (Benedict, 1972), the academic definitions given to ordinary Japanese words appear quite clumsy and dogmatic. In English academic and even popular literature on Japan the same Japanese concepts (*'on'*, *'giri'* and *'gimu'*) Benedict used in her book are still often presented as keywords to penetrate the Japanese mind. Benedict who never visited Japan and who did not speak Japanese, made a lasting contribution to the American scholarship on Japan and her theories are also well known in Japan. The relativist paradigm Benedict adopted for her book helped her to escape much of the bias typical for her own contemporary academic community, and apparently she honestly tried to understand Japanese culture on its own terms, although this book was written at the request of American government agencies in order to help the Americans understand the "enemy alien country". Benedict's book is still surprisingly widely read both in the United States and Japan, although many Japanese scholars, while admitting the merits of the book, have been ready to point out its many shortcomings and plain factual errors (see e.g. Aoki, 1990, p. 30-52, and Aoki, 1994, p. 4-5). Modern Japanologists are usually critical of the way Benedict envisages Japan as a monolithic whole, neglecting the abundance of local variation as well as historical variation in Japanese culture (Kreiner, 1984, p. 40).

I would similarly add that many of the early Japanese as well as Korean examples of a respectful relationship with nature have more than echoes of Buddhist value systems as well as from indigenous Shintô and Shamanist traditions. Furthermore, I suggest that the reason why there have been so many persistent attempts to find the main root of Japanese thought is that among many Western scholars there is a reluctance to identify eclecticism and ideological mixture as the foundation of intellectual and political sophistication in Japan and not as mere aberrations (cf. Najita, 1978, p. 7). In short, Japanese culture is different especially in its rather eclectic mix of traditions. I have noticed very similar problem in the attempt to define and explain the Japanese aesthetic tradition, when both Western and Japanese scholars have been at loss to decide what to include and what to exclude in order to produce a tradition that would somehow correspond with foreign counterparts and include similar elements. Many of the Japanese intellectual traditions are built within intersubjective practices (as I have argued above) or defy grand theories and philosophical systems (while Confucianism clearly is a scholarly tradition based on written sources and academic discourses).

The Japanese language still distinquishes the art forms largely on the basis of technique and material, and shows great concern to "foreign" origins of techniques – after about 150 years of very mixed traditions. Furthermore, both Western and Japanese art communities still find it problematic to locate, for instance, such important parts of Japanese artistic tradition as garden design or tea ceremony within the tradition of Japanese arts. Nowadays it is quite difficult to decide what should be included within the Western art tradition as the borders of expression are all the time deliberately crossed. The often quite rigid categorization used in Japanese language, art education and museums looks rather futile. Furthermore, it is commonplace in Japan to find generalizations about rational world view being the basis of Western arts in a direct contrast to the less dogmatic and less naturalistic world view that defines the Japanese traditions of art, especially the very Japanese *nihonga* – which after all, is also deeply influenced by Western art (Merviö 2013). The point is that in the absence of good native theoretical textual corpus the Japanese traditions, whether they are social or cultural, are not easy to compare with their counterparts elsewhere. Moreover, Japanese researchers themselves often use foreign concepts and theories to make Japanese phenomena fit into global boxes and patterns. When there is no Japanese Confucius or Kant, Japanese will use the original ones even when the Japanese reality does not easily fit in. There is no Japanese Beck, either.

In short, neither Confucianism nor any other simple -ism easily fills the need to explain the Japanese society or risk society. Beck's reflexivity appears as a *deus ex machina* giving meaning and some kind of neat conclusion to the narrative of modernity. In Japan, something else is obviously needed and for me the multiple risk focus would be a good start. In some discourses there are signs of a growing ability to live with Japanese hybrid models, which seemingly are mixing fire with water. Within the discipline of social policy the welfare regime models have become very popular in explaining how welfare services are provided in different cultures and societies. Gøsta Esping-Andersen, who is probably the most famous of the welfare regime theorists, originally proposed three welfare regime variants based on the distinctions among Western societies. Much of East Asia simply does not fit in and Esping-Andersen himself discussed this question and even suggested a fourth regime, that is, the East Asian regime, as a regime for Japan and also for East Asia. Esping-Andersen pays special attention to the social practice of providing welfare services through family care in Japan and points not only to the Confucian traditions and the intergenerational contract for care responsibilities but also the economic factors due to a less abundant social security system (Esping-Andersen, 1997). However, things are not so simple: East Asian historical and cultural narratives are different and if the past is different, so are the models of coping with the modern challenges. When it comes to comparisons of East Asian social security systems, the variety of different national systems is amazing and I wonder how researchers like Esping-Andersen have ever even considered that East Asia must fit into one welfare regime model.

In reference to the contemporary Japanese mix relating to Japanese model of welfare society (and dealing with social risk) Ôsawa Mari comments that the Japanese welfare state since the 1990s has stretched itself in three different directions. Firstly, the so called Scandinavian route is sometimes used to demonstrate how family and working life can be compatible and that the socialisation of care is therefore needed. Secondly, the deregulation of the labour market represents neo-liberalism and, thirdly, the restructuring of employment during economic recession reinforces socio-economic stratification being related to conservatism (Ôsawa 2001: 109-110). Ôsawa catches something significant by demonstrating how the Japanese method of hybridisation works. This balancing act took place at the same time that Japanese welfare state was downsized in the 1980s and 1990s as politicians and bureaucrats became increasingly concerned about fiscal deficits. Takahashi points out that the restructuring of the welfare state is a long-term project that has continued more than two decades in Japan. The Japanese liberalist discourse from the late 1970s to the early 1980s not only emphasised the family obligations for care-giving work but also expected citizens to be strong individuals so that the state would not have to spend public money in the form of social assistance (Takahashi, 2003 and Takahashi, 2004, p. 9-10).

As for commenting why even the pension reform has been such a difficult task for the Japanese state and why a clear welfare regime is nowhere in sight in Japan, Takahashi observes that the leading political parties and technocrats are very reluctant to admit their past policy failures. In a sense the question concerns political arbitrariness, lack of accountability in selecting and deciding the priority, scope and depth of reforms and the absence of self-reflexivity among decision-makers. What has kept Japan's position in welfare regimes ambiguous is closely related to the growing discrepancy in the double standard between policy rhetoric – including policy slogans – and policy implementation in reality. Short-term solutions and strategies have been made merely to suit the occasion, but long-term prospects and policy goals are something hard to achieve. This is because of a lack of consensus on a vision for the future. The decision-makers, who consist of politicians, technocrats, business leaders, experts and so on – hold conflicting views on and interests in the future vision of welfare state (Takahashi, 2004, p. 33). In short, there is no lack of knowledge among Japanese decision-makers or of good models for Japan, but the Japanese model is simply muddling through and people with conflicting views manage to arrive at a solution that is politically, socially and culturally possible, and the reform seems to reach a level of perpetuity. The example of the Japanese welfare society and the East Asian welfare regime tells how eclecticism, pragmatism and ideological mixture linking numerous narratives get together and provide a Japanese risk society model, where even the models and model makers do not take the risk of placing all their eggs in the same basket.

WHEN WE ALL ARE RESPONSIBLE: RISKS BECOMING REALITY IN JAPAN

For Japan year 2011 was the year when risks became reality. In other words, what happened with the triple shocks, earthquake, tsunami and Fukushima nuclear plants, was not something that came as a total surprise. There is well-established pattern of similar size earthquakes and tsunamis in the region and there is plenty of knowledge about risks of nuclear energy and, therefore, we are not dealing with a divine punishment but with a series of tragedies where humans are an active party. The big question is why so little was done to prepare for the kind of disaster that actually struck and what people everywhere in the world can learn from this disaster. Furthermore, the teachings of the crisis are bitter for Japan. What can be done to ensure that Japanese society does not repeat its mistakes and what should be done to make sure that Japanese society uses the opportunity to seriously investigate what went wrong?

Prime Minister Noda told to journalists on the 3rd of March, 2012 that "the government as well as operators and scientists were steeped too deeply in the safety myth" and that "rather than blaming any individual person I believe everyone has to share the pain of responsibility and learn this lesson." Dailymotion video). Punishment should fit the crime, but it seems that the political establishment has decided that responsibility is not an issue and there is no need even to investigate. Well, if someone strikes you on the right cheek, turn to him the other also. Japanese public is expected to be very forgiving. Prime Minister told that everyone is responsible and there was no use to blame anyone, after already having identified the government, operators and the scientists as the ones who shared the same "safety myth". If no individual was responsible one may wonder what was the lesson for those who believed in the "safety myth". Maybe the real insight is that the Prime Minister was thinking that the Japanese decision-making was and is monolithic and the elite has the authority on earth to forgive sins and exonerate responsibility. "Everyone" here does not really cover the unlucky subjects and for the Prime Minister also those people, many of them real specialists, who opposed the fateful decisions do not apparently exist. Or maybe, Prime Minister Noda is part of the great indigenous legal tradition starting from Prince Shôtoku Taishi and his Constitution and its 10th Article: "…The right of others is our wrong, and our right is their wrong. We are not unquestionably sages, nor are they unquestionably fools. Both of us are simply ordinary men. How can anyone lay down a rule by which to distinguish right from wrong? For we are all wise sometimes and foolish at others" (Shôtoku Taishi, 604 A.D. *jûshichijôkempô*, translation: Columbia University, Japanworkbook).

Another way to look at this episode is to regard Prime Minister as a weak politician who did not feel strong enough to antagonize anyone, especially the other members of political elite who kept him in power until the elections that he lost miserably in December 2012 and paved way to a new Abe administration, which is far more friendly to nuclear power and power companies. An administration that uses every opportunity to restart as many nuclear reactors as possible is not the one that will start asking difficult questions about past mistakes and safety myths.

In Japan, it is commonplace that decisions are legitimized by meetings where, in principle, members of the group (workers, residents, etc) can speak out if they have concerns (*nemawashi*, prior consultation or literally "root binding" as in *bonsai* horticulture tradition). This practice usually leads to frequent and long meetings. However, in politics a serious problem of *nemawashi* practice is that decisions are often made behind the scenes, instead of out in the open. Even if *nemawashi* is extended to all people (e.g. workers or residents) it does not mean that all participants are in an equal setting during discussions or that they would dare to say what they think. In fact, the public pressure usually forces the less powerful to obey the leaders. One can see clear parallels with Konrad Lorenz's studies on the Jackdaws, who have a linear hierarchical group structure with higher-ranked birds dominating lower-ranked birds (Lorenz, 1949). When decisions really matter, very often before an open meeting there is an unofficial meeting where the real powerbrokers make their deals. Therefore there is a good reason to regard *nemawashi* as an undemocratic process instead of one promoting participation and consensus-seeking. However, the leaders in Japan tend to expect that all the members of the group stand behind the decisions once they have been "commonly accepted". However, wise leaders in Japan are wise enough to cultivate their own sources of real information as they know very well that they can not expect to hear real opinions in meetings or larger gatherings where most people are saying just what they think they are expected to say.

Of course, no real specialist could ever have taken at face value any childish "safety myth" about earthquakes, tsunamis and nuclear power in Japan. Most who knew better simply kept quiet in public, because they wanted to keep their jobs or in many cases were directly or indirectly rewarded by power companies. It may be that some politicians lacked the basics to understand the risks and never bothered to find out what the real opinions of specialists were. If that is the case, the some politicians may even today fail to understand how the system has failed and what kind of risk society Japan has become.

RISK SOCIETY DISCOURSE AND JAPAN

The word *risuku* (written in *katakana*, to indicate its foreign origin) has gradually become more frequently used and in a great variety of situations in Japan. There are many book titles available with the word and the most usual references are related to risk management or risk assessment. Some refer to operational risk and some others to more exotic risks such as risk diet for women. However, when checking books with *risuku ron* (risk discourse, risk discussion) on their title there are only a handful available. On the contrary, such concepts as *kiken* (danger), *kiki* (crisis) and *anzen* (safety, safe, security) are all much more frequently represented in Japanese book titles. The numbers indicate that risk in the sense of danger and threat is a major issue in contemporary Japanese discourses and that there is still little evidence of risk society discourse becoming part of everyday Japanese parlance.

The contemporary (global) academic risk society discourse has been heavily influenced by the works of Ulrich Beck and, in particular, *'Risikogesellschaft: Auf dem Weg in eine andere Moderne'* (1986). The books of Niklas Luhmann also played a major role in the German discourse (see e.g. Luhmann, 1991). In other words, Beck and Luhmann had a major role in shaping the social risk discourse in Germany. While Luhmann passed away in 1998 Beck has continued to update his theories and has, for instance, in his newspaper articles and TV interviews analysed contemporary events in the context of risk society.

In his 2002 book and subsequent interviews Beck has speculated about the future global institutions and whether effective world government is possible. For Beck the present United States is the closest thing to world government. For the future alternatives Beck presents two scenarios. The first is the European scenario, where "Europe as we have it" is made a general model for all. For Beck it would be like a world imagined by Kant, in the sense of eternal peace and transnational institutions. The other model is the model of the Israel-Palestine conflict, which for Beck is characterised by militarisation of international relations. If the right of the mightier becomes the rule there will be no end to self-fulfilling prophecies of conflicts being solved by military power. In this way terrorism would lead to a militarisation of the world. If these are the alternatives, then the future of the world rests on Europe. The other actors that Beck recognises as the shapers of the future world are the NGOs (such as Greenpeace, Attac and Amnesty International). In short, Beck believes that some kind of cosmopolitan Europe *(das kosmopolitische Europa)* will stand for democratic values and for ideals of peaceful international relations (continuing the tradition of serving as the antithesis to nationalism in Europe) (Beck 2002 and ZDF TV interview by Wolfgang Herles, where Beck explains outspokenly the main ideas of his book soon after it was published, interview removed from the Internet). The way Beck marginalises the rest of the world and selects the "wrong" alternatives while placing his beloved European model in the driving seat of history is at the least simplistic (and reminds me of the end-of-history Fukuyama, who could not see beyond the United

States) but, in addition, will not make too many converts outside his European neighbourhood. The language and tone are somewhat parochial for a person who talks about cosmopolitanism and globalisation.

In some of his less academic German writings such as the article *"Europas Pazifismus ist eine Lebenslüge"* Beck sharply criticises the European peace movements, in particular the citizens' movements, for their opposition to the war in Iraq. The article published in 23 February, 2003 in *Welt am Sonntag*, a conservative Christian Democratic newspaper, argues that the citizens of "old Europe" are living a lie and without American military hegemony Europe could not live in peace and that the pacifist protests are compromising the international fight against terrorism (Beck, 2003). Beck's opinions were quite interesting and demonstrating an independent mind, coming just after some of the largest demonstrations in the history of Western Europe, where only a tiny minority of protesters were hard-boiled pacifists and the majority were against the particular way that the war against Iraq was justified and started. Some of those who reacted to Beck's comments labelled Beck a new breed of Trotskian and Machiavellist, who (with his London School of Economics buddy Giddens) rides the "Third Way" but has no end in his support for even the most extreme examples of neo-conservatism – and himself dreaming about the decline of nation states while dismissing the opinions of millions of people as a mere lie (see e.g. Zeit-Fragen, 2003).

In short, Ulrich Beck is no stranger to healthy political debate and most recently he has also started to comment Japanese situation directly. As Beck was invited to the Safe Energy Ethic Commission (*Ethikkommission für eine sichere Energieversorgung*), which played a significant role in the decision to abandon nuclear energy in Germany in spring 2012 he directly influenced the German policy with such specialists of Japanese environmental policy as Miranda Schreurs and a list of other well-known academic, religious and political thinkers (for the list, Der Tagespiegel, 22 March, 2012). After the Fukushima crisis he has given number of interviews about the situation in Japan.

In his interview to Augsburger Allgemeine Zeitung he told about his trip to Hiroshima peace museum in autumn of 2010 and how he had been wondering how the Japanese can cope with the "cultural schizophrenia" of having the trauma of Hiroshima at the same time with the naïve belief in nuclear energy and that there is no alternative to it in Japan (Augsburger Allgemeine Zeitung, 7 April, 2012). Japanese newspaper Asahi Shimbun interviewed Beck in July 2012 about Fukushima, but did not even mention his recent political role in Germany. In the interview Beck pointed out that the German Green party was was invented as a consequence of Chernobyl and emphasized the role of social movements and civil society. As for the atomic energy in general, Beck argued that the atomic energy and atomic industries are socialist industries because the state, the population, the citizens are paying if something goes wrong. The Fukushima catastrophe was, "on the one hand, man-made, but on the other hand, geographically, socially and in the time dimension, unlimited. It doesn't have a limit." As a new kind risk Beck was comparing atomic energy to climate change, global financial risks and problems of terrorism (Asahi shimbun, 6 July, 2012).

In July 2011 Beck also published as a foreword to a book on a Japanese book on risk society his recent ideas about Japan and especially nuclear power after Fukushima and in his chapter and comments commented about the theory of individualization and its relevance in Japanese context. The book really was focused on individualization and only the title promises a broader analysis of Japanese risk society. The contributors of the book share a belief that Japan and East Asia are good examples how globalization and cosmopolitan era & "cosmopolitanization" (Kosmopolitisierung) have changed societies (Suzuki & Itô (Ed) Risukuka suru nihon shakai; Beck, 2011 b-c). What is striking for me is that for a book published so soon after 3-11 triple catastrophe there is so little about the dramatic events in Japan and about the issues that make Japan different from the rest of the world in terms of risk society.

RISK SOCIETY DISCOURSE AND JAPAN: WHERE IS THE INDIGENOUS DISCOURSE?

Risk society discourse has also gradually started to have an impact in different parts of the world. Among others, the Japanese academic discourses have, of course, closely followed the developments in their respective fields in Europe and in the United States. Beck's books have so far had four translations into Japanese. The first was the *Risikogesellschaft* (1986) that was translated in 1988 by Azuma Ren under the title *Kikenshakai* (danger society) (Beck, 1988). One can hardly think of any worse translation for the title, because after this most Japanese researchers misunderstood the main idea of the book wrong and did not make any distinction between risk and danger – which also meant that the idea of reflexivity was lost in translation. The next translation was that of *Saiki-teki kindaika- kingendai ni okeru seiji-dentô-biteki genri* by Matsuo Kiyobumi (Beck, 1997). Then followed *Kikenshakai- atarashii kindai e no michi* with Azuma Ren and Itô Midori as translators (Beck, 1998b). Among the latest translations are *Sekai risuku shakai ron- tero, sensô, shizenhakai* by Shimamura Ken'ichi in 2003 (Beck, 2003) and *Watakushi dake no kami* by Suzuki Tadashi in 2011 (Beck, 2011a) The 2003 translation was the first of Beck's books with *Risiko* translated as *risuku* in Japanese in its title. The mistranslation of risk in the first translation has clearly been harmful to the reception of Beck's theories in Japan as many researchers in Japan read just what is available in Japanese. In some Japanese books there are brief references to the ideas of Beck, but the whole context is distorted due to the total absence of a risk concept. For instance, Toda Kiyoshi in his excellent book on environmental justice has two brief references to Beck. One just lists him as a sociologist, who has written about environmental destruction and the other notes that Beck has contrasted the class society and danger society *(kiken shakai)* (with reference to the 1988 translation) (Toda, 1994, p. 13,17).

With the latest translations the main works of Beck are already fairly well represented in Japanese. However, Japanese discourses still lack their own Beck or Giddens to give a Japanese face to 'social risk'. The best and most comprehensive account of risk society discourse in Japan is probably Yamaguchi Setsuo's *'Gendai shakai no yuragi to risuku'* (Yamaguchi, 2002). The book presents nicely and precisely the German discourse and what is interesting is that the overwhelming majority of sources are in German. There are a few sources in English but almost none in Japanese. Since there are almost no references to Japan the book serves its purpose of introducing the German discourse to Japanese audience well, but reading the book is like reading a German book that happens to be written in Japanese. Otherwise, to my knowledge the risk society discourses have not yet been a subject of any original book length analysis in Japan. There is, however, another book that in its approach and style is similar to Yamaguchi's book, but focuses entirely on the risk theory of Niklas Luhmann, *'Risuku ron no rûman'* by Komatsu and which unfortunately contains little new for those who have read the German original (Komatsu 2003).

As for other theoretical approaches, in natural sciences and other more empirically oriented sciences, too, there also is remarkably little literature that directly tackles the concept of risk. A major exception is the book *'Risuku, kankyô oyobi keizai'* (Ikeda & Sakai and Tawada, eds 2004). As the title indicates, the book in its thirteen chapters introduces different cases from environment and economy and analyses very real factual risks and dangers. The book also includes a rare case of analysing environmental security and risk in China (Tei 2004: 64-76). Several of the chapters make use of the game theory. The overall approach to the environment is extremely anthropocentric and in most cases environment and economy are literally seen as parts of the same formula. For instance, one chapter with the help of game theory analyses the interaction of economy with environment and such risks as pollution and allergies (Sakai, 2004, p. 14-32).

There is also a book *'Kankyô risuku shinrigaku'* by Nakayachi Kazuya, which focuses on the social psychology of environmental risk. The theoretical framework of the book is based on mainstream behaviouralist theories of social psychology and especially those related to the perception of risk in English. In fact, Chapter Two of the book is devoted to a description of differences in the theoretical approaches of Lennart Sjöberg (of the Stockholm School of Economics) and Paul Slovic (in text they appear in *katakana* forms as Shôberi and Surobikku). Most of the material in the book draws heavily on books written in English but Chapter Three of the book includes original research findings from Nakayachi's studies in Japan (which have previously been published in academic journals). The focus of the chapter is the concept of 'zero risk', but it contains material on risk perception rankings among Japanese respondents. The list includes such 'risks' as blood transfusions, nuclear accidents, bullying at school, surgery, AIDS, vaccinations, air crash, train accident, ozone layer depletion, global warming, terrorism, cancer, etc. Nakayachi also analyses the different types of risks according to their origin, such as 'manmade environmental', 'natural', 'self-behavioural', 'illness' and 'interpersonal conflict'. The differences in rankings are often rather small. However, the general pattern in Nakayachi's findings is that Japanese risk perceptions seem to rank such manmade environmental risks as high as risks related to nuclear power or to the use of various chemicals. On the other hand, Japanese respondents seem to rank relatively low the risks related to personal behaviour (or life-style) such as the risks of smoking, alcohol, mountain climbing or hang-gliding. This finding partly explains why the title of the book is about 'environmental risk' rather than 'risk'. Since the book gives little information on the contributions of other Japanese researchers, Nakayachi's book serves best as an introduction to risk perception theories, with a somewhat short application of these theories in a Japanese context (Nakayachi, 2003).

In some rare cases Japanese researchers have contributed to studies/books written in English where factual risks play a role. Matsuda Noriyuki together with Eugene Rosa and Randall Kleinhesselink have written a comparative study on risk perception in Japan and the United States. The main research finding was that "Americans and Japanese have similar images of dread and catastrophic potential underlying their perceptions of nuclear risks" (Rosa & Matsuda and Kleinhesselink, 2000, p. 207). Furthermore, the study shows that the sample of Japanese college students (studying in the United States) perceived variety of voluntary risks (cycling, hang-gliding, fireworks, downhill skiing, etc) to be less well known than their American counterparts. In the three-page bibliography of this study there is only one risk related article with a Japanese name as the co-writer, suggesting that these authors, too, have had difficulties in finding good Japanese sources to back their argument. While a novice to psychometric sampling, I still find it rather strange that cross-national generalisations are made on the basis of highly selected samples of college students (in the Japanese case, two samples consisting of 62 and 69 students).

In Japan, there is good and easily accessible data available about public perceptions in all walks of life in the form of surveys conducted by the Prime Minister's Office with sufficiently large and representative samples. Furthermore, all types of surveys are regularly conducted in Japan and together they can be used to give some idea about some of the perceptions related to risks and threats in Japan. The problems start if these results are used for comparative purposes when the survey techniques and questions are difficult to replicate in other societies. In any case, comparative risk perception studies including Japan are still rare in any language. In one of the most representative and extensive studies of risk perception in English, Paul Slovic, in a rare reference to Japan, points to three Journal articles, all involving Kleinhesselink alone or with co-authors, Rosa being co-author in two, and no Japanese names appearing in any of the articles (Slovic, 2000, p. xxv). It is safe to conclude that little has been published in English on risk perceptions related to Japanese cases, although, as we have seen, there are researchers such as Nakayachi, who have popularised risk perception studies written in English in Japan.

The absence of a large body of literature on risk in Japanese (or about Japanese risks in other languages) does not mean that different types of dangers and factual risks have not been addressed in Japanese books or journals. There is also an association called *Nihon risuku kenkyûgakkai*, which is affiliated with the American based Society for Risk Analysis (SRA) and works as its Japan Chapter (see SRA and SRA Japan Section homepages). The Japanese chapter in its research activities has largely focused on real and measurable risks reflecting the primary focus of the SRA. Especially in no-non-sense risk management there have been attempts to keep up with foreign research.

In the case reacting to new hazards and threats Japanese researchers and publishers often make great efforts to be the first to satisfy the need to have popularised knowledge of risks that often require quite a detailed understanding of natural science research results. For instance, soon after the SARS epidemic Japanese researchers rushed to publish books on the topic. Similarly, all the influenza epidemics and the BSE and environmental hormones are subjects of good quality natural science discourses in Japan with many good publications. However, such books have so far failed to apply the concept of risk (or come up with their own concepts) and use it to analyse the workings of Japanese society.

When analysing the general picture of Japanese publications related to risk it must be noted that in different disciplines the format of publicising research findings varies considerably and the significance of journal articles and books is perceived very differently by different groups within the academic community. Common sense tells us that risk, risk assessment and risk management show up frequently in very ordinary practical sense in academic journals of various technical, medical and economic fields. Just try writing an article on investment in Greece, futures trading or avian influenza, or, most recently nuclear power in Japan, without using the risk word. In the Japanese language, too, risk has entered the core vocabulary of many disciplines without resulting in any deeper analysis of the meaning of concept itself. Since this article is focused on social risk (although in a multidisciplinary context) I am not even trying to systematically follow the use of the *risuku* word in every discipline or publication in Japan. Such an attempt would already be too late, because *risuku* is everywhere. What I have wanted to do is to have a general understanding how *risuku* is used in different disciplines and to proceed with analysing Japanese risk society, and especially its social dimensions.

RISK SOCIETY AND PUBLIC POLICY

According to Ulrich Beck, late modernity has nurtured individuals who are reasonably ready to acquire and use the best available information and rationalise and regulate themselves and society in order to deal with risks (Beck, 1986). The relationship between risk and reason is most important. Knowledge makes people choose right and rational things. The successes of policy and social or technological progress bring some hope that people may, after all, be able to make rational policy choices before it is too late. In environmental policy there are real measurable issues with real measurable solutions. For instance, in terms of ozone layer treaty or effective measures against air or water pollution there have been clear policy success stories. In Japan, the policies the air and water pollution have been successful. Personally I would still look beyond the numbers and other indicators and see how the nature/ environment in all its diversity actually is coping – and there are lots of problems everywhere. In economic policies it seems that the most widely used yardstick for a policy is whether the markets believe it or not. If it takes only a few cheating Greek politicians and bureaucrats and endemic petty corruption with "small envelopes" (√⟨I∑⌊άl⌈) in one small country to nearly make the whole European and global economy collapse, the world economy is not built on real wealth but on speculation and wishful thinking.

When it comes to health and welfare policies it is even more difficult to measure success beyond numbers. Social problems and societies change all the time and in the case of human rights every case of failure is too much. If there are enough failures, there is a clear need for a reform. This kind of philosophy can be found behind such reforms as the American No Child Left Behind Policy (Congress Act 2001), which was based on wide public concern about the sorry state of education and understanding that the situation had grave consequences for the whole society. This reform had an unusually broad bipartisan support. In that case, the federal role and funding was increased and the actual running of the program was left to the states and local level. While the program hardly solved all the problems in basic education it was the biggest reform for a very long time and certainly has made a difference for many individuals.

Most evaluations of the Japanese health policy start from the basic macro health indices such as the life expectation at birth and infant mortality and then compare the success with expenditure and note that there are no problems in Japan. OECD has mostly advised to do something to the problem of placing elderly patients to long-term care in hospitals as under the current system there is no significant cost to the patients or their families while specialized nursing homes would be difficult to find (see e.g. OECD 2009). The government has, indeed, tried to create new policies to deal with the problems of rapidly ageing society and its challenges to health care. However, the fundamental issue is that it is a difficult equation to maintain the ideology of free access to care and funding structure largely built on fixed income based premiums. Sooner or later the government has to spend much more tax money on health or drastically change the system. Both courses of policy change would be politically very difficult. The present government has been trying to prepare the public for a consumer tax increase (from present 5 percent) by saying that ageing society and the Tôhoku reconstruction require it. This far the public has remained highly suspicious of the motives.

So, the policies can make a difference and rational planning has its place. However, modern societies are far more complex than societies used to be. Modern societies need kind of expertise that simply remains out to reach and beyond understanding of substantial part of population. This is one of the fundamental problems of natural sciences. Much of the knowledge never reaches the non-specialists, not to mention the public. Part of the problem lies with the epistemic communities and the academic community itself. Popularising science is often seen as a demerit within the academic community and taking a clear position is often confused with compromising science. Of course, another way to compromise science is to parrot what the decision-makers want to hear. The latter one proved to be the case with Japanese nuclear "specialists". In short, real specialists have a social responsibility to speak out, when they see a problem.

Another problem is that specialists of narrow fields tend to flock together and often find cooperation with people representing different approaches useless or irritating. This kind of compartmentalization of reality is sometimes made worse by social traditions that do not encourage horizontal cooperation between organization and, instead, favour vertical or hierarchical cooperation and communication. Japanese sociology has for a long time emphasized the tendency in Japan to divide people into different in-groups (*uchi,* literally inside) while the outsiders (*soto,* literally outside) are treated with ignorance or worse. In other words, there are different sets of behavioural and moral codes reserved for people belonging to different groups (cf. Vuori & Merviö, 2007, p. 87). Analyzing what went wrong before the 2011 crisis in Japan with the safety regulations against tsunamis and earthquakes, as well as risks related to nuclear power, would have to take into consideration.

Within Japanese groups there are indeed inter-subjectively accepted social rules which contribute to the neutralising or managing of conflicts but conflicts also exist within most groups and individuals are aware of them, and of the differing interests among the members of the group. The Japanese groups often succeed in keeping their conflicts hidden from outside eyes but it does not mean that conflicts are always neutralised or well-managed, and even less that individuals unquestioningly accept hierarchical power relations. The inter-subjectively accepted social rules are a two-way road and the limits of acceptance are formed in daily life. Anyone who has the skill the use these social rules for manipulative purposes, has the upper hand in social life. "Japanese harmony" is seldom characterised by a blind acceptance of "tradition" and social hierarchy, and if there is a need to continue using such a concept, perhaps the manipulative processes and the perspective of the individuals should also be included in the analysis (Cf. Merviö, 1995, p. 176-177).

It may also be that people are much of the time worried about the wrong things, about things that in the end are lesser risks to people, health and environment than can openly be admitted. Risk has become politicised, and, for instance, the risk of terrorism has fundamentally changed the foreign policies as well as domestic life of many Western societies in just a few years. Measuring a risk that we really do not fully know or understand/grasp is just impossible. Furthermore, it is the very nature of natural sciences that hypotheses are tested and sometimes there are massive mistakes and even the basics may be proved wrong. I have recently written about the relationship between epidemics and environmental change/destruction (I call them *ecodemics*, Merviö 2011), which is a field where risks are huge but risk consciousness is often very low and the policy responses are unpredictable. It is quite understandable that the Hong Kong authorities were first quite unprepared when the SARS crisis emerged. However, no one can claim that the risk of a major earthquake in Japan was really unexpected.

JAPANESE RISK SOCIETY: POLITICAL DIMENSIONS

Japanese society faces a multitude of 'risks' *(risuku)* including those in the fields of politics and international relations, economy, cultural change, social maladies and ecology. However, the public reaction to the existence of these risks varies a lot and the "risk discourses" still seem to be dominated by rather traditional approaches of national security and changing scenarios of international power politics. The everyday life risks are in most cases understood more or less literally in the sense of danger *(kiken)* and sometimes in the sense of calculated risk *(arakajime kôryo sareta kiken)*. What is striking in the Japanese case is that it is one country that has carried furthest the processes of modernisation and industrialisation, yet its people have a major reluctance to go beyond the mind-set of nation-state system and nationalism while the state itself provides rather an undependable safety-net to cushion the risks and dangers of life. In Japan, apparently the idea of controlling and calculating the risk/threat (in the sense of, for instance, the Nordic welfare society) has never been so widespread and people have good reason not to expect much from the faceless authorities doing their job for the citizens. Furthermore, the above-mentioned idiomatic expression of calculated risk (literally something like 'danger coming thought beforehand') can tell as much about a fatalistic acceptance and mental preparation in the face of an unchanging than rationalistic approach to minimise risk by one's own thinking and actions. The phrase may be used as an example of Japanese attitudes of facing risk eye to eye, bravely as individuals in the end, possibly with all the support of their closest in-groups, and believing that the people in charge somewhere know what they are doing and try to do their best and deserve the support of everyone.

Another possibility is that speaking out and complaining aloud is not much valued within Japanese organizational culture and the risk of ostracism is enough to make it appear that people back their leaders and policies. Beck's rather impolite remarks about the naïve beliefs of the Japanese may have a point, when it comes to a lack of open critical discourse about many issues that are very divisive in a German context. It does not necessarily mean that everyone in Japan shared the beliefs that Beck found naïve. It could as well be that many of those who did not agree with the policies did not believe that their dissidence could have made much of a positive difference. Japanese society does not tend to reward its dissidents and it is Beck, who is naïve, if he believes that such German ideas as "*die freischwebende Intelligenz*" (in English, something like "socially unattached intelligentsia") are appreciated or tolerated universally. In Japan the Prime Minister is not going ask opinions any time soon from the known opponents of nuclear energy, especially if their rhetoric gets anywhere close to Beck.

In the European discourses on risk a major starting point has been the assumption that modern societies have reached a stage "where we live in an industrial society organised according to nation-states, but we are already no longer living in it." (Beck, 1999, p. 87). Furthermore, the Beckian understanding of risk is based on such assumptions as risk having become more difficult to calculate and control, crossing national and socioeconomic borders and therefore having become glocal, both global and local at the same time. Risk society is essentially a world risk society and the perspective is global and assumes a certain type of global citizenship or community. With the breakdown of traditional certainties societies have been transformed to something quite new. In the process new risks are created and old ones are given new meanings. Everything from family lives to working life and international relations has been affected by these social changes. Beck makes much use of the concept of individualisation to describe how people deal with risk and have personal concern about risks that have entered their everyday lives. For Beck the natural reaction of people is to seek critical knowledge about risk and make their personal decisions based on the knowledge that they have acquired (see especially, Beck, 1992 and 1995).

Against this background, Japanese society superficially appears as a bastion of trust and obedience to authorities. In other words, European-type of ideas of a post-traditional or cosmopolitan era look strange in a Japanese context and for most Japanese observers. Japanese ideas on nationalism are strongly based on ideologies that emphasise the uniqueness of Japanese society and even its people. The so-called Japaneseness discourse *(nihonjinron)* is one and often quite extreme manifestation of these beliefs, but a far more important role is played by the intersubjective practices that define normal and deviant behaviour. As for changes in Japanese social traditions and institutions, the

Beckian analysis does, indeed, also make sense in the Japanese context: there certainly is an awareness of great transformations taking place in the basic institutions of Japanese society.

However, the political establishment has often tried to slow down the speed of change, whether these are related to the family institution, educational policies or security policy – or policies relating to women and health, as Hara observes in her article elsewhere in this issue. The reasons could be ideological or simply tactical. When the Democratic Party *(minshutô)* was able to topple Liberal Democratic Party *(jiyûminshutô)* in 2009 many of their voters expected that they would try to reform Japanese politics and introduce major social reforms after a long period of nearly one party rule after 1955. It did not go that way: much of time and effort was wasted for futile internal power struggle and the DPJ was not able to pass major reforms when it still had enough votes in Parliament to do so, and once it was weakened in by-elections it lost the real ability to push through reforms and instead has been trying to avoid controversial issues, which could further divide the already weakened party. Many its politicians are originally from the LDP and nowadays the difference between the DPJ and LDP is often difficult to see, if one bases the analysis on policy issues.

DPJ, however, has a fair number of politicians, who have a different background and who at one point also wanted to reform the society. However, a change of government did not prove enough to push through a major change in politics and political culture. The most important social reform that the DPJ-led coalition was able to introduce was the child allowance reform that was intended to encourage families to have more children, as Japan has one of the lowest birth rates in the world. The all time low of 1.25 for total fertility rate per woman was in 2005 and then it has been gradually rising to 1.39 in 2010 (Statistics Bureau 2011, Chapter 2, Section 3: Births and Deaths). While DPJ had been in opposition it constantly criticised the LDP's child-hostile policies. The new DPJ child allowance system did not have any income restrictions and it replaced previous forms of support that provided far less generous support only to those who were the most underprivileged. In short, the DPJ system was similar to the North European systems, which have a very broad and bipartisan support and a long history. In Northern Europe the thinking goes that it is important in the name of public good to make some social benefits (such as free higher education) available to everyone when their needs have positive social impact, while this also makes higher rates of taxation more acceptable among those who pay more. However, the opposition LDP picked up the reform as a symbol of worst kind of waste and the popular opinion and media turned quite hostile to the new child allowance system. Some LDP politicians called it as "socialist" and the media increasingly painted the system as an example of the DPJ populist vote buying and gravy train together with abolishing the highway taxes. After more reformist Prime Minister Kan was replaced by Prime Minister Noda, one of the first major policy revisions was to introduce a 9.6 million yen annual household income restriction for receiving the child allowance together with other restrictions (Mainichi shimbun 14 December, 2011). In short, the system once again targeted only the low-income families and had little to do with encouraging child rearing or changing the image of taxation in Japan. Most of the politics insiders interpreted the policy change as a compromise that was intended to pave way to a Grand Coalition with LDP and/or save the political careers of DPJ politicians and the party itself. As things stand, established political parties offer few visions or real alternatives and voters seem to be increasingly turning to populists with no established party affiliation, who tend to focus on the sorry state of Japanese fiscal policy and would be ready to further reduce spending on such fields as welfare.

Once LDP was back to power in December 2012 the new conservative administration naturally could not change its attitude toward child allowances. However, Prime Minister Abe was fast to realize that Japan had to do something to improve the child care and family policies in order to encourage Japanese to have more children and to free women to work. The concern is presented to the public on the grounds of economic realities rather than equalitarian concerns and it seems that there is some real hope that Japan will adopt policies that are more friendly to children and working mothers.

In terms of risk society, at the end of the day Japan seems to be following the rest of its peers in entering the world risk society, but in a selective way of ignoring some parts of the discourse. Observers of other East Asian countries have likewise pointed out that in some Asian societies and their risk discourses such issues as political stability and economic stability (after the Asian financial crisis) were most visible. Similarly in Japan, the older risk discourses often did not go much beyond the security risks and natural hazards. However, there has also been new research on social risks, such as on so-called new risks associated with family and work, and social change in general. A common theme seems to be that traditional social institutions are eroding while there is a coexistence of both individualization and traditional (family-based) values (see Chan, Takahashi & Wang (Ed.), 2010). Be the risks new or old, there is no denying that East Asian societies are exposed to a very dynamic change and having become the economic dynamo of the whole world and having tasted the benefits of affluence East Asia has no choice to turn back and must accept the erosion of traditions and change of social institutions, which accompany the journey to modern reflexivity. What is troublesome is that the political institutions have proven rather resistant to change in Japan, which already has a long history of multiparty democracy. Japan, indeed, could learn a lesson or two from many of its neighbours, such as Taiwan, South Korea and the Philippines, which have been able to vitalize their societies with more or less successful attempts of democratization and at least have provided real political alternatives.

CONCLUSION

In the words of Ulrich Beck the Fukushima catastrophe was, "on the one hand, man-made, but on the other hand, geographically, socially and in the time dimension, unlimited. It was Germany, which changed its policy regarding atomic energy after Fukushima and Japan still one year after the catastrophe is only slowly wakening to the new reality of a new kind of reflexive relationship with nuclear power and, more generally, the use of modern technology and the social risks linked with modern life. In Japan, the idea that Japan's very own catastrophe is, instead, a global catastrophe has not really sunk in. Coping with the disasters may be the most urgent and visible task of the government, but the Japanese society can hardly wait to find solutions to many long-term policy choices. The "reconstruction" of Tôhoku is not made easier by the aversion of the authorities to critically examine and discuss the past mistakes. The inconvenient truths seem be a taboo for authorities when at the same time they try to show solidarity to victims and avoid admitting responsibility for past mistakes. The result most likely will be stop-gap solutions and half-measures – and, to some extent, repeat of past mistakes. In the words of the now already forgotten Prime Minister the political and scientific elite believed in a mistaken "safety myth", but it has not been made clear what exactly was a myth and what steps have been taken to replace "myths" by more rational approaches. The implementation of evacuation of people from the polluted areas in Fukushima to nearby designated areas tells much about the actual priorities of the national and local authorities: there has been very little open discussion or information about the possibility/

fact that large areas have been made permanently uninhabitable. Instead, the actual de facto policy has been to avoid major economic compensations to victims, give no incentives to relocate to safer areas outside the prefecture and give the impression that things are under control.

This chapter has illustrated both challenges and apparent success stories of Japanese public policy. The present political impasse is not conducive to major policy reforms, but the time will come, when reflexive modernization with its cosmopolitan value system becomes the motor of rational policy-making in Japan. One needs to remember that there is no society on earth where reflexive modernization alone characterizes social development and the recent developments, including an institutional and economic crisis, within the European Union have not helped to convince Europeans or non-Europeans that Europeans have found the right model. Japanese society, with all its insular and parochial features and anomalies of its political system, still arguably represents the most successful East Asian social model and, as such, serves as an important model and contrast to other societies in the region and elsewhere.

REFERENCES

Aoki, T. (1990). *Nihon bunka ron' no hen'yô: Sengo nihon no bunka to aidentitî.* Tôkyô: Chûô kôronsha.

Aoki, T. (1994). Anthropology and Japan: Attempts at writing culture. *The Japan Foundation Newsletter*, *22*, 1–6.

Augsburger Allgemeine Zeitung. (2012). *Soziologe Ulrich Beck im Interview: Katastrophe von Fukushima: Sind die Deutschen hysterisch?* Retrieved from http://www.augsburger-allgemeine.de/politik/Katastrophe-von-Fukushima-Sind-die-Deutschen-hysterisch-id14744351.html

Beck, U. (1986). *Risikogesellschaft: Auf dem Weg in eine andere Moderne*. Frankfurt am Main, Germany: Suhrkamp Verlag.

Beck, U. (1988). *Kikenshakai*. Tôkyô: Niki Shuppan.

Beck, U. (1992). *Risk society: Towards a new modernity*. London: Sage.

Beck, U. (1995). *Ecological politics in the age of risk*. Cambridge, UK: Polity.

Beck, U. (1997). *Saikiteki kindaika- Kingendai ni okeru seiji-dentô-biteki genri*. Tôkyô: Jiritsu-shobô.

Beck, U. (1998a). The challenge of world risk society. *Korea Journal*, *38*(4), 196–206.

Beck, U. (1998b). *Kikenshakai- Atarashii kindai e no michi*. Tôkyô: Hôsei Daigaku Shuppankyoku.

Beck, U. (1999). *World risk society*. Cambridge, UK: Polity.

Beck, U. (2002). *Macht und Gegenmacht im globalen Zeitalter: Neue weltpolitische Ökonomie*. Frankfurt am Main, Germany: Suhrkamp Verlag.

Beck, U. (2002). Europas Pazifismus ist eine Lebenslüge. *Welt am Sonntag*. Retrieved from http://www.welt.de/print-wams/article121610/Europas-Pazifismus-ist-eine-Lebensluege.html

Beck, U. (2003). *Sekai risuku shakai*. Tôkyô: Heibonsha.

Beck, U. (2011a). *Watakushi dake no kami*. Tôkyô: Iwanami Shoten.

Beck, U. (2011b). Kono kikai ni: Fukushima, arui wa: Sekai risuku shakai ni okeru nihon no mirai. In *Risukuka suru nihon shakai*. Tôkyô: Iwanami Shoten.

Beck, U. (2011c). Kojinka suru nihon shakai no yukue. no kikai: Komento ni taisuru komento. In *Risukuka suru nihon shakai*. Tôkyô: Iwanami Shoten.

Bellah, R. N. (1985). *Tokugawa religion: The cultural roots of modern Japan*. New York: The Free Press.

Benedict, R. (1946). *The chrysanthemum and the sword: Patterns of Japanese culture*. Boston: Houghton Mifflin.

Benedict, R. (1972). *Kiku to katana: Nihon bunka no kata*. Tôkyô: Sekai Shisôsha.

Chan, R., Takahashi, M., & Wang, L. (Eds.). (2010). *Risk and public policy in east Asia*. Burlington, VA: Ashgate.

Han, S.-J. (1998). The Korean path to modernization and risk society. *Korea Journal, 38*(1), 5–27.

Harootunian, H. D. (1988). *Things seen and unseen: Discourse and ideology in Tokugawa nativism*. Chicago: The University of Chicago Press.

Ikeda, S., Sakai, Y., & Tawada, M. (2004). *Gendai shakai no yuragi to risuku*. Tôkyô: Keisô Shobô.

Japan Section, S. R. A. (n.d.). *Nihon risuku kenkyûgakkai*. Retrieved on 7 March, 2012 from http://www.sra-japan.jp/cms/

Kim, J.-W. (1998). Korea, land of environmental risk. *Korea Journal, 38*(1), 220–240.

Komatsu, T. (2003). *Risuku ron no rûman*. Tôkyô: Keisô Shobô.

Kreiner, J. (1984). A concrete holistic approach to the study of Japanese culture: An example of civilization studies. In *Japanese civilization in the modern world: Life and society*. Osaka: National Museum of Ethnology.

Lorenz, K. (1949). *Tiergeschichten: Er redete mit dem Vieh, den Vögeln und den Fischen*. Wien: Verlag.

Luhmann, N. (1991). *Soziologie des Risikos*. Berlin: Walter de Gruyter. doi:10.1515/9783110866056

McMullen, J. (1980). How Confucian is modern Japan? *Asian Affairs, 11*(3), 276–338. doi:10.1080/03068378008729995

Merviö, M. (1995). *Cultural representation of the Japanese in international relations and politics: A study of discourses and interpretations between different cultural traditions*. Tampere, Finland: Acta Universitatis Tamperensis.

Merviö, M. (2011). *Ecodemics: Analysing the history of facing and mediating the risks from the wild.* Paper presented at the First Conference of East Asian Environmental History (EAEH2011), Academia Sinica. Taipei, Taiwan.

Merviö, M. (2013). *The re-presentation of Japanese society and its relations with the rest of the world: Japanese visual arts and the mimēsis of the world.* Paper presented at the Asian Studies on the Pacific Coast (ASPAC) Conference at the Monterey Institute of International Studies, a Graduate School of Middlebury College. Middlebury, VT.

Najita, T. (1978). Method and analysis in the conceptual portrayal of Tokugawa intellectual history. In *Thought in the Tokugawa period 1600–1868: Methods and metaphors*. London: The University of Chicago Press.

Nakayachi, K. (2003). *Kankyô risuku shinrigaku*. Kyôto: Nakanishiya Shuppan.

OECD. (2009). *Economic survey of Japan 2009: Health-care reform in Japan: Controlling costs, improving quality*. Retrieved from http://www.oecd.org/document/5/0,3746,en_2649_34587_43791173_1_1_1_1,00.html

Ooms, H. (1984). Neo-Confucianism and the formation of early Tokugawa ideology: Contours of a problem. In *Confucianism and Tokugawa culture*. Princeton, NJ: Princeton University Press.

Ooms, H. (1985). *Tokugawa ideology: Early constructs, 1570–1680*. Princeton, NJ: Princeton University Press.

Ôsawa, M. (2001). Fukushi kokka to byôdô – Shakai seisaku no hikaku jendâ bunseki no tachiba kara. *Shakai Seisaku Gakkaishi, 6*, 99–115.

Reischauer, E. O. (1978). *The Japanese*. Tokyo: Charles E. Tuttle Company, Inc.

Rosa, E. A., Matsuda, N., & Kleinhesselink, R. R. (2000). The cognitive architecture of risk: Pancultural unity or cultural shaping? In *Cross-cultural risk perception: A survey of empirical studies*. London: Kluwer Academic Publishers. doi:10.1007/978-1-4757-4891-8_5

Sakai, Y. (2004). Kankyô ga keizai ka? Risuku no shita no ishikettei. In *Risuku, kankyô oyobi keizai*. Tôkyô: Keisô Shobô.

Shimbun, A. (2012). *Ulrich Beck: System of organized irresponsibility behind the Fukushima crisis*. Retrieved from http://ajw.asahi.com/article/0311disaster/opinion/AJ201107063167

Shimbun, M. (2011, December 14). *Shin kodomo teate: Nenshû 960man-chô, tsuki5000en, zôzei futan ni hairyo - Seifu hôshin*. Retrieved from http://mainichi.jp/life/edu/child/archive/news/2011/12/20111214ddm002010093000c.html

Shindô, M. (2002). *Chihô bunken*. Tôkyô: Iwanami Shoten. Shôtoku Taishi. (604). *Jûshichijôkempô*. Retrieved from http://afe.easia.columbia.edu/japan/japanworkbook/traditional/shotoku.htm

Slovic, P. (2000). *The perception of risk*. London: Earthscan.

Society for Risk Analysis (SRA). (n.d.). Retrieved from http://www.sra.org/

Soeda, Y. (1994). Borantia to fukushi kyôiku no chôryû: Shôgai gakushû shakai no keisei to borantia katsudô. In *Fukushi kaikaku v. sankagata fukushi shakai no kôchiku*. Tôkyô: Zenkoku Shakai Fukushi Kyôgikai.

Statistics Bureau. (2011). *Handbook*. Retrieved from http://www.stat.go.jp/english/data/handbook/c02cont.htm#cha2_2

Suzuki, M., & Itô, M. (Eds.), *(n.d.)*. *Risukuka suru nihon shakai*. Tôkyô: Iwanami Shoten.

Tagespiegel, D. (2012). *Hintergrund, ethikkommission*. Retrieved from http://www.tagesspiegel.de/politik/hintergrund-ethikkommission/3978952.html

Takahashi, M. (2003). Care for children and older people in Japan: Modernizing the traditional. In *The young, the old and the state: Social care systems in five industrial nations*. Cheltenham, UK: Edward Elgar.

Takahashi, M. (2004). *The search for solidarity in Japan's risk society*. Paper presented at ISA RC19: Poverty, Social Welfare and Social Policy. Paris, France. Retrieved from http://www.cevipof.msh-paris.fr/rencontres/colloq/palier/index.html

Tei, S. (2004). Chûgoku no kankyô hozen. In *Gendai shakai no yuragi to risuku*. Tôkyô: Keisô Shobô.

Toda, K. (1994). *Kankyô kôsei o motomete: Kankyôhakai no kôzô to erîtoshugi*. Tôkyô: Shin'yôsha.

Video, D. Afpenglish. (n.d.). *No individual to blame for Fukushima: Japan PM*. Retrieved from http://www.dailymotion.com/video/xp72nb_no-individual-to-blame-for-fukushima-japan-pm_news

Vuori, J., & Merviö, M. (2007). *Japanin ja suomen hyvinvointijärjestelmien vertailtavuus: Vertailu- ja arviointimallin konstruointi erityisesti julkisen ja yksityisen käsitteiden näkökulmasta. Kuopio.* Kuopio University Press.

Yamaguchi, S. (2002). *Gendai shakai no yuragi to risuku*. Tôkyô: Shin'yôsha.

Zeit-Fragen. (2003). Pazifismus- eine Lebenslüge?. *Zeit-Fragen, 9.*

Compilation of References

(1997). Theory and politics of the public/private distinction. InWeintraub, J., & Kumar, K. (Eds.), *Public and private in thought and practice: Perspectives on a grand dichotomy* (pp. 1–42). Chicago: The University of Chicago Press.

Adema, W., & Whiteford, P. (2010). Public and private social welfare. In *The Oxford handbook of the welfare state* (pp. 121–138). Oxford, UK: Oxford University Press. doi:10.1093/oxfordhb/9780199579396.003.0008

Agamben, G. (1998). *Homo sacer: Sovereign power and bare life*. Stanford, CA: Stanford University Press.

Ainsworth, M., Blehar, M. C., Waters, E., & Wall, S. (1978). *Patterns of attachment: A psychological study of the strange situation*. Hillsdale, NJ: Erlbaum.

Allison, G. (1992). Public and private management: Are they fundamentally alike in all unimportant aspects? In J. Shafritz, & A. Hyde (Eds.), *Classics of public administration* (pp. 371–395). Belmont, CA: Wadsworth.

Amsterdam Declaration. (1997). *Amsterdam declaration on the social quality of Europe*. Retrieved on 22 July 2013, from http://www.socialquality.org/site/index.html

Anderson, R. (2009). Social tsunami: Cultural and structural factors in the emergence of welfare. *Social Policy and Administration*, *37*(4), 3.

An, S. et al. (1984). *Study on single mothers in Korea. Korean Women's Development Institute*. KWDI. [in Korean]

Aoki, T. (1990). *Nihon bunka ron' no hen'yô: Sengo nihon no bunka to aidentitî*. Tôkyô: Chûô kôronsha.

Aoki, T. (1994). Anthropology and Japan: Attempts at writing culture. *The Japan Foundation Newsletter*, *22*, 1–6.

Arai, L. (2009). *Teenage pregnancy: The making and unmaking of a problem*. Bristol, UK: Polity Press.

Arendt, H. (1958). *The human condition*. Chicago: The University of Chicago Press.

Aruga, K. (1972). *Ie*. Tôkyô: Shibundô.

Asahi Shimbun. (2009a, March 30). Myanmar people with no work permits or insurance fall through the cracks, illegally working refugees/Ibaraki prefecture. *Asahi Shimbun*.

Asahi Shimbun. (2009b, August 29). Rohingya people/minorities escape persecution and hard life Tatebayashi, Gunma. *Asahi Shimbun*.

Asahi Shimbun. (2009c, June 6). Economic growth with unaccompanied actual situation. *Asahi Shimbun*.

Asahi Shimbun. (2012, November 13). Panel: Shukan Asahi story on Osaka mayor adds to discrimination. *The Asahi Shimbun. Asia and Japan Watch*. Retrieved from http://ajw.asahi.com/article/behind_news/social_affairs/AJ201211130108

Asato, W. (2007). Nippi keizai renkei kyôtei to gaikokujin kangoshi, kaigo rôdôsha no ukeire. In *Kaigo kaji rôdôsha no kokusai idô* [International Movement of Caregivers and Domestic Workers]. Tôkyô: Nihon Hyôronsha.

Aspalter, C. (2001). *Conservative welfare state systems in east Asia*. Westport, CT: Praeger.

Asquith, P. J. (2002). Editor's preface and introduction. In *Imanishi kinji: A Japanese view of nature: The world of living things*. London: Routledge.

Attar Schwartz, S., Tan, J.-P., & Buchanan, A. (2009). Adolescents' perspectives on relationships with grandparents: The contribution of adolescent, grandparent, and parent– grandparent relationship variables. *Children and Youth Services Review*, *31*(9), 1057–1066. doi:10.1016/j.childyouth.2009.05.007

Audit Commission. (1999). *Children in mind: Child and adolescent mental health services*. London: Audit Commission.

Augsburger Allgemeine Zeitung. (2012). *Soziologe ulrich beck im interview: Katastrophe von Fukushima: Sind die Deutschen hysterisch?* Retrieved from http://www.augsburger-allgemeine.de/politik/Katastrophe-von-Fukushima-Sind-die-Deutschen-hysterisch-id14744351.html

Aust, A., & Bonker, F. (2004). New social risks in a comparative welfare state: The case of Germany. In P. Taylor-Gooby (Ed.), *New risks, new welfare: The transformation of the European welfare state*. Oxford, UK: Oxford University Press. doi:10.1093/019926726X.003.0002

Bae, Y. (2001). A study on the temperament and MBTI personality type of unmarried adolescent mothers.[in Korean]. *Journal of the Korea Academy of Psychological Type*, *8*(3), 45–70.

Bailey, J. (2000). Some meanings of 'the private' in sociological thought. *Sociology*, *34*(3), 381–401.

Baldock, J., Manning, N., & Vickerstaff, S. (Eds.). (2007). *Social policy* (3rd ed.). Oxford, UK: Oxford University Press.

Baldwin, S. (1995). Love and money: The financial consequences of caring for an older relative. In I. Allen, & E. Perkind (Eds.), *The future of family care for older people*. London: HMSO.

Baldwin, S., & Twigg, J. (1991). Women and community care – Reflections of a debate. In M. Maclean, & D. Groves (Eds.), *Women's issues in social policy*. London: Routledge.

Barthes, R. (1982). *The empire of signs*. New York: Hill & Wang.

Beck Jørgensen, T., & Bozeman, B. (2007). The public values universe: An inventory. *Administration & Society*, *39*(3), 354–381. doi:10.1177/0095399707300703

Beck, U. (2002). Europas pazifismus ist eine lebenslüge. *Welt am Sonntag*. Retrieved from http://www.welt.de/print-wams/article121610/Europas-Pazifismus-ist-eine-Lebensluege.html

Becker, S., & Bryman, A. (Eds.). (2004). *Understanding research for social policy and practice: Themes, methods and approaches*. Bristol, UK: The Policy Press.

Beck, U. (1986). *Risikogesellschaft: Auf dem weg in eine andere moderne*. Frankfurt am Main, Germany: Suhrkamp Verlag.

Beck, U. (1988). *Kikenshakai*. Tôkyô: Niki Shuppan.

Beck, U. (1992). *Risk society: Towards a new modernity*. London, UK: Sage Publications.

Beck, U. (1995). *Ecological politics in the age of risk*. Cambridge, UK: Polity.

Beck, U. (1997). *Saikiteki kindaika- Kingendai ni okeru seiji-dentô-biteki genri*. Tôkyô: Jiritsushobô.

Beck, U. (1998). *Democracy without enemies* (M. Ritter, Trans.). London: Blackwell Publishers.

Beck, U. (1998). The challenge of world risk society. *Korea Journal*, *38*(4), 196–206.

Beck, U. (1998b). *Kikenshakai- Atarashii kindai e no michi*. Tôkyô: Hôsei Daigaku Shuppankyoku.

Beck, U. (1999). *World risk society*. Cambridge, UK: Polity.

Beck, U. (2000). *What is globalization?* Cambridge, UK: Polity Press.

Beck, U. (2002). *Macht und gegenmacht im globalen zeitalter: Neue weltpolitische ökonomie*. Frankfurt am Main, Germany: Suhrkamp Verlag.

Beck, U. (2003). *Sekai risuku shakai*. Tôkyô: Heibonsha.

Beck, U. (2011a). *Watakushi dake no kami*. Tôkyô: Iwanami Shoten.

Beck, U. (2011b). Kono kikai ni: Fukushima, arui wa: Sekai risuku shakai ni okeru nihon no mirai. In *Risukuka suru nihon shakai*. Tôkyô: Iwanami Shoten.

Beck, U. (2011c). Kojinka suru nihon shakai no yukue. no kikai: Komento ni taisuru komento. In *Risukuka suru nihon shakai*. Tôkyô: Iwanami Shoten.

Beck, U., & Beck-Gernsheim, E. (2001). *Individualization: Institutionalized individualism and its social and political consequences*. London: Sage Publications.

Beck, U., & Beck-Gernsheim, E. (2004). Families in a runaway world. In *The Blackwell companion to the sociology of families*. London: Blackwell Publishing.

Beck, W., van der Maesen, L., & Walker, A. (Eds.). (1997). *The social quality of Europe*. Dordrecht, The Netherlands: Kluwer Law International.

Bellah, R. N. (1985). *Tokugawa religion: The cultural roots of modern Japan*. New York: The Free Press.

Belson, K., & Tabuchi, H. (2013, April 26). In promoting his city for 2020 games, Tokyo's bid chairman tweaks others. *New York Times*. Retrieved from http://www.nytimes.com/2013/04/27/sports/in-praising-its-olympic-bid-tokyo-tweaks-the-others.html?pagewanted=all&_r=0

Benedict, R. (1946). *The chrysanthemum and the sword: Patterns of Japanese culture*. Boston: Houghton Mifflin.

Benedict, R. (1972). *Kiku to katana: Nihon bunka no kata*. Tôkyô: Sekai Shisôsha.

Benn & Gaus. (1983). The public and the private: The concepts and action. In *Public and private in social life* (pp. 3–27). New York: St Martin's Press.

Berman, Y., & Phillips, D. (2004). *Social quality and the conditional factor of social cohesion: 3rd draft*.

Berthoud, R., & Robson, K. (2001). *The outcome of teenage motherhood in Europe* (Innocenti Working Paper No.86). Florence, Italy: UNICEF.

Billis, D. (Ed.). (2010). *Hybrid organizations and the third sector: Challenges for practice, theory and policy*. London, UK: Palgrave MacMillan.

BirdLife International. (2000). *Threatened birds of the world*. Barcelona: Lynx Edicions.

Boardman, A. E., & Vining, A. R. (2010). Assessing the economic worth of public-private partnerships. In G. A. Hodge, G. Greve, & A. E. Boardman (Eds.), *The international handbook on public private partnerships*. London, UK: Edward-Elgar. doi:10.4337/9781849804691.00016

Boas, G. (1969). *History of ideas*. New York: Charles Scribner's Sons.

Bobbio, N. (1992). *Democracy and dictatorship: The nature and limits of state power*. Minneapolis, MN: University of Minnesota Press.

Bonoli, G. (2005). The politics of the new social policies: Providing coverage against new social risks in mature welfare states. *Policy and Politics*, *33*, 431–449. doi:10.1332/0305573054325765

Bonoli, G. (2006). New social risks and the politics of post-industrial social policies. In *The politics of post-industrial welfare states: Adapting post-war welfare states to new social risks*. London: Routledge.

Bonoli, G. (2007). Time matters: Postindustrialization, new social risks, and welfare state adaptation in advanced industrial democracies. *Comparative Political Studies*, *40*(5), 495–520. doi:10.1177/0010414005285755

Bowlby, J. (1969). *Attachment and loss*. New York: Basic Books.

Boyle, G. (2003). *The promotion of quality of life in long-term acre policy*. Paper presented at ESPAnet Conference. New York, NY.

Bozeman, B. (2007). *Public values and public interest: Counterbalancing economic individualism*. Washington, DC: Georgetown University Press.

Brazil, M. (1991). *The birds of Japan*. Washington, DC: Smithsonian Institution Press.

Bream, V., & Buchanan, A. (2003). Distress among children whose separated or divorced parents cannot agree arrangements for them. *British Journal of Social Work*, *33*, 227–238. doi:10.1093/bjsw/33.2.227

Bronfenbrenner, U. (1979). *The ecology of human development*. Cambridge, MA: Harvard University Press.

Buchanan, A., & Flouri, E. (2005). *Father Involvement and outcomes in adolescence and adulthood*. Retrieved on 29 October, 2012 from http://www.esrc.ac.uk/my-esrc/grants/R000223309/outputs/Read/3871fa69-89d7-4d32-9ad2-c5d04d5974f5

Buchanan, A., & Rotkirch, A. (2013). *Fertility rates and population decline: No time for children?* London, UK: Palgrave Macmillan. doi:10.1057/9781137030399

Buchanan, A., & Ten Brinke, J.-A. (1997). *What happened when they were grown up? Outcomes from parenting experiences*. York, UK: Joseph Rowntree Foundation.

Bureau of National Health Insurance. Taiwan. (2012). *Immediate statistics*. Retrieved on 22 July 2013, from http://www.doh.gov.tw/statistic/data

Cabinet Office. (2012). *Heisei 24 nen jisatsu no tôkei*. [Statistics on Suicide, year 24 Heisei]. Retrieved from http://www8.cao.go.jp/jisatsutaisaku/toukei/

Calhoun, C. (2007). *Nations matter: Culture, history and the cosmopolitan dream*. London: Routledge.

Carers National Association. (1999). *Welfare to work: Carers and employment project evaluation report*. London: Carers National Association.

Cartledge, P. (2009). *Ancient Greek political thought in practice*. Cambridge, UK: Cambridge University Press. doi:10.1017/CBO9780511801747

Castells, M. (2000). *End of millennium* (2nd ed.). Oxford, UK: Blackwell Publishing.

Castells, M., & Himanen, P. (2002). *The information society and welfare state: The Finnish model*. Oxford, UK: Oxford University Press. doi:10.1093/acprof:oso/9780199256990.001.0001

Census and Statistic Department. (2012c). *2011 population census household income distribution in Hong Kong*. Hong Kong: Census and Statistics Department.

Census and Statistics Department. (2006). *Hong Kong annual digest of statistics, 2006*. Hong Kong: Census and Statistics Department.

Census and Statistics Department. (2010). *Feature article: Statistics on comprehensive social security assistance scheme, 1999 to 2009*. Hong Kong: Hong Kong SAR Government Census and Statistics Department.

Census and Statistics Department. (2012a). *Hong Kong life tables 2006-2041*. Hong Kong: Census and Statistics Department.

Census and Statistics Department. (2012b). *Hong Kong annual digest of statistics, 2012*. Hong Kong: Census and Statistics Department.

Census and Statistics Department. (2012d). *Feature article: Statistics on comprehensive social security assistance scheme, 2001 to 2011*. Hong Kong: Hong Kong SAR Government Census and Statistics Department.

Central Election Council, Taiwan. (2012). Retrieved on 22 July 2013, from http://web.cec.gov.tw/files/11-1000-1642-1.php

Chang, T. (1997). Taiwan's 1995 health care reform. [in Chinese]. *Health Policy (Amsterdam)*, *39*, 225–239. doi:10.1016/S0168-8510(96)00877-9

Chan, R. K. H. (1996). *Welfare in newly-industrialised society: The construction of the welfare state in Hong Kong*. Aldershot, UK: Avebury.

Chan, R. K. H. (2006). Risk and its management in post-financial crisis Hong Kong. *Social Policy and Administration*, *40*(2), 215–229. doi:10.1111/j.1467-9515.2006.00485.x

Chan, R. K. H. (2009). Risk discourse and politics: Restructuring welfare in Hong Kong. *Critical Social Policy*, *29*(1), 24–52. doi:10.1177/0261018308098393

Chan, R. K. H. (2010). Managing family risk in Hong Kong: How and why. In *Risk and public policy in east Asia*. Aldershot, UK: Ashgate.

Chan, R. K. H. (2011). The politics of health finance reform in Hong Kong. *International Journal of Public and Private Healthcare Management and Economics*, *1*(2), 17–25. doi:10.4018/ijpphme.2011040102

Chan, R. K. H., & Hu, K. (2011). Primary health services utilization and inequality: The emerging symbiotic public/private model in Hong Kong. *Journal of Public and Private Healthcare Management and Economics*, *1*(4), 1–13.

Chan, R., Takahashi, M., & Wang, L. (Eds.). (2010). *Risk and public policy in east Asia*. Burlington, VA: Ashgate.

Chau, R. C. M., & Yu, W. K. (2003). Marketisation and residualisation – Recent reforms in the medical financing system in Hong Kong. *Social Policy and Society*, *2*(3), 199–207. doi:10.1017/S1474746403001222

Chen, F. L. (2000). *Working women and state policies in Taiwan: A study of political economy*. London: Palgrave Publishers. doi:10.1057/9780230508873

Chen, H. L. (2007). Power and autonomy of older people in long-term care: Cross-national comparison and learning. *Social Policy Report*, *19*, 177–203.

Chen, H. L. (2012). Cross-national qualitative research into the long-term care of older people: Some reflections on method and methodology. *European Journal of Social Work*. doi:10.1080/13691457.2012.708903

Cheung, A. B. L. (2009). *Governance in Hong Kong: In search of identity, legitimacy and trust*. Hong Kong: Hong Kong Institute of Education. doi:10.5353/th_b4675579

Child Welfare Bureau. (2013). *Childcare service statistics*. Retrieved from http://www.cbi.gov.tw/CBI_2/internet/main/index.aspx

Chiu, C.-P., & Liu, C.-L. (2012). *A study on childcare insitutions in Taiwan*. Taipei: Research, Development and Evaluation Commission, Executive Yuan. [in Chinese]

Choy, C. C. (2003). *Empire of care*. Manila: Ateneo de Manila Press.

Commission for Social Care Inspection (CSCI). (2004). *Leaving hospital – The price of delays*. London: Commission for Social Care Inspection.

Constable, N. (2007). *Maid to order in Hong Kong*. New York: Cornell University Press.

Coulter, A. (2002). *The autonomous patient: Ending paternalism in medical care*. London, UK: Nuttfield Trust.

Council for Economic Planning and Development. (2011). *Human resource and social welfare*. Retrieved May 10, 2011, from http://www.cepd.gov.tw/m1.aspx?sNo=0012631

Council of Labor Affairs. (2013). *Foreign workers statistics*. Retrieved from http://www.cla.gov.tw/cgi-bin/siteMaker/SM_theme?page=49c05774

Council of Labor Affairs. Taiwan. (2007a). *Monthly bulletin of labor statistics*. Retrieved on 22 July 2013, from http://statdb.cla.gov.tw/html/mon/26080.htm

Council of Labor Affairs. Taiwan. (2007b). *Yearbook of labor statistics*. Retrieved on 22 July 2013, from http://statdb.cla.gov.tw/html/year/year96/rptmenuyear.htm

Council of Labor Affairs. Taiwan. (2009). *Yearbook of labor statistics*. Retrieved on 22 July 2013, from http://statdb.cla.gov.tw/html/year/year96/rptmenuyear.htm

Covell, A. C. (1988). *Folk art and magic: Shamanism in Korea*. Seoul: Hollym.

Cox, R. H. (2001). The social construction of an imperative: Why welfare reform happened in Denmark and The Netherlands but not in Germany. *World Politics*, *53*(3). doi:10.1353/wp.2001.0008 PMID:17595731

Crabtree, B. F., & Miller, W. L. (1992). *Doing qualitative research*. Thousand Oaks, CA: Sage.

Crouch, C. (2011). *The strange non-death of neo-liberalism*. Cambridge, UK: Polity Press.

D'Aunno, T. (2005). Management scholars and public policy: A bridge too far? *Academy of Management Journal*, *48*(6), 949–951. doi:10.5465/AMJ.2005.19573093

Daft, R. L. (2004). *Organization theory and design*. Cincinnati, OH: South-Western Publishing.

Davies, S., Nolan, M. R., Brown, J., & Wilson, F. (1999). *Dignity on the ward: Promoting excellence in care*. London: Help the Aged.

Dent, M., Fallon, C., Wendt, C., Vuori, J., Puhor, M., de Pietro, C., & Silva, S. (2011). Medicine and user involvement within European healthcare: A typology for European comparative research. *International Journal of Clinical Practice*, *65*(12), 1218–1220. doi:10.1111/j.1742-1241.2011.02803.x PMID:22093529

Department of Health (DH). (1997). *The cornerstone of care: Inspection of care planning for older people, CI(97)21*. London: Department of Health.

Department of Health (DH). (2004). *SSI performance assessment 2004: Operating policies*. London: Department of Health.

Department of Health, Taiwan. (2010). Retrieved on 22 July 2013, from http://www.doh.gov.tw/statistic/data/

Department of Health. (n.d.). *The family nurse partnership programme*. Retrieved on 29 October, 2012 from http://www.dh.gov.uk/en/Publicationsandstatistics/Publications/PublicationsPolicyAndGuidance/DH_118530

Department of Household Registration Affairs, Ministry of the Interior. (2009). *Statistics - household registration statistics*. Retrieved from http://www.ris.gov.tw/version96/stpeqr_01_04.html

Department of Household Registration Affairs. (2009). *Fertility rate for women*. Retrieved from http://www.ris.gov.tw/

Department of Household Registration Affairs. (2012). *Total fertility rate*. Retrieved Oct 20, 2012, from http://sowf.moi.gov.tw/stat/year/y02-04.xls

Department of Manpower Planning. (2010). 2010-2060 Taiwanese population estimation. *Taiwan Economic Forum, 8*(9), 66-70.

Dewey, J. (1946). *Public and its problems: An essay in political inquiry*. New York: Henry Holt & Co.

Dilnot, A. (2011). *Fair care funding: The report of the commission onfunding of care and support*. London: The Independent Commission on Funding of Care and Support.

Directorate General of Budget, Accounting and Statistics, Taiwan. (2000). *Household survey statistics in Taiwan*. Retrieved on 22 July 2013, from http://www.stat.gov.tw/public/Data/411716314171.rtf

Directorate General of Budget, Accounting and Statistics, Taiwan. (2003). *Survey of social developmental trend 2003*. Retrieved on 22 July 2013, from http://www.dgbas.gov.tw/public/Attachment/4112911545171.xls

Directorate General of Budget, Accounting and Statistics, Taiwan. (2007). *Quarterly national economic trends, Vol. 117*. Retrieved on 22 July 2013, http://eng.stat.gov.tw/public/Attachm ent/761310155271.xls

Directorate General of Budget, Accounting and Statistics, Taiwan. (2009). *Social indicators 2009*. Retrieved on 22 July 2013, from http://eng.stat.gov.tw/public/data/dgbas03/bs2/socialindicator

Directorate General of Budget, Accounting and Statistics, Taiwan. (2011). *Social indicators 2011*. Retrieved November 17, 2012, http://www.dgbas.gov.tw/public/Attachment/28111192871.pdf

Directorate General of Budget, Accounting and Statistics, Taiwan. (2012a). *Economic statistics indicators*. Retrieved on 22 July 2013, from http://2k3dmz2.moea.gov.tw/gnweb/Indicator/wFrmIndicator.aspx

Directorate General of Budget, Accounting and Statistics, Taiwan. (2012b). *Employment and unemployment statistics*. Retrieved on 22 July 2013, from http://www.stat.gov.tw/ct.asp?xItem=17144&ctNode=517

Directorate General of Budget, Accounting and Statistics, Taiwan. (2012c). *Survey of employee's salary*. Retrieved on 22 July 2013, from http://www.stat.gov.tw/ct.asp?xItem=1135&ctNode=525

Directorate-General of Budget, Accounting and Statistics, Executive Yuan. (1994-2009). *Family income and expenditure survey*. Retrieved from http://win.dgbas.gov.tw/fies/result.asp

Directorate-General of Budget, Accounting and Statistics, Executive Yuan. (2009). *Conditions statistical bulletin*. Retrieved from http://www.dgbas.gov.tw/public/Data/012616104771.pdf

Do, M., & Jeon, E. (2001). Research on issues and welfare policy for teenage single mothers.[in Korean]. *Youth Welfare, 3*(2), 1–11.

Doorslaer, E. V., Masseria, C., & Koolman, X. (2006). Inequalities in access to medical care by income in developed countries. *Canadian Medical Association Journal, 174*(2), 177–183. doi:10.1503/cmaj.050584 PMID:16415462

Doyal, L., & Gough, I. (1991). *A theory of human need.* Basingstoke, UK: Macmillan.

Dunston, R., Lee, A., Boud, D., Brodie, P., & Chiarella, M. (2009). Co-production and health system reform – From re-imagining to re-making. *Australian Journal of Public Administration*, *68*(1), 39–52. doi:10.1111/j.1467-8500.2008.00608.x

Edwards, A., & Elwyn, G. (Eds.). (2009). *Shared decision-making in health care: Achieving evidence-based patient choice*. Oxford, UK: Oxford University Press.

Ehrenreich & Hochschild (Ed.). (2002). *Global women: Nannies, maids, and sex workers in the new economy.* New York: Holt.

Esping-Andersen, G. (1996). Positive-sum solutions in a world of trade-offs? In *Welfare state in transition: National adaptations in global economies*. London: Sage Publications. doi:10.4135/9781446216941.n9

Esping-Andersen, G. (1999). *Social foundations of postindustrial economies*. Oxford, UK: Oxford University Press. doi:10.1093/0198742002.001.0001

EU. (2008). *Council regulation (EC) no 194/2008 of 25 February 2008 renewing and strengthening the restrictive measures in respect of Burma/Myanmar and repealing Regulation (EC) No 817/2006*. Retrieved from http://eur-lex.europa.eu/LexUriServ/LexUriServ.do?uri=OJ:L:2008:066:0001:0087:EN:PDF

Eun, H. (1999). Teen pregnancy & childbirth: Trends and alternatives.[in Korean]. *Journal of the Korean Society of Child Welfare*, *8*, 161–186.

European Foundation of Social Quality. (2006). *Introduction to the theory of social quality*. Retrieved on 22 July 2013, from http://www.socialquality.nl/site/index.html

Ex, C., Gorter, K., & Jansen, U. (2004). Providing integrated health and social care for older persons in The Netherlands. In K. Leichsenring, & A. M. Alaszewski (Eds.), *Providing integrated health and social care for older persons*. Aldershot, UK: Ashgate.

Executive Yuan. (2011). *Population policy guidelines.* Author.

Family Action Building Bridges Evaluation. (2011). *Summary report*. Retrieved on 29 October, 2012 from www.family-action.org.uk/uploads/documents/Building%20Bridges%20Summary%20Evaluation.pdf

Farrington, D., et al. (2001). *Family influences on delinquency.* Retrieved on 29 October, 2012 from samples.jbpub.com/.../60564_CH10_Springer.pdf

Fatherhood Institute. (n.d.). Retrieved on 29 October 2012 from http://www.fatherhoodinstitute.org/

Fei, H. T. (1947). *On particularistic ties*. Hong Kong: Phoenix Publishing Company.

Fenellosa, E. F. (1912). *Epochs of Chinese and Japanese art: An outline history of East Asiatic design*. Berkeley, CA: Stone Bridge Classics.

Fenny, S., & Clarke, M. (2009). *The millennium development goals and beyond – International assistance to the Asia-Pacific*. Hampshire, UK: Palgrave Macmillan.

Finch, J., & Masson, J. (1993). *Negotiating family responsibilities*. London: Routledge.

Flinders, M. (2010). Splintered logic and political debate. In *The international handbook on public private partnerships*. London, UK: Edward-Elgar. doi:10.4337/9781849804691.00014

Food & Health Bureau. (n.d.). *Domestic health accounts (1989/90– 2006/07)*. Retrieved July 21, 2013 from http://www.fhb.gov.hk/statistics/en/dha/dha_summary_report.htm#C

Food and Health Bureau. (2008). *Your health your life: Report on first stage public consultation on healthcare reform*. Hong Kong: Government Printer.

Food and Health Bureau. (2010). *My health my choice: Healthcare reform second stage public consultation*. Hong Kong: Government Printer.

Food and Health Bureau. (n.d.). *Hong Kong's domestic health account (HKDHA) – Estimate of domestic health expenditure,1989/90– 2009/10*. Retrieved from http://www.fhb.gov.hk/statistics/en/dha.htm

Frankenberg, E., Chan, A., & Ofstedal, M. B. (2002). Stability and change in living arrangement in Indonesia, Singapore and Taiwan, 1993–99. *Population Studies*, *56*(2), 201–213. doi:10.1080/00324720215928

Fujishiro, K., Xu, J., & Gong, F. (2010). What does 'occupation' represent as an indicator of socioeconomic status? Exploring occupational prestige and health. *Social Science & Medicine*, *71*(12), 2100–2107. doi:10.1016/j.socscimed.2010.09.026 PMID:21041009

Fuller, E. (2000). *Extinct birds*. Oxford, UK: Oxford University Press.

Fuller, R., & Tulle-Winton, E. (1996). Specialism, genericism and others: Does it make a difference? A study of social work service to elderly people. *British Journal of Social Work*, *26*, 679–698. doi:10.1093/oxfordjournals.bjsw.a011141

Gaus, B. (1983). Public and private interests in liberal political economy, old and new. In *The public and private in social life*. New York: St. Martin's Press.

Gereffi, G. (1999). International trade and industrial upgrading in the apparel commodity chain. *Journal of International Economics*, *48*(1), 37–70. doi:10.1016/S0022-1996(98)00075-0

Giddens, A. (1990). *The consequence of modernity*. Cambridge, UK: Polity Press.

Giddens, A. (2000). *The third way and its critics*. Cambridge, UK: Polity Press.

Glendinning, C. (1992). *The costs of informal care: Looking inside the household*. London: HMSO.

Glenn, E. N. (2000). Creating a caring society. *Contemporary Sociology*, *29*(1), 84–94. doi:10.2307/2654934

Godfrey, A. (2000). What impact does training have on the care received by older people in residential homes? *Social Work Education*, *19*(1), 55–65. doi:10.1080/026154700114658

Gojô, M. (2003). *Kazoku keiei kyôtei no tenkai* [Development of Family Management Agreements]. Tôkyô: Yûhikaku.

Goodman, R., & Peng, I. (1996). The east Asian welfare states: Peripatetic learning, adaptive change, and nation building. In G. Esping-Andersen (Ed.), *Welfare state in transition: National adaptations in global economies*. London: Sage Publications. doi:10.4135/9781446216941.n7

Goodman, R., White, G., & Kwon, H. J. (1998). *The east Asian welfare model*. London: Routledge.

Goodman, R., White, G., & Kwon, H.-J. (1998). *The east Asian welfare model: Welfare orientalism and the state*. London: Routledge.

Goodridge, D., Hawranik, P., Duncan, V., & Turner, H. (2012). Socioeconomic disparities in home health care service access and utilization: A scoping review. *International Journal of Nursing Studies*. doi:10.1016/j.ijnurstu.2012.01.002 PMID:22300550

Goss, R. P. (2003). What ethical conduct expectations do legislators have for the career bureaucracy? *Public Integrity*, *5*(2), 93–112.

Gough, I. (2004). East Asia: The limits of productivist regimes. In *Insecurity and welfare regimes in Asia, Africa and Latin America: Social policy in development contexts*. Cambridge, UK: Cambridge University Press. doi:10.1017/CBO9780511720239.007

Green, M. (2003). *Japan's reluctant realism: Foreign policy challenges in an era of uncertain power*. New York: Palgrave Macmillan.

Gries, P. H. (2004). *China's new nationalism: Pride, politics, and diplomacy*. Berkeley, CA: University of California Press.

Habermas, J. (1989). *The structural transformation of the public sphere: An inquiry into a category of bourgeois society*. Cambridge, MA: MIT Press.

Hall, A. G., Lemak, C. H., Steingraber, H., & Schaffer, S. (2008). Expanding the definition of access: It isn't just about health insurance. *Journal of Health Care for the Poor and Underserved*, *19*(2), 625–638. doi:10.1353/hpu.0.0011 PMID:18469432

Hamaguchi, E. (1982). Nihonteki shûdanshugi to wa nanika. [What is Japanese Groupism?] In *Sono shinka o tou* [Japanese Groupism]. Tôkyô: Yûhikaku.

Hanley, S. B. (1997). *Everyday things in premodern Japan: The hidden legacy of material culture*. Berkeley, CA: University of California Press.

Han, S.-J. (1998). The Korean path to modernization and risk society. *Korea Journal*, *38*(1), 5–27.

Harding, E., & Beresfords, P. (1996). *The standards we expect: What service users and carers want from social services workers*. London: National Institute of Social Workers.

Harootunian, H. D. (1988). *Things seen and unseen: Discourse and ideology in tokugawa nativism*. Chicago: The University of Chicago Press.

Harvard Team. (1999). *Improving Hong Kong's health care system – Why and for whom?* Hong Kong: Government Printer.

Harvey, D. (1989). *The condition of post modernity*. Oxford, UK: Blackwell.

Hasegawa, A. (1993). *Nôson no kazoku to chiiki shakai: Sono ronri to kadai* [Families and Local Community of a Farming Village: Their Logic and Problems]. Tôkyô: Ochanomizu Shobô.

Hatanaka, K. (1986). Tôyôga no fuhenteki shisô o motomete. In *Nihonga: Zairyô to hyôgen*. Tôkyô: Bijutsu Shuppansha.

Health, Welfare and Food Bureau. (2004). *Final report: A study on health care financing and feasibility of a medical savings scheme in Hong Kong*. Hong Kong: Government Printer.

Hempel, H.-P. (1987). *Heidegger und zen*. Frankfurt, Germany: Athenäum Verlag.

Heng, Y.-K. (2010). Mirror, mirror on the wall, who is the softest of them all? Evaluating Japanese and Chinese strategies in the 'soft' power competition era. *International Relations of the Asia-Pacific*, *10*(2), 275–304. doi:10.1093/irap/lcp023

Herrmann, P. (2003). *Social quality and the conditional factor of social empowerment: 3rd draft*. Amsterdam, The Netherlands: EFSQ.

Hesketh, T., Lu, L., & Zhu, W. (2005). The effect of China's one-child family policy after 25 years. *The New England Journal of Medicine*, *353*(11), 1171–1176. PMID:16162890

Himmelweit, S. (2007). The prospects for caring: Economic theory and policy analysis. *Cambridge Journal of Economics*, *31*(4), 581–599. doi:10.1093/cje/bem011

Hirschman, A. O. (1970). *Exit, voice and loyalty: Responses to decline in firms, organisations and states*. Cambridge, MA: Harvard University Press.

Hitt, M. A. (2005). Management theory and research: Potential contribution to public policy and public organizations. *Academy of Management Journal*, *48*(6), 963–966. doi:10.5465/AMJ.2005.19573098

Hitt, M. A., Beamish, P. W., Jakson, S. E., & Mathieu, J. E. (2007). Building theoretical and empirical bridges across levels: Multilevel research in management. *Academy of Management Journal*, *50*(6), 1385–1399. doi:10.5465/AMJ.2007.28166219

Hodge, G. A., & Greeve, G. (2007). Public-private partnerships: An international performance review. *Public Administration Review*, *67*(3), 545–585. doi:10.1111/j.1540-6210.2007.00736.x

Hodge, G. A., Greve, G., & Boardman, A. E. (Eds.). (2010). *The international handbook on public private partnerships*. London, UK: Edward-Elgar. doi:10.4337/9781849804691

Holliday, I. (2000). Productivist welfare capitalism: Social policy in east Asia. *Comparative Political Studies*, *48*, 706–723. doi:10.1111/1467-9248.00279

Hollifield, J. F. (1992). *Immigrants, markets, and states: The political economy of postwar Europe*. Cambridge, MA: Harvard University Press.

Ho, N. et al. (2005). *Study on comprehensive policy for single mother and father*. Ministry of Gender Equality and Family. [in Korean]

Hong Kong Council of Social Services. (2012). *Poverty in figures (2001-2011)*. Hong Kong: Hong Kong Council of Social Services.

Hong Kong Government. (1964). *Development of medical services in Hong Kong*. Hong Kong: Government Printer.

Hong Kong Government. (1974). *Further development of medical and health services in Hong Kong*. Hong Kong: Government Printer.

Hong Kong Government. (1989). *Hong Kong annual report, 1989*. Hong Kong: Government Printer.

Hong Kong Government. (1993). *Towards better health: A consultation document*. Hong Kong: Government Printer.

Hong Kong Government. (2008). *Your health, your life: Report on the first stage public consultation on healthcare reform*. Hong Kong: Hong Kong Government Printer.

Hong Kong Government. (2010). *My health, my choice: Healthcare reform second stage public consultation*. Hong Kong: Hong Kong Government Printer.

Hong Kong Government. (2011). *Hong Kong annual report, 2010*. Hong Kong: Hong Kong Government Printer.

Hong Kong Medical Association. (2010). *Report of doctors' fees survey, 2010*. Hong Kong: Hong Kong Medical Association.

Hong Kong, S. A. R. Government. (2000). Lifelong investment in health: A consultation document on health care reform. Hong Kong: Government Printer.

Hong Kong, S. A. R. Government. (2005). Building a healthy tomorrow: Discussion paper on the future service delivery model for our health care system. Hong Kong: Government Printer.

Hong, S. et al. (2007). *A study of securing rights for adolescent single mothers to receive education*. National Human Rights Commission.

Hosoya, T. (2005). Ie to nihon shakai, saikô. [Rethinking 'Ie' and the Japanese Society]. *Shakaigaku hyôron, 56*(1), 2–15.

Hosoya, T. (1993). Nômin seikatsu ni okeru ko to shûdan. [Individual and Group in the Farmer's life] In *Nômin seikatsu ni okeru ko to shûdan* (pp. 403–445). Tôkyô: Ochanomizu Shobô.

House of Commons Health Committee (HCHC). (2002). *Delayed discharges, third report session 2001-2, vol 1, HC 617-1*. London: The Stationary Office.

Hsueh, C. T. (2008). Taiwan family living patterns change and the elderly: Current status and future. *Community Development Journal, 121*, 47–56.

Huber, E., & Stephens, J. D. (2006). Combatting old and new social risks. In K. Armingeon, & G. Bonoli (Eds.), *The politics of post-industrial welfare states: Adapting post-war welfare states to new social risks*. London: Routledge.

Hughes, C. W. (2004). *Japan's security agenda: Military, economic & environmental dimensions*. Boulder, CO: Lynne Rienner Publishers.

Hugo, G. (2009). Care worker migration, Australia and development. *Population Space and Place, 15*, 189–203. doi:10.1002/psp.534

Hu, K. W. (2001). *Family values, resources and intergenerational support in Taiwan*. Taipei, Taiwan: Academia Sinica.

Hula, E. (2011, September 26). IOC president on 2020 bids, Arab spring, cutting olympic sports. *Around the Rings*. Retrieved from http://aroundtherings.com/articles/view.aspx?id=37990

Hunt, J. (2008). *Family and friends care*. Research in Practice.

Hunt, J., Waterhouse, S., & Lutman, E. (2008). *Keeping them in the family: Children placed in kinship care through care proceedings*. London: BAAF.

Huutoniemi, K. (2010). Evaluating interdisciplinary research. In *The Oxford handbook of interdisciplinarity*. Oxford, UK: Oxford University Press.

Hyde, P., & Davies, H. T. O. (2004). Service design, culture and performance: Collusion and co-production in health care. *Human Relations, 57*(11), 1407–1426. doi:10.1177/0018726704049415

IDA. (2007). *Operational policy and country services (OPCS) and resource, mobilization department (FRM), operational approaches and financing in fragile states, June 2007*. Retrieved from http://siteresouces.worldbank.org/IDA/Resources/IDA15FragileStates.pdf

Iguchi, Y. (2005, February 15). Shôshika nihon ni senryaku hitsuyô. [Need for Strategy in Low Fertility Rate Japan]. *Asahi Shimbun*.

Ikeda, S., Sakai, Y., & Tawada, M. (2004). *Gendai shakai no yuragi to risuku*. Tôkyô: Keisô Shobô.

Imanishi, K. (2002). *A Japanese view of nature: The world of living things*. London: Routledge.

International Herald Tribune. (2007, September 28). China blocks UN effort to condemn Myanmar. *The International Herald Tribune*.

International Herald Tribune. (2013, June 1). Terror in Myanmar. *The International Herald Tribune*.

International Labor Organization (ILO). (2013). *Decent work*. Retrieved from http://www.ilo.org/global/topics/decent-work/lang--en/index.htm

International Olympic Committee. (2011). *Olympic charter: In force as from 8 July 2011*. International Olympic Committee. Retrieved from http://www.olympic.org/Documents/olympic_charter_en.pdf

Iryô Keizai Kenkyû. (2003). *Kateinai ni okeru kôreisha gyakutai ni kansuru chôsa*. [Survey on elderly abuse at home]. Retrieved from www.ihep.jp/publications/report/search.php?dl=170&i=1

ISSA Website (n.d.a). *Family policies*. Retrieved from http://www.issa.int/Topics/Family-policies

ISSA Website (n.d.b). *Technical seminar on family policies - Family policies in the face of changes in family structures and the evolving socio-economic context*. Retrieved from http://www.issa.int/News-Events/Events/Technical-Seminar-on-Family-Policies-Family-policies-in-the-face-of-changes-in-family-structures-and-the-evolving-socio-economic-context

Iwasaki, Y. (1995). Nôson ni okeru josei kigyô no igi to hokosei: Nôson no josei kigyô jittai chôsa o tsûjite. [Significance and Orientations of Female Entrepreneurs in Farming Villages: Through Fact Surveys of Female Entrepreneurs in Farming Villages]. *Nenpô Sonraku Shakai Kenkyû*, *31*, 169–190.

Jacobs, D. (1998). Social welfare systems in east Asia: A comparative analysis including private welfare. *CASE-paper*.

Jae, S. et al. (2008). *Survey of student single mothers. Ministry of Education, Science, and Technology*. MEST. [in Korean]

Japan Nursing Association. (2006). *Nippi EPA firipin-jin kangoshi no ukeire ni kansuru nihon kango kyôkai no kenkai*. [Japan Nursing Association's Position on Acceptance of Filipino Nurses under the Japan-Philippines EPA]. Retrieved from http://www.nurse.or.jp/home/opinion/newsrelease/2006pdf/20060912.pdf

Japan Section, S. R. A. (n.d.). *Nihon risuku kenkyûgakkai*. Retrieved on 7 March, 2012 from http://www.sra-japan.jp/cms/

JICWELS. (2013a). *Keizai renkei kyôtei ni motozuku gaikokujin kangoshi/ kaigo fukushishi kôhôsha to no genjô*. [Current Situation of Foreign Nurse and Caregiver Candidates under the Economic Partnership Agreement]. Unpublished.

JICWELS. (2013b). *Heisei 26 nendo ukeire tebiki kaigo fukushishi course*. [2013 Guide for Acceptance of Caregivers]. Retrieved from http://www.jicwels.or.jp/files/H26E4BB8BE8ADB7E6898BE5BC95E3818D_2.pdf

Jones, C. (1993). The Pacific challenge: Confucian welfare states. In *New perspectives on the welfare state in Europe*. London: Routledge.

Jörg, F., Borgers, N., Schrijvers, A. J. P., & Hox, J. J. (2006). *Variation in long-term care needs assessor's willingness to support client's requests for admission to a residential home: A vignette study*. London: Sage Publications.

Kataoka, M. (2012). Japan, the chaotic, and aida makoto. In *Aida makoto: Tensai de gomen nasai: Monument for nothing*. Tôkyô: Mori Art Museum.

Kataoka, Y. (2012). Japanese individualized family as a form of risk protection and adaption to rural life. *International Journal of Public and Private Healthcare Management and Economics*, *2*(3), 17–26. doi:10.4018/ijpphme.2012070101

Kataoka, Y., & Fukino, T. (2007). Nôson kazoku ni okeru ketsugô patân ni kansuru sûryôteki bunseki: shimaneken chûsankanchiiki de no chôsa deta o mochiite. [A Quantitative Analysis of the Binding Patterns in the Rural Family: Using Survey Data from the Hilly and Mountainous Areas of Shimane Prefecture]. *Shakai Bunka Ronshû*, *4*, 31–39.

Katzenstein, P. J. (1996). *Cultural norms and national security: Police and military in postwar Japan*. Ithaca, NY: Cornell University Press.

Keizer, M., & van der Maesen, L. (2003). *Social quality and the conditional factor of socio-economic security: 3rd draft working paper*. Amsterdam: EFSQ.

Kim, H. (2008). Where should single parent policy go? In Conditions and controversy over single mothers. Korean Women's Development Institute (KWDI). [in Korean].

Kim, C. (2003). *Korean shamanism: The cultural paradox*. Aldershot, UK: Ashgate.

Kim, D. H. (1998). Rush-to growth, economic crisis, limping modernization, and a dual-risk society. *Korea Journal*, *38*(1), 28–45.

Kim, H. et al. (2009). *Korean public opinion survey on unwed mothers and their children. Korean Women's Development Institute*. KWDI. [in Korean]

Kim, H., & Ahn, S. et al. (2009). *Korean attitudes toward unmarried parents and adoption: Improving attitudes towards unwed mothers and promoting support. Korean Women's Development Institute*. KWDI. [in Korean]

Kim, H., & Son, B. et al. (2009). *Unwed mother's life world and policy agenda. Korean Women's Development Institute*. KWDI. [in Korean]

Kim, J. W. (1998). Korea, land of environmental risk. =. *Korea Journal*, *38*(1), 220–240.

Kim, J.-W. (1998). Korea, land of environmental risk. *Korea Journal*, *38*(1), 220–240.

Kim, Y. et al. (2006). *Study on social support for childbirth and childcare of single mothers. Korea Institute for Health and Social Affairs*. KIHASA. [in Korean]

Kim, Y., & Kim, E. (2008). *Life and future of adolescent single mothers*. Nuipun Women Support Centre. [in Korean]

King, D., & Ross, F. (2010). Critics and beyond. In *The Oxford handbook of the welfare state* (pp. 45–60). Oxford, UK: Oxford University Press. doi:10.1093/oxfordhb/9780199579396.003.0004

Kirby, J. B., & Kaneda, T. (2005). Neighborhood socioeconomic disadvantage and access to health care. *Journal of Health and Social Behavior*, *46*(1), 15–31. doi:10.1177/002214650504600103 PMID:15869118

Kirby, J. B., Taliaferro, G., & Zuvekas, S. H. (2006). Explaining racial and ethnic disparities in health care. *Medical Care*, *44*(5Suppl), I64–I72. PMID:16625066

Knijn, T. (2001). Care work: Innovations in The Netherlands. In M. Daly (Ed.), *Care work: The quest for security*. Geneva: International Labour Office.

Knijn, T. (2004). Challenges and risks of individualisation in The Netherlands. *Social Policy and Society*, *3*(1), 57–65. doi:10.1017/S1474746403001490

Knijn, T., & Kremer, M. (1997). Gender and the caring dimension of welfare states: Towards inclusive citizenship. *Social Politics*, *4*(3), 328–361. doi:10.1093/oxfordjournals.sp.a034270

Kochan, T. A., Guillen, M.F., & Hunter, L.W., & O'Mahoney. (2009). Introduction to the special research forum—Public policy and management research: Finding the common ground. *Academy of Management Journal*, *52*(6), 1088–1100. doi:10.5465/AMJ.2009.47084646

Kolvin, I., Miller, F. J. W., Scott, D. M., Gatzanie, S. R. M., & Fleeting, M. (1990). *Continuities of deprivation? The Newcastle 1000 family study*. Aldershot, UK: Avebury.

Komatsu, T. (2003). *Risuku ron no rûman*. Tôkyô: Keisô Shobô.

Korean Unwed Mothers Support Network (KUMSN). (n.d.). Retrieved from http://www.kumsn.org

Kreiner, J. (1984). A concrete holistic approach to the study of Japanese culture: An example of civilization studies. In *Japanese civilization in the modern world: Life and society*. Osaka: National Museum of Ethnology.

Kudo, T. (2008). The impact of U.S. sanctions on the Myanmar garment industry. *Asian Survey*, *48*(6).

Kumagai, S. (1991). Gendai nihon nôson no kazoku. [Families in Japanese Farming Villages Today]. *Japanese Journal of Family Sociology*, *3*, 28–40. doi:10.4234/jjoffamilysociology.3.28

Kumagai, S. (1996). Nôgyô kazoku ni okeru kojinka. [Individualization in Farming Families] In *Ima kazoku ni nani ga okotte irunoka* [What Is Happening to Families Now?]. Kyôto: Mineruva.

Ku, Y. W. (2001). An uncertain age—A balancing act of international social welfare development. In G. Chan, & Y. W. Ku (Eds.), *The new thoughts of social welfare policy*. Taipei, Taiwan: Laureate Books.

Kwon, H. J. (2002). The Korean welfare state: Development and reform agenda. In C. Aspalter (Ed.), *Discovering the welfare state in east Asia*. Westport, CT: Praeger.

Kwon, H.-J. (1997). Beyond European welfare regimes: Comparative perspectives on east Asian welfare systems. *Journal of Social Policy*, *26*(4), 467–484. doi:10.1017/S004727949700514X

Kylänen, M., Vuori, J., & Allen, P. (2012). Exploring theory for citizens' preferences in health policy: The contribution of health policy cultures to understanding the roles of public and private health service providers. *International Journal of Public and Private Healthcare Management and Economics*, *2*(2), 38–57. doi:10.4018/ijpphme.2012040103

Labor Affairs Council. (2009). *Labour statistics*. Retrieved from http://www.cla.gov.tw/cgi-bin/siteMaker/SM_theme?page=41d35566

Langan, M. (1998). *Welfare: Needs, rights and risks*. London: Routledge.

Lan, P. C. (2006). *Global cinderellas: Migrant domestics and new rich employers in Taiwan*. Durham, NC: Duke University Press. doi:10.1215/9780822387787

Larsen, T. P., & Taylor-Gooby, P. (2004). New risks at the EU level: A spillover from open market policies. In P. Taylor-Gooby (Ed.), *New risks, new welfare: The transformation of the European welfare state*. Oxford, UK: Oxford University Press. doi:10.1093/019926726X.003.0008

Lau, K. K., & Yu, S. S. (1999). *The proposal of the harvard expert team and its comparison with other health finance models*. Hong Kong: Research and Library Section, Legislative Council Secretariat.

Lee, M. (2008). The reality of ignoring single mothers in Korea. In Conditions and controversy over single mothers. Korean Women's Development Institute (KWDI). [in Korean].

Lee, C. (1999). Modernity, legality, and power in Korea under Japanese rule. In G.-W. Shin, & M. Robinson (Eds.), *Colonial modernity in Korea*. Cambridge, MA: Harvard University Press.

Lee, M. et al. (2009). *Reviewing issues on unwed mothers' welfare in Korea: Intercountry adoption, related statistics, and welfare policies in developed countries. Korean Women's Development Institute*. KWDI. [in Korean]

Lee, M. et al. (2010). *How to improve government welfare services for low-income unwed mothers in Korea. Korean Women's Development Institute*. KWDI. [in Korean]

Lee, S. et al. (2010). *Critical issues for research promoted in the next five years on low birthrate and aging society. Ministry of Health and Welfare, and Korea Institute for Health and Social Affairs*. KIHASA. [in Korean]

Lee, S. E. (1983). *Reflections of reality in Japanese art*. Cleveland, OH: Cleveland Museum of Art and Indiana University Press.

Leung, G. M., Tina, K. Y. K., & O'Donnell, O. (2009). Redistribution or horizontal equity in Hong Kong's mixed public-private health system: A policy conundrum. *Health Economics*, *18*(1), 37–54. doi:10.1002/hec.1342 PMID:18264997

Levin, E., & Webb, S. (1997). *Social wok and community care: Changing roles and tasks*. London: National Institute of Social Work.

Lewis, J. (2002). Gender and welfare state change. *European Societies*, *4*(4), 331–357. doi:10.1080/1461669022000022324

Lewis, J., & Campbell, M. (2009). The policymaking context: Behaviour and attitudes. In *Work-family balance, gender and policy*. Cheltenham, UK: Edward Elgar. doi:10.4337/9781848447400.00008

Lin, C. Y., Wang, Y. T., & Shi, S. J. (2010). The features of social cohesion in Taiwan: A social quality perspective. *Journal of State and Society*, *8*, 47–98.

Lin, W. Y. (2006). *Social welfare in Taiwan*. Taipei, Taiwan: Wu-Nan Book Co., Ltd.

Lin, W.-I. (2006). *Social welfare in Taiwan: Historical experiences and institutional analysis*. Taipei, Taiwan: Wu-Nan. [in Chinese]

Lister, R. (2003). *Citizenship: Feminist perspectives*. Basingstoke, UK: Macmillan.

Little, M. (2002). *Improving older people's services: Policy into practice, the second phase of inspections into older people's services*. London: Department of Health.

Lo, I.-C. (2011). Ma ying-jeou: Low fertility has become a national security problem. *World Journal*. Retrieved from http://www.worldjournal.com/pages/full_news/push?article-%E9%A6%AC%E8%8B%B1%E4%B9%9D%EF%BC%9A%E5%B0%91%E5%AD%90%E5%8C%96%E6%88%90%E5%9C%8B%E5%AE%89%E5%95%8F%E9%A1%8C+&id=10942140&instance=noon

Lorenz, K. (1949). *Tiergeschichten: Er redete mi dem vieh, den vögeln und den fischen*. Wien: Verlag.

Luhmann, N. (1991). *Soziologie des risikos*. Berlin: Walter de Gruyter. doi:10.1515/9783110866056

Lutman, E., Hunt, J., & Waterhouse, S. (2009). Placement stability for children in kinship care: A long term follow up of children placed in kinship care through care proceedings. *Adoption & Fostering*, *33*(3), 28–39. doi:10.1177/030857590903300304

Mahoney, J. T., McGahan, A. M., & Pitelis, C. N. (2009). The interdependence of private and public interests. *Organization Science*, *20*, 1034–1052. doi:10.1287/orsc.1090.0472

Mainichi Shimbun. (2008, February 14). Tokyo kenbunroku: Visit unrecognized Myanmar refugee mother and child living in Japan/Tokyo. *Mainichi Shimbun*.

Mainichi Shimbun. (2009, July 7). Former diet member secretary running the show? Denies charges of smuggling people at 1.5M yen/person and introducing them to small business. *Mainichi Shimbun*.

Mainichi Shimbun. (2013a, May 1). Tokyo Olympic bid committee chief says Inose's remarks could infringe on IOC rules. *Mainichi Shimbun*. Retrieved from http://mainichi.jp/english/english/newsselect/news/20130501p2a00m0na002000c.html

Mainichi Shimbun. (2013b, May 28). Kûrujapan: Nihon ryôri de shôbu. *Mainichi Shimbun*. Retrieved from http://mainichi.jp/select/news/20130529k0000m040065000c.html

Mansilla, V. B. (2010). Learning to synthesize: The development of interdisciplinary understanding. In *The Oxford handbook of interdisciplinarity (pp-288-306)*. Oxford, UK: Oxford University Press.

Marsilio, M., Cappellero, G., & Cuccurullo, C. (2011). The intellectual structure of research into ppps. a bibliometric analysis. *Public Management Review*, *13*(6), 736–782. doi:10.1080/14719037.2010.539112

Maslow, A. (1943). A theory of human motivation. *Psychological Review*, *50*(4), 370–396. doi:10.1037/h0054346

McGrew, A. (1992). A global society? In *Modernity and its futures*. Cambridge, UK: Polity Press in Association with Open University.

McLaughlin, H. (2009). What's in a name: 'Client', 'patient', 'customer', 'consumer', 'expert by experience', 'service user'—What's next? *British Journal of Social Work*, *39*(6), 1101–1117. doi:10.1093/bjsw/bcm155

McMullen, J. (1980). How Confucian is modern Japan? *Asian Affairs*, *11*(3), 276–338. doi:10.1080/03068378008729995

Mehta, J. (2011). The varied roles of ideas in politics: From whether to how. In D. Béland, & R. H. Cox (Eds.), *Ideas and politics in social science research*. Oxford, UK: Oxford University Press.

Merviö, M. (2001). *Construction of meanings for 'water' in Japanese culture and politics*. Paper presented at the International Water History Association (IWHA). Bergen, Norway.

Merviö, M. (2008). *Domestic violence: Political and ethical analysis of power relationships*. Paper presented at the East Asia Social Policy 5th International Conference. Taipei, Taiwan. Retrieved from http://www.welfareasia.org/5thconference/papers/Mervio%20M_domestic%20violence%20and%20power%20relationships.pdf

Merviö, M. (2011). *Ecodemics: Analysing the history of facing and mediating the risks from the wild*. Paper presented at the First Conference of East Asian Environmental History (EAEH2011), Academia Sinica. Taipei, Taiwan.

Merviö, M. (2013). *The re-presentation of Japanese society and its relations with the rest of the world: Japanese visual arts and the mimēsis of the world.* Paper presented at the Asian Studies on the Pacific Coast (ASPAC) Conference at the Monterey Institute of International Studies, Monterey, CA.

Merviö, M. (1988). *Harmony in the political tradition of Japan*. Tampere, Finland: University of Tampere.

Merviö, M. (1991). Harmony and conflict in the Japanese political tradition. In *Perspectives on Japan and Korea: Nordic proceedings in Asian studies*. Copenhagen: Nordic Institute for Asian Studies.

Merviö, M. (1995). *Cultural representation of the Japanese in international relations and politics: A study of discourses and interpretations between different cultural traditions*. Tampere, Finland: Acta Universitatis Tamperensis.

Ministry of Agriculture. Forestry and Fisheries of Japan. (1998). Kazoku keiei kyôtei suishin no tebiki. [Guide to Promotion of Family Management Agreements]. Tokyo: The Rural Women Empowerment and Life Improvement Association.

Ministry of Education. (2013). *Number of schools, teachers, staff, classes, students, and graduates between 1950 and 2012*. Retrieved from http://www.edu.tw/pages/detail.aspx?Node=4075&Page=20046&Index=5&WID=31d75a44-efff-4c44-a075-15a9eb7aecdf

Ministry of Education. Taiwan. (2010). *Important educational statistics*. Retrieved on 22 July 2013, from http://140.111.34.69/EDU_WEB/EDU_MGT/STATISTICS/EDU7220001/overview/brief-htm/index.htm?open

Ministry of Finance. Taiwan. (2012). *Total tax revenues as percentage of GDP of key countries (not including social security contribution)*. Retrieved November 17, 2012 from http://eng.stat.gov.tw/public/data/dgbas03/bs1/handbook/other/p6-23c.xls

Ministry of Foreign Affairs website Japan's ODA Data by Country. (n.d.). Retrieved from http://www.mofa.go.jp/policy/oda/data/pdfs/myanmar.pdf

Ministry of Gender Equality and Family Website with Mom. (n.d.). Retrieved from http://withmom.mogef.go.kr/supportpolicies/singleParentFamily.doc

Ministry of Gender Equality and Family. (2005). *Guide for single parent policies*. Author.

Ministry of Health Labor and Welfare (MHLW). (1998~2012). *Jinkô dôtai tôkei.* [Statistics on Population Dynamics]. Retrieved from http://www.mhlw.go.jp/toukei/list/81-1a.html

Ministry of Health Labor and Welfare (MHLW). (2007). *Heisei 18 nendo kôreisha gyakutai no boshi, kôreisha no yogôsha ni taisuru shien to ni kansuru hôritsu ni motozuku taiô jyokyô ni kansuru chôsa kekka* (kakutei ban). [2006 = Heisei 18 survey result for the law on elderly abuse prevention and support towards family care givers]. Retrieved from http://www.mhlw.go.jp/houdou/2007/12/h1219-1.html

Ministry of Health Labor and Welfare (MHLW). (2009). *Kôreisha gyakutai boshi taisaku ni tsuite.* [Elderly abuse prevention measures]. Retrieved from http://www.mhlw.go.jp/houdou/2007/12/h1219-1.html

Ministry of Health Labor and Welfare (MHLW). (2010). *Kokumin seikatsu kiso chôsa no gaikyô.* [Survey on the Life of the People]. Retrieved from http://www.mhlw.go.jp/toukei/saikin/hw/k-tyosa/k-tyosa10/index.html

Ministry of Health Labor and Welfare (MHLW). (2011). *Keizai renkei kyôtei ni motozuku gaikokujin kangoshi kaigo fukushishi kôhôsha no ukeire to ni tsuite.* [Acceptance of Foreign Nurse and Caregiver Candidates under the Economic Partnership Agreement]. Retrieved from http://www.mhlw.go.jp/bunya/koyou/other22/index.html

Ministry of Health Labor and Welfare (MHLW). (2012). *Kokumin seikatsu kiso chôsa no gaikyô.* [Survey on the Life of the People]. Retrieved from http://www.mhlw.go.jp/toukei/saikin/hw/k-tyosa/k-tyosa12/index.html

Ministry of Health Labor and Welfare (MHLW). (2013a). *Kaigo hoken seido o torimaku jyôkyô.* [Situations of the Long Term Care System]. Retrieved from http://www.mhlw.go.jp/stf/shingi/2r98520000031zxr-att/2r9852000003202m.pdf

Ministry of Health Labor and Welfare (MHLW). (2013b). *Kaigo jinzai no kakuhô kankei.* [Securing Care Workforce]. Retrieved from http://www.mhlw.go.jp/stf/shingi/2r98520000033t43-att/2r98520000033t98.pdf

Ministry of Health. (1997). *Zorgindicatiebesluit* (White paper). The Hague, The Netherlands: Author.

Ministry of Health. Welfare and Family Affairs. (2008). *White paper on health, welfare and family affairs 2007.* Seoul, South Korea: Ministry of Health, Welfare and Family Affairs.

Ministry of Health. Welfare and Family Affairs. (2009). *White paper on children and adolescents 2009.* Author.

Ministry of Interior. Taiwan. (2006). *Report of the survey of living situation.* Retrieved on 22 July 2013, from http://www.cpami.gov.tw/pwi/ph/ph_14.php

Ministry of Interior. Taiwan. (2010). *Monthly bulletin of the statistics.* Retrieved on 22 July 2013, from http://www.moi.gov.tw/stat/

Ministry of Interior. Taiwan. (2011a). *Monthly bulletin of the registered residence.* Retrieved on 22 July 2013, from http://www.ris.gov.tw/ch4/static/st1-9-95.xls

Ministry of Interior. Taiwan. (2011b). *Social assistance act.* Retrieved on 22 July 2013, from http://law.moj.gov.tw/LawClass/LawAll.aspx?PCode=D0050078

Ministry of Interior. Taiwan. (2012). *Monthly bulletin of the statistics.* Retrieved on 22 July 2013, from http://www.moi.gov.tw/stat/

Ministry of Internal Affairs and Communication. (2013). *Gaikokujin no ukeire taisaku ni taisuru gyôsei hyôka/kanshi.* [Public Sector Evaluation regarding Acceptance of Foreigners]. Retrieved from http://www.soumu.go.jp/menu_news/s-news/73055.html

Ministry of Justice. (2013). *Heisei 24 nen matsu genzai ni okeru zairyû gaikokujinsû ni tsuite.* [Number of Foreign Residents at the end of 2012 = Heisei 24]. Retrieved from http://www.moj.go.jp/nyuukokukanri/kouhou/nyuukokukanri04_00030.html

Ministry of the Interior. (2008). *Interior statistical yearbook.* Retrieved from http://sowf.moi.gov.tw/stat/year/list.htm

Ministry of the Interior. (2008). *Population policy white paper: Strategies towards declining fertility, ageing population, and immigration problems.* Taipei, Taiwan: Ministry of the Interior.

Ministry of the Interior. (2009). *2009 total population.* Retrieved from http://www.moi.gov.tw/news_detail.aspx

Ministry of the Interior. (2009). *Internal statistical bulletin.* Retrieved from http://www.moi.gov.tw/stat/

Ministry of the Interior. (2011). *A century retrospect and prospect of population policy.* Taipei, Taiwan: Ministry of the Interior.

Ministry of the Interior. Ministry of Education, Council of Labor Affairs, & Department of Health. (2006). 2015 economic development visions-The three-year implementation scheme of the great warmth social welfare package: Stage one (2007-2009). Author.

Mitsuoka, K. (1996). *Nôson kazoku no kekkon-nan to kôreisha mondai* [Difficulty of Finding Spouses and Aging Population Problems of Farming Village Families]. Kyôto: Mineruva.

Miyamoto, T. (2011). Hataraku koto no seijigaku. [Politics of Labor] In *Hataraku.* Tôkyô: Fûkôsha.

MNCWA. (2001). *Gender statistics in Myanmar.* Yangon, Myarmar: MNCWA.

Mokomane, Z. (2012). *Anti-poverty family-focused policies in developing countries, department of economic and social affairs, division for social policy and development, family-oriented policies for poverty reduction, work-family balance and international solidarity.* Retrieved from http://www.un.org/esa/socdev/family/docs/WorkFamilyBalanceandIntergenerationalSolidarity.pdf

Morone, J. A. (2000). Citizens or shoppers? Solidarity under siege. *Journal of Health Politics, Policy and Law, 25*(5), 959–968. doi:10.1215/03616878-25-5-959 PMID:11068741

Moss, P., & Cameron, C. (2002). *Care work in Europe: Current understandings and future directions—WP6 care work and the care workforce—Report on stage one and state-of-the-art review.* London: Thomas Coram Research Unit, Institute of Education, University of London.

Nagano, Y. (2004). *Gendai nihon no noson kazoku to noson shakai: Nôson josei no 'ko' no jiritsuka o megutte* [Farming Families and Society of Japan Today: with Focus on Independence of the 'Individuality' of Farming Village Women]. Tôkyô: Waseda Daigaku Shuppankai.

Najita, T. (1978). Method and analysis in the conceptual portrayal of Tokugawa intellectual history. In *Thought in the Tokugawa period 1600–1868: Methods and metaphors*. London: The University of Chicago Press.

Nakayachi, K. (2003). *Kankyô risuku shinrigaku*. Kyôto: Nakanishiya Shuppan.

Naqvi, S. N. H. (2010). *The evolution of development policy: A reinterpretation*. Oxford, UK: Oxford University Press.

Nation (Thailand). (2010, November 11). Not free or fair. *Nation (New York, N.Y.)*.

Nation (Thailand). (2013, June 28). Thein Sein calls for action against poverty. *Nation (New York, N.Y.)*.

National Institute of Population and Social Security Research. (2012). *Nihon no shôrai suikei jinkô*. [Future Population Projection of Japan]. Retrieved from http://www.ipss.go.jp/syoushika/tohkei/newest04/gh2401.pdf

National Institute of Population and Social Security Research. (2013). *Seikatsu hogo ni kansuru kôteki tôkei data ichiran*. [Data on Social Security System]. Retrieved from http://www.ipss.go.jp/s-info/j/seiho/seiho.asp

National Statistics. (2013). *Labor force statistical tables*. Retrieved from http://eng.stat.gov.tw/ct.asp?xItem=12683&ctNode=1609&mp=5

Needham, C. (2006). Customer care and the public service ethos. *Public Administration*, *84*(4), 845–860. doi:10.1111/j.1467-9299.2006.00615.x

Needham, C. (2010). Debate: Personalized public services - A new state/citizen contract? *Public Money & Management*, *30*(3), 136–138. doi:10.1080/09540961003794246

Needham, C. (2011). *Personalizing public services: Understanding the personalisation narrative*. Bristol, UK: The Policy Press.

New York Times. (2010, November 10). In Myanmar, opposition concedes defeat in vote. *New York Times*.

New York Times. (2012, April 5). U.S. moves toward normalizing relations with Myanmar. *New York Times*.

Newman, J., & Kuhlmann, E. (2007). Consumers enter the political stage? The modernization of health care in Britain and Germany. *Journal of European Social Policy*, *17*(1), 99–111. doi:10.1177/0958928707075191

Nihon Keieisha Dantai Renmei. (1995). *Shinjidai no nihonteki keiei* [Japanese Management in the New Era]. Tokyo: Nihon Keieisha Dantai Renmei.

Nolan, B., & Whelan, C. T. (1997). Measuring poverty using income and deprivation indicators: Alternative approaches. *Journal of European Social Policy*, *6*, 225–240.

Nolan, M. R., Davies, S., & Grant, G. (Eds.). (2001). *Working with older people and their families: Key issues in policy and practice*. Buckingham, UK: Open University Press.

Nonoyama Hisaya. (2007). *Gendai kazoku no paradaimu kakushin* [Paradigm change for the modern family in Japan]. Tôkyô: Tôkyô Daigaku Shuppankai.

Nye, J. S. (2004). *Soft power: The means to success in world politics*. New York: Public Affairs. doi:10.1111/j.1540-5842.2004.00673.x

ODonnell, O., van Doorslaer, E., Rannan-Eliya R. P., Somanathan, A., Adhikari, S. R., Akkazieva, B., … Zhao, Y. (2008). Who pays for health care in Asia? *Journal of Health Economics*, *27*(2), 460–475. doi:10.1016/j.jhealeco.2007.08.005 PMID:18179832

ODonnell, O., van Doorslaer, E., Rannan-Eliya, R. P., Somanathan, A., Adhikari, S. R., Harbianto, D., … Zhao, Y. (2007). The incidence of public spending on health care: Comparative evidence from Asia. *The World Bank Economic Review*, *21*(1), 93–123. doi:10.1093/wber/lhl009

OECD. (2007). *Babies and bosses - Reconciling work and family life: A synthesis of findings for OECD countries*. Paris: OECD.

OECD. (2007). *Ensuring fragile states are not left behind*. Retrieved from http://www.oecd.org/dataoecd/34/24/40090369.pdf

OECD. (2009). *Economic survey of Japan 2009: Health-care reform in Japan: Controlling costs, improving quality*. Retrieved from http://www.oecd.org/document/5/0,3746,en_2649_34587_43791173_1_1_1_1,00.html

OECD. (2009). *Factbook*. Retrieved from http://www.oecd-ilibrary.org/economics/oecd-factbook-2009/population-aged-65-and-over_factbook-2009-table4-en

OECD. (2009). *OECD employment outlook 2009: Tackling the job crisis*. Paris: OECD.

OECD. (2011). Executive summary. In *Doing better for families*. Paris: OECD Publishing.

OECD. (2012). *OECD family database*. Retrieved Oct 20, 2012, from http://www.oecd.org/els/familiesandchildren/42293894.xls

OECD-DAC Website. (n.d.). *DAC list of ODA recipients*. Retrieved from http://www.oecd.org/dac/aidstatistics/48858205.pdf

Ogawa, T. (2006). The concept of social quality and its implications for social well-being and aging policy in Asia and the pacific—Developing a social quality approach in Asian types of civil society and its implications for 3S developments. Paper presented in Social Policy Research Workshop--Social Economic Security in Later Life in National Taiwan University. Taipei, Taiwan.

Ogawa, R. (2012). Globalization of care and the context of reception in Japan. *Southeast Asian Studies*, *49*(4), 570–593.

Oguma, E. (2012). *Shakai o kaeru niha* [To Change a Society]. Tôkyô: Kôdansha Gendai Shinsho.

Oishi, N. (2005). *Women in motion: Globalization, state policies and labor migration in Asia*. Stanford, CA: Stanford University Press.

Ooms, H. (1984). Neo-Confucianism and the formation of early Tokugawa ideology: Contours of a problem. In *Confucianism and Tokugawa culture*. Princeton, NJ: Princeton University Press.

Ooms, H. (1985). *Tokugawa ideology: Early constructs, 1570–1680*. Princeton, NJ: Princeton University Press.

Ôsawa, M. (2001). Fukushi kokka to byôdô – Shakai seisaku no hikaku jendâ bunseki no tachiba kara. *Shakai Seisaku Gakkaishi*, *6*, 99–115.

Ôsawa, M. (2008). *Gendai nihon no seikatsu hosho shizutemu* [Contemporary Social Security System in Japan]. Tôkyô: Iwanami Shoten.

Ôuchi, M. (2004). Life course no tayôka to 'ie' seido. [Diversification of Life Courses and the 'Ie' System]. *Nenpô Sonraku Shakai Kenkyû*, *39*, 97–132.

Parrenas, R. S. (2003). *Servants of globalization*. Manila: Ateneo de Manila University Press.

Parsons, T., & Shiels, E. (Eds.). (1951). *Toward general theory of action*. Cambridge, MA: Harvard University Press.

Parsons, W. (1995). *Public policy: An introduction to the theory and practice of policy analysis*. Northampton, MA: Edward Elgar Publishing.

Pedersen, M. B. (2006). A comprehensive international approach to political and economic development in Burma/Myanmar. In T. Wilson (Ed.), *Myanmar's long road to national recongiliation*. Singapore: ISEAS Publications.

Perry, B. D. (2002). Childhood experience and the expression of genetic potential: What childhood neglect tells us about nature and nurture. *Brain and Mind*, *3*, 79–100. doi:10.1023/A:1016557824657

Perry, J. L., & Hondeghem, A. (2009). *Motivation in public management: The call of public service*. Oxford, UK: Oxford University Press.

Phillips, D. R. (2000). Ageing in the Asia-Pacific region: Issues, policies and future trends. In D. R. Phillips (Ed.), *Ageing in the Asia-Pacific region: Issues, policies and future trends*. New York: Routledge. doi:10.4324/9780203463086

Pickard, L. (2001). Care break or carer-blind? Policy for informal carers in the UK. *Social Policy and Administration*, *35*(4), 441–458. doi:10.1111/1467-9515.00244

Pickard, L. (2004). *The effectiveness and cost effectiveness of support and services to informal carers of older people*. London: Audit Commission.

Pierson, P. (2001). Post-industrial pressures on the mature welfare states. In P. Pierson (Ed.), *The new politics of the welfare state*. Oxford, UK: Oxford University Press. doi:10.1093/0198297564.003.0004

Prior, P. M., & Sykes, R. (2001). Globalization and the European welfare states: Evaluating the theories and evidence. In R. Sykes, B. Palier, & P. M. Prior (Eds.), *Globalization and European welfare states: Challenges and change.* Basingstoke, UK: Palgrave.

Quinton, D., & Rutter, M. (1985). Parenting behaviour of mothers raised in care. In R. Nicol (Ed.), *Longitudinal studies in child psychology and psychiatry* (pp. 157–201). Chichester, UK: Wiley.

Rainey, H. G., & Chun, Y. H. (2007). Public and private management compared. In *The oxford Handbook of public management* (pp. 72–102). Oxford, UK: Oxford University Press. doi:10.1093/oxfordhb/9780199226443.003.0005

Ransom, I., & MacNeill, R. (2012, August 9). Medals obscure cost of China's state-run sports regime. *Reuters.* Retrieved from http://uk.reuters.com/article/2012/08/09/uk-oly-chn-state-idUKBRE8781EC20120809

Reischauer, E. O. (1978). *The Japanese.* Tokyo: Charles E. Tuttle Company, Inc.

Research, Development and Evaluation Commission, Executive Yuan, Taiwan. (2012). *2011 survey on individual/household digital opportunity.* Retrieved on 22 July 2013 from http://www.rdec.gov.tw/public/Attachment/222114532071.pdf

Roberts, M. (2006). Philosophy, ethics and societal values in health system reform. In G. M. Leung, & J. Bacon-Shone (Eds.), *Hong Kong's health system: Reflections, perspectives and visions* (pp. 27–40). Hong Kong: Hong Kong University Press.

Roberts, N. C. (2008). *The age of direct citizenship participation.* New York: M.E. Sharpe.

Rosa, E. A., Matsuda, N., & Kleinhesselink, R. R. (2000). The cognitive architecture of risk: Pancultural unity or cultural shaping? In *Cross-cultural risk perception: A survey of empirical studies.* London: Kluwer Academic Publishers. doi:10.1007/978-1-4757-4891-8_5

Roycee, A. (2008). *Burma in turmoil.* New York: Nova Science Publishers.

Rutter, M. (1985). Intergenerational continuities and discontinuities in serious parenting difficulties. In D. Cicchetti (Ed.), *Child maltreatment.* Cambridge, UK: Cambridge University Press.

Rutter, M. (1989). Pathways from childhood to adult life. *Journal of Child Psychology and Psychiatry, and Allied Disciplines, 30*, 23–61. doi:10.1111/j.1469-7610.1989.tb00768.x PMID:2647779

Rutter, M. (1998). Developmental catch-up, and deficit, following adoption after severe global early privation. *Journal of Child Psychology and Psychiatry, and Allied Disciplines, 39*(4), 465–476. doi:10.1017/S0021963098002236 PMID:9599775

Sachs, J. (2004, July 27). Myanmar: Sanctions won't work. *The Financial Times.*

Sakai, Y. (2004). Kankyô ga keizai ka? Risuku no shita no ishikettei. In *Risuku, kankyô oyobi keizai.* Tôkyô: Keisô Shobô.

Sammons, P., Elliot, K., Sylva, K., & Melhuish, M., Siraj-Blatchford, & Taggart, B. (2004). The impact of pre-school on young children's cognitive attainments at entry to reception. *British Educational Research Journal, 30*(5), 691–712. doi:10.1080/0141192042000234656

Samuel, M. (2005, December 15). Profession becoming less focused on clients and more on paper work. *Community Care.*

Samuels, R. J. (2013). *3.11: Disaster and change in Japan.* New York: Cornell University Press. doi:10.1353/jjs.2013.0016

Savas, E. S. (2000). *Privatization and public private partnerships.* New York: Chatman.

Saxonhouse, A. W. (1983). Classical Greek conceptions of public and private. In *Public and private in social life* (pp. 363–384). New York: St. Martin's Press.

Schrijvers, A. J. P., Jedeloo, S., Jorg, F., & Hoogerduin, J. G. (2001). *Rio, the youngest child grows.* Utrecht, The Netherlands: Julius Centre. [in Dutch]

Scott Pty, W. D. Company. (1985). The delivery of medical services in hospitals. Hong Kong: Government Printer.

Scottish Executive. (2006). *Changing lives: Report of the recommendation made by the 21st century social work review group for the future of social services in Scotland.* Edinburgh, UK: Scottish Executive.

Secretary of the National Conference on Taiwan's Economic Sustainable Development. (2008a). *The minute of the national conference on Taiwan's economic sustainable development: Part 1.* Taipei, Taiwan: Council for Economic Planning and Development.

Secretary of the National Conference on Taiwan's Economic Sustainable Development. (2008b). *The minute of the national conference on Taiwan's economic sustainable development: Part 2.* Taipei, Taiwan: Council for Economic Planning and Development.

Semyonov, M., & Gorodzeisky, A. (2008). Labor migration, remittances and economic well-being of households in the Philippines. *Population Research and Policy Review, 27*(5), 619–637.

Shimane Prefecture. (2006). *Shimane-ken no chu-sankan chiiki no teigi.* [Definitions of Hilly and Mountainous Areas of Shimane Prefecture]. Retrieved from http://www2.pref.shimane.jp/teiju/mrteigi/index.html

Shimbun, A. (2012). *Ulrich beck: System of organized irresponsibility behind the Fukushima crisis.* Retrieved from http://ajw.asahi.com/article/0311disaster/opinion/AJ201107063167

Shimbun, M. (2011, December 14). *Shin kodomo teate: Nenshû 960man-chô, tsuki5000en, zôzei futan ni hairyo - Seifu hôshin.* Retrieved from http://mainichi.jp/life/edu/child/archive/news/2011/12/20111214ddm002010093000c.html

Shimizu, I. (2013). Kinsei kindai manga ryakushi. In *Nihon no zushô manga.* Tôkyô: Pai Intânashonaru.

Shin, C. S., & Shaw, I. (2003). Social policy in South Korea: Cultural and structural factors in the emergence of welfare. *Social Policy and Administration, 37*(4), 328–341. doi:10.1111/1467-9515.00343

Shindô, M. (2002). *Chihô bunken.* Tôkyô: Iwanami Shoten. Shôtoku Taishi. (604). *Jûshichijôkempô.* Retrieved from http://afe.easia.columbia.edu/japan/japanworkbook/traditional/shotoku.htm

Shonkoff, J. P., & Phillips, D. A. (Eds.). (2000). From *neurons to neighborhoods*: The *science of early childhood development.* National Academies Press. Retrieved on 29 October, 2012 from http://www.nap.edu/catalog/9824.html

Shutes, I. (2013). Long-term care and migrant labour in the UK. In Europe's immigration challenge: Reconciling work, welfare and mobility. London: I.B.Tauris.

Sidorenko, A. A., & Butler, J. R. G. (2007). Financing health insurance in Asia Pacific countries. *Asian-Pacific Economic Literature, 21*(1), 34–54. doi:10.1111/j.1467-8411.2007.00191.x

Skelcher, C. (2007). Public-private partnerships and hybridity. In *The Oxford handbook of public management* (pp. 317–370). Oxford, UK: Oxford University Press. doi:10.1093/oxfordhb/9780199226443.003.0016

Slovic, P. (2000). *The perception of risk.* London: Earthscan.

Society for Risk Analysis (SRA). (n.d.). Retrieved from http://www.sra.org/

Soeda, Y. (1994). Borantia to fukushi kyôiku no chôryû: Shôgai gakushû shakai no keisei to borantia katsudô. In *Fukushi kaikaku v. sankagata fukushi shakai no kôchiku.* Tôkyô: Zenkoku Shakai Fukushi Kyôgikai.

Soh, H. et al. (2010). *Survey on single mother and father and policy research.* Gyeonggi-do Family and Women's Research Institute. [in Korean]

Soh, H. (2011). *Policy proposal: Support programs of development of children of single mother and father parents.* Gyeonggi-do Family and Women's Research Institute. [in Korean]

Sôma, N., & Park, J. (2007). Korean single mother policy. In Life styles and welfare policies of single mothers: Comparative study of Japan, the U.S., Denmark and Korea. Kyôto, Japan: Minerva. [in Japanese].

Somers, M. R. (2008). *Genealogies of citizenship: Markets, statelessness, and the right to have rights.* Cambridge, UK: Cambridge University Press. doi:10.1146/annurev.lawsocsci.2.081805.105847

Statistics Bureau (Sômushô). (2010). *Rôdôryoku chôsa.* [Labor Survey]. Retrieved from http://www.stat.go.jp/data/roudou/tsushin/pdf/no02.pdf

Statistics Bureau (Sômushô). (2012). *Shûgyô kôzô kihon chôsa, kekka no gaiyô.* [Survey on Labor Force: An Overview]. Retrieved from http://www.stat.go.jp/data/shugyou/2012/pdf/kgaiyou.pdf

Statistics Bureau. (2011). *Handbook.* Retrieved from http://www.stat.go.jp/english/data/handbook/c02cont.htm#cha2_2

Steele, M. W. (2000). The history of the Tama River: Water and rocks in modern Japanese economic growth. *Asian Cultural Studies, 26*, 39–50.

Steinberger, P. (1999). Public and private. *Political Studies, 47*(2), 292–313. doi:10.1111/1467-9248.00201

Stone, R., & Wiener, J. (2001). *Who will care for us? Addressing the long-term care workforce crisis.* Washington, DC: The Urban Institute and the American Association of Homes and Services for the Aging.

Straits Times (Singapore). (2013, May 23). Myanmar economy set to grow 6.75%: IMF, gas production, investment to lead expansion, up from 6.5% last year. *Straits Times.*

Strawbridge, W. J., Wallhagen, M. I., & Cohen, R. D. (2002). Successful aging and well-being: Self rated compared with Rowe and Kahn. *The Gerontologist, 42*, 727–733. doi:10.1093/geront/42.6.727 PMID:12451153

Sumner, A., & Tribe, M. (2008). *International development studies-Theories and methods in research and practice.* London: Sage Publication.

Suzuki, M., & Itô, M. (Eds.), *(n.d.). Risukuka suru nihon shakai.* Tôkyô: Iwanami Shoten.

Swank, D. (2002). *Global capital, political institutions, and policy change in developed welfare states.* Cambridge, UK: Cambridge University Press. doi:10.1017/CBO9780511613371

Tagespiegel, D. (2012). *Hintergrund, ethikkommission.* Retrieved from http://www.tagesspiegel.de/politik/hintergrund-ethikkommission/3978952.html

Taiwan Blood Foundation. (2010). *Yearbook.* Retrieved on 22 July 2013, from http://www.blood.org.tw/index.php?action=sas&PId=28

Takahashi, M. (2004). *The search for solidarity in Japan's risk society.* Paper presented at ISA RC19: Poverty, Social Welfare and Social Policy. Paris, France. Retrieved from http://www.cevipof.msh-paris.fr/rencontres/colloq/palier/index.html

Takahashi, M. (2003). Care for children and older people in Japan: Modernizing the traditional. In *The young, the old and the state: Social care systems in five industrial nations.* Cheltenham, UK: Edward Elgar.

Taleb, N. N. (2010). *The black swan: The impact of the highly improbable* (Rev. Ed.). London: Penguin Books. doi:10.2139/ssrn.1669317

Taylor-Gooby, P. (1997). In defense of second-best theory: State, class and capital in social policy. *Journal of Social Policy, 26*(2), 171–192. doi:10.1017/S0047279497004996

Taylor-Gooby, P. (2004). New risks and social change. In *New risks, new welfare: The transformation of the European welfare state.* Oxford, UK: Oxford University Press. doi:10.1093/019926726X.003.0001

Tei, S. (2004). Chûgoku no kankyô hozen. In *Gendai shakai no yuragi to risuku.* Tôkyô: Keisô Shobô.

The Guardian. (2012, April 24). EU lifts Burma sanctions for one year to support reform. *The Guardian.*

The Japan Times. (2012, October 14). Aiding Myanmar's reforms (opinion). *The Japan Times.*

Thomas, J. A. (2001). *Reconfiguring modernity: Concepts of nature in Japanese political ideology.* Berkeley, CA: University of California Press.

Timonen, V. (2004). New risks: Are they still new for the Nordic welfare states? In P. Taylor-Gooby (Ed.), *New risks, new welfare: The transformation of the European welfare state.* Oxford, UK: Oxford University Press. doi:10.1093/019926726X.003.0004

Ting, K.-F. (2009). *A review on the literature on filial piety.* Central Policy Unity, Government of Hong Kong. Retrieved on 29 October, 2012 from http://www.cpu.gov.hk/chs/documents/new/press/Filial%20Piety%20Literature.pdf

Toda, K. (1994). *Kankyô kôsei o motomete: Kankyôhakai no kôzô to erîtoshugi*. Tôkyô: Shin'yôsha.

Tokyo Council of Social Welfare, Division of Childcare Investigation Committee. (2002). *Report on the study of mothers who gave birth as teenagers, childrearing and childcare support*. Author. [in Japanese]

Torraco, R. J. (2005). Writing integrative literature reviews: Guidelines and examples. *Human Resource Development Review*, *4*(3), 356–367. doi:10.1177/1534484305278283

Totman, C. (2004). Pre-industrial Korea and Japan in environmental perspective. In *Handbook of oriental studies* (Vol. 11). Boston: Brill.

Treat, J. W. (1996). Introduction. Japanese studies into cultural studies. In J. W. Treat (Ed.), *Contemporary Japan and popular culture*. Honolulu, HI: University of Hawai'i Press.

Tsai, P.-Y. (2011b). *The transformation of work-family balance policies in Taiwan*. Paper presented at the The 8th EASP International Conference. Social Policy in East Asia and Beyond: Rethinking Social Policy Strategies in Times of Uncertainty. Hong Kong.

Tsai, P.-Y. (2011a). The transformation of social risks and adaptation of welfare institutions in Europe. In B. Li (Ed.), *European and American welfare systems: Challenges, reforms and constraints*. Beijing: China Social Press.

Tsai, P.-Y. (2012). The transformation of leave policies for work-family balance in Taiwan. *Asian Women*, *28*(2), 27–54.

Tsubota, K., Ogawa, R., Ôno, S., & Hirano, Y. (2012). *Gaikokujin kaigo fukushishi kôhôsha ukeire ankêto kekka*. [Results of the Questionnaire Survey on Acceptance of Foreign Care Workers]. Unpublished.

Tsuji, N. (2005). *Nihon bijutsu no rekishi: Jômon kara manga-anime made*. Tôkyô: Tôkyô Daigaku Shuppankai.

Tsuru, R. (2003). Nôson ni okeru 'ie' no henyô: Nagasaki-ken ikishima no jirei kara.[Transformation of 'Ie' in a Farming Village: Based on Cases at Ikishima, Nagasaki Prefecture]. *Kibi Kokusai Daigaku Shakai Gakubu Kenkyû Kiyô*, *13*, 73–88.

Tuan, C. P. (1992). *The economy in Taiwan after the war*. Taipei, Taiwan: Jen-Chien Publications.

Twigg, J. (1997). Deconstructing the social bath: Help with bathing at home for older and disable people. *Journal of Social Policy*, *26*(2), 211–232. doi:10.1017/S0047279497004960

Umesao, T. (2003). *An ecological view of history: Japanese civilization in the world context*. Melbourne, Australia: Trans Pacific Press.

UN Millennium Project. (2005). *Investing in development - A practical plan to achieve the millennium development goals*. London: Earthscan.

UN. (2012). *The millennium development report 2012*. New York: UN.

UNDESA Website (n.d.). *Tackling family poverty*. Retrieved from http://www.un.org/en/development/desa/news/policy/tackling-family-poverty.html

UNDESA. (2011). *Summary of the proceedings assessing family policies: Confronting family poverty and social exclusion & ensuring work-family balance*. New York: United Nations Expert Group Meeting.

UNDP. (1990). *Human development report 1990 concept and measurement of human development*. UNDP.

UNDP. (2010). *Human development report*. New York: Palgrave Macmillan.

UNFPA. (2008). *Family planning and poverty reduction: Fact sheet 2008*. Retrieved from http://www.unfpa.org/rh/planning/mediakit/docs/sheet4.pdf

UNFPA. (2012). *Impacts of population dynamics, reproductive health and gender on poverty*. New York: UNFPA.

Ungerson, C. (1997). Social politics and commodification of care. *Social Politics*, *4*(3), 362–381. doi:10.1093/sp/4.3.362

Ungerson, C. (2000). *Care work: Gender, labour and the welfare state*. London: Routledge.

Ungerson, C. (2004). Whose empowerment and independence? A cross-national perspective on cash for care schemes. *Ageing and Society*, *24*, 189–212. doi:10.1017/S0144686X03001508

UNRISD Website. (n.d.). *Social policy and development*. Retrieved from http://www.unrisd.org/80256B3C005BB128/(httpProgrammeAreas)/BFA13785EC135F568025718B003C5FA7?OpenDocument

US Department of the Treasury Website. (n.d.). *An overview of the Burmese sanctions regulations title 31 part 537 of the U.S. code of federal regulations*. Retrieved from http://www.treasury.gov/resource-center/sanctions/Documents/burma.pdf

Van den Bovenkamp, H. M. (2010). *The limits of patient power: Examining active citizenship in Dutch health care*. Rotterdam, The Netherlands: Optima Grafische Communicatie.

van der Maesen, L., & Walker, A. (2005). Indicators of social quality: Outcomes of the European scientific network. *European Journal of Social Quality*, *5*, 8–24. doi:10.3167/146179105780337431

van der Wal, Z., Huberts, L. W. J. C., van den Heuvel, J. H. J., & Kolthoff, E. W. (2006). Central values of government and business: Differences, similarities and conflicts. *Public Administration Quarterly*, *30*(3), 314–364.

Van Hooren, F. (2012). Varieties of migrant care work, comparing patterns of migrant labour in social care. *Journal of European Social Policy*, *22*(2), 133–147. doi:10.1177/0958928711433654

Video, D. Afpenglish. (n.d.). *No individual to blame for Fukushima: Japan PM*. Retrieved from http://www.dailymotion.com/video/xp72nb_no-individual-to-blame-for-fukushima-japan-pm_news

Vuori, J. (2013). Citizen participation embedded in public, private and hybrid organizations. *International Journal of Public and Private Healthcare Management and Economics*, *3*(1), xi–xiii.

Vuori, J., & Merviö, M. (2007). *Japanin ja suomen hyvinvointijärjestelmien vertailtavuus: Vertailu- ja arviointimallin konstruointi erityisesti julkisen ja yksityisen käsitteiden näkökulmasta. Kuopio*. Kuopio University Press.

Wagstaff, A. (2005). *Health systems in east Asia: What can developing countries learn from Japan and the Asian tigers?* (World Bank Policy Research Working Paper 3790). Washington, DC: World Bank.

Wahlstedt, P. (2004). Elämme turvallisuusharhassa. *Suomen Luonto*, *4*, 50–51.

Walker, A., & Wigfield, A. (2003). *Social quality and the conditional factor of social inclusion: 3rd draft*. Amsterdam, The Netherlands: EFSQ.

Walker, A., & Wong, C.-K. (2005). Introduction: East Asian welfare regimes. In A. Walker, & C.-K. Wong (Eds.), *East Asian welfare regimes in transition: From Confucianism to globalisation*. Bristol, UK: Policy.

Wallop, H. (2009). Death of the traditional family. *Daily Telegraph*. Retrieved on 29 October, 2012 from http://www.telegraph.co.uk/family/5160857/Death-of-the-traditional-family.html

Wang, F. T. (2010). Globalization of care in Taiwan: From undutiful daughter-in-law to cold-blooded migrant killer. In *Transnational migration from southeast Asia to east Asia and the transformation of reproductive labor: Comparative study between Korea, Taiwan and Japan*. Paper presented at the Kitakyushu Forum on Asian Women (KFAW). Tokyo, Japan.

Wang, Y. T. (2007). *Social quality in Taiwan*. Paper presented in the Second Asian Conference on Social Quality and Sustainable Welfare Societies in National Taiwan University. Taipei, Taiwan.

Wang, F. T. Y. (2002). Contesting identity of Taiwanese home-care workers: Worker, daughter, and do-gooder? *Journal of Aging Studies*, *16*, 37–55. doi:10.1016/S0890-4065(01)00033-0

Wang, K. (2011). Child care and elder arrangements in Taiwan. *Journal of Comparative Social Welfare*, *27*(2), 165–174. doi:10.1080/17486831.2011.567021

Wang, S.-I., & Lai, S.-Y. (1997). The predicament of childcare and role of the state in Taiwan. In *Women, state, and care*. Taipei, Taiwan: Fembooks. [in Chinese]

Wang, S.-Y., & Sun, M.-W. (2003). The role of the state in the childcare policy.[in Chinese]. *National Policy Quarterly*, 2(4), 147–174.

Warner, L. (1952). *The enduring art of Japan*. New York: Grove Press.

Warren, L. (1990). We're home helps because we care: The experiences of home helps caring for elderly people. In P. Abbott, & G. Payne (Eds.), *New directions in the sociology of health*. Baskingstroke, UK: Falmer.

Watanabe, M. (2002). Kazoku nôgyô keiei ni okeru josei no katari ni miru rôdô to jendâ.[Labour and Gender Observed in Talks by Women Engaged in a Family-run Farm]. *Japanese Journal of Family Sociology*, *14*(1), 21–32. doi:10.4234/jjoffamilysociology.14.21

Watanabe, Y. (Ed.). (2008). *Kaisetsu FTA/EPA kôshô* [Commentary FTA/EPA Negotiations]. Tôkyô: Nihon Keizai Hyôronsha.

Waterhouse, S., Hunt, J., & Lutman, E. (2008, May). Keeping them in the family: Neglected and abused children placed with family or friends carers through care proceedings. *Family Law (Chichester)*.

Webster, J., & Watson, R. T. (2002). Analyzing the past to prepare for the future: Writing a literature review. *Management Information Systems Quarterly*, *26*(2), xiii–xxiii.

Weinberg, A., Williamson, J., Challis, D., & Hughes, J. (2003). What do care managers do? A study of working practice in older people's services. *British Journal of Social Work*, *33*, 901–919. doi:10.1093/bjsw/33.7.901

Weingart, P. (2010). A short history of knowledge formations. In *The Oxford handbook of interdisciplinarity* (pp. 3–14). Oxford, UK: Oxford University Press.

Weizsäcker von. E.U., Young, O.R., & Finger, M. (Eds.). (2006). Limits to privatization: How to avoid too much of a good thing. London, UK: Earthscan.

Welsh, E., Buchanan, A., Flouri, E., & Lewis, J. (2004). 'Involved' fathering and child well-being: Fathers' involvement with secondary school age children. *National Children's Bureau for the Rowntree Foundation Parenting in Practice Series*. Retrieved on 29 October, 2012 from http://www.jrf.org.uk/publications/fathers-involvement-with-their-secondary-school-aged-children

White House. (2003). *Speech of President Bush, September 7, 2003*. Retrieved from http://www.whitehouse.gov/news/releases/2003/09/20030907-1.html

Williams, F. (2010). Themes and concepts in migration, gender and care. *Social Policy and Society*, *9*(3), 385–396. doi:10.1017/S1474746410000102

Win, K. Z. (2007). Reality check on the sanctions policy against Myanmar. In *Myanmar state, society and ethnicity*. Singapore: ISEAS Publishing.

Wu, S.-C. (2006). Current childcare services in Taiwan. In *Childcare services*. Taipei, Taiwan: Psychological Publishing. [in Chinese]

Yamada, M. (2004). Kazoku no kojinka.[Individualization in Family]. *Shakaigaku Hyoron*, *54*(4), 341–354. doi:10.4057/jsr.54.341

Yamada, M. (2005). *Meisosuru: Sengo kazoku moderu no keisei to hôkai* [Families in a Runaway World: Formation and Collapse of the Post-war Model of Family]. Tôkyô: Yuhikaku.

Yang, C. L., Chen, K. C., & Li, T. C. (2008). Changes in family structure in nearly two decades: Social changes in Taiwan during 1985 – 2005. *In Proceedings of 11th Symposium on Taiwan Social Change Survey Plans*. Taipei, Taiwan: Institute of Sociology, Academia Sinica.

Yeates, N. (2001). *Globalization & social policy*. London: Sage Publications.

Yeates, N. (2007). Globalization and social policy. In J. Baldock, N. Manning, & S. Vickerstaff (Eds.), *Social policy* (3rd ed.). Oxford, UK: Oxford University Press.

Yeung, R., & Chan, W. S. (2006). Health financing in Hong Kong: The current status. In G. M. Leung, & J. Bacon-Shone (Eds.), *Hong Kong's health system: Reflections, perspectives and visions* (pp. 435–446). Hong Kong: Hong Kong University Press.

Yoder, R. S. (2011). *Deviance and inequality in Japan: Japanese youth and foreign migrants*. Bristol, UK: The Polity Press. doi:10.1332/policypress/9781847428325.003.0001

Youn, M., & Lee, J. (2003). Characteristics of teenage unwed mothers in Korea.[in Korean]. *Korean Journal of Child Studies*, *23*(3), 149–169.

Yûasa, M. (2008). *Han hinkon* [Anti poverty]. Tôkyô: Iwanami Shinsho.

Yu, W. K. (2006). The reforms of health care finance in Hong Kong and urban China: A mixed attitude to social welfare. *Critical Social Policy*, *26*(4), 843–864. doi:10.1177/0261018306068478

Zeit-Fragen. (2003). Pazifismus- eine Lebenslüge?. *Zeit-Fragen, 9*.

Zeng, L. Y., Chang, C. O., & Chen, S. M. (2006). Choose the elderly living arrangements– Discussion of intergenerational relations. *Journal of Housing Studies*, *15*(2), 45–64.

Zimmerman, M. K., Litt, J. S., & Bose, C. E. (2006). *Global dimensions of gender and carework*. Stanford, CA: Stanford University Press.

About the Contributors

Mika Markus Merviö is Professor of International Relations at the Kibi International University, Okayama, Japan. Previously, he worked at the University of Tampere, Finland, from which he also received his Ph.D. (International Relations). Then he moved to the International Christian University, Tôkyô, Japan, as a JSPS researcher and from there to the Miyazaki International University and the University of Shimane, where he worked as a Professor. From 2006, he has been working at the Kibi International University. His research interests include political and social issues, history, art, and environment.

* * *

Sun-Hee Baek is a professor of Seoul Theological University, Korea. She specializes in social welfare, especially childcare policy and family policy.

Ann Buchanan is a Senior Research Associate in the Department of Social Policy and Social Intervention, Professor of Social Work and a Fellow of St Hilda's College. Previously, she was Director of the Centre for Research into Parenting and Children. Before entering academic life in 1990, she spent 10 years working as a child psychiatric social worker in an inner urban area. For more than 20 years, she has been researching parenting and child outcomes, particularly children at risk of social exclusion. She is currently serving on the University of Oxford Research Committee. She was appointed to the Council of the ESRC in 2007 and in 2009 chaired the group responsible for updating the ESRC Framework for Research Ethics. In 2010, she was reappointed to the Council for a further three years and Chairs the Evaluation Committee. She became an Academician of the Academy of Social Sciences in 2009 and was appointed to the Council of the Academy in 2011. She was awarded am MBE by the Queen in 2012 for services to social science.

Raymond K. H. Chan is Associate Professor at the Department of Applied Social Studies, City University of Hong Kong, and Research Fellow, Social Policy Research Centre, National Taiwan University. His research interests are in risk and social policy, comparative social policy, family and labour policies. His articles appeared in *Asian Journal of Public Policy, Asian Journal of Social Science, Critical Social Policy, International Journal of Social Welfare, International Social Work, Journal of Comparative Social Welfare, Social Indicators Research, Social Policy & Administration*, and *Social Policy & Society.*

Fen-ling Chen is Associate Professor in Department of Social Work, National Taipei University and Research Fellow of Social Research Center at the National Taiwan University, Taiwan. She received her Ph.D. in Social Policy at the University of Bath, UK, and in 2007 was affiliated with the Rutgers University, USA, as a Fulbright visiting scholar. Her fields of expertise include comparative social policy, political economy analysis of social policies, issues of employment and welfare issues, especially in connection to women. She is the author of *Working Women and State Policies in Taiwan: A Study of Political Economy* (Palgrave, 2000) and has contributed many book chapters and journal articles within her fields of expertise.

Henglien Lisa Chen qualified and practiced for six years as a social worker (2000-2006) in English local authorities. Lisa teaches the MASW and BASW programs as well as supervising and examining doctoral students in subjects related to, adult care, gerontological social work, and international comparison. Her research interests include: cross-national comparison; social gerontology; ageing care: policies and practice; and ageing care service innovation. Lisa has been invited to present her research in a number of international conferences and universities. She is a referee for a number of international journals. Lisa has a strong involvement in multi-disciplinary research and international social work development. She is an advisor member of the Sussex environment and health research advisor group, a panel member of the Junior Research Associate (JRA) scheme at Sussex and the university representative on the JUCSWEC International Sub-Committee.

Marjory D. Fields, J.D., has served for more than 16 years on the bench, first as a Judge of the Family Court of the State of New York and then as a Justice of the Supreme Court Matrimonial Part. Before being elevated to the bench, she was in private practice, specializing in matrimonial and family law matters. Throughout her entire career, she has been a devoted advocate for the rights of victims of domestic violence and has led efforts to reform and draft new legislation to protect victims' rights. Currently, she is special counsel to Beldock Levine & Hoffman LLP in New York. She has also published and lectured extensively around the world on the topic of domestic violence, human rights of women, other legal issues effecting women, as well as other areas of family law and international jurisprudence.

Kang Hu is Associate Professor at the College of Humanities, Southwestern University of Finance and Economics. He received his PhD in sociology from the City University of Hong Kong. His research interests include social stratification and inequality, social integration, and urbanization in China. His articles have appeared in academic journals such as *International Journal of Public and Private Healthcare Management and Economics, International Journal of Social Quality,* and *Sociological Studies*.

Yoshimi Kataoka is a family sociologist and currently Associate Professor at Shimane University, Japan. Her earlier work experience includes Chief Researcher at Hyôgo Research Institute for Ageless Society (1999-2001) and lecturer at Shimane University (2001-2003). Her main research interest is in changing family life and family perception in contemporary Japanese society. She has actively conducted fieldwork in mountainous communities, mainly in the Shimane Prefecture, and published several academic articles on the theme. In recent years, she has also been participating in the research project of comparative study on international child adaption in Asia and Europe.

Marika Kylänen, MSc (Health Management Sciences), is a Doctoral Researcher at the University of Eastern Finland. She is a Research Coordinator of the International Group for Comparative Studies of Public and Private Management (PubPri Research Group). Her research interests include critical studies of public and private management and publicness, organization theory, comparative methodology, and international comparisons of health service systems. She is Research Fellow and Alumni of the Institute of Governance and Public Management at the Warwick Business School (WBS). In 2010-2011, she did the Research Training Programme at the WBS. Her research is mainly funded by the Academy of Finland.

Akemi Morita is a professor of Tôyô University, Japan. She specializes in social welfare, especially childcare policy, children's rights, local support systems for children and family, and family policy.

Reiko Ogawa has majored in sociology and anthropology and currently Associate Professor at Kyûshû University, Japan. Her research interest is on transnational mobilities of people and images and worked on migration, care work, and popular culture. Her recent publications includes "Conceptualizing Transnational Migration of Care Workers: Between 'Skilled' and 'Unskilled'," *ASIEN: The German Journal on Contemporary Asia*, No. 124 (2012); "Globalization of Care and the Context of Reception of Southeast Asian Care Workers in Japan," *Southeast Asian Studies*, Vol. 49, No. 4 (2012); Eds. Henk Vinken et al., *Civic Engagement in Contemporary Japan: Established and Emerging Repertoires*, Springer, New York (2010); Ed. Reiko Ogawa et al., *Transnational Migration from Southeast Asia to East Asia and the Transformation of Reproductive Labor: Comparative Study between Korea, Taiwan and Japan*, Visiting Researcher's Research Paper, Kitakyushu Forum on Asian Women (2010).

Ji-Yoon Park is Researcher of the Institute of Human Sciences, Tôyô University (Japan), and Researcher of the Monitoring Center for Children's right (South Korea). She specializes social welfare, especially children's right, local support system for children, and support for victims of child abuse and neglect.

Hansdeep Singh, JD, LLM, is Co-Founder and Director of Legal Programs for the International Center for Advocates Against Discrimination (ICAAD), an impact litigation and advocacy center focused on combating structural discrimination globally, and the promotion of human rights norms consistent with public international law. His experiences include work at Human Rights Watch (HRW) women's rights and legal division focusing on domestic violence and religious freedom. At the International Criminal Tribunals of Rwanda and Yugoslavia, he worked with a team of experienced international lawyers in chambers and also with the Office of Prosecution (OTP) to address mass atrocities (i.e. crimes against humanity, war crimes, and genocide).

Jaspreet K. Singh is the Co-Founder and Director of Policy and Advocacy at ICAAD (www.icaadglobal.org). Jaspreet's experience includes successfully litigating several cases before the U.S. Court of Appeals for the Ninth Circuit on issues related to asylum, unlawful deportation, and due process. He has extensive experience in dispute resolution, immigration, asylum, and refugee, civil, and human rights law, and in public relations. Jaspreet graduated from Florida State University College of Law with a Juris Doctorate and Certificate in International law and has his Bachelor's in Philosophy and Political Science from Emory University.

Naoko Sôma is Associate Professor at the International Graduate School of Social Sciences, Yokohama National University, Japan. She specializes in the sociology of citizenship of women and children and family policy in East Asia, especially social care and gender policy in Japan and South Korea from a comparative perspective.

Kana Takamatsu is Associate Professor at Department of Politics and International Relations, International Christian University, Japan. Her research interests include "Gender and Development," "Official Development Assistance Policy," and "Migration and Refugee." Her recent publications are *Official Development Assistance Policy and Human Security* (2011, Nihon hyôronsha, Tôkyô), Double Standard of Refugee Policy (chapter 6) (Ri, Nakamura, Hishiyama ed., *Idô no jidai o ikiru,* 2012, Tôshindô, Tôkyô), and Trafficking in Persons Issues and International Cooperation (Chapter 5) (Ôsawa M. ed., *Jendâ shakaikagaku no kanôsei* Vol.4, 2012, Iwanami shoten, Tôkyô).

Pei-Yuen Tsai is Assistant Professor at the Graduate Institute of Social Work, National Chengchi University, Taiwan. He is Researcher of the National Taiwan University Children and Family Research Center. His research interests cover issues of new social risks, work-family balance, family policies, and welfare restructuring, with particular reference to East Asia. He is currently working on a research project on the comparison of child-related leave between Taiwan and OECD countries. Recent publications include: The Transformation of Leave Policies for Work-Family Balance in Taiwan, *Asian Women, 28*(2).

Jari Vuori is a professor at University of Eastern Finland. He is currently Head of Health Management Sciences at the Department of Health and Social Management. He is Research Fellow of Warwick Business School (WBS). His research focuses mainly on the differences between public and private organizations and sectors at macro-and micro levels. He is head of the International Group for Comparative Studies of Public and Private Management (PubPri Research Group). His research and PubPri research group is mainly funded by the Academy of Finland. His educational and scientific background stems from public management, business administration, and economics. He acts as the Editor-in-Chief of the *International Journal of Public and Private Healthcare Management and Economics*.

Lih-Rong Wang is professor of Department of Social Work and Deputy Dean of Social Science College National Taiwan University. She was academic visitor of University of Oxford (07/2011-06/2012). Recently, she finished two National Gender-Based Violence/Domestic Violence Survey; two waves of East-Asia Social Quality Survey and Gender, Community Resilience after Disaster. Her recent papers have been published in *Global Social Work Practice, Journal of Social Work in Disability and Rehabilitation,* and *Social Indicator Research.* Her books such as *Women and Social Policy and Risk &Public Policy in East Asia* (co-authored with Dr. Raymond Chan and Dr. Mutsuko Takahashi) have been published locally and internationally. She has been serving in several international journals' editorial board such as *Planet@Risk and Asia Women, Journal of Social Quality,* and as chief editor of *NTU Social Work Review.*

Yun-Tung Wang, Associate Professor in National Taiwan University, Department of Social Work, got his Ph.D. degree from Columbia University, School of Social Work in 2001. His major research interests focus on welfare policy for people with disabilities, gerontology, and cost-benefit analysis in social policy. His recent representative publications include: "Job Coach Factors Associated with

Community-based Employment Service Program Outcome Measures for People with Disabilities – A Taiwan Case Study," *Disability and Rehabilitation*, 32(19)(2010); "Multimedia education program for patients with a stoma: effectiveness evaluation," *Journal of Advanced Nursing*, 67(1)(2011); and "Are Adults with Intellectual Disabilities Socially Excluded? An Exploratory Study in Taiwan," *Journal of Intellectual Disability Research* (accepted).

Peishan Yang is Associate Professor of National Taiwan University, Department of Social Work, also Deputy Director of National Taiwan University Social Policy Research Center. Before receiving her Ph.D. from Columbia University, School of Social Work, she had worked as Social Worker at Jewish Home and Hospital for the Aged in New York, USA, for about 7 years, thus acquiring substantial cross-national and cross-cultural experiences. Her main research interests are social gerontology, domestic violence against older adults, and long-term care. Her recent publications in English include "Surviving Social Support: Care Challenges Facing Taiwanese Centenarians" (*International Journal of Social Welfare*, 2012), "An Evaluation Study of a Dementia Screening Program in Taiwan: An Application of the Theory of Planned Behaviors" (*Journal of Gerontological Social Work, 55*[7], 2012, coauthored with Tang and Chen) and "Revitalizing Roles of Older Adult Citizens: Successful Stories of History Alive Project" (*Ageing International, 38*[1], 2012).

Index

G

H

I

J

K

L

M

N

O

P

www.ingramcontent.com/pod-product-compliance
Lightning Source LLC
LaVergne TN
LVHW060420300926
849162LV00006B/1484
9781466650312